A GUIDE TO THE ANTIQUITIES OF UPPER EGYPT

Designed as a guide for visitors to the Egyptian monuments from Abydos to the Sudan frontier, this book contains a wealth of archaeological information, as well as practical advice for those who plan to visit the sites described. The book's contents are arranged usefully, by location, and are illustrated with informative diagrams and maps.

THE KEGAN PAUL LIBRARY OF ANCIENT EGYPT

The Amarna Age • *James Baikie*
Ancient Egypt the Light of the World • *Gerald Massey*
Ancient Egyptian Literature • *Adolf Erman*
Ancient Egyptian Scarabs and Cylinder Seals • *Percy Newberry*
Arts and Crafts of Ancient Egypt • *W. M. Flinders Petrie*
Burial Customs of the Ancient Egyptians • *John Garstang*
The Cat in Ancient Egypt • *N. Langton and B. Langton*
A Century of Excavation in the Land of the Pharaohs • *James Baikie*
Egyptian Art • Gaston Maspero
Egyptian Mummies • *G. E. Smith and Warren R. Dawson*
Egyptian Papyri and Papyrus-Hunting • *James Baikie*
Egyptian Temples • *Margaret Murray*
Everyday Life in Ancient Egypt and Assyria • *Gaston Maspero*
First Steps in Egyptian • *E.A. Wallis Budge*
From Fetish to God in Ancient Egypt • *E. A. Wallis Budge*
The Gods of the Egyptians • *E. A. Wallis Budge*
A Guide to the Antiquities of Upper Egypt • *Arthur E. P. Weigall*
Index of Names and Titles of the Old Kingdom • *Margaret A. Murray*
The Lost Pharaohs • *Leonard Cottrell*
Luxor and Its Temples • *A. M. Blackman*
The Mechanical Triumphs of the Ancient Egyptians • *F. M. Barber*
Notes for the Nile • *Hardwicke D. Rawnsley*
Notes for Travellers in Egypt • *E. A. Wallis Budge*
Osiris • *E. A. Wallis Budge*
Pharaohs, Fellahs and Explorers • *Amelia B. Edwards*
A Popular Account of the Ancient Egyptians • *J. Gardner Wilkinson*
The Pyramids and Temples of Gizeh • *W.M. Flinders Petrie*
Researches in Sinai • *W. M. F. Petrie*
In Search of the Woman Pharaoh Hatshepsu*t* • *H.E. Winlock*
Seventy Years in Archaeology • *W. M. F. Petrie*
Travels in the Upper Egyptian Deserts • *Arthur E. P. Weigall*
Tutankhamen and the Discovery of His Tomb • *G. Elliot Smith*

A GUIDE TO THE ANTIQUITIES OF UPPER EGYPT

From Abydos to the Sudan Frontier

ARTHUR E. P. WEIGALL

Routledge
Taylor & Francis Group
LONDON AND NEW YORK

First published in 2004 by
Kegan Paul Limited

Published 2016 by Routledge
2 Park Square, Milton Park, Abingdon, Oxfordshire OX14 4RN
711 Third Avenue, New York, NY 10017

First issued in paperback 2016

Routledge is an imprint of the Taylor and Francis Group, an informa business

© Taylor and Francis, 2004

Distributed by:
Extenza-Turpin Distribution
Stratton Business Park
Pegasus Drive
Biggleswade
SG18 8QB
United Kingdom

All Rights reserved. No part of this book may be reprinted or reproduced or utilised in any form or by any electric, mechanical or other means, now known or hereafter invented, including photocopying or recording, or in any information storage or retrieval system, without permission in writing from the publishers.

British Library Cataloguing in Publication Data
A catalogue record for this book is available from the British Library.

Library of Congress Cataloging-in-Publication Data
Applied for.

ISBN 13: 978-1-138-97557-6 (pbk)
ISBN 13: 978-0-7103-1002-6 (hbk)

TO

JAMES HENRY BREASTED
PH.D., ETC.

PROFESSOR OF EGYPTOLOGY
AND ORIENTAL HISTORY IN THE UNIVERSITY
OF CHICAGO

THIS BOOK IS DEDICATED

PREFACE

THIS volume has been prepared for the use of visitors to the monuments of Upper Egypt, that is to say, all those situated between Balianeh, the southernmost town of Middle Egypt, and Adendân, the last Egyptian village on this side of the Sudan frontier. The majority of visitors, after leaving Cairo and its neighbourhood, do not make more than one or two excursions in Middle Egypt; and the fact that the present writer has not the opportunity to describe the ancient sites between Cairo and Balianeh, will not be found greatly to lessen the scope of the book.

The only claim which is made for this Guide is that each chapter has been written actually in, or in a few cases a stone's throw away from, the temples or tombs therein described. The information supplied is derived from careful and prolonged personal observation and thought, checked and augmented by the study of the handful of pertinent books which alone could be carried; and there is no antiquity or ancient site, however small, here recorded which has not been personally seen and examined.

The object of the Guide being alone the describing of the ancient remains and the explaining of their purpose, no other information has been given, except a few hints as to the best methods of visiting the various sites.

A. E. P. W.

Luxor, 1909

CONTENTS

CHAP.		PAGE
I.	ABYDOS	1
II.	HOU AND KASR ES SAYÀD—DENDEREH	26
III.	KOPTOS—OMBOS—KUS—SHENHÙR—MEDA-MÙT	47
IV.	THEBES	60
V.	THE TEMPLE OF LUXOR	70
VI.	THE TEMPLES OF KARNAK	84
VII.	MORTUARY CHAPELS OF THE NOBLES	114
VIII.	THE TOMBS OF THE KINGS	184
IX.	THE MORTUARY TEMPLES OF THE KINGS OF DYNASTIES XVIII TO XX	229
X.	THE TWO MORTUARY TEMPLES OF DÊR EL BAHRI	261
XI.	DÊR EL MEDINEH—THE TOMBS OF THE QUEENS—THE PALACE OF AMENHOTEP, KASR EL AGUZ, AND OTHER ANCIENT SITES	276

CHAP.		PAGE
XII.	From Thebes to Esneh on the West Bank: Arment, Rizakát, Gebelên, Asfun—From Thebes to Esneh on the East Bank—Tûd, Dababiyeh—The Temple and Cemeteries of Esneh—From Esneh to El Kâb on the East and West Banks.	293
XIII.	The History of El Kâb (Eileithyiapolis) and Kôm el Ahmar (Hieraconpolis)—The Ruins at Kôm el Ahmar and at El Kâb—From El Kâb to Edfu	307
XIV.	The Temple of Edfu.	330
XV.	The Cemeteries of Edfu—Edfu to Gebel Silsileh on the West Bank—Hasiyeh—Shutt er Rigâl—The Temple of Redesiyeh—Edfu to Gebel Silsileh on the East Bank—Bueb	347
XVI.	Gebel Silsileh, West Bank—Gebel Silsileh, East Bank—From Gebel Silsileh to Kôm Ombo	356
XVII.	The Temple of Kôm Ombo—From Kôm Ombo to Aswân	374
XVIII.	The History of Aswân and Elephantine	391
XIX.	The Temple of Aswân—The Granite Quarries—The Rock Inscriptions and other Antiquities on the East Bank	

CONTENTS

CHAP.		PAGE
	OF THE RIVER—THE ISLAND OF ELEPHANTINE—THE ISLAND OF SEHEL	404
XX.	THE TOMBS OF THE PRINCES OF ELEPHANTINE—THE MONASTERY OF ST. SIMEON—OTHER TOMBS AND ROCK INSCRIPTIONS ON THE WEST BANK—THE NUBIAN HIGHROAD	423
XXI.	THE HISTORY OF LOWER NUBIA	440
XXII.	FROM SEHEL TO PHILÆ	464
XXIII.	FROM PHILÆ TO KALÁBSHEH	490
XXIV.	FROM KALÁBSHEH TO MAHÁRAKA	511
XXV.	FROM MAHÁRAKA TO KASR IBRÎM	532
XXVI.	KASR IBRÎM — ABU SIMBEL — FROM ABU SIMBEL TO ADENDÂN	557
	INDEX	583

LIST OF MAPS AND PLANS

Map of Upper Egypt . . . . . . *Frontispiece*	
	PAGE
The Temple of Sety I. at Abydos	11
The Temple of Rameses II. at Abydos	21
The Temple of Dendereh	37
The Temple of Luxor	73
General Plan of the Temples of Karnak	85
The Temple of Khonsu, Karnak	89
The Great Temple of Amen-Ra, Karnak . . .	93
The Mortuary Chapel of Rekhmara	116
The Mortuary Chapel of Sennefer	118
The Mortuary Chapel of Sumnut	120
The Mortuary Chapel of a Chief Archer . . .	122
The Mortuary Chapel of Amenneb	122
The Mortuary Chapel of an Unknown Official . .	123
The Mortuary Chapel of Pehsukher	124
The Mortuary Chapel of Ramenkheper-senb . .	125
The Mortuary Chapel of Amenemheb	127
The Mortuary Chapel of Amunezeh	130
The Mortuary Chapel of Amenemhat	132
The Mortuary Chapel of Anena	135
The Mortuary Chapel of Tehutinefer	138
The Mortuary Chapel of Menkheper	139
The Mortuary Chapel of Horemheb	141
The Mortuary Chapel of Thenuna	143

xiv ANTIQUITIES OF UPPER EGYPT

	PAGE
The Mortuary Chapel of Amenhotepsase	144
The Mortuary Chapel of Zenuni	147
The Mortuary Chapel of Ra	148
The Mortuary Chapel of Menna	150
The Mortuary Chapel of Aimadua	153
The Mortuary Chapel of Antefaker	155
The Mortuary Chapel of Khaemhat	157
The Mortuary Chapel of Userhat	159
The Mortuary Chapel of Rames	161
The Mortuary Chapel of Amenemhat	166
The Mortuary Chapel of Nekht	167
The Mortuary Chapel of Userhat	169
The Mortuary Chapel of Huy	171
The Mortuary Chapel of Aba	174
The Mortuary Chapel of Amenmes	177
The Mortuary Chapel of Bak	178
The Mortuary Chapel of Amenneb	179
The Mortuary Chapel of Panehesi	181
Sketch Map of the Valley of the Tombs of the Kings	187
The Tomb of Rameses IV.	197
The Tomb of Rameses X.	200
The Tomb of Merenptah	203
The Tomb of Rameses V. and Rameses VI.	205
The Tomb of Rameses III.	207
The Tomb of Tausert and Setnekht	210
The Tomb of Sety I.	214
The Mortuary Temple of Amenhotep Ist and Thothmes I., and Pavilion of Rameses III. at Medinet Habu	233
The Great Mortuary Temple of Rameses III. at Medinet Habu	237
The Mortuary Temple of Sety I.	257
The Temple of Dêr el Bahri	267

LIST OF MAPS AND PLANS

	PAGE
Plan of Dêr el Medineh .	278
The Tomb of Nefertari .	282
The Tomb of Amenherkhepeshf	285
The Tomb of Khaemuast	289
The Temple of Edfu	337
The Temple of Kôm Ombo .	381
Plan of the Island of Philæ .	469
Temple of Kalâbsheh	506
The Temple of Dendûr .	515
The Temple of Dakkeh .	521
Sketch Plan of Amâda Temple	537
The Temple of Dêrr	545
The Great Temple of Abu Simbel .	567
Abahûdeh Temple .	579

A CHRONOLOGICAL TABLE OF THE PHARAOHS OF EGYPT

(*The dates here given are those of Professor Breasted*)

DYNASTY O

At this period Egypt was divided into the two kingdoms of the Upper and Lower country. The names of several of the Kings of the Delta are known, and those of two or three of the Upper Egyptian kings have been found. The latter dynasty seems to have ended with :

Selk .	B.C. 3450
Narmer .	B.C. 3425

DYNASTY I

Narmer and his son (?) Mena united the two kingdoms, and their successors reigned over Upper and Lower Egypt, their capital being Memphis.

1. Mena . . . . B.C. 3400
   Seven other kings.

DYNASTY II

Nine kings who reigned at Memphis. . B.C. 3200

DYNASTY III

Nine kings who reigned at Memphis	B.C. 3000
3. Zeser .	B.C. 2980
10. Sneferu	B.C. 2900

DYNASTY IV

This was the great age of the pyramid builders of Gizeh.

1. Khufu .	B.C. 2900
3. Khafra	B.C. 2850
4. Menkaura .	B.C. 2825
7. Shepseskaf .	B.C. 2750

DYNASTY V

The kings of this dynasty are said to have been of Heliopolitan origin.

1. Userkaf	.	B.C. 2750
2. Sahura	.	B.C. 2743
3. Neferarkara	.	B.C. 2731
8. Asesa	.	B.C. 2683
9. Unas	.	B.C. 2655

DYNASTY VI

During this dynasty, which ruled at Memphis, the princes of the various provinces of Egypt obtained a degree of power which they had never before possessed ; and the period has a distinctly feudal character.

1. Teta	.	B.C. 2625
2. Userkara	.	B.C. 2600
3. Pepy I.	.	B.C. 2590
4. Merenra I.	.	B.C. 2570
5. Pepy II.	.	B.C. 2565
6. Merenra II.	.	B.C. 2475

DYNASTY VII

Very little is known of this dynasty, which ruled at Memphis.
B.C. 2475

DYNASTY VIII

Very little is known of this dynasty, which also ruled at Memphis . . . . B.C. 2450

DYNASTY IX

This dynasty is also very obscure. The family is said to have been of Herakleopolitan origin . . . B.C. 2445

DYNASTY X

This dynasty, though obscure, is better known than the last. It was also Herakleopolitan . . . . B.C. 2300

A CHRONOLOGICAL TABLE

DYNASTY XI

This is the first Theban dynasty, the ruling family being originally princes of Thebes.

1. Antef I.   ⎫
2. Antef II.   ⎬ B.C. 2160–2110
5. Nebtauira Mentuhotep . . . B.C. 2076–2030
6. Nebhapetra Mentuhotep . . . B.C. 2030–2002
7. Seankhkara Mentuhotep . . . B.C. 2002–2000

DYNASTY XII

Egypt was very prosperous under this second Theban dynasty; and the ruins of many buildings of this period are known.

1. Amenemhat I. . . . . . B.C. 2000–1970
2. Senusert I. . . . . . B.C. 1970–1935
3. Amenemhat II. . . . . . B.C. 1935–1903
4. Senusert II. . . . . . B.C. 1903–1887
5. Senusert III. . . . . . B.C. 1887–1849
6. Amenemhat III. . . . . B.C. 1849–1801
7. Amenemhat IV. . . . . B.C. 1801–1792
8. Sebekneferura . . . . . B.C. 1792–1788

DYNASTY XIII

This dynasty is still rather obscure. It was also Theban.

Sebekhotep II. . . . . ⎫ Between
Neferhotep . . . . . ⎬ B.C. 1788
Sebekhotep III. . . . . ⎪ and
Sebekemsaf. . . . . ⎭ B.C. 1700
Many other kings.

DYNASTY XIV

Very little is known of this dynasty, which is said to be of Xoïte origin . . . . About B.C. 1700

DYNASTIES XV AND XVI

These are the Hyksos, or " Shepherd," dynasties, when Egypt was under the dominion of Asiatics.

Khyan . . . . B.C. 1700
Apepa I. . . . . . . B.C. 1650

DYNASTY XVII

This was the Theban dynasty which revolted against the Hyksos.
3. (?) Sekenenra III. . . . . B.C. 1600
4. (?) Kames . . . . . B.C. 1590

DYNASTY XVIII

Under this Theban dynasty the power of Egypt reached its zenith.
1. Aahmes I. . . . . . B.C. 1580–1557
2. Amenhotep I. . . . . ⎫
3. Thothmes I. . . . . ⎬ B.C. 1557–1501
4. Thothmes II. . . . . ⎫
5. Hatshepsut . . . . ⎬ B.C. 1501–1447
6. Thothmes III. . . . . ⎭
7. Amenhotep II. . . . . B.C. 1447–1420
8. Thothmes IV. . . . . B.C. 1420–1411
9. Amenhotep III. . . . . B.C. 1411–1375
10. Amenhotep IV.: Akhnaton . B.C. 1375–1358
11. Smenkhkara . . . . ⎫
12. Tutankhamen . . . . ⎬ B.C. 1358–1350
13. Ay . . . . . . ⎭

DYNASTY XIX

After the reign of Rameses II. the power of Egypt began to decline. This dynasty was also Theban.
1. Horemheb . . . . . B.C. 1350–1315
2. Rameses I. . . . . . B.C. 1315–1314
3. Sety I. . . . . . B.C. 1313–1292
4. Rameses II. . . . . B.C. 1292–1225
5. Merenptah . . . . . B.C. 1225–1215
6. Amenmeses . . . . B.C. 1215
7. Septah . . . . . B.C. 1215–1209
8. Sety II. . . . . . B.C. 1209–1205

DYNASTY XX

This was the last Theban dynasty. Except for Rameses III. the Pharaohs were nonentities.
1. Setnekht . . . . . B.C. 1200–1198
2. Rameses III. . . . . B.C. 1198–1167
3. Rameses IV. . . . . B.C. 1167–1161
4. Rameses V. . . . . B.C. 1161–1157

A CHRONOLOGICAL TABLE

5. Rameses VI.	⎫
6. Rameses VII.	⎬ B.C. 1157–1142
7. Rameses VIII.	⎭
8. Rameses IX.	B.C. 1142–1123
9. Rameses X.	B.C. 1123–1121
10. Rameses XI.	B.C. 1121–1118
11. Rameses XII.	B.C. 1118–1090

DYNASTY XXI

This dynasty was Tanite. The power of the High Priests of Amen was now at its height.

1. Herhor	⎫ B.C. 1090–1085
2. Nesubanebded	⎭
3. Pasebkhennu I.	B.C. 1085–1067
4. Painezem I.	B.C. 1067–1026
5. Amenemapt	B.C. 1026–976
6. Seamen	B.C. 976–958
7. Pasebkhennu II.	B.C. 958–945

DYNASTY XXII

This dynasty was Bubastite, but some traces of its activities are found in Upper Egypt.

1. Sheshonk I.	B.C. 945–924
3. Takeloth I.	B.C. 895–874
4. Osorkon II.	B.C. 874–853
6. Takeloth II.	B.C. 860–834
Other kings.	

DYNASTY XXIII

This dynasty was Tanite, but it is somewhat obscure.
B.C. 745–718

DYNASTY XXIV

This dynasty, which was Saïte, is of little importance.
B.C. 718–712

DYNASTY XXV

We here have three Ethiopian kings, during whose rule Egypt was invaded by the Assyrians.

1. Shabaka	B.C. 712–700
2. Shabataka	B.C. 700–688
3. Taharka	B.C. 688–663

DYNASTY XXVI

During this dynasty, which was of Saïte origin, there was an attempt to remodel the country on the lines of the Old Kingdom.

1. Psametik I. . . . . B.C. 663–609
2. Necho . . . . B.C. 609–593
3. Psametik II. . . . . . . B.C. 593–588
4. Apries . . . . B.C. 588–569
5. Aahmes II. . . . . . B.C. 569–525
6. Psametik III. . . . . . . B.C. 525

DYNASTY XXVII

During this dynasty Egypt was under the rule of the Persian kings, who were regarded as Pharaohs . . B.C. 525–415

DYNASTY XXVIII

This was a Saïte dynasty of no importance . B.C. 415–399

DYNASTY XXIX

This dynasty was of Mendesian origin . . B.C. 399–378
2. Hakar . . . . . . B.C. 393–380

DYNASTY XXX

This is the last Egyptian dynasty. It was of Sebennyte origin, and attained to some power.

1. Nectanebo I. . . . . . . B.C. 378–361
2. Nectanebo II. . . . . . B.C. 359–342

DYNASTY XXXI

This marks the second dominion of the Persians over Egypt.
B.C. 342–332

DYNASTY XXXII

During this period Alexander the Great, Philip Arrhidæos, and Alexander II. ruled over Egypt as Pharaohs . B.C. 332–305

A CHRONOLOGICAL TABLE

DYNASTY XXXIII

This is the well-known Ptolemaic period, when Egypt once more became a nation of some power.

1. Ptolemy I., Soter I. . . . . B.C. 304–283
2. Ptolemy II., Philadelphus . . . B.C. 283–246
3. Ptolemy III., Euergetes I. . . . B.C. 246–222
4. Ptolemy IV., Philopator. . . . B.C. 221–205
5. Ptolemy V., Epiphanes . . . . B.C. 205–181
6. Ptolemy VI., Philometor
7. Ptolemy VII., Eupator . . . . } B.C. 181–170
8. Ptolemy VIII. . . . .
9. Ptolemy IX., Euergetes II. . . } B.C. 170–116
10. Ptolemy X., Soter II. Lathyrus . . B.C. 117–106
11. Ptolemy XI., Alexander I. . . . B.C. 106–87
12. Ptolemy XII., Alexander II. . . . B.C. 87–80
13. Ptolemy XIII., Neos Dionysos . . B.C. 80–51
14. Ptolemy XIV. . . . . .
15. Ptolemy XV. . . . . . } B.C. 51–23
16. Ptolemy XVI., Cæsarion . . .

DYNASTY XXXIV

Egypt was ruled by the Emperors of Rome, each of whom became Pharaoh . . . . . B.C. 30–A.D. 394

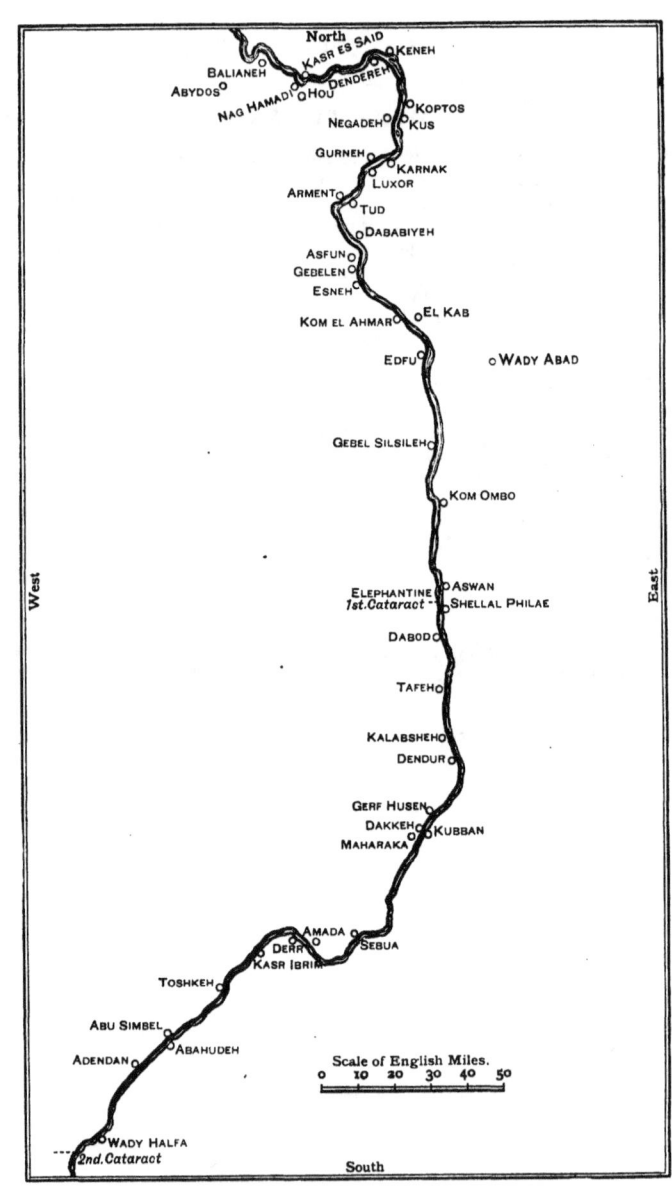

MAP OF UPPER EGYPT

A GUIDE TO THE ANTIQUITIES OF UPPER EGYPT

CHAPTER I

ABYDOS

THE temple of Sety Ist at Abydos is of such beauty and interest that it should be visited by all those who are able to undertake the somewhat tiring excursion. Most of the tourist-steamers stop at Balianeh, the nearest town on the river, sufficient time to allow of a visit being made to Abydos, which lies some six or seven miles west of the Nile. Good donkeys are to be obtained at Balianeh, and there are also one or two carriages for hire. The excursion may be made by train from Luxor with comparative ease. One leaves Luxor early, reaching Balianeh at about mid-morning, and one returns by the train which passes Balianeh about 8 P.M., arriving at Luxor just before midnight.

Methods of visiting Abydos.

THE HISTORY OF ABYDOS

Near the site of the later Abydos there stood at the dawn of history a city named This or Thinis,[1] in which resided the powerful chieftains who ruled the land for many miles to the north and south. Several of these chieftains having reigned in succession, there arose a ruler named *Selk*, "the Scorpion," who conquered all the country as far south as Edfu, or Gebel Silsileh, and perhaps as far north as Assiut. He built for himself a southern capital at Kôm el Ahmar (p. 307), where he was

[1] The city of Thinis is sometimes thought to be situated farther to the north, and not on the site of Abydos; but this is highly improbable.

acknowledged by the local title of "Hawk-Chieftain," and assumed the name of Ka. He continued to reside at Thinis also, and when he died he was buried in the western desert behind Abydos. His successor, Narmer, extended his conquests towards the north, and presently came into collision with the kings of Lower Egypt, who reigned at Buto, not far from the sea. Narmer seems to have forced a marriage between the heiress of that kingdom and himself; and in the person of the son of this union, Mena, Upper and Lower Egypt were united. King Mena for political reasons was obliged to found for himself another capital, which he named Memphis, and placed at the point where the Nile valley opens into the wide plain of the Delta. He was, however, crowned at Kôm el Ahmar, and he still resided for part of the year at Thinis, where it is probable that he was buried. The fragment of a vase bearing his name was found amongst the ruins of the latter city.

These ruins are situated in that part of the site known as the Temenos or Enclosure of Osiris—an open space at the north-west of the modern village of El Arâbah el Madfûneh. Here there was a small mud-brick temple, dedicated to the jackal god Wepwat, "the Opener of the Ways," who was the primitive deity of the district. The royal residence was probably situated in the desert, a short distance back from the town; and still farther westward there was the royal burying-ground. The objects found in the town show that already a high state of civilisation had been arrived at, and an ivory statuette of a king of this period found here is executed with a degree of artistic skill never surpassed at any time in Egyptian history.

The Ist and IInd dynasties.

As each of the kings of the Ist dynasty died he was buried here at Thinis, which was now a city of some size. Of King Zet, the third Pharaoh[1] of the dynasty, part of a slate-stone bowl has been found in the town; while many other objects undoubtedly dating from this period have come to light. Two large fortresses were now erected in the desert, and here the troops of the province were quartered. In the IInd dynasty, Kings Khasekhemui and Perabsen resided at Thinis, and clay sealings bearing their names have been found in the fortress, known as the Shunet es Zebîb, and in the town. The Pharaohs of this dynasty were still buried here with their ancestors, although they had now come to regard Memphis as their home.

[1] The word *Pharaoh* was the title of the Egyptian kings, just as *Mikado* is the title of the Japanese emperors, or *Khedive* that of the modern rulers of Egypt.

ABYDOS 3

In the IIIrd dynasty the custom of burying the Pharaohs here ceased, though the place had now gained such fame as a royal necropolis that it had become the chief seat of the priesthood of the dead. With the primitive god Wepwat, the god Khentamenta, "the Chieftain [1] of the Underworld," was now worshipped ; and in the IVth dynasty a temple of some size was erected in their honour. Here King Khufu left a small ivory statuette of himself, which was recently found ; while of King Menkaura a sealing has been unearthed.

<small>The IIIrd and IVth dynasties.</small>

In Lower Egypt, and especially at Memphis at this time, the god Osiris was held in high honour, and traditions seem to have been already in circulation, relating how this deity once ruled as king of Egypt, and taught the arts of civilisation to his subjects. The first king of Egypt was naturally the greatest of the inhabitants of the Underworld, and thus he came to be identified with Khentamenta of Thinis. Tradition stated that Osiris had been murdered, and that his body had been torn into many fragments ; and since at Thinis the early and now half-forgotten kings of Egypt had been buried, and the city had become famous for its necropolis, it is not surprising that gradually there grew up the belief that the mutilated body of Osiris himself had been interred here. This god now took his place beside Wepwat and Khentamenta in the affections of the people of Thinis. Great honour was paid, in consequence, to the tombs of the archaic kings, for one of them sheltered the body of Osiris ; and soon the tomb of King Zer of the Ist dynasty came to be regarded as the actual divine sepulchre, for what reason we do not know. Meanwhile, however, other cities were also making claim to the possession of the body of Osiris ; and although this fact never wholly banished the belief of the Thinites that the corpse of their god lay here, it became more generally acknowledged that the *head* only of Osiris was buried in this necropolis. One now begins to hear of another deity also, Anhur, who seems to have been one of the early gods of Thinis ; but as yet his power does not seem to have been great.

<small>The god Osiris.</small>

In the Vth dynasty the head of Osiris came to be the recognised emblem of the district, and while the site of the old city retained its name of Thinis, the neighbourhood was now known as *Abdu*, "The Mound of the Osiris-head Emblem." This word *Abdu*, or per-

<small>The Vth and VIth dynasties.</small>

---

[1] Literally, "First of the West," the Underworld being in the western hills.

4   ANTIQUITIES OF UPPER EGYPT

haps *Abidu*, was altered in Greek times to Abydos, in memory of the Abydos in Greece. The province, however, was still named after Thinis. The name of King Userkaf of the Vth dynasty was found on a sealing in the town ; of Neferarkara, another king of this dynasty, a decree has been found allowing the priests to be exempt from forced labour; there is a sealing inscribed with the name of King Shepseskaf; an alabaster vase bearing the name of Userenra was also discovered ; while of about this date there is an inscription referring to a " Prince of Abdu," which is the earliest instance of the use of this name. A decree dating from the reign of Teta of the VIth dynasty was found here ; King Pepy Ist seems to have built a temple on the site of the early shrine of Wepwat; King Merenra restored or added to this temple ; and of Pepy IInd an inscribed vase has been unearthed, and a statue is referred to in an inscription. Nothing is heard of Thinis or Abydos during the obscure period of the VIIth–Xth dynasties ; but in the XIth dynasty we find the kings carrying on extensive building operations here. A king of Thebes, named Nubkheperra Antef, states that he extended his dominions as far north as the northern frontier of the Thinite nome, conquering the troops of a Lower Egyptian king with whom he was contesting the Egyptian throne. This King Antef undertook large building works here, dedicating them to Anhur, Lord of Thinis, and also left a stele in the temple. King Sankhkara Menthuhotep built or repaired a temple ; and King Nebharpetra Menthuhotep also built here. Senusert Ist of the XIIth dynasty swept away a large part of the early temple, and erected a much larger edifice in its place. The work was carried out by a certain Menthuhotep, who says, " I conducted the work in the temple, I built the god's house, dug the sacred lake, and built the well." He also built the sacred barge of the god, erected altars adorned with lapis lazuli, bronze, electrum, silver, and copper, and made ornaments of malachite and costly stone. This temple seems to have been dedicated either to Osiris of Abydos or to Anhur, who had now become a deity of much importance in Thinis ; for elsewhere one reads that Senusert Ist erected temples to these two gods, and placed therein costly gold, silver, copper, and bronze utensils. During this reign also we read of an official who visited Abydos on his way to collect recruits for the army in the oasis of El Khârgeh, to which a good road runs from Abydos.

The XIth and XIIth dynasties.

Senusert IIIrd.

Under the great King Senusert IIIrd extensive works were carried on at Abydos. This king, desiring to be buried beside the archaic kings of Egypt and their chief Osiris, and yet feeling it incumbent upon him to erect a pyramid at Memphis, resolved to be interred at both places. He therefore constructed a huge rock-cut tomb for himself at Abydos, and here it is probable that he was buried for a short space of time, his body afterwards being removed to his northern pyramid. The officials whom he sent to superintend the temple works have left some records of themselves. We read of one who erected a statue of the king. Another tells us how he was sent to adorn the secret place of Osiris with gold obtained in the king's Nubian wars. A portable shrine of gold, silver, lapis lazuli, *carob*-wood, *meru*-wood, and other costly materials was made; and the official in charge states that he also decked the statue of Osiris with electrum, malachite, lapis lazuli, and every precious stone.

At this time the god Osiris had become the chief deity of Abydos, and the ceremonies in connection with his worship were of an elaborate nature. In the reign of Senusert IIIrd we read of a kind of religious drama which was here enacted, and which purposed to relate the story of the conflict between Osiris and his enemies. The first ceremony was "The Going Forth of Wepwat when he proceeds to Champion his Father"; and the priests then repelled the attacks of the enemies upon the sacred barque. Then came the feast called "The Great Going Forth," when the sacred barque was carried to the supposed tomb of Osiris in the western desert. Here a mimic battle was fought, and very possibly "the slaying of the enemies" was represented by actual human sacrifices. The sacred barque was then carried around the upper desert, was conveyed to the east bank of the river, and finally was brought back to the temple. The official in charge of this ceremony then tells us how he followed the statue of the god into his house, "to tend him when he resumed his seat." In this drama we catch a glimpse of the prehistoric history of Egypt, for in the partisans of Osiris one must see an early conquering tribe who defeated the aboriginal races. In the temples of Hieraconpolis (Kôm el Ahmar) and Edfu one again meets with traces of this tradition, which will be discussed in their correct place.

The worship of Osiris.

King Amenemhat IIIrd of the XIIth dynasty sent an official to Abydos to assist at some such festival as the above, and this personage also conducted work on the sacred barge, "fashioning its colours"; and, by virtue of his office as Master of Secret Things, he clothed the statue of the god with its ceremonial robes. In the XIIIth dynasty Sebekhotep IIIrd built onto the temple of

The XIIth and XIIIth dynasties.

Osiris, and also restored the tomb of Senusert IIIrd. In the second year of Neferhotep the king states that, finding Abydos in ruins, he searched in the library of Heliopolis, and there found documents relating to the Osiris temple, from which he was able to reconstruct the ceremonies and re-establish the priesthood of Abydos. When his orders had been carried out he visited Abydos in state, sailing up the canal which connected the town with the Nile. In his fourth year he issued a decree regulating the boundaries of the necropolis, and ordering all trespassers to be branded. The name Abdu or Abydos seems now to have become the general name for the double city of Thinis and Abydos, though in speaking particularly of one or the other part of the city their individual names were used. King Sebekemsaf built onto the temple; an otherwise unknown sovereign named Penthen left his name here; and under King Khenzer[1] a certain Amenysenb cleansed the temple of Senusert Ist, renewed the painting of the reliefs and inscriptions, and rebuilt the altars of the god with cedar-wood.

The XVIIIth dynasty.

Aahmes Ist, the first king of the XVIIIth dynasty, restored the ruined temples of Abydos, and also erected a pyramid here for himself, in order that he might be buried temporarily beside his ancestors before being interred in Thebes. He also constructed a mortuary chapel near this pyramid for his grandmother Tetashera. The next king, Amenhotep Ist, built a temple in honour of his father Aahmes. Thothmes Ist, the succeeding Pharaoh, ordered a barque to be built for Osiris, made of cedar, the bow and stern being of electrum. A portable barque was also made, being decorated with gold, silver, black copper, lapis lazuli, and other precious stones; and he ordered statues to be erected, their standards being of electrum. He further presented the temple with offering tables, sistrums, necklaces, censers, and dishes. The name of Thothmes IInd is found in the temple together with that of Thothmes IIIrd.

Thothmes IIIrd.

This latter king took much interest in Abydos, and built largely onto the ancient temples, setting up also the statues of Senusert IIIrd, his ancestor. The high priest of Osiris at this time, named Nebuana, states that he conducted many works in the temple of Osiris, using gold, silver, malachite, lapis lazuli, and "every splendid and costly stone" in the decorations. "I was summoned," he writes, speaking of himself, "to the god's golden house, and my place was amongst his princes. My feet strode in

[1] Sometimes called Nezerra.

the splendid place; I was anointed with the finest ointment; and a wreath was around my throat." The yearly tax which had to be paid into the treasury at this time by the four chief officials of Abydos consisted of three *debens*[1] of gold, a quantity of linen, honey, and grain, and some oxen. The tax of Thinis was six debens of gold and half a deben of silver, together with bread, grain, honey, and cattle in vastly larger quantities than those demanded from Abydos. For example, 62 sacks of grain were asked of Thinis and only 3 sacks of Abydos; 17 head of cattle were asked of Thinis and about 4 or 5 of Abydos; while 20 sacks of unknown contents were demanded from Thinis and none from Abydos. Thus it is seen that still in the XVIIIth dynasty the city of Thinis was very wealthy, and was the actual, as well as the nominal, capital of the province. In this reign we read of a prince of this Thinite province, named Antef, who controlled the entire oasis region of the western desert; and the products of these oases must have been a source of considerable wealth. At this period, then, we are to imagine the administration of the province as being conducted from within the walls of the enclosed city of Thinis, at the north-west end of the modern village; and here we may picture the rich temples rising amidst the houses, their altars blazing with gold, and their halls ringing with the noise of sistrums and the sound of the chants of Osiris. To the south of this enclosure, and possessing the tombs of the archaic kings in the desert, was the city of Abdu or Abydos, and perhaps it already was enriched with temples dedicated to Osiris and Khentamenta, besides those dedicated to these gods within the enclosure of Thinis. Another deity had now been joined to the company of gods worshipped in Thinis and Abydos. This was Unnefer, who was identified with Osiris, and who afterwards came to be one of the greatest gods of Egypt.

King Thothmes IVth appears to have taken great interest in Abydos. He presented 1200 *stat* of land to the temple, and regulated the supply of cattle, poultry, &c., for its altars. He also made endowments for the tomb of Aahmes Ist. Amenhotep IIIrd erected a large temple in Thinis; but this was abandoned during the heretical period which followed on the death of this king. Of Akhnaton a scarab was found in the town. *The end of the XVIIIth dynasty.*

King Rameses Ist of the XIXth dynasty, and King Sety Ist restored some of the buildings within the Thinis enclosure; but the energies of the latter were mainly given to the erection of his *The XIXth dynasty.*

[1] A *deben* of gold weighed about 100 grammes.

splendid temple in Abydos proper, dedicated to Osiris, Isis, and Horus, and also to other gods not closely connected with the district. It is this temple which forms the main objective of the modern visits to Abydos, and it may be said to be perhaps the most beautiful temple in Egypt. Here the mysteries of Osiris were performed, and the souls of the dead kings were worshipped. Rameses IInd built another temple near that of Sety Ist, and he also restored some of the ancient buildings. His activity here was due to the fact that when he visited Abydos in his first year, he had found the funds of his father's temple misappropriated, and parts of it still unfinished. With the assistance of his vizir, Parahotep, and the high priest of Osiris, named Unnefer, he soon placed matters here upon a sound basis; and during his reign Abydos may be said to have reached the height of its power and wealth. The high priest Unnefer was a personage of great importance at Abydos, and came of a family of high sacerdotal dignitaries. His father was high priest of Osiris before him; his step-father and half-brother were in turn high priest of Anhur, at Thinis; while his grandfather seems to have been a high priest of Amen. Numerous statues and steles inscribed with his name have been found at Abydos, where he seems to have ruled in undisputed power. A certain interest attaches to his half-brother, who was named Minmes; for, besides the office of high priest of Anhur here, he held the position of chief ritual-priest, or in other words chief magician, of the king. As Rameses IInd is generally regarded as the Pharaoh of the oppression, this chief magician will be a personage of some interest to Biblical students.

The worship of Osiris.

At the back of the temple of Sety Ist, King Merenptah constructed some underground chambers, in the darkness of which the mysteries of Osiris were performed; and perhaps human sacrifices were here made. By this time Osiris had become one of the most important deities of Egypt, and Abydos was regarded as the chief seat of his worship. We now hear little more of the primitive god Wepwat; and the other deities, Khentamenta and Unnefer, are at this time merely names of Osiris. The traditions relating to him have so far developed that his enemies are now designated as the worshippers of the god Set; his wife is the goddess Isis; and his son, who avenged his murder, is the god Horus. The power of Osiris covered a wide province in the religion of Egypt. He was a sun-god, a moon-god, a god of vegetation, a god of the Nile, and, above all, the great god of the Dead and of the Underworld. Every person who died in the

ABYDOS 9

faith, so to speak, was identified with Osiris; and one spoke of "Osiris" So-and-so in the same way that nowadays we would use the words "the late."

The Chancellor Bey, on behalf of King Septah of the XXth dynasty, left his name at Abydos. King Rameses IIIrd built a temple in Thinis for the god Anhur, and seems to have erected a palace for himself in or near it. He speaks of having built a large enclosing wall also, with ramps and towers, and with doors of cedar fitted onto doorways of stone. This is perhaps the great wall which still rises to a great height around the ruins of Thinis. Rameses IVth added to this temple; and he also erected a stele on which is inscribed a prayer to Osiris that he may grant a long reign to the king. Another Pharaoh of the name of Rameses, sometimes called Rameses VIIth, also erected a stele here, praying in very humble terms, and in beautiful language, that his life may be spared—a prayer, however, which was of no avail. King Paynezem IInd of the XXIst dynasty is stated to have sent a statue of a great Libyan chieftain named Namlot to be erected at Abydos. <small>The XXth and XXIst dynasties.</small>

Inscriptions of Kings Takeloth Ist and IInd have been found in the Thinite enclosure. During the reign of Taharka the vizir Menthuemhat visited the royal tombs at Abydos, and inscribed his name on the rocks near by. King Haabra of the XXVIth dynasty undertook some building works here, as did his successor Aahmes IInd. The latter king sent an official named Pefnefdeneit to superintend the work, and this personage records that he restored the ruins of earlier temples, re-established the priestly revenues, planted arbours of date palms, and made vineyards. These vineyards he supplied with foreign slaves, and they then yielded 30 *hin* of wine per day. He confiscated the property of the local prince, who apparently had been held responsible for the disorder which obtained; and he applied this income to meet the burial dues of the necropolis, in order that all persons might be freely interred in the holy ground. He also states that he arranged and conducted a performance of the Osiris drama, which has been mentioned above. Kings Nectanebo Ist and IInd also turned their attention to Abydos, and the former Pharaoh erected a temple of some size. <small>The XXIInd to XXXth dynasties.</small>

The Ptolemies do not seem to have given much attention to Abydos, and the Romans also omitted to build here. This must have been due to the decline of the power of Osiris at Abydos, or rather to the change of the seat of his worship to Philæ. Very <small>The later period.</small>

little more is heard of the once wealthy city. The temples fell into ruins, and the unchecked town rose over them. The graves in the necropolis were looted for the gold which they contained, and the once holy tombs of the archaic kings were given over to the thieves. Even the god Osiris, who in Ptolemaic times had become the hero of many complicated legends, gradually lost favour in late Roman days, and finally became a demon of minor but hostile power.

The Temple of Sety Ist

When Sety Ist, the second king of a new dynasty, came to the throne, he must have realised that he could offer no better proof of the legitimacy of his descent from the ancient Pharaohs of Egypt than by displaying an active regard for their souls' welfare. In building this temple at Abydos, dedicated to the main gods of Egypt, and especially to Osiris, he caused the worship and ceremonies to centre around the paramount fact of his descent from the archaic kings, and of these kings' collective identity with Osiris. Sety Ist selected a stretch of desert land behind the town of Abydos for the site of his temple, about a mile east of the city of Thinis. If the reader will look at the plan of the building he will see that, unlike all other Egyptian temples, this building has a wing or annex on its east side; and all those who have studied the building have come to the conclusion that the chambers forming this wing were originally intended to be built onto the south end of the axial line, but that for some unknown reason they were finally placed at the side. Mariette stated that the builders had struck rock at this point, and had had to extend their work eastward to avoid it; but recent excavations behind the temple have shown that there is no such rock here, and indeed there is none within a mile of the spot. These recent excavations have disclosed a number of subterranean chambers and passages built at a later date in more or less the axial line, and these are evidently the buildings referred to by Strabo, who states that they led down to a spring which, rising here in the sand, discharged itself into a small channel, and so finally joined the Nile. The reason, then, for the turning aside of the back rooms of the temple is surely obvious: the builders found that they were approaching moist, unstable sand, upon which the foundations could never rest secure, and they were obliged to abandon all hope of building in this direction. Owing to the delay thus caused, the temple was many years in process of

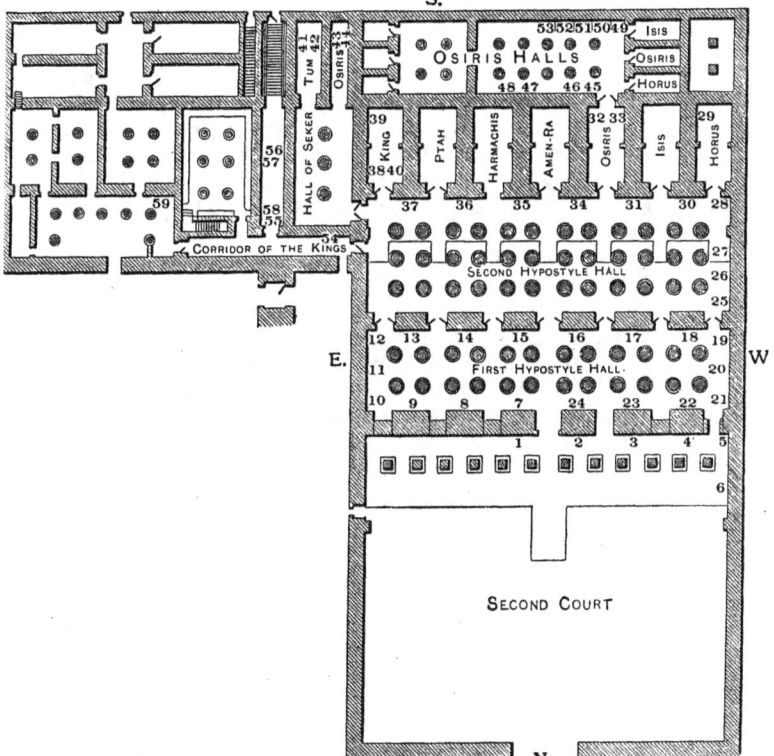

THE TEMPLE OF SETY I. AT ABYDOS

building, and was still unfinished at the death of Sety. It was completed, however, by Rameses IInd, his son, who, in spite of his many protestations of filial piety, placed his own name and figure as conspicuously as possible on all the walls, and even renamed the building after himself.

ANTIQUITIES OF UPPER EGYPT

The fore-court and second court.

The Pylons and Forecourt of the temple are still buried under the houses of the village, and the visitor first enters the open Second Court, of which only the southern end is now preserved. At this end there is a raised terrace, approached by a gently graded stairway; and on this terrace rise the stumps of twelve square pillars, built, like the temple, of limestone, but having sandstone bases. These pillars supported a roof which has now disappeared, and thus a kind of portico or pronaos was formed along the front of the main building. The reliefs on the pillars show Rameses IInd embraced by the principal gods of Egypt. On the outer walls of the main temple there is at the east end a long inscription which tells how Rameses IInd came to Abydos, and, finding the temple unfinished, decided to continue the building. Farther along (1) one sees a large figure of the king offering the symbol of Truth to Osiris, Isis, and his father Sety Ist. Next (2) there are the figures of Horus, Isis, and Sety Ist, after which (3) Rameses is shown standing beside a sacred tree, on the leaves of which Ptah writes his name, while Thoth records the number of his years. He is presented at the same time with the royal crook and flail by Harmachis, behind whom Osiris stands. Rameses is next (4) led forward by Horus(?) and Khnum, preceded by the standards of the Jackal which represents Wepwat of the south, and that of the uninterpreted emblem of Thebes. The king then (5) addresses Osiris; and on the west wall (6) there is a damaged scene in which he is shown slaughtering Asiatic prisoners before Amen-Ra.

The first Hypostyle Hall.

One now enters the first Hypostyle Hall, the roof of which is supported by two rows of twelve columns. To obtain some idea of the magnificence of this hall, the visitor should look at it from the extreme east or west end, allowing the eye to travel down the whole length of the rows of columns. In the original plan this hall was entered from the Second Court through seven doorways, but all but two were later blocked up by Rameses IInd. Seven corresponding doors lead from this hall into the second Hypostyle Hall, from which again seven shrines open. These shrines from east to west are dedicated to Sety Ist, Ptah, Harmachis, Amen-Ra, Osiris, Mut, and Horus; and thus the two Hypostyle halls are also divided into seven sections, each dedicated respectively to one of these gods. The visitor, however, will find it best to examine all the main reliefs in this first Hypostyle Hall without regard to these divisions. Commencing from the first scene on the east side of the main entrance (7) one sees Rameses between

ABYDOS 13

Amen-Ra and Tum of On, who throw over him the signs of "life" and "stability." Above this the king is shown offering vases before a ram-headed form of Amen-Ra. Next (8) Rameses holds a religious standard before the shrine of Ptah; and above this scene he kneels upon the symbol of the union of Upper and Lower Egypt, while the stems of the papyrus and lotus plants, emblematic of the two countries, are interlaced by Wepwat and Horus(?). Rameses is then (9) shown worshipping Min, behind whom are the mystical insignia of his cult; and above this the king draws by a rope the sacred barque of Seker, which rests upon a sledge. On the east wall (10) Rameses is purified with the water of life by Thoth and Horus; and above this he performs a ceremonial dance[1] before a seated figure of Ptah, behind whom stands the lion-headed consort of that god, Sekhmet. Next (11) he is suckled by Hathor of *Per-Kau*, Hathor of Alabastronpolis, Hathor of Diospolis Parva, and Hathor of Dendereh; and he is dandled by Isis(?). This scene is intended to demonstrate the divine upbringing of the king; and the next scene (12), which represents the god Khnum, who made man on a potter's wheel, presenting the newly-fashioned child to Ptah, is intended to show his divine origin. On the south wall between the doorways the reliefs continue. First (13) Rameses is introduced by Mut to Ptah and Sekhmet, and Ptah records his royal name. Above this he stands before a shrine containing the barque of Seker. Then (14) he is blest by Harmachis, while behind him stand two goddesses, one of which is Hathor. Above this he offers a figure of Truth to Amen-Ra and Hathor. Next (15) he makes an offering to Amen-Ra and Mut; and above there is a variation of the same subject. Next (16) he offers kneeling statuettes to Amen-Ra and Mut; and above this he burns incense before Amen-Ra and Khonsu. He is then (17) seen receiving the symbol of Jubilees from Osiris, and behind him stand Harseisis and Isis. Above this his name is inscribed upon his shoulder by Thoth, in the presence of Osiris. He next (18) receives the royal cobra, the Hathor symbol, and a necklace from Isis, and the double crown from Horus. Above this he is suckled by Isis in the presence of Horseisis. On the west wall (19) Rameses offers various golden symbols to Osiris, Isis, and Horseosiris; and above this his name is written on the sacred tree by Thoth, he himself kneeling amidst the foliage. He is then (20) led by Wepwat of the south and by Harendotes to Hathor of Dendereh; and (21) he is purified with

[1] The reader will remember that David *danced* before the ark of the Lord.

the water of life by Thoth and Horseisis; while above this he dances before a god and is embraced by other deities. On the north wall (22) he performs one of the well-known but little understood foundation ceremonies before Horseisis, who projects towards him the symbols of "power," "stability," and "life." Above this he worships Horseisis. He then (23) performs the foundation ceremony of pegging out the limits of the temple in the presence of Osiris; the goddess Safkhet, the patron deity of archives and records, assisting him. Above this he breaks ground with a hoe before Osiris. Finally he receives life from Amen-Ra, while Osiris stands behind him; and above this he offers incense and a libation to Amen-Ra.

The second Hypostyle Hall.

The visitor has now seen the main reliefs in this hall, and should pass through one of the seven doorways into the second Hypostyle Hall. The roof is supported by three rows of twelve columns, of which the third row stands on a raised platform or terrace, which forms the threshold of the seven sanctuaries. The reliefs on the east and north wall of this hall do not attract one's attention. Those on the west wall, however, are perhaps the most beautiful temple reliefs now preserved in Egypt. From this point onwards practically all the workmanship is that of the reign of Sety Ist, and the superiority of these reliefs over those of Rameses IInd, which have already been seen, is at once apparent. Under Sety Ist Egyptian art reached one of its highest levels; and the delicate cutting of the stone displayed here, and in his tomb and temple at Thebes, is worthy of the best periods of the old kingdom.[1] The scenes on this west wall have lost their original colour, but the white limestone only serves to increase their beauty. We first see Sety Ist (25) burning incense and pouring a libation before Osiris and Harendotes. Above this he kneels before a god. He next (26) presents offerings before (27) a shrine containing Osiris seated between the goddesses Maat and Renpet on the one side, and Isis, Amentet-Hapet, and Nephthys on the other. Above this he pours

[1] The art of this period may be traced in its development from that of the early XVIIIth dynasty with considerable clearness. One first finds a softening influence, perhaps due to Syria, in the art of Thothmes IVth, which becomes very marked in the late years of Amenhotep IIIrd. Then follows the exaggeration of the new characteristics under Akhnaton, and the attempted return to the old canons under Tutankhamen. Under Horemheb the influence of Akhnaton is still marked, though, in the main, the style has returned to that of Amenhotep IIIrd. These varying characteristics are, however, solidified under Sety Ist; but after this the art steadily deteriorates under the Ramesside Pharaohs.

ABYDOS 15

a libation before Osiris and Isis. He then (28) offers a figure of Truth to Osiris, Isis, and Horseisis; while above this he kneels before Horus and Isis, receiving the curved sword, the crook, and the flail from the former.

One should now enter the first sanctuary at the west end, which was dedicated to Horus. On its walls Sety is shown worshipping that god; and especially noticeable are the beautiful reliefs on the east side (29), where one sees the sacred barque of Horus standing in its shrine, the king burning incense before it, while below he makes various offerings to Horus and Isis. At the end of the sanctuary is a false door which was heavily inlaid with metal, as is shown by the deep cutting between the ornamentation. One may notice the grass mats rolled up at the top of each panel of the door, as was the custom in the case of real doorways. Between the entrance of this sanctuary and that of the next there is a recess in which the deities Isis, Unnefer, and Horseosiris are shown; and above this there is a large relief (30) showing the king receiving emblems of royalty from Horus and Isis. The second sanctuary is dedicated to Mut, and on either wall one sees the sacred barque of the goddess, before which the king burns incense. The rest of the reliefs show him making various offerings to Mut. The recess between this and the next sanctuary contains figures of Nut, Osiris, and Isis; and above it (31) the king is seen kneeling and burning incense between Osiris and Isis. The third sanctuary is that of Osiris, and through it one passes into the chambers specially dedicated to his worship, which will be described later. On the east wall (32) the king is seen burning incense before a shrine containing the emblem of Abydos: the wig and head of Osiris raised upon a pole. In front of the shrine are five standards, namely, the Jackal Wepwat of the south, the Jackal Wepwat of the north, the Ibis of Hermopolis, the Hawk of the Horus tribes, and the figure of Anhur of Thinis. On the opposite wall (33) there is the sacred barque of Osiris; and one may here notice the rich and elaborate ornamentation: the coloured fans and plumes, the head of Osiris above the shrine in the barque, and the fruit offerings of grapes, pomegranates, figs, &c. Between this and the next sanctuary the recess in the wall is decorated with the figures of Mut, Amen-Ra, and Khonsu; and above (34) the king is seen kneeling between Amen-Ra and Osiris, bedecked with the magnificent insignia of royalty. The next sanctuary, which lies in the axial line of the temple, is dedicated to Amen-Ra, the great god of the empire. In the reliefs he is sometimes shown in the form of

The sanctuaries, and south wall of the second Hypostyle Hall.

16 ANTIQUITIES OF UPPER EGYPT

Min, as at the Luxor temple and elsewhere. One sees the sacred barque of the god, accompanied by those of Mut and Khonsu ; and again one observes the gaudy fans, plumes, and insignia. Fruit and flowers are heaped before the barque : grapes, figs, pomegranates, trailing vines, festoons of flowers are shown ; and jars of wine, golden statuettes, &c., are here seen. Outside this sanctuary the next recess in the wall contains the figures of Harmachis, Amen-Ra, and Mut; and the relief above it (35) shows the king kneeling between Amen-Ra and the ram-headed Harmachis, receiving from the former a curved sword and a mace. The king holds a tame bird in his hand. The following sanctuary is that of Harmachis, and the reliefs are not unlike those already seen. The next recess contains the figures of Sekhmet, Ptah, and Harmachis ; and the large relief above it (36) shows the king in the sacred tree, on the leaves of which Ptah and Horus(?) write his name. The next sanctuary is dedicated to Ptah, but it is much ruined. One here notices again the clean white of the walls, which so admirably shows off the fine workmanship of the reliefs. Between this and the next sanctuary the recess in the wall contains the figures of the king with Thoth ; and above this (37) he is seen offering to Ptah (damaged) and Sekhmet. The last sanctuary is dedicated to Sety Ist himself. On its walls we see (38) the king enthroned and carried by three hawk-headed beings called "The Spirits of Pe" (a city in the Delta), and three jackal-headed beings called "The Spirits of Nekhen," *i.e.* Kôm el Ahmar (p. 307). These two cities were the archaic capitals of Lower and Upper Egypt. Before him go the standards of the shield and crossed arrows of Neith, the so-called scorpion sign, the emblem of Thebes, the disc and feathers of Amen-Ra, the hawk of the Horus tribes, the ibis of Hermopolis, and the jackals, Wepwat, of the south and north. Above this the king, holding the crook and flail, stands between Thoth and Nekheb on the one side and Horus and Uazet on the other. The goddesses Uazet and Nekheb are the patron deities of the two above-mentioned capitals. We next (39) see the barque of the king ; for, like the gods, he possessed an image which was carried in this portable vessel in the temple processions. Another interesting scene here (40) shows him seated above the sign of union between Nekheb and Uazet, while Horus and Thoth lace together the stems of the papyrus and lotus plants, and Safkhet records the ceremonial union.

The Hall of Seker.
Between this last sanctuary and the passage on the east side, closed with an iron door, there is an open doorway leading into a

ABYDOS

three-columned hall, known to the Egyptians as the Hall of Seker. On the north wall the reliefs show the king worshipping the hawk-headed Seker and the human-formed Tum. On the east wall are four recesses, of which the first contains the figures of Tum, Thoth, and Seker; the second of Osiris, Min-Ra (?), and a god whose name is now lost; the third of Seker, Ptah, and Seker again; and the fourth of Osiris, Tum, and Hor-ur of the south. Between these recesses the king is shown worshipping the gods. On the west wall he offers four times to the hawk-headed Seker.

Two rooms lead off the southern end of this hall, the first having a vaulted roof, and the second being now roofless. The first is the chamber of Tum, and in the reliefs one sees the king adoring that god and the associated deities. On the east wall (41), at the top, the king kneels before a shrine containing the humanly-formed Ptah-Thenen, a disk-headed Amen-dwelling-in-Aten, a ded^1-headed Osiris-Unnefer, a sphinx representing the king, and the lion-headed Sekhmet. Below this the king kneels before the lion-headed Tum, on whose head is his distinctive symbol of a hawk and lotus-flower, Ptah-Osiris, Shu, the hawk Horus perched upon the *uazet* sign, Isis, Nephthys (?), Nekheb, and a woman-headed hawk of Hathor. On the opposite wall (42), at the top, he worships before a shrine containing the mummified hawk of Seker, the lion-headed Tum, the ibis-headed Thoth, a naos in which is a lotus and a crescent-moon connected with the worship of Tum, a sphinx representing the king, and the lion-headed Tum holding a flail and sacred eye. Below this the king burns incense before a shrine containing a figure of Tum with a hawk and lotus upon his head, Nu the primeval water, Khepera, the dawn, with a scarab on his head, Thoth, and damaged figures of Neith and Uazet.

Chamber of Tum.

The second room, the Chamber of Osiris, has upon its walls some curious reliefs. On the east wall (43) we see the king kneeling before a naos containing the two hawks of Seker, and behind this is a representation of the sarcophagus of Osiris. The god, crowned with the crown of Upper Egypt, lies upon a bier, and Isis in the form of a hawk hovers over him, while the goddess in human form and Horus stand at either end of the body. Above this relief one sees Osiris holding a crook and flail, the jackal-headed Anubis, Nekheb wearing the crown of Upper Egypt, and three unnamed figures holding snakes and lizards, who are said to be giving life, might, and strength to the king. On the opposite

Chamber of Osiris.

---

[1] The symbol *ded* will be seen at (52). It perhaps represents the backbone of Osiris, and has the meaning of "stability."

wall (44) one sees a shrine containing two hawks, one representing Isis and the other Horus; and behind this is the sarcophagus of Osiris again. He lies on the lion-couch, so common in Egyptian tombs, while Isis and Horus bend over him. Behind this again is a shrine in which a now damaged figure of the hippopotamus goddess Taurt is shown. From these reliefs it is clear that in this chamber were celebrated the mysteries connected with the resurrection of Osiris. Tradition stated that the god, after his murder and burial, came to life for a short time and had intercourse with his wife Isis, who afterwards gave birth to Horus.

The Osiris Halls. Behind the sanctuary of Osiris, which, it will be remembered, is the third from the west end, there is a portion of the temple especially dedicated to Osiris. The visitor should enter it through the Osiris Sanctuary, and he will then find himself in a hall, the roof of which was supported by eight columns. On the north wall the reliefs have been intentionally damaged, but are still good. The first relief at the top (45) shows the king offering before the shrine of Anubis, containing a jackal; and below this he worships at the shrine of Harendotes, in which is the figure of a hawk. The third relief (46) shows him opening the door of the shrine of Horus, which contains a hawk. The eighth relief (47) shows at the top the shrine of Heket, in which is the figure of a frog; and below this the king opens the door of the shrine of Min-Horseisis. The ninth relief (48) represents him worshipping at the shrine of the cow *Shentait*. On the south wall (49) is the great emblem of Abydos, the head of Osiris, having a large ornamental wig, placed upon a pole, while the king and Isis worship it. Next (50) is the ibis-standard of Thoth; then (51) the great *kherp* or bâton of Thoth and the hawk-standard; next (52) the *ded*-symbol of Osiris clothed with a girdle and skirt; and (53) the king and Isis lift the same symbol. On the rest of the wall the reliefs show the king worshipping various gods. We see, then, that the reliefs in this hall were intended to give a kind of catalogue of the larger shrines and emblems employed in the Osiris worship. Three sanctuaries lead off the west end of the hall. The first is dedicated to Horus, and the fine coloured reliefs show the king offering to that god, with whom are associated Osiris and Isis. The second chamber is dedicated to Osiris, and to the king who is here identified with that god. The brilliant reliefs show the king crowned and enthroned, wearing the insignia of Osiris, while Anubis, Isis, Thoth, and Horseosiris salute him; and on the end wall he is embraced

ABYDOS

by Osiris, with whom are Isis and Horus. The third sanctuary is dedicated to Isis, and the reliefs show the king worshipping her with Osiris and Horus. The four-columned hall with its three sanctuaries, which forms the east end of the Osiris Halls, is now so much ruined that it does not repay a visit.

One now returns to the second Hypostyle Hall, and enters the passage at the east side, closed by an iron door. On the south wall of this passage (54) is the famous list of kings. One sees Sety Ist holding a censer, and the young prince Rameses, afterwards King Rameses IInd, reading from a papyrus; and before them in two rows are the cartouches of a large number of the Pharaohs of Egypt, beginning with Mena and ending with himself. The third row of cartouches is a repetition of his own names. This list has been of great value to Egyptologists in fixing the position of certain of the less known Pharaohs; but it does not give the names of all the monarchs, and the spelling of some of the earlier names is defective. *(The list of kings.)*

A passage leading towards the south, and ending in a stairway, once led out to the desert at the back of the temple; and it seems to have been used at the festivals in which the processions visited the tomb of Osiris. The reliefs date from the reign of Rameses IInd. On the west wall (55) that king and his son, Prince Amenherkhepshef,[1] are seen catching a bull for sacrifice; and farther along (56) the king drags forward the elaborate barque of Seker. On the east wall (57) he and four genii pull at a rope which is attached to a net in which many wild duck have been caught. These he and his son present to Amen-Ra and Mut. At the other end of the wall (58) he drives four sacrificial calves to Khonsu, and dances before a god whose figure is now destroyed.

Returning to the passage in which the list of kings is shown, one may pass through the iron door at its east end into several ruined and unfinished chambers. One first enters a hall of ten columns, in which the reliefs have never been completed. Those at the south-west corner, showing the slaughtering of cattle, are of good workmanship, and especially one figure (59) is noticeable for its spirited action. It represents a man pulling at a rope attached to the hind leg of a bull, and one can well see the tension of his muscles. The other chambers are hardly worth visiting. One hall contains reliefs representing the sacred barques, and a bench or shelf running around the walls seems to have been the resting-

---

[1] This prince, who was the heir-apparent, seems to have died early, for Rameses IInd was succeeded by another son, Merenptah.

place of the actual barques. Foreign inscriptions of the 6th century B.C., and later Coptic inscriptions, are scrawled upon the walls.

The Temple of Rameses IInd

The richness and beauty of the temple.
The temple of Rameses IInd, which was erected early in that king's reign, lies a short distance to the north-west of that of Sety Ist. It is very much ruined, and only the lower parts of the walls and the bases of the pillars remain; but even from this remnant one may learn how costly and beautiful was the original building. In describing the edifice, Rameses IInd states that he built this "august temple, established for eternity," for the god Unnefer; and that it had "portals of granite, the doors thereto of copper, wrought with figures in real electrum; a great sanctuary of alabaster set in granite"; and other costly features. He also states how "he established for the god permanent daily offerings. . . . He filled the temple with everything; it was overflowing with food and provisions, bulls, calves, oxen, geese, bread, wine, fruit; it was filled with slaves, doubly supplied with fields, made numerous with herds; the granaries were filled to overflowing, the grain-heaps approached heaven. . . . The treasury was filled with every costly stone, silver, gold in blocks; the magazine was filled with everything from the tribute of all countries. He planted many gardens set with every kind of tree, all sweet and fragrant woods, and the plants of the Land of Punt." One sees, then, in these ruins, the remains of a temple of exceptional richness and beauty. The few remaining reliefs upon the walls display a delicacy of workmanship far removed above that shown in most of the temples of this period; and the visitor will find it worth his while to devote some time to an examination of the ruins. The modern gate of the temple has been affixed to the doorway leading into the Second Court; and the Forecourt lies half buried in rubbish outside the protected area.

The Second Court.
One enters the Second Court through a pink granite portal, on which one sees the king offering to Osiris, while Thoth and Safkhet record his jubilee. Around three sides of this court ran a covered gallery, the roof of which was supported by rectangular pillars, having on their outer sides colossal figures of the king in the form of Osiris. At the fourth or northern side these figures were con-

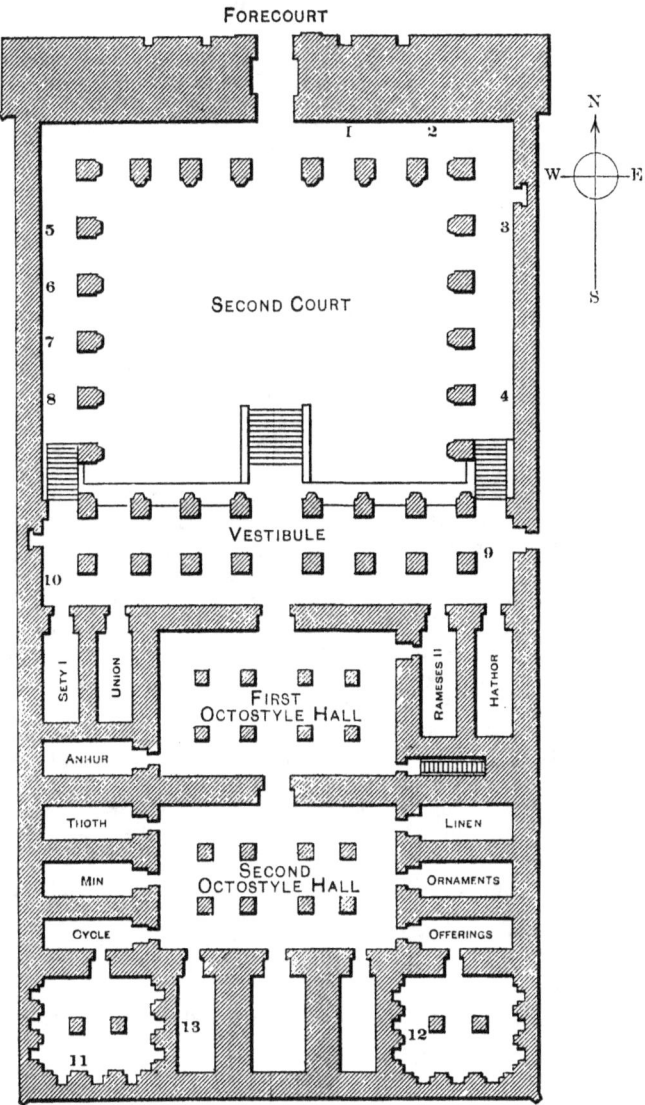

THE TEMPLE OF RAMESES II
AT ABYDOS.

tinued, but here they stood upon a raised platform, and, together with a second row of square pillars, served to support the roof of a kind of vestibule. The reliefs in the Second Court are of considerable interest. At the east end of the north wall we see (1) a number of priests carrying flowers, and leading towards the temple a bull, fattened for sacrifice and bedecked with flowers, an oryx, and a gazelle. Coming from the temple to meet these sacrificial gifts there is (2) a procession headed by men clapping their hands, singing, blowing trumpets, and carrying festal banners. Behind them there is a chariot, the horses of which are held by a groom, while another holds the reins. Then follow a group of nobles, behind whom are soldiers with feathers in their hair who play upon castanets. Other soldiers, carrying shields, spears, and axes, follow; and more standard-bearers are then seen; while finally there are negroes, one of whom has a tom-tom slung behind him, and Asiatics clad in long robes. The scenes along the east wall show (3) a number of priests leading to the temple fatted bulls and a calf, while others carry offerings of geese, pigeons, bread, fruit, &c. Farther along this wall one sees only the lower part of reliefs, representing persons carrying offerings; but towards the end (4) the masonry is less ruined, and one sees the temple servants bearing dishes of food on their heads, the procession being led by one who carries on his shoulders a statuette of the king, preceded by a Ritual-Priest burning incense before it. The scribe of the temple, with pen and writing-tablet in hand, and a priest displaying his bâton of office, receive the offerings.

Turning to the other side of the court, the west wall is just high enough to allow of the lower reliefs being seen. Butchers (5) are shown slaughtering and cutting up the sacrificial bulls; and (6) servants are seen running forward with the joints of meat, each of which has been purified by the Libation-Priest, who carries the vase of holy water, and presents the offerings to the scribe whose business it is to record them. Bulls, antelopes, and geese (7) are brought to the temple, and (8) are received by a scribe who writes their number upon a tablet, a priest who burns incense, another who extends his hand, and a Ritual-Priest who holds the bâton of his office.

The Vestibule.

One now ascends the low steps to the raised Vestibule. On the east wall (9) nine captive southern tribes are represented, their names written in ovals, above each of which rise the head and shoulders of a typical negro. With the exception of Wawat, or Lower Nubia, these tribes are all located above the Second Cataract.

ABYDOS

On the west wall (10) a similar scene shows nine captive Asiatic tribes. From this Vestibule four small chambers lead off. In the Room of Hathor there is a scene (11) in which the king is shown holding out the bâton towards a now damaged barque containing a statue of the cow of Hathor suckling a small figure of the Pharaoh. In the Room of Rameses IInd (12) the king, seated in a sacred barque which rests upon a sledge, is drawn along by six figures, representing the spirits of Eileithyiapolis or Nekheb (El Kab) and the spirits of Pe, a city in the Delta. The Room of the Union is too much damaged to be of interest; but in the Room of Sety one may distinguish the lower part of a barque which contained a figure of Sety Ist. These four rooms, then, which are dedicated to the father of Rameses IInd, to himself, to the Union, and to Hathor, the goddess of birth and of maternity, are evidently intended to demonstrate the fact of the succession of Rameses IInd to the divine rights of his father; and they are thus a fitting introduction to the scenes in the inner chambers, where he stands in the presence of the gods.

One passes now through a ruined grey-granite doorway into the first Octostyle Hall, the roof of which was supported by eight square pillars of sandstone. Only the lower parts of the walls remain, and here one sees a line of kneeling Nile-deities, each bearing a tray of offerings. A narrow stairway, once ascending to the roof, leads from the east side of this hall. On the west side there is a chamber (Room of Anhur) in which only the lower part of the reliefs can be seen. *First Octostyle Hall.*

One next enters the much ruined second Octostyle Hall, from which three chambers lead on either side. The three on the east side are for Osiris. In the Room of Linen a relief represents a number of priests carrying necklaces and a casket containing fine linen. The king walks behind them, pouring out a libation. The Rooms of Ornaments and of Offerings are much ruined; but in the Room of Thoth a relief shows the king, wearing the crown of Upper Egypt, offering a pot of incense to a seated figure of Osiris. In the Room of Min the king is seen pouring libations and burning incense before the sacred barques, while on the west wall he worships the god Min; but these scenes are much damaged. In the Room of the Cycle of Horus Gods one sees the king, wearing the crown of Lower Egypt, dancing before the gods, and holding in each hand a symbol composed of three vases. On the opposite wall he is given life by a damaged figure of Horus. Two once splendid, but now much ruined, chambers lead respectively from the *The second Octostyle Hall.*

24   ANTIQUITIES OF UPPER EGYPT

third chamber on either side of the hall. In each of these chambers a series of recesses around the walls have once contained statues of the various gods. In the west room the first recess in the south wall (11) is less ruined than are the others; and here one sees the king making the mystical sign of holding up the little finger before a figure of Osiris standing in front of a winged *ded*-symbol, which is thought to be a conventionalised representation of the backbone of Osiris. The room on the east side of the sanctuary has upon its west wall a relief (12) showing three deities, of which the first is nameless, the second is the goddess Heket of Abydos, and the third is the god Anubis of the necropolis. The room on the west side of the sanctuary has at its south end a shelf on which offerings were placed. On the west wall (13) three goddesses are shown: the first is nameless, the second is the scorpion goddess Selk, and the third is Hathor of Dendereh.

The Sanctuary.

The Sanctuary is so much ruined that it is difficult now to picture it in its original magnificence. The great pink-granite doorway has now fallen, but originally it is said to have been fitted with splendid doors of beaten bronze. The walls of the chamber were made entirely of alabaster, resting on a foundation of sandstone, and were covered with reliefs and inscriptions, of which only a few traces are now left. At the end of the chamber there was a now much broken group of five seated figures sculptured in grey granite. These represented Sety Ist, a Queen, Osiris, Rameses IInd, and another god or personage whose name is lost; and in this group the purpose of the temple is shown. Osiris, who embodied the personalities of the dead Pharaohs of Egypt, was here worshipped as the king's ancestor, having the same spiritual relation to Rameses as had his father Sety Ist in actual fact. In one of the rooms of the temple a list of kings was found, and was carried out of the country many years ago. One sees, then, that, like the temple of Sety Ist, this also was a shrine of the dead monarchs, whose virtues and divine rights were inherited by Rameses IInd.

Other Remains

The numerous other remains at Abydos need only be recorded briefly here, as they are rarely visited. The remains of the city of This and of the "Temenos of Osiris" are to be found to the

ABYDOS

north-west of the temple of Rameses. Here mounds and pits of rubbish, with some fragments of masonry showing above the surface, mark the site of the once famous place. High walls of crude brick are seen around it, and on the east side is the sacred lake. In the desert behind this site lies the necropolis, one of the most extensive in Egypt. Tombs of almost all periods have here been found. Some distance back towards the western hills two low mounds of a red colour will be seen. These are composed of the fragments of the offering-pots placed upon the tombs of the earliest kings of Egypt by later generations; and beneath the mounds M. Amelineau and Professor Petrie discovered these early royal sepulchres, dating from the Ist and IInd dynasties. The tombs are now not worth visiting, for they are half-covered by debris. Some distance to the north-west of these tombs stands a large and imposing brick building, now known as the Shunet es Zebîb. The walls still stand to a height of over 40 feet. The length of the building is about 400 feet, and its breadth over 200. It was evidently a fortress of the Ist or IInd dynasty; but in later times it was used as a burial-place for ibis-mummies, that bird being sacred. Hence it received in ancient Egyptian the name Shenet Debhib, "The Storehouse of the Ibis-mummies," and this is evidently the origin of the meaningless modern name which would be translated "The Raisin Magazine." Another somewhat similar fortress lies to the west, and is now used as a Coptic monastery, known as Anba Musas. In the desert to the south of the necropolis is the temple and "false"-tomb of Senusert IIIrd. The temple was discovered by Dr. Randal MacIver, and the tomb by the present writer. Here the body of Senusert was probably laid previous to its final burial at Dashour, in order that it might be near Osiris for a while. Other "false"-tombs are here found, and there is a "false"-pyramid of Aahmes Ist farther to the south.

Between Abydos and Nag'-Hamâdi the only site of interest is that of the prehistoric cemetery of El Amrah, 5 miles south of Abydos, on the west bank. This is now entirely excavated. A few graves of this and later periods are the only remains until Hou is reached.

CHAPTER II

HOU AND KASR ES SAYÂD—DENDEREH

Methods of visiting Hou and Kasr es Sayâd.

AFTER passing the railway bridge of Nag'-Hamâdi, the first ancient remains which are met with are situated in the neighbourhood of the modern town of Hou on the west bank of the river, and Kasr es Sayâd on the east bank. The tombs of Kasr es Sayâd are decorated with reliefs which are only rather poor copies of those found at Sakkâra and elsewhere, and the traveller will not find them quite worth a visit while there are other and better things to be done. Nor are the antiquities at Hou of any general interest. Those who wish to visit the tombs[1] of Kasr es Sayâd should take the early train from Luxor to the station of El Dabbeh, which is reached about 9 A.M. Donkeys must here be procured, and the traveller is advised to bring his own saddle with him from Luxor. The path runs direct from the station to the cliffs, which are here of magnificent form and colour, and thence bears off to the right, round the corner and straight ahead for two miles or so. The return journey to Luxor can be made by the train; or the visitor can arrange with one of the excursion steamers to stop to pick him up at Kasr es Sayâd. For a visit to Hou, Nag'-Hamâdi is the nearest station.

THE HISTORY OF HOU AND KASR ES SAYÂD

Hou.

The modern town of Hou marks the site of the ancient Diospolis Parva, the capital of the province of that name. In early days the city was named *Het-Sekhem*, "The House, or Fortress, of the Hathor-totem," and thus, like Dendereh, it was presided over by the goddess Hathor. Very little is known of its history. The prehistoric cemeteries near by indicate that it already existed at that period. The cemeteries also show that it was flourishing

[1] See p. 28.

HOU AND KASR ES SAYÂD

during the Old and Middle Kingdoms. During the XVIIth dynasty there was here a settlement of those Nubian tribes who buried their dead in what are called "pan-graves," and who, perhaps, were retained here as soldiers. As there was a fortress here in Roman times, it is quite possible that there was one in early days also. Cemeteries of the XVIIIth dynasty have also been found, and that the city was at this time flourishing is shown by the size of the tax which the officials were called upon to pay each year to the crown. In the reign of Thothmes IIIrd the tax paid by the Recorder of the city consisted of five *debens* of gold, a large quantity of grain, and other items now unreadable, while the Scribe of the Recorder paid three *debens* of gold. In the XXIInd dynasty we read of a Priest of Hathor, Lady of Diospolis Parva, who was made Governor of the Oases. The Oasis of El Khârgeh is most easily reached by the caravan route from Hou, the journey on camels taking about four to five days. The remains of the temple at Hou bear the names of Ptolemy VIIth, Philometer Ist, Ptolemy Xth, Philometer IInd, the Emperor Nerva, and the Emperor Hadrian. The fortress built here in Roman times may have been used as a basis of communication with the oasis.

The name of the city of Khenoboskion in early times is not known with certainty. Its Greek name Khenoboskion, however, which means "geese-pasture," suggests that large numbers of geese were here reared. Now, in the list of town taxes of the reign of Thothmes IIIrd, one reads that a certain city situated north of Dendereh and not far from Hou, and named Heturt-Amenemhat, was called upon each year to provide 500 geese (?), amongst other items. It is therefore possible that Heturt-Amenemhat is the name of Khenoboskion. In early times it was perhaps the terminus of one of the many eastern trading roads or caravan routes to the gold-mines, and it is not unlikely that it was originally an offshoot from the city of Diospolis Parva. In the VIth dynasty two of the princes of the province of Diospolis Parva, and other nobles whose names are now lost, where buried in the cliffs behind Khenoboskion, which suggests that at this date the daughter city had become equal in size to the parent. The name Heturt-Amenemhat, "The great enclosure of Amenemhat," seems to indicate that a fortress was erected here by one of the kings of the XIIth dynasty named Amenemhat; and, if this is so, one may draw a close parallel between the twin cities of Diospolis Parva and Khenoboskion and those of Hieraconpolis and Eileithyiapolis, Elephantine and Syene, Hierasycaminos or Pselchis and Contra Pselchis (Kubbân), and

Khenoboskion.

28   ANTIQUITIES OF UPPER EGYPT

others. In each of these cases the parent city of great antiquity is situated on the west side of the river, and its trading centre, fortified under the XIIth dynasty, is situated on the east bank.[1] In the XVIIIth dynasty the heavy tax imposed upon the Mayor of Heturt-Amenemhat is a proof of the wealth of the city at that time. This tax consisted of 5 *debens* of gold, 1 *deben* of silver, over 1000 loaves, many sacks of grain, &c., 5 calves, 3 yearlings, 3 two-year-olds, 2 full-grown oxen, and the 500 geese mentioned above. In later times Khenoboskion is mentioned in the Itinerary of Antonine, a list of Roman stations, and elsewhere, and was then still of importance. The high mounds of ruins and debris which marked the site in modern times have been almost entirely dug away by the *sebakhîn*, or peasants who use the remains of ancient towns as manure, there being certain beneficial chemicals in the decayed rubbish.

The Antiquities of Hou and Kasr es Sayâd

Hou.

The town of Hou is a large, untidy place rising high upon the ruins of the ancient city. These ruins consist of mounds, composed of collapsed brick buildings, broken pottery, and the usual debris of a town. They are being dug away by the *sebakhîn*, and in places these excavations are so extensive that one may stand on some high eminence and watch the people digging through the same broken bricks and potsherds thirty feet below. The remains of a sandstone temple are to be seen among these mounds, not far from the market-place. On the bank of the river there are traces of an ancient quay wall. On the edge of the desert behind the town stands the Roman fortress, the brick walls of which are still some fifteen feet high in places. Near this fort the cemeteries of the prehistoric period, the XIIth dynasty, and the XVIIIth dynasty, excavated by Professor Flinders Petrie, extend over the desert.

The tombs of Kasr es Sayâd.

As has been said, nothing now remains of the ruins of Khenoboskion itself. The two rock tombs which are cut into the cliffs date from the VIth dynasty—that period of Egypt's many-phased history when, under the strong rule of the Pepys, the organisation of the Upper Egyptian provinces was practically for the first time undertaken. In many of the provincial towns the local princely family became elevated to a considerable degree of importance,

[1] See also the history of Ombos, opposite to Koptos.

HOU AND KASR ES SAYÂD

and at several district capitals there remain fine tombs of these families, dating from just this one dynasty. These two tombs were the burial-places of Prince Zauta and Prince Adu, who were both princes of the province of Diospolis Parva. Prince Zauta seems to have been the founder of the family, and the workmanship shown in his tomb is better than that in the tomb of Adu, who probably succeeded him. Zauta held the titles of Prince of the Province, Governor of the South, Keeper of the Door of the South (*i.e.* of the Nubian frontier), Master of the Secrets of the Door of the South, *Erpa-ha*-Prince, Governor of the Fortress,[1] Sole Companion, Royal Registrar, Ritual-Priest, and Overseer of the Priests of the Pyramids of Meryra, Merenra, and Neferkara. Adu's titles were the same, with the omission of those relating to Nubia and the south, probably owing to the fact that this office had been handed over to the prince of some other province. A prince of Dendereh held the title at about this period, and princes of Elephantine are also known to have held it. The fact that Zauta and Adu are both connected with the pyramids of King Neferkara Pepy IInd and his predecessors shows that they lived at the end of the dynasty, and it is possible that in the troubled times which followed, the Nubian frontier was not protected.

On the way to these two tombs the visitor will pass five rock tombs of no interest. The sixth tomb is that of Adu. On either side of the broken entrance of this tomb there are inscriptions cut into the rock, giving the titles of the prince. On entering, the tomb is seen to consist of a rectangular chamber, from the back wall of which a sloping passage leads down into the actual sepulchre, now blocked with rubbish. The walls of the chamber are decorated with coloured reliefs similar to those found at Sakkâra and elsewhere. Upon the inner side of the front wall immediately to one's right on entering is a much damaged scene showing Adu harpooning fish, and to one's left is the corresponding scene showing him hunting birds with a boomerang. The rushes amongst which the hunt is taking place are full of birds of various kinds, and a butterfly is also seen. The lower part of the scene is destroyed.[2] The left end wall of the chamber has upon it the figure of the prince standing before the usual offerings, and there

Tomb of Adu.

---

[1] Heqhet.
[2] It is necessary to state that an interpretation of this scene given in another guide-book, in which Adu becomes a warrior with weapon uplifted to slaughter his enemies, is as incorrect as the general description of the two tombs there given.

is also part of a stele or false-door depicted, above which is an inscription of some length giving the usual laudatory comment on his life. The reliefs on the corresponding wall at the right end of the tomb are destroyed. The back wall has upon it a large quantity of offerings, while at the far end, to one's left, are scenes in five registers. The first two from the top contain hunting incidents; the third shows tame animals being fed, &c.; the fourth contains some interesting cooking scenes, in two of which a man is seen fanning the food or the fire over which it is being held; and in the fifth row one sees a number of slaughtered gazelles.

Tomb of Zauta.

The second tomb, that of Prince Zauta, has had a large part of its front wall quarried away by some unscrupulous persons in need of easily obtained slabs of stone.[1] The reliefs which are still to be seen on the inner side of this wall show the slaughtering of cattle, and a figure of the owner with the titles inscribed above it. The tomb, although much damaged, is seen to have consisted of three main rooms, the entrance-door having led into the middle room; but the partition walls are now destroyed. From the back wall of this middle room the shaft descends, in the form of a sloping passage, to the burial chamber, now blocked with debris. From the left-hand chamber a small undecorated room leads, in which are four niches only large enough to have contained small objects of funeral furniture. From the right-hand chamber a small recess leads, now much damaged. On the far wall of this right-hand chamber are reliefs showing the prince seated before a number of persons who are bringing offerings to him, and some figures of ritual-priests near by are engaged in a well-known ceremony, described elsewhere (p. 274). On the corresponding left wall are hunting scenes, and representations of servants bringing offerings. On the sides of the entrance to the shaft the prince is seen seated to receive more offerings.

In the neighbourhood of these two tombs there is a cemetery of the same period, which seems to have been almost entirely dug out by tomb-plunderers.

From Hou to Dendereh, on the East Bank

Between Khenoboskion and Keneh on the east bank there are the mounds of an old town at Deshneh and at Fou, which was the ancient Bopos; and there is a small plundered cemetery at El

[1] Probably early in the nineteenth century.

DENDEREH

Kenawieh. The town of Keneh marks the site of the ancient Kainepolis, which being thus in Greek times called "New-town," cannot date earlier than that period. Neither on this nor on the west bank will the visitor find anything to interest him.

The Ancient Sites on the West Bank

Riding along the desert southwards from Hou one passes several prehistoric cemeteries, mostly dug out, while a small Roman fort is also seen. Near Wakf there are prehistoric cemeteries, and also a few graves of the New Empire. The city known in the XVIIIth dynasty as Wahast, and seemingly connected with the oases, is listed as being situated next to Hou and Khenoboskion; and is probably to be located somewhere near Wakf. Other prehistoric cemeteries lie some six miles south of Wakf; but near Dendereh there is little of value or importance. There do not seem to have been any prehistoric settlements nearer Dendereh, which at that time was a kind of no-man's land between the territory of the tribes of Diospolis Parva and that of the Set-worshippers of Ombos.

DENDEREH

The temple of Dendereh is usually visited by persons travelling in Upper Egypt, as it is one of the best preserved of the ancient edifices. It stands on the edge of the western desert opposite Keneh, about half-an-hour's ride from the river. The tourist steamers allow the passengers sufficient time to visit the temple, but one may also make the excursion with ease from Luxor by railway. At Keneh station one may obtain a carriage in which to drive to the bank of the river, where a ferry-boat will be found. Donkeys should have been sent on from the station to meet one on the west bank, and the ride through the fields to the temple is usually enjoyable.

Methods of visiting the temple.

The History of Dendereh

In ancient times the official name of this place was Ant, but it was also known vulgarly as Tantarer, from which the Greek

Tentyra and the modern Dendereh are derived. It was the capital of the VIth Province of Upper Egypt, which was bounded on the north by the province of Diospolis Parva—the tombs of whose princes have been described above, and on the south by the province of Thebes. In the last chapter the visitor will have read how the archaic kings of Thinis, who reigned before Mena, pushed their way southwards, and founded a capital for themselves at Kôm el Ahmar near Edfu. A tradition states that at the beginning of things the followers of the god Horus defeated those of the god Set in a fierce fight at Dendereh, and finally crushed them in a desperate battle at Edfu ; and there is reason to suppose that one may see in this tradition a reference to the conquests of these Thinite chieftains. Dendereh was throughout its history considered to be the place at which the preliminary battle to that at Edfu took place, and the god Horsmataui, "the hawk who unites the two lands," who represents the unity of Upper and Lower Egypt brought about by the conquests of the archaic kings, is described as the child of Dendereh and Edfu, or rather of Hathor and Horus, the gods of those places.

Hathor, the patron deity of Dendereh, was a goddess of very high standing in Egypt ; but in the mythology of the best periods of Egyptian history she is evidently composed of a combination of several independent forms. Sometimes she is the cow which issues forth from the western hills ; sometimes she is the fairy godmother, who is present at childbirth ; and sometimes she is the fair goddess from the land of Punt. But here at Dendereh she appears in her original form. She is the beneficent goddess of maternal and family love, of beauty, of light, and of joy. Her form is generally that of a woman, above whose head rises the sun's disk, fixed between a pair of cow's horns. The totem by which in prehistoric times she was represented consisted of a cow's head fixed upon a pole, having above it a casket or shrine. In later times the cow's head gave place to the model of a woman's head with cow's ears ; and in this form we see the totem used as a column in the great Hypostyle Hall of the temple. The trinity of Dendereh consisted of Hathor, Horus of Edfu, and their son Horsmataui, and was thus identical with that worshipped at Edfu, with the difference that the chief deity was there Horus instead of Hathor.

The earliest temple at Dendereh is said, in the inscriptions in the existing building, to have been built by those archaic kings who were known as the "followers of Horus." A temple was then built here by Khufu, the Pharaoh who erected the great pyramid at

DENDEREH

Gîzeh. A plan of the building, drawn upon hide, is said to have been found in the archives of the royal palace during the reign of King Pepy of the VIth dynasty; and that king thereupon rebuilt the temple which had fallen into ruins.

At this period Dendereh was a place of considerable importance. The tombs of the nobles, which lie in the desert behind the temple, were excavated by Professor Flinders Petrie some years ago, and many inscriptions bearing on the history of the VIth dynasty were discovered. So many of these persons held the title of *Heq het*, "Ruler of the Fortress," that one is led to suppose that there must have been a fortified enclosure here in which a part of the Upper Egyptian army was stationed. One reads of a "steward of the magazine of stores of war," and again of a "captain of the host"; while, like the prince of Diospolis Parva, whose tomb has been described above, and some of the princes of Elephantine, a prince of Dendereh held the title of "Governor of the South," which entailed the guarding of the Lower Nubian frontier against the negro invasions. One noble, named Merra, tells us that he laboured all his life for the furtherance of the interests of Dendereh, and that he was praised not only by the citizens, but by "the travellers and the negroes of foreign lands." This indicates that the negroes of Lower Nubia were in the habit of entering Egypt peaceably and penetrating as far north as this province. The tombs of six probably successive princes of the province of Dendereh have been found, and most of them seem to have held high offices in the Government; while their wives and daughters acted as priestesses in the temple of Hathor. *The VIth dynasty.*

Some of these nobles speak of themselves as having conducted the "Voyage of Hathor," in which ceremony one may recognise the voyage of the sacred barge, containing the image of Hathor, to Edfu to visit the temple of Horus, her consort. This festival was one of considerable importance in Upper Egypt, and seems to have dated from the earliest times. The barge was towed up the river by numerous galleys, and on nearing Edfu it was met by the barge of Horus. The images of the two deities were carried up to the temple, and, after some days, the goddess was taken down stream again to Dendereh. Inscriptions from these tombs also refer to the sacred kine of Hathor, which seem to have been kept near the temple; but their burial-place has not yet been found. *The worship of Hathor.*

At Gebelên an inscription of King Nebhotep Menthuhotep of the XIth dynasty refers to him as "son of Hathor, Lady of Dendereh." At Dendereh the cartouche of a King Menthuhotep was found, *The XIth, XIIth, and XIIIth dynasties,* which indicates that Dendereh continued to flourish at this period. At about this time a queen, named Neferukayt, held large properties in this neighbourhood, and the tomb of her steward was found in the cemetery. From Senusert Ist of the XIIth dynasty the temple of Hathor received rich presents of golden ornaments; and traces of a temple built by Amenemhat Ist have been found. A vase of a little-known king of the XIIIth dynasty, Khaneferra Sebekhotep IIIrd, was recently found near the temple.

The XVIIIth dynasty.   In the XVIIIth dynasty Thothmes IIIrd restored the temple, and is said to have rebuilt the original shrine of the days of Khufu. The festival of the Voyage of Hathor to Edfu, which seems to have fallen into abeyance, was revived by this king. At this time the tax which had to be paid to the Crown by the chief official of Dendereh consisted of one *deben* of gold, a little silver, some grain and honey, five calves, one ox, and a few two-year-olds; and the smallness of this tax indicates that the town was not very rich. The name of Thothmes IVth has been found on a stone in the temple; and a colossal statue of Queen Mutemua, his wife, was recently unearthed. In this dynasty the general custom of regarding certain animals as sacred led to the building of catacombs for their interment in the desert. Gazelles, cats, ichneumons, birds, and snakes were here buried, though of these species only the snake is known to have been specially sacred to the goddess Hathor.

Later history.   Except for the traces of the work of Rameses IInd[1] and Rameses IIIrd,[2] nothing more is seen of Dendereh until the days of the Ptolemies. This does not mean that the place fell into insignificance, but rather that the remains of this date still lie hidden under the mounds of ruins which have collected around the temple. The present edifice seems to have been begun sometime previous to the reign of Ptolemy Xth Soter IInd, as the building was sufficiently advanced for that king to place his cartouches in the crypts. Ptolemy XIth Alexander and Ptolemy XIIIth Neos Dionysos also inscribed their names here. Some of the inscriptions outside the temple refer to Ptolemy XVIth Cæsarion and to the Emperor Augustus. On the rear wall Cæsarion and Cleopatra VIth are shown. The Greek dedicatory inscription states that the great

---

[1] A block of stone bearing the cartouche of one of the Rameses is built into the pavement at the mouth of the crypt in the small court to the west of the second vestibule.

[2] In a recent visit to Denderch the writer noticed a brick to the south of the temple stamped with the cartouches of Menkheper-Ra, the Priest-King of the XXIst dynasty.

DENDEREH 35

Hypostyle Hall was finished in the twentieth year of the Emperor Tiberius, while another inscription states that the decoration of the outer walls had been finished in that sovereign's second year. Thus the temple as it stands dates from about B.C. 125 to 60 A.D., its building occupying about 185 years. It was not, however, regarded as finished; for the priests had, no doubt, the intention of adding a forecourt and pylons in front of the main building, and erecting an enclosing wall around it, as at Edfu. Money, however, was not forthcoming, and it was not till the time of the Emperors Domitian and Nerva Trajan that even the entrance-gate in the brick enclosing wall in front of the temple could be built. Coins have been found here extending down to the reigns of Theodosius IInd and Valentinian IIIrd, and the extensive mounds left by the ancient town show that it was still a place of some considerable size.

In the days of the Romans the goddess Hathor was identified with Venus and Aphrodite. The Greek dedicatory inscription states that the temple was erected for "the great goddess Aphrodite and her fellow-gods." Terra-cotta statuettes of Aphrodite, modelled in the usual Greek style, with one arm raised above the head, are sometimes found near the temple. *Hathor in late times.*

DESCRIPTION OF THE TEMPLE

The visitor on approaching the temple passes through the much-ruined masonry gateway of Domitian and Trajan, which formed the main portal in the brick-enclosing wall around the temple-buildings. The mounds of the ancient town rise around this doorway, but a space in front of the temple has been cleared, across which one passes to the main temple. The façade of the temple is imposing, and being well preserved a good idea of the appearance of the building in ancient times may be obtained, though originally the brilliant colouring of the reliefs must have given a far less sombre tone to the whole. This façade is formed of six Hathor-columns, with screen-walls between them. The reliefs, which are much damaged, show "The Prince of Princes, Autocrator Tiberius Claudius[1] Cæsar," before the gods of Dendereh. *The approach to the temple.*

One passes through the doorway into the great Hypostyle Hall, known to the Egyptians as the *Khent* or First Hall. Eighteen columns support the lofty roof. These columns are shaped in the *The great Hypostyle Hall.*

---

[1] Spelt T-b-r-s K-l-u-t-i-s.

form of the totem of Hathor, described above, which is often represented by itself as the emblem of Hathor. Painted in brilliant colours and used as a column, its decorative merits are obvious; but its use thus in the temple is not due to the good taste of the Egyptian architect, but to the piety of the priests. The faces of the Hathor heads have all been intentionally damaged by Christian fanatics, and the reliefs on the walls have also been badly mutilated. These reliefs, which date from the reigns of Augustus, Tiberius, Caligula, Claudius, and Nero, are of no great interest. On the screen walls at the west of the entrance (1) the Pharaoh, crowned as King of Lower Egypt, leaves his palace to visit the temple. Before him walks a small figure of a priest burning incense, and one also sees five tribal standards moving in procession before him. These standards are the Jackal Wepwat of Thinis, the Ibis of Hermopolis, the Hawk of Edfu and Hieraconpolis, the emblem of Thebes, and the complicated symbol of Dendereh. The first four of these standards are almost invariably shown at this ceremony of "going forth from the palace," and even as early as the archaic period one sees them preceding the king in a ceremonial relief of the reign of Narmer, with the difference, however, that the ibis there gives place to a second hawk. The next scene (2) shows the king being purified by Thoth and Horus of Edfu, but the relief is much damaged; and thirdly (3) we see him crowned by Nekheb and Uazet. These two goddesses were the patrons respectively of Eileithyiapolis (El Kâb) and Buto, the archaic capitals of Upper and Lower Egypt. This series of reliefs is continued on the west wall, where (4) the king is led by Menthu, the war-god of Thebes, and Tum the god of Heliopolis (called, in the Bible, On), to Hathor of Dendereh; (5) he marks out the limits of the temple by driving in the boundary posts, while Safkhet, the goddess of Records, and Isis, assist him; (6) he presents the temple—here represented by a single shrine—to Hathor; (7) he worships Hathor, Horus of Edfu, and their small son Horsmataui; (8) he offers a figure of Truth to Hathor, facing whom is a small figure of Horsmataui; and finally (9) he presents the symbol of "fields" or "estates" to Hathor and Horsmataui. On the east side of the doorway the first scene (10) shows the Pharaoh, now crowned as King of Upper Egypt, leaving his palace as before. The rest of the scenes on this and on the east wall are too damaged to be of interest. Those on the south wall show the Pharaoh in the presence of the gods of Dendereh.

The scenes in this hall are thus mainly concerned with the

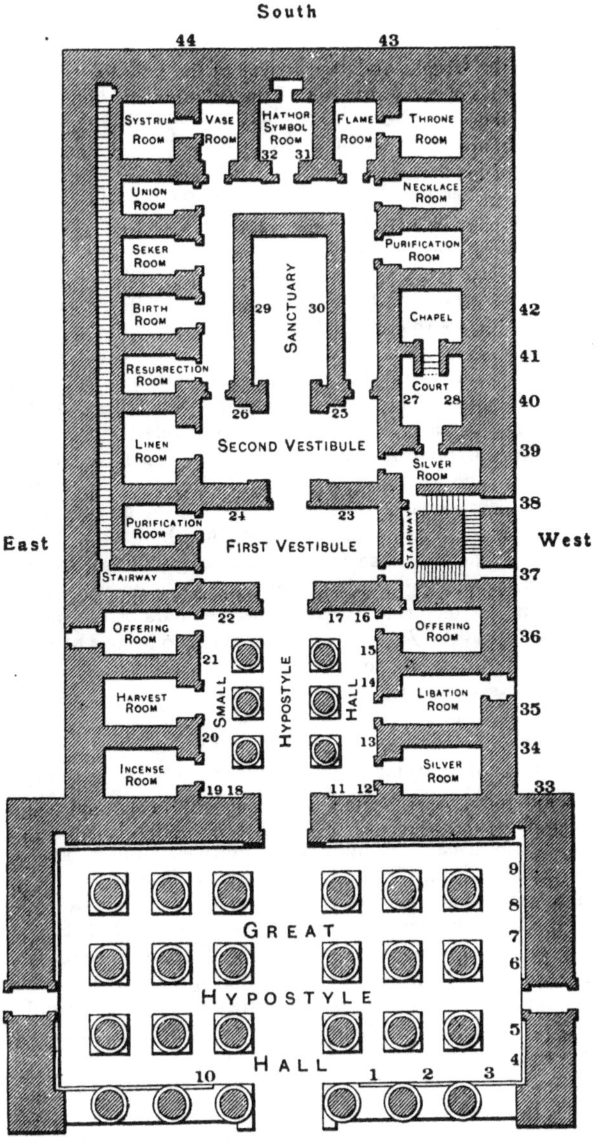

THE TEMPLE OF DENDEREH

building of the temple, and the arrival of the king to visit it. On the upper parts of the walls, and on the columns, the king is shown presenting flowers, chaplets, fine linen, incense, sistrums, and so forth to Hathor and to other gods. In the inscriptions this hall is spoken of as the place in which the sistrums and the tambourines were sounded ; and one may picture the groups of priestesses passing between the columns, and may hear in the imagination the echoing sounds of their barbaric music.

<small>The ceiling of the great Hypostyle Hall.</small>
The ceiling of this hall is decorated with an elaborate series of astrological scenes. The ceiling will be seen to be divided by the architraves into seven sections. In the westernmost section one sees an elongated figure of the goddess Nut, who is supposed to be resting her hands and feet on the ends of the world, her body thus forming the arch of heaven. A long line of figures is here seen, and amongst them one may notice at intervals the northern six signs of the Egyptian Zodiac—the lion, the serpent, the balances, the scorpion, the archer, and the goat. A second line here contains eighteen ships, in which are the *Decani* or presidents of the eighteen sections of ten days into which the half year was divided. In the second section of the ceiling there will be seen at either end a winged figure which represents the wind, while amongst the various astrological figures the twelve hours of the night will be noticed, and the *Decani* here arranged into groups of three, to represent the space of one month, will be observed. In the third section the scenes refer chiefly to the moon, which is here represented by the sacred eye. First we see the fourteen days of the waning moon ; then the fourteen days of the waxing moon ascending the steps of heaven ; and lastly the god Osiris, in his capacity as a moon god, is seen seated in a boat with Osiris and Nepthys floating above the heavens. The fourth or middle section of the ceiling is, as usual, decorated with alternate vultures and disks with spread wings. The fifth section is decorated with three rows of figures, amidst which one may discern the twelve boats of the hours of the day, each having in it the sun's disk and the figures of the divinities to which each hour was sacred. The sixth section has at either end a winged figure of the wind, while numerous astrological figures are represented. The seventh section of the ceiling is decorated, like the first, with an elongated figure of Nut. At the north end the sun pours down its rays upon the shrine of Hathor ; while at. intervals along the line of figures one sees the southern six signs of the Zodiac—the crab, the twins, the bull, the ram, the fishes, and the water-carrier. The eighteen

ships of the *Decani* of the second half of the year are here also shown.

One now passes into the small Hypostyle Hall, the roof of which is supported by six columns, clumsily decorated with the Hathor head and shrine above the ordinary floral capital. The bases of these columns are of granite, such as is quarried at Aswân. This hall was known to the Egyptians as the "Hall of the Appearance." The reliefs on the lower parts of the walls relate to the ceremonies in connection with the founding of the temple. The first scene at the west of the entrance (11) shows the Pharaoh (whose cartouches have been left blank, as though the Egyptians had found themselves unable to keep up with the rapid changes of rulers at the end of the Ptolemaic dynasty) crowned as King of Lower Egypt, leaving his palace to visit the temple. He is preceded by the standards of the Jackal of Thinis and the emblem of Thebes, while a priest burns incense before him. He then (12) breaks the ground for the new temple with a hoe, in the presence of Hathor. Next, on the west wall (13), he kneels before the goddess and shapes the first brick for the building. This is an indication of the antiquity of the ceremony, for it dates back to the archaic days when the temples were built of brick instead of stone. The next scene (14) shows the king placing the foundation stone in position, or performing some similar building ceremony, before the goddess. Then (15), with a gesture of the hand, he presents the temple to Hathor and Horsmataui. On the south wall (16) he presents a metal-headed spear to Horus of Edfu ; and in this connection it may be noticed that the troops of Horus, who defeated those of Set at Dendereh and Edfu, are said to have been metal workers, whereas the weapons of their enemies were made of flint, wood, and stone. Lastly (17) the king burns incense before Hathor.

The small Hypostyle Hall.

At the east side of the entrance (18) we see the Pharaoh, crowned as King of Upper Egypt, leaving his palace, preceded by the standards of the Jackal of Thinis, the Hawk of Edfu and Hieraconpolis, the Ibis of Hermopolis, and the emblem of Thebes. He then (19) presents blocks of gold and silver to Hathor for the decoration of the temple. On the east wall (20) he performs an obscure ceremony of throwing balls of perfume over the temple in the presence of Hathor and Isis. Next (21) he presents the temple to Hathor and Horus of Edfu, before whom stands the "child of Hathor." Finally, on the south wall (22), the god Ptah introduces the king into the presence of Hathor and Horus, while their youthful son shakes a sistrum before them.

Chambers leading from small Hypostyle Hall.

From this hall six chambers lead off, three on either side; but at the time of writing no steps have yet been taken to exclude the bats from the temple, which therefore congregate in hundreds in these dimly lighted rooms. The first chamber on the west side was known as "the Silver Room," and the representations show the Pharaoh offering various ornaments to Hathor. At the side of the doorway he is seen entering the chamber, and offering a casket to Hathor, said to contain gold, silver, lapis lazuli, and malachite. An inscription in this chamber states that the chamber was filled with "a multitude of stones, and with all the splendid gems of the mountains." The second chamber, from which a doorway, now closed, led out of the temple, was used for the storing of the jars of holy water obtained from the seven most sacred reaches of the Nile. Through this chamber the Libation-Priest passed each day on his way to perform the ceremony of purifying the temple. The third chamber seems to have been used for the storing of various offerings. The first chamber on the east side of the hall was that in which the incense and unguents were prepared or kept; and the reliefs show the Pharaoh offering these to the gods of Dendereh. In the second room on this side the harvest products of the fields were kept, *i.e.* the fruit, flowers, plants, &c., which were offered as sacrifices to the goddess. Lastly, the third room was used for the housing of the various offerings which were brought into the temple by the side door leading from this chamber.

The First Vestibule.

The First Vestibule which one now enters was known to the Egyptians as the "Hall of the Altar." It was here that the great sacrifices were offered to the gods. One must, of course, imagine each of these halls as having been separated from those before and behind it by great double doors of cedar wood, ornamented with shining metal and with painted designs. At these sacrificial ceremonies the priestesses and privileged worshippers were assembled in the great Hypostyle Hall. From here one might see through the open doors into the small Hypostyle Hall, where the priests were gathered. At the hour of sacrifice the doors of the First Vestibule were opened, and one then saw the priests of high rank at the altar. The doors of the Second Vestibule and of the Sanctuary were probably seldom opened, and none but the priests and nobles of highest rank were ever permitted to see these inner chambers.

DENDEREH

The reliefs upon the walls of this First Vestibule show a Pharaoh, whose cartouches have been left blank, offering libations and sacrifices before the gods of Dendereh. On the south wall, at the west and east end (23 and 24), one sees two damaged figures of a ram-headed and a bull-headed demi-god assisting the king to make offerings to Hathor and Horus. Two doorways in the west wall of this vestibule lead to a stairway ascending to the roof, which will be described later. Of the two doorways in the east wall the first also leads to a stairway to be described later, and the second admits one to a chamber, called, according to one interpretation of the inscription, the "Room of Purification." The reliefs here, however, are not of particular interest.

The Second Vestibule, named the "Hall of the Cycle of the Gods," being never entered by the public, or even by the priests of lower rank, contained reliefs in which some of the mysteries of the Hathor religion were revealed. In these reliefs Hathor is represented in her capacity as a sun-goddess, the patron deity of life and light. On the south wall at the west and east sides of the doorway of the Sanctuary (25 and 26) the king is seen offering two mirrors to the goddess, she being the deity of Beauty. These mirrors are round plates of polished copper, with wooden handles carved in the form of Hathor heads. Above the cornice of this Sanctuary-doorway Hathor is represented as a human-headed hawk standing within the disk of the sun, which rises above the horizon. *The Second Vestibule.*

On the east side of this Vestibule there is a chamber which was known as the "Linen Room," and which was used for the storing of the garments with which the statue of Hathor was clothed on festal occasions. On the west side a passage leads into a small open court, at the south end of which there is a small chapel raised upon a platform. This passage was known as the "Silver Room," and the reliefs indicate that it was used for the storing of precious metals and stones. The reliefs in the court are of some interest. On the two main walls (27 and 28) one sees a long list of offerings, each object being carefully drawn in miniature; and above this the king is seen slaying with a spear the crocodile of Set in the presence of Horus of Edfu, and he also is shown offering to various gods. The small chapel was used for the services in connection with the ceremonies of "the Day of the Night of the Child in his Cradle"—a celebration relating to the birth of Horus, which was solemnised at the end of the Egyptian year. On the ceiling of this chapel there is a relief of considerable interest. The goddess Nut is here shown in a grotesque, *Chambers leading from the Second Vestibule.*

though conventionally correct, attitude, in which her hands and feet touch the two sides of the world, and her body is arched above it. A somewhat similar but much elongated figure of Nut will have been observed on the ceiling of the great Hypostyle Hall. In this goddess the Egyptians saw the progenitor of all things. She is here shown standing on the primeval waters under the earth; her robe is decorated with the zigzag lines by which the Egyptians pictured water, and thus she seems to be clothed in the rain and dew of heaven which made the earth fertile, while from her body the sun and moon issue forth, the former pouring its rays upon the hills of the world, from which the trees spring up. A Hathor-headed shrine rises in the valley between the hills, and above it a group of hieroglyphs gives the name of the goddess, " Nut the Unknown."

The Sanctuary. One now returns to the Second Vestibule, and enters the Sanctuary, a chamber which, when its doors were closed, must have been quite dark. To the Egyptians it was generally known as the "Dwelling Place of the Golden One." The inscriptions tell us that the doors were closed and sealed for the greater part of the year, and were only opened at the great festivals. The reliefs show the Pharaoh in the presence of Hathor and other gods. On the west and east walls (29 and 30) he burns incense before a shrine containing the sacred barques of Hathor and Horus.

Chambers behind the Sanctuary. From a passage which runs around the back of the Sanctuary several chambers lead off. Entering this passage on the west side, the first chamber on the right was known as the "Purification Room." The next chamber was called the "Necklace Room," and in the doorway one sees a representation of the king presenting a necklace to Hathor. The third room was named "The Flame Room," and leading from this was "The Throne Room of Ra." The next chamber lies immediately behind the Sanctuary, and was one of the most sacred rooms in the temple. Here the golden images of Hathor were preserved in a recess high up in the south wall. On the north wall on either side of the entrance we see the king led by the goddess of Lower Egypt, Uazet (31), and the goddess of Upper Egypt, Nekheb (32), to Hathor. Two other reliefs represent King Pepy of the VIth dynasty kneeling before Hathor. An iron stairway leads up to the recess in which the golden images were kept. On its south or back wall there is a representation of the totem of Hathor, over which the sun spreads its wings, while two winged female figures, corresponding very closely to the Hebrew cherubim, are repre-

DENDEREH 43

sented. The next chamber was known as "The Vase Room"; after which follows "The Sistrum Room," in which there are two recesses for the storing of the golden sistrum-symbols so frequently seen in the temple reliefs. The following four chambers were called respectively "The Room of the Union of the Two Lands"; "The *Seker* Room," the god Seker being a form of Osiris; "The Birth Room," in which the birth of Horus was celebrated; and lastly, "The Resurrection Room." In all these chambers there are at present so many bats, that the visitor is advised to do no more than to make the tour of the passage, without entering the rooms leading from it.

Before quitting the temple the visitor should not fail to ascend to the roof, from which a splendid view of the surrounding country may be obtained. A winding stairway leads from the west side of the First Vestibule, and a straight stairway from the east side ascends in an easy gradient to the roof. These stairways were used by the priests of Hathor at the great festival of the New Year, when the image of the goddess was carried around the temple and up on to the roof, in order to gaze upon all her possessions. A great procession was then formed, the king sometimes taking part in it. At the head were the standard-bearers carrying the standards of the primitive provinces. The king then followed, holding in his hand the standard of Dendereh, and behind him walked a number of priests bearing the standards of all the provinces of Egypt. Then came the Chief Ritual-Priest, chanting from a papyrus; and behind him walked a priest wearing a mask in the form of a lion. A priestess bearing two caskets followed next, and then the High Priest, the Second Priest, the Third Priest, and the Fourth Priest walked in succession. Several priests dressed to represent certain demi-gods came next, and behind them the king and queen sometimes walked, when the former was not heading the procession. The casket or shrine in which the image of the goddess was placed then followed, being carried by several priests; and behind it walked ten priests, each carrying a casket containing some image or symbol which was held to be sacred. The reliefs on the walls of the stairways show this procession ascending and descending to and from the roof. At the south-west corner of the roof there is a twelve-columned chapel, which was used as a halting-place at the processional festival. A flight of iron steps, in place of the damaged original stone steps, ascends to the highest part of the roof. At the northeast corner of the lower level there is a small chapel in which the

The stairways to the roof.

44 ANTIQUITIES OF UPPER EGYPT

mysteries of the resurrection of Osiris were performed. In the inner chamber Osiris is seen lying on, or rising from, his bier. This chapel may be compared with that on the roof of the temple of Isis at Philæ (p. 485).

The crypts. The visitor is not advised to visit more than one of the twelve crypts which are built below the temple, the most easily accessible being that leading from the third room behind the Sanctuary. Here on the walls of the passages are representations of the temple statues and paraphernalia which were perhaps kept in these crypts. The workmanship is excellent, and the plumage of a hawk here represented should be particularly noticed. A statue of King Pepy, the original builder of the temple, is also seen.

Reliefs on the outside of the temple. Persons wishing to examine the reliefs on the outside of the temple should commence from the north-west corner, proceeding southwards along the path over the mounds of debris left by the ancient town. The first relief of interest (33) shows the Pharaoh standing in the presence of Horsmataui, the tunics of both figures being beautifully carved to represent elaborate embroidery. Next (34) the king is seen leaving his palace, crowned as Pharaoh of Lower Egypt, the usual standards preceding him. He is then (35) purified by Thoth and Horus of Edfu; he is (36) crowned by Nekheb and Uazet; (37) is led by Menthu and Tum to Hathor and Horsmataui; (38) pegs out the limits of the temple; (39) breaks the ground in the presence of Isis and a snake-headed form of Horus; (40) shapes the first brick for the temple; (41) throws perfume over the building; (42) presents the finished temple to Hathor and Horsmataui; and along the remainder of the wall he is seen making various offerings to the gods of Denderêh. On the south or rear wall of the temple the large reliefs represent (43) the famous Cleopatra and her son Cæsarion—whose father was Julius Cæsar — worshipping Hathor, Horsmataui, Unnefer, Horus Behudet (a form of Horus of Edfu), and Isis; and farther along the wall (44) Cleopatra and Cæsarion are again shown worshipping Hathor, Horus Behudet, Horsmataui, the Child of Hathor, and Hathor again. Between these two groups there is a large Hathor-head, now much damaged. The reliefs on the east wall of the temple are still partly buried in rubbish, but apparently they were much the same as those on the west wall.

The Birth-House at the south. Returning the same way as he has come, the visitor should enter the small Birth-House, which stands at the south-west corner of the temple. This building consists of a sanctuary on either side of which is a narrow chamber, while in front of the

DENDEREH

sanctuary there is a roofed vestibule. The reliefs, which were worked in the reign of the Emperor Augustus, are of little interest. We see Hathor suckling the child Horus, and on the east and west walls of the sanctuary the cow of Hathor is shown. In the rear wall a recess has been cut in which, in high relief, stands a figure of the god Bes, the patron deity of childhood. On either side of the recess a figure of the cow-headed Hathor is cut in relief, but the arms of these figures have been so carved that they grasp the hands of Bes. Higher up one sees the totem of Hathor cut in high relief, while at the base of the wall there is a figure of the goddess, now headless.

At the north-west of the main building, the visitor approaching the temple will have noticed a small edifice partly buried in rubbish. This is again a Birth-House, and was erected by the Emperor Trajan. It is here necessary to explain what is meant by the term "Birth-House." In the temples of Ptolemaic date there is almost invariably a small temple attached to the main building, and in the reliefs on its walls there are always scenes relating to the birth of Horus. Here were celebrated the ceremonies based on the tradition which relates how the child Horus grew to the stature of manhood, and, making himself Pharaoh of Egypt, overthrew the enemies of his father. The main point which the reliefs seem to be intended to demonstrate is that Horus, as first Pharaoh of Egypt and ancestor of all later Pharaohs, was the offspring of the gods, specially commissioned by them to unite the contending factions of the country, and to evolve law and order out of the chaos. In uniting Egypt the first Pharaoh had to be recognised as the local king or chieftain of every tribe, and had to be crowned, nominally, at many different places. To recognise any later sovereign as Pharaoh, the priests of each city had to assume that he was the true descendant of Horus, and had been chosen for the throne by the gods themselves. Hence, at the sovereign's accession, in every large temple the story of the divine birth of Horus had to be repeated, the new king had to be acknowledged as the physical or spiritual descendant of Horus, and the crowning of the Pharaoh both as king of the province and as the ruler of Upper and Lower Egypt had to be performed. For this purpose the Birth-Houses came to be built, and sometimes, as at Dendereh, a Coronation-House also.

The Birth-House at the north.

The Birth-House in question was decorated with reliefs showing the birth of Horus, and the suckling of the baby by Hathor and other goddesses seated upon couches. We see the gods

46   ANTIQUITIES OF UPPER EGYPT

fashioning the child and his *ka* or double in heaven, and contemplating their work on earth. The temple, however, is at present so much filled with rubbish, and harbours so many bats, that a visit to it cannot be recommended.

<small>The Coronation-House; and the doorways.</small>
Just to the south of this temple there are the partly buried ruins of a small shrine built by the late Ptolemies, in which the reliefs show the king leaving his palace, and crowned by the goddesses Nekheb and Uazet. This seems to have been a kind of Coronation-House, in which the new Pharaoh was recognised as such by the priests. There are on the east side of the temple enclosure two masonry doorways, one bearing the cartouches of the Emperor Antoninus, and the other those of Tiberius Claudius and Nero. A Greek inscription on the latter mentions the twenty-first year of Tiberius.

<small>The Coptic Church.</small>
Between the northern Birth-House and the Coronation-House there stand the half-buried ruins of a very fine church, built of sandstone. It is large and roomy, and has several chapels. The recesses are decorated with very excellently carved designs; and when fully excavated one may hope to see in it one of the finest of the early Christian buildings of Egypt. It is possible that this church marked the famous centre of Christian activity in the fourth century, known as *Tabenna* or *Tabennesch*. At Tabenna, which is known to have been located somewhere in this neighbourhood, fifty thousand monks are stated by St. Jerome to have assembled to celebrate the Easter festival. It is to be hoped that this building will soon be cleared of debris.

<small>The cemeteries of Dendereh.</small>
In the desert behind the temple lie the cemeteries of the VIth dynasty, but the large brick tombs of the princes of the province are now much ruined, and the inner chambers are inaccessible, while all inscriptions and reliefs have been removed. Some two or three miles back in the desert there are several small tumuli graves of Ptolemaic or Roman date, in which the Beduin of the period were perhaps buried. Some ancient quarries are to be found some miles farther to the south-west. Between Dendereh or Keneh and Koptos there is nothing of interest.

CHAPTER III

KOPTOS—OMBOS—KUS—SHENHÛR—MEDAMÛT

THE ordinary traveller in Egypt will not find it worth his while to visit the ruins of Koptos, which stand near the site of the modern village of Kuft; but persons who are particularly interested in antiquities will perhaps desire to visit the small temples here. Those who are travelling by dahabiyeh, and who are moored near Kuft, will find the excursion an easy one. The trains from Luxor are fairly convenient; and, if a dragoman has been sent on ahead with a good donkey, it is possible to leave Luxor by the morning train, to pay a visit to the ruins, and to return to Luxor in time for lunch.

Methods of visiting Koptos.

THE HISTORY OF KOPTOS

The history of *Koptos*, the Greek form of the ancient Egyptian *Kebt*, carries us back to archaic times. On the west bank of the river there was the predynastic settlement of Ombos (p. 53); and it would seem that the inhabitants of that town were engaged in mining gold in the eastern desert, as the original name of the place, *Nubi*, "gold," indicates. They therefore required a mining station on the east bank of the river, and the foundations of the future Koptos were thus laid. It is usually thought that Koptos itself dates back to the earliest known period; but this is not so. Except for a few small prehistoric cemeteries in the hills several miles from the town no trace of anything earlier than the Ist or IInd dynasty has been found. Ombos, on the opposite bank, judging by its vast prehistoric cemeteries, is a much more ancient settlement; and just as Hieraconpolis on the west bank is a more ancient city than El Kâb on the east bank (p. 307), Elephantine than Aswân (p. 391), Koshtâmneh than Kubbân (p. 525), and so on, so here the western city is more ancient than the eastern. This is due to the fact that the main lines of communication from end to end of Egypt are upon the west bank of the river, which was thus populated first ; and wherever a city is found on the east bank opposite to an early settlement on the west bank, one generally finds that it is an offshoot or mining station of a date later than that of the western city. From Koptos a road ran to the breccia quarries of Wady Fowakhieh, and to the gold-mines of the Wady Hammamat district. Archaic inscriptions in the quarries show that they were already being worked in the Ist and IInd dynasties, and it was probably the miners and quarrymen who founded the city of Koptos. Wady Fowakhieh is half-way between Koptos and the Red Sea, and before long the Egyptians penetrated through to the coast along this route, and possibly began already to open up communication with Sinai, Arabia, and the land of Punt. It may be presumed that the men of the desert, the forerunners of the Beduin, were an important element in the early population of the station ; and it is not surprising, therefore, to find that the early god of the place was Min, the patron deity of the eastern desert, whose totem was an object built up of Red Sea shells and the like. Professor Petrie found three archaic statues of this god in Koptos, upon which the figures of various desert animals were rudely cut. In the IVth dynasty the town had already begun to rise into importance, and a ceremonial jar bearing the name of King Khufu (B.C. 2900) indicates that the temple services flourished at this time. In the VIth dynasty Pepy Ist and IInd erected or restored a temple here; and in the XIth dynasty it was already a place of considerable importance. In the eighth year of the reign of Sankhkara Mentuhotep (B.C. 2030), an official was sent along the road to the Red Sea to obtain myrrh and incense from the land of Punt (p. 269), and he is said to have set out from Koptos with an army of 3000 men. In the XIIth dynasty, Amenemhat, a noble of Beni Hasan, states that he went to Koptos at the orders of Senusert Ist (B.C. 1970), with an army of 600 men, to bring gold from the mines near that place. Senusert Ist is known to have repaired the temple at Koptos, as also did Amenemhat Ist before him. The quarries behind Koptos were worked by Senusert IIIrd (B.C. 1887), who is there called, "Beloved of Min, Lord of Koptos"; and under Amenemhat IIIrd there are various traces of activity in the city, which by this time must have been a place of great importance, eclipsing the mother city Ombos on the west bank. The site was probably enclosed with walls early in this dynasty, as were El Kâb, Aswân, and perhaps Karnak, for fear of the negroes who were expected to invade Egypt at any moment from the desert

KOPTOS

(p. 447). In the dark ages of the XIIIth and XVIth dynasties occasional light is shed upon the history of the city. Under King Nubkheperura Antef, an official of the temple of Min, named Teta, was found guilty of treason (?), and all his goods were given to the *ha*-prince of Koptos. The same king undertook some work in the temple, as blocks bearing his name indicate. Another king of this period, Ra-hotep, states that the doors of the temple had decayed, and were restored by him; and of the Pharaoh Sebekhotep IIIrd scarabs have been found here. During the Hyksos period Apepa Ist connected himself with the town; and when the kings of the XVIIIth dynasty came to the throne, the city came in for considerable attention. Thothmes IInd carried on some works here, and objects bearing the name of Hatshepsut have been found. Thothmes IIIrd rebuilt the temple, and we learn that in his reign the tax collected from the city was one deben of silver and half a deben of gold, ten measures of grain, some honey, and a number of calves. The smallness of the gold tax indicates that the gold-mines were not being vigorously worked in this neighbourhood. On the other hand, in the chapel of Menkheperrasenb (p. 125), we see the reception of the gold from the captain of the police of Koptos, and from the governor of the "gold country" of Koptos. The names of Thothmes IVth and Akhnaton have been found in the city; and we know that the latter king worked the quarries. Under Sety Ist and Rameses IInd (B.C. 1300) various building works were carried on; and a tablet found at Koptos relates how certain Hittite princes and a princess came to Egypt, apparently *viâ* Koptos, with horses, goats, cattle, gold, silver, and greenstone. Merenptah and Rameses IIIrd undertook building works here, and under the latter king an expedition was sent to Punt which returned in safety to Koptos, where the goods which they had brought were loaded on to Nile vessels amid rejoicings. The king is said to have presented thirty-nine people to the temples of the city. Rameses IVth seems to have paid a visit to the town on his way to the breccia quarries; and Rameses VIth seems to have been connected with the place. In later times Painezem, Osorkon, Shabaka, Psammetik Ist (or IInd), Aahmes IInd, and Nectanebo have all left their names here.

In Ptolemaic times the trade with the east brought considerable wealth to Koptos. The city was now the capital of the fifth nome of Upper Egypt, of which the standard was two hawks. Queen Arsinoë, the daughter of Lysimachus of Thrace, was banished by her husband, Ptolemy Philadelphus, to Koptos, where she held her court for some years. A curious story dating from this period relates how Prince Setna, the son of Rameses IInd, heard from a ghost at Koptos how a certain book of magic had been dropped into the river at that place, how its owner and child had been drowned there, and how they desired to be reburied at Memphis. Many of the Roman emperors have left their names at Koptos, for during that age the trade-route with the East was much in use, and the breccia and granite quarries were worked from this base. The Imperial porphyry quarries of Gebel Dukhan and the white granite quarries of Um Etgal (Mons Claudianus) also used Koptos as a base. In the ninth year of Domitian an interesting tariff of taxes on goods passing in and out of the city across the desert was drawn up, and a copy has fortunately been preserved. An inscription of the eighth year of Trajan has also been found here; and another inscription of this period tells us that there was now a senate at Koptos, as at many of the other Egyptian towns. The city rebelled against Diocletian in 292 A.D., and was utterly destroyed by him in punishment. Both Strabo and Pliny tell us that the population was very mixed, and had Arabic and Phœnician elements in it; and one may thus suppose that the city had for long been a seat of disaffection. The worship of Min continued down to late times, but now Osiris, Isis, and various forms of Horus were also worshipped. Aelian states that the inhabitants crucified the hawk and worshipped the crocodile; but he must have been thinking of Ombos on the other side of the river, where such customs might be expected. The city recovered from the blow inflicted by Diocletian, and in the Middle Ages was a place of considerable importance; but it finally fell into disrepute, and Kus took its place as the terminus of the desert routes. The Christians have left traces of their churches amidst the ruins of the old temples; and the name Koptos is still preserved in the word Copt (a native Christian), as also it is in the word Egypt (Greek: *Aiguptos*).

THE ANTIQUITIES OF KOPTOS

The ruins in the town enclosure. Passing through the town of Kuft a large open space is reached, covered with enormous quantities of potsherds, with here and there mud-brick walls rising to some height. This is the site of the ancient Koptos, and of the excavations of Prof. Flinders Petrie in 1893-4. Amidst the chaos of ancient rubbish various remains of stone-work stand out, and attract the visitor's eye. The largest group of such ruins lies at the west end of the site. Here may be seen a number of sandstone and granite blocks dating from various periods, and re-used in the building of an early Christian church. Three square granite pillars still stood in position until recent years, while others lie on the ground, and these seem to have been built into the doorway and the choir of the church. The pillars originally dated from the reign of Thothmes IIIrd, and were decorated with fine reliefs in the best XVIIIth dynasty style; but all except one panel have been carefully chiselled out by the unconsciously barbarous Christians. The one remaining panel seems to have been hidden by a wall, and therefore escaped destruction, and solitarily remains to tell of the beauty of the early temple which stood here.[1] Upon it Thothmes IIIrd is seen standing, while beneath him runs an inscription relating to the jubilee-festival. The name of Amen, which also occurs, has been erased by King Akhnaton who worshipped the god Aton; but it has been carefully rewritten at a later date, probably by order of Sety Ist. These pillars have been erected by the Copts upon a platform composed of fragments of a Roman temple, on one of which the cartouches of Augustus Cæsar may be seen.

A few yards to the south of this group of ruins lie a number of Ptolemaic and Roman inscribed blocks of stone, built into a later wall. Farther to the south is a granite block inscribed with the name of Ptolemy IVth, Philopator; and near it is a colossal granite statue of a queen, much battered and worn. At the south-west end of the site there stands a sandstone door with some small panels of relief upon it, some of which still remain coloured. The reliefs show Claudius Cæsar worshipping Horus, Isis, Sebek, Min, and other gods. Near this is a stone tomb, from which a granite sarcophagus and a stele were removed a few years ago to the Cairo Museum. A similar tomb to the east of this now stands open. It consists of a small sandstone chamber, standing above ground, and roofed with sandstone blocks, one of which has been removed. Through the aperture one sees a stone sarcophagus lying empty, the lid being tipped over to one side. There are no inscriptions, but the form of the tomb shows it to have been Ptolemaic or Roman. Just near this tomb is a small granite temple or shrine, dating from the reign of Ptolemy XIIIth Neos Dionysos, the father of the famous Cleopatra. The reliefs show the king worshipping various gods, but only a small part of them remains. A few yards to the south is another small temple, now

---

[1] This pillar has now been removed to the Cairo Museum.

forming part of a native house, and harbouring goats and chickens. The reliefs are bold and well executed, especially noticeable being a fine scene of four priests carrying a throne or shrine, upon which a lion is represented. The cartouches seem only to give the title Autocrator Cæsar, which was held by all the Roman Emperors in Egypt. Prof. Petrie's excavations were made at about the middle of the east end of the site, and the works are marked by the usual pits and rubbish mounds. A few stone blocks and some Coptic pillars are to be seen; and a broken basalt naos of Ptolemy XIIIth of fine workmanship lies half buried in the ground. The east end of the site is covered with the ruins of small mud-brick houses of the old town.

The temple of Kaleh. The most interesting ruin in the neighbourhood is a small Roman temple standing at the corner of the village of Kaleh, less than a mile north of Kuft, by a path across the fields. The temple consists of a forecourt and second court, with a chamber on either side, and a sanctuary with a passage running around it, from the south side of which another chamber leads. The entrance to the forecourt abuts the houses of the village towards the east, but the temple may be entered by another doorway upon the south side of the second court. The roof has entirely disappeared, and all the reliefs seem much worn and weathered. The walls, however, are very perfect, and the general plan of the temple is extremely clear. In the main sanctuary the main wall is dedicated to Min, but the little chamber at the back of this is dedicated to Isis. Here are the best preserved reliefs, and the visitor will note the rich colouring which is still to be seen. In the forecourt is a scene showing the king, wearing the crown of Lower Egypt, leaving his palace. The reliefs outside the temple are boldly executed, but are much damaged. The cartouches throughout are those of the Emperor Tiberius Claudius. Observed from the back the temple is seen to stand upon a high platform of very solid masonry, which raised the west end above a moat or lake, now dried up, into which it projected. The ruin has not yet been excavated or cleared by the Department of Antiquities, but its interests are protected by the Department's gaffir, and as it is very rarely visited by tourists, its walls have escaped the scribbles so commonly seen in other temples.

A few tombs of no importance at the edge of the desert are the only other ancient remains in this locality.

OMBOS

OMBOS

Before describing the antiquities of Ombos, which lies on the west bank of the river at a point equidistant between Kuft and Kus, mention must be made of those ancient sites which lie between Dendereh and Ombos. Riding along the edge of the desert southwards from the temple of Dendereh one passes only meagre traces of one or two cemeteries until the village of Dêr is reached. Here there are the ruins of an ancient Coptic monastery; and a short distance to the south rises a mound of mud-bricks, which appears to be a ruined *mastaba* or pyramid. Not far from here are the extensive prehistoric cemeteries of Ballas, now mostly dug out. Passing a few XIIth and XVIIIth dynasty tombs, excavated by Professor Petrie, one reaches the site of Ombos. The traveller will not find much to attract him to this place, and the excursion, which is best made from the station of Kus, on the opposite bank of the river, is long and tiring.

Antiquities between Dendereh and Ombos: west bank.

THE HISTORY OF OMBOS

Like the ancient town of Kôm Ombo, near Aswân, this city was named *Nby*, "The Golden"; and from this word the Coptic *Ombo* and Greek *Ombos* were derived. The extensive prehistoric cemeteries which lie to the north and south of the site speak for the great antiquity of the place; and it may be that its name is derived from the fact that, before the foundation of Koptos, it was the treasury to which the gold was brought from the Eastern mines. When two cities of high antiquity are in close proximity to each other on opposite banks of the river one often finds—at any rate in Upper Egypt—that the city on the western bank is in each case the more ancient of the two. In the case of Diospolis Parva and Khenoboskion, which stand opposite to one another, the former, on the west bank, is the more ancient, and is the capital of the province; while the latter, on the east bank, does not rise until the VIth dynasty. Hieraconpolis and Eileithyiapolis stand opposite one another, and the former, which is on the west bank, is certainly the more ancient. Of Elephantine and Aswân, the former is the older city. In the case of Dakkeh and Kubbân, the former, on the west bank, has near it an archaic fortress; while the latter, on the east bank, does not date earlier than the XIIth dynasty. The reason for this is obvious. Most of the cities of Upper Egypt in archaic times traded in gold, and despatched caravans into the eastern desert. These cities were usually built on the western bank of the river, owing, perhaps, to the fact that the main routes of communication from end to end of Egypt passed along the western desert. Mining stations had, therefore, to be founded on the eastern bank, opposite to the parent cities, and these stations soon became cities as large as those on the western bank. It is certain that Diospolis Parva, Hieraconpolis, Elephantine, and Dakkeh were settlements of great antiquity, and that originally the *raison d'être* of their offshoots Khenoboskion, Eileithyiapolis, Aswân, and Kubbân, was the gold-mining in the eastern desert; and therefore, since Koptos was the terminus of several trade routes and gold-mining routes in the eastern desert, since no antiquities have been found there earlier than the Ist dynasty, and since Ombos undoubtedly dates to the prehistoric period, one may safely say that Koptos was an offspring of the city of Ombos, and that Ombos was the original repository of the gold from the eastern mines, its name being derived from this fact.

The god Set.

The patron deity of Ombos was the god Set, one of the aboriginal gods of Egypt. When the army of the Horus-worshipping tribes invaded the southern provinces of Egypt (which invasions are perhaps to be identified with the wars of the archaic kings of Thinis), it was the army of the Set-worshipping tribes which was defeated at Dendereh and at Edfu. The presence of this stronghold of Set here at Ombos accounts for the first battle having been fought at Dendereh; and, arguing in the opposite direction, the fact that the battle with Set was fought here shows that Ombos was already in existence at this very early date. After these wars between Horus and Set, the two nations seem to have entertained nothing but respect for one another, and while the victories of Horus were celebrated at Dendereh, Edfu, and elsewhere, the god Set continued to be worshipped by the conquered aborigines, who now intermarried with their conquerors. One of the early kings of Egypt seems to have been crowned both at Ombos and Hieraconpolis, for above his name as Hawk-chief of Hieraconpolis there is drawn both the hawk and the figure of Set; or it may be that through his mother this king inherited the actual chieftainship of the Set tribes, just as he inherited the hawk chieftainship. In later times Set is often spoken of as a valiant fighting god, warring on the side of the Egyptians against their enemies; and on an XVIIIth dynasty relief he is seen in the act of giving life to the

Pharaoh as King of Hieraconpolis. In early prayers for the dead he is invoked together with Horus. Even at Edfu, the place of his defeat, Set is spoken of as assisting King Thothmes IVth, along with the other Egyptian gods. And in the XIXth dynasty Kings Sety Ist and IInd were named after him. Set, then, although originally the enemy of Horus, reigned throughout the best part of Egyptian history as the equal of that god; and it was only in Ptolemaic times that the traditions of the archaic wars, in the light of the development of the worship of Horus, Osiris, and Isis, came to be the basis of a persecution of Set which ended by converting him into Satan, Prince of Evil. It is difficult to say from whence the god Set came in early times; but it cannot be denied that he was originally connected with the Asiatic god Sutekh, with whom he was in later times identified. He is always represented either as a fabulous monster having upright, square-topped ears, a long snout, and a rigid tail, or else as a human-bodied creature having the head of that monster.

The temple of Set at Ombos seems to have been in existence in the earliest times, and pottery and sealings of the period previous to the IVth dynasty have been found there. Scarabs of Senusert Ist and Senusert IIIrd of the XIIth dynasty and of Sebekhotep IIIrd of the XIIIth dynasty have also been discovered there. In the XVIIIth dynasty Thothmes Ist built here, and the beautiful relief of that king which adorned this temple will perhaps have been noticed by the visitor in the Cairo Museum. Later Thothmes IIIrd rebuilt the temple on more extensive lines, and this work was finished by his son Amenhotep IInd. Rameses IInd undertook some restorations to the temple, and Merenptah added his name to the new reliefs. Rameses IIIrd states that he restored the temple, building up its ruined walls. He placed slaves and captives there to tend it, endowed it with the revenues from certain lands and islands, presented it with herds of cattle, and increased the offerings at its altars. Nothing more is heard of the temple until the XXIInd dynasty, when one of the Sheshonk kings left his name here. The only other reference to Ombos dates from the Roman occupation, when Juvenal in his fifteenth Satire describes a fight which took place between the people of Dendereh and those of Ombos. At Ombos the crocodile was held sacred, owing to its (now obscure) relation to Set; while for the same reason it was held in abhorrence at Dendereh. During a feast at Koptos it seems that some persons from Dendereh killed one of these animals, and a fight ensuing, they captured and

The temple of Ombos.

56 ANTIQUITIES OF UPPER EGYPT

actually devoured an Ombite citizen. Thus, as in the first glimpse which we obtain of Ombos, so in the last, we see the gods Horus and Set fighting with one another.

THE ANTIQUITIES OF OMBOS

The temple, town, and pyramid.

Little now remains to be seen of the once prosperous town and its fine temple. Amidst the heaps of debris one may see here and there some of the limestone walls of the temple, and the cartouches of Merenptah are conspicuous. The town was never very large, but it seems to have been closely compacted. The temple had in front of it a mud-brick pylon, with recesses for flagstaffs: and the main chambers, built of stone, were surrounded by a brick-enclosing wall. A short distance to the north there are the remains of a pyramid, which, by the rough workmanship displayed in its building, seems to date from a very early period. From this point for several miles towards the south there extend the famous prehistoric cemeteries known as the cemeteries of Nekâdeh. Thousands of prehistoric and archaic graves have been opened here, both by authorised and unauthorised excavators ; and from the pottery here found Professor Petrie was first able to draw up his—to Egyptologists—famous sequence of pot-shapes, by which the prehistoric period in Egypt is now dated. At the southern end of these cemeteries, a short distance north-west of the town of Nekâdeh, Monsieur de Morgan in 1897 discovered a large brick tomb, containing various inscribed objects which prove it to be the burial-place either of King Menes himself, the first king of the Ist dynasty, or of his wife or daughter. The brick ruin is not now worth visiting, as it is too much damaged to be intelligible. Archæologists, however, who are anxious to see it will find the excursion from *Kus* railway station neither difficult nor tedious, while for those persons who are travelling by dahabiyeh and are moored a short way below Nekâdeh the excursion may be made on foot.

The tomb of Menes.

KUS AND SHENHÛR

Methods of visiting Kus and Shenhûr.

Returning once more to the east bank of the river the traveller's attention may be called to the ruins of Kus and Shenhûr, which lie to the south of Koptos, and almost opposite to Nekâdeh. Neither of these places possess ruins of sufficient interest to make a visit to them worth the traveller's while, unless he is particularly interested in antiquities ; but those who wish to make the excursion,

KUS AND SHENHÛR

and do not own a dahabiyeh, should travel by the early train from Luxor to Kus, taking their donkeys with them. Shenhûr lies some $3\frac{1}{2}$ miles to the south of Kus, and the train which passes Kus at noon on its way to Luxor may be caught.

KUS

The modern town of Kus is built upon the ruins of the ancient city of Keskes, of which the patron deity was the god Hor-uar, "Horus the Elder," who was also god of Kôm Ombo. Hor-uar, or as the Greeks called him, Arueris, is usually identified with Apollo, and hence the city was known to the Greeks as Apollinopolis Parva. Its history, however, is entirely unknown until the period of the Ptolemies, of which date a Greek dedicatory inscription was observed at Kus. The only remains to be seen are the extensive mounds of debris, and a block or two of stonework from the temple. In the mosque there is a granite basin inscribed with the name of Ptolemy IInd Philadelphus. One fragment of stone construction has upon it a Ptolemaic or Roman relief, representing a Pharaoh sacrificing a gazelle; and near this it is evident that the ruins of the temple are buried. Keskes, or Kus, rose in importance as Koptos declined; and in the Middle Ages it is said to have been second in size only to Cairo. It was then the chief terminus of the trade routes with the East, but in more modern times it gave place to Keneh, and sank to its present insignificant size.

The ruins in the town.

SHENHÛR

The modern village of Shenhûr marks the site of the ancient town of *Senhor*, a place which has no history earlier than the Roman period. At this date a small temple was erected here, which exists in fairly good preservation at the present day. This temple consists of three much ruined halls or forecourts, the second of which has the bases of eight columns, and behind these courts is the main temple, still partly roofed and not extensively ruined. It is oriented from south to north, and on its west side is an open space, in which are the potsherds and other remains of the ancient town; while on its east side stands the modern village buried amidst the trees. The first court of the temple is entirely ruined, and has no inscriptions. The second court, in which are the columns, has a fragment of an inscription on the north door-

The temple of Shenhûr.

way, giving the cartouche of the Roman Emperor Nerva. The third court is mainly filled with rubbish, but part of an inscription can be seen on the south wall. A ruined gateway leads from this court into the first hall of the temple, of which the side walls alone are standing. In the north wall are two small doorways leading into side chambers, both roofed, but much filled with rubbish, and a main gateway leading into the second hall. From this hall a door in the west wall leads into the side chamber, and one at the west end of the north wall leads into another chamber, now choked with rubbish. The main doorway in the north wall brings one into the partly roofed pronaos, from which a door leads off to the south. In front of one is the sanctuary, with the usual passage leading round the back of it, partly roofed. The sanctuary is the only part of the inner chambers of the temple decorated with reliefs. The outer face of the doorway has the usual winged disk upon the lintel, while to right and left are small reliefs showing the Pharaoh worshipping Min, Horus, Thoth, Amen-Ra, and other gods. The outer face of the front wall shows on the right a bigger relief of the king worshipping Isis, and on the left a similar scene with Mut as the deity. Entering the chamber, which is much choked with rubbish, on the north wall the king is seen before Mut and Isis, while on the side walls similar reliefs show him before Isis, Khonsu, Horus, Thoth, &c. All these reliefs are much weathered, and are not very clear. All the cartouches which are to be seen here read simply "Autocrator Cæsar." The passage around the sanctuary is partly roofed. From the west wall a doorway leads into a small chamber, while in the middle of the north wall there is an opening from which a small passage in the thickness of the wall goes off to right and left.

The reliefs upon the outside of the temple are much blurred, except those on the back wall. In the middle of this wall there is a false door with a winged disk above, and some small side-reliefs showing the king in the presence of Isis, Thoth, Khonsu, and other deities. To the west of this false door there are some large reliefs representing the king worshipping Amen-Ra, Mut, Khonsu, and Isis; and to the east similar reliefs show him worshipping Min, Mut, Khonsu, and Isis. These must be regarded as the main deities of the place; but the name *Senhor* suggests that *Hor* or Horus was also a patron of the town.

Just to the north of the temple there is a mound of ruins upon which is built a mosque, the minaret of which now leans dangerously. The mosque is a decidedly picturesque building, and,

KUS AND SHENHÛR

together with the temple and the background of trees, forms a picture of great charm. The minaret will serve as a landmark to those who are riding from Kus. A few remains of a Coptic church are to be observed in the neighbourhood, and near the edge of the desert, some miles to the east, there are two or three mounds which mark the sites of ancient towns.

FROM KUS TO THEBES

After leaving Shenhûr, a person riding on the eastern side of the river towards Luxor passes no ancient sites—except one or two insignificant cemeteries, entirely plundered, and some ancient stone blocks near the railway—until he reaches the village of Medamût, which is supposed to mark the site of the Christian town of Maximianopolis. The remains of the temple, which once stood at Medamût, are sometimes visited from Luxor by persons who are desirous of a long donkey-ride. The road passes to the east of the railway line, and with a good donkey the ruins may be reached in about an hour. They are, however, of little interest. A temple once stood here, built by Amenhotep IInd, and enlarged by Sety Ist and Rameses IInd, and dedicated to the god Mentu. The present remains of columns, &c., mostly date from Ptolemaic and Roman days, and the cartouches of Ptolemy Euergetes Ist, Ptolemy Euergetes IInd, Ptolemy Lathyros, Ptolemy Auletes, Antoninus Pius, and Tiberius are to be observed. *[East bank. Medamût.]*

Between Nekâdeh and Thebes, upon the west bank of the river, there are several plundered cemeteries, but no sites of interest to the ordinary traveller are found. Between Nekâdeh and the village of Kamuleh there are four Coptic convents, which are said to date from the time of the Empress Helena. These are Dêr el Melak, Dêr es Salîb, Dêr Mari Girgis, and Dêr Mari Bokli. *[West bank.]*

CHAPTER IV

THEBES

Situation, &c.
THE modern town of Luxor, which word is a corruption of El Uksur ("The Castles"), stands on the site of the southern portion of the ancient city of Thebes. The visitor arriving by railway drives from the station through the native streets to the Europeanised portion of the town, which is mostly situated on or near the river front. Those arriving by steamer or dahabiyeh find themselves at once in this part of the town, and the native quarter remains to be seen later. Here the beautiful temple of Luxor stands, backed by the town. Unfortunately there are a few houses between it and the river, but it is hoped that some day these will disappear. To the south of the temple is the entrance to the Luxor Hotel, beyond which is a row of shops, &c., leading along to the huge building of the luxurious Winter Palace Hotel. To the north of the temple stand the Karnak, Savoy, and Grand Hotels, hidden amidst the trees. The house and offices of the Inspector-General of Antiquities stand on the edge of the river some distance farther to the north, the approach being along the Luxor-Karnak road.

Luxor is 454 miles south of Cairo, and 136 north of Aswân. A comfortable night journey from Cairo in the *wagon-lit* brings the traveller to this the ancient capital of Egypt; and no one who has found his way to Cairo should fail to travel up to this interesting centre of antiquities. Nor should he allow but a few days for his visit. There is so much of importance to be seen here that he should arrange to make a prolonged stay. Luxor, with its fine hotels, is a good centre for the excursions to all the ancient sites from Abydos in the north to Edfu in the south.

The name "Thebes."
The name of the province of which Thebes was the capital was Wast or Tjamet, which in later times came to be known as the Thebaïd. The two towns occupying the sites of Karnak and Luxor were known as "the two Apts," the word Apt signifying "a

THEBES

harîm." Karnak was often called Apt-asut, "the thrones of Apt," while Luxor was called Apt-reset, "the southern Apt." The word Apt was pronounced, in the New Empire at any rate, Ape; and the feminine article *Ta*, "the," was often placed before it, thus giving Tapé. The Greeks corrupted this into Thebai or Thebes, thus identifying it with the name of cities of their own in Bœotia, Attica, Thessaly, Cilicia, Asia Minor, &c., just as they had done in the case of the Egyptian Abdu, which they had altered to Abydos. In the days of Homer the name Thebes had already come into use; and the lines are well known which thus refer to the city:—

> "By the fertile stream
> Where, in Egyptian Thebes, the heaps of precious ingots gleam,
> The hundred-gated Thebes, where twice ten score in martial state
> Of valiant men with steeds and cars march through each massy gate."

To the Egyptians Thebes was known by many names. It was "Victorious Thebes," "The Thrones of the Two Lands," "The Mysterious City," "The City of the Hidden Name," "The City of the Lord of Eternity," "The Mistress of Temples," "The Mistress of Might," and so on. It was also called simply Nu, or Nut, "the City"; and from this is derived the No or No-Amon which is so often spoken of and which the Assyrians changed to Ni. The western bank of the river, where lay the Necropolis, was often called simply Wast or Tjamet Amentet, "Western Thebes"; but in later times it was generally called Pa-Hathor, "the house of Hathor," she being patron goddess of the western hills; and hence the Greek Pathyris. As late as the seventh century A.D., however, the name Tjeme is found as the designation of the western desert at this point. The Greeks also called Thebes Diospolis Magna, Amen being identified with Zeus; and Diodorus indicates that the Egyptians preferred this name to that of Thebes.

Diodorus says that Thebes is the most ancient city of Egypt, and, though this is evidently not correct, it may well be *one* of the most ancient cities of the country. There are some traces of prehistoric remains on the west bank of the river opposite Karnak, and at Karnak itself relics of a period as early as the IInd dynasty have been found. The cultivated land on the east bank of the Nile valley is particularly wide at this point, and the site of Thebes was the centre of what must always have been a populous district. The site, being on the river bank at about

History.

the middle point of this wide area, could not well avoid becoming the market-centre; and thus one may suppose that there was a settlement here from the earliest times. The beginning of the history of the town is, of course, lost in obscurity. In all probability there were three small towns in early times which later became amalgamated. The first of these was situated on the west bank, probably in the neighbourhood of the later palace of Amenhotep IIIrd, and the town of Medinet Habu, for near this point some early tombs and pottery fragments have been observed. The second stood at Luxor, near the later temple of Amenhotep IIIrd, and the third was situated at Karnak. These three towns, being some miles apart, were quite separate so long as they remained of small size. It is probable that Karnak was the most ancient of the three; for, as has been said, there are indications that the place was in existence in archaic times. Throughout the main part of the Old Kingdom the place remained of no importance, and the capital of the province was Arment, some distance to the south on the west bank of the river. In the VIth dynasty (B.C. 2500), however, the local princes of Thebes obtained some degree of power, as did so many provincial families at this time. The tomb of a certain Ahy, who was "Great Chieftain of the Province," was discovered some years ago in the Theban necropolis; but, although he was buried in Thebes, the inscriptions do not mention the name of that city, though there is a reference to Arment and to Dendereh. This family of princes seems to have retained its power during the confused period which followed, for in the XIth dynasty we again catch sight of them (B.C. 2100). One of the princes of this line was named Antef or Antefaa, and under one of the Pharaohs of dynasty X. he seems to have held the important appointment of "Keeper of the Frontier of the South" (see p. 29), which title generally indicates that the possessor was the most powerful of the Upper Egyptian nobles. The successor of this prince, also named Antef, having further increased his sphere of influence, declared himself Pharaoh, and managed to extend his kingdom from the Theban province to the First Cataract on the south and to Abydos on the north. This king seems to have been closely connected with Karnak, for he was buried at Dra abu'l Neggar, exactly opposite that place, and particular reference is made to him in a list of kings at Karnak. The first really great Pharaoh of this line, however, was Nebhapetra Mentuhotep, whose temple and tomb at Dêr el Bahri are described in Chapter X. This

THEBES

king's reign lasted for nearly fifty years, and under his rule Karnak enjoyed the greatest prosperity, while the two neighbouring towns may have also increased in size and wealth. At about this period the glory of Thebes, "like a splendid sea," is referred to.

At the beginning of the XIIth dynasty Amenemhat Ist (B.C. 2000–1970) erected a temple at Karnak, which was enlarged by his successor, Senusert Ist; and the walls of other buildings of this dynasty have recently been discovered. Senusert IIIrd (B.C. 1887–1849) restored Dêr el Bahri, and undertook other building works. As the capital of Egypt, Thebes must now have been a place of considerable wealth and size; and although the Pharaohs of this dynasty lived mostly in the north, they did not neglect the southern metropolis. It is at about this date that large tombs were made in the hills to the north of the Theban necropolis, which perhaps indicates that the town on this side of the river had now attained some size. At the beginning of this period a certain noble named Antefaker constructed for himself a tomb which may now be seen at Shêkh abd' el Gûrneh (p. 155).

In Dynasty XIII. Sebekhotep IIIrd (?) built a temple at Luxor, a fact which shows that this town was also now of considerable size. During the chaotic period, between Dynasties XIII. and XVII., one hears practically nothing of this neighbourhood. Some of the kings were buried at Dra abu'l Neggar (p. 186) in small brick pyramids. While the Shepherd Kings were reigning in Lower Egypt, the remnants of the old line of kings seem to have held a precarious sway at Thebes; and under three kings, Sekenenra Ist, IInd, and IIIrd of Dynasty XVII., the power of the old capital began to be won back. King Kames, who succeeded to the third Sekenenra, made himself master of Upper Egypt practically as far south as the Second Cataract. He likewise seems to have been buried at Dra abu'l Neggar, and his and his wife's jewels, discovered in that neighbourhood, form one of the richest "finds" ever made in Egypt.

Aahmes Ist (B.C. 1580–1557) restored the temple at Luxor, and his successor, Amenhotep Ist, conducted extensive works at Karnak, and on the edge of the western desert at Dra abu'l Neggar and Medinet Habu. Thothmes Ist and Thothmes IInd built at Karnak and elsewhere; and under the succeeding Pharaohs, Hatshepent and Thothmes IIIrd, Thebes became the most important city in the world. Vast wealth had been brought here from the Pharaohs' trading expeditions or victories in Asia and the Sudan, and enormous numbers of foreign slaves were now compelled to work for the beautification of the city. At Karnak the great festival hall of Thothmes IIIrd, and the obelisks and buildings of his predecessors, formed a group of temples of great magnificence. They were surrounded by gardens filled with the flowers and trees both of Egypt and of Asia. These extended to the south towards the modern Luxor, where there were other temples. The houses of the town clustered around these two groups of buildings; and on the other side of the river there were, no doubt, many villas. At the edge of the western desert there were the temples at Medinet Habu, Dêr el Bahri, and elsewhere; and a small town inhabited by the priests and other persons connected with the necropolis began to grow up at Dêr el Medineh.

Thothmes IIIrd went regularly every summer to the wars, and returned to Thebes at the end of September or beginning of October, bringing with him the wealth which he had captured in Syria or the Sudan. It was then that the people of Thebes obtained their glimpses of the outside world, and learned to admire the luxury of conquered Syria and to despise its people. Each year the fleet of war galleys moored in front of the city and discharged onto the crowded quays the wretched, bedraggled prisoners who had been brought here to work for the rest of their lives as slaves. Each year the loot from the Syrian cities—golden vases, fine linens, splendid arms and armour, gilded chariots, and numbers of horses—was conducted through the thronged streets to the palace. Each year the soldiers of the victorious army paraded through the city, and the sounds of martial music were as frequently heard as were the chants of the priests.

Thothmes organised regular "Feasts of Victory," which were conducted in the most gorgeous manner; and presentations of the loot were then made to the temples. In recording these gifts the king says: "My majesty gave [to the temple] three Asiatic cities. . . . My majesty presented gold, silver, lapis lazuli, malachite, copper, bronze, lead, colours, &c., in great quantities. . . . I set aside numerous fields, gardens, and ploughed lands of the choicest." The king also presented the temple with 1578 Syrian slaves, and of course numerous negroes. During the cool winter season the court remained for the most part of the time at Thebes; and the city was the centre to which the traders and ambassadors of the countries of the whole known world converged. In the spring Thothmes went away to the wars again; and Thebes, sweltering under the summer sun, remained quiet until the autumn.

Amenhotep IInd (B.C. 1448), the successor of Thothmes IIIrd, carried on the same aggressive policy; but by this time Egypt had learnt to adopt some of the barbarous methods of her enemies, and we are told how the Pharaoh slaughtered his captives in the temples. Six princes of Tikhsi, whom he had captured, were hanged head downwards on the walls of Thebes, while a seventh was taken up to the Sudan and there executed in a similar manner. Still the wealth of the world poured into the city, and still the temples were enlarged and beautified. After the short reign of Thothmes IVth, Amenhotep IIIrd came to the throne; and the luxury and wealth of Thebes may now be said to have reached its height. This king built the temple of Luxor, and from it to the temples of Karnak he constructed a wide road bordered with sphinxes. This road passed along more or less the same line as that of the modern Luxor-Karnak road. The river was probably closer to it than it is now (p. 87), but there was room, no doubt, for the villas of some of the nobles between it and the water. The two towns of Luxor and Karnak were now amalgamated, and the town on the west bank of the river was probably linked to the main city by a chain of villas and by a good highroad. The king erected his mortuary temple on the west bank, and the two colossi remain to this day to tell of its magnificence. South of this temple he constructed for himself a beautiful palace on the edge of the desert, and just to the east of it he made an enormous pleasure lake, where he and his famous queen, Thiy, could sail together in a golden barge. Here he held his court in the shadow of the magnificent Theban hills; and hither came the ambassadors of Asia, and even of the Greek islands, to do him homage. The three towns, now amalgamated into the one city of Thebes, became the wonder of the world; and there appear to have been not a few foreigners who deserted their own countries in order to live here. The climate, of course, was only tolerable from September to May each year; and during the summer months it must have been the custom to move to the north.

The next Pharaoh, Akhnaton, owing to his religious beliefs, found Thebes an objectionable place to live in, and built himself a new capital at Tell el Amarna in Middle Egypt. Here he reigned for a dozen years or so, while Thebes lay under a cloud, her temples closed, and her wealth diverted. But at the death of Akhnaton the court returned to the old capital, and Thebes once more became the proudest city of the world. The kings of the new dynasty, Horemheb, Rameses Ist, and Sety Ist, built at Karnak on an unprecedented scale. Th evast Hypostyle Hall was now erected, and numerous pylons and other buildings were set up. Karnak was now becoming the religious quarter of Thebes, and Luxor the secular; and there is reason to suppose that the king's palace was now situated at Luxor. This new dynasty was of Memphite origin, and there was now a tendency to spend the greater part of the year in the north. Rameses IInd (B.C. 1292 to 1225) does not seem to have lived here much, and thus Luxor became somewhat weakened in power; and Karnak, the religious centre, became the most important of the three quarters of Thebes. After the time of Rameses IInd practically no building was undertaken at Luxor, but a great deal was done at Karnak. The palace of Rameses IIIrd (B.C. 1198-1167) was situated near that of Amenhotep IIIrd on the west bank, and here he built his great temple—Medinet Habu. This king, being of a religious disposition, seems to have lived at Thebes for considerable periods, but the city was now beginning to be a sort of Rome of the Middle Ages, dominated by the priests. We read how the king "planted Thebes with trees, shrubs, isi-plants and menhet-flowers"; but this was done not so much for the glory of the city as for that of its religion. During the reigns of the later Ramesside kings the power fell more and more into the hands of the high priest at Karnak, and finally the High Priest Herhor dethroned the unfortunate Rameses XIIth, and made himself Pharaoh (B.C. 1090). From that moment Thebes ceased to be the real royal city, and became the centre of the religion. Karnak was now the Vatican or the Canterbury of Egypt; Luxor was fast becoming a mere village; and the town on the western bank was now the centre of the mortuary worship. The Pharaohs of the succeeding dynasty—Sheshonk, Osorkon, Takeloth, and others—did not reside at Thebes, but they added certain buildings to those already existing at Karnak. Then followed the Ethiopian dynasty (B.C. 712 to 663), during which Thebes came in for considerable attention, and was regarded more as an administrative centre than it had been for some hundreds of years. Lower Egypt was at this time exposed to the invasions of the Assyrians, and the Pharaohs were thus obliged to reside in the upper country. In the year B.C. 661 the generals of

Ashurbanipal razed the city to the ground, and stripped the precious metal from the temples. "Two enormous obelisks, wrought of bright silver, whose weight was 2500 talents," were carried to Nineveh. Many of the inhabitants were slain, and for many years the fate of the city was the talk of the world. The words of the prophet Nahum will be remembered : " Art thou better than No-Amon, that was situate among the rivers, that had the waters round about it, whose rampart was the sea (river ?), and her wall was from the sea ? Ethiopia and Egypt were her strength, and it was infinite ; Put and Lubim were thy helpers. Yet was she carried away, she went into captivity : her young children also were dashed in pieces at the top of all the streets : and they cast lots for her honourable men, and all her great men were bound in chains."

A century later (B.C. 525) Thebes was again stripped by Cambyses, who, however, could not have found much left to carry away with him.

For the next three hundred years the city remained in some obscurity ; and very little was done to beautify her temples, or to restore to them the wealth which they had lost. In Ptolemaic times there was a considerable revival, and Karnak received much attention. The city, however, revolted against Ptolemy Epiphanes and was severely chastised. Diodorus, who visited Thebes about B.C. 57, writes as follows concerning its origin and size : " Afterwards reigned Busiris, and eight of his posterity after him ; the last of which " (of the same name with the first) " built that great city which the Egyptians call Diospolis, the Greeks Thebes ; it was in circuit 140 stadia " (about twelve miles), " adorned with stately public buildings, magnificent temples, and rich donations and revenues to admiration ; and he built all the private houses, some four, some five stories high. And to sum up all in a word, he made it not only the most beautiful and stateliest city of Egypt, but of all others in the world. . . . And we have it related that not only this king, but the succeeding princes from time to time, made it their business to beautify the city ; for that there was no city under the sun so adorned with so many and stately monuments of gold, silver, and ivory, and multitudes of colossi and obelisks."

In B.C. 24 Strabo visited Thebes, and describes it as follows : —" Next to the city of Apollo is Thebes, now called Diospolis, ' with her hundred gates, through each of which issue 200 men, with horses and chariots,' according to Homer. . . . Other writers use the same language, and consider Thebes as the metropolis of Egypt. Vestiges of its magnitude still exist, which extend 80 stadia" (about 9 miles) "in length. There are a great number of temples, many of which Cambyses mutilated. The spot is at present occupied by villages." He then goes on to describe the monuments on the other side of the river, and speaks of the colossi, the Ramesseum, the tombs of the kings, &c.

Under Roman rule Thebes appears to have been but a collection of villages built over and around the ruins of the old temples. Roman tourists came here in considerable numbers to see its wonders, of which perhaps the most attractive was the musical Memnon (p. 248). In early Christian times the western bank of the river at Thebes became famous as a monastic settlement, and hundreds of anchorites lived in the tombs. The Bishop Pisentius, who was one of the founders of this settlement, is said to have lived in a tomb in which were several mummies, and to have held converse with their souls. The great monastery of Dêr el Bahri ("the northern monastery"), dedicated to St. Phoebammon, and that of Dêr el Medineh, were now founded; and both on the east and west bank of the river many of the old temples were converted into Christian churches. Around the temple of Medinet Habu there grew up a large Christian town; at Luxor the village spread itself over the ruins of the temple; and at Karnak the ancient buildings were surrounded by the hovels of the natives. Thus Thebes became divided once more into its three original parts.

The gods. In early times the god of Thebes was Mentu, whose original seat of worship was Arment. In the tomb of the VIth dynasty prince of Thebes, mentioned above, no reference is made to Amen, who was then evidently a god of no importance. He was probably a minor local god: perhaps a deified hero, or perhaps originally but a spirit or bogie which haunted the neighbourhood. In the XIth dynasty he had risen to some power, and in the XIIth dynasty he was more important than Mentu. The rise of Thebes necessitated the rise of its local god, and when the city became the proud metropolis, Amen became the state god. A local goddess, Mut, "the Mother," was now raised to a degree of great importance by being associated with Amen as the wife of that god. To complete the trinity the local moon-god, Khonsu, possibly a form of Horus, was named the son of Mut and Amen.

The old state god of Egypt was Ra, the sun-god, whose chief

seat of worship was Heliopolis, near Cairo. In order to make Amen acceptable to the nation as the royal god he was identified with Ra under the name Amen-ra seten neteru, "Amen-Ra, king of the gods," which was contracted into Amonrasonter, the famous name of later times. Amen was sometimes identified with Min, the god of Koptos, and under the name Min-Amen he received much worship in Roman and Ptolemaic times.

The goddess of the western hills opposite the city was Hathor. Sometimes she was regarded as a beautiful woman; sometimes she was a cow which could be seen coming forth from the hills; and sometimes again she was a serpent. The main seat of her worship was Dendereh, but all these western hills belonged to her, and she was certainly the most important mortuary deity of Thebes. There were many other gods worshipped in Thebes, but none which belonged primarily to the city.

CHAPTER V

THE TEMPLE OF LUXOR

THE temple of Luxor stands on the river bank, a few minutes walk from the imposing Winter Palace Hotel. Visitors will find it best to examine the temple in the afternoon, for the lights are then very beautiful; while by moonlight the colonnades are perhaps more impressive than any other buildings in Upper Egypt.

HISTORY OF THE TEMPLE

On the site of the temple there seems to have stood during the Middle Kingdom a small building erected by King Sebekhotep IInd; for a block of stone bearing that Pharaoh's name has been employed in the foundations of the later edifice. A shrine of Thothmes IIIrd was built on the site of the later Forecourt of Rameses IInd, and it is probable that the original shrine of the Middle Kingdom stood here. The famous Senmut, the supporter of Queen Hatshepsut, states that he conducted all the works of the queen and of Thothmes IIIrd at Luxor. The south end of the temple which is seen to-day, that is to say, the colonnaded Forecourt and the chambers leading from it on the south, was erected by King Amenhotep IIIrd of the XVIIIth dynasty, and was dedicated by him to the great Theban trinity—Amen-Ra, Mut, and Khonsu. In ancient times the temple was generally known as "The Temple of Amen in the *Apts* of the South"; and in mediæval times it came to be known as *El Uksûr*, "The Castles," from which the modern name of the town "Luxor" is corrupted.

The reign of Amenhotep IIIrd marks the zenith of Egyptian wealth and prosperity, and the king had not been long upon the throne before he felt it incumbent on him to erect in the city of Thebes a temple worthy of the most wealthy metropolis of the world. At Karnak there was already the temple of Thothmes

THE TEMPLE OF LUXOR

IIIrd and his predecessors, and on the west bank of the river numerous temples studded the edge of the desert. But in the heart of the city there was no edifice of any magnitude to be shown with pride by the Thebans to the numerous foreigners who now visited Egypt. In erecting the temple the king took the opportunity of placing before the Theban populace upon its walls a series of scenes relating to, and justifying, his accession to the throne. Egyptian law decreed that the king should either be the son or the husband of a Pharaoh's eldest daughter; but Amenhotep IIIrd was neither. His father, Thothmes IVth, seems to have had no daughter to whom Amenhotep could have been married in order to become legal king; and his mother, Mutemua, was in all probability the daughter of the king of a small North Syrian country called Mitanni. Moreover, the wife whom he had married when he was still young—the famous Queen Thiy—was not royal at all, and very possibly was not Egyptian. The erection of the temple at Luxor, therefore, was undertaken probably for the purpose of conciliating the people and priesthood of Thebes; and the reliefs, which demonstrate the miraculous birth and divine coronation of the king, were intended to set at rest any doubts as to the legality of his accession. The temple is thus an entirely personal monument, and the glorification of the king is its evident *motif*. Speaking of this building the king says: "Amenhotep IIIrd, Ruler of Thebes, is satisfied with the building made for his father Amen-Ra. . . . When the people see it they give praise to His Majesty. It is Amenhotep IIIrd who hath satisfied the heart of his father Amen."

When Akhnaton, the son of Amenhotep IIIrd, came to the throne and renounced the worship of Amen, he ordered that god's name to be erased wherever it occurred; and one may see to this day how it has been chiselled out in all the inscriptions. A small shrine of Aton, the new god, was erected within the precincts of the Luxor temple.[1] The next king, Tutankhamen, who returned to the worship of Amen, destroyed this shrine; and continued the building of the original temple which Amenhotep IIIrd had left unfinished. Horemheb and Sety Ist of the XIXth dynasty proceeded with this work. Rameses IInd much increased the size of the temple by adding to it the pylons and Forecourt at the north end, and a few small additions were made shortly afterwards by Merenptah, Sety IInd, Rameses IIIrd, Rameses IVth, and Rameses VIth. The architect of the work of Rameses IInd

[1] Fragments from this temple are (1907) preserved in the Luxor temple.

was a High Priest of Amen named Bakenkhonsu, who tells us that he erected obelisks "whose beauty approached heaven," and that he laid out a "garden planted with trees" in front of the pylons. "I made," he continues, "very great double doors of electrum; their beauty met the heavens. I hewed very great flagstaffs, and I erected them in the august court in front of the temple." The temple was now at the height of its glory. A broad and magnificent avenue of sphinxes extended from its pylons to the temple of Karnak, along which the great processions of priests passed on festal occasions. Around the temple were beautiful gardens, and on its west side were the extensive quays of Thebes, always crowded with galleys. So great was the wealth of the priesthood that the walls of the temple were inlaid with electrum, the doors were studded with gold, and it is said that even parts of the pavements were covered with sheets of silver.[1] Under Rameses IIIrd there were 2623 servants in the temple; and a herd of 279 head of cattle supplied the altars, according to a list of this date. Menkheperra, the son of King Painezem Ist of the XXIst dynasty, restored parts of the temple which were ruined.

In the reign of Smendes one reads of a flood which destroyed or endangered the building (p. 301), and another flood in the reign of Osorkon IInd is recorded. In the XXVth dynasty Kings Shabaka and Shabataka restored parts of the building; and in the XXIXth dynasty King Hakar[2] added to it, as did also Nectanebus IInd in the XXXth dynasty. Finally, Kings Alexander and Philip built here; but by that time the riches of the temple had probably been carried off during the various invasions and revolutions of later Egyptian history. In Christian times churches were constructed inside the temple, and after the Mohammedan conquest houses were erected in the once sacred courts, which, falling and being rebuilt, soon filled the place with debris. A mosque, dedicated to a much honoured saint, was built in the Ramesside Forecourt, and still stands there, although the main part of the temple has now been cleared and walled in.

DESCRIPTION OF THE TEMPLE

The Forecourt of Amenhotep IIIrd.
On passing through the modern gate one enters the Forecourt of Amenhotep IIIrd, around which runs the famous colonnade, so often portrayed. The columns are still almost perfect except for

[1] Breasted, *Records*, ii. 886.
[2] Weigall, Report on the Temple of Luxor, *Annales du Service*.

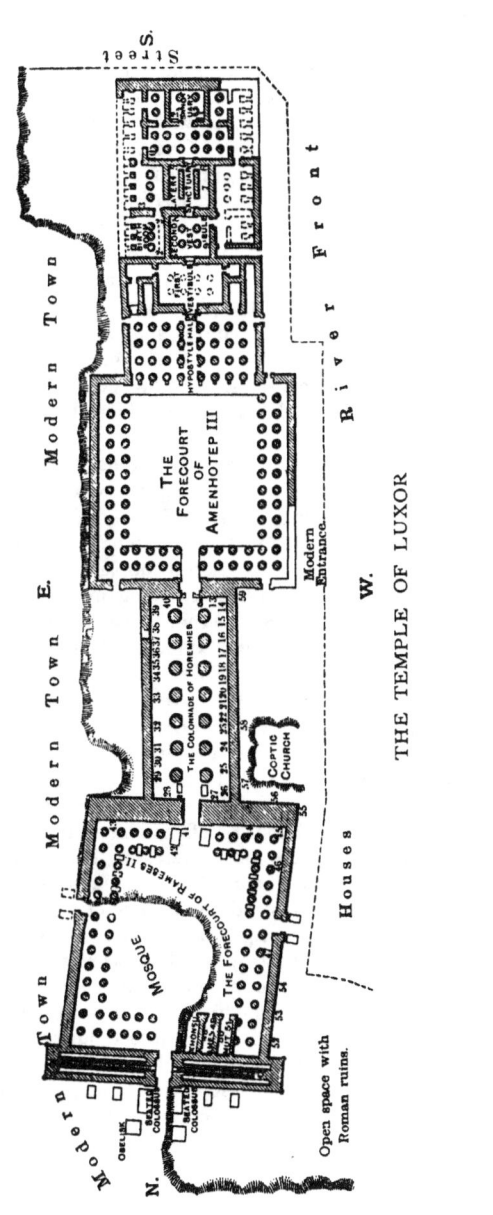

THE TEMPLE OF LUXOR

those at the north end, where originally the first gateway of the temple stood. The roofing blocks, which lay across the architraves, and thus connected them with the now much damaged back walls, have all disappeared. One must imagine this court in its original state as being smoothly paved, and, as now, open to the sky, the colonnade, however, casting more shadow than it does at present. On the columns, architraves, and walls the inscriptions and reliefs were highly coloured, and the effect of this must have been brilliant. At the north end of this court, in the original design of the temple, was the front gateway, and beyond this stretched an avenue of sphinxes which, on nearing Karnak, led one to the various buildings of Amenhotep IIIrd in that temple. Later in his reign the king perhaps added in front of the Forecourt a grand colonnade, which, however, remained unfinished at his death.

The Hypostyle Hall. At the south end of the Forecourt stands the Hypostyle Hall, the roof of which was supported by eight rows of four columns, on the lower parts of which Rameses IVth and Rameses VIth have placed their cartouches. On the now much damaged walls the reliefs of Amenhotep IIIrd have been supplemented by a series of cartouches of Rameses IIIrd, and a long inscription at the top dates from the reign of Sety IInd. Inscriptions also mention repairs executed by Sety Ist and Rameses IInd in this hall.

The First Vestibule. One now passes into the First Vestibule, which originally possessed eight columns. The vestibule has been re-used as a Roman temple, and an apsidal recess has been constructed at the south end, flanked by two granite pillars. The walls have been covered with plaster, and elaborate scenes of men and horses have been painted on them. These are now in a very bad state of preservation, and the original reliefs can here and there be seen. Of these original reliefs the most interesting is a group at the east end of the north wall (1). One there sees a throne, ornamented with the figure of a lion, carried on the shoulders of several nobles. On the throne there was originally a figure of Amenhotep IIIrd, but this is now entirely destroyed. Fan-bearers walk by the side of the throne in an attitude of humility. A group of nobles follows behind, and in front are soldiers armed with spears, shields, and sickle-shaped swords; while a priest burning incense, and musicians singing and clapping their hands, proceed at the head of the company. The king is supposed to be going in procession to worship Amen-Ra, and at the corner of the wall here one sees him in the presence of that deity pouring out a libation upon some

THE TEMPLE OF LUXOR

bunches of flowers. On the north wall the king is seen kneeling inside the shrines of the various forms of Amen. The first of the temple chambers is, thus, appropriately decorated with scenes showing the arrival of the Pharaoh at his temple and his introductory worship of the god Amen.

Returning to the Hypostyle Hall, since the original doorway leading towards the Sanctuary is now blocked by the Roman altar, one may enter the small chapel on the east side, on the walls of which Amenhotep IIIrd is shown worshipping the goddess Mut. A similar chapel on the west side was dedicated to Khonsu. Passing out by the doorway on the east wall of the Hypostyle Hall, and skirting the foot of the rubbish mounds which here encroach on the temple precincts, one turns to the right and enters the Birth-Room. The roof of this chamber was supported by three columns, but it has now collapsed. On the west wall (2) are the well-known reliefs relating to the pretended divine birth of the king. There are here three series of scenes, the story commencing at the north end of the bottom series. In the first scene one sees Queen Mutemua, the mother of Amenhotep IIIrd, embraced by Isis in the presence of Amen. The god Amen is here supposed to have met Mutemua by chance, and to have loved her; while Isis tells him who she is and how she may be approached. The next scene shows Amen being led by Thoth to the queen's chamber, the latter god having suggested a means by which King Thothmes IVth, the queen's husband, may be temporarily got out of the way. In the next scene Amen and the queen are seated together, and are borne aloft by the goddesses Selket and Neith, while the god puts the breath of life into her nostrils. Amen had disguised himself as the king, and had found the queen asleep in her chamber; and she, awakened by the fragrance which filled the room, and believing him to be her husband, had led him to her couch and had listened to his words of love. Before leaving her the god revealed himself, and told her that the child of their union should be named Amenhotep. In the next scene we see Amen giving instructions to the god Khnum, whose duty it was to fashion man upon a potter's wheel. Finally, at the end of this series, Khnum is shown modelling two figures, one of the king's physical body and the other of his *ka* or spiritual double, while Isis gives life to the figures. In the second series, higher up on this wall, the scenes run from south to north. First, the god Thoth is seen announcing to the queen that her confinement approaches. Next, Mutemua is seated upon a stool, while

The shrines of Mut and Khonsu.

The Birth-Room.

ANTIQUITIES OF UPPER EGYPT

Isis and Khnum chafe her hands. Taurt and Bes, the patrons of childbirth, and many demi-gods, are grouped around the queen. In the following scene Isis is shown presenting the new-born infant to Amen, its father; and, finally, the child is nursed by Amen on his knees in the presence of other gods. In the uppermost series we see the child in the presence of the gods, nursed by the nine Hathors and by the queen; while the last scene at the top north corner shows the now grown man as Pharaoh. Upon the other walls of this room the king is represented as being blessed by various gods.

Passing through a door in the south wall one enters a much ruined chamber, built on a plan similar to that of the Birth-Room. The reliefs are badly damaged and are difficult to distinguish. On the north wall there is an interesting and better preserved scene (3), representing the king standing in a boat plucking reeds, which he afterwards presents to the god Min. This is doubtless some Nile ceremony connected with the king's birth or coronation, the actual significance of which is now lost; but those who have been to the temple of Kom Ombo will remember that this same ceremony is there represented in the Birth-House (p. 389) in a ridiculously exaggerated form.

The later Sanctuary. A doorway in the west wall leads into a chamber which was originally one of the vestibules before the Sanctuary, but which in later times was itself converted into a sanctuary. A masonry naos or shrine, erected by Alexander the Great, occupies the main part of the chamber. The doorways in the north and south walls have been blocked up, though one may now pass through a small opening in the former. The reliefs on the walls of the original chamber represent King Amenhotep IIIrd in the presence of the gods. On the east wall (4) the king is seen presenting slain bulls and other offerings to the sacred barque of Amen, which stands in a shrine. On the south wall, at the east end (5), he kneels, as King of Upper Egypt, to receive life from Amen-Ra, while the goddess Urthekau stands behind him. At the west end of this wall (6) he kneels, as King of Lower Egypt, for the same purpose. On the west wall (7) we see him presenting flowers to Amen-Ra and Mut, and making offerings again to the sacred barque. This barque was probably made of cedar of Lebanon covered with gold-leaf, and in it was a shrine in which a portable image of Amen-Ra could be deposited. It was regarded with the utmost reverence, and was only shown in public at great festivals or in times of distress. One reads, for example, how in the reign of Osorkon IInd it was brought out in

THE TEMPLE OF LUXOR

order to appease the waters of a flood, one of the priests addressing a long hymn to it. The shrine of Alexander the Great is dedicated to Amen-Ra, Mut, and Khonsu. The reliefs are carefully executed, but already one begins to see in the modelling those exaggerations which give so grotesque an appearance to later Ptolemaic reliefs. An inscription inside the shrine states that Alexander "made it as a monument for his father Amen-Ra, in white stone, with doors of acacia inlaid with gold, as it had been in the time of Amenhotep IIIrd"; and one is thus led to suppose that a shrine of some kind existed in this chamber in the XVIIIth dynasty.

The visitor should now enter the Second Vestibule, the roof of which is supported by four graceful columns. The scenes on the walls show the king in the presence of Amen-Ra and other gods. At the east end of the south wall (8) one sees the king embraced by Amen-Ra, from whom he receives "life," while behind him stands the goddess Ament and the goddess Mut. On the west wall (9) there are much damaged scenes representing priests bringing offerings to Amen; and the visitor should especially notice the fine ram-headed vases which they carry. The ram, of course, was the sacred animal of Amen-Ra. *The Second Vestibule.*

Leaving this chamber by the door in the west wall, and turning to the left, one passes through two ruined and open rooms into the long hall which runs transversely behind the later, and before the original, Sanctuary. Twelve columns support the roof, most of which have collapsed. The reliefs are much damaged, and the visitors' attention need only be called to one scene (10) at the north end of the east wall. Here we see the king, holding the crook, led by Horus to Amen-Ra, while behind the king are two goddesses, Mut and Uazet. The faces of these two should be observed, as they are typical of the period, and have considerable artistic merit.

The original Sanctuary of the temple is a small four-columned chamber opening from the middle of the south wall of this hall. On the north wall, to the west of the doorway (11), we see Amenhotep IIIrd dancing before Amen-Ra, holding two vases in his hands; and to the east of the doorway (12) he is seen led by Tum and Horus to Amen-Ra. Both here and in the later Sanctuary, which is said to be a copy of an earlier monument, the god Amen-Ra is closely identified with the god Min, in whose form he is most frequently shown. This is something of an innovation; for, although the identification of Min with Amen-Ra may date from an earlier period than that of Amenhotep IIIrd, the predominance of *The original Sanctuary.*

the Min form in the heart of the temple of the original Amen-Ra is unexpected. We may, perhaps, see in this the influence of Queen Thiy, the wife of Amenhotep IIIrd; for her father, Yuaa, was a priest of Min and at the same time a keeper of the sacred cattle of Amen. Queen Thiy may have learnt to worship Min as a child; and her husband, who seems to have acted on her every wish, may have insisted on the prominence of that god in his new temple in order to please her.[1]

The Colonnade of Horemheb.
The visitor should now return to the Forecourt of Amenhotep IIIrd, and should pass northwards into the Colonnade of Horemheb, which is the most imposing part of the whole temple. Fourteen columns, in two rows, supported the lofty roof, which has now disappeared; and on the side walls, now much damaged and reduced to less than half their original height, there were superb reliefs, brilliantly coloured. The hall was perhaps designed by Amenhotep IIIrd, but it was incomplete at his death. His successor Akhnaton, having renounced the worship of Amen, did not continue the work; but the next king, Tutankhamen, decorated the walls. His successor Horemheb, however, imposed his cartouches over those of Tutankhamen. These reliefs are of particular interest, and give one a clear insight into the ancient ceremonies of the temple. The most important celebration of the Theban year was the "Feast of Amen in the Apts," in which the god was brought from Karnak to Luxor. His sacred barge, accompanied by many galleys, was towed up stream, while on shore the portable sacred barques were carried, amidst a procession of priests and nobles, to the temple. After great sacrifices had been made in the Luxor temple the procession returned to Karnak, where further ceremonies were performed. This festival was particularly honoured each year by Horemheb, for it was during its celebration that he had been chosen king by the priesthood of Amen. Horemheb was not of royal birth, but as commander-in-chief of the army he had risen to such a degree of power that he was selected to fill the vacant throne. Coming to Thebes to be crowned, he arrived just as this festival was in progress; and the reliefs on the walls of this colonnade give one a good idea of its nature.

The festival scenes.
The visitor should first look at the reliefs at the west end of the south wall; then those on the west wall, north wall, and east wall;

[1] It may be noted in passing that Min, as god of vegetation and generation, is precisely similar to the North Syrian god Adon, who again is identified with Aton. The son of Amenhotep IIIrd and Queen Thiy renounced the worship of Amen for that of Aton.

THE TEMPLE OF LUXOR

and finally those at the east end of the south wall. At the west end of the south wall (13) a much damaged relief shows the king holding the *kherp* or baton towards Amen-Ra and Mut, while four priests pour water or wine from large amphoræ into tall jars which stand before the shrine. At the beginning of the west wall (14) we see all manner of offerings and temple paraphernalia—standards, sacred barques, vases, chests, fruit, flowers, geese, &c.—which are supposed to be heaped up before the shrine of Amen in the Luxor temple on this festal day. Next (15) we see twelve dancing girls, drawn in small size. They are bending themselves backwards till their hands touch the ground behind them, and are evidently supposed to be performing various contortions for the edification of the persons attending the festival. Four girls shake sistrums beside them, and above are men beating castanets and drums. Next (16) there are the representations of a number of booths in which the slaves of the temple busily prepare meat, incense, flowers, fruit, wine, and so forth for the "beautiful festival of the Apt." Butchers are seen slaughtering and cutting up the oxen, and their active figures are drawn with unusual skill. There now begins a long procession which is supposed to be coming along the river bank from Karnak. It is headed (17) by a company of soldiers bearing shields, battle-axes, and spears, and accompanied by standard-bearers. We next (18) see the two chariots of the king, led, empty, by grooms, who turn to watch the crowds behind them. Then follows (19) an animated group of men who pull at a rope which extends into the scenes on the now destroyed upper part of the wall, where it was shown to be attached to the sacred barge which was being towed up the river from Karnak. Next (20) we see a group of five negroes, four carrying bludgeons and one a drum; and behind them there is a much damaged group of negroes wearing feathers in their hair, and playing castanets. Eight women (21) shake sistrums, and behind them a group of men clap their hands in rhythm to the song which the whole company is singing. One must imagine the road lined with people as this noisy procession goes by, and the houses were no doubt decorated for the occasion. Then follows (22) another group of men pulling at a rope, and this time sufficient of the wall remains to permit one to see that this rope is attached to an elaborate sacred barge, which is also towed by a many-oared galley. Next (23) there is a group of soldiers bearing standards, followed by others who beat castanets and drums, clap their hands, and blow trumpets. Three groups of priests (24) are next shown, each group bearing on its shoulders a portable sacred barque, while incense is burnt before each of them. The last of these three groups has as a background a representation (25) of the doorway of a temple flanked by flagstaffs. This is evidently one of the gates of Karnak temple, from which the procession is issuing. Finally (26) there are offerings and temple furniture, which are supposed to be placed before the shrine of Amen at Karnak.

At the west end of the north wall (27) we see the king standing before Amen-Ra and Mut, and offering incense and a libation to Amen-Ra. Crossing now to the opposite side of the Colonnade, we see on the east end of the south wall (28) these two scenes repeated. Those who are acquainted with the style of art which obtained under Akhnaton, the heretic king, will see at once that his influence is still felt in the art of this period. The head of the king, especially the modelling of the mouth, chin, and throat, shows distinct traces of the Akhnaton style.

On the east wall we first see (29) the usual temple paraphernalia and offerings, here supposed to be before the Karnak shrine of Amen. Next (30) a spirited group of bulls with decorated horns awaits sacrifice. Then (31) the three sacred barques are carried at the head of the procession returning to Karnak. These are followed by standard-bearers and a well-drawn group (32) of negroes, who dance, blow trumpets, and appear to be half mad with excitement. Higher up on the wall many-oared galleys are shown, floating down the river towards Karnak. Then follow (33) the king's two chariots, behind which is a guard of soldiers. A group (34) of girls shaking sistrums, and men clapping their hands, is now seen; after which more standard-bearers and soldiers (35) are shown. Then follow (36) minstrels playing on lutes, others beating castanets, and others clapping their hands. Above these we see the barges floating down the river, and it will be observed that since they are now going down with the stream they no longer require to be towed by ropes. Next (37 and 38) there are more sacred barques carried by the priests, and below these the booths of the butchers are again seen. Finally (39) we see the king offering a last sacrifice at Luxor before passing out of the doorway, which is shown behind him. At the east end of the south wall (40) the king is seen offering bouquets of flowers to Amen-Ra and Mut. The much damaged statues in white marble at the north end of the Colonnade represented Rameses IInd and the goddess Mut on the one side, and Amen and Mut on the other.

One now enters the Forecourt of Rameses IInd, the greater portion

THE TEMPLE OF LUXOR 81

of which is still filled with the ruins and rubbish of the mediæval village. The mosque of Abu'l Haggâg stands on the top of this mound, and the Department of Antiquities is therefore unable to clear this part of the temple. On entering the Forecourt the visitor should first look at the two damaged grey granite colossal figures of Rameses IInd, which are seated on either side of the entrance. On the throne of the east, or right hand, colossus (41) there is a symbolical representation of the union of Upper and Lower Egypt. Two figures of the Nile are seen binding together the stems of the lotus and papyrus plants, which are the symbols of the two countries. Below this there is a series of captive Asiatic nations, the name of each being written in an oval from which the upper part of a typical Asiatic figure rises. On the opposite colossus a similar series of negro tribes are shown. Against the right leg of the eastern colossus (42) there is a beautifully modelled figure of Queen Mut-Nefertari, the wife of Rameses IInd, and a similar but damaged figure is to be seen at the side of the western colossus. Between the columns in the front row on the east side of the Forecourt there are five colossal statues of Rameses IInd, the third of which, stepping out as it does from the dark recess between the columns, is particularly impressive. By the leg of the first statue there is a small figure of Queen Mut-Nefertari; on the plinth of the second statue is the figure of the "king's daughter and king's wife," Amenmerit; beside the third statue Mut-Nefertari is again shown; and on the plinth of the fifth statue is the figure of the "king's daughter and king's wife," Banutanath. Both Banutanath and Amenmerit were daughters and at the same time wives of Rameses IInd. The reliefs on the walls behind these statues show Rameses in the presence of the gods. At the east corner (43) he is seen led forward by Menthu of Thebes, Wepwat, and Thoth.

Turning now to the west side of the court, six much damaged colossi are seen standing between the columns as before. The reliefs on the walls behind are of interest. In the middle of the south wall (44) there is a small representation of the actual front gateway of the temple, which the reader will presently visit. One sees the two seated colossal figures at the sides of the doorway, the four standing colossi, the two obelisks, the pylons, and the flag-staffs from which flutter pennants. Walking towards this doorway are seventeen of the sons of Rameses IInd; while behind them (45 and 46) various nobles lead forward enormously fatted bulls, whose horns are fantastically decorated. Those of one of the bulls which

82   ANTIQUITIES OF UPPER EGYPT

were naturally "crumpled" were fitted with metal tips in the form of hands, while a metal head was fastened between them, thus giving the effect of a figure with waving arms. It will be observed how the hoofs of the bulls have grown upwards, as is often the case with prize cattle which are not properly exercised. Some of the bulls have heavy earrings in their ears, and others are bedecked with flowers. Farther along the west wall, beyond the doorway, Queen Mut-Nefertari is seen shaking two sistrums, while behind her are the damaged figures of many of the sons and daughters of Rameses IInd. The king is known to have had 111 sons and 67 daughters at least, and it is probable that he had many more than this.

<small>Three chapels in the Forecourt of Rameses IInd.</small>   The three small chapels at the north end of this Forecourt are dedicated respectively to Mut, Amen, and Khonsu. On the east wall of the middle chapel, *i.e.* that of Amen (48), Rameses is shown offering incense to a figure of Min, and on the west wall, opposite (49), he makes an offering to the sacred barque of Amen-Ra. On the east wall of the chapel of Mut (50) he burns pellets of incense before the shrine of Mut and Neith; and on the west wall (51) there is the barque of Mut, and a figure of that goddess in a shrine before which Rameses worships. The elegant pink granite columns in front of these chapels seem to have belonged to an edifice earlier than the rest of the temple, for the name of Thothmes IIIrd of the XVIIIth dynasty is seen on one of the blocks. Fragments of stone bearing this king's name were recently found by the present writer a few yards to the west.

<small>The pylons and front entrance.</small>   The visitor should now leave the Forecourt by the door on the west side, and should pass round to the front of the temple. The gateway between the two pylons is now partly filled with rubbish, over which the roadway to the mosque passes. At present only the western pylon is freed from the debris of the village. Two colossal figures of Rameses IInd are seated at the front entrance, that on the east side being still partly buried. Of the four standing colossi which flanked the gateway, only one now remains; while of the two obelisks one has been removed to the Place de la Concorde in Paris, and the other, in its original position, is now partly encumbered with debris. The inscriptions on the obelisks give the titles of Rameses IInd, and state that he made these monuments for his father Amen-Ra. The scenes on the front of the pylons are somewhat difficult to distinguish; and as very similar reliefs are to be found on other temples where they can more easily be seen, only the general significance need here be noticed. In the fourth year of his reign Rameses IInd advanced into Syria to

THE TEMPLE OF LUXOR

make war on the Hittites, and by rapid marches he quickly penetrated as far as Kadesh, one of the enemy's capitals. Here he was out-manœuvred by the Hittite king, who attacked him in the rear, separating his advance column from the main army. Rameses saved the situation by his bravery and dash, keeping the Hittites engaged until his reinforcements arrived. The battle was a victory for neither side, and led to the making of an offensive and defensive alliance between the Hittites and Egyptians. On the north face of the east pylon the Battle of Kadesh is represented, and one sees Rameses IInd charging the enemy in his chariot. On the west pylon the Egyptian camp is shown, and Rameses is seen holding a council of war.

Returning now towards the modern gateway along the outside of the west wall of the temple, several reliefs relating to the wars of Rameses will be observed. First (52) we see the king storming a fortress near Tunip, in the land of Naharin. Then (53) in his chariot he charges the enemy, and his horses are shown biting at his foes. Below this we see him receiving the prisoners who are brought in. Next (54) he rides back in triumph amidst a train of captives. A much damaged scene at the end of the wall of the Forecourt (55) shows the king in his chariot charging the enemy, who fall back on their city. Some of the inhabitants fly from the city, and drive their cattle into the marshes. Round the corner (56) the king in his chariot, followed by his soldiers, attacks the city of Saturna. Beyond this (57) there is a striking representation of a devastated country. A dismantled and ruined fort stands empty upon a hill, while around it one sees the bare fields and the fallen trees, all of which have been cut down. Not a living thing is shown in this scene, but farther along the wall one observes the army of Rameses, in perfect order, returning from the land which they have laid waste. At about a third of the distance along the wall (58) the army is shown climbing the eastern slopes of the Lebanon, while below on the sea-coast another contingent of Egyptian troops is coming to meet them. At the end of this wall (59) the sons of Rameses are shown bringing in the Asiatic prisoners which they have taken.

The outer west walls of the temple.

Before leaving the temple the visitor should look at the small Coptic Church which stands outside the west wall of the Colonnade of Horemheb, near the reliefs which have just been described (55 to 58). The columns which supported the roof lie scattered over the site; and at the north-east corner the well-preserved baptismal tank is worthy of notice.

The Coptic Church.

CHAPTER VI

THE TEMPLES OF KARNAK

VISITORS to Luxor will do well to pay at least two or three visits to the great temples of Karnak, and it will be as well not to attempt to see all the ruins at one time. The temple of Khonsu (p. 88), the great temple of Amen-Ra (p. 92), and the northern and eastern buildings may be visited in one morning. The southern ruins (p. 108) should be reserved for an afternoon visit. A view of the temples at sunset and by moonlight should be obtained if possible. A drive or donkey-ride of less than half-an-hour takes one from Luxor to Karnak. The word *Karnak* means in Arabic "a window," and seems to have been applied to the temples and to the surrounding village from the fact that the great windows of the Hypostyle Hall were a conspicuous feature of the ruins.

HISTORY OF KARNAK

The history of Karnak is largely the history of Thebes. Thebes does not appear to have been a city of any particular importance before Dynasty XI. (B.C. 2160-2000), and the temple of Karnak, though it existed previous to that date, was probably of unpretentious size. The tribal god of Thebes was Amen, "The Hidden"; and here at Karnak it is possible that a shrine was dedicated to him in archaic times, though as yet no antiquities of that date have been found to confirm this supposition. In Dynasty XI. the princes of Thebes became, by conquest, the Pharaohs of all Egypt; and Amen thus became the royal or state god of the country. Ra, the sun-god of Heliopolis, had been the patron deity of the royal house previous to this; and the tradition was so firmly established that Amen in his new rôle was identified with the sun under the name Amen-Ra. Besides Amen there were two other tribal deities of Thebes: Mut, the "Mother," and Khonsu, a beautiful young man who seems to have been connected

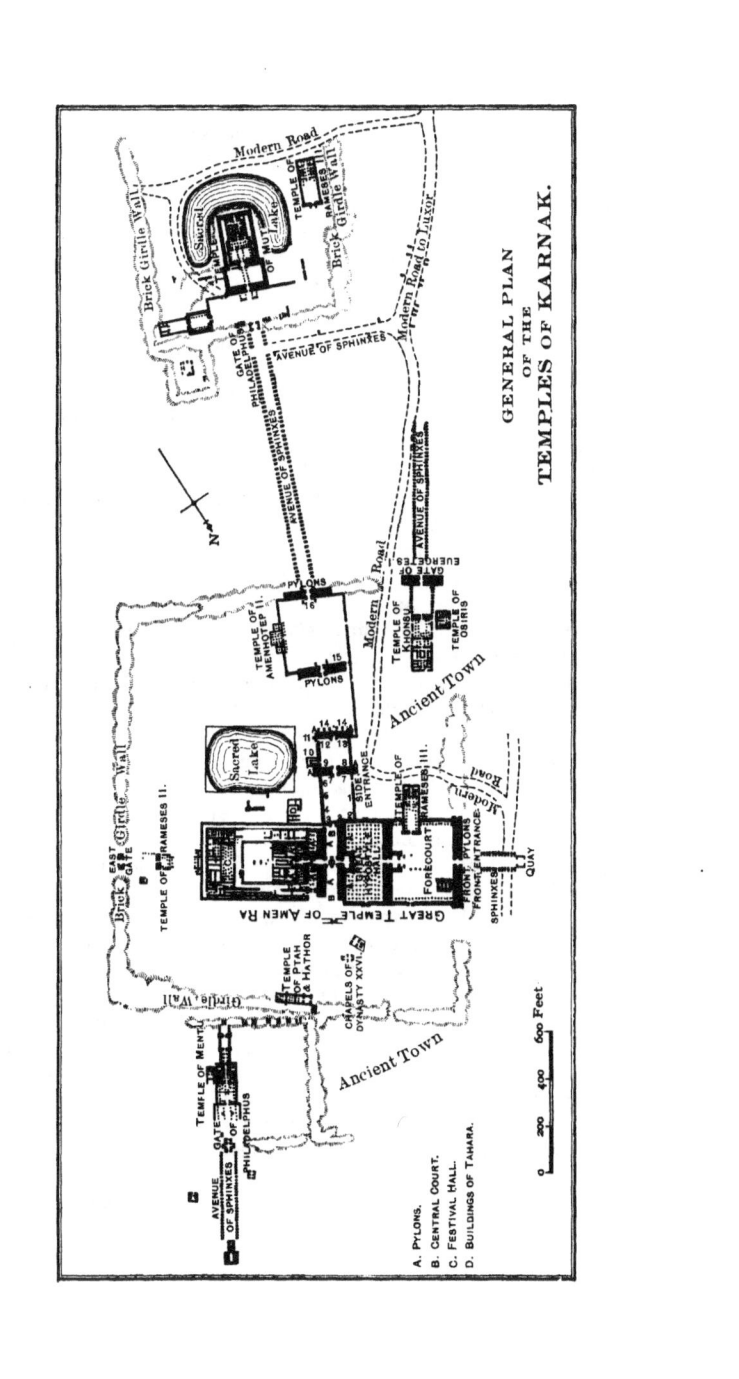

originally with Horus. These three quite separate tribal gods of
the peoples of the Theban district were now formed into a definite
trinity. Amen-Ra became the father, "the king of the gods";
Mut, the mother, was his wife; and Khonsu, soon identified with
the moon since Amen-Ra was the sun, became their offspring.
When the great kings of Dynasty XII. came to the throne about
B.C. 2000, and Thebes became the mighty capital of a nation once
more. united and consolidated after generations of internal strife, a
large temple was erected to this trinity, and traces of it have been
found at Karnak. It is probable that Karnak at this time was the
actual site of the city, and that Luxor was a suburb. This temple
of Dynasty XII. seems to have stood not far from where now
stands the sanctuary of Philip Aridaeus (p. 99), for just to the
south of that building a pedestal was found bearing the name of
Amenemhat Ist, the founder of the dynasty; while Amenhotep,
the high priest under Rameses IXth (p. 109), states that a
sanctuary was built in the time of Senusert Ist. Fragments of
Nubian ("pan-grave") pottery of this date have been found to the
east of the temple, and suggest that a Nubian garrison was
stationed here, or that Nubian slaves were in residence. Statues
and other remains of the succeeding dynasties have been found;
and the temple seems to have existed throughout the troubled
times of the Hyksos rule which followed. When, with Dynasty
XVIII., the power of Thebes was restored, the great temple once
more began to flourish. An inscription in the quarry of Ma'sara
near Cairo records the fact that Aahmes Ist in his twenty-first year
(B.C. 1559) was cutting stone for one of the temples of Thebes; and
another inscription records his splendid gifts to Karnak. Amenhotep Ist erected some beautiful buildings of white limestone, of which
many blocks have been recently unearthed. Thothmes Ist, the next
king, also built here; and Anena, the noble whose tomb (No. 81)
is to be seen at Shêkh abd'el Gûrneh (p. 133), records the erection
of two great pylons still existing (p. 99), a doorway named "Amen-mighty-in-wealth," of which the door was of Asiatic copper inlaid
with gold, and two obelisks, one of which still stands (p. 98).
Thothmes IInd continued the work at Karnak, and a statue of this
king has recently been found (p. 99). Thothmes IIIrd and
Hatshepsut (B.C. 1501–1447) both built here, and the former
Pharaoh undertook such extensive works that the temples now
began to assume something of their present form. The temple in
general was now called "the Throne of the World" or "the
Glorious Building." At this time the reader must remember that

THE TEMPLES OF KARNAK

the Great Hypostyle Hall, the Forecourt, and the huge pylons which now stand at the entrance of the main temple, did not exist ; and if he will lay his hand over these buildings upon the general plan of the temple he will be able the more readily to understand the appearance of the site in Dynasty XVIII. It is possible that the river ran through what is now the Forecourt, and that the buildings were pushed westward as it receded. To Thothmes IIIrd is due the Festival Hall at the east of the main temple, the temple of Ptah and Hathor, and other buildings. Amenhotep IInd and Thothmes IVth, the succeeding Pharaohs, both added to the now glorious temple, and Amenhotep IIIrd (B.C. 1411-1375) also built extensively, erecting, amongst other buildings, two pylons which now form the east wall of the Great Hypostyle Hall. The temple of Mut (p. 111) was built for the most part by this king, and a small temple of Mentu to the north of the main buildings was also erected by him. Then followed the great religious revolution of Akhnaton (B.C. 1375-1358) and the temporary downfall of Amen-Ra. Previous to the revolution Akhnaton set up a small temple to Ra-Horakhti Aton, the new god, at Karnak ; and after his death this was utterly destroyed by the once more triumphant priests of Amen-Ra, and the fragments were used by Horemheb (B.C. 1350-1315) in the building of his pylons. When Amen-Ra had thus returned to power, the priests decided that his glory should be made known to the world by the erection of the largest temple in his honour in existence. The Great Hypostyle Hall was therefore planned, which was to be a vast portico or pronaos in front of the temple of Dynasty XVIII. Built almost entirely in the reign of Horemheb, it was so far finished by the reign of Rameses Ist (who held the throne only from B.C. 1315 to 1314) that that king was able to inscribe his name upon one of the pillars and upon the doorway through the front pylons. Horemheb also connected the temple of Mut with the main temple by means of two pylons and an avenue of sphinxes (p. 111). Sety Ist (B.C. 1313-1292) and his successor Rameses IInd (B.C. 1292-1225) undertook the decoration of the Great Hypostyle Hall, but neither of these two kings built extensively at Karnak, though many reliefs and inscriptions date from their reigns. At this time the front pylons and Forecourt did not exist, and the temple began with the Hypostyle Hall. In the open space in front of it Sety IInd (B.C. 1209-1205) erected a small temple (p. 92) and also a quay (p. 92) at the edge of the Nile. The river, however, has now receded 500 or 600 yards, and the quay stands in the midst of the dry land. Rameses IIIrd (B.C. 1198-1167) erected a temple in this open space where the Forecourt was later laid out (p. 94), and another temple was placed by him close to that of Mut (p. 113). He also began the temple of Khonsu (p. 88) upon the site of an earlier edifice. Under the later Ramesside kings little building was undertaken, but in the reign of Herhor (B.C. 1090-1085) the temple of Khonsu was completed. From this time onwards for many years no great works were undertaken at Karnak. It already composed such an enormous mass of buildings that no attempt was made to increase its size at all considerably. The Bubastite kings (B.C. 945-745) added a doorway here and there, and a few reliefs and inscriptions were carved upon the walls. The Ethiopian Pharaohs (B.C. 712-663) added some columns in front of the Great Hypostyle Hall, and erected one or two small shrines. The Assyrian invasions at this time stripped Karnak of much of its wealth ; but, thanks to the energies of the governor of Thebes, Mentuemhat, the wrecked buildings were restored. In the succeeding dynasty the Forecourt appears to have been planned, but the building of the great pylons which now form the front entrance of the main temple does not seem to have been undertaken until Ptolemaic times (B.C. 300 onwards). The Ptolemies restored and added to the various temples, and their handiwork is to be seen in all directions, though nothing very large was undertaken by them. The Roman emperors do not seem to have carried on any works of importance at Karnak, and the place must have largely fallen into ruins. The early Christians converted many of the temples into churches, and their rude paintings are to be seen on many of the walls (as, for example, p. 104). The village soon spread over the ruins, which gradually became buried beneath the debris. Excavations during the last half century have cleared most of the buildings, and these works are now being carried on with energy by the Department of Antiquities, under the superintendence of Monsieur Legrain.

THE TEMPLE OF KHONSU

The first temple which one reaches when approaching Karnak from Luxor is that of Khonsu, begun by Rameses IIIrd (B.C. 1198), on the site of an earlier temple. Khonsu, god of the moon, was the son of Amen and Mut, and was the third member of the Theban trinity. He is generally represented as a young man wearing the side-lock of hair which generally denotes a youth of

THE TEMPLES OF KARNAK 89

princely rank. The temple stands on the left of the main road, and the great gateway which rises before its pylons forms the terminus of the famous avenue of sphinxes. These sphinxes will have been observed on either side of the modern road for some distance back, though originally they ran all the way from the temple of Luxor. The isolated gateway in front of the temple of Khonsu was erected by Ptolemy IIIrd Euergetes (B.C. 247-222), and originally walls ran from right and left of it enclosing the temple; but these have been entirely destroyed. Upon the gateway we see Ptolemy IIIrd offering to his ancestors and to the various gods, in company with Queen Berenice.

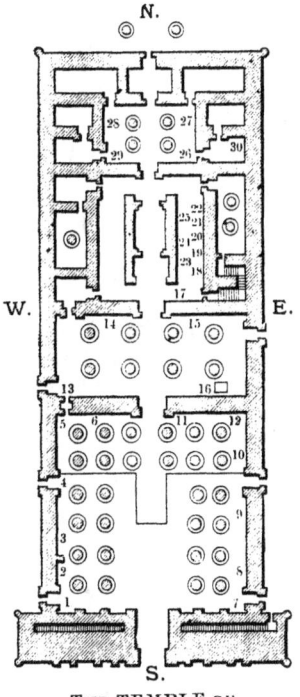

THE TEMPLE OF KHONSU: KARNAK

Passing across the open court beyond this gateway, we enter the temple through a doorway between the pylons, and so reach the Forecourt, on the west, east, and north sides of which there are two rows of heavy columns, those on the north side being raised on a low terrace. The inscriptions and reliefs on the columns and walls of this hall were made during the reign of Herhor (B.C. 1090-1085). At the south end of the west wall, above the doorway, we see (1) two galleys being rowed up-stream to Luxor, and towing behind them the sacred barque (2), now somewhat difficult to distinguish. Between the second and third columns (3) the king is shown standing on board the galley upon which the portable sacred barque has been placed. Above the second doorway (4) other galleys are shown. At the end of the wall (5) more barques are seen, and behind them is a row of princes. This procession of galleys from Karnak to Luxor formed the main incident of the great yearly festival, at which the image of Amen was conveyed from its sanctuary at Karnak in order that the god might behold his temple at Luxor. The festival is

The Forecourt.

shown in greater detail on the walls of the Luxor temple (p. 78). At the west end of the north wall (6) we see priests bearing along the barques of Mut, Khonsu, and Amen (the Theban trinity); and above this the king is shown praying before Ptah, dancing before Harmachis, and worshipping various other gods. On the east wall, over the first doorway (7), the king kneels before Khonsu, and higher up worships other gods. An interesting representation of the gateway and pylons of this temple (8) is next shown. Eight flagstaffs are seen in front of the pylons, heavily clamped with bronze. Next (9) the king is seen worshipping before the large sacred barque of Amen-Ra, and the smaller ones of Mut and Khonsu. At the end of the wall are priests carrying upon their shoulders a standing figure of the god Min (10), to whom the king offers flowers. Priests carrying standards march before the god. At the east end of the north wall (11) the barque of Amen is again shown, carried on the shoulders of the priests; while in the corner (12) the king receives jubilee gifts from the hawk-headed Khonsu. The doorway leading into the Hypostyle Hall was erected by Nectanebo Ist (B.C. 382–364).

The Hypostyle Hall. The Hypostyle Hall is not a building of great size. Four large and four small columns support the roof, and one may still see how the hall was lighted by grated windows above the side architraves. There were several statues of the sacred apes of the moon in the hall, but only two are now left. These date from the reign of Sety Ist (B.C. 1313–1292), and therefore belonged to the earlier temple which stood on this site before Rameses IIIrd erected the existing edifice. The reliefs and inscriptions upon the walls of the hall date from the reign of Rameses XIIth (B.C. 1118–1090), the last of the Ramesside Pharaohs, whose throne was seized by the high priest of Amen, Herhor. Above the doorway at the west end of the south wall (13) we see him purified by Thoth and Horus of Edfu before Amen-Ra and the goddess Ament. At the west end of the north wall (14) the king burns incense before the barques (15), which are carried on the shoulders of the priests. On the south wall, at the east side of the doorway (16), he makes offering to Amen-Ra, Mut, and Khonsu, who are seated in a shrine. The doorway leading into the next hall was built by Herhor and restored by Nectanebo Ist.

The Sanctuary and inner chambers. One now passes into a hall in the middle of which are the ruins of the red granite sanctuary originally built by Amenhotep IInd (B.C. 1448–1420), incorporated in the new temple by Rameses IIIrd, and reinscribed by Rameses IVth, but very little of it now remains.

THE TEMPLES OF KARNAK 91

The walls to right and left are partly constructed of blocks taken from an earlier shrine of Thothmes IIIrd (B.C. 1501–1447) which seems to have stood here. In the corridor on the left or west of the sanctuary the reliefs show King Rameses IVth in the presence of the gods. The reliefs of this king in the east corridor have considerable merit. Here on the south wall we see the king (17) offering to Amen-Ra, Mut, and Khonsu. On the east wall (18) he offers flowers to Khonsu; (19) he offers a statuette to Ament; (20) he is purified by Thoth and Horus of Edfu; (21) he is led forward by Menthu and Tum; and (22) he offers the figure of Truth to Amen-Ra and Mut. On the west wall (23) he offers a figure of Truth to Amen-Ra; (24) he burns incense before Mut; and (25) he offers food to Khonsu. The chapels on either side are dark, and are of no interest. A stairway leads to the roof from that on the east side. We now pass on into a small four-pillared hall. The earliest reliefs here date from the reign of Rameses IVth, but others have been added in Ptolemaic and Roman times. At the east of the entrance (26) we see one of the Cæsars offering to the gods. On the east wall (27) the upper panels show Rameses IVth offering to the sacred barque, and below this a Roman Pharaoh kneels before Khonsu, Thoth, Unnefer, and a number of minor gods. The damaged reliefs on the north wall are Ramesside. Those on the west wall (28) show a Roman emperor offering to Amen-Ra, Ptah, Hathor, and a number of small gods. The reliefs at the west end of the south wall (29) show a Roman Pharaoh offering to Amen-Ra. It is interesting to notice the graceful movement of the Ramesside figures, as compared with the stiff upright postures of those of Roman date. From this hall five doorways lead into chapels, of which those in the north wall are dedicated to Amen, Mut, and Khonsu by Rameses IIIrd. In the chapel leading from the east side of the hall a relief, showing Rameses IIIrd before Ptah (30), retains part of its colour.

To the west of the temple there is a little shrine of Ptolemaic date which is hardly worth a visit. The shrine was dedicated to Osiris, and on the sides of the doorway the king appears before Osiris and other gods. One passes through a two-columned portico lit by grated windows, and through a vestibule, and so reaches the little sanctuary, at the end of which is a recess. In this recess the king is seen worshipping the figure of Taurt on one side, and the standard of Hathor on the other. Below this there was a crypt, from which a passage passed into the main temple.

The temple of Osiris.

THE GREAT TEMPLE OF AMEN-RA

The pylons and entrance of the great temple.

Having visited the Temple of Khonsu, one proceeds along the road to the north, which presently bends to the west, and later to the north again, bringing one finally to the front of the huge pylons of the Great Temple of Amen-Ra. Leading up to the gateway there is a well-preserved avenue of ram-headed sphinxes, which were erected by Rameses IInd. At the west end of this avenue there is a rectangular terrace which in ancient times was washed by the river. Records of the height of the inundation under the XXIst–XXVIth dynasties are marked on the front of this terrace. There were here two small obelisks dating from the reign of Sety IInd, but only one now remains. To the south of the entrance there is a small, half-buried shrine built by Harkar (B.C. 390). The two front pylons date from the Ptolemaic era, but they were never completed; and the great mounds of mud-bricks on their east and west sides are evidently the ruins of the scaffolding used by the builders in their construction. The larger of the two pylons is nearly 150 feet in height. Visitors are strongly recommended to ascend the north pylon, from which a fine view of the ruins may be obtained. It is approached through the doorway in the north side of the Forecourt, an ascending pathway and modern steps leading up to the summit.

The Forecourt of the great temple.

One now passes into the large Forecourt, which was laid out in about the XXVIth dynasty. It covers an area of nearly ten thousand square yards; but it is now difficult to picture the place as it appeared originally, when a level pavement was to be seen, instead of the irregular bramble-covered earth which now takes its place. On the north and south sides of the court there is a much-ruined gallery of columns, which have not yet been fully excavated. On the left or north of the entrance there is a large altar of late date, and farther to the north stands a partly unexcavated building consisting of three shrines dedicated to Amen-Ra, Mut, and Khonsu, and dating from the reign of Sety IInd. The reliefs on the walls are of no particular interest, and only show the king worshipping the sacred barques, and in the presence of the gods. Behind this building there is a row of ram-headed sphinxes, which seem to have been placed here for future use during the building of the pylons. Leading up to the entrance of the Great Hypostyle Hall there were two rows of five columns connected by screen-walls, but only one of these columns

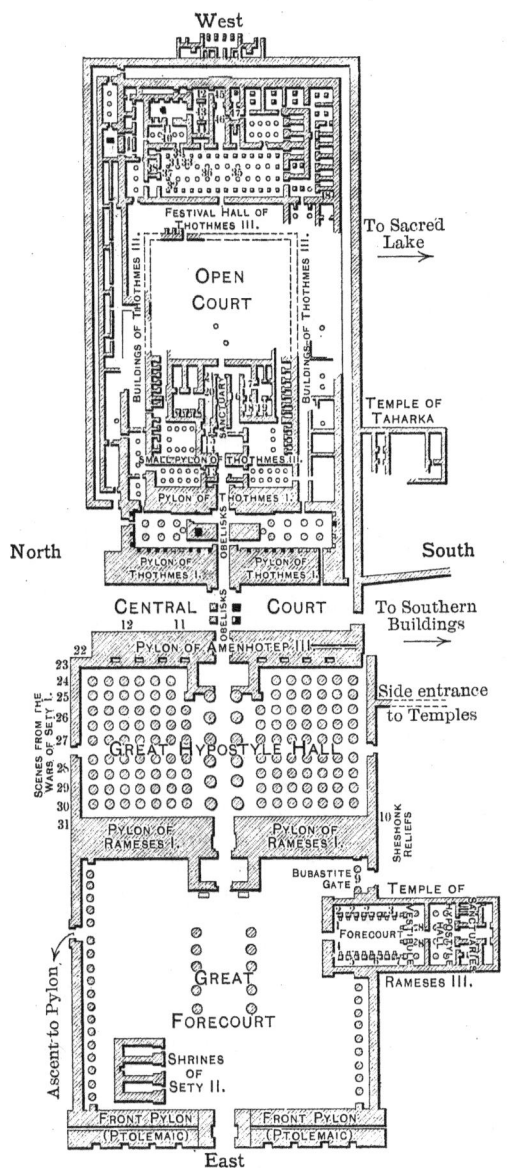

THE GREAT TEMPLE OF AMEN RA: KARNAK.

now remains standing. They were erected by the Ethiopian Pharaoh Taharka of the XXVth dynasty, but they also bear the names of Psametik IInd of the XXVIth dynasty, and of Ptolemy IVth Philopator, the latter king being responsible for the screen-walls. The two pylons which formed the east wall of this Forecourt, dividing it from the Great Hypostyle Hall, have both fallen; and the mass of tumbled blocks of sandstone gives one, perhaps, a clearer idea of the size of the pylon than would the perfectly preserved building have done.

<small>The temple of Rameses IIIrd.</small>

On the right or south side of the Forecourt there is a small temple built by Rameses IIIrd of the XXth dynasty, and which consequently stood here before the Forecourt was built. On either side of the entrance is a badly proportioned statue of the king, standing upon a high pedestal. Both figures are made of sandstone, and have been coloured. On the two small and ruined pylons behind them we see the king slaughtering captives, whom he grasps by the hair, in the presence of Amen-Ra. This god delivers to him a series of captive cities, each represented by the upper part of a figure rising from an oval in which the name of the place is written. One now enters the small, open Forecourt, on three sides of which there runs a covered gallery, its roof being supported by square pillars, having against their front sides colossal Osirid figures of the king. These are now much damaged, and only three of them still retain their heads. The scenes on the walls of this little Forecourt are of some interest. At the east side of the doorway (1) the king is seen receiving from Amen-Ra the symbols of jubilees, indicating that the god will grant him a long reign. From the east end of this wall a scene extends along the east wall to the side doorway, (2) representing the king leading a procession of priests, who carry to the temple the sacred barques of Amen-Ra, Mut, and Khonsu upon their shoulders, while others waft fans. Beyond the doorway (3) the king burns incense and pours a libation before the sacred barque, which is now supposed to have been placed in its shrine. At the west end of the north wall (4) the king again receives jubilee-symbols from Amen-Ra. At the north end of the west wall (5) he burns incense before a statue of Min which is carried to the temple on the shoulders of the priests, a cloth embroidered with the cartouches of the king being thrown over the wooden structure on which the statue stands. Above the now blocked doorway walk many priests, bearing the three standards of the hawk, the emblem of Thebes, and the Disk and Feathers of

<small>Forecourt of the temple of Rameses IIIrd.</small>

Amen. Beyond the doorway (6) the king is shown worshipping the statue of Min, which has now been placed in its shrine, the priests bowing around it. The last scene on this wall (7) shows the king making offerings to Amen-Ra, Mut, and Khonsu.

Ascending a slight slope at the south end of the Forecourt, the visitor finds himself in a Vestibule, the roof of which is supported by a row of four columns. The reliefs are much damaged, but show the king in the presence of Amen-Ra, Mut, Khonsu, and other gods. The lower parts of two black granite statues dedicated to Sekhmet, the lion-headed goddess, by Rameses IIIrd, will be observed. The figures of the king on the two jambs of the doorway leading into the next hall (8) will be seen to have once been inlaid with bronze or gold, for the marks of the pins which held the metal in place are still noticeable. One passes now into a small eight-columned Hypostyle Hall. The reliefs here, which are of no particular interest, show the king in the presence of the various gods. From this hall three sanctuaries, with adjoining rooms, lead off, and in each shrine the king is seen making offerings before the sacred barques of the gods. The middle shrine is, of course, dedicated to Amen-Ra; that on the east to Mut; and that on the west to Khonsu. *The Vestibule, Hall, and Sanctuaries of the temple of Rameses IIIrd.*

Leaving the temple of Rameses IIIrd, the visitor should give a few moments to the examination of the gateway (9) just to the east of that building (see plan). This gateway, now in ruins, was erected by the Pharaohs of the XXIInd dynasty. There was a two-columned portico before the gateway, and it should be noticed that the square stones above the capitals of the columns were covered with gold or bronze, as is indicated by the nail-holes which are still to be seen. There is here a closed gateway, and beyond it (10) upon the left are the famous reliefs and inscriptions of Sheshonk Ist, the Shishak of the Bible, which commemorate his victory over Rehoboam, king of Judah, about B.C. 926. These are carved upon the south face of the pylon of Rameses Ist, and visitors who wish to see them must approach from the outside of the temple. It will be remembered that the Bible refers to this war in the following terms (1 Kings xiv. 25-26) : " And it came to pass in the fifth year of King Rehoboam, that Shishak king of Egypt came up against Jerusalem : and he took away the treasures of the house of the Lord, and the treasures of the king's house ; he even took away all ; and he took away all the shields of gold which Solomon had made"; and (2 Chron. xii. 2-4 and 9) : " It came to pass, that in the fifth year of Rehoboam, Shishak, king of Egypt, *The Bubastite gateway.*

came up against Jerusalem because they had transgressed against the Lord, with twelve hundred chariots, and threescore thousand horsemen; and the people were without number that came with him out of Egypt; the Lubim, the Sukkiim, and the Ethiopians. And he took the fenced cities which pertained to Judah, and came to Jerusalem." The reliefs here show the king smiting a group of kneeling Asiatics. On the left Amen is seen extending the sword of victory to the king. Behind and below him there are the names of the captured Palestinian towns in several rows. Many of these are now lost, but originally there were 156 names, some of which are well known to Bible students. Perhaps the most interesting amongst them is " The Field of Abram," and the name " Jordan" also occurs. The inscriptions give no details regarding the campaign, but only in vague terms record the king's victory over the Asiatics.

Returning now to the Forecourt we proceed towards the Great Hypostyle Hall, which is entered through a partly ruined doorway of Ptolemaic date. The pylons on either side of this doorway, built by Rameses Ist, are ruined, and at the time of writing (1908-9) work is being carried on by the Antiquities Department with the object of rebuilding them. At present the pressure upon the sides of the doorway is so great that it has been necessary to hold them back by means of wooden beams; but these will be removed as soon as the pressure has been relieved and the masonry solidified. On either side of the gateway stood a colossal figure of Rameses IInd, but only the south figure now remains standing.

The Great Hypostyle Hall. The visitor now passes into the Great Hypostyle Hall, the largest hall of any temple in the world, covering as it does over 50,000 square feet. The roof, now fallen in, was supported by 134 columns in 16 rows, the two middle rows being higher than those at the sides. These larger columns are some 33 feet in circumference, and about 80 feet in height. When the hall was roofed it must have been in perpetual semi-darkness, for the light appears to have been admitted only through the grated windows, one of which is to be seen on the right-hand side behind the large columns. At present the hall cannot be seen in its entirety, as the work of consolidating the columns is proceeding; but the visitor will be able to reconstruct the edifice in his imagination without difficulty. The enormous circumference of the columns and their closeness one to another does not permit one to appreciate the spaciousness of the hall from all points of view; but here and there the eye may travel down the whole length of one of the aisles, and

THE TEMPLES OF KARNAK

it is then that the vastness of the building is seen. In all directions there are reliefs and inscriptions which were once highly coloured, and the Pharaohs who built the hall are seen in the presence of Amen-Ra and other gods. It has already been stated at the beginning of this chapter that the Pharaoh who planned and conceived this great building was probably Horemheb (B.C. 1350-1315). The hall was so far finished in the reign of Rameses Ist (B.C. 1315-1313) that that king was able to inscribe his name on one of the columns. The reliefs were added during the reigns of Sety Ist and Rameses IInd (B.C. 1313-1225); and Rameses IIIrd, IVth, VIth, and XIIth added their names upon the walls and columns. The pylons which form the east end of the hall had been erected by Amenhotep IIIrd (B.C. 1411-1375) in front of the temple of the XVIIIth dynasty, which lies beyond; and the Great Hypostyle Hall was in reality an enormous portico or pronaos built in front of these pylons, corresponding to the great hall at Esueh (p. 302), or that at Dendereh (p. 35). As the reliefs upon the walls of the hall are at present not easily seen, the visitor will do well to give his time to the more general contemplation of this huge ruin, and then to pass on through the pylons of Amenhotep IIIrd into the earlier temple.

Let the visitor now forget the existence of all the temples of Karnak so far described, and regard them as non-existent; for here he stands at the original front gateway of the temple of the XVIIIth dynasty, and nothing but an open court lay before it. When the Pharaohs of the XIXth dynasty added the Great Hypostyle Hall this earlier temple became the inner sanctuary; but originally it was a complete temple in itself. We first find ourselves in a transverse court, generally called the Central Court, the walls in front of us being ruined. On our right is an obelisk of Aswân granite, 76 feet in height, erected by Thothmes Ist (B.C. 1535-1501). There were originally four obelisks here, but the other three have fallen; they stood at what was the entrance of the temple. On the left, on the east face of the pylon of Amenhotep IIIrd (11), there is a fine relief showing a great galley rowed by long oars. Soldiers and priests stand on the deck. This galley tows the sacred barque of Amen, which is seen farther along the wall (12), and upon which King Amenhotep IIIrd is shown worshipping before the shrine. We now pass on through the ruined pylons built by Thothmes Ist, and so enter a court, around the sides of which there were a series of Osirid figures, like those we have already seen in the temple of Rameses IIIrd (p. 94) and else-

The earlier temple.

where. This court is somewhat difficult to understand, owing to the various additions and alterations which were made to it. Originally, in the reign of Thothmes Ist, it was simply an open court lying between the inner and outer pylons erected by that king. Then, in the same reign, a roof supported upon columns was added, so that the court became a pillared hall. Next, Hatshepsut appears to have removed part of the roof and to have placed two great obelisks here, one on either side of the middle aisle. Thothmes IIIrd, after Hatshepsut's death, was anxious to obliterate all traces of the queen's work, but at the same time did not care to destroy such fine monuments as these two obelisks of hers. He therefore surrounded them with masonry up to the roof of the hall, thus completely hiding them from persons inside that building; but it would seem that he permitted their upper parts to project uncovered above the roof, where they could only be seen at a distance, and the name of the queen upon them could not be read. This masonry casing has now partly fallen, and thus the one obelisk which still remains standing (on the left) can be seen in its entirety. It is a magnificent monument of Egyptian ingenuity; although it is a monolith, its height is no less than 97½ feet. Both obelisks were quarried in the granite hills of Aswân, were floated down the river to Karnak, and were then erected, trimmed, and inscribed; and it is definitely stated that the entire work took only seven months to accomplish. In the inscription the queen addresses herself to the visitors of all ages who shall admire her work, and she says of it: "I will make this known to the generations which are to come, whose hearts will inquire after this monument which I have made, and who will talk inquiringly and gaze upon it in future. I was sitting in the palace, I was thinking of my creator, when my heart urged me to make for him (these) two obelisks whose points reach unto the sky, in the noble hall of columns which is between the two great pylons of Thothmes Ist. O ye who see my monument in the course of years, and converse of what I have done, beware of saying, 'I know not, I know not why these things were done.' Verily the two great obelisks which my majesty has wrought, they are for my father Amen, to the end that my name should remain established in this temple for ever and ever." The queen was evidently fearful lest persons should not believe that the work had been accomplished in so amazingly short a time as seven months, and she therefore makes an oath that she speaks the truth, the nature of which is so terrible that there can be no possibility of the statement being inaccurate. In conclusion she says: "Then

The Obelisk of Hatshepsut.

let not him who shall hear this say it is a lie which I have spoken, but let him only say 'How like her!'"

The visitor should walk round to the back of the obelisk, where he will see more clearly the manner in which Thothmes IIIrd hid it with masonry. If he enters the opposite side of the hall, where stood the second obelisk, he will see how that great monolith has crashed down, destroying the roof and columns. We now pass through the next ruined pylon of Thothmes Ist, and on through a shattered gateway. This brings us into another transverse hall of columns, erected by Thothmes Ist. It was, however, blocked up by Thothmes IIIrd, who placed a small shrine on either side of the middle aisle. We next reach a great granite doorway erected by Thothmes IIIrd, on the walls at either side of which are lists of conquered states. Just to the left, in the shrine built by Thothmes IIIrd (13), there is a recently discovered statue of Thothmes IInd, which is interesting since there are but few such relics of him now known. Passing through the gateway we come to another transverse court which lies before the main sanctuary. Before us there are two most graceful granite pillars, erected by Thothmes IIIrd, that on the left having a papyrus design upon it and that on the right a lotus, symbolic of Lower and Upper Egypt. On the left (14) there is a fine head of Amen-Ra in quartzite sandstone, and opposite it (15) there are portions of a statue of the goddess Ament in the same material. These were erected by Tutankhamen (B.C. 1355), the Pharoah who came to the throne at the death of the "heretic" Akhnaton; but Horemheb erased the royal name and wrote his own over it. Beyond these statues to the north or left there is a ruined hall of the time of Thothmes IIIrd, in which the lower parts of delicate columns are to be seen, beyond which are shrines. On the right or south through a ruined gateway we see a corresponding pillared hall, at the end of which are sanctuaries.

The granite sanctuary is in so ruinous a state that it cannot now be entered without great difficulty. It was erected in the reign of Philip Arrhidaeus (B.C. 318) to replace the original sanctuary which had fallen into ruins. The reliefs inside the chamber are without interest. The visitor should pass round to the right or south side in order to examine the scenes upon this outside wall. Here in the top row (16) Philip is crowned by the gods, and led into the presence of Amen-Ra. In the second row the festal barques of the gods are carried upon the shoulders of the priests; and the visitor should observe the white screens in

The sanctuary.

100 ANTIQUITIES OF UPPER EGYPT

the form of wings, which hide from view the shrines in which the statues of the gods are kept. In the third row there are more barques to be seen. We may now enter the door on our right at the end of the wall which runs parallel with the sanctuary. This brings us into some ruined chambers dating from the reign of Thothmes IIIrd. On our right (17) there is a limestone figure of Amenhotep IInd, who has been seated beside a god now destroyed. In the next chamber on the left wall (18) Thothmes IIIrd is seen making offerings to Amen. The offerings consist of beautiful vases and ornaments which deserve close inspection. (They can best be seen by morning light.) Opposite there are some steps, from the top of which the south wall of the sanctuary can be seen. Through a doorway (at 17) we pass on southwards into a small chamber, and before us is a granite altar approached by steps made by Thothmes IIIrd. There are two chambers to the west or right of this. In the first, on the left wall (19), we see Thothmes IInd with arms raised pouring holy water over a figure of Amen; and at the end of the wall he stretches out his hands in the performance of some unknown ceremony before that god.

The chambers at the sides of the sanctuary.

The visitor should now return to the sanctuary and should walk round the back of it. On the right, *i.e.* eastward, there is an open court in which traces of the temple of the XIIth dynasty have been found. Beyond it stands the imposing Festival Hall of Thothmes IIIrd, which will be described later (p. 103), since it does not actually form part of the main temple of Amen-Ra. The visitor should now pass round to the north side of the sanctuary. Here (20) on its outer wall we see Philip in the presence of the gods. In the middle he dances before Amen, holding two flagons in his hand. At the west end of the wall, just above a small flight of steps, we see the representation of a large statue of the god Min standing on a portable erection, behind him being the curtained shrine in which the statue stands when not exhibited. To this figure Philip is seen offering two model trees, symbols of the god. Running parallel with this wall of the sanctuary there is another wall, dating from the reign of Thothmes IIIrd, in which is a fine black granite gateway. On the wall (21) Thothmes IIIrd is seen offering to Amen-Ra. The offerings include two obelisks and numberless vases, chests, &c. Passing through the doorway we reach a small court from which leads a chamber recently rebuilt. It contains some highly coloured reliefs of the time of Hatshepsut; but it is now closed to the public.

We may now return past the front of the sanctuary and past

THE TEMPLES OF KARNAK

the obelisk of Hatshepsut to the central court. Here we may turn to the right or north, and pass round to the outer wall of the Hypostyle Hall in order to inspect the reliefs which are to be found there.

These reliefs represent scenes from the wars of Sety Ist (B.C. 1313–1292). Under the heretic King Akhnaton the Egyptian possessions in Asia had been totally lost, and the succeeding kings, Horemheb, Rameses Ist, &c., had been too busily occupied with the reorganisation of the country to make any definite attempt to regain them. Sety Ist, however, in the first year of his reign entered upon the series of campaigns which are represented in these reliefs, and recaptured the greater part of the lost territory. The scenes commence on the east face of the projection of the wall beyond the pylon of Amenhotep IIIrd. Here (22) we see at the top of the wall a figure of Sety Ist standing beside his chariot receiving the submission of the chiefs of the Lebanon, whom he compels to cut down cedar trees for him. We see the Syrians felling the trees, while an Egyptian officer reports the progress of the work to the king. Below this scene the king is shown in his chariot attacking a hill fortress of Canaan. The ground is strewn with the dead which have fallen to his arrows. This was the culminating victory of the campaign in the first year of his reign against the Beduin, whom he pursued from the Eastern Delta across the desert to this city on the frontier of Canaan. Turning the corner of the wall we next see at the top (23) a damaged scene showing the king in his chariot charging into the enemy who are flying towards their city of Zenoam, which is seen upon a hill surrounded by forests, amidst the trees of which some of the fugitives hide. The city of Zenoam lies a short distance inland from Tyre. Below this scene he is shown in his chariot on the march from Egypt across the desert to Zenoam. Above him two of the fortified outposts which he had to pass are shown, and below the horses a lake called " Sweet " is represented. Next (just above the stump of a broken column) we see him (24) in his chariot shooting his arrows at the Beduin, who appear to have attacked him on his march across the desert. Beyond this in the lower part of the wall (25) he is seen in his chariot returning triumphant to Egypt after this campaign. He leads a number of prisoners towards the canal which runs beside the frontier city of Tharu, and which is seen to be full of crocodiles. On the opposite side of the canal the Egyptian officials are waiting to receive him with bouquets of flowers. Next in the lower row (26)

The reliefs on the outer walls of the Great Hypostyle Hall.

he presents captives to a seated figure of Amen-Ra, in front of whom the booty of beautiful vases, &c., is piled up. Above this is a similar scene of the presentation of the booty to Amen. There then follows a large scene showing the king slaughtering his captives in the presence of Amen-Ra, who presents the sword of victory to him. The god holds a number of ropes which are attached to the series of ovals in which are written the names of the captured nations. The words of Amen to the king, in the form of a poem, of great impressiveness, refer to him as "a circling star which scatters its flame," as a "young bull ready horned and irresistible," as "a crocodile lying on the shore, terrible and unapproachable," and as "a fierce-eyed lion amongst the corpses in the valleys."

A doorway leading into the Hypostyle Hall is now passed, and beyond it (28) there is a similar scene of the slaying of prisoners before Amen. Next (29) at the bottom of the wall he presents Hittite prisoners to a shrine in which are Amen-Ra, Mut, Khonsu, and Maat. It should be observed that the goddess Mut has the form of Sekhmet (see p. 112, where the subject of the identification of these two goddesses a hundred years earlier is discussed). Above this scene he presents Libyan prisoners to Amen-Ra, Mut, and Khonsu. Farther along, in the lower row (30), the king is stepping into his chariot after a battle with the Hittites, dragging prisoners after him by the hair. Above this he is seen returning in his chariot from the Libyan war, driving prisoners before him. Next at the bottom of the wall there is a large scene (31) representing a battle with the Hittites. He charges into their midst in his chariot and they fly before him. This is the earliest battle with the Hittites known to history. This warlike people were already pushing southwards from Asia Minor into Syria, and Sety probably encountered them behind the Lebanon. Those who have seen the monuments of Sety's son, Rameses IInd, will be familiar with the representations of the desperate battle of Kadesh fought between the Egyptians and Hittites only a few years later, by which time the domination of Syria hung in the balance between them. Above this scene there are two representations of the battles with the Libyans. On the left the king on foot is seen in the thick of the battle attacking his adversaries with a spear. On the right he is in his chariot with his sword raised, and about to strike down a Libyan chieftain. It should be noticed that his horse's reins are tied round his waist. Above this again, at the top of the wall, there are the remains of a scene representing the capture of a

THE TEMPLES OF KARNAK

Galilean city named, like its more powerful neighbour in the north, Kadesh. The city stands on a hill, at the foot of which the cattle of the inhabitants are driven away to a place of safety. This completes the series of reliefs here, and the visitor may now take one of three directions: either he may ascend the inclined path which leads up to the pylon, or he may enter the main temple again through one of the doors in the wall just described, or he may choose to cross the open ground to the north in order to visit the temple of Ptah, which stands immediately under the brick girdle wall (p. 106).

THE FESTIVAL HALL OF THOTHMES IIIRD

The temple or festival hall of Thothmes IIIrd stands behind, *i.e.* at the east of the main temple of Amen-Ra (p. 93). Behind the sanctuary of Philip Arrhidaeus there is an open space, where, perhaps, once stood a temple of the XIIth dynasty. Thothmes IIIrd converted this space into a level court, and built a series of chapels on either side of it, and his Festival Hall at the east end of it. These chapels are much ruined on the north side, and on the south side they have almost entirely disappeared. We cross this open court, and so reach the hall. Entering, the visitor finds himself in a spacious building, the roof of which is supported by two rows of ten columns. The capitals are curious, and appear at first to be inverted; but in reality they are representations in stone of the knobs of the tent-poles used in a festival marquee. It should perhaps be stated here that the forms of all stone columns in Egyptian architecture (except the simple square pillars and their elaborations) are derived from earlier columns of wood and other such materials. Thus the stone column with the papyrus capital is derived from a palm-trunk, or similar support for the roof of an archaic shrine, surrounded by a cluster of papyrus-reeds, the flowers being bunched at the top. Again, the column with the palm-capital has its origin simply in a palm-tree used to support the roof of a mud-built house. Egyptian festivals are known to have taken place in elaborate tents; and such tents, it would seem, were held up by poles not unlike walking-staves. Thus in this festival hall a column was used which represented such a pole. A gallery of square pillars passed around the sides of the hall, the roof of the gallery being lower than that of the hall. The outer wall of this gallery is now destroyed, and the hall thus appears to be open. Above the gallery there were apertures

The Egyptian columns.

The Hall.

in the wall of the hall, through which the light passed into the building. Upon the square pillars there are reliefs showing the king embraced by various gods : for example, on the east face of the north-west pillar (32) he is embraced by Amen-Ra; on the south face of the third pillar on the east side of the hall (33) he is embraced by Mut ; and on the north face of the same pillar (34) by Horus. The names, and often the figures also, of Amen-Ra, and of many of the other gods, have been erased, either by Akhnaton, the "heretic" king who abandoned the worship of the old gods of Egypt, or perhaps by the Christians. The hall was used later as a Christian church, and one may see traces of Coptic paintings of saints on the columns (as for example at 35 and 36). Three ruined statues, one sitting, one kneeling, and one standing, are to be seen at the north-west end of the hall, the kneeling figure being of King Merenptah. The north wall of the hall, between the doorways of three sanctuaries which are here built, is partly ruined ; but there still remains a scene upon it (37) showing Thothmes IIIrd standing in the presence of the god Min. The three sanctuaries are almost entirely destroyed, except for the west wall of the middle chamber. Here (38) one sees the king making offerings to a seated figure of Mut, while behind him three women clap their hands and chant. Upon the rest of the wall there are figures of priests who carry the ceremonial paraphernalia, consisting of small figures of the king, batons, censers, &c.

The visitor should leave the hall by the doorway near the north end of the east wall (39), which leads into a ruined chamber of which two columns and part of their architrave alone remain standing. On the left as one enters (40) there is the fragment of a granite altar of the time of Thothmes IIIrd. One now steps across the ruined wall ahead (41), and turns to the right, entering a small hall in which stand four delicate and almost perfectly preserved columns, spanned by their architrave. The walls of this little hall are much damaged, but enough remains upon them to repay a visit. Upon them the king caused to be carved a catalogue of the flowers, plants, birds, and animals, which were to be found in the temple gardens, and which had mostly been brought by the king from Syria in the twenty-fifth year of his reign. On the east wall (42) we have a view of the garden, and one may see the splendid flowers, some shown in various stages of their development ; while amongst them are gazelle and various birds. On the south wall (43) there are representations of fruit, flowers, birds, and cattle ; and on the west wall (44) there are again birds, flowers,

THE TEMPLES OF KARNAK 105

and animals, some of which are particularly well drawn. We now leave this hall by the steps at the south-east corner (45), and, passing through two ruined rooms, we enter a doorway upon the left (46) which leads us through another ruined chamber to a well-preserved sanctuary. Upon the front wall of this (47), above the doorway, Thothmes IIIrd is seen standing while the jackal-headed Anubis offers him a pot of ointment and a strip of linen. Behind him is a green-coloured figure of Hapi, the god of the Nile, bearing offerings signifying "plenty." Farther to the left the king is seen being kissed by Hathor, the Egyptian Venus. Entering the shrine we find that the reliefs date from the time of Alexander, who states in an inscription here that he rebuilt the original sanctuary of Thothmes IIIrd. In the middle of the room there has been a huge statue of a hawk in crystalline limestone, but only the pedestal now remains. On the walls the king is seen before the gods. On the right-hand side, commencing from the entrance and continuing to the middle of the back wall, the scenes are as follows:—First (in the corner) he is purified with water by Horus of Edfu; next he robes himself with the sacred skirt; next he sits on a throne and purifies his hands in a basin; then he walks forward holding a staff; next he holds up a pellet of some unguent or incense; then he stands in the presence of Min-Amen-Ra; then before Amen-Ra; on the next wall he pours holy water over a statue of Amen-Ra; and finally he makes an offering to Amen-Ra.

We now return to the Festival Hall, and turn to the left or south. Presently on the left we pass two small shrines erected by Thothmes IIIrd. The next building on the left is a hall in which seven of the columns and part of the roof are standing. At the north end of the Festival Hall there is a series of small shrines. Only the first of these is now properly accessible (48). On the walls Thothmes IIIrd is seen before the gods. Near here the famous Table of the Kings, now in the Bibliothèque Nationale in Paris, was found, which gives a list of fifty-six of the king's ancestors. Around the Festival Hall Rameses IInd built a stone girdle wall, upon the outer side of which are reliefs showing him in the presence of the gods. To the east of this wall, *i.e.* behind the hall, the same king erected a small colonnade, now ruined. Farther to the east there is a fine gateway built in the girdle wall by Nectanebo, and finished by the Ptolemies. Not far from here are the remains of several uninteresting buildings of various dates. From the south-west of the Festival Hall a path leads up to the Sacred Lake, which will be described later (p. 111).

The Temple of Ptah and Hathor

Visitors should not fail to pay a visit to this little temple which lies a short distance to the north of the main temple, just inside the brick boundary wall. The building was erected in honour of the Memphite god Ptah, the Vulcan of the Egyptians, and his consort Hathor, by Thothmes IIIrd, upon the site of a XIIth dynasty temple. Some building had been done here by Hatshepsut during her sole reign, but Thothmes IIIrd erased her cartouches. The building was enlarged under the Ptolemies. A path leads across the open ground from the large temple to this little shrine. One enters the building through a series of six gateways, built close together, but now considerably ruined. The first (*i.e.* most western) of these was erected under the Ptolemies.

The second gate, however, is much earlier, dating from the reign of the great queen Hatshepsut, whose cartouches have been erased from the building probably by her successor Thothmes IIIrd. The queen is seen to be making offerings to Ptah, Hathor, the goddess Ament, Amen-Ra, Mut, and others now destroyed. The third gate was erected by Ptolemy Neos Dionysos. The fourth gate, again, was built by Hatshepsut, whom we see on either side dressed as a king of Upper and Lower Egypt, the cartouches, however, being erased. The fifth gate dates from the reign of Ptolemy IIIrd. One then passes into a little four-pillared court with screen-walls on either side. The sixth gate was erected by Thothmes IIIrd, but inscribed upon it also are the cartouches of Rameses IIIrd and of Ptolemy IIIrd Euergetes.

On one's left there is a scene showing Thothmes IIIrd worshipping Amen-Ra and Ptah, Ptah (with his consort Hathor) being the patron god of this temple and Amen-Ra the presiding deity of all Karnak. We now enter a hall, the roof of which was supported by two pillars. On the left, above a small doorway, Ptolemy XIth and his wife Arsinoë are seen worshipping Ptah and Hathor. At the side of this some steps lead up to an undecorated chamber. In the north wall of the hall there is a doorway inscribed with the cartouches of Thothmes IIIrd, who evidently is the builder of the original temple here. Above this a scene has been added by Ptolemy XIIth, who is seen worshipping Ptah, Hathor, and Imhotep. The last-named deity was in Ptolemaic times identified with Asclepius, the god of medicine (see remarks on him in the section on Gebelên, p. 297). To the right of this there are

THE TEMPLES OF KARNAK 107

two niches in the wall in which temple utensils or papyri were kept. Above them one sees Thothmes IIIrd burning incense before a damaged figure of Ptah. On the next wall above two more niches the same king is seen in the presence of Amen-Ra and Ptah. Returning to the right side of the doorway through which one entered this hall one sees Ptolemy XIth worshipping Hathor. On the adjoining wall there are the figures of the gods Amen-Ra, Ptah, Khonsu, Mut, and Hathor, that is to say, a combination of the Theban Trinity Amen-Ra, Mut, and Khonsu, with the Memphite Ptah and Hathor. The cartouche inscribed beside this scene is that of Horemheb. A list of priests connected with this temple is here inscribed. It mentions one high priest of Ptah and Hathor, four ritual priests of those deities, and twelve libation priests. On the left of this one sees two niches as on the opposite wall, and above them Thothmes IIIrd is shown making an offering to Ptah. On the next wall, above another niche, there is a figure of Thothmes IIIrd adoring Amen-Ra and Ptah, but it is much damaged.

In this hall there stand three altars upon which the sacrifices to Ptah and Hathor were made. That in the middle was set up by Thothmes IIIrd when he erected the temple; but that on the southern side dates from the reign of Amenemhat Sehetepabra, who seems to have been the builder of an earlier temple on this site, now entirely vanished. The northern altar is uninscribed.

We now pass into the sanctuary and see before us a headless statue of Ptah, probably contemporaneous with the building of the temple. On the walls of this room are figures of Thothmes IIIrd adoring Ptah and Hathor. In the chamber on one's right there is a fine standing statue of the goddess Sekhmet. The light in this chamber is dim; and the statue, with its lion face staring through the darkness, inspires the visitor with a certain amount of awe even at the present day, the natives being often actually afraid to enter the temple. One can therefore well imagine that in ancient times, when the goddess was believed to have been the bloodthirsty agent of the sun-god in the great massacre of mankind, this sanctuary must truly have been a place of terror. The room on the opposite side of the building does not repay a visit.

THE RUINS NORTH OF THE MAIN TEMPLE

With the exception of the temple of Ptah and Hathor the ruins to the north of the main temple of Amen-Ra need not be visited.

The shrines of Dynasty XXVI. On the left of the pathway from the Great Hypostyle Hall to the temple of Ptah there are the remains of three small shrines of Dynasties XXV. and XXVI. The southernmost of the three was built for King Psammetichus IIIrd and Queen Ankhnes-neferabra (B.C. 526) by their major-domo Peduneit. In the four-columned hall which stands before the sanctuary, King Aahmes IInd (B.C. 570–526) is seen on the left, and Queen Neitaqert (Nitocris) on the right. The middle shrine was built by a prince Sheshonk in the reign of Aahmes IInd. The northern shrine was built by Taharka (B.C. 688–663).

The temple of Mentu. Near the temple of Ptah there is a gateway passing through the brick girdle wall. Outside this gateway one traverses the mounds of debris of the ancient town, and presently reaches the ruins of the temple of Mentu. This temple was once an imposing building, but it is now almost entirely destroyed. It was erected by Amenhotep IIIrd in honour of the war-god Mentu, and was enlarged by Rameses IInd and by later kings. Two obelisks once stood at its doorway. A fine granite gateway was built in front of this temple by Ptolemy Philadelphus, leading to which was an avenue of sphinxes.

To the west of this temple there is a small Ptolemaic chapel; and farther to the south, against the brick girdle wall which surrounded these temples, there are six little chapels erected at various dates between the third and eighth centuries B.C. None of these are of interest to any but archæologists.

THE RUINS SOUTH OF THE MAIN TEMPLE

Those who wish to see the temple of Karnak at all thoroughly should make a special visit to the buildings to the south of the main temple. These ruins look their best in the late afternoon, and the reader is therefore advised to see them at that time. One enters the temple by the smaller gateway, which will be found on the right-hand side of the main road at the point where it turns to the left to skirt round to the great gateway. One thus passes into a rectangular court, on the left of which is a doorway giving access to the main temple. It was under the north-east end of this court that the great *cache* of statues was found in 1903-4. It would seem that at some time, when the destruction of the temple at the hands of foreign invaders was feared, the priests removed most of the statues which adorned the halls and courts and buried them here, where M. Legrain (who is in charge of the

THE TEMPLES OF KARNAK 109

excavations which the Department of Antiquities is carrying on at Karnak) had the good fortune to find them. On the west wall of the court[1] (1) there are some damaged scenes showing the Pharaoh Sety IInd (B.C. 1209) in the presence of the gods. On the north wall (2) there is a long historical inscription of Rameses IInd. On either side of the entrance to the main temple (3) there are reliefs showing Rameses IXth (B.C. 1142) in the presence of the gods. On the east wall, near the north corner (4), Merenptah (B.C. 1225) is seen kneeling between the forepaws of a ram-headed sphinx (symbolic of Amen-Ra), over which the hawk of Edfu hovers. Farther along this wall (5) there are lengthy historical inscriptions of Merenptah and Rameses IIIrd, the former referring to his wars with the Libyans and the people of the Mediterranean. Still farther along (6) there is a fine representation of Merenptah in the act of slaying a group of enemies. The south side of this court is formed by a pylon built by Thothmes IIIrd, upon the walls of which (7) are lists of nations conquered by him. On either side of the doorway through it there are granite statues of Amenhotep IInd, Rameses IInd, and other Pharaohs. The doorway, though ruined, is very fine. It is made of granite, and the lintel, now lying on the left of the path, was of alabaster. In the right-hand wall there are two niches in which the water of purification, or some other ceremonial accessory, was kept. On the right and left of the doorway as we pass out into the next court there are the lower parts of two enormous granite statues of Thothmes IIIrd, upon which later kings have placed their names. Two obelisks stood before them, but these are now destroyed. On the right the face of the pylon (8) is decorated with a relief showing the king slaying large numbers of foreigners. At the north corner of the east wall of this court Rameses IIIrd is shown adoring Amen-Ra. Behind the king is the hawk-headed Khonsu. Near this (10) there is a small doorway of the time of Thothmes IIIrd, through which one enters an alabaster corridor which leads to the sacred lake (p. 111). A corresponding doorway at the other end of the wall (11) also dates from the time of Thothmes IIIrd. Inside this doorway, on the left, there is a figure of Rameses IXth, and before him the figure of the High Priest of Amen, Amenhotep. The high priest offers flowers to the king, but since he is drawn on the same scale as his master, it is evident that the Pharaoh was but a figure-head, as indeed the whole history of these last Ramesside kings makes

[1] See the general plan of the temples of Karnak, p. 85.

clear. Outside the doorway, a few yards to the left, the high priest is again seen in the presence of the king, and two servants deck him with fine linen. Beyond this there is a still larger figure of Amenhotep, cut upon a scale which no noble of earlier times would have dared to aspire to; and one sees how these high priests were gradually gathering to themselves the power which actually set them upon the throne of Egypt a few years later. Returning to the court, we come next to the pylon which forms its southern side. This was built by Thothmes Ist and Hatshepsut (B.C. 1500), but the queen's names were erased by Thothmes IInd, whose own cartouches were placed there. In later days Sety Ist (B.C. 1200) added considerably to the scenes and inscriptions upon its walls. On the left, or east, pylon (12) Sety Ist is seen sacrificing to the gods, and the earlier Pharaohs are also shown. On the right, or west, pylon (13) there is a large figure of Rameses IIIrd standing between the gods Thoth and Horus of Edfu, who pour the water of life over him. Farther along he stands between Tum and Harmachis. Above this, high up, the sacred boat of Amen is carried along on the shoulders of the priests, with King Sety Ist marching before it.

We pass on through the doorway of this pylon, which was built by Thothmes IInd and Thothmes IIIrd. On the right side of the doorway Rameses IInd is seen led forward by Mut and Khonsu, and standing in the presence of Amen. Against the south face of the pylon there are, on the west, a seated statue of Thothmes IInd in quartzite sandstone, and another of Amenhotep Ist in crystalline limestone, while on the east there is another statue of Thothmes IInd. On the walls of the pylon behind these statues Thothmes IInd is seen slaying his enemies. Looking at the pylon from this side in the late afternoon, with the green brambles and grasses in the foreground, the visitor will agree that there are few ruins in Egypt which offer so picturesque a grouping. We now find ourselves in a ruined court; on our left is the sacred lake, beside which is the modern pump-house; on our right is a gate of exit to the road; and before us is a pylon built by Horemheb, which is almost entirely destroyed. Across this we may walk to the next court, in which many palms now grow. It is interesting to observe, on the south-west corner of the pylon (15), a Christian recess cut into the old wall. There are other similar relics of early Christianity in various parts of the neighbouring ruins. We now have on our right, across the road, the temple of Khonsu; and on our left there are the ruins of a

THE TEMPLES OF KARNAK   111

little temple built by Amenhotep IInd (B.C. 1448), on the square pillars of which that king is seen before the gods. In design this temple is not unlike that of Thothmes IIIrd behind the main temple (p. 103); but it is now too ruined to be of much interest. The south side of the court is formed by a second pylon built by Horemheb, largely out of the blocks of the shrine of Harmachis erected by Akhnaton, the "heretic" Pharaoh. Before it stand the much damaged colossi in crystalline limestone of Rameses IInd. The splendid granite doorway which leads through the pylon is now much ruined; but on the right (16) there are four panels of reliefs which should be observed. At the bottom Horemheb stands before Amen-Ra; above this he is seen before Min; still higher before Amen-Ra again; and at the top he stands before Mut and Khonsu, the figures here being now headless. A paling across the doorway brings our walk in this direction to an end: beyond it we see amidst the palms the avenue of sphinxes which led to the temple of Mut. On the east of this avenue there is a small chapel of Osiris-Ptah, erected by Tanutamen and Taharka (B.C. 688-663).

In returning to the main temple the sacred lake may be visited. Almost every Egyptian temple had a lake at its side, upon which certain ceremonies were performed. The sacred barques of the gods were floated upon its waters; and to this day there is a native tradition that upon this Karnak lake a golden boat may sometimes be seen, which is evidently the barque of Amen. The lake was surrounded by a terrace of masonry, and originally must have been most imposing. We have already seen how it was approached on the west side by an alabaster passage (p. 109). On the north side there are traces of buildings of the time of Rameses IInd. *The sacred lake.*

THE TEMPLE OF MUT IN ASHER

From the pylon of Horemheb (see above) an avenue of sphinxes leads southwards to the temple of the mother-goddess Mut, the consort of Amen, which is situated in a part of Karnak known in ancient days as *Asher*. From the main road from Luxor to Karnak there is a branch road which runs off to the right or east at a point not far beyond the European cemetery. This takes us to the south end of the temple of Mut, which stands on the left, projecting into a lake; and, passing round it to the north end of the temple we may enter the ruins by the gateway at the end of the avenue of sphinxes.

ANTIQUITIES OF UPPER EGYPT

History of the temple. The temple dates for the most part from the reign of Amenhotep IIIrd (B.C. 1411–1375), but an earlier building, dating from the reigns of Hatshepsut and Thothmes IIIrd (B.C. 1500), had occupied the site previous to this; and Amenhotep IIIrd used many of its stones in its foundations. It is interesting to note that Senmut, whose chapel at Shêkh abd' el Gûrneh is numbered 71, was concerned in the building of this earlier edifice. The temple was much defaced during the persecution of Mut and Amen in the reign of Akhnaton (B.C. 1375–1358), but one of the successors of the "heretic" Pharaoh, Tutankhamen, seems to have undertaken some repairs. Rameses IInd, Sety IInd, Setnekht, Rameses IIIrd and Rameses IVth, covering the period from B.C. 1292 to 1161, each undertook work here. Pinezem IInd, Shashank Ist, Piankhi, and Taharka (B.C. 1000 to 663) have left traces of their work in the temple; and Ptolemy Ist added considerably to the buildings. The temple is now almost entirely destroyed, and is in no part more than a few feet in height, the ground plan of the buildings being thus alone visible. It is, however, well worth a visit, as its situation is most picturesque.

At the south end of the avenue of sphinxes there is the main doorway to the temple, built by Ptolemy Ist. On the left there is a relief showing the king shaking two sistrums before Mut and the lion-headed goddess Sekhmet, while behind him the queen plays a harp and a princess beats a tambourine. We now pass through the first court which is still unexcavated. Here there were lines of ram-headed sphinxes, some of which may still be seen, while an overturned colossal figure of a king is to be noticed on the left. The second doorway is then reached. On either side there is a figure of the bearded dwarf Bes, a god almost as closely connected with womanhood and maternity as was Mut herself. This gateway is said in the inscription to have been built by Amenhotep IIIrd and Rameses IInd, and to have been restored in Ptolemaic times. We next pass into the second court, around which are numerous seated statues of the lion-headed goddess Sekhmet, many of which bear the name of Amenhotep IIIrd, while others are dedicated by Pinezem IInd and Sheshonk Ist. The goddess Sekhmet was the wife of Ptah, the great Memphite deity, and thus bore to him the same relationship that Mut did to Amen, the Theban god. She was identified with Hathor; and there seems little doubt that she was also identified with Mut in some of her forms. In the reign of Amenhotep IIIrd there was a tendency to introduce features of the religions of the north into the Theban

THE TEMPLES OF KARNAK 113

worship. Rames, the vizir at the end of the reign (p. 160), seems to have been a Memphite noble ; and it is known that the kings of this period themselves lived for part of the year at Memphis. The free introduction of these Sekhmet figures into the temple of Mut may thus be accounted for by the supposition that Mut of Thebes and Sekhmet of Memphis were identified as one goddess by those who were desirous of uniting the thought and policy of Upper and Lower Egypt (see also p. 162).

We pass on through a ruined doorway into the third court. On our left there is a large statue, probably of Amenhotep IIIrd, and on the right is a fine figure of Sekhmet in large size, bearing a dedication by Sheshonk Ist. The walls of this court have the name of Rameses IInd inscribed upon them. Ascending now to the main temple, which is almost totally destroyed, we find ourselves in what was once an eight-columned hall, beyond which is the sanctuary, while on either side the ruins of small chapels are to be seen. On the right of the sanctuary four baboons in sandstone, two of which are still standing, form the side-ornaments of a doorway leading into a gallery in which there is a long row of Sekhmet figures. Beyond the main temple, to the south, there is a Ptolemaic gateway overlooking the horse-shoe shaped lake which spreads round this end of the building. It is perhaps not an accident that the lake is shaped like one of the hieroglyphs connected with womanhood. The whole temple and lake are surrounded with brick walls. In the south-west corner of the enclosure there is a ruined temple of Rameses IIIrd. On the west exterior wall there are some scenes from that king's campaigns in Syria and Libya.

CHAPTER VII

MORTUARY CHAPELS OF THE NOBLES

THE mortuary chapels of the great nobles of the XVIIIth dynasty, which are excavated in the sides and at the foot of the low hills known as Shêkh abd' el Gûrneh, Gurnet el Murrai, El Assasif, and Dra abu'l Neggar, do not receive as much attention from the visitors to Thebes as they deserve. They are of extreme interest. Nowhere else can one obtain so clear an idea of the manners and customs of the ancient Egyptians as in these chapels. The walls of each chapel are covered with paintings depicting scenes from the everyday life of the people, as well as of the grandees; and although they have suffered very severely at the hands of the natives, one may still find representations of enthralling interest, which are as pleasing to the ordinary traveller as they are valuable to the archæologist. The chapels usually consist of two or more chambers cut into the rock, the walls of which are decorated with paintings. Sometimes a well leads down from one of these rooms, or from the courtyard in front, to the chamber in which the mummy was buried; but often there is no such burial-place, the bodies having been laid to rest in small pits in the Valley of the Tombs of the Kings. Thus, just as the kings were buried in the valley, but built their mortuary temples on the edge of the cultivation, so the nobles were often buried beside their royal masters, but constructed their mortuary chapels in the main necropolis. Thus it would be incorrect to use the word "tomb" in describing these chapels; for often the tomb is not here at all, and in almost every other case it is at least some yards distant from the chambers visited by us. The chapels on the hill of Shêkh abd' el Gûrneh may be described first. The hill is situated immediately behind the Ramesseum, the majority of chapels being on its east and north sides, enclosed by a wall. The enclosure is entered on the east side, opposite the Ramesseum; and from the gateway paths lead in all directions to the various chapels.

MORTUARY CHAPELS OF THE NOBLES

NO. 100. THE MORTUARY CHAPEL OF REKHMARA

This important chapel, which faces one on entering the enclosure, is of peculiar form. One first enters a transverse corridor, and thence passes into a long, narrow passage, the roof of which slopes upward to a considerable height. All the walls are covered with paintings, but these are much blackened by the smoke of the fires of the natives who used to live in this chapel until recent years.

Rekhmara was vizir during the latter half of the reign of Thothmes IIIrd, and was thus at the head of the government at a time when Egypt was at the zenith of its power. He came of a noble family, his uncle having been vizir before him. His duties were manifold, and comprised the superintendence of almost every branch of government work, the Pharaoh and the Chief Treasurer being the only two persons with whom he was required to consult. It is said that "there was nothing of which he was ignorant in heaven, in earth, or in any quarter of the underworld." The inscriptions in the tomb are of very great importance, for they give a detailed account of the duties of a vizir, and state the moral principles which guided his administration. One of the last duties in the life of Rekhmara was the crowning of Amenhotep IInd as king after the death of the great Thothmes IIIrd; and his decease must therefore have occurred not long after B.C. 1447. As there is no burial-chamber in the chapel, it may be supposed that he was buried in one of the pits in the Valley of the Tombs of the Kings. *The career of Rekhmara.*

Amidst the many scenes depicted on the walls of this chapel, it will only be necessary here to draw the visitor's attention to the ten representations of the greatest interest. At the north end of the west wall of the first room, one sees (1) a wine-press, near which are numerous jars of grape-juice. The grapes have been placed in a kind of trough, and the workmen tread them with their feet, supporting themselves by means of ropes hung from a cross-bar. The juice passes out by a drain, and is received in the large jars here shown. On the east wall, just to one's left on entering (2), there is a scene showing the reception of the tribute of cattle, rings of gold, chests of linen, &c. Farther along the same wall (3) there is a representation of the court of law in which the vizir sat to dispense justice. Four rugs or mats indicate the foot of the throne; and up the central aisle one sees the prisoners brought forward by the police. Attendants stand on either side *The scenes in the first room.*

of the court, and outside there are messengers, and persons who do obeisance before entering. At the south end of the west wall (4) one sees the arrival of the tribute from Nubia and Asia. The negroes bring giraffes, cattle, leopards, baboons, monkeys, elephants' tusks, gold, &c.; and the long-robed Asiatics bring

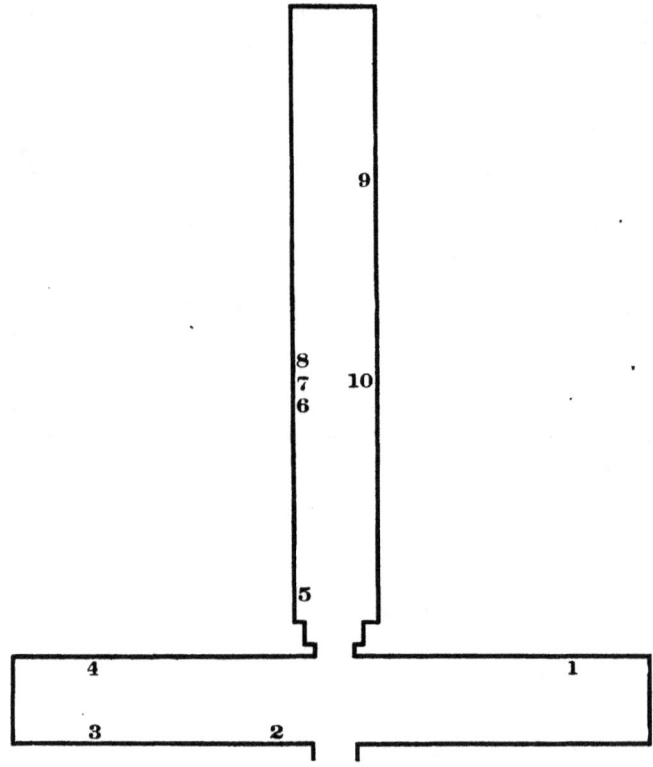

chariots, vases, jars of wine, and other costly articles, all of which are recorded by the scribes of the vizir before being placed in the Treasury.

The scenes in the second room.

Passing into the second room, on the south wall (5) Rekhmara is shown seated upon a chair watching various craftsmen at work; and farther along (6) one sees two men fetching water from a

MORTUARY CHAPELS OF THE NOBLES 117

square lake surrounded by trees. One of the men stands up to his waist in the water, and holds the water-pot upon his shoulder. A short distance farther on (7), just beyond a break in the wall, there is an interesting representation of a seated and a standing colossal statue, to which the finishing touches are being put by workmen who stand on scaffolding. Above this Rekhmara watches the weighing of gold, the making of a statue of the king, and other works. One next (8) sees a series of the usual funeral scenes, which, however, can be better studied in other tombs. The bier is dragged towards the tomb; the boats cross the Nile to the necropolis; and the funeral furniture is borne along. On the north wall (9) an interesting painting represents a pond with trees growing around it, and a boat sailing upon it. This is supposed to be in the "happy land" to which the soul of Rekhmara had gone. On this wall the visitor should also particularly notice (10) a scene representing a feast, at which men and women are present. Musicians play upon the harp and lute, and the guests are waited upon by male and female servants, wreaths being placed around their necks, and dishes of food handed to them. The other scenes in this chapel will be best appreciated by those who will closely examine them, after seeing the similar representations in the various chapels which are about to be described.

Chapels 99, 98, and 97 are without interest, and have hardly any of their paintings preserved.

NO. 96A. THE MORTUARY CHAPEL OF SENNEFER

Travellers should make a point of visiting this chapel, as the paintings are particularly fresh, and the scenes depicted are of much interest. The noble for whom the chapel was made was named Sennefer. He was entitled *Ha*-Prince of Thebes, Superintendent of the Granaries of Amen, and Superintendent of the Cattle of Amen; and since mention is made of the funeral temple of Thothmes IIIrd, and the name of Amenhotep IInd is inscribed upon one of his amulets, one may suppose that he lived in, or not long after, the reigns of those Pharaohs.

The chapel is entered by a steep tunnel, which opens into a low chamber covered with paintings. On the right one first sees (1) the figure of Sennefer entering, so the inscription says, into the Underworld after a happy old age. Near by servants are shown carrying boxes and a bed for his use in the tomb. Farther along

The first room.

118   ANTIQUITIES OF UPPER EGYPT

(2) other servants are seen carrying the cartonnage head which fits over the mummy, the *ushabti* figures which were supposed to act as servants in the next world, collars, and other paraphernalia. Sennefer and his daughter Muttuy, who was a songstress of Amen-Ra, stand near to receive these articles. We next see (3) Sennefer's sister, the king's nurse Sentnefert, holding a sistrum and a necklace : she has just risen from her chair, which stands beside her. On the opposite side of the doorway into the next room (4) there are figures of Sennefer and his sister. Beyond this (5) he is shown, baton in hand, seated upon a chair, while a woman and several men make offerings to him. The ceiling of this room has been painted to represent a cluster of vines.

The second room.   We now pass into the second room, which is of some size, the

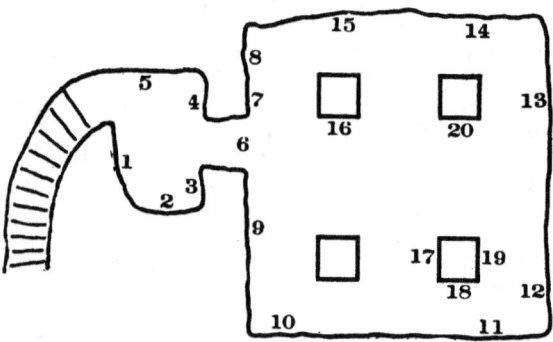

roof being supported by four pillars. Above the doorway through which we pass (6) two jackals, symbolising the necropolis, are shown seated upon their shrines, and the inscription gives a prayer for the soul of Sennefer, that he may come forth from, and go into, his temple. Turning to the left (7), Sennefer and his sister Meryt are shown walking towards the doorway, "coming forth to earth to see the *Aten*-disk every day." Next (8) one sees Sennefer and Meryt seated. On the right of the entrance (9) Sennefer and Meryt, the former smelling the fragrance of a lotus-flower, sit before a quantity of offerings presented by a priest clad in a leopard-skin. Then (10) Sennefer and Meryt are purified with holy-water by a priest connected with the mortuary temple of Thothmes IIIrd. Strange to say, on one of the amulets around the neck of the figure of Sennefer is the name "Alexander," written

MORTUARY CHAPELS OF THE NOBLES 119

in hieroglyphs; and one must therefore suppose that the tomb was open in the Greek period, and was visited by a person of that name. At the far end of this wall (11) Sennefer and his sister make offering before a shrine in which Osiris and Anubis are shown. On the next wall (12) a funeral boat, containing the statues of Sennefer and Meryt, is towed across the river, accompanied by other vessels. A damaged figure of Sennefer is here represented, a mirror and pot of ointment being under his chair, and many offerings heaped up before it. Farther on (13) one sees Sennefer seated to receive the offerings brought to him by male servants. Next (14) there is a damaged representation of Sennefer and Meryt in the presence of Osiris and Hathor, the latter having a hawk upon her head. Finally (15) servants bring furniture for the tomb, oxen are slain as offerings, and in the lowest row we see workmen setting up two obelisks at the door of the chapel. To one side of this there is a woman offering two vases, and on the other side there is a scene possibly representing a human sacrifice—a man partly wrapped up crouching on a table or stand. The scenes on the pillars are of interest. In one of these (16) Sennefer sits amidst the foliage of the sacred tree with his wife beside him, and vases of wine before him. In another scene (17) Sennefer, seated, receives a bowl of wine from Meryt, "to make a happy day," as the inscription phrases it. Elsewhere (18) we see Sennefer purified by Ritual-priests; and (19) he is shown, receiving from Meryt a necklace with a scarab-pendant, and another with pendants of the so-called girdle, backbone, and snake amulets. Finally we may notice a scene (20) in which Sennefer and Meryt are seated before a sacred tree, amidst whose boughs a small figure of Isis is represented. The ceiling pattern in this room is partly that of the vines which has been seen in the first room. It is painted over the rough, unsmoothed rock, which increases its effectiveness, and at the same time must have been a considerable economy to Sennefer.

This chapel is situated in the court of a larger chapel, No. 96B, the entrance of which is to be seen a few yards distant. At present it is closed to the public. The owner was the same Sennefer who lived under Amenhotep IInd, but the scenes on the walls are much damaged, although once of very considerable interest. Mounting the stairway at the side of the court, we pass on our right the chapel of Rames, surnamed May, No. 94, the scenes in which are now destroyed for the most part. Continuing

120 ANTIQUITIES OF UPPER EGYPT

to ascend the stairway we reach another large court, at the end of which is the mortuary chapel of Ken-Amen, No. 93, now closed.

NO. 92. THE MORTUARY CHAPEL OF SUMNUT

The path continues up the hill, winding slightly to the south, and presently we reach the tomb of Sumnut, a prince who held the important Court appointment of "Washer of the King's Hands," during the reign of Amenhotep IInd. Entering the first room, one sees on the right (1) an unfinished painting in outline, and the red squares employed by the artist in order to fix his proportions are still to be seen. On the north wall (2) numerous funeral offerings are depicted, amongst which are statuettes of the king and queen. On the left of the entrance (3) the souls of Sumnut and his wife, holding two braziers on which pigeons are burning, stand facing a number of offerings which they have come forth from their tomb to receive. On the south wall (4) there are some much damaged scenes representing various works which Sumnut is inspecting. Jars are filled with grain; others containing wine are standing in shady booths; trays of grain, meat, flowers, and fruit are carried by servants. Passing into the next room, one sees on the right (5) an unfinished representation of Sumnut and his wife seated before offerings made by their son. On the opposite wall (6) another unfinished scene shows the harpooning of fish and hunting of birds with boomerangs in the marshes, the bag being presented to Sumnut and his wife. In the third room,

The first room.

The second room.

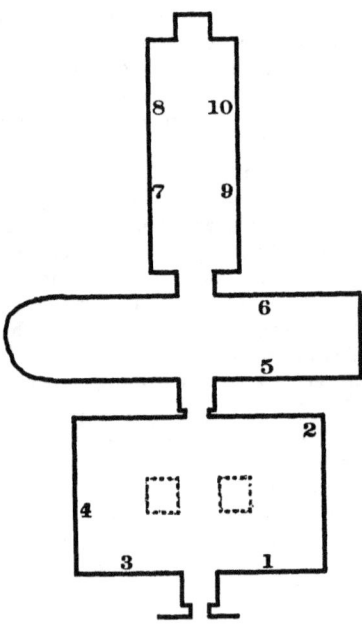

MORTUARY CHAPELS OF THE NOBLES 121

on the north wall (7) there are funeral scenes, in four rows. At the top five shrines for holding religious images are shown, and men are seen carrying the burial paraphernalia to the tomb. In the second row a bundle, probably representing the victim of a human sacrifice, is dragged on a sledge. A chest for holding the canopic jars is dragged along; and the coffin, beside which are images of Isis and Nephthys, is also drawn towards the tomb. In the third row one sees funeral chests, sacred barques, shrines of Anubis, a hawk-standard symbolic of the west, and other objects. Two men are shown performing the funeral dance, which was an integral part of the burial ceremonies, and which is already seen in the tombs of the VIth dynasty at Sakkâra. An ox is then represented being slain before the door of the tomb. In the lowest row are funeral boats, and sledges upon which are statues of Sumnut and his wife. Farther on (8) we see the damaged figures of Osiris and Hathor, and at the end of the wall Sumnut and his wife are seated before a quantity of offerings. On the opposite wall various ceremonies are performed before the two mummies. Food and drink offerings are made to the embalmed bodies, and the ceremony of "opening the mouth" of the mummy is shown, a priest touching the mouth of the body with a carpenter's tool. Lastly, one may observe the scene representing the funeral feast (10), at which Sumnut and his wife are seated, while facing him is his son Amnefer, who was *Ha*-prince of Neferusi, and Superintendent of the Priests of Thoth of Hermopolis. Various male and female relatives are present, and women entertain them by dancing and playing harps. The pathway continues up the hill, and presently divides, the southern path leading to

The third room.

No. 91. THE MORTUARY CHAPEL OF A CHIEF ARCHER

The name of the person buried here is now lost, but his titles were *Erpa-ha*-Prince, and Chief of the Archers. The chapel is unfinished, and is in a much damaged condition. At the north end (1) one sees Asiatics clad in white robes, bowing and presenting beautiful vases as tribute. Farther along the king, who is either Thothmes IIIrd or Thothmes IVth, is seen seated under a canopy to receive these gifts. At the south end of the chapel (2) negroes are shown bowing to the ground, and bringing in their tribute of tusks, animals, &c. Negro soldiers, carrying shields, are also seen, these probably being some of the famous

122 ANTIQUITIES OF UPPER EGYPT

Mazoi troops which formed the backbone of the Egyptian army. There is little else of interest in the chapel.

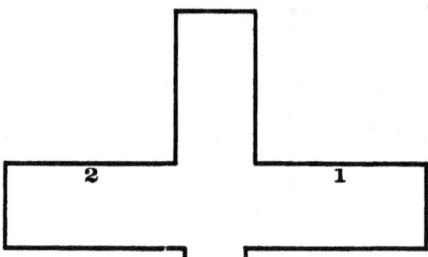

The northern path leads past two or three undecorated chapels, and presently brings us to

NO. 90. THE MORTUARY CHAPEL OF AMENNEB

The personage for whom this chapel was made was entitled *Erpa-ha*-Prince, Fanbearer, Chief of the Soldiers, "watching the king's footsteps in the lands of the north and south." His name is erased wherever it occurs, but traces which remain indicate that it read Amenneb. The king whom he served was either Amenhotep IInd or Thothmes IVth, as the damaged cartouche

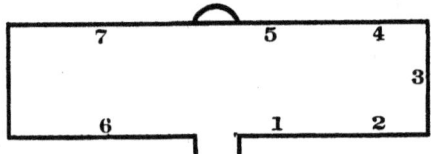

ends with the word *kheperu*. Turning to the right on entering the chapel, one sees (1) the owner and his wife standing before a number of offerings. On this wall (2) there has also been the scene of a feast, but it is much damaged. Women can still be seen dancing, and men are depicted playing on the lute. On the north wall (3) there is the much damaged funeral stele. At the north end of the west wall (4) one sees, in the top corner, a representation of the pylons of a temple decorated with two flagstaffs. The sacred lake and garden are seen near by; and butchers are

MORTUARY CHAPELS OF THE NOBLES 123

shown cutting up the meat for the sacrifices, while others bring geese for the same purpose. Below this a house, with door and windows, is seen standing amidst the palms. A wine-press elegantly decorated is seen near by. Below this again soldiers are shown walking towards the house; and at the bottom there is an interesting representation of the branding of cattle. A man heats the stamp in the fire, in the presence of Amenneb, who is seated on a stool, with his servants behind him. Farther on (5) one sees a damaged figure of Amenneb holding the standard of the royal *dahabiyeh*, and leading captive several Asiatics from Naharin, who bring tribute of horses and various articles. On the left of the entrance (6) Amenneb and his wife are seated, and are presented with exquisite golden bowls by two of their daughters, whose figures are now much damaged. Near by women dance and play upon the lute and harp; and there have been representations of women squatting on the floor, playing pipes and singing. It is unfortunate that these are partly destroyed, for they were depicted full-face, which was not at all a common manner of representing the human form. On the opposite wall (7) the captain of the *Mazoi*, or negro troops, of Thebes, and other officials, present to Amenneb the troops under their charge, armed with bows and arrows, spears, and shields; and conspicuous amongst them are the standard-bearers and a trumpeter.

NO. 89. THE MORTUARY CHAPEL OF AN UNKNOWN OFFICIAL

Descending somewhat and turning northwards, one soon reaches this chapel, the name of the owner of which is now lost. Turning

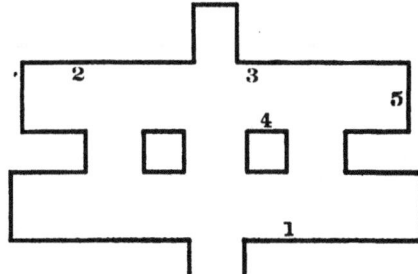

to one's right on entering, there is (1) an unfinished representation of a funeral feast. Offerings are made to the *Ka* of Amen-Ra,

ANTIQUITIES OF UPPER EGYPT

Harmachis, and Thothmes IIIrd. At the south end of the west wall (2) one sees the ceremonies performed before the mummy before burial. A damaged scene (3) shows King Amenhotep IIIrd seated with Hathor, while Asiatics, Negroes, and Egyptian soldiers bring offerings of vases, gold, &c.; but the drawing is poor and is much faded. On the west side of the northern pillar (4) there is an unfinished representation of Thothmes IIIrd drawn in outline with red paint. On the north wall (5) soldiers are seen running in front and behind a chariot, which is not now very clear.

NO. 88. THE MORTUARY CHAPEL OF PEHSUKHER

The pathway continues northwards to the chapel of Pehsukher, who was a high official of the XVIIIth dynasty, the name of the actual Pharaoh whom he served not being preserved in the inscrip-

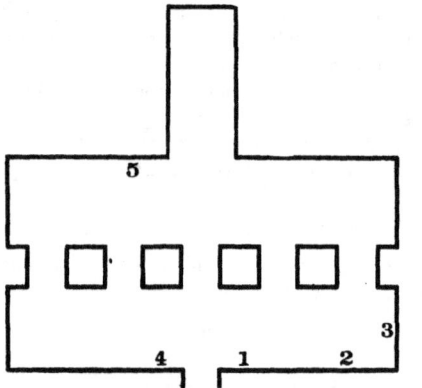

tions. Amongst Pehsukher's many titles may be mentioned that of *Erpa-ha*-Prince, Royal Registrar, Watching the King's footsteps in the Lands of the North and South, and Standard-bearer of the King. On one's right on entering (1) Pehsukher and his wife are seen standing before a heap of offerings. Farther along (2) the Second Priest of Amen, named Mahui, offers Pehsukher flowers, &c. On the north wall (3) there is a damaged stele. At the left of the entrance (4) Pehsukher stands before the door of his house, and makes a list of men, chariots, and horses which are brought before him. Below this there are damaged scenes of harvesting,

MORTUARY CHAPELS OF THE NOBLES 125

ploughing, &c. On the opposite wall (5) a scribe makes lists of men who are recruited for military service. Much of the decorations remain unfinished.

Chapel No. 87 is not worth visiting. One passes from No. 88 around the bend northwards to this chapel. It belonged to a Superintendent of the Granaries of the South and North, named Min-nekht; but not much of the original decoration now remains, except in the innermost chamber, where on one wall there are funeral scenes. A pathway now runs up and down the hill, and, descending by it to a somewhat lower level, we pass on our left the following chapel.

NO. 86. THE MORTUARY CHAPEL OF RAMENKHEPER-SENB

This tomb is historically one of the most important at Thebes. Ramenkheper-senb was High Priest of Amen, and at the same time held the important posts of Superintendent of the Gold and

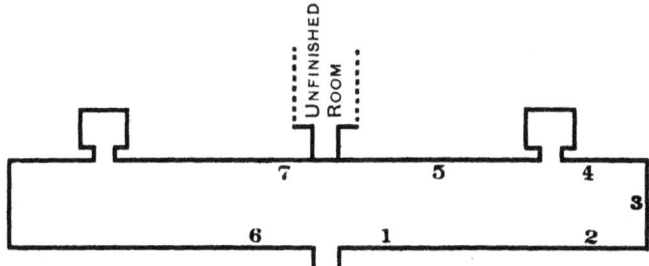

Silver Treasuries, and Chief of the Overseers of Craftsmen, under Thothmes IIIrd; and that king's great building works at Karnak seem to have been under his direction in part. On entering the chapel one observes on the right-hand side (1) a scene showing cattle and geese being led in. Farther along (2) we see in the top row a number of chariot-makers busily at work; in the second row men are making bows and arrows; and in the third row vases, chess-boards, &c., are being made. The necessary amount of gold for these works is being weighed out. The inscription states that Ramenkheper-senb is "inspecting the workshop of the temple of Amen, the work of the craftsmen, in real lapis lazuli, and in real malachite." On the north wall (3) gold is brought in by the captain of the *Mazoi* of Koptos and the Superintendent of the Gold-Country of Koptos; and the inscription reads, "The reception of the gold of the highland of Koptos, as well as the gold of Kush." Persons are shown bringing bows and arrows, ostrich feathers and eggs, an ostrich, a hare held by the ears, a gazelle with long ears, and other creatures of the desert. At the north end of the west wall (4) there is a small representation of a two-doored magazine, containing rows of jars. Farther along (5) an important scene shows two lines of Asiatics bringing forward the most beautiful vases and ornaments of gold and silver, which speak of the luxury of the Orient at that time. Plumed helmets of bronze, chariots, bows and arrows, weapons, children as slaves, and horses, are brought in by these Asiatics. The inscription states that amongst these persons are "the Chief of Keftiew, the Chief of the Hittites, the Chief of Tunip, and the Chief of Kadesh." On the left of the entrance (6) are scenes of harvesting; and finally on the opposite wall we may observe (7) a damaged representation of the canopy under which the king was seated. Much of the chapel is unfinished.

Descending the pathway and turning slightly to the south, one reaches

NO. 85. THE MORTUARY CHAPEL OF AMENEMHEB

Career of Amenem-heb.

This chapel is famous for its historical inscriptions which throw light on the campaigns of Thothmes IIIrd. Amenemheb was an *Erpa-ha*-Prince and Royal Registrar, and he also held a high position in the army during the king's Asiatic campaigns. In the king's VIth Campaign Amenemheb was present at the capture of Kadesh, and took prisoner two nobles of that city. The king presented to him a lion-shaped ornament, two pendants in the form of flies, and four bracelets, all of the finest gold, as a reward for his bravery. In the VIIIth Campaign he captured three prisoners in Naharin, and near Aleppo he captured thirteen men, seventy asses, and thirteen bronze spears inlaid with gold. Several prisoners fell to him at the battle of Carchemish; and he was richly rewarded by the Pharaoh. At the battle of Senzara he killed a man in single combat, and was rewarded with two silver rings and some other objects in gold. At an elephant hunt which the king organised during this campaign, Amenemheb saved his master's life. The

MORTUARY CHAPELS OF THE NOBLES 127

king was attacked by a large elephant, but Amenemheb, running forward, drew the animal's attention to himself, and was pursued into a river, where he took refuge between two rocks. When the elephant attacked him, he cut off its trunk with a blow of his sword, and managed to escape. The king rewarded him with gold, and with three sets of clothing in place of the one damaged during his

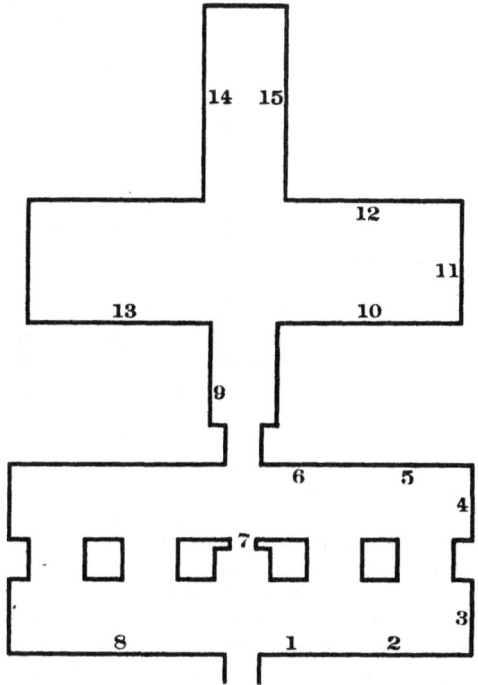

adventure. In the Xth Campaign Amenemheb captured three men after a hand-to-hand fight, and received from the king two gold necklaces, four bracelets, two fly-shaped pendants, a lion-formed ornament, and a male and female slave. In the XIVth Campaign against the Beduin he captured three men; and in the XVIIth Campaign he was the first to scale the walls of Kadesh, capturing two of the enemy, and being rewarded by the king with various presents. During this siege the Prince of Kadesh sent out a mare towards the Egyptian chariots in order to disturb the line of battle ; and the stallions were already becoming restive when Amenemheb rushed forward on foot, pursued the mare, and killed her with his sword, thus saving the situation. After the death of Thothmes IIIrd, Amenemheb lived a retired life for a short time ; but one day while rowing a sacred vessel at one of the religious festivals on the Nile, the new king, Amenhotep IInd, observed him and invited him to the palace. On reaching the throne-room Amenemheb bowed low ; but the king spoke in a most friendly manner to him, saying, "I know your character: I was but a fledgeling in the nest when you were in my father's retinue. I give you the office of deputy of the army. . . . You shall inspect the personal troops of the king." So in this important position Amenemheb remained for the last years of his life.

First room. On entering the chapel one sees on the right (1) Amenemheb and his wife Bakt, the former holding two braziers in each of which a dead dove or pigeon lies. Farther on (2) the usual funeral feast is depicted. He and his wife are seated, while their son offers them bouquets of flowers. The guests sit near ; musicians play upon harps and lutes ; and there are traces of women dancing. On the north wall (3) there is the partly-destroyed funeral stele, on which some Coptic hermit who used this chapel as a dwelling-place has painted Christian crosses in red. A damaged scene near this (4) shows Amenhotep IInd presenting Amenemheb and his wife to Thothmes IIIrd, who is dressed as Unnefer, the god of the dead. This is interesting as being a clear instance of the identification of the king with Osiris (or Unnefer) in the underworld; and of the living king's duties as mediator between man and god. On the west wall (5) Asiatics are seen, clad in white ornamented robes, bringing offerings and paying homage. Their red beards are noticeable, and it is to be observed that they bring some of their children with them. Farther along (6) there is a damaged scene representing Thothmes IIIrd seated under a canopy, while Amenemheb presents to him these Asiatic prisoners. On the west side of the lintel between the two middle pillars (7) there is a curious hunting scene showing a man striking an enormous female hyæna with a stick ; and it probably refers to some incident in Amenemheb's life, when he was attacked by a hyæna and defended himself in this manner. The size of the hyæna is suggestive of the exaggerated dimensions of the proverbial angler's fish. On the left of the entrance (8) Amenemheb stands before the door of a

MORTUARY CHAPELS OF THE NOBLES

house, and soldiers are brought forward to him, and are listed by his scribes. On the left of the passage into the next room (9) there is a scene representing the offering of ornaments, vases, statuettes, &c.

On the right as one enters the second room (10) one sees the netting of birds ; and on the north wall (11) the spearing of fish is shown. On the west wall (12) the funeral feast is shown. Male and female servants offer food and drink to the guests ; and male and female harpers are seen, while women are shown playing on the pipes. On the left of the entrance (13) offerings are brought to the tomb, and placed in booths, in which servants prepare them for consumption. Funeral boats cross the Nile; the bier is drawn along on a sledge to the sepulchre ; bows and arrows, shields, a chariot, and other warlike objects are brought to be buried in the tomb of the old warrior; and women are seen wailing with arms raised. On the left wall of the recess at the west of this room (14) the mummy stands, while before it are laid out the insignia necessary at the funeral. A ritual-priest reads the formulæ, and behind this the coffin is dragged on a sledge by men and kine. Jars of wine for the funeral feast stand in decorated booths. On the opposite wall (15) more offerings are brought, and a garden is shown with a lake in it, surrounded by trees, this perhaps being the estate for the endowment of the tomb.

The second room.

No. 84. THE MORTUARY CHAPEL OF AMUNEZEH

This chapel lies just to the south of No. 85. It is not of general interest, though to archæologists it is of some importance. Amunezeh was an *Erpa-ha*-Prince, the Chief Royal Herald, and Steward of the Palace, during the reign of Thothmes IIIrd. On one's right on entering (1) the guests are seen at the funeral feast. On the north wall (2) is the much broken funeral stele ; and on the west wall (3) there are scenes showing the Asiatics bringing in their tribute, but these representations are very much damaged. Some of the Asiatics are coloured red-brown like the Egyptians, and wear short skirts, but have beards and longish hair. Others are yellow-skinned, and wear long white robes, ornamented in colours. At the opposite end of the wall (4) Negro tribes are seen bringing in their tribute of leopards, leopard-skins, giraffes, baboons, and gold-rings. A monkey clings round the neck of the giraffe. On the south wall (5) there is again a damaged stele, through

The first room.

130   ANTIQUITIES OF UPPER EGYPT

which a later tunnel has been pierced. On the east wall (6) Amunezeh is depicted seated before a quantity of offerings.

The second room.   On the north wall of the second room (7) there is a damaged but interesting scene showing Amunezeh in his chariot, galloping towards an enclosure into which many wild animals have been driven. Here one sees antelopes, wild bulls, ostriches, and other creatures of the desert; and into their midst Amunezeh shoots

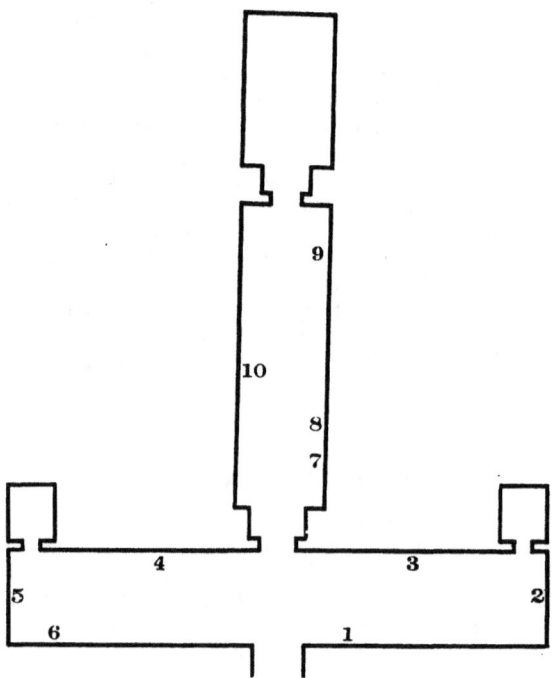

arrow after arrow as he gallops around the outside of the stockade, his chariot reins tied around his waist. Farther along (8) he inspects the produce of his farms; and still farther (9) he and his wife are seen seated before a number of offerings. On the opposite wall (10) there are scenes from the funeral ceremonies. The last chamber in the chapel is vaulted, and has an elaborately decorated ceiling. A niche at the west end was the receptacle of the *Ka*-

MORTUARY CHAPELS OF THE NOBLES 131

statues. The place has been used by Coptic hermits, who have left rough paintings on the walls.

Chapel No. 83 is reached by retracing one's steps northwards, and continuing by the path which leads to the conspicuous ruined brick tower. This chapel was constructed for a judge named Aahmes, but only the ceiling pattern now remains. To the north of the chapel of Minnekht, No. 87, and just to the south of, and above, this chapel, No. 83, the visitor will find

NO. 82. THE MORTUARY CHAPEL OF AMENEMHAT

This chapel dates from the middle of the XVIIIth dynasty. Amenemhat was the Steward of the Vizir, and Scribe of the Grain of Amen under Thothmes IIIrd. The Vizir was perhaps User, who is shown in the wall-paintings here, and who was probably related to Amenemhat.

On the north wall of the first room (1) there have been hunt- First room. ing scenes, but one only now sees a few antelopes in an enclosure such as has been observed in the tomb of Amunezeh. On the west wall (2) there is a fragmentary scene representing birds and butterflies delicately drawn and coloured, reminding one of Japanese workmanship. On the left of the entrance (3) the Vizir User and also his wife Thuau are shown seated. On the south wall (4) Amenemhat is seen offering a sacrifice to his dead relations. Near this on the west wall (5) there is a damaged scene representing the funeral feast. Amenemhat and his wife are seated before numerous offerings; guests are seated near by; women play upon the pipes, clap their hands, and dance; while a man plays a harp. Below this bulls are brought to the butchers, and one bull is seen to toss another with which it has been fighting.

On the south wall (6) there are the usual funeral scenes, here Second more clear than in some of the other chapels. Along the top row room. from east to west one sees the funeral boat towing another vessel, containing the Ka-statues, across the Nile. Offerings are brought to the tomb, and two oars—having a religious significance—are offered at the tomb door. In the second row there are more boats, and an object dragged upon a sledge, which is possibly the victim of a human sacrifice wrapped in a cloth or skin. Farther on two men are seen performing the funeral dance, and near this meat is offered at the door of the tomb. In the third row the mummy is shown lying on a bier which is being dragged to the sepulchre by men and oxen, while before it walk a priest and the widow. A ritual-priest reads a long prayer from a papyrus. A casket is brought to the door of the tomb, and two women bewail.

Behind the tomb stands the goddess Hathor with a hawk-standard on her head. On the opposite wall (7), passing from west to east, we see Amenemhat and his wife Bakt seated, while in the upper registers before them the funeral of Amenemhat is represented. Bakt, who was then still alive, is shown twanging a harp and wailing a funeral dirge. She is depicted with her mouth open, and there is an expression of grief on her face which is cleverly, if grotesquely, portrayed. Their son, also named Amenemhat, plays a lute behind Bakt, and their daughter makes sad music upon the double-pipes. The various relations who have gathered together to bewail the deceased noble sit on stools, while servants offer them drink and put ointment on their heads. In the lower register there are some much 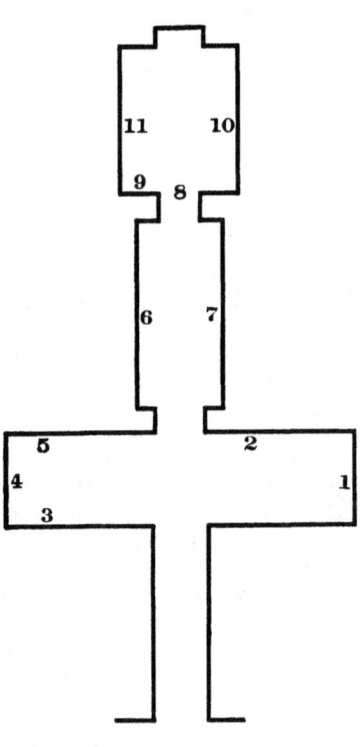 damaged scenes showing the priests making offerings to the mummy and performing the mystic ceremony of "opening the mouth" of the dead man so that he may breathe in the underworld. Passing into the last room one sees over the doorway (8) a group of women wailing and tearing their hair in front of Amenemhat's coffin, the first two women having allowed the hair to fall over their eyes. On one's left (9) there is a funeral stele which has been painted over figure-scenes now visible in

Third room.

MORTUARY CHAPELS OF THE NOBLES

places beneath. The inscription on the stele gives prayers for the benefit of the great Vizir User, who was probably a relation of Amenemhat; and here the twenty-eighth year of the reign of Thothmes IIIrd is given as the date. On the north wall (10) there is a list of offerings, and below it there are the figures of the ritual-priests performing a funeral ceremony very commonly represented upon the monuments. Two priests stand praying, one reads from a papyrus the magical formula, another kneels in prayer, and one turns round to perform the "banishing" rite. Below, again, one sees Amenemhat's relations, and servants are depicted bringing offerings to the tomb. On the opposite wall (11) one sees at the top the ritual-priests making offerings to the dead; below these the friends and relations are again shown; and below, again, one sees a festival in honour of Hathor, the Golden One of Dendereh, as she is here called. Men and women jump and dance, some of the men click castanets, and three women hold necklaces, which are always acceptable to this goddess. Below one sees cows, antelopes, &c., brought as offerings.

NO. 81. THE MORTUARY CHAPEL OF ANENA

This chapel is one of the most interesting in the group. It was made for a noble who held the offices of Superintendent of the Granaries, Superintendent of the Workmen in the Karnak Treasuries, Superintendent of the Royal Buildings, *Ha*-Prince of the City, &c., during the reigns of the Pharaohs Amenhotep Ist, Thothmes Ist, Thothmes IInd, Thothmes IIIrd, and Hatshepsut. An historical inscription of considerable value was cut upon a stele at the end of the outer chamber of the tomb; but this is now quite destroyed. Fortunately a good copy had been made. From it we learn that Anena inspected all that the king received in the way of metals and jewels; and superintended the building of all public monuments. He was in charge of the building of the now ruined hall at Karnak in which stands the obelisk of Hatshepsut. He superintended the excavation of the tomb of Thothmes Ist, the first royal tomb which was cut in the Valley of the Tombs of the Kings; and under the following Pharaohs he rose to such power that he cannot find words to tell it. "I increased beyond everything," he says. "I cannot tell it. But I will tell you this, ye people: hear, ye. Do the good that I did, do ye likewise. My years were passed in gladness, because I showed no treachery, I did not inform against any one, I did no evil. I was devoid of hesitancy, I was devoid of blasphemy towards sacred things." The chapel consists of a front gallery cut in the rock, the roof being supported by six square pillars. One enters through the aperture between the south wall and the first of these pillars, all the other apertures being now closed. The roof of the gallery has partly fallen, and has been replaced by woodwork. From this gallery there leads a chamber, at the far end of which are four seated statues.

<small>The gallery.</small> The paintings in the gallery are of considerable interest, and deserve to be examined with some care. On our right as we enter (1) there are scenes from the hunting field. The large figure of Anena is partly destroyed; but one may still see his legs, which show that he was running; and the lower part of a bow is to be observed with which he was shooting arrows at a number of wild animals. The most striking figure in the picture is that of a female hyæna which rears itself on its hind legs and bites with its teeth at one of the arrows, breaking it off with its fore paw. One of Anena's hounds rushes forward to attack the infuriated beast. It is probable that this incident actually occurred, and was described by Anena to the artist engaged upon the painting of his tomb in order that a record of it should be made. In the lower part of the scene are three figures of huntsmen, painfully inactive and stupid in comparison with the spirited drawing of the hyæna, and with the equally clever drawing of a dog which is shown in the act of biting the stomach of a rearing animal. The head and ears of this dog are drawn in correct perspective, and its attitude as it makes an upward bite, its tail tucked well between its legs and its hind quarters drawn in to avoid the kick of its victim's hoofs, is true to nature. The artist whose work this scene is, was evidently original, though he was by no means great. His animals as they gallop are extremely stiff, and prance like the conventional chariot horses one so often sees on Egyptian monuments; and his human figures are poorly executed. But the above-mentioned dog and the hyæna are to be ranked high amongst the specimens of Egyptian art which have come down to us, if only as indications of their author's momentary freedom from convention.

Upon the next pillar (2) there is an interesting representation of Anena's garden. At the top are seen ten *dôm* palms, and here we see the gardener taking his orders from Anena who is seated with his wife in an arbour. In the middle of the garden, below a number of small trees, there is a pond (now much damaged), and beside it another gardener stoops down. At the bottom of the

MORTUARY CHAPELS OF THE NOBLES 135

scene one can just make out the front wall of the garden, at one end of which is a small wooden door. Rising above the wall the store-houses and granaries can be seen. At the top of this picture there is an inscription which gives the number of trees possessed by Anena : 73 sycamores, 31 acacias, 170 palms of one kind, 120 palms of another kind, and so on.

On the third pillar (3) there is the figure of Anena seated upon a chair, a large number of offerings being placed before him, including baskets of grapes, bread, meat, vases of wine, and a censer in the usual form of an arm. On the fifth pillar (4) two scenes remain. The upper scene shows the ploughing of Anena's fields ; and the lower scene shows the same fields at harvest-time,

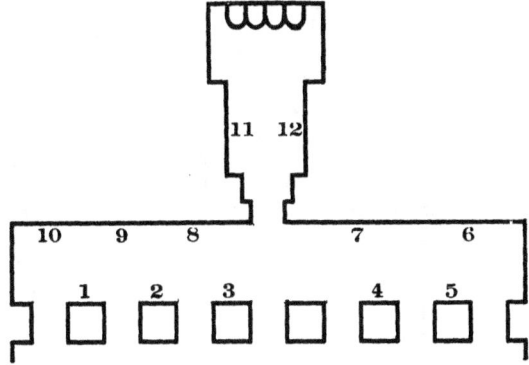

a fine crop of *durra* (such as may be seen at the present day) having grown up. Upon the sixth, and last, pillar (5) three scenes remain. The uppermost shows us a group of labourers working with the pitchfork ; below this one sees the corn carried away in rope nets ; and at the bottom three men and a black woman are seen working at harvest-time.

Opposite these scenes, on the west wall (6), there is the usual representation of the harpooning of fish in the marshes, a sport much indulged in by the ancient Egyptians. Below this some servants bring in the produce of the estate, and notice should be taken of the prettily decorated baskets. Farther along this wall (7) there are painted five rows of animals farmed upon the estate. The wall is much damaged, but it can be seen that these animals were being led towards the seated figure of Anena, who, with his dog under his chair, and his relations around him, watches the parade of his possessions. In the top row one sees geese and flamingoes; in the second row are donkeys, one of which is depicted in the act of braying, with its ears thrown back; in the third row are sheep and goats, two of which are seen to be butting one another, a man carrying a lamb, and behind him some indistinct swine; in the fourth row are oxen; and in the fifth row there is a spirited drawing of cattle being led in by farm-hands, a calf trying to run away and an old man of ample girth being noticeable for their execution.

On the continuation of this wall beyond the door (8) one observes Anena and his wife and relations watching the parade of foreign tribute brought to Egypt from the wars of Thothmes Ist. There are here five rows of figures. In the top row an Egyptian soldier, armed with a battle-axe and stick, is driving in a group of Nubian women, who are carrying their children in cow-hide baskets upon their backs; in the second row one sees the soldiers bringing in the spoil; the third row is destroyed, but in the fourth there are fair-skinned Asiatic women carrying their children upon their shoulders, and an Asiatic man leading a bear (?); and in the lowest row tribute of vases, baskets, and other goods, is brought in. Farther along (9) there is a figure of Anena, who is supposed to be engaged in his official work of inspecting the cattle and grain of the temple estates. In the third row offenders are brought for trial, and one man is receiving a sound beating. Farther along this wall (10) there is an interesting scene representing the weighing of the jewellery, necklaces, and other treasure belonging to Karnak. A large pair of scales is seen; one man watches the indicator, while another writes down the record. The weights are here to be seen in the form of oxen and trussed ducks. Many weights in these forms have been found in Egypt, oxen and ducks having been the medium of exchange before weights were invented. The ox-weights appear in Egypt for the first time in the XVIIIth dynasty; but it may be mentioned that the custom of regarding an ox as a monetary unit was so widespread that in Rome, for example, the word for a head of cattle, *pecus*, originated the word *pecunia*, money. An inscription near this scene gives a list of the donations to the various gods at Karnak, but it is now almost unreadable.

The inner chamber.

We now enter the inner chamber. On our left (11) at the end of the wall there are large figures of Anena and his wife; but the paintings have been maliciously rubbed and blurred in ancient

MORTUARY CHAPELS OF THE NOBLES

times. Offerings are presented to the deceased couple by a male figure, perhaps that of their son. The rest of the wall is occupied with funeral scenes in four rows. In the top row one sees the mummy of Anena lying under a canopy; and a boat in which are the *Ka*-statues of the deceased is seen crossing the Nile from the city to the Necropolis. Below this, women are shown pouring dust upon their heads and weeping; and two other boats are seen crossing the water. In the third row there is a plan of a house and garden, a lake with palms around it (drawn as though the lake were in mid air), and some squares of irrigated land. This scene occurs on several tombs, but it is impossible to say what it represents. It may perhaps be the estate from which the tomb derives its endowment; or perhaps again it may be the temple grounds in which the funeral ceremonies took place. In the lowest row we see three men performing the funeral dance which was one of the oldest ceremonies of the mortuary ritual. Other figures carry to the tomb the funeral furniture which is to be buried with the deceased.

On the opposite wall (12) the funeral ceremonies are again shown. Here we see on the lower part of the wall the ceremony always performed by the ritual-priests at funerals, in this case led by Anena's brother, who was a priest of the goddess Mut.

In the recess at the end of this chamber there are four much damaged seated statues. From left to right these are Anena's wife Thuau, Anena himself, his father also called Anena, and his sister (?) Aahhotep. On the walls at either side are paintings showing Anena and his relations. His favourite dog is seen behind his chair.

No. 80. THE MORTUARY CHAPEL OF TEHUTINEFER

This chapel is situated to the south of that of Anena (No. 81). The paintings in it are somewhat rough, but they have several points of interest. Tehutinefer was a Prince by rank, but he held the office of Scribe of the Treasury, under one of the Pharaohs of the XVIIIth dynasty. His sister was named Takhat, and was a musician of Hathor of Denderah. It is possible, therefore, that their residence was at that city.

On the right as one enters (1) there are figures of servants bringing offerings to the tomb; and a woman is seen shaking a sistrum. On the opposite wall (2) Tehutinefer and Takhat are shown seated, while their daughter stands behind them, and

Second room. their son makes offerings before them. Behind this group one sees the guests seated at the funeral feast, while a man plays a harp and some women dance for their entertainment. Under the chair of Tehutinefer there is a much damaged representation of his pet monkey eating from a dish. The walls at the other end of the chapel have never been decorated with paintings; but passing into the inner chamber there are some scenes of interest to be observed. On the left (3) there are representations of scenes from Tehutinefer's official work as Scribe of the Treasury. In the top row we see gold brought in and weighed; and a servant is beaten for some negligence in his duties. In the second row gold is again weighed, and a scribe writes down its value; a servant, bowing, announces the arrival of booty, consisting of tusks of elephants, skins, a casket slung upon a pole, and other articles. In the third row, grain is heaped up and measured; and again one of the men is beaten for some offence against the rules. On the opposite wall (4) there are scenes from the funeral. In the uppermost row the mortuary priests perform ceremonies before the mummy of the dead noble. In the second row the mummy is drawn to the tomb upon a sledge pulled by men and oxen; women weep and tear their hair; and the priests perform the ceremony of sacrificing a cow and pouring out a libation before the mummy. In the third row servants are seen bringing offerings to the funeral. Near this there is a scene representing Tehutinefer's house amidst the trees at the edge of the river. His boat waits for him on

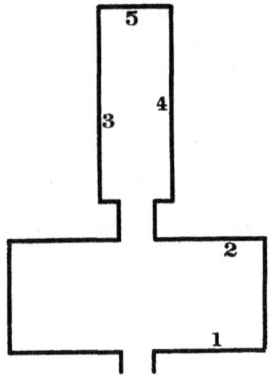

the water, and on shore his chariot is standing in charge of a groom. At the end of this wall we see him sitting in his spirit form with his wife and daughter, while a woman on earth stands before him, her hair disordered by her demonstrations of grief. On the end wall of this chamber (5) Tehutinefer is shown worshipping Osiris Unnefer, the god of the dead.

NO. 79. THE MORTUARY CHAPEL OF MENKHEPER

Menkheper, sometimes called Ramenkheper-senb, was the son of Minnekht, whose tomb (No. 87) is to be seen upon this hill. He was a noble, who held the offices of Scribe of the Granaries of the King, and libation-priest in the mortuary temple of Thothmes IIIrd. This temple was excavated by the present writer a few years ago. It is situated on the edge of the cultivation, not far north of the Ramesseum. Menkheper evidently lived quite shortly after the death of that great Pharaoh, though the exact date is not known. On one's right on entering the chapel (1) Menkheper is seen with his wife and daughter standing in a boat which has pushed its way amidst the reeds. In one hand he holds a boomerang, and in the other a decoy. The reeds are full of nests, in some of which

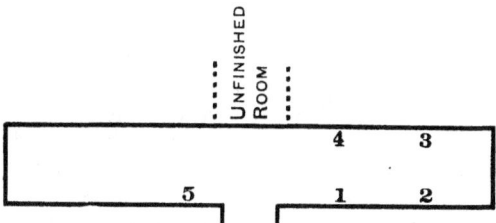

are eggs and in others young birds; and above the reeds a flight of birds rises, some being at once struck down by the boomerangs. Farther along this wall (2) we are introduced to Menkheper's farms and estates. At the top a bull is led along; and servants carry a jar of grape-juice from his vineyards, a group of similar jars being shown near by. Below this geese, flowers, fruit, and more jars are brought in. A wine-press is here seen, in which men tread the grapes with their feet, holding on to ropes hanging from a cross-bar in order to support themselves. The juice runs out of the press and is caught in a jar by a man (in the painting the jar is destroyed). Below this again is the vineyard, and one sees the labourers plucking the bunches of grapes and carrying them in. The wines of ancient Egypt were famous, and Greek writers state that wine was first invented in the valley of the Nile. It is said that the Egyptians were addicted to systematic intemperance; and certainly these statements find some confirmation in the tomb-paintings, which so frequently represent wine-making and wine-drinking. On the opposite wall (3) we see a quantity of offerings, including funeral furniture, vases, sandals, bow and arrows, shields, tunics, jewellery, *ushabti*-figures, canopic jars, &c., placed before the seated figure of Menkheper, beside whom are his parents, now once more united with him in the Underworld. Beyond this one sees the funeral feast in progress. Servants offer food and drink to the assembled guests; a man plays a harp; women play on the pipes, dance, or clap their hands in unison with the music. On the right of the entrance into the unfinished chamber (4) Menkheper is represented seated to receive the homage of his son, who was a scribe in the mortuary temple of Thothmes IIIrd, where the father had served. On the left of the entrance to the tomb (5) there have been some rustic scenes, and one may still see well-executed geese driven in, and eggs carried in baskets.

NO. 78. THE MORTUARY CHAPEL OF HOREMHEB

At the top of the hill, above the chapel of Anena (No. 81), and just to the left of the chapel of Thenuna (No. 76), there is the mortuary chapel of Horemheb, an official who lived during the reigns of Thothmes IIIrd, Amenhotep IInd, Thothmes IVth, and Amenhotep IIIrd, *i.e.* from some time previous to B.C. 1447 to some time after B.C. 1411. He held the offices of Superintendent of the Sacred Cattle, Superintendent of the Workmen of Amen, Superintendent of the Military Scribes, Superintendent of the Recruits, Superintendent of the Horses, Captain of the Archers, and Royal "Nurse" or Guardian to one of the Princesses. The chapel was decorated for the most part during the reign of Thothmes IVth, and must have been finished early in that of Amenhotep IIIrd.

Entering the tomb, a scene is observed on the right (1) showing the usual funeral feast. The guests are seated and servants offer them food, while women dance and play upon lutes for their amusement. Lower down there are some blind minstrels; a fat old man plays a harp; others sing and clap their hands. Horemheb himself nurses a young princess upon his knee. Butchers are seen busily cutting up oxen for the feast. On the opposite wall (2) the foreign tribute is brought in. At the top Asiatics are shown leading horses decked with gay plumes. Fine vases, orna-

MORTUARY CHAPELS OF THE NOBLES 141

ments, and rings of gold are also brought in. Lower down, negroes are seen arriving from the Sudan. Amongst them there are some women who carry their babies in baskets upon their backs; these are represented in a very lifelike manner. At the bottom some of the negroes dance, and one beats a drum in honour of the occasion. Cattle are driven in, and soldiers are seen armed with shields and axes. At the end of the wall there is a much-damaged figure of King Thothmes IVth, to whom this tribute is supposed to be brought. On the left of the entrance (3) there is another feast scene. Women are seen presenting beautiful golden bowls to the now obliterated figures of Horemheb and his wife. Two women play upon lutes: one has been drawn in a full-face

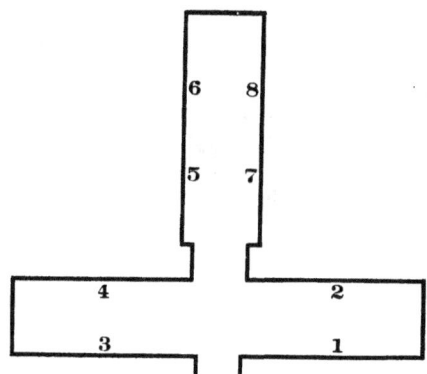

view, which is very rare in Egyptian painting. Another woman plays upon a harp. The pretty transparent garments which these women wear should be noticed. Below this fattened bulls are led to the slaughter. On the opposite wall (4) Thothmes IVth is shown enthroned beneath a canopy, while two servants fan him with plumes. Horemheb has been presenting flowers to the king, but his figure is here, and in many other parts of the tomb, erased. We next see troops, led by the regimental standard-bearers, being listed by the military scribes. Persons bring in produce from the fields and carry it to the storehouses, which are entered through a doorway inscribed with the name of Thothmes IVth. One figure, with unusual naturalism, is seen passing through this doorway, and half hidden by it. Below this there are persons bringing in fattened oxen, antelopes, birds, &c.

Inner chamber.

We now pass into the inner chamber, and on the left (5) funeral scenes are to be observed. At the top the coffin (much damaged) is dragged by oxen towards the tomb. A bundle dragged along upon a sledge possibly contains the body of a human victim sacrificed to the soul of Horemheb, but this is not a certain interpretation of the scene. Women mourners wail as they walk along. In the second and third rows all the objects which are to be buried with Horemheb are carried to the tomb—ornaments, bows, arrows, boxes, his chariot, &c. In the lowest row are the funeral boats crossing the Nile from the city of Thebes to the necropolis. Farther along the wall (6) an obliterated figure of Horemheb is seen praying to the gods; and his heart is weighed in the balances before Thoth, Shu, and various seated gods, while Osiris, the great judge of the dead, is seen seated in his shrine. Above the balances are the well-drawn insignia of his office. On the opposite wall (7) there are damaged funeral scenes; and farther along (8) there are much faded representations of Horemheb and his son in a boat, engaged in boomeranging birds and spearing fish. Below this there is a charming little scene showing an old trapper, named Ptahmes, kneeling beside a group of well-drawn pelicans. His hand is at his mouth, as though to indicate to his assistants that they must be silent as they await the signal to shut the trap.

NO. 77. THE MORTUARY CHAPEL OF REY

This chapel is to be found a short distance above the chapel of Ramenkhepersenb (No. 79). The personage for whom it was made was named Rey, and held the office of Superintendent of the Engravers of the King. He was also connected with the mortuary temple of Thothmes IVth. The scenes are very much damaged, and but little remains. One observes the usual representation of a feast, and there are some soldiers to be seen; but the chapel does not repay a visit.

NO. 76. THE MORTUARY CHAPEL OF THENUNA

At the top of the hill, above the chapel of Anena (No. 81) and north of the chapel of Horemheb (No. 78), there is the chapel of Thenuna, who was Standard-bearer of the King, Superintendent

MORTUARY CHAPELS OF THE NOBLES 143

of the Sacred Cattle of Amen, and Steward of the Palace, probably in the reign of Thothmes IIIrd or Amenhotep IInd. One enters a large hall, the roof of which is supported by four square pillars. On the right (1) there are some well-drawn scenes, showing cattle being listed by scribes. The figures of the scribes are very animated, and are suggestive of the energy with which their work was supposed to be conducted. On the adjoining wall (2) offerings

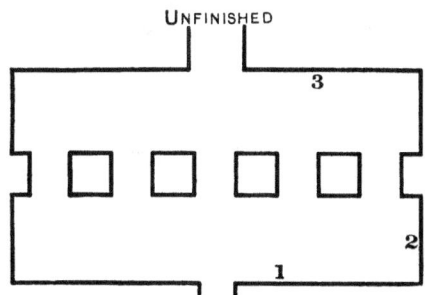

are made to the soul of Thenuna by his son or relative. On the next wall (3) there has been a figure of the king seated under a canopy, with Hathor behind him. A magnificent series of vases, &c., supposed to be the tribute of Asia, is shown before the king. The paintings are unfinished in this chapel, and the excavation of a further chamber has been abandoned. From this chapel one enters the chapel of Amenhotepsase, which is about to be described, through a hole in the wall.

NO. 75. THE MORTUARY CHAPEL OF AMENHOTEPSASE

Amenhotepsase was Second Priest of Amen in the reign of Thothmes IVth, and appears to have been a dignitary of great importance at court. Those who have visited the chapel of Razeserkasenb (No. 38) will remember that that official was Steward of the House of Amenhotepsase, which indicates that the Second Priest was a wealthy man. In the priesthood of Amen there were the High Priest, the Second Priest, the Third Priest, and the Fourth Priest at the head of the religion, and Amenhotepsase was thus a priest of almost the highest possible rank.

The chapel is entered by a hole in the wall leading from

No. 76, and the real entrance is now closed with an iron grating. On the right of this closed entrance (1) Amenhotepsase and his wife (both figures erased) are seen seated before a heap of offerings, amongst which some wine jars hung with garlands of flowers are noticeable. Above them is an inscription giving the name and titles of the deceased noble. Before them are scenes in five registers, representing a feast given in honour of Amenhotepsase. In the uppermost row are men-servants bringing food, &c. In the second row are guests seated while others offer them food; in the third the official, Bak, offers flowers to his late master, and behind him are some well-drawn women playing harps, guitars, &c. In the fourth stands the

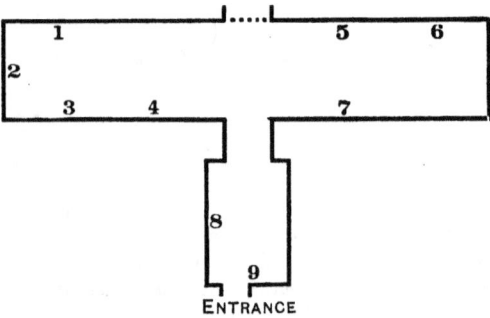

steward Razeserkasenb, while behind him are three seated women, one playing a double-pipe and the others clapping their hands as an accompaniment to the music; and in the fifth row there are men and women seated at the feast, while waitresses offer them dishes of food. A continuation of the last row along the bottom of the wall shows the chariot, and its horses, which has brought Amenhotepsase to the feast. In front are two outrunners, and behind are other servants, one of whom has the honour of carrying his master's shoes. The next wall (2) has upon it some mystical scenes, mostly erased. The middle part of the wall shows a cavity from which a painted plaster stele of the usual type seems to have been removed by robbers. Above is an erased figure over which holy water is being thrown by small figures on either side, while mythical figures composed of the *ded* and *shu* symbols are making offerings. A small inscription in the lower corner of the scene

MORTUARY CHAPELS OF THE NOBLES 145

says that the offerings are "for thy spirit, O Second Priest of Amen, Amenhotepsase." At the north end of the adjoining wall (3) there is an interesting scene representing the two pylons and main doorway of a temple, on either side of which is a colossal statue (one erased), and an obelisk, or ceremonial post. Over the doorway is a cartouche of a king, in which the name has unfortunately never been written. Fourteen trees stand near the temple, and sixteen male figures approach towards it. This scene evidently shows the temple of Amen at which Amenhotepsase officiated, and in all probability it may be identified either with that part of Karnak which was adorned by Thothmes IVth, or with the now destroyed temple of that king at Gûrneh. In both cases there were pylons and colossi, and Amen was the presiding deity. The scene which occupies the rest of this wall (4) is much damaged, and some of the figures are chiselled out. There are three men walking side by side, and behind them two others, while before them stand seven women holding sistra in their hands. These are the deceased's wife, his three daughters, and three women unnamed. On the left of the entrance (5) is a scene showing the weighing of gold in the scales by Razeserkasenb in the presence of Amenhotepsase, the large figure of the latter being, however, erased. The gold is in ring form, and the weights are in the form of lying bulls, while one is shaped like a frog. Specimens of the weights of the bull-form are fairly well known, and are almost always made of bronze. In Egypt they do not appear before the New Empire, the weights of the Old and Middle Empires being almost always simply rectangular in shape. A few specimens of the frog-form are known, but these are rare. Watching the operation of weighing are six figures (which appear at first sight to be only two, as they stand one behind the other), and the inscriptions call them the "Masters of the workmen of the temple of Amen," and "the Superintendents of the workmen of the temple, taking the silver and gold." Behind this scene are four rows containing representations of the workmen of the temple, for whose use the gold and silver has been weighed out. In the first row are carpenters engaged in making symbolical figures; in the second row are a sculptor carving a sphinx, and a vase-maker modelling a vase; in the third are vase-makers, and the method of work should be noticed; and in the fourth chests, collars, &c., are being made. The third man is using a bow drill. A chariot is being made in separate parts, for use in the religious processions. Behind these scenes is a large erased figure of Amenhotepsase with his titles displayed near him, and a statement of how greatly he pleased the Pharaoh as "the eyes of the king in Thebes." He is here (6) seen to be inspecting the harvest produce, shown in four rows, and scribes are seen recording the amount of grain brought in. In the lowest row three men carry a measuring-rope, a coil of which is wound round the arm of the first and third man, each coil being surmounted by a gold or gilt ram's-head with the uraeus on the forehead. This rope must have been the standard measure of the Amen temple, and these rams'-heads the two knobs with which the rope was ended. The opposite wall (7) is unfinished, and the two main figures, one carrying a tall fan, have been erased. There is a good drawing of a servant bending forward and probably putting a collar around his master's neck. Behind these is a large quantity of temple furniture, the painting of which is unfinished. There are sphinxes, collars, staves, statues of the king, vases, tables, a harp, shrines, fans, dishes, &c. The cartouche upon the statues is that of Thothmes IVth, and it is from this that we can date the tomb. At the north end of this wall is a very much damaged figure of what was probably the king seated under a canopy, with Amenhotepsase bowing before him. In the inner room, the right wall (8) has upon it some much damaged and unfinished scenes showing the deceased and his wife seated, while before them are offerings. There have been funeral scenes on the rest of this wall, and the funeral boats can be seen crossing the water. At the end of the chamber (9) there is a plastered niche for the *Ka*-statue to stand in, and it is through this that the hole into the next chapel has been forced.

NO. 74. THE MORTUARY CHAPEL OF ZENUNI

This chapel is situated near the top of the hill, at its northern side. From the chapel of Thenuna (No. 76) one passes over the summit of the hill and descends somewhat, this chapel being found upon one's left, a few yards from the boundary wall of the enclosure. It was made for the Superintendent of the Military Scribes and Scribe of the Recruits, Zenuni, who lived during the reign of Thothmes IVth (B.C. 1420). Upon the right on entering (1) there is a figure of Zenuni making an offering to Osiris, who is seated beneath a canopy. Zenuni's wife, who was a songstress in the temple of Thoth of Hermopolis, stands behind him. On the adjoining wall (2) there is a damaged funeral stele upon which the cartouches of Thothmes IVth appear. On the next wall (3) ser-

MORTUARY CHAPELS OF THE NOBLES 147

vants, cattle and horses, are listed; and at the other end of the wall (4) there is an interesting representation of a military parade. In the second row a portly standard-bearer should be observed. Upon his standard there are the figures of two men wrestling, this

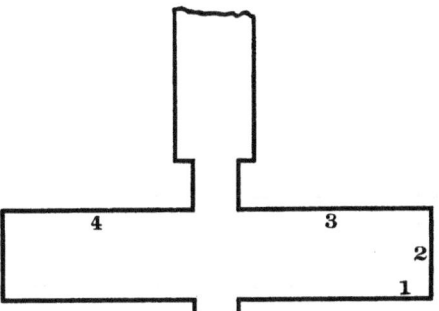

evidently being the sign or crest of the regiment. Below this there are some negro troops with feathers in their hair, for in old days, as at the present time, the Egyptian army was largely drawn from the Sudan.

NO. 73. THE MORTUARY CHAPEL OF A MASTER BUILDER

This chapel lies a few yards from No. 74, just described. It was never finished, and such scenes as were completed have been much damaged. The owner was a master builder in charge of the work upon the two great obelisks in the temple of Amen; but both his name and that of the king he served are lost. There have been scenes of fishing and bird hunting, and much temple furniture is depicted.

NO. 72. THE MORTUARY CHAPEL OF RA

A short way above No. 73 is the chapel of the High Priest of Amen and of Hathor in the mortuary temple of Thothmes IIIrd (p. 255), who bore the unusual name of Ra (the Sun). He was the son of a priest named Aahmes, and lived during the reign of Amenhotep IInd. The chapel was never finished, and is now very much damaged. Before us on the left as we enter (1) there is a much damaged figure of Amenhotep IInd seated beneath a canopy. On the right wall of the inner room (2) funeral cere-

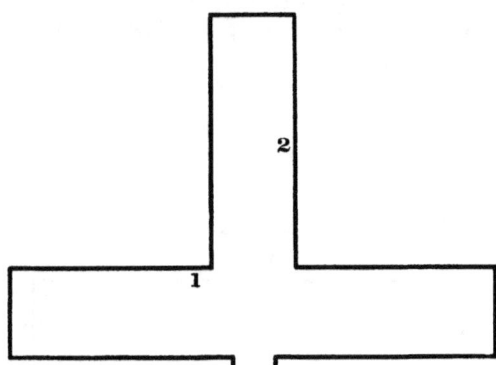

monies are performed before the mummy of Ra. Above, there is a curious pattern composed of cartouches of Thothmes IIIrd.

NO. 71. THE MORTUARY CHAPEL OF SENMUT

This chapel is to be found on the north side of the hill, somewhat below No. 72. It is distinguished by the white wall which is built before it. Senmut was steward of the palace of Hatshepsut, and was the chief power behind that queen's throne (B.C. 1500). He seems to have opposed the claims of Thothmes IIIrd to the throne; and when, at the death of Hatshepsut, that king came into his own, Senmut fell into disgrace. His name and figure were everywhere erased, and, no doubt, this chapel of his was much damaged. The chapel consisted of a front gallery, from which a passage penetrated into the rock. Only a few fragments of the paintings now remain. At the right end of the gallery some of these fragments have been protected by a wall and iron door. These consist of the historically important figures of Mycenæan envoys who bring tribute or presents of fine Cretan vases. In the passage which leads into the hillside, it will be noticed that there are a number of small tablets cut in the rock, upon which the name (afterwards erased) of Senmut was written. The plastered surface, upon which the scenes which adorned the walls were painted, must have covered these tablets; and it would seem that Senmut had

MORTUARY CHAPELS OF THE NOBLES 149

caused them to be placed here, fearing that his name might be erased from the inscriptions upon the plaster when the regime which he supported should fall, and hoping that this hidden record of his identity might be overlooked by the destroyers.

Chapel No. 70, belonging to a noble named Amenemheb, is too much damaged to require a description here.

NO. 69. THE MORTUARY CHAPEL OF MENNA

This is one of the most interesting of the mortuary chapels, and visitors should make a point of seeing it. It is situated at the north-east corner of the enclosure, at the bottom of the hill; and is just inside the small gateway which leads into the enclosure from the back of the native houses behind the tomb of Nekht (No. 52). Menna was superintendent of the estates of the king and of Amen, and scribe of the estates of the king in the north and south. He lived at about the middle of the XVIIIth dynasty, but the actual king whom he served is not known. The colouring of the paintings is extremely fresh and bright, and much of the work has evidently been executed by an artist of high standing. A curious feature of the tomb is the fact that some personage, perhaps from motives of revenge, has carefully and systematically destroyed in the paintings most of the essential things which would make for Menna's happiness. By depicting on the walls of a chapel of this kind the scenes from the life of the deceased, it was thought that a permanency was given to them. Menna is here shown in the act of throwing a boomerang at a flight of duck, and he would thus be able to indulge in this sport throughout eternity. He is shown overlooking the agricultural work on his estates, and thus would always be able to entertain himself in this manner. But an enemy, entering the chapel, has cut the pictured boomerang in half, so that for ever the hunting is spoilt; and has broken out the eye of the figure inspecting the estates, so that never again will Menna be able to see his possessions. Throughout the chapel the destruction of these essentials is to be observed; and, according to Egyptian beliefs, the happiness of Menna would thus have been much impaired. Entering the tomb, one sees on the right (1) the figure of Menna and his wife standing before a heap of offerings. Menna carries two braziers upon which birds are sacrificially burnt in the flames. Behind are male and female relations bearing flowers and food. At the far end of the wall sit the souls of Menna and his

First chamber.

wife, while a relation offers them bouquets of flowers. On the adjoining wall (2) there is the funeral stele, at the sides of which two male and two female relatives pray. On the next wall (3) the relatives are seen seated at the funeral feast in honour of the souls of the dead; while in the two lower rows funeral offerings are brought and priests perform the last ceremonies. The ordinary priests, it may be noticed, are clad in leopard-skins, while the Ritual-priests, or wise men, have a white band across their shoulders. At the opposite end of the tomb (4) Menna and his wife worship Osiris, below whom burnt offerings of geese and other flesh are consumed in the flames. On the adjoining wall (5) there are some charming rustic scenes, which should be carefully examined. The figure of Menna, with eye destroyed, overlooks these scenes. In the top row, from left to right, a slave is seen kissing the foot of the overseer; the lands are measured by means of a rope, from which, however, the knobs which assured the correctness of the measurement have been struck out by the avenger, in order that Menna may never again count his acres; a boy walks along driving an animal, also destroyed, and carrying a small kid; Menna stands under a canopy to watch the arrival of a boat from some other part of his estates; the passengers from the boat come ashore and are received by a servant; and sailors are beaten for being late of arrival. In the second row, from left to right, Menna's chariot and servants await to carry him to his fields; the quantity of his grain is recorded by the scribes; Menna stands under a canopy while servants bring him drink; and lastly there are scenes of winnowing and threshing. In the third row, Menna sits under a canopy, outside of which is a tree with birds' nests built in it; scenes of reaping follow; a girl brings a jar of water to a labourer who drinks from it, but the avenger has destroyed his mouth, so that, being thirsty, he will fail to do the work which Menna requires of him; a woman, nursing a baby, sits under

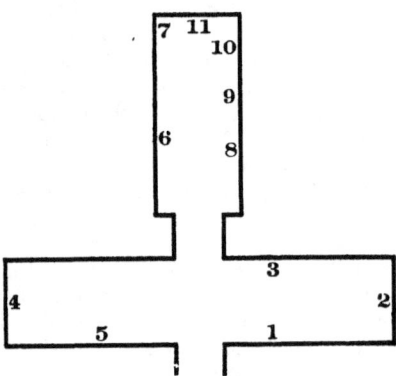

MORTUARY CHAPELS OF THE NOBLES 151

a tree; a girl, naked save for a belt, assists in the work; men carry away the corn in nets slung on poles; two girls quarrel and tear one another's hair; two men sit in the shade under a tree, the one piping a tune upon a flute; and a water-skin hangs on a branch to cool in the breeze. In the bottom row there are ploughing scenes, and the sowing of seed is shown; a girl takes a thorn out of another's foot; the heads of the flax are removed from the stalks by means of combs or forks fixed to the ground. At the end of the wall nearest to the door Menna is shown seated, while his three daughters, gorgeously arrayed, shake sistrums before him. Observe how the curls of their hair fall prettily across the face, and notice their elaborate head-dresses of gold.

On the left wall of the inner chamber (6) there are funeral scenes of considerable interest. In the top row, furniture is brought to the tomb to be buried with the deceased—beds, chests, chairs, *ushabti* figures, vases, &c.; and cows for sacrificial purposes are brought along, together with offerings of food. In the second row the funeral boat, containing the bier and the mourning women, is rowed across the river to the western side. The procession then moves up to the tomb. In the third and fourth row an ox is purified and sacrificed; funeral boats cross the river; boxes of various goods are carried along towards large figures of Hathor, the goddess of the western hills, and Anubis, the god of the necropolis. Farther along the wall (7) the heart of Menna is weighed in the balances in the presence of Osiris, while Thoth records the good and bad deeds of the deceased. The avenger has destroyed the plumb of the scales and the eye of the figure which is holding them, in order that they may weigh falsely, and that Menna may thus be "found wanting." On the opposite wall (8) funeral boats are seen sailing on the Nile, and certain ceremonies by which the mummy was endowed with life are shown in a series of scenes. Many of these ceremonies have been rendered ineffective by the destruction of parts of the figures. At the end of the wall a figure clad in yellow is thrice seen upon a chair. This is probably the *sem*-priest, who, according to religious papyri, performs a mystical ceremony at the funeral, clad in a cow-skin. Farther along the wall (9) Menna and his family are seen amongst the reeds in a boat, first spearing fish (and it is to be observed that his hand directing the spear is destroyed, so that his aim may be bad) and then boomeranging birds, which are retrieved by a cat and an ichneumon. The boomerang has been carefully cut in two, so that the sport may be spoilt. Butterflies are seen over-

Inner chamber.

ANTIQUITIES OF UPPER EGYPT

head, while in the water fish and crocodiles are shown. Upon the surface the duck swim amongst the lotus-flowers. There is here a charming figure of a girl leaning from the boat to pluck one of these luxuriant water plants. The face has been destroyed, but the figure is graceful and dainty in spite of the conventionalities of the artist. Farther along the wall (10) Menna and his wife receive offerings. At the end of the room (11) there is a niche in which are the lower parts of the statuettes of Menna and his wife. The figures were probably smashed by the same hand which damaged the scenes.

No. 68. THE MORTUARY CHAPEL OF NESPANEFERHER

This chapel dates from the XXIst dynasty, or even later (about B.C. 1000). It was made for a priest of Amen and Chief Scribe of the Temple of Amen, named Nespaneferher. The scenes in it are much damaged and are of little interest, but the ceiling is worthy of notice.

No. 67. THE MORTUARY CHAPEL OF HAPUSENB

Hapusenb, who caused this chapel to be made, was one of the nobles of the court of Queen Hatshepsut. The chapel is so much destroyed that it has not been necessary to close it with a wall or door. Part of this destruction may have been due to the persecution of his memory instituted by Thothmes IIIrd at his succession, just as in the case of Senmut (No. 71).

No. 66 does not contain the name of the personage for whom it was made. It is almost entirely destroyed.

No. 65. THE MORTUARY CHAPEL OF AIMADUA

This large chapel is situated a short distance above No. 67, and is approached by a pathway skirting the wall of the enclosure. It was originally made for a noble of the XVIIIth dynasty, but was re-used by Aimadua, the chief of the scribes of the temple of Amen under Rameses IXth (B.C. 1142). One enters a large six-pillared hall, the walls of which were originally sculptured with scenes; but these have been covered with plaster and other representations have been painted over them. On the right (1) the sacred barque of Amen is seen carried by priests, the king burning

MORTUARY CHAPELS OF THE NOBLES 153

incense before it. At the points where the plaster has fallen off the original reliefs can be seen underneath. On the end wall (2) priests are seen bringing offerings. On the adjoining wall (3) priests carry sacred vessels, and Aimadua is seen offering to Amen-Ra, Mut, and Khonsu. On the left of the entrance (4) the sacred barque of Amen is carried by priests and censed by the

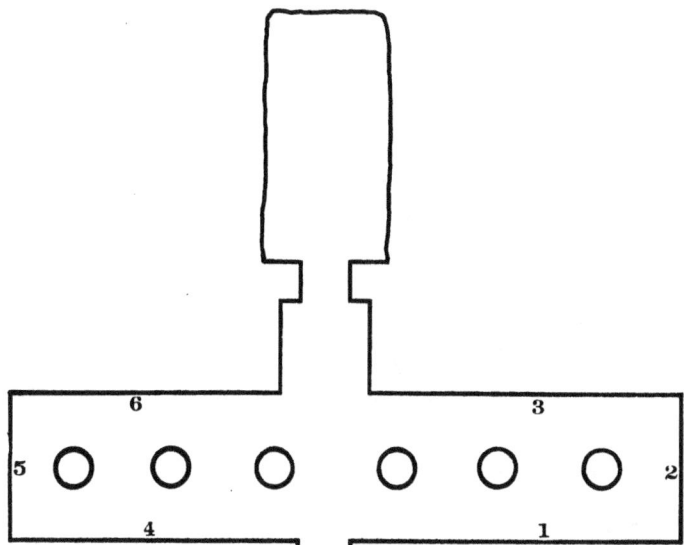

Pharaoh. A series of beautiful vases should here be noticed. On the next wall (5) the barque of Amen is again depicted, and behind it walk the souls of dead kings. On the adjoining wall (6) Aimadua and his relations make offerings to Osiris and Maat. In the inner room there are mythological scenes, and Aimadua makes offerings to the gods of the Underworld.

NO. 64. THE MORTUARY CHAPEL OF HEQERHEH

This chapel is situated at the foot of the enclosure on the north side of the hill. It was made for a noble named Heqerheh, who lived in the reign of Thothmes IVth (B.C. 1420), and was tutor

154   ANTIQUITIES OF UPPER EGYPT

and guardian of that king's son, Prince Amenhotep, afterwards Amenhotep IIIrd, and of other princes. The tomb is much damaged, but there are some scenes of interest still left in it. On the end wall, west side, there is a much broken scene showing Heqershau, probably the father of Heqerheh, nursing the young king Thothmes IVth upon his knees. His feet rest upon a footstool on which nine captives are shown. Heqerheh stands near by, and behind him there are two princes.

NO. 63. THE MORTUARY CHAPEL OF SEBEKHOTEP

Just to the west of No. 64 is another much damaged chapel, which was made for a certain Sebekhotep who was "Prince of the Territory of the South and the Territory of Sebek," and held the office of Royal Registrar, Superintendent of the Seal, and Superintendent of the Priests. One of his daughters appears to have been one of the secondary wives of Thothmes IVth, for Sebekhotep calls himself the father-in-law of the king, and he mentions the Princess Thaa, the daughter of Thothmes IVth, who was probably his grand-daughter. The only scene in the chapel which calls for attention is to be found on the right side of the inner corridor. Here there is a garden of Paradise in which is a lake. There are fishes in the water, and lotus flowers float upon the surface. Sebekhotep and his wife walk beside this lake, and drink of its pure water, raising it to their lips in the hollow of their hands. Seated under the shady trees they eat food given to them by the tree-goddess, Isis, whose body seems to grow out of the trunk of a persea tree. This was the heaven in which the Egyptian prayed to rest; he always asked that his soul might be refreshed with water, that he might be fanned by the cool north wind blowing through the trees beside a lake, and that there might be flowers and scents to soothe him.

NO. 62. THE MORTUARY CHAPEL OF AMENEMUSEKHT

Prince Amenemusekht was a Superintendent of the Court, and a Royal Registrar, but it is not known what king of Dynasty XVIIIth he served. His mortuary chapel, situated not far from No. 63, is so much damaged that it is practically without interest.

MORTUARY CHAPELS OF THE NOBLES

NO. 61. THE MORTUARY CHAPEL OF USER

Like No. 62, this chapel is almost entirely destroyed. It was made for a vizir named User, the son of the Vizir Aahmes, whose chapel, it would seem, is No. 83. The chapel appears to date from about the reign of Thothmes IIIrd.

NO. 60. THE MORTUARY CHAPEL OF ANTEFAKER

This is the oldest chapel on the hill of Shêkh abd' el Gûrneh, dating as it does from the XIIth dynasty. It is situated high up on the hillside, above and to the north of the brick ruins of Wilkinson's house. One enters a long passage, the walls of which are covered with coarse plaster crudely painted with scenes relating to Antefaker, the Theban noble for whom the chapel was made. On the right we see (1) three men pulling at the cord which is connected with a bird-trap. Higher up others catch fish in a net. Farther along (2) Antefaker is shown shooting his arrows into an enclosure in which are antelopes of various kinds, wild cattle, hares, &c., pursued by hounds. Farther along again (3) there are some interesting cooking scenes. A man cooks some food over a fire which he fans into flame; pots are filled; a woman grinds grain; and so on. Still farther (4) Antefaker and his wife are seen receiving offerings. On the opposite wall near the door (5) the funeral boats are seen crossing the river from Thebes to the necropolis. The coffin is drawn along by men and oxen. Farther along (6) four men with curious head-dresses dance the funeral dance, and higher up women and girls also go through the steps of this ceremonial measure.

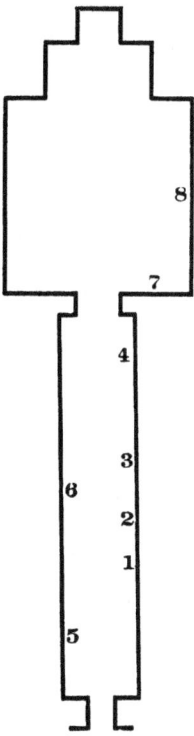

In the inner room on the right (7) male and female harpers are seen. On the adjoining wall (8) offerings are shown. In the floor of this room the shaft goes down to the tomb where Antefaker was buried. Beyond it there is a niche for the statue of the deceased.

NO. 59. THE MORTUARY CHAPEL OF KEN

Somewhat higher, and slightly to the south of No. 60, there is the small chapel of Ken, a High Priest of Mut. Little is to be seen here except the usual representation of the funeral feast.

NO. 58. THE MORTUARY CHAPEL OF AMENHOTEP

On a level with the brick ruins of Wilkinson's house, but a short distance northwards, there is the small chapel of the Superintendent of the Priests of Amen, Amenhotep, who seems to have lived during the reign of Amenhotep IIIrd (B.C. 1411). The chapel is much damaged, and is not of interest.

NO. 57. THE MORTUARY CHAPEL OF KHAEMHAT

This beautiful chapel, made for Khaemhat, the Superintendent of the Granaries during the reign of Amenhotep IIIrd, is situated between the Ramesseum and the enclosure of Shêkh abd' el Gûrneh just to the south of the large chapel of Rames (No. 55). Visitors should not fail to see this chapel, which has upon its walls some of the finest reliefs in the necropolis. It was made at a time when the Egyptian art of the New Empire was at its height. The grace and delicacy of the work of this period is such that, in spite of the conventionalities which so limited the capacities of the artists, no one can look upon it without pleasure.

One enters a small transverse chamber, and upon the left wall Khaemhat (1) is seen standing, while before him are persons who have brought offerings, and a portly butcher holds the leg of an ox which is being cut up. We next (2) see three beautifully executed male figures bringing offerings to a shrine in which the snake goddess Rennut, "the Lady of the Granaries," is seated nursing an infant. Farther along (3) a large number of ships are seen at anchor, moored to the Theban quays, having brought the grain for the royal granaries from the length and breadth of Egypt. The elaborate masts, and the great rudders ornamented with the head of the Pharaoh carved in wood, should be observed. In a niche at the end of the room (4) there are the much-damaged statues of Khaemhat and his wife. On the adjoining wall (5) servants are seen bringing in a number of bulls of a remarkably small variety. The wavy hair of the figures in the lowest row (see p. 163) has a very

MORTUARY CHAPELS OF THE NOBLES 157

pleasing effect. Farther along (6) there is a damaged figure of Khaemhat presenting a statement of the produce of the country to a figure, also damaged, of Amenhotep IIIrd. The king's throne should be observed. It is supported by lion legs, between which are a captive negro and a captive Asiatic, symbolic of the king's conquests in the south and north. On the arm of the throne the Pharaoh is shown as a lion slaying an Asiatic.

Turning now to the wall at the right of the entrance (7) many interesting rustic scenes are to be observed. At the top Khaemhat

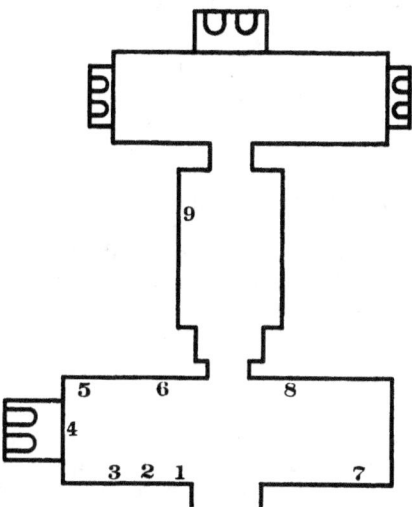

goes to measure his lands. In the third row his chariot is seen waiting for him, tended by grooms. Refreshments are seen standing in the shade of a tree, and a servant takes some food from the box in which it was packed. In the fourth row there are scenes of sowing and reaping. Two men press the corn into a net to carry it away. A boy sits upon a stool and plays a tune upon a flute. Near him Khaemhat's chariot is again seen. The driver sits half asleep in it, the groom crouches in the shade of the tree, and the horses quietly graze. In the lower rows there are scenes of ploughing. One of the workmen is shown drinking from a water-skin hung on the branch of a tree to be cooled by the breeze. On the opposite wall (8) the king, now headless, is shown seated under a canopy, while Khaemhat and his friends and assistants bow to him. At the top Khaemhat is decorated with golden necklaces by order of the king as a reward for his faithful services. This event occurred in the thirtieth year of the reign, *i.e.* B.C. 1381.

The scenes in the inner room are not of much interest. At the end of the left wall the god Osiris and the goddess Hathor are seen. In the innermost room there are statues of the deceased and his relations, now much damaged.

NO. 56. THE MORTUARY CHAPEL OF USERHAT

Visitors to No. 57 will have noticed that at one corner of the first chamber there is a hole in the wall through which a second chapel can be seen. The actual entrance to it is in an adjoining hollow, approached by a somewhat circuitous path. This chapel was made for Userhat, a tutor and scribe in the reign of Amenhotep IInd (B.C. 1448). On the outside of the doorway there are damaged figures of Userhat and his wife offering sacrifices to Osiris. On our right upon entering (1) Userhat and his wife are seen standing before offerings which their son presents to them. On the opposite wall (2) Userhat offers an elaborate table of fruit and garlands of flowers to King Amenhotep IInd, who is seated upon his throne. The king, whose face is destroyed, wears a fine red tunic spotted with yellow, and holds a little ceremonial battle-axe in his hand. Farther along (3) we see at the top two rows of bakers seated beside tables upon which are loaves of bread and cakes. In the third and fourth row the friends and relations of Userhat sit beside other tables of bread and baskets of provisions, while jars of wine are placed upon stands near by. A waiter offers a bowl containing some drink to one of these guests. In the fifth and sixth rows servants are seen bringing the baskets of bread and cakes to the door of the house, where an overseer with whip in hand counts them. Farther along again (4) men bring in bags of gold-dust from the mines, and these are counted by overseers. By this scene Userhat wishes to illustrate his great wealth. In the two bottom rows men are seen sitting upon stools under the trees in the garden. Some have fallen asleep, and their heads are buried on their arms. Two barbers are at work cutting the hair and shaving the heads of some of these men, while others sit waiting their turn. This scene seems to be representative of Userhat's kindness to his servants, who, when their above-shown work is finished, may sit and enjoy his bounty in the garden.

MORTUARY CHAPELS OF THE NOBLES 159

Turning now to the wall at the left of the entrance (5) Userhat and his wife and daughter stand before offerings. It will be observed that the two female figures have been rubbed out; and it may here be pointed out that in early Christian times this chapel was used as a dwelling-place by some monk who, for fear lest he should be tempted as was St. Anthony, obliterated every female figure in the wall-paintings throughout the chapel. Some rough crosses and drawings are to be seen here and there, which are also to be attributed to this pious hermit. Farther along the wall (6) at the top there are rural scenes showing cows pastured amongst the trees. One of the cows licks her calf. In the third row the cows are thrown down and branded. In the fourth row

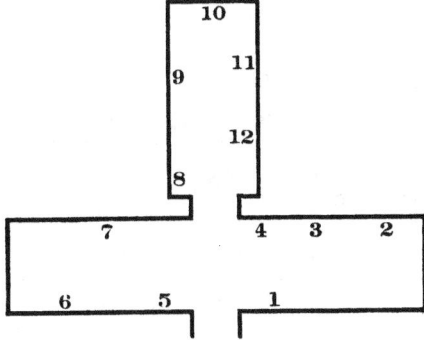

men bring in baskets of grain which are heaped up and measured. On the opposite wall (7) there is a large feasting scene in which all the female figures have been destroyed by the Christian hermit, as is also the harp belonging to the squatting figure of a harper. Under the chair of the large figures there is a monkey eating, and near it are a looking-glass and other articles. Over the seated figure of Userhat to whom women (destroyed) and a man are making offerings, runs the inscription : "For the sake of thy soul, make a happy day in thy beautiful house of eternity which is thy dwelling for ever. Thou art seated in it, thy heart being happy, whilst thou followest this good god Osiris, Lord of Eternity, who grants that thou shalt receive food in his presence at all times of the day." Passing into the inner room we see on the left (8) a fine hunting scene. Userhat in his chariot, the reins tied round his waist, shoots his arrows into a mass of gazelle, hyænas, jackals, hares, &c. Note especially at the bottom right-hand corner of the scene the well-drawn jackal entangled and caught in the low branches of a tree, while blood flows from its mouth. The rest of the wall is occupied with the usual scenes of snaring and boomeranging birds, harpooning fish, &c.; but in the bottom row (9) there are some spirited figures treading grapes in a wine-press. At the end of the wall (10) there have been seated statues, but only part of one remains. On the right wall (11) there are a number of women wailing at the funeral, and below them offerings are being brought to the tomb; while at the bottom funeral boats are seen crossing the Nile. Farther along the wall (12) more offerings are being brought to the tomb, and it is interesting to notice that a horse as well as the chariot of the deceased is led along. The coffin is dragged along by five men and some oxen.

NO. 55. THE MORTUARY CHAPEL OF RAMES

Situation and history.

Visitors should not fail to see this, the most important of the Theban mortuary chapels. It is situated amidst the mounds of debris between the Ramesseum and the hill of Shêkh abd' el Gûrneh, a few yards to the south of the chapel of Khaemhat (No. 57). It was made for Rames, the Vizir of Egypt during the early years of Amenhotep IVth (Akhnaton). Rames was a personage of great importance at this period. It seems probable that he already held the office of vizir at the close of the reign of Amenhotep IIIrd. His mortuary chapel appears to have been begun at about the commencement of the reign of Amenhotep IVth (B.C. 1375), and it is thus almost contemporaneous with that of Khaemhat, in which mention is made of the thirtieth year of the reign of Amenhotep IIIrd (B.C. 1381). Rames appears to have died childless, and the chapel seems to have been made for him by his brother Amenhotep, who held the offices of Steward of the King's Palace at Memphis, and Superintendent of the Royal Craftsmen. This Amenhotep has caused his own figure to appear almost as prominently as that of Rames in the chapel; and one may therefore perhaps suppose that Rames was already dead when it was made. His death, it may be conjectured, occurred about the second year of the reign of Amenhotep IVth, and he was perhaps buried, as were many of the great nobles, in the Valley of the Tombs of the Kings. The chapel which we now see, or at any rate its decoration, was

MORTUARY CHAPELS OF THE NOBLES

executed soon after this date. The scenes on the east wall (1 to 7) seem to date from the second or third year of the reign of Amenhotep IVth; those at the south end of the west wall (13) probably date from the fourth year of the reign; and those at the north end of the west wall (16) from the fifth or sixth year of the reign. It may be remembered that Amenhotep IVth abandoned the worship of Amen-Ra and the old gods of Egypt in about his fifth year, and adopted the worship of Aton, whose symbol was the sun's disk, from which many rays, each ending in a human hand, projected. He then changed his name from Amenhotep to Akhnaton. At the same time the king rid himself of the old art, and adopted entirely new canons. This change

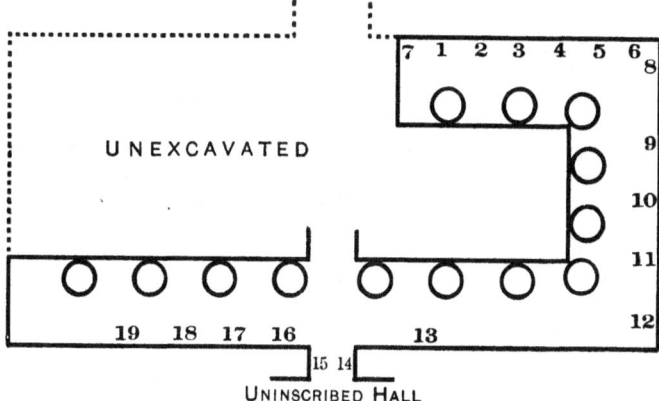

took place while the chapel of Rames was still in the hands of the craftsmen, and the last scenes are executed in the new style. Visitors should certainly read some account of the artistic and religious revolution before seeing the monument.[1] Rames is said to have been "a doer of truth, a hater of deceit," and the king is said to have loved him "because of his remarkable traits." Besides being vizir he also held the offices of "Chief of the Works Amongst the Great Monuments, Superintendent of the Priests of the North and South, Judge, Master of the Wardrobe, Master of the Secrets of the Palace, and Head of the Entire

[1] In Professor Breasted's "History of Egypt" a good account of the period is given. See also the present writer's "Life of Akhnaton" (Blackwood & Son).

Land." He was probably of Memphite origin, for his wife has a Memphite name, and his brother was in charge of the palace at Memphis. The latter was thus an early convert to the new religion which originated in Heliopolis, not far from Memphis, and which, therefore, might be expected to appeal to him more than did the Amen religion of Thebes.

The chapel has not yet been entirely cleared. There was probably an open court in front of the pillared hall, but it is now buried beneath the rubbish. The hall is only partly exposed, though it is probable that the portion still buried is largely undecorated. The chapel was discovered in 1860, and was partly opened by Ebers in 1872 and by Villiers Stuart in 1879. It has been numbered 108 and 112 by early Egyptologists. The present writer discovered the beautiful reliefs upon the east wall, and enclosed them, in 1908, partly at the expense of the Department of Antiquities and partly at that of the Metropolitan Museum of New York, U.S.A.

The east wall. Upon entering the tomb the visitor should pass round to the eastern wall, the reliefs on which, being earlier in date than those on the other walls, should be seen first. Upon this wall one sees a series of beautifully executed reliefs, cut in the natural limestone, all the flaws in which have been filled with white plaster. In the lower row there are four groups of figures facing two other groups. From north to south these are (1) an official of Amen named Keshy and his wife, who is not named; (2) the Master of the King's Horses, May, and his wife, the priestess of Mut at Karnak, Urnure; (3) the father of Rames, named Neby, and his wife Apuaa; (4) the brother of Rames, Amenhotep, the Steward of the King's Palace at Memphis and Master Craftsman, and his wife May. These four groups are faced by (5) Rames and his wife Ptahmeryt, behind whom are (6) Amenhotep again (the brother of Rames), his daughter Ptahmeryt, and his wife May, under whose chair there is a pet cat killing a bird. Above these figures there are others, now much damaged by the breaking of the stone. Here, about half-way along the wall, a man is seen seated with a little girl by his side. This is the Superintendent of the Recruits, Amenhotep, probably a relation of Rames. The prominent jaw and strong features shown in the profile indicate that this is a careful portrait. Behind him the brother of Rames, Amenhotep, is again seen with his wife. Facing this figure Rames and his wife are represented, and it will be noticed that a pet goose is shown under his chair. Behind him the father and

MORTUARY CHAPELS OF THE NOBLES 163

mother of Rames, Neby and Apuaa, are again represented. At the north end of the wall (7) there are small, unfinished figures bringing offerings, and above them two beautifully executed male figures are to be seen. The wig of the foremost should be observed: it undulates in the same manner as does that of one of the figures in the tomb of Khaemhat (p. 156), a peculiarity of this period.

The visitor should notice certain points in the scenes upon the wall. It will be observed that the reliefs have never been painted, although it was the usual custom to do so.[1] This was perhaps due to the good taste of the sculptor, or more probably to the fact that the work was never completed. In each case, however, the eyes have been painted in in black, the eye being the essential feature. It is a curious fact that the eyes and eyebrows of the third group (3), which represents the parents of Rames, are painted heavily and with square ends to the lines, that being the fashionable way of painting the living feature at the beginning of the reign of Amenhotep IIIrd at which time they lived. The eyes of all the other figures, however, are painted in thinner lines, pointed at the ends, according to the fashion of the younger generation, who evidently did not plaster their eyes and eyebrows with *kohl* as their fathers had done. The eyes of the three figures at the south end of the wall (6) have been sponged out, perhaps by some tomb-robber afraid of being observed by the souls of the deceased, who were supposed to see from out of the eyes of their portraits. To this day the Egyptian tomb-robber believes that if he breaks the eyes of the first figure which he encounters on an ancient monument, his actions will go unpunished by the occult powers. It should also be noticed that the names of Amen and Mut, and the word "gods," have been cut out by the agents of the new religion of Aton, who had instructions from Akhnaton to obliterate the names of the old deities of Egypt. These have been reinserted about the time of Sety Ist after the reversion to the old religion of Amen.

We now turn to the south wall, upon which there have been two rows of paintings representing the usual funeral scenes. The upper scene appears to have represented that part of the funeral procession in which the sarcophagus of the deceased, presided over by the figures of Isis and Nephthys, and the so-called human sacrifice (according to Maspero) are depicted. When the new religion

The south wall.

---

[1] The reliefs in the tomb of Khaemhat, although now almost devoid of colour, have still traces of the paint which covered them.

was introduced the king appears to have banned these ceremonies; and in this tomb it would seem that he is responsible for the careful plastering over of the whole scene with mud. In the lower row one sees (from left to right) first a group of mourners (8), then a number of retainers carrying the funeral furniture: jars of wine, boxes, beds, chairs, &c. Objects very similar to these were found in the tomb of Yuaa and Thuau at the tombs of the kings (p. 226), and are now to be seen in the Cairo Museum. Next (9) there are some well-grouped women wailing and gesticulating. Then we see a number of servants bringing offerings of flowers, wine, &c. Next (10) there are some more weeping women, from whose eyes the tears flow; and in front of them there are the yellow- and red-clad figures of priestesses or funeral-dancers. In front of them there has been the figure of a priest making an offering, but it has been erased, possibly owing to the fact that Akhnaton did not tolerate the ceremony which he was performing. We then see (11) a damaged representation showing the mummy of Rames standing before the door of the tomb, while priests perform the last ceremonies before it. Behind the tomb is a large figure of Hathor, the lady of the western hills. Next (12) a damaged figure of Rames is seen, behind whom is that of his wife Ptahmery. Below them there are some unfinished figures of Rames and others.

The west wall.

We now come to the last scenes executed previous to the change in the art. In an elaborate shrine (13) sits the young king Amenhotep IVth, represented with somewhat boyish features. Behind him sits the goddess Maat. Below the throne are the names and symbolic representations of the vassal nations of his empire. Rames stands before the king holding the standard of his office. Other figures follow, but the work is unfinished, and it is interesting to notice the methods employed by the craftsmen. We may see that the drawings of the figures are first outlined in black paint; then the surface of the stone is lowered around these drawings in order that they may stand out in relief. Next, the hard edges are rounded off; and lastly the detail is cut in with a fine chisel. We now come to the doorway leading into the inner hall. On either side Rames is seen, on the left (14) coming forth from the underworld as a spirit, and on the right (15) entering again into the "Hills of the West." Farther along the wall of the outer hall (16) we see the scenes executed in the new style. Here, instead of the conventional figure of the Pharaoh which we noticed on the opposite side of the doorway, the king and his young queen

Nefertiti are shown in what appears to be fairly close portraiture. The rays of the Aton, the new god, stream around them. Behind them are courtiers and attendants. In front (17), executed only in black outline, there are figures of nobles prostrating themselves before the king. In the top row Rames is decorated with gold collars as a reward for his diligence, and he is then seen turning to his friends to display to them these collars around his neck. Below this he, or some other official, is seen introducing Egyptians, Asiatics, Negroes, and Libyans, to the glories of the king and of the new religion. These foreigners are not bound, and do not crawl up to the throne in humiliating attitudes as do the captives seen in reliefs of other periods. The king no longer decorates his throne with the representations of these bound foreigners which he did before the change in the religion, as we may see in the reliefs on the opposite wall (13); for the new religion was essentially humane. Still farther along the wall there are some unfinished scenes (18) showing various persons carrying bouquets of flowers. Lastly, (19) low down on the wall there is a representation of the little temple of Aton at Karnak, built by the king at the beginning of his reign. ·

Thus in this mortuary chapel we have a complete record of the change of religion and art which caused such an upheaval in Egypt. The chapel was left unfinished, for soon after the fifth or sixth year of the young king's reign the whole court was transferred to Tell el Amarna. As has been said, Rames was probably already buried ; and, after the names of Amen and Mut and certain scenes had been erased, the mortuary services in honour of his soul were no doubt continued here. In the reign of Rameses Ist or Sety Ist the names of Amen and Mut were restored, and the figure of Amenhotep IVth (16) was erased. Thereafter the chapel soon fell into disuse, and about three hundred years later it was used by other persons as a place of burial.

NO. 54. THE MORTUARY CHAPEL OF HUY AND KENURE

This chapel is situated a few yards outside the enclosing wall of Shêkh abd' el Gûrneh, at the foot of the hill below and somewhat to the north of the main entrance. It was made for a standard-bearer of Amen named Huy who lived in the XVIIIth dynasty, but it was usurped by an official of the temple of Khonsu, named Kenure, in the XIXth dynasty. On the left as we enter are some interesting funeral scenes, including a curious representation of a figure of

Anubis, the funeral god, dragged along on a sledge, preceded by wailing women. On the opposite wall the cow of Hathor is seen emerging from the western hills, to receive the offerings of the deceased noble and his wife. On the right of the entrance, at the top, are the seated figures of the deceased King Amenhotep Ist and Queen Aahmes-nefertari, who are worshipped by Huy and his relations.

NO. 53. THE MORTUARY CHAPEL OF AMENEMHAT

This little chapel is situated between those of Rames (No. 55) and Nekht (No. 52) outside the enclosure of Shêkh abd' el Gûrneh. It was made for a noble named Amenemhat, who seems to have lived during the reign of Amenhotep Ist (B.C. 1557). On the right of the entrance (1) Amenemhat is seen shooting bulls, ostriches, antelopes, hares, porcupines, and other animals which have been driven into an enclosure and are hunted by dogs. On the end wall (2) is the funeral stela. At the top Amenemhat makes offerings to two princesses, one of whom is Aahmeshenttameh, the sister of Amenhotep Ist, while the other is a "royal wife," whose name is now lost. On the adjoining wall (3) Amenemhat spears a hippopotamus in the marshes. Farther along (4) he harpoons fish and brings down birds with his boomerangs. On the left of the entrance (5) the usual funeral feast is shown, and one of the male guests is seen to be overcome with nausea. Below this women contortionists perform their tricks to amuse the guests.

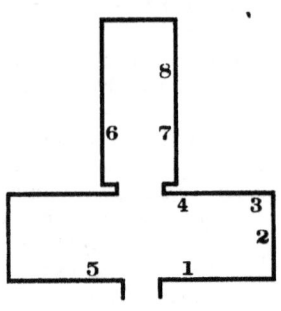

In the inner room on the left wall (6) the usual funeral procession is seen wending its way to the necropolis where Hathor and Osiris await to receive the deceased into his rest. On the opposite wall (7) funeral ceremonies are performed before the mummy of Amenemhat, and farther along there are figures of himself and his relations (8).

MORTUARY CHAPELS OF THE NOBLES

NO. 52. THE MORTUARY CHAPEL OF NEKHT

This little chapel is one of the best known to tourists in the necropolis. It is situated on the left of the path from the Ramesseum to Dêr el Bahri. The colouring is very well preserved, and there is a dainty quality in the paintings which makes them particularly attractive. The chapel was made for a certain Nekht, a scribe of the granaries at the middle of the XVIIIth dynasty. On the left as we enter (1) Nekht and his wife are seen with a heap of offerings piled before them. A bull is slain as a sacrifice to them. Upon the rest of this wall, (2) there are agricultural scenes which are worthy of close observation. At the top there are scenes of winnowing and measuring the grain, in the presence of Nekht, who sits in an elegant bower. Observe the quails hung up by their legs outside. Below this reaping is shown, and the corn is pressed into nets to be carried away. Below this again the land is ploughed, and trees are cut down where new ground is being reclaimed. The attitude of the old ploughman bending over his plough is particularly spirited.

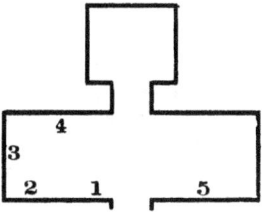

A man is shown drinking from a water-skin which has been hung on a tree to cool in the breeze. Upon the next wall (3) there is the usual funeral stela. On the adjoining wall (4) the scenes represent the mortuary feast. The guests are seated upon grass mats, and the women are seen to be talking to one another. A nude waitress puts a collar of flowers around the neck of one of the guests. Three women entertain the company by playing upon the lute and harp, and by dancing; while a blind harper also makes music for their edification. At the bottom right-hand corner the favourite cat of Nekht is seen under the chair, devouring a fish. Beyond the doorway (5) Nekht is seen hunting birds amongst the reeds, into which he has penetrated in his boat. His family are enjoying the sport with him. In one hand he holds a decoy, and in the other a boomerang. Farther along he spears fish from a boat; but the spear has never been painted in, the scene being quite unfinished. There is here a charming figure of his little daughter who points to the fish and looks up at her father. Below this there is the representation of a vineyard and a wine-press; and poultry is plucked. The other scenes in the chapel are mostly unfinished, Nekht having died before the completion of the work.

NO. 51. THE MORTUARY CHAPEL OF USERHAT

This chapel is situated on the right-hand side of a hollow not far to the east of No. 52 (Nekht). One passes it on the left when riding from the Ramesseum to the chapel of Nekht. It was made for a certain Userhat who was High Priest of the deified King Thothmes Ist during the reigns of Rameses Ist and Sety Ist. On the right, as we enter (1), in the upper half, Userhat is seen kneeling before twenty-four judges of the dead who sit in front of a shrine in which Osiris is enthroned between the standing figures of the ibis-headed Thoth and the jackal-headed Anubis. Farther along (2) Ra-aakhepersenb, the father of Userhat, and also High Priest of Thothmes Ist, kneels while priests pour holy water over him from two golden vases, saying as they do so, "Twice pure is the Osirian High Priest of Thothmes Ist." At the end of the wall (3) Userhat (?) says prayers before a heap of offerings. Along the lower half of the wall there are figures of Userhat and his relations, who bring flowers and offerings to place them before a shrine of Harmachis, behind whom is the goddess of the Underworld called "The Lover of Silence." Userhat himself pours wine over the heap of offerings which they have brought. On the adjoining wall (4) there is a painting which is one of the finest in the necropolis. We see Userhat with his wife and sister (?) seated in Paradise in the shade of a fig-tree burdened with fruit, amidst which the wagtails flit. They sit on elaborate chairs, their feet resting on wooden boards, and drink the water of life from golden cups. Under the chairs are garlands of flowers with which they may deck themselves. Above the two women their souls flutter in the form of human-headed birds. A tree goddess (see pp. 119, 154), rising out of the lake which lies before them, pours from a vase the water which they are drinking, and offers them bread, figs, grapes, and a honeycomb. Userhat stretches out his hand to take one of the figs. Between him and the goddess the T-shaped lake is to be seen at which the souls of Userhat and his wife in the form of semi-human birds drink the water from the hollow of their hands. The scene is not quite finished, but as it stands it is of wonderful beauty and grace. On the next wall (5) there are four

MORTUARY CHAPELS OF THE NOBLES 169

little funeral scenes one above the other. At the top Userhat, the son of the owner of the chapel, together with another man and some wailing women, makes a funeral offering to the seated ghosts of his father and mother. This scene is repeated twice below; in the third, the twisted candles should be noted burning in honour of the dead. Still lower a man and woman make offerings to the shades of two deceased relatives. Farther along the wall (6) we see various members of the family making offerings to Osiris and to Thothmes Ist, each seated in a shrine. It should be noticed that the woman in the upper row carries a long papyrus-reed, drawn naturally and not conventionally as it always appears upon the monuments. Beyond the doorway into the inner room

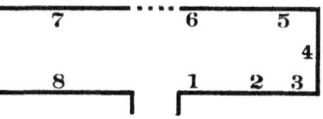

(7) the visitor should notice in the middle row the black stone statue of Thothmes Ist drawn on a sledge with women singing before it, and fans wafted over it. It is dragged towards the lake of the temple upon which is a barque (now damaged) ready to receive it. On the opposite wall (8) in the top row there are scenes illustrating the judgment of the soul. Near the entrance we see the heart of Userhat weighed in the heavenly scales against the figure of a man. Userhat stands in the presence of Osiris, with whom is the hawk of the Western Hills. Below this the funeral boat is dragged by oxen towards the tomb, wailing women preceding it. In the corner we see the mummies of Userhat and his wife standing up, while a priest offers to them, and another reads the ritual of the funeral from a papyrus.

Chapel No. 50, belonging to Neferhotep, the poet who wrote the well-known "Harper's Lament," is at present closed while being repaired. It is situated next door to No. 51.

NO. 49. THE MORTUARY CHAPEL OF NEFERHOTEP

This chapel is situated at the north-east face of the low mound which rises at the mouth of the bay known as El Assasif. It is not yet open to the public. Upon its walls there are some beautiful paintings, which are now so blackened by smoke that the closest scrutiny is required in order to appreciate them. The chapel was made for a certain Neferhotep, and for a relative of his named Amenhotep, during the reign of Amenhotep IIIrd or Horemheb.

NO. 48. THE MORTUARY CHAPEL OF SURERE

A short distance to the south of No. 49, not far from the house of the Omdeh of Gûrneh, and next door to No. 32, is the chapel of Surere, a noble of the court of Amenhotep IIIrd. The chapel consisted, like that of Rames (No. 55), of a pillared court, and some internal chambers excavated in the rock. These inner chambers now appear as a vast cavern half filled with debris. The carved doorways of the innermost chambers are remarkable for the cats sculptured in high relief on the lintels. Only a portion of the pillared court has been excavated. Here there are reliefs showing the figure of Amenhotep IIIrd, but the inscriptions are for the most part erased.

No. 47 is an unexcavated chapel not far from the house of the Omdeh. It was made for a certain Userhat, a noble of the court of Amenhotep IIIrd, and once contained some beautiful reliefs representing Amenhotep IIIrd, Queen Thiy, &c.; but these have been hacked out by robbers and sold.

No. 46 is the chapel of a certain Rames, of the XVIIIth dynasty, but it is without interest. It is situated immediately below Wilkinson's house on Shêkh abd' el Gûrneh.

No. 45 is the little chapel of Tehutiemheb, an official of the XIXth dynasty, who usurped it from its original owner Tehuti, a steward of the previous dynasty. At present it is not open to the public. It is situated not far to the north of the chapel of Khaemhat (No. 57).

No. 44 is the chapel of Amenemhat, a noble of Dynasty XXIInd. It has only just been opened.

No. 43 is that of Neferrenpet, also just opened.

No. 42 is the chapel of Amenmes, now being opened (1909).

No. 41 is the large chapel of Amenempt, of the early part of Dynasty XIXth. This fine chapel is now open to the public, too late, however, to be described here.

We may now turn to the chapels in other parts of the necropolis; and first we may describe the chapel of Huy at Gurnet el Murrai.

NO. 40. THE MORTUARY CHAPEL OF HUY

This chapel is situated upon the low hill which rises behind the Colossi, that is to say, south of the hill of Shêkh abd' el Gûrneh. It was made for Huy, who with his brother Amenhotep was joint-

MORTUARY CHAPELS OF THE NOBLES 171

Viceroy of Ethiopia in the reign of Tutankhamen (B.C. 1355). On the right on entering (1) the Pharaoh is seen seated under a canopy, while officials come towards him bowing, and Huy receives a ring of gold. The inscription says that this ring is the seal of the viceregal office, and it states that the territory under the control of Huy runs from Napata in the Sudan to El Kab (p. 312). On the opposite wall (2) the Pharaoh is again seated on his throne, and Huy stands before him (much damaged) to present the fine vases which are here depicted. These represent the tribute captured in Asia, for Huy as Viceroy of the Sudan was perhaps the commander of the Ethiopian soldiers of which the Egyptian

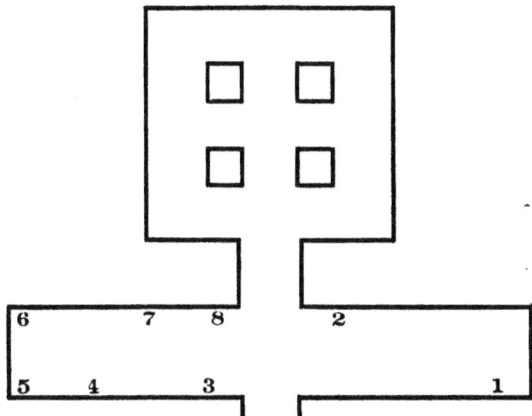

army mainly consisted. On the left of the entrance (3) Huy watches the arrival of two great boats which probably bring the tribute of the south. Next (4) Huy watches the weighing of gold and other produce of Nubia. Boats (5) are launched, and (6) others arrive from Nubia with the tribute. We now come to the well-known scenes (7) representing the arrival of a deputation from Nubia and Ethiopia. At the top we see the chiefs of Lower Nubia (Wawat) and the prince of Maam (Ibrim, p. 553) bowing before Huy. Then follows a prince riding in a chariot drawn by bulls. Negroes follow behind : one is a woman who brings her children with her. In the next line are princes of Ethiopia bringing gold, a giraffe, bulls with decorated horns (p. 81), and other kind of tribute. The various objects are placed before the throne (8) of the Pharaoh. The inner room does not repay a visit.

We now come to the chapels in the district known as El Assasif, *i.e.* those in or at the mouth of the bay of Dêr el Bahri.

Chapel No. 39 belonged to a certain Puamra, the Second Priest of Amen in the reign of Thothmes IIIrd. The chapel is large, and is decorated with very fine reliefs. The present writer has only just opened it (1908–9), and a description of it is not yet practicable.

NO. 38. THE MORTUARY CHAPEL OF RAZESERKASENB

Visitors who have seen Chapel No. 75 at the top of the hill of Shêkh abd' el Gûrneh, will remember that Amenhotepsase, the personage for whom it was made, held the office of Second Priest of Amen during the reign of Thothmes IVth, and that a certain Razeserkasenb was steward of his household. It is the chapel of this steward which is now to be recorded. It is situated not far north of the chapel of Nekht (No. 52) in a hollow behind the modern houses. On the left on entering Razeserkasenb and his wife and son stand before a heap of offerings which are presented to Amen, Harmachis, Osiris, and Hathor. Some smaller figures behind represent, at the top, two sons and, lower, servants. A figure carrying a jar of wine is noticeable for its spirited drawing. At the bottom are butchers cutting up oxen for the funeral feast. Upon the adjoining wall, at the top, are scenes showing the measuring of the fields with a measuring-rope. First walks an old farmer with long hair, then three retainers, then Razeserkasenb holding his palette (observe the curious shin-pads upon his legs), then a man with a writing tablet, and lastly a servant holding a pair of sandals. Refreshments are to be seen in a box under the shade of a tree. In the next row farmers bring offerings to a bower in which Razeserkasenb is sitting. A white goat here seen is drawn with great freedom and spirit. At the left Razeserkasenb makes an offering to the serpent Rennut, the goddess of the harvest. In the third row on the left the crops are harvested, and on the right the grain is winnowed. Below this again are ploughing scenes, and on the left a water skin from which the labourers may drink hangs on a tree, while refreshments are seen under it in the shade. On the right of the entrance there is an unfinished scene showing Razeserkasenb and his wife standing before offer-

MORTUARY CHAPELS OF THE NOBLES 173

ings. On the opposite wall there is a damaged figure of the owner seated in what was once a bower, while his two daughters present to him a collar of flowers and a dish of ointment. The dresses of the two women are somewhat peculiar, and are arranged around the breast in an unusual manner. Behind these two figures there are jars of wine decorated with vine leaves, and dishes of food and ointment. Below are female musicians, and amongst them is a delightfully drawn figure of a young dancing girl. The harps and other instruments held by these women should be noticed. Beyond this there are the usual feasting scenes. The guests are waited upon by nude waitresses. In the bottom row at the far corner a man is seen to turn in discomfort from the feast, being overcome with nausea, while his companion touches him on the arm to know what troubles him. This scene, which also occurs in other chapels, is supposed to be indicative of the plenteousness of the repast; and it seems to have been the height of good manners for the guests to eat and drink until nature thus revolted.

Chapel No. 37 is not yet open to the public. It was made for a certain Horua who lived during the reign of Amenartas.

NO. 36. THE MORTUARY CHAPEL OF ABA

This chapel was made for a noble of the XXVIth dynasty named Aba, the son of Ankhhor and Taari, who held the office of Steward of the Palace of Queen Netakret (Nitocris), the daughter of Psamtek Ist. He was also Master of the Wardrobe, and "Nurse" (*i.e.* Guardian) of the Queen. He is said to have been acquainted with the secret rites performed for the late Queen Shepenapt in her temple, by which is meant the little temple at Medinet Habu (p. 245). At the period at which Aba lived there was a tendency in art and religion to return to the style and customs of the classical period of the Pyramid Age. Thus in this chapel we shall notice many scenes which remind us of the reliefs in the tombs at Sakkâra.

The chapel is entered by a broad flight of steps at the foot of which an iron door has recently been placed. One then enters an anteroom, the walls of which, though much damaged, still bear some interesting scenes. On the right as we enter (1) there is a much damaged scene showing Aba as a priest adoring the hawk-headed Harmachis. The careful modelling of the limbs of the god should be observed. The figures are reminiscent of early work, but the scene is not early in character: it will be recognised by

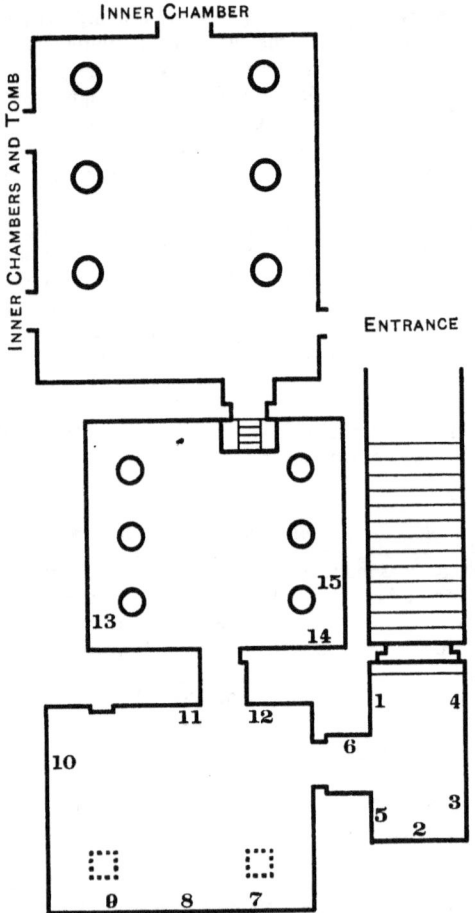

those who have visited the tombs of the kings as being that which is almost always found at the doorways of the royal tombs of the XIXth and XXth dynasties, where the king is seen making an

MORTUARY CHAPELS OF THE NOBLES

offering to Harmachis. At the end of the room (2) there is a "false door" modelled more or less on the old Sakkâra design : it is through this door that the soul of the dead man was supposed to pass in and out of the tomb. In the niche in the middle of the "false door" there probably stood a statue of the deceased. On the left wall (3) there is a damaged figure of Aba seated before offerings, above which is a list of supplies of all kinds which are to be at the disposal of the dead man. Walking towards them (4) there are rows of men and women bringing offerings of provisions, live animals, &c., to place before the shrine. This scene is copied very closely from early mortuary decorations, and the women in the lowest row are especially reminiscent of the work of the classical period. On the right wall (5) Aba has been shown seated before offerings, a pet gazelle under his chair. Below him three men make offerings to a standing figure of his *Ka*, clad in the simple skirt of early days and holding the long staff of that period. The ceiling of this room is coloured blue and is decorated with yellow stars. An inscription along the middle gives the cartouches of Queen Netakret, and the name of Aba.

We now pass through a doorway, on the right of which (6) is a fine figure of Aba holding two braziers, upon which offerings of birds, &c., are burning. We then reach a hall, the roof of which has been supported by square pillars with Hathor-head capitals not unlike those at Dendereh. They are here introduced perhaps in connection with Aba's office of Steward of the Queen's Palace, Hathor being the patron lady of Egyptian queens. Upon the left wall as we enter (7) there are a number of roughly cut scenes representing various arts and crafts. At the top left-hand corner shoemaking and leather-cutting are shown ; and below this chariot-making is represented. A large and well-drawn figure of Aba (8) watches these scenes. He is clad in the Old Kingdom style. Farther along the wall (9) at the top men and women dance and clap their hands in honour of the deceased. On the west wall (10) there is a second "false door," on which there are inscriptions of some historical importance, stating that Queen Netakret was the daughter of Psamtek, and that her mother was Shepenapt. On the sides of the doorway leading into the next hall (11 and 12) there are the figures of the three jackal-headed and three hawk-headed spirits of Nekhen and Pe (p. 212). Eight sacred bulls and cows are also shown, and there are the sacred oars to be seen, as at Medinet Habu (p. 240) and elsewhere.

We now enter a pillared court which was originally open. On

the left (13) there is a third "false door." On the right (14) one sees Aba and his father Ankh-hor sitting together before offerings. Above them Aba and his wife receive the adoration of their son. Upon the adjoining wall there is (15) an interesting hunting scene in which various animals are being shot. Below this, at the bottom, Aba's chariot is noticeable. On the rest of this wall there are many small figures bringing offerings, &c., to the tomb, which should be carefully examined both on account of the neatness of the work and also because of the interest of the scenes represented.

One may now pass into the inner hall from which small chambers lead. The tomb where Aba was buried is entered from one of these chambers. On the right, near the entrance to this hall, there is some coarse painting surrounding a low tunnel cut in the wall. This dates from Ptolemaic times, when some personage of that period used this place as a convenient sepulchre.

Chapel No. 35 is not yet open to the public. It is situated not far from the temple of Dêr el Bahri. It was made for a noble of the XXVIth dynasty.

Chapel No. 34, not yet open to the public, is situated just to the east of this. Originally it was a most imposing chapel, and the brick pylons are still to be seen; but now the inner chambers are closed. It was made for the famous Mentuemhat, a governor of Thebes at the time of the Assyrian invasions (XXVth dynasty), who carried on great works of restoration at Karnak and elsewhere (p. 88).

Chapel No. 33 is that of Peduamenemapt, a noble of the XXVIth dynasty. It is situated in the plain in front of the temple of Dêr el Bahri, and consists of an enormous open excavation in which are shrines dedicated to the worship of the deceased, and from which the actual tomb leads down into the depths of the rock. This subterranean portion is now closed. It is extremely deep, and the walls are covered with mortuary texts now much damaged.

No. 32, near the house of the Omdeh of Gûrneh, and next door to No. 49, was made for a certain Thothmes, a Steward of a Queen's Palace. It is not yet open to the public.

No. 31 is the chapel of Khonsu, of Dynasty XXth, just opened (1909).

No. 30 is that of Khonsumes, leading from No. 31.

Nos. 29–20 are reserved for chapels in the neighbourhood not yet opened. We may now turn to the chapels in that part of the necropolis known as Dra abu'l Neggar, *i.e.* the district north of

MORTUARY CHAPELS OF THE NOBLES

El Assasif. Here were buried many of the kings of the XIIIth–XVIIth dynasties in tombs above which were brick pyramids; but these are now destroyed and their exact location lost.

NO. 19. THE MORTUARY CHAPEL OF AMENMES

This small chapel, only recently excavated, is situated on the hillside between the entrance to the Valley of the Tombs of the Kings and the northern rest-house of the Department of Antiquities (a conspicuous pink-washed building). It was made for a certain Amenmes, who was the High Priest of the deified Amenhotep Ist at about the time of Rameses Ist. The paintings in this tomb are much damaged, but they are exceedingly well executed, and should be seen by all those who are particularly interested in Egyptology. On the left wall as one enters (1) at the top, the sacred barques of Amenhotep Ist are seen taking part in some festival in honour of the god. In the second row the sacred barque is placed upon a sledge and is dragged along towards the king's mortuary temple, the pylons of which are seen near by. In the third row there are scenes from the funeral of Amenmes. Women are wailing as the coffin is dragged towards them by men and oxen. On the

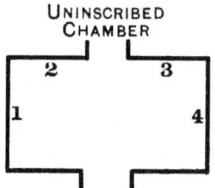

next wall (2), in the top row, the festival scenes are continued. There is the figure of the deified Thothmes IIIrd in a shrine, near the pylons of the temple, and in the presence of this image of the great warrior-king the soldiers hold fencing and wrestling matches. The figures, though so much damaged, are seen to be wonderfully drawn: notice especially the muscles of the legs of the combatants. In the second row the lake of the temple is seen, and on it floats a barque in which is a shrine containing a statue of the deified Queen Aahmes-nefertari, before which a priest burns incense. The barque is towed by a galley towards the quay, where priests stand awaiting its arrival in order to carry the statue to the temple which is seen behind them. Below this the scenes from the funeral of Amenmes are continued. The mummies of himself and his wife stand before the door of the chapel or tomb, while two male relatives weep beside them, and a woman hugs the feet of the mummy in the excess of her grief. Beyond the door of the tomb are the pink hills of the west, and

178 ANTIQUITIES OF UPPER EGYPT

into these the souls of Amenmes and his wife and son are seen to be walking. The cow of Hathor, the lady of the western desert, appears before them.

On the opposite side of the doorway (3) the statue of Amenhotep Ist, gorgeously decorated and carried in a high chair of gold, is carried along by the priests, while magnificent fans are wafted over it. The temple is seen near by. Below this are more funeral scenes, his soul and that of his wife being worshipped by relations. On the next wall (4) in the top row there are some much damaged gods and goddesses. In the lower row Amenmes and his wife are seated in Paradise while relatives adore them. Before them there is a palm-tree decorated with flowers, which is interesting as being an example of the design from which some forms of decorated stone columns were derived. Behind the figures of Amenmes and his wife their two souls in the form of birds drink the water of life which flows from a vessel held by a now destroyed tree goddess (p. 168). The rest of the paintings are too much damaged to permit of description.

No. 18. THE MORTUARY CHAPEL OF BAK

This chapel is situated somewhat to the north of that just described, at the side of the pathway leading from the rest-house of the Department of Antiquities to the mouth of the Valley of the Tombs of the Kings. It was made for an untitled personage named Bak, who was the son of a Scribe of the Cattle of Queen Nefertari, and lived somewhere about the time of Thothmes IIIrd. The chapel hardly repays a visit, as the paintings are quite conventional. On the right as we enter (1), at the top, Bak and his wife receive offerings from their son. Their little daughter is seen by their side, and a pet goose is shown under the chair (as in the tomb of Rames, p. 163, and elsewhere). In the lower row, his father and mother receive offerings. On the next wall (2) is the funeral stele. On the adjoining wall (3), at the top, Bak hunts birds with the boomerang, and spears fish in the marshes. Lower down there are scenes from his vineyards, and a wine-press is shown. At the other side of the doorway into an inner room (4) there are much damaged scenes showing the listing of the jars of wine, and the weighing of precious metals. A weight in the form

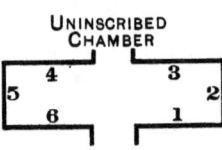

MORTUARY CHAPELS OF THE NOBLES

of a hippopotamus should be noted. On the next wall is a funeral stele again; and to the left of the entrance (6) there is the usual funeral banquet.

NO. 17. THE MORTUARY CHAPEL OF AMENNEB

This chapel is of considerable interest, but it is little visited, as it is somewhat off the beaten track. It is situated amidst the modern houses on the hillside above the pink-washed rest-house of the Department of Antiquities. It was made for a noble who lived somewhere about the time of Thothmes IIIrd, or perhaps slightly earlier. He was a scribe and "doctor," and is said to have "accompanied the king's footsteps in foreign lands." His name is everywhere erased, but it can be seen to have been Amenneb. He was the son of a personage named Nebsenuy. On the left as we enter (1) Amenneb and his wife are seen standing at the door of the chamber. Next to this (2) their brother offers flowers to them. On the next wall (3), in the top row, we see on the left the deceased and his wife seated; and under the chair their daughter is seen holding a mirror. On the right the deceased is seated on a chair, while his daughter offers vases to him. 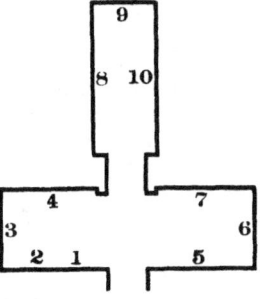 In the second row three women sit, two on a reed-mat and one on a chair. The figure seated upon the chair holds out a drinking cup into which a waitress pours some pleasant mixture composed of several ingredients. To the left three women clap their hands and sing, another plays a harp, and a man plays a guitar. In the third row the relations of the deceased are seen feasting. On the adjoining wall (4), on the right, there is a large figure of the deceased with his staff in his hand. On the left he is seated on a chair while a waitress mixes a drink for him. In the middle, between the two above-mentioned figures, there are representations of granaries, and servants are seen walking up the stairs to them. In the lower row we see on the left the bakers with their round loaves of bread. Farther along are jars of wine, and servants are seen with provisions which are to be brought as offerings to the chapel. On the right side of the entrance doorway (5), on the left, there is a large figure of Amenneb seated with his palette in his hand. The figure offering to him has been erased, and restored in later times. On the next wall (6) the deceased worships Anubis and Osiris. On the adjoining wall (7), to the left, the deceased is seated to receive the offerings made by his son. The scenes on this wall are unfinished, but they are extremely important to the archæologist on account of the foreigners depicted in them. At the top we see Cretan men and Asiatic women bringing to the Egyptian court the tribute of their countries. In the second row an Asiatic chieftain, clad in flowing white robes, sits on a chair, while his wife, with heavy, flounced skirts, stands beside him. An Egyptian official, standing in front of him, holds a vase which he seems to have received from the chieftain, judging by the latter's gesture; and other vases are shown near by. The scene perhaps represents the receiving of presents by an Egyptian envoy which are to be conveyed by him to his court.

In the inner room there are some interesting funeral scenes. On the left wall (8), at the top, the mummy of Amenneb is dragged along on a bier. A ritual-priest reads the funeral service from a long papyrus, as he walks before it. In the second row the funeral boats are seen crossing the river, and at the right end of this row the door of the chapel is seen, before which an ox is slain as a sacrifice. A priest offers a leg of the victim at the door, and a priestess kneels holding two jars of wine. In the third row the funeral boats are again shown. At the right end of the fourth row two dancing figures should be observed, as in the chapel of Anena (p. 137) and elsewhere. At the right end of the wall there is a large figure of Hathor, the goddess of the western hills. On the end wall (9) there are the figures of Anubis and Osiris, one on either side of a niche in which a statue of the deceased once stood. On the remaining wall (10) priests are seen performing the last rites before the mummy, as in the chapels of Menna (p. 151), Sumnut (p. 121), and elsewhere; and at the end of the wall the souls of the deceased and his wife, and his mother and father, are seen seated before numerous offerings which have been made to them by their relatives.

No. 16. THE MORTUARY CHAPEL OF PANEHESI

This chapel is situated just to the south of the southern resthouse of the Department of Antiquities, not far from No. 17. It was made for a certain Panehesi, a priest of Amenhotep Ist, who

MORTUARY CHAPELS OF THE NOBLES 181

lived about the time of Sety Ist. The excavation of the chapel and the paintings are very rough, but they are not without interest. On our right on entering (1) the two bottom rows of paintings represent rustic scenes. In the upper of these two rows, on the left, we see the cutting of the corn which is carried away on donkeys. Farther to the right the ploughing of Panehesi's fields is seen. One of the cows has refused to draw the plough, and has lain down, thereby almost dislocating the neck of its mate, to which it is connected by the yoke (here not drawn). The farmer vainly attempts to set matters to rights. Behind the plough a woman sows the seed. In the lower row cattle trample on the grain to thresh it, while Panehesi watches them, seated in the shade of a tree. Behind him is a box containing refreshments, beside which a servant stands. Farther on, a tree is cut down, and there are more ploughing scenes. Above these two rows a priest is seen making offerings to the souls of Panehesi and his wife who are seated beneath a tree of Paradise from which a goddess leans forth to pour out the water of life for the benefit of another figure of Panehesi's soul. Under the tree the two souls, 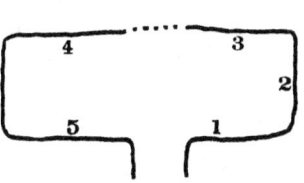 now in the form of birds, are shown. On the next wall (2), in the top row, the deceased man and his wife stand before a now destroyed figure of Osiris, the god of the underworld. In the bottom row there is a representation of one of the great festivals in honour of Amenhotep Ist, at which Panehesi officiated in his lifetime (see the chapel of Amenmes, p. 177). From the gateway and pylons of a temple, decorated with eight flagstaffs, issues a procession of priests bearing vases and other ceremonial utensils. Some carry a huge vase on a portable shrine upon their shoulders. The vase has a lid in the form of a ram's head, the sacred animal of Amen. A great bunch of flowers is borne before it, and a priest burns incense in front of it. On the next wall (3), at the top, there is seen, on the left, a statue of Amenhotep Ist seated upon a splendid portable throne. Fans are wafted before and behind it, and flowers are seen in profusion. It rests upon an altar or pedestal, before which Panehesi and his wife sacrifice. Below this are figures of Amenhotep Ist and Queen Aahmes-nefertari seated in a shrine, adored by Panehesi and his wife. The right half of the wall, where was a splendid sacred barque, is almost

ANTIQUITIES OF UPPER EGYPT

entirely destroyed. On the farther side of the doorway into the inner room, now closed (4), Panehesi makes a libation and sacrifice at the gate and pylons of the temple. On the opposite wall, along the top row, he and his wife adore various demi-gods in Hades (5); and below this there are some unfinished funeral scenes, showing the bier dragged along towards the tomb.

Chapels Nos. 15 to 11 are situated in this neighbourhood, but have not yet been opened. Nos. 10-1 are situated at Dêr el Medineh (p. 279).

LIST OF MORTUARY CHAPELS ACCESSIBLE IN NOVEMBER 1909
(with permanent numbers)

The mortuary chapels of Thebes are being excavated and safeguarded continuously, and many have been found since the above descriptions were written. The following is the present list :—

1. Sennezem. Dêr el Medineh.
2. Pashedu. ,, ,,
3. Sennezem. ,, ,,
4. Ken. ,, ,,
5. Neferaabt. ,, ,,
6. Neferhotep. ,, ,,
7. Rames. ,, ,,
8. Kha. ,, ,,
9. Amenmes. ,, ,,
10. Penbuy. ,, ,,
11. Tehuti. Dra abu'l Neggar.
12. (Leading from 11). ,, ,,
13. Shuroy. ,, ,,
14. (Near No. 13). ,, ,,
15. Tetaky. ,, ,,
16. Panehesi. ,, ,,
17. Amenneb. ,, ,,
18. Bak. ,, ,,
19. Amenmes. ,, ,,
20. Mentuher Khepeshef. ,, ,,
21. User. Shêkh abd' el Gûrneh.
22. Uah. ,, ,,
23. Zai. ,, ,,
24. Nebamen. Dra abu'l Neggar.
25. Amenemheb. Assasif.
26. (Near No. 36). ,,
27. (Pylons near Assasif). Assasif.
28. (Near No. 25). ,,
30. Khonsumes.
    Shêkh abd' el Gûrneh.
31. Khonsu. ,, ,,
32. Thothmes. Assasif.
33. Peduamenemapt. ,,
34. Mentuemhat. ,,
36. Aba. ,,
37. Horua. ,,
38. Razeserkasenb.
    Shêkh abd' el Gûrneh.
39. Puamra. Assasif.
40. Huy. Gurnet Murrai.
41. Amenemapt.
    Shêkh abd' el Gûrneh.
42. Amenmes. ,, ,,
43. Neferrenpet. ,, ,,
44. Amenemhat. ,, ,,
45. Tehutiemheb. ,, ,,
46. Rames. ,, ,,
47. Userhat. Assasif.
48. Surere. ,,
49. Neferhotep. ,,
50. Neferhotep.
    Shêkh abd' el Gûrneh.
51. Userhat. ,, ,,

MORTUARY CHAPELS OF THE NOBLES 183

52. Nekht. Shĕkh abd' el Gûrneh.
53. Amenemhat. ,, ,,
54. Huy and Kenure. ,, ,,
55. Rames. ,, ,,
56. Userhat. ,, ,,
57. Khaemhat. ,, ,,
58. Amenhotep and Amenemhat.
                Shĕkh abd' el Gûrneh.
59. Ken. ,, ,,
60. Antefaker. ,, ,,
61. User. ,, ,,
62. Amenemusekht. ,, ,,
63. Sebekhotep. ,, ,,
64. Heqerheh. ,, ,,
65. Aimadua. ,, ,,
66. Hapu. ,, ,,
67. Hapusenb. ,, ,,
68. Nespaneferher. ,, ,,
69. Menna. ,, ,,
70. Suaniamen (?). ,, ,,
71. Senmut. ,, ,,
72. Ra. ,, ,,
73. No name. ,, ,,
74. Zanuni. ,, ,,
75. Amenhotepsase. ,, ,,
76. Thenuna. ,, ,,
77. Rey. ,, ,,
78. Horemheb. ,, ,,
79. Menkheperrasenb. ,, ,,
80. Tehutinefer. ,, ,,
81. Anena. ,, ,,
82. Amenemhat.
           Shĕkh abd' el Gûrneh.
83. Aahmes. ,, ,,
84. Amunezeh. ,, ,,
85. Amenemheb. ,, ,,
86. Menkheperrasenb. ,, ,,
87. Minnekht. ,, ,,
88. Pehsukher. ,, ,,
89. Amenmes. ,, ,,
90. Nebamen. ,, ,,
91. No name. ,, ,,
92. Sumnut. ,, ,,
93. Kenamen. ,, ,,
94. Rames May. ,, ,,
95. Mery. ,, ,,
96. Sennefer. ,, ,,
97. Amenemhat. ,, ,,
98. No name. ,, ,,
99. Sennefera. ,, ,,
100. Rekhmara. ,, ,,
101. No name. ,, ,,
102. Imhotep. ,, ,,
103. No name. ,, ,,
104. Tehutinefer (?). ,, ,,
105. Amenemant. ,, ,,
106. Paser. ,, ,,
107. Nefersekheru. ,, ,,
108. Nebseni. ,, ,,
109. Min. ,, ,,
110. Hor. ,, ,,
111. Amenuahsu. ,, ,,

CHAPTER VIII

THE TOMBS OF THE KINGS

THE valley in which the tombs of the Pharaohs of Dynasties XVIII., XIX., and XX. are situated, known to the natives as *Bibân el Molûk*, lies amidst the limestone hills behind the temple of Dêr el Bahri and the Theban plain. There are several ways of approaching it. The main road leads north-west from the temple of Sety at Gûrneh, and, turning west, soon passes in between the hills, where it is clearly marked, and cannot be mistaken. A ride of less than half-an-hour through rugged desert scenery brings one to the wooden barrier which marks the entrance of the royal necropolis. There is a bridle-path over the hill, leading from Cook's rest-house at Dêr el Bahri; a steep path, somewhat dangerous for inexperienced climbers, leads from immediately above the north galleries of the temple of Dêr el Bahri; there is a third path between the two above mentioned; and from the south of Dêr el Medineh a long but easy track leads over the hills. The visitor, however, will find it best to ride up the long valley road and to return over the hill by the path which leads to Cook's rest-house. As the tombs are lit by electricity from 9 A.M. to 1 P.M. (after about March 15 from 8 A.M. to 12 P.M.), and are closed in the afternoons, the visitor will find it best to bring the excursion to an end at Cook's rest-house at lunch-time. In or near the valley there are the tombs of all the Pharaohs of the three above-mentioned dynasties, from Amenhotep Ist to Rameses XIIth, with rare exceptions. The tomb of Tutantkhamen has not yet been found (1908). The tombs of Rameses VIIIth and Rameses IXth have not been found, and probably are not situated in this valley at all, these Pharaohs having reigned in the north for but a year each. Akhnaton was buried at El Amarna, and his successor Smenkhkara's tomb has not yet been discovered. The position of the tombs will be seen upon the accompanying map. The list is as follows:—

THE TOMBS OF THE KINGS

*1. Rameses VIIth.
*2. Rameses IVth.
*3. Rameses IIIrd (abandoned).
*4. Rameses XIth.
5. Uninscribed.
**6. Rameses Xth.
7. Rameses IInd (blocked).
**8. Merenptah.
**9. Rameses Vth (usurped by Rameses VIth).
10. Amenmeses (lunching tomb).
**11. Rameses IIIrd (begun by Setnekht).
12. Uninscribed.
13. The Chancellor Bey (blocked).
*14. Tausert (usurped by Setnekht).
*15. Sety IInd.
**16. Rameses Ist.
**17. Sety Ist.
18. Rameses XIth (electric engine).
*19. Prince Mentuherkhepeshef.
20. Queen Hatshepsut.
21. Uninscribed shaft.
22. Amenhotep IIIrd (west valley).
23. Ay (west valley).
24. Uninscribed (west valley).
25. Uninscribed (west valley).
26. Uninscribed shaft.
27. ,, ,,
28. ,, ,,
29. ,, ,,
30. Uninscribed shaft.
31. ,, ,,
32. Uninscribed.
33. ,,
*34. Thothmes IIIrd.
**35. Amenhotep IInd.
36. Prince Maherpra.
37. Uninscribed.
38. Thothmes Ist.
39. Amenhotep Ist.
40. Uninscribed shaft.
41. ,, ,,
42. Probably Thothmes IInd.
43. Thothmes IVth.
44. The Lady Tentkaren.
45. Prince Userhat.
46. Yuaa and Tuau.
*47. Septah.
48. The Vizir Amenemapt.
49. Uninscribed.
50. ,,
51. ,,
52. ,,
53. ,,
54. ,,
55. Queen Thiy, and later Akhnaton.
56. Uninscribed.
57. Horemheb.
58. Uninscribed.
59. ,,
60. ,,

Tombs marked with two asterisks are lit by electricity. Those marked with one asterisk are open to the public, but are not lit. All other tombs are closed to the general public.

Those who only have a short time to spend in the valley are advised to visit as many of the seven best tombs as they can in the following order :—

35. Amenhotep IInd, as an example of a mid-XVIIIth dynasty tomb. The king's mummy still lies in this tomb.
16. Rameses Ist, which, though small, shows the development of the entrance and passage, and the extension of the painting.
17. Sety Ist, the largest and finest tomb in the valley, and a good example of the art of the XIXth dynasty.
8. Merenptah, in which is the Pharaoh's great sarcophagus.
11. Rameses IIIrd, showing the developments of the XXth dynasty.
9. Rameses Vth and VIth, a good example of late Ramesside work.
6. Rameses Xth, one of the last tombs in this valley.

186 ANTIQUITIES OF UPPER EGYPT

In the following pages the tombs are described in the order of their numbers, but by examining the best ones in the above chronological order the visitor will obtain a better understanding of the points which have now to be discussed.

<small>The history of the valley.</small>
Thebes became the residence of the Pharaohs of Egypt in the XIth dynasty, when the princes of this locality made themselves rulers of all Egypt. These kings were buried in rock-cut tombs in various parts of the Theban necropolis; and the visitor may perhaps have seen the sepulchre of Mentuhotep IIIrd at Dêr el Bahri. Some of the other kings of this house were buried in the face of the hills just to the left, or south, of the entrance to the valley, a part of the necropolis now known as Dra abu'l Neggar. The Pharaohs of the XIIth dynasty were buried near Memphis; but some of those of the XIIIth to XVIIth dynasties were again interred at Dra abu'l Neggar, and here the immediate ancestors of the great kings of the XVIIIth dynasty lay. King Amenhotep Ist (B.C. 1557) decided to be buried in quite new ground. He selected a desolate hillside above the cliffs which form the southern end of the valley of the Tombs of the Kings, and not far from the summit of the range of cliffs which rises behind Dêr el Medineh. During the

<small>First use of the valley.</small>
reign of his successor Thothmes Ist there lived a noble named Anena, whose tomb (No. 81) is to be seen on the hillside of Shêkh abd' el Gûrneh. This noble seems to have advised his royal master to place his tomb down in the desolate valley which subsequently became the royal necropolis, but which at this time was absolutely devoid of tombs of the dead or habitations of the living. In his biographical inscription Anena says: "I saw to the excavation of the rock-tomb of his majesty, alone, no one seeing, no one hearing." Thus, with the utmost secrecy, the Pharaoh Thothmes Ist was buried in his tomb which is now numbered 38, deep in the valley below the place at which his father lay; and from that time onwards for four and a half centuries the Pharaohs were buried in the valley, Rameses XIIth, the last king of the XXth dynasty (B.C. 1100) being the last monarch to be interred here (No. 4).

<small>The personages buried in the valley.</small>
As a general rule in the XVIIIth dynasty only the Pharaohs themselves, or queens who reigned in their own right, constructed large tombs here, the bodies of their nearest relations being buried with them. Generally also a favourite vizir or noble was allowed to be buried in a little rock chamber excavated near the tomb of his master. Amenhotep IIIrd, however, allowed Queen Thiy both to bury her non-royal parents Yuaa and Tuau here in a large tomb (though on the outskirts of the royal area), and also to

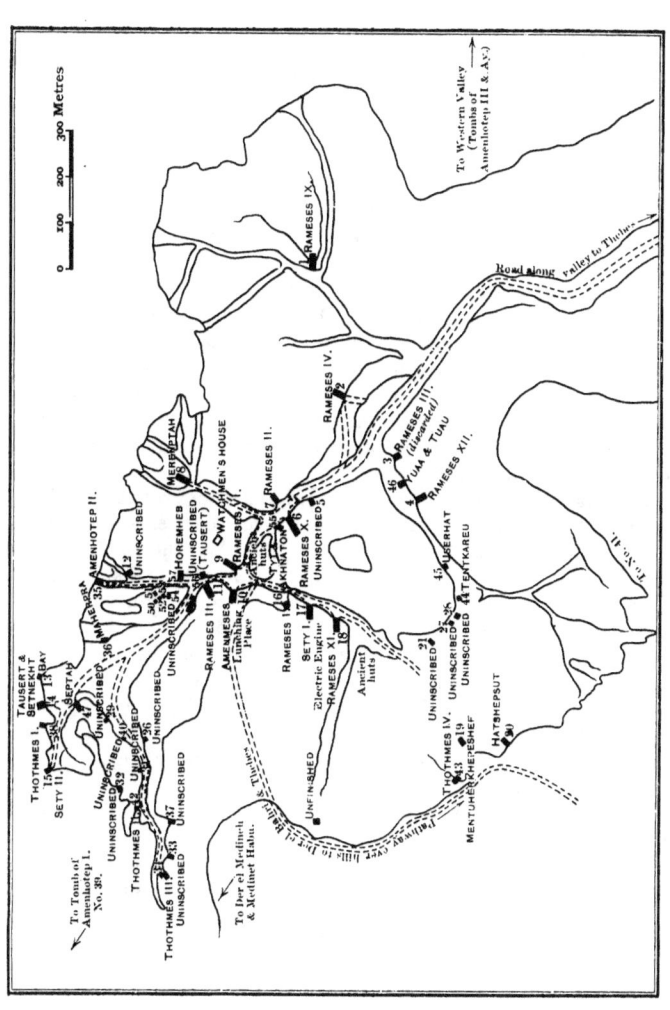

SKETCH MAP OF THE VALLEY OF THE TOMBS OF THE KINGS

construct a sepulchre for herself near them (No. 55); but he only permitted this because he did not intend to place his own tomb in the valley at all. There is another great valley leading westwards from a point a short distance north of the modern barrier; and far up this he excavated his own tomb (No. 22). His son and successor was buried at Tell el Amarna, though his body was later brought to this necropolis; but one of the succeeding kings, Ay, was likewise buried in this western valley (No. 23). King Horemheb, however, returned to the earlier site, and cut his tomb not far from that of Amenhotep IInd. His relations seem to have been buried with him. Rameses IInd buried his queen in the valley now known as the Valley of the Tombs of the Queens, and from that time onwards for some generations many of the queens and princes were there interred. Queen Tausert, who reigned in her own right at the end of the XIXth dynasty, following the example of Hatshepsut, constructed her tomb in the Valley of the Tombs of the Kings, and, against all tradition, allowed her favourite chancellor, Bey, to excavate a tomb of the large type for himself there. After this, however, only the Pharaohs seem to have been buried here.

The tomb-robbers.
As it was the custom to bury jewellery and other precious articles with the kings' bodies, there was always great danger of robbery; and it was for the sake of security that Amenhotep Ist and Thothmes Ist excavated their tombs in this remote region. They each constructed their tombs with but a small and rough entrance; and this entrance was hidden by debris as soon as the king had been buried. It is probable that the overseers of the work were bound by the most solemn oaths to keep the secret of the location of the tomb, and it may be that the slaves employed in its construction were afterwards killed, though it must be said in fairness to the ancients that there is no direct evidence to confirm this supposition. Unless all the workmen were thus silenced, however, it is difficult to understand how it came about that Setnekht in excavating his tomb (No. 11) drove it straight into the tomb of one of his predecessors, Amenmeses (No. 10), the location of which it would seem that he did not know, although Amenmeses had been dead but a half-dozen years. Here it is probable that six years after the making of a tomb there was no one alive to tell of its existence. The rough entrance-passage of the royal tombs from the time of Thothmes IIIrd to the end of the XVIIIth dynasty led down to a deep well, which served two purposes. In the first place it carried off any infiltrations of rain-water which might

penetrate into the tomb; and in the second place it acted as a blind to those robbers who did not know that the passage continued behind the apparently solid wall on the opposite side of the well, and it wasted the time of those who should guess this simple device, but who nevertheless would have to descend the well on the one side, ascend it on the other, and discover what part of the sheer wall was to be tapped to find the blocked opening to the farther passages. Should these difficulties be overcome and an entrance effected, the robbers would presently find themselves in a pillared hall, which would appear to form the end of the tomb. But in the floor of this hall there was a stairway leading downwards which was filled with debris to the surface of the floor, the whole area being then plastered over with mud, so that no trace of this farther extension of the tomb could be detected. It was only when the robbers had found, and had dug their way down, these stairs, that they would reach the real burial-chamber, where the king lay in a stone sarcophagus heavily lidded. In the early tombs it was generally only the last two chambers which were decorated with inscriptions and paintings, all the previous chambers and passages being roughly cut in the rock, and untrimmed; no vestige of the king's name being anywhere inscribed. Sometimes the walls of the well were decorated, so as to assist the confusion of the robbers. Towards the close of the XVIIIth dynasty, however, it became the custom to decorate some of the first chambers and corridors, and to make the mouth and entrance-passage somewhat larger and more imposing. It was felt that the rabbit-hole of an entrance (such as the visitor will find in No. 35), if it helped to hide the tomb, certainly did not assist in the magnification of the king's glory. The entrance to the tomb of Horemheb is thus much more imposing, while in the case of the tomb of Sety Ist the inscriptions and reliefs actually begin at the entrance; and, since that entrance was supposed to be well hidden by the mounds of debris which were always thrown over the mouths of these tombs of the XVIIIth and XIXth dynasties, this piece of vanity did not much endanger the mummy's safety. In every case the greatest secrecy was exacted from all those who had anything to do with the tombs, and it is probable that no post-funerary ceremonies of any kind were performed in the valley. The funeral temples of the Pharaohs, where their souls might be worshipped, were for this reason placed far away from their sepulchres, on the edge of the cultivation, instead of at the mouth of the tomb as in earlier times (for example, the temple of Mentuhotep IIIrd at Dêr el Bahri). The two most famous of these mortuary temples, of course, are the Ramesseum and Medinet Habu ; and the visitor will have seen the temple of Sety at Gûrneh, and the much-ruined temple of Thothmes IIIrd. Sety IInd was the first Pharaoh to excavate his tomb in such a manner that the entrance-passage led into the hillside without much gradient, all tombs previous to his having descended into the rock at a fairly steep incline. After the reign of Rameses IIIrd the Pharaohs seemed no longer to take much trouble to hide their tombs. As they ceased to build temples for themselves at the edge of the cultivation, it is possible that the ceremonies in honour of their souls were now performed at the mouths of their tombs ; and the appearance of these mouths leads one to suppose that they were not totally hidden, but were only closed with stones and debris. Much larger sarcophagi were now employed, and each Pharaoh's body lay under several tons of granite. The kings of this age, however, knew quite well that several of the tombs of their ancestors had been robbed, and it is probable that they did not bury so much jewellery with them now as formerly.

The great robberies. There must have been large numbers of police and watchmen stationed in and around the valley, and there were numerous officials and priests connected with the necropolis. The temptation to rob the tombs in their charge must have been very great, and, either by these men themselves or by organised gangs of thieves, practically every tomb was in time looted. A series of great robberies was detected during the reign of Rameses Xth, and a fairly complete account of the trials has come down to us. The governor of the eastern bank of the river at Thebes first detected the robberies, and made use of them to bring trouble upon the governor of the western bank. The latter, however, managed to save his face by acting with energy himself in the detection of the robbers, and by stating that the evidence produced in the first instance by his colleague was incorrect. The records which we possess show clearly the quarrel between these two officials ; but as it was the policy of each of them to find the offenders as quickly as possible, it came about that a very large number of persons, innocent and guilty, were brought to trial. Some of the confessions of the robbers, in which they describe how they burst their way into the tombs, tore the jewellery from the bodies of the dead kings, and burnt their coffins, are of very great interest, and tell a very vivid story of the destruction of which we at the present day see so many traces. During the following dynasty the robberies had become so alarming that the priests decided to take from every tomb the mummies which still remained in them, and to hide them elsewhere. A large number of royal mummies were therefore carried to the tomb of Amenhotep IInd (No. 35), which happened to be known to some of the officials, and were there hidden; others were secreted in the tomb of Amenhotep Ist (No. 39). A few years later (about B.C. 960) many more royal bodies were carried to a small tomb near Dêr el Bahri and were buried there. Two of these hiding-places were discovered in recent years, and the mummies were taken to the Cairo Museum, where they now lie. At the time when these removals were undertaken a few of the early tombs were still unknown, or had again been forgotten after being once robbed; and these are the only tombs in which the excavators of the present day discover, or hope to discover, royal remains which are worth the finding. All the other tombs stand open, or half choked with rubbish, and contain no antiquities. Many of them have stood thus for several hundred years, and Greek and Roman travellers have left their names upon the walls, while in some cases Coptic hermits have used them as dwelling-places. In the time of Strabo forty tombs stood open; Diodorus speaks of seventeen, but says that forty-seven were recorded in the official register kept by the priests; which would mean either that they knew of more royal tombs than we do now, or that they counted in some of the small pits. Napoleon's archæologists mention eleven. In modern times robberies sometimes occur here; and in the one instance in which the Department of Antiquities has ventured to place the mummy of a Pharaoh in the tomb where he was originally buried (No. 35), a daring robbery was effected. It would be very desirable to replace the mummies of the Pharaohs in their tombs; but after some years' experience the present writer feels that he at any rate would not be inclined to urge this undertaking, for their ultimate destruction, at some time when the hands of the law were momentarily impotent, would be inevitable. No native robber would be satisfied that splendid jewels were not secreted in the bodies until he had broken every royal mummy to pieces.

The visitor who has seen the tombs of the nobles at Shêkh abd' el Gûrneh, or elsewhere, will remember that it was the Egyptian custom to cover the walls with representations of scenes from the life of the dead man; and our museums are full of the objects of everyday use which were buried with him. This custom seems to have originated in the desire to display the possessions of the owner of the tomb, in order that there might be a continuation of them in the underworld. In the case of the king, however, this was unnecessary. His future life and all his possessions were assured to him, for he was immortal. As Pharaoh he was a god; and although the creed was not closely adhered to, it was believed that as long as his name was inscribed upon his mummy he need not ever fear poverty or annihilation. The Egyptians thought that their Pharaohs were the descendants of Ra, the sun-god, and that the divine spirit passed from one ruler to his successor from age to age. Thus, all he required in his tomb was the ritual and mythology of the underworld; and, with a few notable exceptions, neither were scenes from his life painted upon the walls of his sepulchre, nor were the comforts of life, in the shape of house furniture, buried with him. In the tomb of Thothmes IVth some of the king's weapons were buried with him, and in that of Rameses IIIrd these and a few other objects are represented upon the walls. But these instances are probably exceptional. It must also be remembered that the tombs in the valley correspond to the actual burial-pits at Shêkh abd' el Gûrneh, the painted chambers which we see at the latter place being really the chapels above the tombs, and they therefore correspond to the royal mortuary temples. Thus, just as one does not expect biographical paintings in the burial-pits of the tombs of the nobles, but only in their chapels above, so one does not expect anything except religious scenes and texts in the royal tombs, but may look for the goods of this world in the mortuary temples to a certain extent. There some of the possessions of the king are recorded, and his deeds are often mentioned, but such records were not really necessary for his soul's welfare. In earlier times it is probable that this mortuary ritual was written upon a roll of papyrus which was buried with the body; but in the XVIIIth dynasty, when the kings began to be buried in this valley, the custom had developed, and the walls of the funeral chamber were painted drab colour to represent in enlarged form this papyrus of earlier days. Upon this surface the ritual was inscribed in more or less cursive characters, such as would be written with the pen upon the papyrus; and just as the vignettes to the scribe-written papyri were roughly drawn in outline, so on the walls of the tomb the figures of the gods were merely sketched in, with but a touch of colour here and there. Towards the end of the XVIIIth dynasty, this custom, which the visitor will observe in No. 35, died out, and it became usual to paint more elaborately the gods and

THE TOMBS OF THE KINGS

hieroglyphics of the ritual. This stage in the development, introduced by Thothmes IVth, may be observed in the tomb of Rameses Ist (No. 16). About this period (to be precise, in the time of Horemheb) the custom of executing these figures in low relief came into existence; and thus in the tomb of Sety Ist (No. 17) one finds the walls decorated with elaborate scenes and inscriptions beautifully cut upon the stone and afterwards richly coloured. There is now no trace of the connection between these figures and those drawn with the pen upon papyrus; and from henceforth the walls are decorated with the same manner of work as are those of the great temples.

According to the ritual of Ra, the great sun-god each evening descended behind the horizon and passed in his boat through the twelve divisions (*i.e.* hours) of the underworld; and so ascended again triumphant next morning. The identification of the king with Ra led very naturally to the application of this myth to the soul of the dead monarch. As the sun set at night, so the king died; as the sun passed through the underworld at night, so the king had to make his way past the twelve divisions of that dark land during the night of death; and as the sun rose in the morning once more, so the king would come back to earth again when the long night was passed. It was necessary, therefore, to supply the royal soul with all those religious formulæ which would assist him to pass through the darkness and would permit him to enter the twelve portals, each of which was guarded by a terrible serpent. It is not always clear whether the king travels *with* the sun, or actually *as* the sun; and so little is the ritual understood, and so tedious are the formulæ when translated, that the visitor need not trouble himself to examine the scenes before him too closely. "The Book of that which is in the Underworld," "The Book of the Twelve Portals," "The Book of the Sun's Journey through the Underworld," and "The Book of the Praisings of the Sun," supply the bulk of the inscriptions and scenes. Besides this doctrine of the king's identification with the sun after death, there was another, and quite separate, series of beliefs which came to form part of the ritual of the royal tombs. The great god Osiris was believed to have lived upon earth in the far past, and to have been murdered by the god Set, his death being later revenged by his son Horus. When the king died he was believed to be absorbed into Osiris, in just the same way that, according to the solar doctrine, he was absorbed into the sun; but in this case he required to be "justified" before he could come into his kingdom,

The Solar Mythology.

though, being a god already, this was but a formality. The king on earth was the incarnation of Horus, as he was also of Ra: he was in fact the son of Osiris during his life, and Osiris himself after his death. Thus we find some of the chapters of "The Book of the Dead" in the royal tombs, which belong to the Osirian and not the solar series of myths. In each case countless spirits and demigods address the king, and are answered in correct terms; countless prayers and praisings are spoken; countless names called and responses given; and countless ceremonies are performed. Often it is obvious that the ancient scribe himself does not know the sense of what he is writing, and it would thus be futile for any one at the present day to attempt a detailed explanation of the ritual.

The construction of the tombs.
The question is sometimes asked as to how many years these great tombs occupied in the making. From the shortness of the reigns of some of the kings who have fairly large tombs in the valley it would seem that they were excavated with great rapidity. Rameses VIIth reigned about one year, but his tomb (No. 1), although small as compared with some others, is of fair size. Amenmeses probably reigned only a year or so, but his tomb (No. 10), which is now reserved for visitors to take their luncheon in, will be seen to be by no means small. The work seems to have been commenced immediately upon the accession of the Pharaoh; and, if he lived to reign for several years, the tomb was sometimes lengthened and elaborated, until, as in the case of that of Sety Ist (No. 17), it reached enormous dimensions. The tombs, it is thought, were excavated by means of flint tools, the final dressing being done with copper chisels. Slaves, Egyptian and foreign, were employed upon the work; and the rapidity with which the rock was tunnelled suggests that the overseer's whip was in constant use. It was important that good virgin rock should be selected. Setnekht commenced a tomb (No. 11) beside that of Amenmeses (No. 10), the location of which was hidden and unknown to him. After tunnelling for a short distance his workmen cut their way right through into the tomb of Amenmeses; and therefore the work had to be abandoned. Setnekht then usurped the tomb of Tausert (No. 14), his predecessor. Rameses IIIrd at the beginning of his reign cut a sepulchre at the north end of the royal area (No. 3), but abandoned it after the work had continued for some time, owing to the poor quality of the rock. He then took possession of this abandoned tomb of Setnekht, deviated its course so that it might run clear of the

THE TOMBS OF THE KINGS 195

sepulchre of Amenmeses, and made it into a quite satisfactory piece of work. There is only one other instance of usurpation in the valley, namely, that of Rameses VIth, who is seen to have usurped the tomb of Rameses Vth[1] (No. 9).

The question as to how the workmen lit the tombs while they were engaged upon their decoration is often asked. It would seem certain that sunlight (reflected into the tomb by mirrors) and small oil lamps were the only two methods of lighting employed; but by the latter method a very pure non-smoke-giving oil would have had to be used. *The lighting of the tombs.*

Modern excavations have been conducted on this site by various persons. M. Loret, then Director of the Department of Antiquities, made some valuable finds here at the end of the last century; but the importance of these discoveries has been eclipsed by those of Mr. Theodore M. Davis, who for some years has superintended and financed the excavations here on behalf of the Department. *Excavations.*

NO. 1. THE TOMB OF RAMESES VIIth

The Pharaoh Ra-user-mery-Amen-setep-en-Ra Rameses-at-Amen-neter-heq-an, generally called Rameses VIIth, but sometimes, and probably incorrectly, known as Rameses Xth, only reigned for about one year (B.C. 1150), and hence did not have time to excavate a tomb of large size. This tomb is situated up a small valley which leads westwards from the right of the main road somewhat before reaching the point at which one first comes in sight of the wooden barrier. It has not been cleaned out in modern times and is not yet closed with a door. Being small and not very interesting it is seldom visited. On the right as one enters, the king is seen worshipping a seated figure of Ptah-Seker-Ausar (a combination of the three gods Ptah, Sokaris, and Osiris), and on the left he worships Harmachis-Tum. Mythological figures are seen on either side as we pass on; and presently to right and left there is the figure of the god "Horus-supporter-of-his-mother," or of the priest or prince who acts the part of that god at the funeral, who holds up a bowl from which the water of purification streams over the deceased Pharaoh, clothed as Osiris. We now pass into the burial-chamber, in which stands a rough, unfinished granite sarco-

---

[1] In the tomb of Sety IInd the cartouches are written over other erased cartouches; but this is not a case of usurpation.

196   ANTIQUITIES OF UPPER EGYPT

phagus. On the walls of this chamber are the usual scenes, here much damaged. On the roof there is that curious elongated figure of the goddess Nut, which the visitor will perhaps have seen elsewhere (Dendereh, p. 41; Edfu, p. 341, &c.). In the recess at the end of this chamber, on the right, the king offers "Truth" to Osiris-Unnefer, the god of the dead. The mummy of this Pharaoh has never been found. The tomb was perhaps unknown to the priests who transferred the royal mummies to their hiding-places, and it may have been found and robbed at a later date. In Greek times it was standing open, for there are some graffiti of that age upon the walls.

NO. 2. THE TOMB OF RAMESES IVth

The Pharaoh Ra-heq-maat-setep-en-Amen Rameses-maa-maat-mery-Amen (Rameses IVth) reigned for half-a-dozen years, about B.C. 1170. This tomb is situated on the right, or west, of the main road, just outside the barrier. It must have been robbed not many years after the king's burial, for when the priests removed the first batch of royal remains to the tomb of Amenhotep IInd, they could only find the coffin of the Pharaoh, and this they religiously hid. The mummy had probably been broken up already. The tomb was open in Ptolemaic times, and there is a Latin inscription dating from the Imperial age scribbled upon the wall, while from the Coptic age there is a graffito on the right wall behind the entrance-door, reading "Ammonios, the martyr." It is now closed with an iron door; but it is not sufficiently interesting to be much visited. Curiously enough, the architect's original plan of this tomb, drawn on papyrus, is still preserved (at Turin). Above the main entrance the visitor sees the sun's disk within which are the figures of the ram-headed god of the setting sun and the scarab-shaped deity of the rising sun. Isis and Nephthys are shown, one on either side. In the first corridor on the left the Pharaoh is shown adoring the hawk-headed Harmachis; and the sun is represented passing between the two horizons. Beyond this in forty-five lines is inscribed "The Book of the Praising of Ra." The second corridor contains long inscriptions, relating to the worship of Ra. In the third corridor are mythological figures and texts. Passing into the fourth section of the tomb, the visitor will see upon the walls the long inscriptions which constitute chapters cxxiii., cxxv., and cxxvii. of "The Book

The corridors.

THE TOMBS OF THE KINGS 197

of the Dead." These are the chapters which refer to the "justification" of the dead.

One now enters the burial-chamber, in the middle of which stands the large granite sarcophagus in which the Pharaoh was buried. It has been broken by the early robbers who stole the body of the king as mentioned above. It measures 11½ feet by 7 feet at the sides, and is over 9 feet in height. On the walls of this chamber there are some scenes which call for remark. On the left walls chapters i. and ii. of "The Book of the Portals" is inscribed with appropriate scenes. Illustrating chapter i., we see the king kneeling before the sun-god, who is towed in his boat through the first division of the underworld, and offering him the symbol of "Truth." The souls of the wicked (?), in charge of the god Atum, are seen bound and fettered, and some are lying dead. In chapter ii. one again sees the sun-god in his boat, which has now passed through the serpent-guarded portal into the second division of the underworld. The god Atum is now leaning upon his staff watching the wicked serpent Apophis who has been rendered harmless by means of certain spells. On the right walls of this chamber chapter iii. of the same book is inscribed and illustrated. The boat of the sun has now entered the third division of the underworld. Here, among other figures, twelve goddesses divided by a serpent into two rows of six, are seen to represent the six hours of the night before and after midnight. This part of the ritual ends here in the middle of chapter iv., when the sun-boat has passed into the fourth division of the underworld. Upon the roof of this chamber is the figure of the goddess Nut, and upon her body are marked the constellations of the heavens.

Beyond the burial-chamber there is a corridor on the walls of which "The Sun's Journey through the Underworld" is inscribed. On the lintel of the door leading into the last chamber the visitor will notice a representation of the boat of the sun resting upon a double sphinx. Upon the walls of this last chamber there are representations of a bed, a chair, two chests,

THE TOMB OF RAMESES IV.

The burial-chamber.

The innermost chambers.

and the usual four canopic vases. These objects were, perhaps, actually placed in this room at the time of the funeral, though this was somewhat against the custom of earlier times.

NO. 3. THE DISCARDED TOMB OF RAMESES IIIrd

This tomb is now partly choked. It runs into a spur of rock to the left, or east, of the main road, a short distance outside the barrier. It was excavated for Rameses IIIrd, but was abandoned, probably owing to the poor quality of the rock; and the king was finally buried in No. 11.

NO. 4. THE TOMB OF RAMESES XIIth

This was the last tomb to be excavated in the valley, being made for Rameses XIIth, the last king of the XXth dynasty, who signed away one by one all his rights to the High Priest of Amen-Ra, finally losing his throne to him about B.C. 1100. The mummy of the Pharaoh was carried to the hiding-place at Dêr el Bahri by the priests of the next dynasty, where it was found in recent times. The tomb is unfinished and undecorated, except for some figures beautifully outlined in red paint at the entrance. The king is here seen worshipping a god who is represented as having four rams' heads (see p. 199); Harmachis; and Mersergert, the goddess "who loves silence." The poverty and insecurity of the court at this period is clearly shown by the fact that, although the king reigned twenty-seven years, the painting and sculpturing of the tomb was hardly begun.

NO. 5. AN UNINSCRIBED TOMB

This tomb lies on the left or east of the road near the wooden barrier. It probably dates from the XVIIIth dynasty, and may have been excavated for a queen or some great noble.

NO. 6. THE TOMB OF RAMESES Xth

This tomb was made for the Pharaoh Nefer-ka-Ra-setep-en-Ra Rameses-kha-uas-merer-Amen, who for some time was called Rameses IXth, but who, there seems little doubt, should really be numbered as Rameses Xth. He reigned about 1140 B.C., and it was during his lifetime that the great trial of tomb-robbers,

THE TOMBS OF THE KINGS 199

mentioned above, took place. His own mummy, however, did not escape the hands of the thieves. It seems already to have been lost when the priests hid the various royal mummies, for it was not found in either of the two hiding-places, although a casket belonging to his burial was carried by them to Dêr el Bahri. The tomb lay open in Ptolemaic times ; but in recent years it has been cleaned up, and closed by an iron gate, while electric light has been installed in it. It is situated on the left of the road immediately inside the wooden barrier. The entrance is imposing, and it is at once apparent that it could not have been entirely hidden from sight at any time with much success. The tomb passes into the hillside with little slope, and it is only in the innermost corridors that the descent, so usual in all the corridors in earlier tombs, is observed.

Entering the tomb one observes on the right (1) the figure of the king burning incense and offering a vase to Amen-Ra-Harmachis [a combination of the great Theban deity and the Heliopolitan sun-god, here shown as having four rams' heads], and to the goddess Mersergert, "The Lover of Silence, daughter of the Underworld." On the opposite wall (2) the king performs the ceremony known as the *seten de hotep* before Harmachis and Osiris, the former being the Heliopolitan form of Ra with whom the king became identified after death, and the latter being the great god of the dead. Somewhat farther along on the right side (3) nine serpents, followed by nine bull-headed demons, nine figures each enclosed in an oval, and nine jackal-headed figures, are to be seen. These are triple trinities, or cycles, of creatures of the underworld, shown in illustration of the book of "The Sun's Journey through the Underworld" which is here inscribed. On the opposite wall (4) is the text of chapter cxxv. of "The Book of the Dead," and beneath it there is a figure of the god "Horus-supporter-of-his-mother," or the priest or prince who performed the rôle of that deity at the funeral ceremony, pouring the water of life over the deceased king who is represented in the form of Osiris, having been absorbed into that god after death. In explanation of this scene, it should be mentioned that the god Horus, after the death of his father Osiris, was said to have "supported" his mother, assisted her to bury the dead god, and to have overcome her enemies. In the same way, when the king died and was absorbed into Osiris, his son was expected to "support" the royal house, and to see to the funeral-rites of the dead king. It is not clear whether this figure of " Horus-supporter-of-

The first corridor.

his-mother" is that of the god himself, or that of the king in the guise of Horus, performing for Osiris the rites which he wishes to be performed for himself in similar manner, or again of the priest or relative who actually performed the funeral ceremony. Symbolically, however, it certainly was intended to indicate that the rites of burial had been performed for the king which Horus and Isis were thought to have performed for Osiris. In the scene before us it will be observed that Horus wears the side lock which signified the rank of a royal prince. Four uninscribed chambers, two on either side, are here seen; these being used for the storing of funeral offerings.

The second corridor. Passing on into the second corridor, one sees on either side (5) the serpent which guards the door. That on the left is said to "watch the door for him who dwells in the tomb"; and that on the right is said to "watch the gate of Osiris." On the left (6) the king is seen advancing into the tomb, a goddess carrying his names before him and acting as his herald. Farther along, on the left (7), there is an inscription from "The Book of the Dead," beyond which the king is seen worshipping Khonsu-Neferhotep-Shu, a hawk-headed deity who addresses the king in the following words: "I give thee my power, my years, my seat, my throne upon earth, to become a soul in the Underworld. I give thy soul to heaven, and thy body to the *Duat* (Underworld) for ever."

The third corridor. One now enters the third corridor; and on either side, behind the doorway, one again sees the guardian serpents. On the right wall (8) the king is seen offering a figure of Maat, the goddess of Truth, to Ptah, before whom in smaller size Maat herself stands. Farther along (9) there is a mystical representation of the dead king as Osiris, stretched along the hills of the world, above

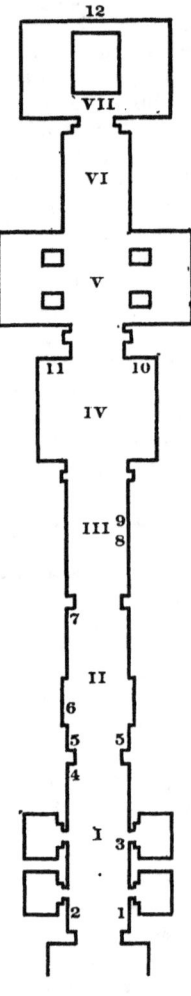

THE TOMB OF
RAMESES X.

THE TOMBS OF THE KINGS 201

which the disk of the sun rises. The beetle, symbolic of new creation, comes from out the disk to bring life once more to the earth ; and as the sun thus renews the activities of the world each morning, so the king's mummy will be revivified at its resurrection. On the remainder of this and the opposite wall are mythological figures ; and one sees the boat of the sun sailing across the heavens.

The passage now opens into a chamber, and before us on the right (10) we see the figure of " Horus-supporter-of-his-mother " with arms raised, holding four instruments of religious significance above a religious standard of the ibis of Thoth, the god of wisdom. On the opposite side (11) a similar figure holds a bowl of water which flows over the standard of the ram of Khnum, the god of the Cataracts, from whence the pure and sacred water of the Nile was thought to spring. These two figures are clad in the priestly leopard-skins, and it is evident that they are intended to endow the king with wisdom and purity. The drawing of the profile, with its strong features and hooked nose, is remarkable. Passing on through a pillared chamber, and down the wooden gangway to the burial chamber, one sees the tank in the floor, in which the granite sarcophagus, now lost, stood. The only scene which calls for remark in this chamber is to be seen behind this tank (12). A figure of the infant Horus is shown seated within the winged disk of the sun ; and it seems probable that this figure is symbolic of the renewal of life and youth after death. *The inner chambers.*

NO. 7. THE TOMB OF RAMESES IInd

Opposite the tomb last described, on the right of the main road just inside the barrier, there is the tomb of the famous Rameses IInd ; but for the present it is closed both owing to its dangerous condition and to the fact that it is not properly cleared. It is of vast size, being of the same length, and of larger area, than the great tomb of Sety Ist (No. 17). The tomb was robbed during the reign of Rameses Xth, the trial of the thieves being on record ; and Herhor, the first king of Dynasty XXI., removed the mummy of the Pharaoh to the tomb of Sety I., about B.C. 1100. The wrappings were there renewed, and about B.C. 1065 a new coffin was supplied. The body, being again in danger of robbery, was removed to the tomb of Anhapu about B.C. 973, and thence to the tomb of Amenhotep about B.C. 963. Finally it was hidden at Dêr el Bahri about

B.C. 960, and there it was found in modern times. It is now exhibited in the Cairo Museum.

NO. 8. THE TOMB OF MERENPTAH

A few yards beyond tomb No. 7 a path leads to the right, or west, and brings one to the tomb of Ba-en-Ra-mery-Amen Hotep-her-maat-Merenptah, commonly called simply Merenptah. This Pharaoh was the son of Rameses IInd, and reigned from B.C. 1230 to 1215. The tomb was robbed not very long after the king's death; and his body was carried by the priests to the tomb of Amenhotep IInd (No. 35), where it was deposited by mistake in the coffin of Setnekht. When this hiding-place was found in recent years the mummy was identified by the rough inscriptions upon the bandages. The tomb was cleaned out a few years ago, and under the rubbish in the burial chamber the great sarcophagus lid was discovered, which is now exhibited *in situ*. The tomb was closed with an iron door, and electric light was installed. Visitors are recommended to see this tomb, as the sarcophagus is of great beauty; but it should be remarked that the descent and ascent of the long corridor is somewhat tiring. Merenptah is usually said to have been the Pharaoh in whose reign the Exodus took place, but this is not certain. The Bible does not, as is generally thought, tell us that the Pharaoh was drowned in the Red Sea; and, even if the Exodus was as disastrous a catastrophe to the Egyptians as the Hebrew tradition indicates, there is no reason why the monarch should not have been comfortably buried in his tomb.

The first three corridors. On the lintel of the door one sees the disk of the sun in which are the beetle which represents the dawn and the ram-headed figure typifying sunset. Isis and Nephthys worship, one on either side. Entering the passage, which descends at a sharp angle, one sees on the left (1) a fine coloured relief representing the king worshipping Harmachis. Three perpendicular lines of hieroglyphs farther along give the titles of the "Book of the Praising of Ra," which is inscribed upon this wall in tolerably complete form, and is continued on the opposite wall. One then sees a symbolical representation of the sun's disk passing between the two horizons. Entering the second division of the corridor there is to be seen on the left (2) a figure of Isis kneeling, and near her the jackal, Anubis, the god of the Necropolis. Isis tells the king that she extends her protection over him, and gives him

THE TOMBS OF THE KINGS   203

breath for his nostrils. On the opposite wall (3) there is a similar scene in which Nephthys takes the place of Isis. In the third corridor on the right (4) there is an interesting representation of the boat of the sun passing through the underworld towed by the gods. On the opposite wall (5) is the boat of the sun again, and in it stand Horus and Set. The latter god was still regarded as a good deity; but in later times he came to be the Prince of Evil.

The corridor now widens into a chamber (IV) in which there are figures of various genii and gods of the underworld. To the left, on the back wall of this room (6), is a figure of Anubis before whom are two of the four genii who serve Osiris. On the opposite side (7) there is the figure of "Horus-supporter-of-his-mother," of which an explanation has been given in the description of tomb No. 6. Before him the remaining two genii are shown. One now passes into a chamber, the roof of which is supported by two columns. Immediately to one's left (8) the king is seen before Osiris. Above the adjoining wall (9) it is interesting to notice a great block of flint protruding from the roof, which the workmen have not troubled to cut away. The chamber (X) which leads off to the right is unfinished. A stairway passes down through the floor of Chamber V, which brings us presently to the room (VII) in which lies the outer lid of the great granite sarcophagus. This great lid seems never to have been carried down to the burial chamber, but to have been left here owing to the difficulties of moving it farther. One now passes on through a corridor (VIII) to the much-ruined burial hall (IX), the vaulted roof of which

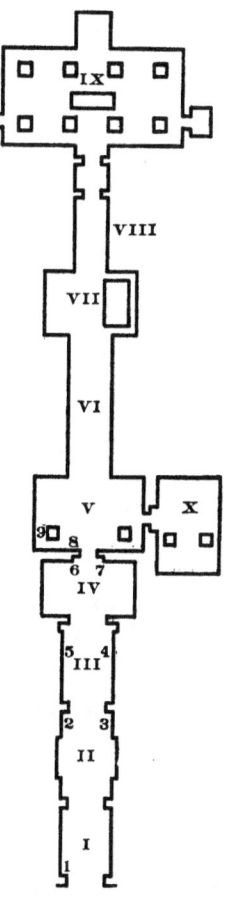

THE TOMB OF MERENPTAH

was supported by eight now much damaged columns. The scenes in this hall are too much damaged to be of interest; but the visitor's attention will naturally be claimed by the beautifully sculptured inner lid of the granite sarcophagus, which lies here in its original position. The mummy of the king was placed in a wooden coffin, and this coffin was placed in a now destroyed granite sarcophagus, of which the recumbent figure before us formed the lid. It was intended that this should then be placed inside an outer sarcophagus, the lid of which has been seen in Chamber VII; but there does not seem to have been time for the accomplishment of this difficult task. The electric light is effectively thrown on to the figure, and the visitor cannot fail to be impressed by its grandeur and dignity.

NO. 9. THE TOMB OF RAMESES Vth AND RAMESES VIth

This tomb, which was erroneously called by the Greeks the tomb of Memnon, runs into the hillside immediately under the custodians' shelter, on the right of the main road. It was excavated for Ra-user-maat-sekheper-en-Ra Rameses-Amen-khepeshef-mery-Amen—that is to say, Rameses Vth (B.C. 1160). His successor was Ra-neb-maat-mery-Amen Rameses-Amen-her-khepeshef-neter-heq-an, Rameses VIth. The first part of this name, Ra-neb-maat, is the same as that of Amenhotep IIIrd, who was called "Memnon" by the Greeks. Rameses VIth seems to have failed to find opportunity in his troubled reign for the making of a tomb for himself; and when he died, therefore, the priests placed him in the tomb of his predecessor, changing the cartouches from the former to the latter names. The tomb was robbed shortly afterwards, and when the priests came to transfer the royal mummies to the tomb of Amenhotep IInd in order to hide them, they could only find the body of Rameses Vth. This and the empty coffin of Rameses VIth they carried away, and these were found in the hiding-place in recent years. The tomb was standing open in Greek times, and a graffito on one of the walls reads "Hermogenes of Amasa has seen and admired the tombs, but this tomb of Memnon, after he had examined it, he more than admired." The tomb is now lit with electric light, and is a good example of the work of the period. It should certainly be visited.

Upon entering the first corridor one sees upon the left (1) a figure of the king in the presence of Harmachis and Osiris-Chieftain-of-the-Underworld; and upon the opposite wall (2) a

similar scene occurs. Farther along, on the left (3), the boat of
the sun is seen between the twelve hours of
the night, inverted to indicate that they are
on the underside of the world, and the
twelve hours of the day. On the right wall
of the second corridor (4) there is a figure
of Osiris enthroned, and towards him ascend
nine figures. Above floats the boat of the
sun, and from it a pig, representing a wicked
being, is driven by the holy apes of Harmachis. In these sections of the tomb there
are many representations of the enemies of
the sun which he meets and overpowers on
his journey through the night. Passing
through the third corridor one enters a
chamber (IV) which leads into a four-pillared hall (V). Here above the farther
door (5) one sees the king burning incense
before Osiris. On the pillars there are the
figures of various gods ; and on the ceiling
there is an elongated figure of the goddess
Nut (the Heavens). Stretching from this
room downwards there are to be seen to left
and right the two winged serpents of the
underworld. We pass through the sixth
and seventh corridor, and so enter an antechamber (VIII) in which chapter cxxv. of
" The Book of the Dead " is inscribed.
The burial hall (IX) is now reached, in the
middle of which the broken sarcophagus of
granite stands. The astronomical figures
upon the ceiling of this hall are of considerable interest. On the right wall (6) there
is a representation of the boat of the sun in
which the god stands in the form of a beetle
(the rising sun) with a ram's head (the setting sun). The boat is drawn across the sky,
which is supported by two lions. Two birds
with human heads, the usual form in which
a soul is represented, are seen worshipping
the sun as he passes. These are the souls
of the gods of the sunset and sunrise.

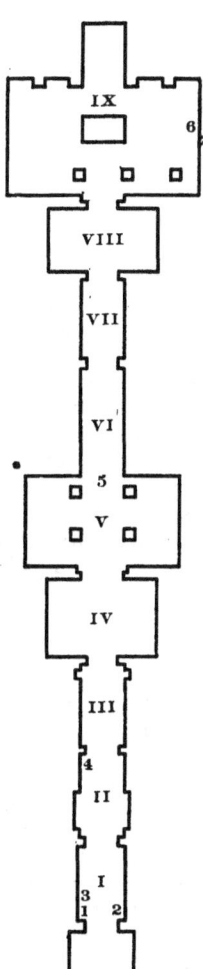

THE TOMB OF RAMESES
V. AND RAMESES VI.

NO. 10. THE TOMB OF AMENMESES

The full name of Amenmeses (B.C. 1215), one of the successors of Merenptah, was Ra-men-ma [1]-setep-en-Ra Amenmeses-heq-uas. The tomb which he made for himself faces the visitor as he walks southwards along the main road, not far inside the barrier. The claim of Amenmeses to the throne was not recognised by later kings ; and one of these deliberately erased the inscriptions and figures upon the walls of his tomb, so that now almost nothing is to be seen. It has already been stated at the beginning of this chapter that the tomb was so successfully hidden after the burial of the king that Setnekht (No. 11), six years later, drove his own tomb right into it by mistake, not knowing that it existed. It may have been Setnekht, or his son Rameses IIIrd, who destroyed the inscriptions, and it is possible that the mummy was at the same time carried out of the royal valley and deposited in some more humble tomb, for it has never been found. The tomb has not been entirely cleared in modern times, and it is possible that the body still lies beneath the debris. It may, however, have perished at the hands of the robbers. The tomb is now used as a lunching-place for tourists who have brought their refreshments with them, and tables and forms are provided.

NO. 11. THE TOMB OF RAMESES IIIrd

This tomb was begun by Setnekht, the father of Rameses IIIrd, about B.C. 1200. The work was abandoned, however, when the tunnel was found to have cut into the tomb of Amenmeses (No. 10), the existence of which had not been known to the workmen ; and Setnekht then usurped the tomb of Tausert (No. 14). When Rameses IIIrd came to the throne (B.C. 1198) he excavated tomb No. 3, but abandoned this owing to the bad quality of the rock. He decided that it would be cheapest to continue the tomb discarded by his father, changing its course so that it should avoid the tomb of Amenmeses. Here he was ultimately buried ; but the priests who are responsible for the hiding of the royal mummies carried his body to Dêr el Bahri, where it was found in modern times. His granite sarcophagus is now exhibited in the Louvre at Paris, while the lid is in the Fitzwilliam Museum,

[1] Later changed to *maat*.

THE TOMBS OF THE KINGS 207

Cambridge. The tomb was open in Greek times, and there are several graffiti upon its walls. It was reopened by the traveller Bruce, and hence is sometimes called "Bruce's tomb." It is situated on the left side of the road, between the custodians' house and the fork of the roads. It is now lit by electric light.

One enters the tomb down a flight of steps, and on either side of the doorway there are two bull-headed totem standards sculptured in the rock. One observes at once the great development made in the style of the entrance, which is far more imposing than in the case of the tomb of Merenptah who had reigned but a few years previously. On the left (1) the king is seen before Harmachis, and farther on the sun is shown passing between the two horizons, as we have already seen in other tombs. "The Book of the Praising of Ra" is inscribed upon this and the opposite wall. Leading from this and the next corridor there are a series of ten small chambers, five on either side, which were used for the storing of offerings and funeral paraphernalia. In Chamber A there have been scenes showing persons cooking and preparing provisions for the tomb, but these are much damaged. On the right wall (2), at the top, a cauldron is seen boiling upon the fire, tended by two men. In Chamber B funeral boats with elaborate sails are seen passing across the Nile. Chamber C is decorated with a series of figures of gods of the harvest and of plenty, some with ears of corn rising from their heads. In Chamber D on the right wall (3) there are military standards; on the middle wall (4) there are arrows, sheaths, bows, and other weapons; and on the left wall (5) there are the four tribal standards which, since archaic days, had gone before the Pharaoh at certain ceremonies and functions. In Chamber E one sees the gods of the Nile and of the fields bringing offerings of flowers, fruit, and birds. Chamber F contains representations of jars of

The first two corridors and side chambers.

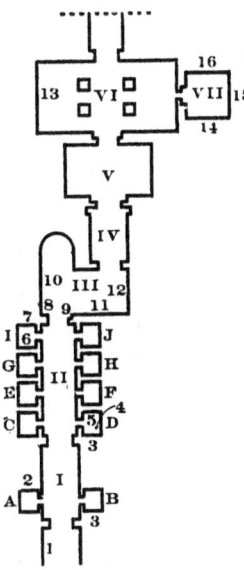

THE TOMB OF RAMESES III.

208   ANTIQUITIES OF UPPER EGYPT

wine, vases, skins, furniture, &c. Chamber G is decorated with representations of sacred animals, and sacred symbols. In Chamber H one sees the canals of the underworld which traverse the fields of the blessed; and on these the king is seen floating in his boat. In Chamber I there are the two famous representations of Egyptian harpers. On the left (6) the harper plays before the gods Anhur and Harmachis; on the right (7) before Atum and Shu. The refrain of their song is: "Receive the blessed King Rameses'!" It is probable that harpers of this kind played at the funeral ceremonies, singing the praises of the deceased and lamenting their death. Finally, in Chamber J there are representations of twelve forms of Osiris. As has been said before, it was against earlier custom thus to portray material things upon the walls of the tombs; but Rameses IIIrd seems to have been unwilling to rely entirely on the power of his godhead for his soul's comfort after death.

The inner rooms.   At the end of this corridor, beyond the series of side chambers, there is on the left (8) the figure of Isis with the jackal Anubis, and on the right (9) the figure of Nephthys also with Anubis. Farther along, on the left (10), the king is seen standing before Atum and before Ptah. It was at this point that the tomb ran into that of Amenmeses; and it now deviates, therefore, to the right. On our right (11) we see the king pouring out a libation before Ptah-Seker-Ausar (a combination of Ptah, Sokaris, and Osiris) who is guarded by the wings of Isis. Before us (12) the king is seen in the presence of Osiris and Anubis. We now pass through Corridor IV. on the walls of which the journey of the sun through the underworld is shown with texts from "The Book of that which is in the Underworld," and so enter Chamber V. This leads into a pillared hall (VI), through the floor of which the passage leads downwards. At the bottom of the left wall (13) there are representations of the four great races of mankind known to the Egyptians: the Temehu, or Libyans, with pointed beards and light brown skins; the Nehesu, or Negroes, with black skins; the Amu, or Semites, with yellow skins; and the Remitu, or Egyptians, with dark brown skins. A chamber (VII) leads from this hall to the right, but the scenes in it are much blackened by smoke, and are not of interest. On the right wall (14) the king is led forward by Thoth and Harmachis, to be presented to Osiris. On the middle wall (15) the king is in the presence of Osiris. On the left wall (16) the king offers an image of "Truth" to Osiris.

THE TOMBS OF THE KINGS

The remaining chambers of this tomb are now closed to the public. The scenes are much damaged, and they are not of great interest.

NO. 12. AN UNINSCRIBED TOMB

This tomb is situated a few yards from the tomb of Amenhotep IInd (No. 35). It is not inscribed, and its date cannot be stated with certainty. It is now blocked with debris.

NO. 13. THE TOMB OF THE CHANCELLOR BEY

This tomb is excavated at the south end of the valley, on the right of the path leading to the tomb of Tausert (No. 14) and Sety IInd (No. 15). It is interesting as being the only tomb in the valley of royal size made for a non-royal personage. The noble for whom it was excavated was named Bey. He held the position of Chancellor during the reign of Queen Tausert (No. 14), and rose to very great power (about B.C. 1210). The tomb has not been cleared in modern times, and is now almost totally blocked with debris.

NO. 14. THE TOMB OF TAUSERT AND SETNEKHT

This tomb is situated at the extreme south of the royal necropolis. From the custodians' house one walks southwards, keeping to the right at the junction of two paths which is presently reached. One now passes the tomb of Septah (No. 47) on the left, and the tomb of Bey (No. 13) on the right. The path now leads round to the left, and this tomb is to be seen on the right, closed by a small iron door. It was excavated for Queen Tausert, who reigned in her own right about B.C. 1210, and therefore was entitled to a tomb in this valley. In the first passages she is seen with her husband Septah; but by the time that the tomb had penetrated to the inner halls, Septah had died and Tausert had married Sety IInd. The figure of the latter king is, thus, to be seen in these inner halls with Tausert. After the death of Tausert there was general disorder in Egypt, and it may be supposed that the tomb was then plundered. The following king, Setnekht, when he had restored order, began the excavation of tomb No. 11, but abandoned it as recorded above. He then usurped this tomb of Tausert, and changed the figures and inscriptions accordingly. Some of the jewels of the queen had survived the destruction; and these were placed, perhaps at the orders of Setnekht, in a convenient rock chamber (No. 56) where they were recently found in 1908 by Mr. Theodore M. Davis. Her body, however, seems to have been left in the tomb. The body of Setnekht seems to have suffered destruction at the hands of later robbers, for it has not been found. The priests who were hiding the royal remains in the tomb of Amenhotep IInd seem to have entered this tomb, and to have found a mummy there which they believed to be that of Setnekht. The tomb was evidently in great disorder, but they placed this mummy in the empty coffin of Setnekht and carried it to the hiding-place, where it was discovered in modern times. When it was unrolled, however, it was found to be that of a woman; and one must therefore suppose that it was in reality the body of Queen Tausert, since all other queens of this period were buried in the Valley of the Tombs of the Queens. The tomb then remained open and was visited by travellers in Greek times. It has now been cleaned, and may be visited by candle-light.

Entering the first corridor one sees on the right (1) the figures of Tausert and Septah in the presence of Ptah, Harmachis, and other gods. On the opposite wall (2) Tausert and Septah stand before Harmachis, Anubis, Isis, and others. The second corridor is damaged. In the third corridor to right and left we see the cartouches and figure of Setnekht superimposed on plaster over the earlier figures. We now pass into a small chamber (IV) which leads into a larger room (V), above the door of which Anubis and Horus are seen worshipping Osiris. Continuing on our way downwards we pass through Rooms VI and VIII, the walls of which are covered with crude paintings of the time of Setnekht superimposed over those of Tausert. Hall IX is now reached, the roof of which is supported by eight pillars. This was the original burial chamber of Tausert; and it is clear that when the hall was made the queen's consort Septah had already died and Sety IInd

THE TOMB OF TAUSERT AND SETNEKHT

THE TOMBS OF THE KINGS

had taken his place; for the figure of the latter king is to be seen on one of the far pillars to the left. Two further corridors, added by Setnekht when he usurped the tomb, bring us to the final hall (XIII) where he was buried. In the middle, lying upon its side, is the lid of the granite sarcophagus of Setnekht, beautifully sculptured to represent a recumbent figure of Osiris. The body of the sarcophagus is broken. It does not seem to have been usurped from the original burial of Tausert, but appears rather to have been made for Setnekht.

NO. 15. THE TOMB OF SETY IInd

This tomb is situated not far to the east of No. 14, at the top of the pathway. It was made for King User-kheperu-ra Sety-mer-en-ptah, commonly called Sety IInd, who reigned B.C. 1209-1205. The king's mummy was carried to the tomb of Amenhotep IInd by the priests of B.C. 960, and it was there found in modern times. This is the first tomb to be cut into the rock without much downward gradient; and in other ways the style of the work shows a considerable advance on previous customs. It is a curious fact that the cartouches and figures near the doorway have been erased and re-executed. There seems little doubt, however, that the same cartouches (*i.e.* those of Sety IInd) were erased and were rewritten, and the plan of the tomb seems to preclude the possibility of its having been commenced by an earlier Pharaoh. It seems more likely that Sety IInd was for a time exiled, his name being erased; and later was reinstated, his name being then reinscribed.

The sculpture in the first corridor of the tomb is beautifully executed. On the left as one enters the king is seen worshipping Pa-Ra "The Sun," and Nefertum. On the right he worships Ra and Seker. We now pass through corridors, upon the plastered walls of which the paintings have never been finished; and presently we reach a small chamber, on the walls of which there are various figures of the king and of many sacred symbols each resting in its shrine. We then enter a four-pillared hall, from which a further passage descends. On the pillars are the deities Nefertum, Horus, Harmachis, Ptah, Anubis, Horus-supporter-of-his-mother, Maat, and Seb. The tomb comes to an abrupt end a short distance farther on, the king having died. The walls have been hastily painted, and on the ceiling a large figure of Nut has been rapidly put in. Fragments of a sarcophagus are here to be seen.

No. 16. THE TOMB OF RAMESES Ist

This tomb is situated to the east of the lunching tomb (No. 10). It was made for Ra-men-pehti Ramessu (Rameses Ist) who reigned about B.C. 1315. A mummy which appears to have been his was found at Dêr el Bahri in the royal hiding-place. The tomb is now lit by electric light, and is worthy of a visit. It is much more imposing at the entrance than those of all earlier kings except Horemheb (the immediate predecessor of Rameses Ist). The visitor will remember how small and rough the first stairways and passages are in the tomb of Amenhotep IInd; but here they are wider and more carefully worked. The king reigned so short a time that the tomb was never finished, and he had to be buried in the chamber at the bottom of the second flight of steps, which, if the tomb had been continued, would have been developed into the well. In this little chamber stands the large sarcophagus of granite in which the royal mummy rested. The walls around are covered with well-preserved paintings. It will be remembered that in the tomb of Amenhotep IInd (No. 35) the figures of the king and gods were painted in outline only. The next king, Thothmes IVth, first originated the custom of colouring the figures as completely in the tomb as they were coloured in the temples; and here we see the last phase of this custom. In the next tomb which we shall visit they will be found to be executed in coloured relief.

On the right as one enters the goddess Maat, Truth, is seen, and the king is shown offering to Nefertum, a deity usually distinguished by the lotus which rises from his head. On the west wall the boat of the sun is seen drawn by four figures; and other mythological scenes are here represented, illustrating chapter ii. of "The Book of the Portals." Below the boat the god Tum is seen slaying the evil serpent Apophis. On the south wall, behind the sarcophagus, one sees on the right the god Horus-son-of-Isis leading the king, behind whom are Tum and Neith, towards Osiris, before whom stands the figure of Horus-supporter-of-his-mother (see page 195). At the other end of this wall the king makes an offering to the beetle-headed Tum-Ra-Khepera; and over the door of the recess he kneels between a kneeling jackal-headed figure and a kneeling hawk-headed figure, representing the spirits of the two ancient cities of Pe and Nekhen, the primitive capitals of Lower and Upper Egypt. In

THE TOMBS OF THE KINGS 213

the recess a figure of Osiris-Chieftain-of-the-Underworld is shown, supported by the ram-headed god of the sunset and of death. Before them the cobra Nesert, the deity of the harvest, is coiled, typifying the renewal of life. On the east wall the king is seen between the jackal-headed Anubis and the hawk-headed Horus. Near by are various mythological figures, amongst which we may notice the twelve hours of the night in the form of goddesses ascending the steps to the apex of the midnight. At the left of the entrance the goddess Maat is seen again, and the king is represented in the presence of Ptah, near whom is the *ded*-symbol, so commonly used in ancient Egyptian religion.

NO. 17. THE TOMB OF SETY Ist

This tomb, excavated for Ra-men-maat Sety-mer-en-Ptah (Sety Ist), who reigned B.C. 1313-1292, is the most imposing sepulchre in the valley. Sety Ist was the son of Rameses Ist, whose tomb has just been described; and the development in style is very striking. No longer are the first corridors roughly cut and left undecorated; but now the inscriptions and figures begin from the entrance, and continue uninterrupted down the whole length of the tomb. Sculptured reliefs, brilliantly coloured, now take the place of the paintings seen in earlier tombs; and those who have visited the great temple at Abydos will recognise the beautiful workmanship which they have admired on the walls of that ruin. The mummy of Sety Ist was removed by the priests to Dêr el Bahri, where it was hidden with many more royal bodies; and thus it has been preserved to us, being now exhibited in the Cairo Museum. The tomb was apparently open in Greek times, but it became silted up, and was rediscovered in 1817 by Belzoni. It was then said to be quite undamaged; but from that time, until it was closed with an iron door in recent years, it was left open, and consequently was much cut about by thieves and early archæologists (it would be difficult to say which of the two did the greater damage). The great alabaster sarcophagus found *in situ* by Belzoni was taken to the Soane Museum in London, where it now stands.

Entering the tomb, the visitor observes upon the left (1) the figure of the king standing before Harmachis, while just beyond it (2) the sun's disk, in which are the figures of the ram-headed god of the setting sun and the beetle-shaped god of the dawn, is shown passing between the two horizons. The long texts which

The first corridors.

follow are from the "Book of the Praisings of the Sun." One now passes down a stairway, and on the left, at the top of the wall, thirty-seven forms of the sun-god are shown, while on the right thirty-nine are seen. Near the bottom of the steps one sees on the left (3) a kneeling figure of Isis, and on the right (4) a similar figure of Nephthys. The fine profiles of these figures should be noted. Corridor III is now reached. On the right wall (5) the scenes represent the journey of the boat of the sun through the fourth division of the underworld, *i.e.* the fourth hour of the night. On the left side (6) the boat passes through the fifth division, drawn by seven gods and seven goddesses. The inscriptions on these walls are taken from the fourth and fifth chapters of the "Book of that which is in the Underworld." One now passes into a chamber (IV) upon the walls of which various gods are shown. On the right (7) the king is seen in the presence of Hathor, Isis, Hathor again, and Osiris. On the adjoining wall (8) Osiris, Anubis, and Horus are shown. On the left (9) the king is shown in the presence of Isis, Hathor, and Osiris.

The middle halls and corridors.

Hall V is now entered, the roof of which is supported by four columns. On the right wall of this hall (10) the sun's journey through the fifth division of the underworld, from the "Book of the Portals," is shown. On the left wall the journey through the fourth division, from the same book, is to be seen. On the lower part of the wall (11) the god Horus is shown, and standing before him are the four divisions of mankind, each represented by four figures. First there are four Egyptians, then four Asiatics with beards, then four negroes, and finally four Libyans

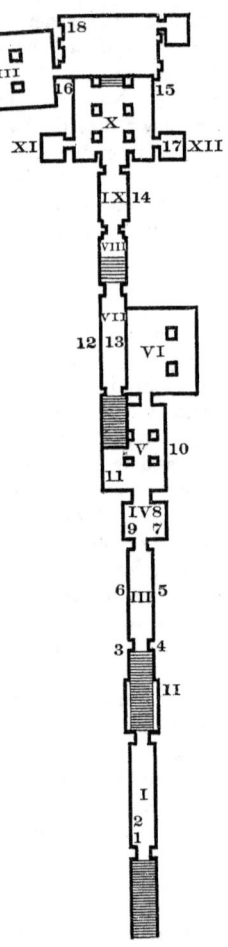

THE TOMB OF SETY I.

THE TOMBS OF THE KINGS

with feathers in their hair. On the pillars the king is seen in the presence of various gods, some of whom embrace him. From this hall a second pillared room (VI) leads; but here the scenes, which represent the journey of the sun through the ninth to eleventh divisions of the underworld, are only sketched in outline, the chamber never having been finished. It was intended only as a blind for any robbers who might penetrate into the tomb. The main chambers are reached down a stairway descending through the floor of Hall V, which was entirely closed after the funeral. Robbers would thus think that this Hall VI formed the end of the tomb. The ruse only partially succeeded; the robbers did not detect the stairway, but, finding that the walls of Hall VI rang hollow, they broke through into Corridor VH below, as may now be seen. This corridor, now approached down the stairs, has some interesting scenes upon its walls. On the left (12), along the top of the wall, one sees a series of statues of the king represented as standing upon pedestals, while priests make offerings and perform ceremonies before them. Such statues were placed in royal and in other tombs as a place of habitation for the *Ka* or "double" of the deceased. The accompanying texts are taken from the "Chapter of the Opening of the Mouth," *i.e.* the ritual relating to the endowing of the statues and mummy of a dead person with life. On the opposite wall (13) there are similar scenes, which are also continued into Corridor VIII. We now enter Room IX. On the right wall (14), from north to south, the following gods are seen to be worshipped by the king—Hathor (the corner figure), Anubis, Isis, Horus, Hathor again, with a beautifully executed profile, and Osiris.

The great burial-hall (X) is now reached. Six pillars support the roof; and at the farther end the floor descends to a lower level. The scenes and inscriptions in the first part of the hall describe the sun's journey through the first and second divisions of the underworld. On the right wall (15) we may notice the twelve black-headed hours of darkness. On the opposite wall (16) there are twelve hour-figures, which are noteworthy by reason of the unconventional manner in which they are drawn. The shoulders are almost correctly drawn; and the contrast between these and the other figures in the hall is striking. In the side-room (XII) there is an interesting representation (17) of the cow of Hathor standing across the heavens, with the stars and planets of the universe spread under her. The texts in this room tell the story of the destruction of mankind by the sun-god, then king of

The burial-hall and adjoining rooms.

Egypt, after which that deity retired to the heavens. The king's sarcophagus stood at the lower end of the hall, but it has now been removed, as stated above. This portion of the hall has an arched roof, which is decorated with a series of astronomical figures. On the left there is a recess (18) in which the figure of the king identified with Osiris is seen. Two religious symbols, connected with the god Wepwat stand beside him; and on the right Anubis performs a mystical ceremony; while on the left are the four genii of the underworld. Further passages and chambers were cut in the rock beyond this, but they are now in a ruinous state. Room XIII remains to be visited. Here the sun's journey through the sixth, seventh, and eighth divisions of the Underworld is recorded. One of the pillars has fallen: on the other there are figures of the king, Ptah, and Osiris. A shelf runs around the room, upon which the paraphernalia of the funeral was placed.

NO. 18. THE TOMB OF RAMESES XIth

The tomb of Ra-kheper-maat-setep-en-ra Rameses-Amen-her-khepshef-mery-Amen, known as Rameses XIth (B.C. 1120), is situated just to the east of No. 17. It contains practically no inscriptions or reliefs, and the electric engine has been housed in it. It is therefore closed to the public. The mummy of the Pharaoh was found at Dêr el Bahri (?) in the coffin of a certain Nesikhonsu.

NO. 19. THE TOMB OF PRINCE MENTUHERKHEPESHEF

This tomb, which has recently been cleared, is situated between the tombs of Thothmes IVth (No. 43) and Hatshepsut (No. 20), under the eastern cliffs of the valley. It was made for "the Eldest Royal Son of the King, the *sem*-priest, Chief Royal Scribe of the Two Lands, Great Superintendent of the Troops," Mentuherkhepeshef, who lived towards the close of the long line of Ramesside kings. The tomb, which is obviously unfinished, consists of but a single corridor, at the end of which a recess for the coffin has been sunk. On entering the tomb one notices on either side the drawings of the swing doors, which, as may be seen from the pivot-holes at the top, actually stood here. On either side of the corridor there are delicately executed paintings representing the prince in the presence of various gods. On the right wall, from west to east,

THE TOMBS OF THE KINGS

these gods are—Ptah, Thoth, Khnum, Hapi, Duamutef, Mersegert ("the-Lover-of-Silence"), and Sekhmet. On the left the gods are—Osiris, Ptah, Khonsu, Bast, Amseth, Kebh, and Amen-Ra. The luxury of the period can be seen in the costly and elaborate robes which the prince wears ; while the delicacy of the colouring suggest considerable refinement in artistic taste.

NO. 20. THE TOMB OF HATSHEPSUT

The famous queen, Ra-maa-ka Hatshepsut (B.C. 1500), constructed the great temple of Dêr el Bahri as her mortuary temple. She therefore cut her tomb into the cliffs of the valley at a point immediately behind this temple, so that, penetrating far into the rock, her body might lie deep below the shrines where her soul would be worshipped. The rock, however, was very bad at the point selected, and the workmen had to turn their tunnel to one side. The tomb was discovered in recent years, but was found to be in a most ruinous condition. The passages are very long ; but, like the tombs of Amenhotep Ist, Thothmes Ist, and Thothmes IInd, it has no well. In the burial-chamber the sarcophagus of the queen was found, but her body has been lost. The sarcophagus of Thothmes Ist, her father, was also found here ; and it would seem that the queen had removed the Pharaoh from his own tomb, No. 38, and had placed his body beside her.

NO. 21. AN UNINSCRIBED TOMB

This small tomb, which is situated not far down the valley from the tomb of Hatshepsut, may have belonged to a noble of her reign, but there is no direct evidence as to its identification.

NO. 22. THE TOMB OF AMENHOTEP IIIrd

This tomb is situated in what is known as the western valley, that is to say, the great gorge which opens to the west from the main road, some four hundred or five hundred yards before the main valley is reached. Far up this gorge, in virgin ground, King Neb-maa-ra Amenhotep-heq-uast (Amenhotep IIIrd) excavated his tomb ; and here, after a brilliant reign, from B.C. 1411 to 1375, he was buried. The tomb does not seem to have been known to the priests who transported the royal mummies to other hiding-places, for the body of Amenhotep IIIrd was not thus rescued, but fell a victim to later robbers. The tomb was known to Napoleon's expedition, and it lay open until a few years ago, when an iron door was affixed to the entrance. It is not open to the general public.

One first passes down a long passage cut in three sections which slopes rapidly downwards. The well is then reached, around the walls of which there are paintings showing the king in the presence of various gods. Crossing this well, one enters a two-pillared hall, through the floor of which a stairway leads down to further chambers, exactly as in the case of earlier tombs of the XVIIIth dynasty. This presently brings one to a small chamber on the walls of which are some much-damaged paintings representing the king before the gods. One now passes into a pillared hall, at the far end of which, in a sunken recess, the broken fragments of the sarcophagus are to be seen. One or two much-damaged chambers complete the tomb.

NO. 23. THE TOMB OF AY

After the death of Amenhotep IIIrd the Court was removed for a short time to Tell el Amarna, where, under the direction of the Pharaoh Akhnaton, a new religion absorbed its attention. Smenkhkara and Tutankhamen were the succeeding Pharaohs, but neither of their tombs have yet been found (1908). They were succeeded (B.C. 1350) by Ay (Ra-kheper-kheperu-ari-maat, Neter-at-Ay-neter-heq-uast), who was not of royal birth. The tomb of this Pharaoh was excavated in the western valley near that of Amenhotep IIIrd. Entering the tomb, one walks down a passage and a flight of steps, past a small chamber, and so reaches a larger room, on the walls of which are paintings. On the right there are some figures of apes, after which the tomb is sometimes called "the Tomb of the Apes." On the east wall the king, with his wife, is seen boomeranging birds. Again, he stoops down to pluck reeds. On the left wall the king and his *Ka* stand before Nut, Hathor, and Osiris. The broken sarcophagus, once very fine, lies here in the burial-hall. The visitor will notice in this tomb a great freedom from the conventional Egyptian type of paintings, and it would seem that Ay did not regard himself exactly as a royalty.

THE TOMBS OF THE KINGS 219

NOS. 24 AND 25. UNINSCRIBED TOMBS

These two tombs are situated in the western valley not far from the two royal sepulchres just described. They contain no inscriptions, but they probably belonged to princes or nobles of the end of the XVIIIth dynasty.

NOS. 26 TO 31. UNINSCRIBED TOMBS

These six tombs are situated in various parts of the main valley. They are mostly pit-tombs, and contain no inscriptions. They probably belonged to princes or viziers of the XVIIIth dynasty, who were buried near the Pharaohs they had served.

NOS. 32 AND 33. UNINSCRIBED TOMBS

The first of these is situated just to the west of No. 42 (Thothmes IInd?), and is devoid of inscription. The second tomb is situated immediately to the left of the tomb of Thothmes IIIrd (No. 34). It was perhaps used as a burial-place of one of his family, or perhaps for a vizir such as Rekhmara, whose tomb-chapel is to be seen at Shêkh abd' el Gûrneh, but whose burial-pit is not known.

NO. 34. THE TOMB OF THOTHMES IIIrd

This tomb is excavated in a "chimney" of rock at the southeast corner of the valley. From the custodians' house one walks southwards, turning to the left at the junction of the paths, and thus leaving the tombs of Septah (47), Bay (13), and Tausert (14) on one's right. The path terminates in a flight of steps leading up the "chimney." Ascending these, and crossing a platform of rock, one finds in the far corner the mouth of the tomb, which is approached by a steep flight of steps. The situation is most impressive, and repays a visit; but the descent of the tomb is somewhat difficult. The coffin and mummy of the great Pharaoh, Ra-men-kheper Thothmes IIIrd (B.C. 1501-1447), were found at Dêr el Bahri, where they had been hidden by the priests. The tomb is now open to the public, but it is not lit with electric light, and candles have therefore to be used. Passing into the tomb one descends a steeply sloping passage, which brings one to a second flight of steps. At the bottom of these one enters a second passage, which terminates in the well, now crossed by a bridge. Thothmes IIIrd is the first king to have used a well in his tomb. All his successors employed the same device until the end of the dynasty. This well was made partly for the purpose of deceiving would-be robbers, for the entrance to the chambers on the opposite side was blocked, and was not visible to the eye. The robbers would thus descend the well in search of the burial, and, finding none, would think that the tomb had never been used. The well was also intended to carry off the torrents of water which the king knew would be likely to rush down this rock "chimney" on rainy days, and might penetrate into the burial-chamber. So far the tomb is almost precisely like that of Amenhotep IInd (No. 35). We now enter a two-pillared hall, upon the walls of which there is a long list of 741 gods and demi-gods. There is a similar hall in No. 35, but it is not decorated. As in No. 35, one now passes down a flight of steps in the left-hand corner. This flight was originally blocked up, so that a robber would believe this hall to be the end of the tomb. Descending the steps one reaches the large burial-hall, which is of oval shape, probably to suggest a cartouche; and at the far end, behind the two pillars which support the roof, the royal sarcophagus is to be seen. This again is like that of Amenhotep IInd. Upon the walls of this chamber there are the texts and illustrations of the "Book of that which is in the Underworld," executed in outline as in No. 35. On the left face of the nearer pillar there is an interesting scene very roughly executed, showing the king being suckled by Isis, here shown as a tree-goddess, of whom only the breast and arm are depicted as though growing out of the trunk. Behind the king stand his queens Ramery and Aahset, his secondary wife Nebtkheru (whose name is not enclosed in a cartouche, as are those of the two first named), and his daughter Nefertari. Above this scene one sees the king and his mother floating through the underworld in a boat. This mark of filial piety is the more appreciated when one remembers that the king's mother was a woman named Ast, who was not of very lofty origin. The tomb has been left partly unfinished, as though the king, occupied by the administration of the great empire he had built up, had not bothered to give much attention to his last resting-place.

THE TOMBS OF THE KINGS

NO. 35. THE TOMB OF AMENHOTEP IInd

The tomb of Ra-aa-kheperu Amenhotep-neter-heq-an, the son and successor of Thothmes IIIrd (B.C. 1448-1420), is situated at the west side of the royal area. A pathway leads westwards from near the custodians' house, and brings one to the mouth of the tomb. This sepulchre was so well hidden that the priests of the ninth century B.C., who possessed the secret of its location, decided to use it as a hiding-place for the royal mummies which, in their own tombs, were in danger of destruction at the hands of robbers. Here the bodies of many of the Pharaohs were found in recent years, as well as that of Amenhotep IInd himself. The latter body was left in the tomb, and may now be seen there by visitors. The tomb is lit by electric light, and is perhaps the most impressive in the valley. Those who desire to see only the six or eight best tombs should visit this sepulchre first. Chronologically it is the earliest of the group of tombs now lit by electric light, and previous to it in date there is only the tomb of Thothmes IIIrd open to the public.

One descends a flight of steps, and passes down a sloping corridor roughly cut out of the rock. A second flight of steps and a second corridor brings one to a deep well, across which a modern bridge has been placed. As has been said at the beginning of this chapter, the purpose of the well was twofold. In the first place, it carried off the rain-water which otherwise might soak into the tomb; and in the second place it led the tomb-robbers astray. The entrance to the farther chambers on the opposite side of the well was blocked, and hidden by plaster, across which the painting was extended, and thus the tomb appeared to end at the bottom of the well, where a little chamber was cut as a further blind. Crossing the bridge, one passes into a two-pillared hall, which is devoid of decoration. A stairway descends through the floor at the left-hand corner of the hall. These stairs were filled up after the funeral, and the robbers who penetrated as far as this would be likely to believe that they had reached the end of the tomb. Descending the stairs one passes into a six-pillared hall, all the walls of which are covered with inscriptions and scenes from the "Book of that which is in the Underworld," roughly painted upon drab-coloured stucco to represent papyrus. (See introduction to this chapter, p. 192.) Upon the pillars one sees the king in the presence of various gods, boldly drawn in outline. At the far end of the hall, the floor of which is here at a deeper level, the sarcophagus stands, and in it lies the mummy of the Pharaoh himself. The native custodian generally turns out all the lights except that which falls upon the mummy, and the effect thus produced is most impressive. The king appears to be lying peacefully asleep. The likeness, however, has not been very closely preserved by the embalmers, for the nose was evidently more aquiline in life, and the mouth not so wide. The limbs, now thin and withered, were in life robust and muscular; for this king was a man of great physical strength, and is said to have been able to draw a bow which none of his soldiers were strong enough to use. He was a strong and powerful ruler, who consolidated the many kingdoms and races which his military genius and that of his father had incorporated in the Egyptian empire. He was perhaps less humane than his temperate father; and on one occasion he is said to have slain in cold blood with his own hands a number of rebel princes, while another was tied head downwards to the prow of his dahabiyeh when he returned from the wars. It is interesting to recall these and other scenes from his life of thirty-three centuries ago, as one looks upon his actual body; and the visitor will find it worth his while to read something of the king's history before coming to see his body. The wonderful preservation of the hall in which he lies, the fresh colouring on the undamaged walls, and the newly polished appearance of the quarzite-sandstone sarcophagus, give the impression that Ancient Egypt is not as far removed from us as we had thought.

In a side chamber to the right there lie three bodies which were found in the tomb, without names upon them. One of these is the mummy of an elderly woman, whose brown hair, however, had not yet been silvered by age. This is possibly the body of Amenhotep's wife, Queen Taa, though it is perhaps that of some other queen, such as Hatshepsut, who had been removed here for safety. The second mummy is that of a young boy of about fourteen years of age, who wears the side-lock of hair indicative of youth. This young prince may have been one of the elder sons of Amenhotep IInd, who died before his father, thus leaving Thothmes IVth to succeed to the throne, which he had never expected to do. The third body is that of a young woman, probably under thirty years of age, who was perhaps a daughter or secondary wife of Amenhotep.

THE TOMBS OF THE KINGS

NO. 36. THE TOMB OF PRINCE MAHERPRA

This tomb lies between Nos. 13 and 35. It was made for a noble named Maherpra, who held the offices of royal tutor and royal standard-bearer during the reign of Hatshepsut. It was discovered a few years ago, and was found to contain many antiquities which are now exhibited in the Cairo Museum.

NO. 37. AN UNINSCRIBED TOMB

This tomb lies on the left-hand side of the foot of the steps which lead up to the tomb of Thothmes IIIrd (No. 34). It is uninscribed, and probably belonged to some noble of the reign of Thothmes IInd or IIIrd.

NO. 38. THE TOMB OF THOTHMES Ist

This is the earliest tomb actually in the valley, being made for King Ra-aa-kheper-ka Thothmes Ist (B.C. 1535–1501), apparently at the suggestion of one of his nobles named Anena. It is situated between the tomb of Tausert (No. 14) and that of Sety IInd (No. 15). It is not open to the general public. One passes down a flight of steps and presently enters a square room. A second flight of steps leads on into the burial-hall, the roof of which is supported by one column. The walls have been covered with stucco, but this has now fallen. In this hall stand fragments of the base of the sarcophagus of quartzite-sandstone. In seems probable that Queen Hatshepsut, his daughter, transferred the king's body from this insignificant tomb to her own more elaborate sepulchre, for a sarcophagus bearing the king's name was found in her tomb. The mummy was later hidden at Dêr el Bahri, where it was found in modern times.

NO. 39. THE TOMB OF AMENHOTEP Ist

The situation of this tomb is remarkable. It lies high up on the hillside above the royal valley, at its extreme south end. By the pathway which passes above the tomb of Thothmes IIIrd one ascends the sloping side of the hill until the summit of the cliffs overlooking Dêr el Medineh is almost reached. Here some houses used by the watchmen who guarded this tomb are seen, and about

200 feet to the west, in the gully, the entrance to the tomb will be found. The Abbot Papyrus, in which a record of the Ramesside inspection of certain tombs is given, describes the position of the tomb accurately, stating that it is 120 cubits (*i.e.* about 200 feet) down the hill from these houses ;[1] and we are here told that it belonged to King Zeser-ka-ra Amenhotep (Ist) who reigned about B.C. 1557–1545. The tomb was then found to be intact; but the priests who hid the royal mummies six hundred years after the death of Amenhotep Ist, removed the body of that king to Dêr el Bahri, where it was found in modern times. The tomb is entered down a rough flight of steps which brings one to a low doorway. Passing through this, one enters a chamber from which a tunnel leading to the ruined burial-hall is cut. A further chamber contains some bones and other fragments of the burial. No inscriptions remain, and the tomb has no interest to the visitor, except as being the earliest sepulchre in the vicinity, and the precursor of the tombs in the valley below.

NOS. 40 AND 41. UNINSCRIBED TOMBS

These two tombs are uninscribed and are of no particular interest. They were probably made for nobles of the XVIIIth dynasty, who desired to be buried near the kings they had served.

NO. 42. THE TOMB OF THOTHMES IInd (?)

This tomb is situated on the right-hand side of the path which leads to the tomb of Thothmes IIIrd (No. 34), at the foot of the steps which give access to the crevice in the rocks where that tomb is excavated. One descends a rough flight of steps leading down to the door; passes along a sloping passage; enters a small chamber in which are stacked some pots; and thence one passes into the burial-hall. This hall is oval, or cartouche-shaped, and the roof is supported by two pillars. The walls have been plastered and tinted drab-colour, but no inscriptions or figures have been painted there. The *kherker* ornamentation around the top of the walls has been put in, but the tomb was left unfinished. A coffin of quartzite-sandstone, like that of Thothmes IIIrd, but entirely uninscribed and unpolished, stands at the far end of the hall, the lid lying beside it.

[1] See the present writer's article regarding its identification in *Les Annales*.

THE TOMBS OF THE KINGS

There seems little doubt that this tomb was made for a Pharaoh, but was left unfinished owing to his sudden death, though it was certainly used as his burial-place, since pots and other articles from the burial have been found. It is similar in style to the tomb of Thothmes IIIrd, but is smaller in size. It is probably earlier than the time of Thothmes IIIrd, for it has no well, and in this it is like the tombs of Thothmes Ist and Hatshepsut. It is not later than the reign of that king, for the custom of shaping the burial-hall into an oval died out after that time. Now the tomb of Thothmes IInd has not yet been identified, though the king's mummy and inner coffin were found at Dêr el Bahri, where they had been hidden by the priests. Thothmes IInd, after a short reign, died in a somewhat sudden manner at the height of the great feud which so confused the reigns of Thothmes Ist, IInd, and IIIrd, and Hatshepsut; and it would thus seem very likely that this tomb was rapidly made as his burial-place. In the event of no other tomb being found which can be proved to belong to Thothmes IInd, one may say that this sepulchre may be regarded as belonging to him.[1]

NO. 43. THE TOMB OF THOTHMES IVth

The tomb of Ra-men-kheperu Thothmes-kha-khau (Thothmes IVth) is excavated at the foot of the south-east cliffs of the valley, above and to the right of the tombs of Mentuherkhepeshef (No. 19) and Hatshepsut (No. 20). Thothmes IVth died at the age of about twenty-six years, in B.C. 1411, but before B.C. 1350 the tomb had been robbed. In the eighth year of the reign of Horemheb (B.C. 1342) the tomb was entered by Maya, "Superintendent of Works in the Necropolis," and the rifled mummy of its occupant was placed once more in its coffin, from which the plunderers had dragged it. In about B.C. 960 the mummy was carried to the tomb of Amenhotep IInd and there hidden. At the time of writing (1909) the tomb is closed to the public. One enters the tomb down the usual flight of steps, and passes into a corridor, at the end of which a second flight of steps leads to a second corridor. The well is then reached, and upon its walls are some interesting paintings representing the king in the presence of the gods. In the tomb of Amenhotep IInd, the father of Thothmes IVth, it will be

[1] It would seem that the modern excavators found traces of the burial of a noble named Sennefer in this tomb. But this must have been due to some later shifting, for the tomb is certainly royal.

remembered that the gods were drawn in outline. Here we have them completely painted for the first time in this necropolis. Crossing the well one reaches a pillared hall; and it is particularly interesting to observe the ancient rope by which the plunderers ascended, fastened round one of these columns, and still hanging down the well. A further flight of steps, a corridor, and again another flight of steps, brings one to a chamber, on two of the walls of which are paintings showing the king with the gods, while on the third wall is the inscription stating that the above-mentioned Maya had entered the tomb. Then follows the four-pillared burial-hall, in which the fine sarcophagus of the king still lies. The sarcophagus is much bigger than that of Amenhotep IInd, but the burial-hall is of somewhat the same shape. Chambers leading off to either side contain remains of the original burial.

NO. 44. THE TOMB OF THE LADY TENTKAREU

This tomb is situated between the tombs of Hatshepsut (No. 20) and Rameses XIIth (No. 4). In it the remains of a lady named Tentkareu were found, she having been one of the women of the court.

NO. 45. THE TOMB OF PRINCE USERHAT

This tomb lies not far from No. 44. It was made for a noble of the XVIIIth dynasty, but it is not inscribed or decorated.

NO. 46. THE TOMB OF YUAA AND TUAU

Between the tomb of Rameses XIIth (No. 4) and that of Rameses IIIrd (No. 3) a small tomb was discovered in 1905, which was approached by a flight of steps and a sloping passage. It was found to contain the bodies of Yuaa and Tuau, the parents of Queen Thiy, the consort of Amenhotep IIIrd (B.C. 1411–1375). With them was a number of interesting antiquities, now exhibited in the Cairo Museum (the Davis room). The tomb itself is uninscribed and is of no particular interest.

NO. 47. THE TOMB OF SEPTAH

The tomb of King Akh-en-ra-setep-en-ra Mer-en-ptah-Septah (B.C. 1215–1209) lies on the left of the path which leads up to tombs 14 and 15. Septah was the Pharaoh who was married to

THE TOMBS OF THE KINGS

Queen Tausert (No. 14) previous to her marriage to Sety IInd (No. 15). His figures are seen beside those of the queen in the first corridors of her tomb. Soon after the burial had taken place, agents, perhaps of Sety IInd, entered the tomb and erased the name of the Pharaoh wherever they found it. Later, the priests who were transporting the royal mummies to a place of safety entered the sepulchre and carried the body of the king to the tomb of Amenhotep IInd, where it was found in recent times. They, or some other well-wishers, restored the erased cartouches of the king. The inner chambers collapsed at some time or other; and the first corridors alone remain at the present day.

On the right and left as we enter the figure of the goddess of Truth (Maat) is seen with wings outstretched. On our left there is a fine representation of Septah addressing Harmachis; and beyond this is the usual representation of the sun passing between the two horizons. Near the bottom of the accessible portions of the tomb, on the left, there is a scene showing the mummy of the king, or of Osiris, tended by Isis, Nephthys, and the jackal-headed Anubis, while above and below are the jackals of the Necropolis, seated upon the gates of the underworld. The ceiling, which, though much damaged, is very fine, should be observed.

NO. 48. THE TOMB OF THE VIZIR AMENEMAPT

This small undecorated tomb contained the well-preserved body of the Vizir Amenemapt, who lived during the XVIIIth dynasty.

NOS. 49 TO 54. UNINSCRIBED TOMBS

These small tombs have been discovered during the last few years, but they were mostly empty. One tomb contained the mummies of monkeys and a dog, perhaps the pets of Amenhotep IInd, near whose tomb they were found. They are of no interest to the visitor.

NO. 55. THE TOMB OF QUEEN THIY

This tomb is situated just to the south of that of Rameses Xth (No. 6). It seems to have been made for Queen Thiy, the wife of Amenhotep IIIrd (B.C. 1411–1375); but it would appear that her body was removed from it to make room for that of the " heretic "

King Akhnaton which had been brought back to Thebes from Tell el Amarna, probably by Tutankhamen. The latter body was found in the tomb when it was opened in 1907, but some of Queen Thiy's funeral furniture still remained there. The tomb is not inscribed, and now that the antiquities have been removed, it is not of much interest.

No. 56. AN UNINSCRIBED TOMB

This tomb, situated just to the north of No. 57 and almost opposite No. 4, is not inscribed, and there is no clue as to whom it was made for originally. In it was found the jewellery of Queen Tausert (No. 14), which had perhaps been placed here by Setnekht, who usurped her tomb.

No. 57. THE TOMB OF HOREMHEB

At the time of writing (1908-9) this tomb has not been opened to the public. It was discovered recently; and as the publication of the discovery has not yet been made, an account of it would be premature. A long series of passages and steps lead down to a well, on the opposite side of which there is a pillared hall, and beyond it a further passage leads down to the burial-hall, where stands the sarcophagus. Some excellent paintings adorn the walls.

CHAPTER IX

THE MORTUARY TEMPLES OF THE KINGS OF DYNASTIES XVIII. TO XX.

IN the last chapter the visitor has been introduced to the Valley of the Tombs of the Kings, in which lie the sepulchres of the Pharaohs of Dynasties XVIII. to XX. ; and it has been pointed out that the mortuary temples of these sovereigns were erected at the edge of the desert some distance from their tombs. It is now necessary to describe this line of temples, which runs the whole length of the necropolis on the border-line of the fields. The mortuary temples now known are the following :—

Amenhotep Ist	(p. 243),	whose tomb is No.	39 (p. 223).
Thothmes Ist	(p. 243),	,, ,, ,,	38 (p. 223).
Thothmes IInd	(p. 243),	,, ,, ,,	42 (p. 224).
Thothmes IIIrd	(p. 255),	,, ,, ,,	34 (p. 219).
Amenhotep IInd	(p. 255),	,, ,, ,,	35 (p. 221).
Thothmes IVth	(p. 249),	,, ,, ,,	43 (p. 225).
Amenhotep IIIrd	(p. 245),	,, ,, ,,	22 (p. 217).
Sety Ist	(p. 256),	,, ,, ,,	17 (p. 213).
Rameses IInd	(p. 249),	,, ,, ,,	7 (p. 201).
Merenptah	(p. 248),	,, ,, ,,	8 (p. 202).
Septah	(p. 255),	,, ,, ,,	47 (p. 226).
Tausert	(p. 249),	,, ,, ,,	14 (p. 209).
Rameses IIIrd	(p. 229),	,, ,, ,,	11 (p. 206).

Besides these there is the mortuary temple of Queen Hatshepsut at Dêr el Bahri, which will be described in the next chapter; and there are also the minor temples of other queens, which will be noted in the present chapter. We may describe these temples in the order of their situation from south to north.

THE MORTUARY TEMPLES AT MEDINET HABU

The group of temples known as Medinet Habu lies at the south of the Theban necropolis, about ten minutes' ride from the colossi.

230 ANTIQUITIES OF UPPER EGYPT

From Luxor one rides along the path which passes the colossi, and one turns sharply to the left immediately after reaching the rest-house of the Department of Antiquities, which stands amidst the trees at the edge of the cultivated land. The road, which is clearly marked by stones, then leads southwards, turning presently to the left, and later to the right again around the front of the ruins. Here on certain days there are a few natives to be found who have small antiquities for sale. The visitor will do well to note that legal vendors should have upon their arm a brass badge with their licence number upon it, by which they can be identified should they give trouble.

The history of Medinet Habu. The temples at Medinet Habu are entirely mortuary in character, and form the southernmost group in the long line of royal funeral temples which runs the whole length of the necropolis. The history of the ruins upon this site dates back to the reign of Amenhotep Ist (B.C. 1557). The tomb of that king (No. 39, above the Valley of the Kings) lies to the north-west of Medinet Habu, upon the hills above Dêr el Medineh, and, judging by the custom obtaining during subsequent generations, the royal mortuary chapel would be situated on the edge of the cultivation more or less opposite the tomb. Now the small temple of Dynasty XVIII. inside the enclosure of Medinet Habu, is to be dated to the reign of Amenhotep Ist, that king's name having been found there, and it is therefore very probable that that building was his mortuary temple. It may, in fact, be the "temple of Amenhotep of the garden," referred to in the Abbot papyrus in connection with the tomb of Amenhotep Ist. It was usurped by Thothmes Ist, the next king, who probably used it as a mortuary temple for himself. The following sovereigns, Thothmes IInd, Hatshepsut, and and Thothmes IIIrd, added to the buildings, but Hatshepsut and Thothmes IIIrd made other mortuary temples for themselves, the former at Dêr el Bahri, and the latter to the south of the Ramesseum. The buildings were further restored by later kings, and Rameses IInd, who buried his wife Nefertari in the valley immediately west of this site (p. 281), built what appears to be a little mortuary chapel for her here. Rameses IIIrd (B.C. 1198–1167) some generations later built the great temple here as a place of worship for his soul, thus carrying on the mortuary traditions of the site. It is thought that his palace was situated just to the south of the temple, but this is not certain, though, as the palace of Amenhotep IIIrd is situated not far away, it is quite probable. The kings of the Ethiopian Dynasty XXV. added to the temple of Amenhotep Ist, and the queens of this dynasty (Amenartas and her successors) erected mortuary shrines near by. Later Pharaohs built here, or inscribed their names upon the walls. In Christian times one of the courts of the temple was converted into a church, and a town grew up around it upon the ruins of the priests' houses of earlier days. The place was called in dynastic times *Thamu*, and in Coptic days this name had become *Tjēme*, or *Pkastron n Tjēme*, "The Castle of Tjēme." When the Christians were persecuted by the Arabs the town fell into ruins, and so remained. The origin of the modern name "Habu" is not known.

At Medinet Habu there are three distinct temples and a pavilion. At the present time, when riding to Medinet Habu from the north, one skirts the enclosing wall, passes a walled-in pylon and gateway, and enters the enclosure through the pavilion of Rameses IIIrd. One then sees straight ahead the great pylons of the large temple of the same Pharaoh. On the right there is the temple of Amenhotep Ist, enlarged by the Ptolemies, who added to it the pylons which have been seen from the roadway. On the left is the small temple of Amenartas. The ruins will, therefore, be described in four sections—

1. The Mortuary Pavilion of Rameses IIIrd.
2. The Mortuary Temple of Rameses IIIrd.
3. The Mortuary Temple of Amenhotep Ist.
4. The Mortuary Temple of Amenartas.

THE MORTUARY PAVILION OF RAMESES IIIrd AT MEDINET HABU

Rameses IIIrd lived at a time when there was considerable intercourse between Egypt and Asia, and there were many Asiatics attached to the court. It was only natural, therefore, that the Egyptian architects should be influenced by their ideas, and should sometimes erect buildings which resembled those of Syria. The pavilion of Rameses IIIrd, which we now approach, is built in the style of the Syrian citadels, which we see so often represented in the war scenes upon temple walls in Egypt. The main building consists of two crenellated towers, which rise above a gateway, and contain several apartments. There is an enclosed courtyard in front of this, at the entrance of which, on either side, is a guard-room.

Passing between these two rooms or lodges, one sees on the left

The walls. (south-east wall of the Pavilion) a scene (1) showing the king slaying his enemies, the Nubians and Libyans, in the presence of Amen-Ra, the state god of Thebes. On the right (2) he performs the same ceremony before Harmachis, the sun-god of Heliopolis, the enemies here being the Hittites, Amorites, Thakari, Sardinians, Sicilians, Tyrrhenians, and Philistines. Passing in between the two high walls of the Pavilion, one sees on the left (3) and right (4) a representation of the king leading prisoners into the presence of Amen-Ra, to become slaves in the temple. A seated granite figure of the goddess Sekhmet is now seen on either side. This goddess was said to have been the agent of the sun-god in the massacre of mankind which had occurred in the young days of the world; and it is probable that her presence here was intended to be a further indication of the warlike character of the building. On the walls behind these two statues the king is seen (on the left) before Thoth, the god of wisdom; Safkhet, the goddess who records the great historical events; Ptah, the Memphite Vulcan; and Sekhmet; and (on the right) before Tum, one of the forms of the sun-god of Heliopolis, originally connected with Aton or Adonis, the great Syrian deity; Anhur, the ancient god of This, the early capital of Dynasty I.; and other gods. In the doorway itself, on the left (5), the king is seen bringing prisoners to Amen-Ra; and on the right (6) he smites down his enemies, while a symbolical lion attacks them with tooth and claw. On the west face of the Pavilion (7 and 8) the king is seen presenting his captives to the gods of Egypt.

The upper chambers. Thus we see that the Pavilion forms a kind of triumphal entrance to the temple, and to the palace at the south of the temple, and was built in order to perpetuate for his soul's delight the victories won upon earth by the king. Its martial character, as we have seen, is indicated by its similarity in construction to the forts and citadels of Asia; by the reliefs upon its walls, and by the two figures of Sekhmet. The scenes upon the rooms inside the Pavilion, however, are of a very different character, and are intended to represent the pleasures of home comforts to which the victorious king returned in life, and to which his soul in the underworld would return. We ascend the steps on the south side of the tower, and presently reach a chamber, the roof of which is destroyed, thus exposing the room above. It is on the walls of this upper chamber that one sees the famous *harêm* scenes, so often mentioned in Egyptological works. On the west wall the king, seated, catches hold of the arm of one of his ladies,

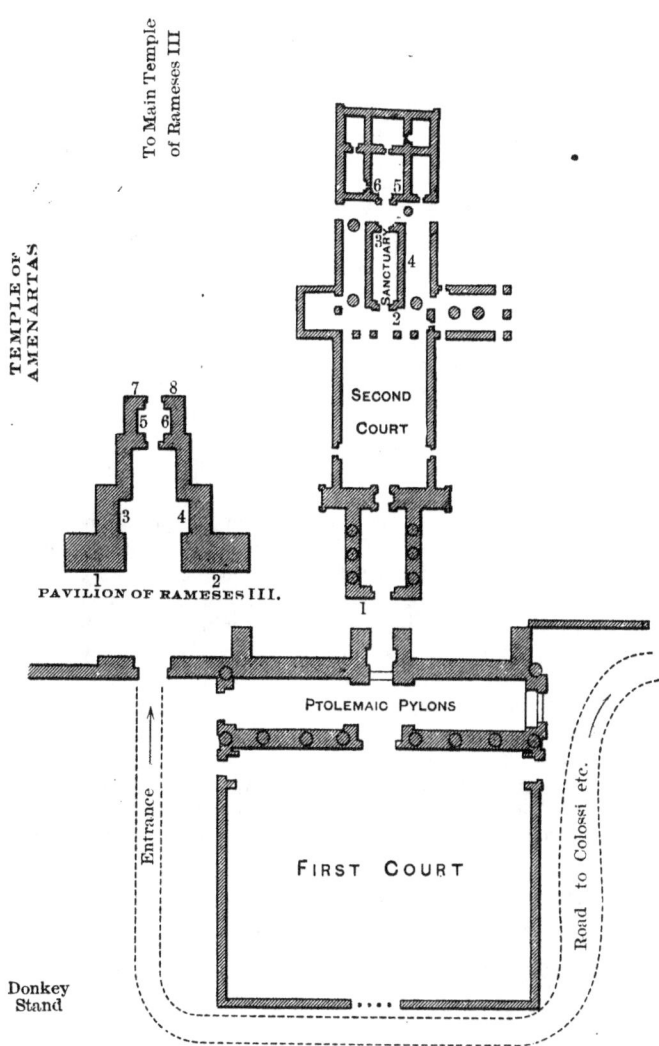

THE MORTUARY TEMPLE OF
AMENHOTEP 1ST AND THOTHMES I,
AND PAVILION OF RAMESES III, AT MEDINET HABU

and strokes her chin with his finger. On the south wall other women play tambourines to amuse him. The scenes on the other walls are somewhat similar, but all are in bad preservation. Women are seen with flowers in their hands, while others wave fans to and fro; and it soon becomes apparent that behind the stiff conventionalities of the artist a scene of Oriental palace life is to be traced as profligate as it is luxurious. These were the scenes which Rameses IIIrd wished to perpetuate for the benefit of his soul; and these were the rooms where that soul would lodge until born again in human form. Looking eastwards out of the windows of the chamber, the royal soul would see the sunrise, thought to be so essential to happiness in the underworld, and the city of Thebes would be in full view. He would look to right and left on the scenes of his triumphs carved upon the walls of the Pavilion, and the nations whom he had conquered would, for him, remain conquered as long as figures of the captives were preserved upon these stones. The visitor looking from this window will notice some curious brackets projecting from the walls, carved in the form of the heads and shoulders of foreign captives, who appear to be lying on their faces pinned down by the weight of the masonry above. Over each of these brackets (which have no architectural use) there is an open space or recess in the wall where a stone has been inserted after the completion of the building. It is possible that slain foreign captives were really placed here above their images, and were built into the wall, for the custom of thus burying human beings in or under a building is not uncommon as a foundation ceremony in other countries. Their souls would thus remain for ever the slaves of the king's soul; and when he was tired of the amusements of the *harêm* within, he had but to look out of the window to feast his eyes upon these wretched representatives of the nations he had conquered.

THE GREAT MORTUARY TEMPLE OF RAMESES IIIrd AT MEDINET HABU

The Pylons.

From the Pavilion one passes across an open court to the main temple which stands before one, its great pylons rising to an impressive height. Originally four masts of wood clamped with shining copper stood in front of the pylons, and at their tops long streamers of coloured linen fluttered. The recesses in which these masts stood may be seen let into the masonry of the pylons, two on either side of the gateway. The usual scenes are sculptured

MORTUARY TEMPLES OF THE KINGS 235

upon the face of the two pylons, showing the king slaying his enemies before Amen-Ra and Harmachis. Between the two recesses for the masts, at the foot of the right pylon (39), there is a scene showing the king smiting two captives in the presence of Amen-Ra; and beneath this there is an inscription which tells us in bombastic language how Rameses IIIrd overthrew the Libyans in the eleventh year of his reign. Here the king is said to have been "like a plundering lion, terrifying the goats," and again he is said to have fallen upon the Libyans "like a mountain of granite" so that "their blood was like a flood, and their bodies were crushed on the spot." Below this the gods Ptah and Thoth are seen inscribing the king's name on a leaf of the sacred tree, while the king himself kneels before Amen.

We now enter the First Court of the temple, which is peculiar in that the galleries to left and right have their roof supported on the one side by columns with calyx capitals, and on the other side by square pillars against which Osirian figures stand. The court has thus a somewhat unbalanced appearance, but it is nevertheless impressive. The Osirian figures have been much damaged in Christian times, but otherwise the court is in good preservation. Turning to the left as we enter, we see on the face of the left or south pylon (1) a great battle picture, representing the defeat of the Libyans in the eleventh year of the reign. The king in his chariot charges into the midst of the enemy, who are scattered or slain before him, and it is said that he pursued them for "sixty miles of butchery." Being Libyans they are represented as having beards, long hair, and the heavy sidelock. Other Egyptian chariots charge with the king, and in the lowest row we see Egyptian infantry, assisted by Sardinians (in horned helmets) and Philistines (in feathered head-dresses), who acted as Egyptian mercenaries. At the end of this wall, behind the corner pillar (2), the king is seen walking with fan bearers wafting their long fans before and behind him. On the south wall there are several apertures which seem to have given access to this court from the royal palace, which probably stood amidst gardens at the south of the temple. This fact seems to explain the presence of the columns only on this side of the court: they formed a kind of portico in front of the entrance to the palace, and it was from this portico that one was supposed to look across at the Osirian figures on the opposite side of the court. The main entrance was on the east side, but the royal entrance was on this south side. On this wall there are several scenes of interest.

THE INTERIOR. The first court.

First (3) we see the king in his chariot returning from the wars, his pet lion running by his side. Fan bearers walk before and behind him, while soldiers, nobles, and priests are grouped around him. Beyond a doorway (4) the king is seen slaying Asiatics. Under his feet are the heads of four foreigners sculptured in the round, forming a kind of bracket such as we have noticed in the Pavilion. Below this we see soldiers at their sports in the presence of the royal princes. First two men fight with singlesticks, and it will be observed that they wear a shield on the arm. Then two Egyptians are seen wrestling. Next a negro wrestles with an Egyptian; and farther on we see that the Egyptian (coloured red) has thrown the negro, and holds up his hands in appeal to the umpire. There is here a window, at the opposite side of which (5) the king again slays Asiatic prisoners, standing upon a bracket formed of three sculptured heads representing foreign types. Below this the sports are continued. First, an Egyptian who has thrown his negro adversary appeals to the umpire. Second, an Egyptian wrestler bodily lifts an Asiatic slave who has been made to fight with him. Next, two men wrestle, and one catches the other's leg to throw him. Then an Egyptian wrestler flings an Asiatic over his head. Next, two men fence with singlesticks, their forehead, chin, and knuckles being protected by pads. Lastly, the victorious fencer raises his hands in appeal to the umpire, and his opponent staggers off with his hand to his face, as though his nose were bleeding. Prince Rameses, the king's son, who was a military commander, watches the sports with his suite. Farther along the wall (6) the king, accompanied by his nobles, inspects his horses which are held by the grooms, one of whom blows a call upon his trumpet. On the west wall, left side (7), the king is seen presenting to Amen-Ra and Mut three rows of captives. In the top row the prisoners are probably Sagalassians of Pisidia; those in the second row are the Danaans; and those in the third row Philistines. The Philistines occupied the sea-coast towns of Palestine, and while some of their communities, as we have seen, fought as mercenaries for the Egyptians, others leagued themselves with the Pharaoh's enemies, as is here indicated. On the opposite wall (8) there is a long inscription giving an account of the king's war in Syria in the eighth year of his reign. Here he had to meet and scatter a league of Greek and Asiatic nations who were threatening Egypt from this direction. The great battle on the coast of Palestine is described, and the Egyptian victory is triumphantly recorded. On the north wall, behind the

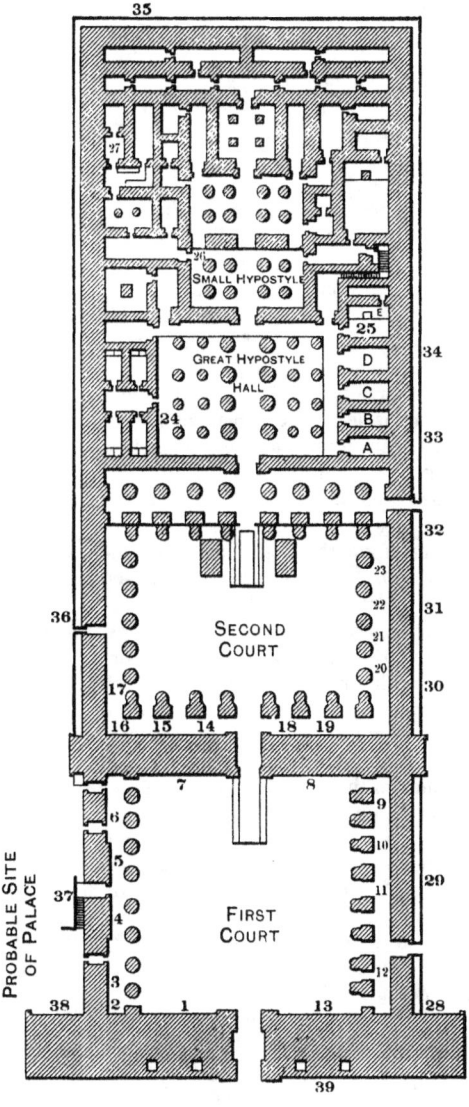

THE GREAT MORTUARY TEMPLE OF
RAMESES III AT MEDINET HABU

Osirian pillars (9), the king is seen presenting to Amen-Ra, Mut, and Khonsu (the Theban trinity), two rows of prisoners; and the inscription records the king's speech to the gods, in which he says, with reference to the captives: "I carried off their people, all their possessions, all the splendid precious stones of their country, they are placed before thee, O Lord of Gods. . . . I have carried them away: the males thereof to fill thy storehouse, their women to be the servants of thy temple." Farther along (10) the king, in his chariot, drives before him Libyan, Syrian, and Philistine captives. His pet lion trots by his side, and fan-bearers walk behind. Next (11) the king is seen attacking an Amorite city. He has alighted from his chariot which has been left in charge of the grooms, and standing upon the corpses of his fallen enemies he shoots his arrows at the defenders of the fortress. The Egyptian attack is led by Sardinian mercenaries who carry round shields, and wear horned helmets. Scaling ladders have been placed against the walls of the city, and the attacking party has already gained a footing on them. Farther along, beyond a doorway (12), the king is seen standing on the balcony of his palace, his arm resting upon the cushioned balustrade, while fan-bearers stand behind him, and officers and priests are in attendance. The king addresses the nobles who bring to him the Asiatic captives which they have taken, and they reply in the usual laudatory manner. On the adjoining wall, or pylon (13), the king is again seen on his balcony receiving the officials who bring the hands of the slain Libyans which had been cut off on the battlefields of the Libyan war as a means of counting the dead. Prisoners are also brought before him. A sloping causeway now leads the visitor to the granite doorway, through which one passes into the Second Court.

The second court. This court has a gallery on each of its four sides, the roof of which is supported by five columns on the north side, five columns on the south, eight square pillars with Osirian figures before them on the east, and eight on the west. Behind these pillars on the west side there are eight columns, for the gallery is here deep. One of the columns on the north side has been pulled down in Christian times to make room for the altar of the church into which the court was then converted. The Christians destroyed the Osirian figures, and covered the ancient reliefs with plaster. They then closed the court in, supporting the roof with columns which may now be seen on the south side of the temple. Turning to the left the visitor will find some scenes of interest upon the

MORTUARY TEMPLES OF THE KINGS 239

walls. The king (14) leads Asiatic prisoners to Amen-Ra and Mut. The king (15) in his chariot drives prisoners before him, while fan-bearers walk behind, and below him his bodyguard of Egyptian and Philistine soldiers are seen. Next (16) the king in his chariot shoots arrows at a horde of flying enemies, many of whom have been slain. The colour on this scene is partly preserved, and one may notice the elaborate blue robes of the foreigners. Philistines, distinguished by their feathered caps, are here again seen assisting the Egyptians. High up above this scene the king is shown walking towards the temple doorway with the four standards of the four primitive tribes of Egypt before him. On the adjoining wall (17) he is seen in his chariot, the horses of which are held by grooms, turning round to inspect the heaps of hands, cut off from the slain, which are brought in by the soldiers together with some prisoners. The number of hands is recorded by scribes. On the right-hand side of the entrance (18) Amen-Ra, Mut, and Khonsu are seen; and coming towards them hand in hand (19) there are three hawk-headed figures representing the spirits of Hieraconpolis (the first capital of Upper Egypt), the goddess Nekheb, lady of that city, the king, the goddess Uazet, lady of Buto (the first capital of Lower Egypt), and three jackal-headed figures representing the spirits of that city. The corner of the court here has been screened off, in order to form a little chapel in which offerings might be made. Upon the adjoining wall (20) the king is seen purified by Thoth and Horus of Edfu as an opening ceremony at a religious festival in which he took part and which is represented upon this north wall. We see him (21) walking behind a sacred boat which is carried on the shoulders of the priests to meet (22) the great barque of Amen-Ra, which is also carried on the shoulders of the priests. High above this we see a representation of the festival of the god Min. The statue of the god is shown borne on a structure covered with a great canopy, almost hiding the priests who are carrying it. On the lower part of the wall the barque of Amen-Ra is now placed in its shrine, and the king (23) makes offerings to it. Above this we see the king at the festival of Min carried upon his portable throne by soldiers whose heads are decked with feathers while courtiers walk behind. Returning to the middle of the court we now ascend a slope to the gallery which passes along its west end. On either side of this slope there is the pedestal of a great colossal statue now totally destroyed. The reliefs on the west wall of the gallery show the king in the presence of the gods, and along the lower row there are figures of his sons and daughters.

<small>The great Hypostyle Hall.</small>
We now enter the Hypostyle Hall, which is far more ruined than the two preceding courts. The Christian village was built over this hall, and as much of the twenty-four columns as showed above the then level of the ground was destroyed. Thus only their lower part now remains. The scenes upon the walls show the king in the presence of various gods, but they are not of much interest. On the left or south side (24) he is seen with bow in hand leading behind him a number of captives. At the same time he presents some beautiful Asiatic vases to Amen-Ra, Mut, and Khonsu. On either side of the hall there are several small chapels, dedicated to the worship of particular gods. Chapel A is dedicated to the worship of the deified Rameses IIIrd. Here we see princes and princesses (his sons and daughters) bringing offerings to him and to his queen who stands behind him. Chapel B is dedicated to Ptah, the Memphite Vulcan; C to Osiris; and D to Ptah again. Here there is a headless statue of that god sculptured in alabaster. Chapel E is dedicated to Amen-Ra, and upon the right wall (25) the bringing in and slaughtering of fatted bulls for sacrifices should be noticed.

<small>The first small Hypostyle Hall.</small>
Along the middle aisle we now pass into the first small Hypostyle Hall, the roof of which was supported by eight columns. Through a doorway on the left (26) one passes into a series of six small chambers, where certain mysteries connected with the king's life in the underworld were performed. Passing through the first of these chambers, one enters a two-columned room, which leads into a chamber in which there is a stone bench passing around the wall, upon which offerings might be placed. From this room two chambers lead. On the right one enters an arched chapel dedicated to Osiris. On the left one passes into a chamber, on the right wall of which (27) are some interesting scenes. Here the king in the underworld is seen ploughing and reaping the fields. The canals and pools of Paradise are shown, and the figures of the gods of the underworld are seen seated beside the water. On the opposite wall the king addresses Osiris, before whom are the four genii who serve him rising from a lotus-flower. From this chamber one passes into the final room, where a number of sacred emblems and sacred cattle are seen.

<small>The second small Hypostyle Hall, &c.</small>
Returning, one enters the second small Hypostyle Hall. On the right of the aisle there is a sculptured red granite group representing the king seated with the ibis-headed Thoth; and on the

MORTUARY TEMPLES OF THE KINGS 241

left a somewhat similar group shows him seated with the goddess Maat. The king was thus shown to be the mate of Wisdom and Truth. The remaining chapels and chambers have little of interest to show to the ordinary visitor.

The scenes upon the exterior of the temple are of considerable interest. The visitor should return through the Second and First Courts, turning to the left or north upon leaving the temple. Walking round to the back of the pylon he will find upon its west face (28) at the top a scene showing Rameses in his chariot attacking two Hittite cities, on the walls of which the defenders are seen. Some fall from the battlements, and many lie slain around. Below this there is a scene from the Libyan war. The Egyptian archers and light infantry attack the enemy, numbers of whom are slain. Rameses has alighted from his chariot and binds two Libyans. The inscription here speaks of the king as being "like Baal in his hour of wrath, raging like a hawk amongst the sparrows." On the adjoining wall (29), at the top, there are five scenes from the Amorite war. The king in his chariot attacks a city of the enemy. Before him Egyptian archers and Sardinian infantry make the assault, and effect a footing upon the walls, where an Egyptian trumpeter blows a triumphant call. Next, the king, having left his chariot, attacks the fortress. Then, standing alone, he receives three lines of prisoners, who are to be placed as slaves in the temple of Amen-Ra. Then, riding in his chariot, with his lion trotting beside him, he drives two lines of prisoners before him. Next, the king leads two lines of captives, and presents them, together with a number of fine vases, to Amen and Khonsu. Below these five scenes from the Amorite war there are five others from the Libyan war of the eleventh year of his reign. First, Rameses is seen charging the Libyans in his chariot. The Egyptians are supported by archers who shoot their arrows from the walls of two Egyptian fortresses near by. Then we see the king dragging captives by the hair towards him. Then, accompanied by two sunshade-bearers and an officer, he inspects three lines of captives, and says to the officer, "Say to the vanquished chief of the Libyans, 'See how thy name is obliterated for ever and ever.'" Next, Rameses, driving in his chariot, with two lines of Libyan captives before him, approaches a group of priests. Then he leads two lines of captives to Amen and Mut. We now pass the projection made by the second pylon, and come to seven scenes relating to the war with the "Peoples of the Sea" in the eighth year of the king's reign. As these scenes run from

THE EXTERIOR WALLS.
The north wall.

west to east, they should be seen in that order. First (34) the king is seen standing on a balcony, fan-bearers being behind him. He reviews the recruits levied for the coming war, and distributes arms to them. Next, the king in his chariot sets out for the war, accompanied by Egyptian and Sardinian infantry. Then Rameses (33) is seen charging into the enemies' ranks. These are seen to consist mostly of Philistines, distinguished by their feather head-dresses. The two-wheeled ox-carts in which are the enemies' families are seen to be waiting near the scene of the battle. Next (32) there is the representation of a great sea battle between the Egyptians on the one hand and the Sardinians and Philistines on the other. From the shore the king and the Egyptian archers pour volleys of arrows into the enemy's fleet. Then (31) the king is seen standing in the balcony once more to receive the Philistine prisoners. Next (30) the king is seen bringing prisoners to present them to Amen-Ra, Mut, and Khonsu. Finally we see Amen presenting the sword of victory to the king who brings three rows of captives to his shrine. The rest of the wall has upon it three scenes from the first Libyan war, but they are somewhat damaged and are not of great interest.

<small>The west and south walls.</small>
The back or west wall has upon it no scenes of much interest. At its south end (35) there are scenes from the Negro wars, but they are much damaged. We now pass round the corner to the south side of the temple. Here there are long lists inscribed relating to the temple supplies; and the king is seen in the presence of the gods. Outside the Second Court of the temple (36) there are the remains of the Coptic church, thrown out from inside the temple in modern times. Not far from this, amongst the mounds of rubbish, a passage was recently found descending into the earth, and leading to the temple well. The stone walls of the passage are inscribed with the names of Rameses IIIrd, and with figures of the water-gods. Farther along (37) there is a stairway leading up to a window overlooking the First Court. On the sides of this the king is seen slaying a Negro and an Asiatic prisoner. The visitor will now see before him on the west side of the projecting pylon (38) a magnificent hunting scene. The king in his chariot spears wild bulls who run towards a reed-covered swamp. The bulls are splendidly drawn, and the scene is perhaps one of the finest examples of Egyptian animal portraiture in existence. Two bulls have been killed, and one falls wounded at the edge of the lake, disturbing the duck and the fish in the water.

MORTUARY TEMPLES OF THE KINGS 243

Below are the huntsmen. Above this scene the king is shown hunting antelopes and wild asses.

The visitor now finds himself back once more in the court at the front of the temple, and he may now wish to visit the Temple of Amenhotep Ist which stands to the north of the Pavilion.

THE MORTUARY TEMPLE OF AMENHOTEP Ist AND THOTHMES Ist AT MEDINET HABU

The First Court, Vestibule, and Pylons of this temple are of Ptolemaic and Roman date. A large number of blocks from earlier temples have been used in their construction, and the work is in places very rough. But if the visitor will enter the First Court, and will look back at the Pylons and Gateway, he will be duly impressed by the beauty and elegance of the building. The front gate of this First Court, now walled up, bears the cartouches of Antoninus Pius (A.D. 138-161), and the same emperor set up two rows of eight columns here, only two of which are now complete. A large red-granite funerary stele of Thothmes IIIrd is here to be seen. The First Pylons bear the names of Ptolemy Lathyros (B.C. 117-106) and Ptolemy Auletes (B.C. 80-52). We now pass between the pylons and approach a small hypæthral court and pylons which were erected by Shabaka (B.C. 712-700) and Taharka (B.C. 688-663). The sides are formed by four columns to right and four to left, joined by screen walls. Nekhtnebef (B.C. 361-343) here imposed his name over those of the original builders; and the names of Ptolemy Lathyros are also seen. On the front wall, left side (1), Nekhtnebef is seen slaying foreign prisoners as his greater ancestor Rameses IIIrd had done in the main temple. We now pass on through a small doorway upon which are the names of Ptolemy Lathyros and of Taharka, and so enter the Second Court, on either side of which stood a row of nine columns. This court appears to have been built during the reign of Thothmes IIIrd (B.C. 1501-1447) and to have formed an integral part of the original temple. To the right there is a gateway upon which is the name of Pedeamenapt, a noble of the XXVIth dynasty whose tomb is described on p. 173. On its west wall, which is the front wall of the main building, there are inscriptions of the time of Thothmes IIIrd, Horemheb (B.C. 1350-1315), Sety Ist (B.C. 1313-1292), Rameses IIIrd, and Painezem Ist. The latter king has left an inscription saying that he found the temple

<small>The later additions.</small>

in ruins and restored it, and he gives the name of the temple as "The Splendid Throne of Amen-Ra."

The original temple. We now enter the main temple, and find ourselves in a gallery surrounding a sanctuary. This part of the building was begun by Amenhotep Ist (B.C. 1557), and continued by Thothmes Ist, Thothmes IInd, Hatshepsut, and Thothmes IIIrd. It was, doubtless, intended to be the mortuary temple of Amenhotep Ist, but was usurped by his successor Thothmes Ist, as has been pointed out in the introduction to this chapter. Upon the doorway of the sanctuary there is an inscription dated in the second year of Merenptah (B.C. 1223) stating that that king had given orders to the Chief Ritual Priest to restore the temple. On the right-hand side of the sanctuary doorway (2) King Thothmes IIIrd is seen receiving life from Amen-Ra. Entering the sanctuary one observes on the walls the original reliefs of Thothmes IIIrd to which Sety Ist has added. On the left (3) Amen-Ra writes upon the leaves of the sacred tree, and Thothmes IIIrd is led towards him by Tum and Hathor. Above this he dances before Amen-Ra. Outside the sanctuary on the north side (4) there are some much-damaged reliefs relating to the foundation ceremonies. The king is seen breaking the ground with a hoe, kneeling to fashion the first brick, and so on. These foundation ceremonies will be seen to better advantage at Dendereh (p. 36) and Edfu (p. 338). In the inner chambers behind the sanctuary the king is seen in the presence of various gods: (5) he is kissed by Amen-Ra. Additions were made to this main part of the temple by Hakar (B.C. 400) and by Ptolemy Physkon (B.C. 171-130).

About thirty yards to the north of this temple there is an open tank in the ground, the sides of which are constructed of masonry. This seems to have been the site of the performance of that part of the funeral ceremonies which were concerned with the launching of the mortuary barque upon the waters. It may also have served for the irrigation of the garden which seems to have been laid out around it. There is also a smaller tank in the neighbourhood connected with the temple by an underground passage. From this tank the water for the temple seems to have been brought, just as that for the temple of Rameses IIIrd was brought from the well on the south side, mentioned above. To the west of these tanks there is a small brick chapel which contains fragments of statues of Rameses IInd and his wife Nefertari, and may perhaps be the funeral shrine of Nefertari, who was buried in the Valley of the Queens, just to the west of this place. There are also some

MORTUARY TEMPLES OF THE KINGS

Christian columns to'be seen here, and other objects found in the neighbourhood. The masonry and brick walls which surround the enclosure were probably built by Rameses IIIrd; but the cartouches of Rameses Vth have been inscribed upon the stonework.

THE MORTUARY TEMPLE OF AMENARTAS AT MEDINET HABU

This little temple, which is distinctly called a *Ka*-chapel in the inscriptions, stands just to the south of the main pathway from the Pavilion to the great temple. Persons entering Medinet Habu through the Pavilion pass this building upon their left. The builder was the well-known Queen Amenartas, the daughter of Kashta, and wife of Piankhy IInd, who reigned about B.C. 700. Upon the right and left sides of the doorway the queen is seen in the presence of Amen-Ra and Mut. We pass into a four-columned hall which stands before the sanctuary. Facing us to the left and right the queen is seen performing the usual foundation ceremonies. The sanctuary is surrounded by an ambulatory, upon the walls of which there are many mystical funeral inscriptions. On the right side of the doorway into the sanctuary the queen is seen led forward by Thoth and Anubis, and below this Prince Piankhy's wife Shepenapt, the succeeding queen, makes offerings to the queen's Ka. On the left side the queen presents offerings of three bulls to Anubis, and below this Queen Shepenapt makes offerings to Hathor on behalf of Amenartas. Additions were made to this building (on the west side) by Queen Neitakert, the grand-daughter of Amenartas. On the wall of the first of three additional chambers this queen is seen receiving the devotions of three ritual-priests. The third chamber is dedicated to a queen named Mehtenusekht. In this chamber there was a crypt, which now lies open.

THE MORTUARY TEMPLE OF AMENHOTEP IIIrd AND THE COLOSSI

The Mortuary Temple of Amenhotep IIIrd (B.C. 1411-1375) lies to the north of Medinet Habu, a stone's-throw from the rest-house of the Department of Antiquities, which stands amidst the trees at the desert end of the pathway across the fields from Luxor. The temple is almost totally destroyed, and but a few bases of pillars and fragments of stone, flooded each year by the inundation, now remain of the main building. The two great colossi which sit side by side amidst the fields, and which are perhaps the most famous relics of ancient Thebes, flanked the front entrance of this temple. They are thus similar, for example, to the two colossi which sit in front of the Luxor Temple, or to those in front of the Horemheb colonnade of that temple (p. 81). Behind them there were perhaps two pylons of crude brick, as in some of the other mortuary temples of the XVIIIth dynasty; and behind these again there was perhaps an open court, or two courts, surrounded with a brick wall. The pylons and walls, being of brick, have disappeared, owing to the rise in the level of the floods of the inundation which now cover the surrounding fields each year, but which in ancient times did not penetrate nearly so far westwards. In one of these courts there was a great stone stele upon which was an inscription referring to the dedication of the temple. This stele, now overthrown, is still to be seen lying some distance behind the colossi. Behind this again there was the main temple, which, as has been said, is now entirely ruined. It was once a rich and gorgeous monument worthy of the great king who built it, who has rightly been called "Amenhotep the Magnificent." The king says of it that he "made it as a monument for his father Amen . . . ; an everlasting building of fine white sandstone, wrought with gold throughout, its floor adorned with silver, and all its portals with electrum. . . . It is numerous in royal statues . . . of every splendid, costly stone. It is supplied with a 'station of the king'" (marked, probably, by the fallen stela), "wrought with gold and many precious stones. Flagstaves are set up before it wrought with electrum. It resembles the horizon of heaven when the sun rises therein. Its storehouse is filled with slaves, with the children of the princes of all the countries made captive by his majesty." In another inscription the king says: "My majesty filled the temple with monuments, and with my statues" (probably the colossi are meant). "When they are seen in their place there is great amazement because of their size. . . . Great was all that which I made, of gold, stone, and every splendid and costly stone, without end." All this has now gone, and the two great colossi alone remain.

The colossi.

The two colossi represented King Amenhotep IIIrd seated upon his throne. Beside the legs of the statue there is in each case a small figure of Queen Thiy, his wife, on the right, and of Mutemua, his mother, on the left. On the sides of the throne there are

MORTUARY TEMPLES OF THE KINGS

figures of the Nile-gods of Upper and of Lower Egypt uniting the two lands by plaiting together the stems of the lotus- and papyrus-plants, symbolic of the two divisions of Egypt. This design is often found upon the royal throne, and dates back to early times. The colossi are made of sandstone, probably quarried at Gebel Silsileh (p. 356). They were both monoliths originally; but the northern colossus partly fell and was restored with sandstone blocks in the reign of Septimius Severus. The southern figure measures 52 feet in height, or 65 feet including the pedestal, or again about 70 feet including the now destroyed crown which probably surmounted the head. Each foot is $10\frac{1}{2}$ feet in length; the breadth across the shoulders is 20 feet; and the middle finger of the hand is $4\frac{1}{2}$ feet long.

The northern colossus, which, as it afterwards partly fell, may have been cracked by the great earthquake of B.C. 27, became famous in the days of the Roman occupation on account of a curious noise which came from it in the early mornings. This noise was first observed by Roman travellers of about the reign of Nero (A.D. 54–68), and so strange was the sound that the colossus became the most important monument to be visited in Upper Egypt. It was perhaps due to the slight expansion of this crack in the stone when the rays of the sun fell upon it after the contraction due to the coldness of night; or again the breath of wind which comes with the dawn may have whistled through the crack. A large portion of this colossus seems to have fallen about A.D. 200, and the restoration now seen was made soon afterwards by the Emperor Septimius Severus (A.D. 193–211).[1]

The two colossi are sometimes called *Es Sanamât*, "the Idols," by the natives; and early modern travellers state that they are called respectively *Tama* and *Shama*. In Greek times the northern figure was thought to be a statue of Memnon, the son of Tithonus or Dedun, a Nubian god, and of Eos, the Dawn. This Memnon was one of the great heroes of the Trojan war, who was said to have led an army of Ethiopians to the siege of that city.

The names of the colossi.

---

[1] That the sound was due to a crack in the stone as stated above seems probable. The great earthquake of B.C. 27 is known to have shaken the Theban monuments very considerably. The sound was first noticed a few years later. A portion of the colossus was restored about A.D. 200, and hence probably fell just before that time. The fact that it fell indicates that there were cracks; and the fact that the sound was not heard before the earthquake, and ceased after the restoration, suggests that a crack produced the sound.

The Greeks misread the names of Amenhotep IIIrd (who erected the colossi) as "Memnon"; and, knowing that the Trojan hero of that name came from this part of the world, they identified the two Memnons, and regarded the colossus as the figure of the Trojan hero. The sound emitted from it was then said to be the cry of Memnon to his mother Eos, when she appeared each day as the dawn above the eastern horizon.

The vocal Memnon. Strabo visited the colossi about B.C. 24, three years after the earthquake, and states that the upper portions of the northern statue had been shattered. He heard a sound issue from the remaining portion of the figure, but he was not convinced that he had not been imposed upon by some of the natives. In the eleventh year of the reign of Nero, about A.D. 65, a traveller scratched a record of his visit to the colossus upon its pedestal; and from that time onwards it became customary to write verses or epigrams upon the pedestal. Eight governors of Egypt thus inscribed their names, and several other persons of distinction recorded the fact of their visit. Hadrian with his wife Sabina stayed several days (A.D. 130) at the foot of the colossi in order to hear the sound. The vain court poetess, Balbilla, wrote several verses here, including one in sixteen very bad hexameters in honour of Hadrian. Some good lines were written by a certain Asklepiodotus, in which he refers to the Memnon legend. Pausanias, Pliny, and Juvenal in their writings refer to the phenomenon. The sound was said to be like a gong or like the blast of a trumpet, while others describe it as being similar to the singing of human voices. It was heard only at or just after sunrise, but often visitors were disappointed and failed to hear it, in which case they considered that Memnon was angry. It may have been in order to propitiate him, after failing to hear the sound, that orders were given by the officials of Severus that the figure should be restored.

THE MORTUARY TEMPLE OF MERENPTAH

The ruins of this temple are situated just to the north of the above-mentioned temple of Amenhotep IIIrd, on the edge of the desert. Only a few stones and some unsightly heaps of debris now remain, and the road from Medinet Habu to the Ramesseum passes right across them. Originally two pylons stood in front of the building, but these have now disappeared. Beyond them there was a court which had a colonnade of six pillars on either side.

MORTUARY TEMPLES OF THE KINGS 249

In this court a great stela stood, famous to antiquarians as having upon it a reference to the defeat of the Israelites by Merenptah. A second court can still be traced, and behind this the main body of the temple stood. The ruins were excavated by Professor Petrie in 1896 ; and it is hoped that the Department of Antiquities at some future date will be able to clear away the debris from them as has been done at the Ramesseum.

THE MORTUARY TEMPLE OF TAUSERT

Queen Tausert, the daughter of Merenptah (B.C. 1225), caused her mortuary temple to be placed just to the north of that of her father. It is now almost entirely ruined, and is covered with debris. It lies within a levelled area which has been cut out of the rock. It was excavated by Professor Petrie in 1896.

THE MORTUARY TEMPLE OF THOTHMES IVth

North of the temple of Tausert and immediately south of the Ramesseum are the ruins of the mortuary temple of Thothmes IVth (B.C. 1420–1411), now too much destroyed to require a visit. The temple was enclosed by a stout wall, and had the usual pylons before it, but these are now destroyed. The site was excavated by Professor Petrie in 1896.

A little chapel dedicated to the worship of Uazmes stands between this temple and the Ramesseum, but it is now almost completely destroyed.

THE RAMESSEUM, OR MORTUARY TEMPLE OF RAMESES IInd

The Ramesseum is situated on the edge of the cultivation south of Dêr el Bahri and north of Medinet Habu. Although largely destroyed, it is of great interest, and its beauty as a ruin is considerable. The temple should be visited in the afternoon in winter, when the lighting is most effective. The pathway which leads across the cultivation from the canal to the colossi should be followed ; and usually there is a small track across the fields branching from the pathway and leading directly to the temple.

As has been said before, the tombs of the Pharaohs of the early part of the New Empire were hidden in the Valley of the Tombs of the Kings, and the temples at which their souls were worshipped were placed at the edge of the cultivation. The temples of

Medinet Habu (p. 234), the temple of Sety Ist (p. 256), and the other more ruined buildings which are to be found along the whole length of the necropolis at the border of the cultivated fields are all mortuary temples at which the souls of the kings buried behind the western cliffs were adored. The Ramesseum, in the same way, is the mortuary temple of Rameses IInd, whose tomb (No. 7) is situated in the Valley of the Tombs of the Kings (p. 201). Here the soul of that famous Pharaoh, who reigned from B.C. 1292 to 1225, was supposed to come to receive its offerings. Upon the walls Rameses caused to be sculptured various scenes from his wars, and especially those illustrating the adventures which befell him at the battle of Kadesh, when he was forced to make a desperate charge through the ranks of the enemy. Various gods are seen upon the walls, especially Amen-Ra, the presiding deity of Thebes, to whom the temple was dedicated; and Rameses is shown in their company.

Around the back of the temple there are a number of brick buildings, most of which date from the reign of Rameses IInd. These were used as storehouses and places of residence for the priests and slaves attached to the temple; and it is thought that there was a school or seminary here for the priests. Merenptah and Rameses IIIrd added somewhat to these buildings, but they seem to have fallen into ruins not long afterwards, though the temple itself remained in good preservation. They were partially excavated by Professor W. M. Flinders Petrie in 1895-96, and are now (1909) being cleared of rubbish. The earth and debris removed from the site has been formed into an embankment which passes around the whole area; and, though it may perhaps be contended that this gives too tidy an appearance to a ruin whose chief beauty lies in its picturesque disorder, it should be remembered on the other hand that any other plan for the disposal of these tons of rubbish was fraught with difficulties.

In Greek times the temple was called the Memnonium or the Tomb of Osymandyas (the Greek rendering of one of the names of Rameses IInd), but it is now generally known as the Ramesseum, a name given to it by Champollion. Diodorus, the Sicilian geographer, describes this temple as he saw it about 60 A.D. It was then in good preservation, and the great colossal figure of Rameses, which is now overthrown, was still without "a crack or a flaw."

At the time of writing the main entrance for the public is at the east end of the south side of the temple, while a second entrance

MORTUARY TEMPLES OF THE KINGS 251

is situated at the west end of the area ; but for the purpose of this description it will be supposed that the visitor at first is standing in the First Court, between the ruined pylons which edge the cultivation and the main ruins of the temple. Upon the west face of the two pylons there are some interesting scenes from the battle of Kadesh, which was fought between the Egyptians under Rameses IInd and the Hittites about the year B.C. 1388. Rameses IInd had marched into Syria to oppose the southern advance of the Hittites, and the armies came into touch not far from the city of Kadesh, which stood upon an island in the Orontes river. Rameses IInd, then a youth, hearing that Kadesh had been evacuated, pushed on with a division of his army and camped to the west of the city ; but the Hittites in reality had made a great flanking movement to the east, and managed to push in between the camp and the remaining Egyptian divisions. They then stormed the Egyptian camp, and Rameses only cut his way out by desperately charging through the enemy's ranks in his chariot. He, and those of his soldiers who thus cut their way out, effected a juncture with the advancing divisions, and after a pitched battle, he was left in possession of the field. Rameses all his life lived on the reputation of this one wild charge which he had made to escape from the massacre of his entrapped division; and representations of the scene are recorded on the walls of several temples. In the glory of this one act of the bravery of despair, the fact that he and his army were very nearly annihilated is quite forgotten ; but since Rameses almost at once returned from Syria, bringing little if any booty with him, and made an alliance with the Hittites (of which both the Hittite and the Egyptian copies are now known), it is obvious that his ultimate victory was in no way complete.

The first court.

On the north pylon, at the extreme north end, there was a list of eighteen towns captured by Rameses in the eighth year of his reign, only fourteen of which now remain. Amongst them one notices Jerusalem, Damascus, Askelon, Beth-Anath, and Merom. In the middle of the pylon, at the top, the ill-fated Egyptian camp is seen. A wall of shields has been placed around it, and a wicker doorway in it is protected by a group of sentries. Inside the enclosure animated scenes of camp life are represented. The horses have been unharnessed from the chariots, and near by are the baggage-waggons with their teams. Soldiers are seen talking together, and some amuse themselves by fencing with one another. To the right the sudden and unexpected attack of the Hittites is shown. Farther to the right the king is seen seated, while his generals stand around him. He is here taking council as to what course he should adopt. On the south pylon Rameses is seen escaping from the camp in his chariot, driving the enemy before him. Behind him his charioteers gallop along; but in reality they no doubt formed up around him, to protect him from injury. Farther to the right the king is seen grasping his enemies by the hair and slaying them.

The colossus. The visitor should now walk across the court to the fallen granite colossus, which is the largest statue in Egypt. It was seated at the left side of the entrance to the Second Court, and, no doubt, a similar figure was intended to be placed at the right side. Attempts have been made to quarry away the great figure, as may now be seen. When complete the statue must have weighed over a thousand tons. It was 57 or 58 feet in height; the length of the ear is $3\frac{1}{2}$ feet; the breadth of the face from ear to ear is $6\frac{3}{4}$ feet; the breast from shoulder to shoulder is $21\frac{1}{2}$ feet; the circumference of the arm at the elbow is $17\frac{1}{2}$ feet; the length of the index finger is $3\frac{1}{2}$ feet; the breadth of the foot across the toes is $4\frac{1}{2}$ feet; and the area of the nail upon the middle finger is about 35 square inches. When it is remembered that this colossus was made of a single piece of granite quarried at Aswân, shipped down the Nile to Thebes, and dragged across the fields to its present position, the visitor will be able to appreciate something of the stupendous nature of the work. This is the statue of Osymandyas, of which Shelley writes in his well-known sonnet:

> " I met a traveller from an antique land
> Who said: ' Two vast and trunkless legs of stone
> Stand in the desert. Near them on the sand,
> Half-sunk, a shattered visage lies. . . .' "

The legs, still standing when these lines were written, are now also shattered.

The second court. We now ascend into the Second Court, only a portion of the front wall of which now stands, this being supported by brick buttresses recently built by the Department of Antiquities. On the west side of this wall there was a row of Osirian figures standing against square pillars, but only four of these now remain. The north and south sides of the court have almost entirely disappeared; but the bases of the double row of columns may be seen. The west side of the court was formed, as at Medinet Habu, by a gallery or terrace, the roof of which was supported by a row

MORTUARY TEMPLES OF THE KINGS

of Osiris statues and a row of columns, only a few of these now remaining. On the west face of the front wall of this court there are some interesting scenes from the above-mentioned battle of Kadesh. These are seen to best advantage early in the afternoon, when the sunlight strikes the wall. To the left the king in his chariot charges through the chariots of the enemy in his escape from the beleaguered camp. Below him to the right runs the river Orontes, and into it the enemy is driven headlong. On the opposite bank the Hittite troops try to rescue some of their drowning comrades, and the king of Aleppo, one of the vassal sovereigns of the Hittite power, is turned upside down by his rescuers in order to relieve him of the water he has swallowed. Half-way up the wall at the extreme right the city of Kadesh is seen standing on a round island in the river Orontes. This was the city which Rameses had hoped to capture, but which remained in the hands of the Hittites at the close of the war. Above these scenes, at the top of the wall, there are representations of the festival of Min. These will be seen to better advantage at Medinet Habu, and there is no need to describe them here.

We now pass across the open court, in which lie fragments of statues, blocks from the fallen columns, and other debris of the once imposing temple. The visitor should particularly notice the colossal head of a black granite statue of Rameses, which is of fine workmanship. Three flights of steps lead up to the raised terrace at the west end, where stand the Osiris pillars corresponding to those which we have seen in front of the above-mentioned scenes from the battle of Kadesh. On the backs of these pillars the king is seen in the presence of the gods. To the left, or south, there is a portion of the temple wall which has not fallen. On the east face of this wall, to the right, the king is seen kneeling before the seated figures of Amen-Ra, Mut, and Khonsu, while Thoth, the god of wisdom, records his name in order that it may be perpetuated. To the left he is led forward into the divine presence by Menthu, the Theban war-god, and Tum. In the bottom row a number of the king's many sons are shown.

We now enter the ruins of the great Hypostyle Hall, which originally was entered through three doorways placed at the head of the three above-mentioned flights of steps. The roof of the hall was originally supported upon forty-eight columns. The calyx capitals of the columns in the middle aisle are well preserved, and are of very graceful form. The visitor will not fail to be impressed

The Great Hypostyle Hall.

by the beauty of the ruins if he will stand in the middle of this hall and will look westwards through the doorway to the Theban hills or eastward to the fallen colossus and the fields beyond. On the west face of the wall described above there is an important scene representing the siege of the Amorite fortress of Zapur. Rameses is seen charging towards the doomed city in his chariot, which is driven over the corpses of the slain. An overturned chariot, from which the occupant is seen to be falling, is crushed beneath the royal car. Along the lower line two sons of the Pharaoh stab and slay, while old men, women, and children beg piteously for mercy. The enemy in the beleaguered fortress appears to be making a stubborn defence. The banner or standard which rises above the citadel is pierced through and through with arrows; the walls are crowded with warriors, and dead bodies hang over the walls. The Egyptians, assisted by Sardinian mercenaries in horned helmets, place ladders against the walls, and attempt to mount; while at the bottom four princes, protected by testudos, assist in the attack. At the opposite end of the hall, on the left of the doorway, the king is seen receiving the royal insignia from Amen-Ra, behind whom is the goddess Mut. Below is a row of the king's sons. On the right of the doorway Rameses receives the symbol of life from Amen-Ra, who is seated. Behind the god stands Khonsu, while behind the king is Sekhmet. Below is a line of princes again.

The first small Hypostyle Hall.

We pass on into the first small Hypostyle Hall, the roof of which was supported by eight papyrus-bud columns. Part of the roof still remains in position, and on the ceiling astrological figures may be seen. It would appear from the inscriptions that the sacred books of Thoth, the god of wisdom, were kept in this hall. To the right and left of the entrance the sacred barques of the Theban trinity are shown carried in procession. At the farther end of the hall, on the right, there is a large scene showing the king seated amidst the foliage of the Heliopolitan tree of life. Atum (seated), Safkhet, the goddess of history, and the ibis-headed Thoth, write the king's names upon the leaves of the tree, in order that they may never be forgotten.

The second small Hypostyle Hall.

Entering the second small Hypostyle Hall, one sees on the right the king making offerings to Ptah and Sekhmet. This hall is much ruined, and only four of its columns remain. There were other halls and chambers beyond, but these are totally destroyed. The visitor passes across an open space and, traversing the streets between the ancient brick buildings, soon reaches

MORTUARY TEMPLES OF THE KINGS

the western doorway of the area, where he will find himself facing the tombs of Shêkh abd' el Gûrneh.

THE MORTUARY TEMPLE OF AMENHOTEP IInd

Immediately to the north of the Ramesseum are the ruins of the mortuary temple of Amenhotep IInd (B.C. 1448-1420); but the building is almost completely destroyed. The site was excavated by Professor Petrie in 1896.

THE MORTUARY TEMPLE OF SEPTAH

King Septah, the husband of Tausert (B.C. 1215-1209), placed his temple to the north of that of Amenhotep IInd. The site was excavated by Professor Petrie in 1896, and some interesting objects were found amidst the ruins of the building; but the place is too much destroyed to repay a visit.

THE MORTUARY TEMPLE OF THOTHMES IIIrd

The next temple to the north is that of Thothmes IIIrd (B.C. 1501-1447). It was excavated by the present writer in 1905 at the expense of Prince Djemil Pasha Toussoun.

The temple is built in the usual oblong form, running from due east to west. This is divided into three sections or courts. The first or outer court is entered between two ruined pylons of unbaked bricks; this court was left almost entirely unexcavated. An opening in the west wall, in the axial line, leads into the second or fore court, which is built upon a higher level; the pavement to the east of this doorway is made of limestone slabs. An inclined causeway constructed of bricks leads up to the third section of the temple, which again is on a higher level. At the foot of this ascent, upon the left hand, is a trough or basin of sandstone. Upon the right hand, opposite the trough, there is an indication of a stone construction which may have been an altar. At the entrance of the third court, where the causeway passes the brick crosswall, there are on either side of it a series of brick niches in which small statues may have stood. The third court, in which stood the main temple, was completely excavated to the pavement level. On the south and south-west sides of this court the natural limestone had been quarried away in order to give a level surface, and the face of the rock remained as a wall upon these sides.

Upon the north and north-west sides, however, a brick enclosing wall had been constructed. Towards the north-east of this area the ground dips, but rises somewhat again before the north boundary is reached, and the high level had been kept by the introduction of a large quantity of sand, held in place on the north side by a brick containing-wall running from east to west. In the middle of the now level courtyard the main temple was built.

This temple was constructed partly of sandstone and partly of limestone. It is so entirely ruined that little idea can be obtained of its original appearance. The main features now seen are the bases of a sandstone doorway and part of the adjoining wall upon the south side; the bases of two or three limestone columns; the pedestals probably of two colossal statues on the north-west side —a fragment of a colossal crown was found near by; and an indication of some of the main walls. The pavement of limestone remains intact in places, and towards the north-east it is seen to have been built over the sand filling and its containing wall. Most of the fallen blocks of relief are of limestone. The hieroglyphs and figures are of excellent workmanship, and some of the colouring is well preserved. A magazine built at the west end of the enclosure contains most of the fragments of the reliefs found during the excavation.

Some distance to the north of this temple there are some ruins which are thought to have been those of the palace of Hatshepsut. Farther to the north-east there are some remains of a small building of Amenhotep Ist, which was perhaps a mortuary temple for one of the members of that king's family, or for one of his ancestors. Just to the south of the temple of Sety Ist there are the remains of a temple begun by Rameses IInd, but abandoned when he decided to build the larger edifice now known as the Ramesseum.

THE MORTUARY TEMPLE OF RAMESES Ist AND SETY Ist

The temple in which the deified Pharaoh Sety Ist (B.C. 1313-1292) together with his father Rameses Ist (B.C. 1314-1313) was worshipped, is situated at the north extremity of the line of mortuary temples, not far from the point at which the road to the Valley of the Tombs of the Kings enters between the hills. It is therefore generally visited on the way to the tombs. It is generally called the temple of Gûrneh, but the name is not very

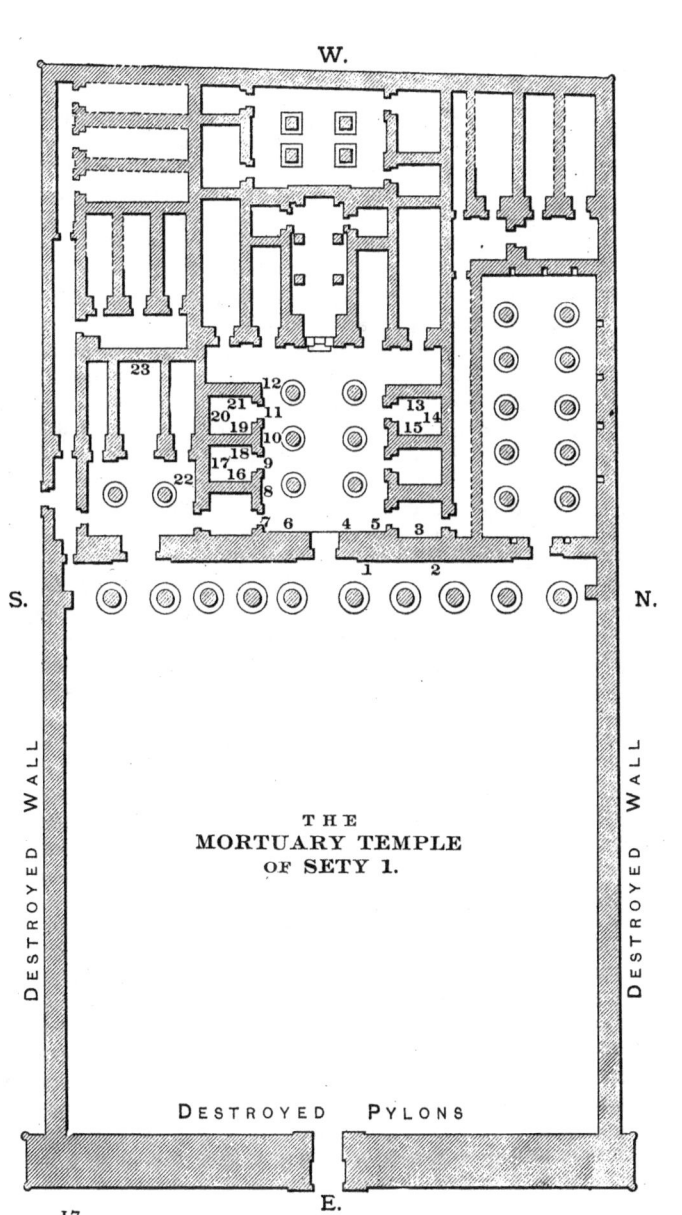

17

happy, as there are so many temples in Gûrneh. The tomb of Sety Ist in the valley (No. 17) is perhaps the largest and finest of all the royal sepulchres, and although this mortuary temple is not so large as those of later kings—for example, those of Rameses IInd and Rameses IIIrd—it was a more imposing structure than any built by previous kings. At the present time the entire court in front of the main temple, which was entered through the usual pylons, is destroyed, and thus the building has lost more than half its extent. The temple, however, possesses in beauty and elegance what it lacks in size, and the visitor will not fail to appreciate its graceful proportions. It was built towards the close of the reign of Sety Ist, and was never finished by him, being completed by his son Rameses IInd. Rameses Ist, the father of Sety Ist, had reigned for so short a time that he had made for himself only a small tomb (No. 16) and had erected no mortuary temple. Sety Ist therefore included his name in the inscriptions in this temple, and his figure is to be seen here and there upon the walls. Rameses IInd showed his filial piety in completing the temple, though probably he was only using funds specially left by Sety Ist for that purpose. The names of Kings Merenptah and Septah have been inscribed here; but no later king touched the temple, which must have soon fallen into disuse. At the time of writing the temple is much encumbered by fallen stones, but the Antiquities Department proposes to clear them away within the next few years. On certain days the vendors of small antiquities are authorised to ply their trade at a bench in front of the temple; and visitors are again reminded that only those who bear a brass badge exposed upon their arm are licensed, and that it is against the rule, made for the comfort of visitors, for these merchants to offer their goods to tourists upon the pathways or highroads.

We first enter the colonnade in front of the temple. Upon the façade, along the lower row, the figures of the provinces of Egypt, each in the form of the Nile god Hapi, are seen bearing the produce of the country towards the main door. Above this, to the right of the middle doorway (1), there is a large figure of Rameses IInd, who decorated the whole of this wall, sacrificing to Amen-Ra seated within a shrine. Behind the god there are standing figures of Mut, Khonsu, hawk-headed, and the king again. Beyond this (2) the king dances before Min. We now enter the northernmost of the three doors, and find ourselves in a large roofless hall, which originally contained ten columns, the back portion being divided into several chambers. These columns

MORTUARY TEMPLES OF THE KINGS

and dividing walls are now destroyed, and one sees but a large open area, on the surrounding walls of which Rameses IInd is shown offering to various gods. We pass through the door on our left and enter a small chamber. On the left wall (3) Rameses IInd is seen dancing before Min, behind whom stands the goddess Ament. Between the king and the god there are two tall stands upon which are two sacrificial vessels and a bunch of lotus flowers. We now pass through this chamber into the central Hypostyle Hall, the decorations of which were almost completed by Sety Ist. Just to the north of the main doorway (4) that king is led forward by Mentu and Tum, the former giving him the symbol of life. Next to this (5) he receives the symbol of many jubilees from a seated figure of Amen-Ra, behind whom is Khonsu. On the opposite side of the doorway (6) Rameses kneels before the seated figures of Amen-Ra and the deified Sety Ist. Behind the king is Mut, who raises her arms to bless him. Along the upper part of the south wall (7) Sety Ist makes an offering to Amen-Ra, while the vulture goddess of Nekheb hovers above him. Next (8) a now headless figure of the king is shown leading cattle to sacrifice to Min. Then (9) with arms raised he presents the harvest (represented by four stacks of corn decorated with feathers) to the now headless figures of Amen-Ra and Mut. Next (10) the king, again headless, offers flowers to Min and Isis. Then (11) he sacrifices to Amen-Ra, Mut, and Khonsu; and at the end of the wall, lower down (12), he is suckled by Mut, the mother goddess. In the third room on the north of the hall, on the left wall (13), Sety pours out a libation to Osiris, Isis, and Horus; on the end wall (14) he burns incense and pours out a libation to Amen-Ra, Mut, and Khonsu, who are in a shrine; and on the right wall (15) he makes an offering to Osiris enthroned, behind whom are Isis, Hathor, and Nephthys. We now enter the second, or middle, room on the south side of the hall. On the left wall (16) the jackal-headed Wepwet makes an offering to the enthroned and deified Sety Ist, behind whom is the goddess of the Theban nome. On the end wall (17) the enthroned figure of Sety is purified with holy water by Horus-Supporter-of-his-Mother (p. 199) and Thoth. On the right wall (18) the former offers to Sety who is enthroned with the goddess Maat. Passing into the next room we see on the left wall (19) the figure of Thoth standing before the sacred barque in which the image of Sety was carried at the memorial ceremonies. On the end wall (20) Sety is seen enthroned between Amen-Ra and Mut, the patrons of Thebes, on the one side, and Ptah and Sekhmet, the patrons of Memphis, on the other. On the left wall (21) Horus-Supporter-of-his-Mother makes an offering to the soul of Sety, behind whom is a goddess, on whose head is the name of this temple.

We now pass out into the front gallery and enter the temple again by the southernmost of the three main doors, which leads us into a two-pillared hall dedicated to the worship of Rameses Ist. On the right wall (22) Rameses IInd is seen kneeling before Amen-Ra, who gives him the symbol of jubilees. Behind the king is Mut ; and behind Amen is Khonsu and the deceased Rameses Ist. Three sanctuaries lead off this hall. In the two side ones are reliefs showing Rameses before the gods. In the middle sanctuary we see Sety on either side offering to the sacred barques of Amen-Ra. On the end wall (23) Sety is twice seen, in the guise of Osiris, in a hawk-topped shrine. The back chambers of the temple are much ruined and do not repay a visit.

CHAPTER X

THE TWO MORTUARY TEMPLES OF DÊR EL BAHRI

ALTHOUGH the smaller of the two temples at Dêr el Bahri is not often visited, the large temple is to be regarded as one of the finest ruins in Egypt. It is built against the cliffs at the western end of a bay not far north-west of the Ramesseum. There is a rest-house near the temple at which visitors travelling under the arrangements of Thos. Cook & Son, or those staying at the Winter Palace Hotel or Luxor Hotel, may take their lunch. At the gates of the rest-house the vendors of small antiquities are authorised to sell their goods to the tourists (see p. 258). It is usual for parties of tourists to visit the Tombs of the Kings in the morning, to lunch at this rest-house, and then to visit Dêr el Bahri in the afternoon; but those who have the time to spare will find it best to combine the excursion to this temple with something less fatiguing than a visit to the royal valley. The name *Dêr el Bahri*, "The Northern Monastery," has reference to the Christian monastery erected on the site of the large temple in about the seventh century A.D. In ancient days this district was known as *Zesret*, "the Holy," and the two temples were called *Zesreti*, "The two Holy [Places]."

THE MORTUARY TEMPLE OF NEBHAPETRA

King Nebhapetra Mentuhotep (XIth dynasty), who is generally known as Mentuhotep IIIrd but is perhaps to be regarded as Mentuhotep IInd, reigned for forty-six years from B.C. 2076 to 2030; and we have here his tomb and funeral temple. In causing his body to be buried here Nebhapetra was following the example of his predecessor Nebhotep Mentuhotep Ist, whose tomb,[1] now filled up, was discovered not long ago just near the house which stands in front of the temple which we are about to describe. This tomb does not seem to have had a mortuary temple attached to it; but

---

[1] Called *Bab el Hosan* by the natives.

Nebhapetra, being a much greater and more powerful king, was not satisfied with the construction of a tomb for himself, and caused a pyramid to be built in front of it and a mortuary temple around about, called by the ancient Egyptians *Akhaset*, "The Glorious Seat." These buildings are situated at the foot of the cliffs just to the south of the large temple. They were discovered by Professor Naville and Mr. H. R. Hall (Egypt Exploration Fund) in 1903; and though of great importance to archæologists the visitor will not find the ruins of much interest now that the most valuable objects have been taken to the Cairo Museum. One ascends to the platform upon which the pyramid is built by a sloping ramp, flanked by colonnades of square pillars. One of the original beams of wood will be noticed (under foot) as one ascends the ramp. At the top the visitor finds himself upon a paved platform from which rises the ruined base of a pyramid, about 60 feet square, which was once cased with fine stonework, though the filling was of the roughest material. Around the pyramid there was a colonnade, the walls of which were once covered with reliefs. If the visitor will walk round to the back of the pyramid he will find a row of pits sunk in the pavement and originally surmounted by decorated shrines. In these pits were buried the favourite ladies of the king's *harêm;* and those who have visited the Cairo Museum may remember the beautiful white limestone sarcophagus of a woman named Kauit, which stands in a corner of the great central hall there, and which was discovered in one of these pits. Behind this row of graves the visitor will see the entrance of the tunnel-like tomb of the king himself which runs down into the rock for 500 feet, and ends in a granite chamber in which an alabaster shrine or sarcophagus was found wherein the royal mummy had been laid to rest. After the king had been buried the temple, originally intended solely for the benefit of his soul, began to be used as a place of more general worship, and the goddess Hathor seems to have been especially reverenced here. Dudumes, a king of the XIIIth dynasty, has left his name in the temple, showing that it was at that time a place of worship. On the right of the entrance to the tomb, a few yards from the north-west angle of the pyramid, the famous shrine containing a figure of the Hathor cow was discovered. It is now to be seen in the Cairo Museum. The shrine was made during the reign of Thothmes IIIrd, and the cow was sculptured at the orders of his successor, Amenhotep IInd, who caused it to be placed here in honour of Hathor, the goddess of the Western Mountains. At this time the pyramid was still standing, for as late as the reign of King Septah (B.C. 1215) an inscription was cut upon the casing stones. In the papyri and tomb paintings of this period there is often a representation of a pyramid and tomb standing in front of the hills from which the Hathor cow looks out. This will have been noticed perhaps in the mortuary chapels of the Theban nobles. It is possible that this conventional representation of the tomb (with the pyramid and the Hathor cow) has as its prototype this mortuary temple of Nebhapetra. It was the earliest building of any size in the necropolis, and Nebhapetra, either on his own merits or on those of his temple, became a sort of patron-saint of the cemetery; and thus it is not surprising that the priests should regard the building as the purest example of what a tomb should be. As a matter of fact, the type is not a pure one; for the pyramid, which in earlier days was the actual burial-place, is here an architectural feature without meaning, since the actual tomb lies behind it in the rock. In the reign of Rameses IXth (B.C. 1142–1123) an inspection of the royal tombs was made, and the "pyramid" tomb of Nebhapetra was found to be intact. But in later years the king's mummy was robbed; and no traces of it, save only a few fragments of the embalming cloth, were found by the modern archæologists. The temple fell into ruins before the end of the Pharaonic age, and the pyramid was no doubt destroyed for the sake of its stone.

THE MORTUARY TEMPLE OF HATSHEPSUT

In the last chapter the mortuary temples of the Pharaohs of the XVIIIth, XIXth, and XXth dynasties were described; and it was seen how these buildings stood upon the edge of the cultivation, while the royal tombs were hidden away in the distant valley. Queen Hatshepsut's tomb was cut in the cliffs on the east side of this valley, and was intended to run directly eastwards into the great ridge of rock which, like a natural wall, separates the valley from the Theban plain. Thus, if her mortuary temple was placed at the opposite side of this wall, that is to say, against the eastern face of the cliffs, the priests who worshipped her soul there would be standing almost above the place where her body lay. In the days of the old kingdom the mortuary temples of the kings stood upon the east side of the pyramids in which they lay; and here the cliffs took the place of the pyramid, under which the body was buried, and on the east side of the cliffs the temple would stand.

History of the temple.

The queen therefore decided to build her mortuary temple close up against that of her ancestor Nebhapetra, which has just been described. To a large extent she copied this earlier building, though she dispensed with the pyramid. One ascended a similar ramp, flanked by colonnades, and there were chapels in which the cow of Hathor was worshipped; but her building was on a far larger scale, and entirely eclipsed that of her ancestor. An avenue of sphinxes led from the temple down to the edge of the cultivation, and at the east end of this there was a building which may have been used as a palace by the queen. As this neighbourhood was known as *Zesret*, "the Holy," she called her temple *Zeserzesru*, "the Holy of Holies." The archæologist is confronted with a very serious difficulty upon the walls of this great temple, for he has to find his way through the confusion of cartouches which is always met with in dealing with monuments of this period. Queen Hatshepsut was the daughter of Thothmes Ist. When Thothmes Ist died he was succeeded by his son Thothmes IInd, who was, perhaps, married to his sister, Hatshepsut. Thothmes IInd was succeeded after a short reign by his half-brother, or possibly son, Thothmes IIIrd, who thereupon married Hatshepsut. At first the power was almost entirely in the hands of the king; but it soon shifted to those of the queen, and Thothmes IIIrd appears upon the walls of the Dêr el Bahri temple in a very inferior position. It was only when the queen died that he again obtained absolute control of the government and showed himself to be one of the greatest of Egypt's Pharaohs. So furious was he at the years of suppression which he had suffered during Hatshepsut's lifetime, that in revenge he erased her name from all her monuments. This he did in the temple of Dêr el Bahri; but we are now confronted with the difficulty. Over the erased name of the queen are written the names of Thothmes Ist and Thothmes IInd. Is it possible that these two kings were not dead, and, after years of exile, came back to power? Or are we to suppose that Thothmes IIIrd inserted their names over that of Hatshepsut? We know that kings sometimes did insert the names of their dead predecessors on erased cartouches: for example, the name of Amenhotep IIIrd, erased by the heretic king, was rewritten in full (upon the sarcophagus of Queen Thiy) by Tutankhamen, or some other king. On the other hand, why should Thothmes IIIrd have particular feelings of respect for the first two kings of that name? For the purposes of this guide, fortunately, an answer need not be given to the question, nor need the reader confuse himself further in the

MORTUARY TEMPLES OF DÊR EL BAHRI

matter. It is only necessary for him to remember that the temple was built by Hatshepsut during the reign of Thothmes IInd, and at the beginning of her joint reign with Thothmes IIIrd (about B.C. 1500), when the king was in an inferior position; that it was still unfinished at her death; and that at some time or other her name was everywhere erased. As Hatshepsut was a queen regnant, she was generally represented upon the monuments as a king, and is often spoken of as "he" instead of "she." This was merely a convention however, and there is no reason to suppose that she actually assumed male costume in real life, as is so often stated. The architect of the temple was probably the famous Senmut (p. 148), who was one of the queen's great supporters, and fell with her. Some additions were made by Rameses IInd; Merenptah inscribed his name on the walls; and in Ptolemaic times the innermost sanctuary was repaired by Physkon and Lathyros, who, however, seem to have mistaken the nature of the building, as we shall see later. A Christian monastery was erected upon its ruins, and soon little of the temple remained visible. Mariette excavated a portion of the building, and the rest was cleared by the Egypt Exploration Fund, under the direction of Professor Naville. The restoration of the terraces was undertaken as the only practical means of protecting the paintings from rain.

Before ascending the ramp a visit may be made to the lower colonnade on the south side. That on the north side is uninteresting. The scenes are mostly erased, and the figure of Hatshepsut is everywhere destroyed; but half-way along the wall (1) there is a fine figure of Thothmes IIIrd dancing before Min. Farther to the south (2), in the lower row, there is an interesting line of soldiers carrying, besides their axes, branches of trees and standards, this being the festival of the dedication of the queen's obelisks. The troop on the right is met by a company of archers led by a bugler. Farther to the left we see butchers and priests preparing offerings for the festival, and at the end of the wall there are more troops. Above this are boats sailing down the Nile, bringing the obelisks, which were finally set up at Karnak (p. 98), from the quarries at Aswân. We now ascend the ramp, and, reaching the middle court, we bear off to the right. Here the view is very fine; the beautiful colonnade on our right, with its sixteen-sided columns standing out delicately against the towering rocks behind, affords a composition of the greatest charm. Crossing the court a small, twelve-pillared hall is entered, which forms the pronaos to a chapel of Anubis, the jackal-god of the necro- *The lower court.*

The middle court.

The chapel of Anubis.

266   ANTIQUITIES OF UPPER EGYPT

polis. Here the colour is very well preserved, but the figures of Hatshepsut have been erased, only those of Thothmes IIIrd remaining. On our right (3) the jackal-headed Anubis stands looking towards a little niche, in which are figures of the three deities, Nekheb, Anubis, and Uazet. Above this niche there is a strongly coloured figure of Thothmes IIIrd offering two cups of wine to the hawk-headed Seker. At the other end of this wall (4) there has been the representation of a shrine, in which is the standard of Wepwet (a skin hung upon a pole), and before it there was a figure of Hatshepsut, but this has been destroyed. Above the shrine the visitor should notice the very decorative vulture painted in red, blue, and white. On the adjoining wall (5) Anubis sits enthroned, and receives a mass of offerings presented by the now erased figure of Hatshepsut. Above the queen the beautifully coloured hawk of Edfu hovers. On the far side of the doorway leading into the inner chambers (6) Amen-Ra is seen enthroned, and before him are offerings presented by the queen. Above the queen is the vulture of El Kâb, again noticeable for its fine colouring. On the next wall (7) are the hawk-headed Harmachis and the goddess Nekheb, and above them is another fine vulture with spread wings. Farther to the left (8) Anubis is seen looking towards a niche, in which are the figures of Nekheb (here identified with Mut), Uazet, and Amen-Ra. Above the niche is a figure of Osiris. The visitor should now enter the inner chambers of this chapel. On the end wall of the first room the standard of Wepwet is seen, but the figure of Hatshepsut before it is erased. On the side walls Anubis and Amen-Ra are seen. A second room leads off to the right, and in it there are representations of Anubis and other gods. On the right is a good figure of Thothmes IIIrd pouring holy water over Seker, the god of the dead. From this room another shrine leads off, very dark, and evidently intended to be very secret.

The Birth Colonnade. Returning to the court, one should now enter the Birth Colonnade, upon the walls of which the immaculate conception and birth of Queen Hatshepsut are recorded. The visitor will remember a somewhat similar series of scenes in the Luxor Temple (p. 75) referring to the birth of Amenhotep IIIrd. The scenes now before us are badly damaged; for not only did Thothmes IIIrd erase the figures of the queen throughout, but in later years Akhnaton erased the figures of Amen-Ra. Rameses IInd recoloured a large part of the erased scenes, but his work is very crude. The series begins at the south end of the colonnade (9).

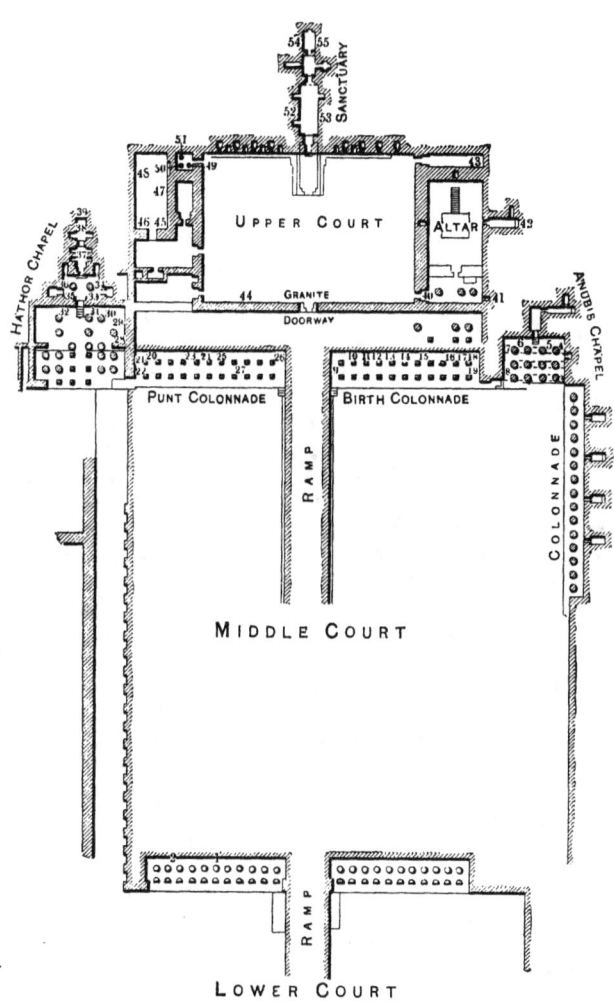

THE TEMPLE OF DÊR EL BAHRI

Here at the top of the wall, in the middle of the portion which is sculptured, Amen-Ra is seen with the *Ka* or astral body of the unborn queen upon his knee, while before him and below him are the gods who have come to see the child. It was the desire of Amen to find a woman who should give birth to a child which should be the human counterpart of the astral child whom he was nursing. He therefore questioned the gods, and learnt from Thoth that Queen Aahmes, the beautiful wife of the old King Thothmes I., was a fitting mother for the child; and the god of wisdom advised him to enter the queen's chamber while the king was out. Acting upon this advice, Amen-Ra came down to earth, penetrated to the queen's chamber, and seated himself beside her. Thereupon two goddesses transported them to the clouds, where we see them (10) seated opposite each other while the god places the symbol of life to her nostrils, and the queen becomes pregnant with the divine breath. The inscription tells us that the god at first assumed the form of the absent husband, in order that the queen should receive him as he desired. He found her asleep, but the fragrance of his presence awoke her. It was not until he had accomplished his purpose, however, that the queen realised that she had been transported to the heavens and had been mated with a god. Amen-Ra then told her that in due course she should give birth to a daughter, who should be named Hatshepsut, and should rule the land of Egypt. He then returned to heaven, and the queen found herself once more in her palace. Amen-Ra then sent for the ram-headed Khnum, the potter of the gods, and (11) told him to fashion the daughter whom he had created so that her form should be as exalted as that of a god. We then see Khnum (12) seated before a potter's wheel, upon which he is fashioning the human body of the child as an exact replica of the astral child which is seen beside it. The frog-headed goddess Heket is seen putting life into the nostrils of the divinely created babe. The ibis-headed Thoth (13) now appears to the queen, and warns her to prepare for her confinement. Queen Aahmes, now big with child (14), is led forward to her accouchement by Heket and Khnum. The scene in which the queen is brought to bed (15), like all other scenes in this series, is treated with delicacy and modesty. It is difficult to make out the various figures, but by close examination the visitor will see the queen seated on a chair, her hands chafed by the midwives. The chair stands upon a great couch with lion-legs, and this again stands upon another larger couch. Below

MORTUARY TEMPLES OF DÊR EL BAHRI 269

the bed, as though supporting it in the heavens, are various gods, including the genii of the north, south, east, and west. The midwife on the right of the queen should be especially noticed. She kneels upon one knee, and her hands are outstretched towards the queen. Her figure is beautifully drawn, and quite lacks the conventional faults which so often minimise the artistic value of Egyptian drawings : it might have been the work of a Greek. At the extreme right sits Meskhent, the goddess of births, who directs the midwives. We next see (16) the queen seated on a great bed, while two Hathors, with cow-heads, suckle the baby and its astral body. It is curious to notice that the child, being of divine parentage, has actually twelve *Kas* or astral bodies, and these (17) we see being nursed by twelve goddesses. At the end of the wall (18) the child and its *Ka* (erased) are presented to the gods, the scene ending with an interview between Thoth and Amen, at which the child's future is perhaps arranged. On the end wall of the colonnade (19), in the lower scene, the child and its *Ka* (erased) are seen in the hands of kneeling goddesses; and Safkhet, goddess of History, dips her pen in the ink-pot to write a record of the birth.

The visitor should now walk round to the colonnade on the south side, where the famous scenes from the expedition to the land of Punt (pronounced Pount) are to be seen. The country of Punt was situated on the shores of the Red Sea, and probably embraced the whole area between Ras Ruway and Somaliland. It was believed by the Egyptians to be the home of their ancestors, and they seem to have regarded it with considerable respect on that account. Several expeditions thither are known to have been made at various periods ; and Queen Hatshepsut, in sending her ships there to obtain the gums and spices for which parts of the country were famous, was only following the example of many of her predecessors. The expedition seems to have been fitted out upon the Nile, and to have passed into the Red Sea by way of the Wady Tumilât Canal, which had connected the two waters since the days of the XIIth dynasty ; but it is possible that the ships were built at Kossair or some other port, the materials having been transported across the desert from Thebes. The exact destination of the expedition is not known, but a luxuriant, marshy country at the edge of the sea or at the mouth of a river is indicated by the reliefs. The series of scenes begins at the south end of the colonnade, at the south end of the west wall (20). Here we see two rows of boats.

The Punt Colonnade.

The lower row represents the Egyptian ships arriving at their destination. The sails are spread, but the men are rowing to help them along. The inscription states that the ships are "arriving at the goodly way into God's Land, journeying in peace to the land of Punt." The complicated rigging and tackle of the vessels is most clearly shown, and will be easily understood by those who are acquainted with the rig of sailing-vessels. In each case the captain of the ship and first officer are seen standing in the enclosure which corresponded to the bridge. In one case the captain calls, "Steer to port!" In front of these large vessels there is a small rowing-boat, which seems to have been sent ahead in order to replenish the empty water-jars from the streams or wells of the mainland, thus indicating that the journey has not been without its hardships. Leaving the upper row for the present, we pass on to the south wall (21). Here (bottom row) the Egyptians have now landed, and a small force of soldiers, heavily armed with spears, axes, and shields, in case of attack, is led into the interior by an officer. They have brought with them a few objects with which to trade with the natives: strings of beads, an axe, a dagger, some bracelets, and a wooden chest. The chieftain of Punt, named Parahu, with arms raised in salutation, steps forward to parley with the Egyptian officer. The representation of the enormously fat wife and daughter of the prince is now to be seen in the Cairo Museum, the block of stone having been stolen from the wall many years ago, and later recovered. Two sons, and three servants driving a donkey on which the queen was wont to ride, have now disappeared altogether. The village from which the prince and his family have come is seen to the left (22). Here are houses built on piles under the trees, with ladders leading up to them. A dog is seen (high up on the wall), and cattle are shown grazing under the trees. The water, in which are all manner of fishes, seems to approach close to the houses. The inscription tells us that the men of Punt addressed the Egyptians in the following words: "Why have ye come hither unto this land, which the people of Egypt know not? Did ye come down the ways of heaven, or did ye sail upon the sea and upon the waters of God's Land? Or have ye trodden the path of the sun? Lo, as for the King of Egypt, is there no way unto his majesty that we may live by the breath which he gives?" In the upper rows, just above the group of soldiers (21), there is a tent, and before it incense, gold rings, and other valuables are piled, these having been presented by the

MORTUARY TEMPLES OF DÊR EL BAHRI

men of Punt. In this tent the Egyptian officers gave a feast of "bread, beer, wine, meat, fruit, and everything that is found in Egypt," for the edification of the chieftain. Above this, again, we see the Egyptians carrying off the incense trees in baskets; and on the next wall, upper row (20), the ships are seen being loaded. Men walk up the gangways carrying the trees, and above this more trees, apes, and other marvels from this strange land, are carried on board. The inscription describes this scene in the following words: "The loading of the ships very heavily with marvels from the land of Punt; all goodly fragrant woods, heaps of myrrh-resin, with fresh myrrh-trees, with ebony and pure ivory, with green gold of Amu, with cinnamon-wood, *khesyt*-wood, with *ahmut*-incense, *senter*-incense, eye-cosmetic, with apes, monkeys, dogs, with skins of the southern panther, and with natives and their children." Farther to the right we see the ships returning, laden with their strange cargo. The inscription tells us that they are now supposed to be upon the Nile again, nearing Thebes. On arrival at the capital the produce of Punt (23) is displayed. At the bottom of the wall are three great incense trees, representing the thirty-one trees which arrived safely, and under these are cattle. Above are skins, chests of gold, bows, &c.; and higher up are panthers, a now headless giraffe, and other animals. Great heaps of incense leaves (24) are being measured in wooden measures; and above this gold rings are weighed in the balances against weights in the form of oxen (p. 136). The inscription tells us that "silver, lazuli, malachite, and every splendid costly stone" was also weighed. Farther along the wall (25) there is a fine figure of Thothmes IIIrd, with his large, characteristic nose. He offers two jars of incense leaves to the erased barque of Amen-Ra, which was carried on the shoulders of the priests. Amen-Ra then makes a speech, saying that he will open up the land of Punt to Egyptian enterprise. On the end wall (26) an erased figure of Hatshepsut is seen in a kiosk or shrine, below which is a striking decoration of two lions and the symbol of the union of Upper and Lower Egypt. Before her were the figures of three nobles, one of whom was the great Senmut, but these have been erased. The queen announces to them the success of the expedition, and, in a bombastic speech, testifies to her own glory. This brings the series of scenes to a close. On the north side of the fourth pillar from this end (27) there is an excellent portrait of Thothmes IIIrd, who is embraced by Amen-Ra.

The Hathor Chapel.

The visitor should now walk round to the Hathor Chapel, which stands to the south of the Punt Colonnade, corresponding in situation to the Anubis Chapel, which has already been seen on the north side of the temple. We first enter a hall, the columns of which are now for the most part destroyed. Some of these had Hathor capitals (see Dendereh, p. 32). On the wall to our right (28) there are some interesting festival scenes. In the bottom row soldiers, carrying branches of trees as well as their arms, run forward to the sound of the tom-tom. At the right end two men dance and others beat castanets. Above are the festal boats, upon which are vacant thrones under canopies, which will be occupied by the king and queen. Farther to the left (29) Thothmes IIIrd presents a sacred oar to Hathor. On the adjoining wall (30) Hatshepsut, whose name is changed to that of Thothmes IInd, dances before Hathor; and farther along (31) the goddess, in the form of a cow, licks the hand of the enthroned Pharaoh. This scene is repeated (32) on the opposite side of the doorway. Passing through this doorway we enter the inner chambers. The first of these rooms is a small two-pillared hall, from which four little shrines lead off. On the right wall as we enter (33) Thothmes IIIrd is seen offering a curious symbol to Hathor. On the next wall (34) there is an erased figure of Hatshepsut making offerings to Hathor. On the left side of the entrance doorway (35) an erased figure of Hatshepsut is seen offering harvest sheaves decorated with feathers to Hathor. On the adjoining wall (36) the lion-headed goddess Urthekau offers her necklace to an enthroned figure of Amen-Ra. A fine doorway, with Hathor totems painted on either side, leads into the inner sanctuary. Here on either side (37) there is a fine figure of the Hathor cow standing under a canopy in its sacred barque, heaps of offerings being placed before it by erased figures of Hatshepsut, in front of whom is the nude boy-deity Aha, son of Horus. We then enter the innermost vaulted shrine. On either side (38) the Hathor cow is seen, and Hatshepsut is shown drinking from its udder. At the end wall (39) is a figure of the queen between Amen-Ra and Hathor. In this shrine there probably stood a figure of a Hathor cow, such as that found in the temple of Nebhapetra.

The upper court.

We now return to the middle court and ascend the ramp which leads up the hill. At the top of this a granite doorway, erected by Hatshepsut, whose name has been replaced by that of Thothmes IIIrd, is passed, and we find ourselves in the upper court

MORTUARY TEMPLES OF DÊR EL BAHRI

of the temple. Before us is a series of niches in the wall, and in the middle is the doorway leading to the inner sanctuary. On either side of the court are chambers in which the mortuary services were performed. We may first enter the doorway upon our right. Inside this doorway, on the left (40), there is a figure of Hatshepsut, altered to Thothmes IInd, standing between Harmachis and Amen-Ra, to which gods this portion of the temple seems to have been dedicated. In a niche in the opposite wall (41) a little figure of Amen-Ra is seen. In the middle of the hall, on our left, there is a great limestone altar, at the far side of which are steps leading up to it. This altar was dedicated to Harmachis, the great sun-god of Heliopolis, who in the form of Aton became the sole god of Egypt in the reign of Akhnaton (p. 161). There is a little shrine leading off this hall to the right of the altar; but its close proximity to the place where Harmachis was worshipped caused it to suffer heavily under Akhnaton, who, believing that Harmachis was the only god, destroyed all the figures of other gods carved upon its walls. As Thothmes IIIrd had already erased the figure of Hatshepsut in it, we now find only few of the reliefs intact. Entering, we see on the right and left walls the figures of Hatshepsut (erased by Thothmes IIIrd) and those of the gods (erased by Akhnaton). On the end wall (42) there is a well-preserved figure of Thothmes Ist, and an erased figure of Hatshepsut adoring at a shrine in which is a standard or totem of Wepwet. A recess leads off to the left. On the right wall of this Thothmes Ist and Queen Senseneb, his mother, make offerings to an erased figure of Anubis. On the left wall Queen Aahmes, mother of Hatshepsut, and an erased figure of Hatshepsut herself, make offerings to an erased figure of Amen-Ra. On the end wall an erased Anubis salutes the erased Hatshepsut. The representations of Senseneb, Thothmes Ist, and Aahmes in this shrine indicate that the souls of Hatshepsut's ancestors were here adored, and her royal descent celebrated. The colour upon the walls is wonderfully fresh, but it has been somewhat spoilt by a coating of varnish, which has turned yellow with time.

Returning to the court, we may enter the second door upon our right, which admits us to a shrine dedicated to Min-Amen. On the right and left walls are large erased figures of Hatshepsut and figures of Thothmes IIIrd (not erased) offering to Min and Amen-Ra. On the end wall (43) there is a damaged scene showing Hatshepsut, whose name has been changed to that of Thothmes IInd, embracing Min. Crossing to the other side of the court we may notice on the east wall (44) a troop of soldiers bearing festal standards, &c. Some are leading panthers along, and others carry the two portable thrones of Hatshepsut and Thothmes IIIrd. We may then enter the chapel on our left, *i.e.* the second door on the south side of the court, which was set apart for the funeral services in honour of Hatshepsut. This chapel is modelled on the form of the Old Kingdom mastaba chapels, the arrangement being much the same as that, for example, in the chapel of Aba (p. 173). Against the end wall stood the stela, but this is now destroyed. The vaulted masonry roof should be noticed. To right and left as we enter (45 and 46) butchers are seen cutting up the meat which is to be sacrificed before the stela. On the right wall (47) there are well-preserved rows of servants bringing all manner of offerings towards the stela. On the opposite wall a similar scene is represented, and the visitor may particularly notice the servants who lead along a crane with its beak tied to its neck. This method of securing a crane is well known: the bird has to thrust its head forward in order to obtain the impetus to begin to fly, and this being rendered impossible, it can only walk. On this wall, just below the point at which the roofed portion begins (48), there is a series of small figures, some kneeling, and some pouring out libations. This represents the well-known funeral service performed by the "Reader-priests," which occurs constantly on the Old Kingdom monuments, and continues throughout Pharaonic times. At the end of the wall, on either side of the chamber, is an erased figure of Hatshepsut seated upon the throne, symbolical of the union of Upper and Lower Egypt. This symbol, so commonly seen, consists of the intertwining of lotus and papyrus stalks, each held by a figure of the Nile-god Hapi.

Returning through the court we now visit the next shrine on our left, dedicated to Amen-Ra. Here we have figures of Hatshepsut (whose cartouches have been converted into those of Thothmes Ist and Thothmes IInd) and Thothmes IIIrd offering to the gods. On our left (49) Hatshepsut is embraced by the goddess Uazet. On the adjoining wall (50) the queen offers cups of wine to Min-Amen, and on the next wall (51) the queen on the left and Thothmes IIIrd on the right offer the symbol of fine linen to Amen-Ra.

The visitor should now enter the main sanctuary of the temple, which opens from the middle of the west wall of the court. Before its granite doorway is a portico built in Ptolemaic times. Here, in a rough red-paint inscription, mention is made of

Amenhotep IIIrd and of Amenhotep, son of Hapu, the wise man of that reign. Entering the first chamber we may notice at the bottom of the wall on the left (52) some well-drawn ducks and other birds supposed to be in a lake. To one side are the squares which represent the irrigated fields. High above this Hatshepsut kneels, and beside her stands her daughter Raneferu. They present offerings to a much-damaged barque of Amen-Ra. On the right wall (53) Hatshepsut, Thothmes IIIrd, and the Princess Raneferu sacrifice to this barque, behind which stood Thothmes Ist, Queen Aahmes, and the little Princess Batineferu. We pass on through the next chamber and reach the innermost shrine, which was entirely rebuilt in Ptolemaic times. On the left and right are various ill-proportioned figures of gods, those on the left wall (54) being led by the deified philosopher Imhotep, and those on the right (55) by the deified Amenhotep, son of Hap (p. 276). It would seem that in Ptolemaic times the priests no longer remembered that this building was the mortuary temple of Hatshepsut, but regarded it as some mystical sanctuary connected with these two great wise men.

A few yards to the north of the Lower Court there is the tomb in which one hundred and sixty-three mummies of priests were found in the year 1891. These are now in the Cairo Museum. In the valley to the south of the temple, behind the hill of Shêkh abd' el Gûrneh, is the tomb in which the great find of royal mummies was made in 1881 (p. 191).

CHAPTER XI

DÊR EL MEDINEH—THE TOMBS OF THE QUEENS —THE PALACE OF AMENHOTEP, KASR EL AGUZ, AND OTHER ANCIENT SITES

DÊR EL MEDINEH

THE temple of Dêr el Medineh, though of small size, is a building of considerable beauty; and visitors should not fail to see it. From Luxor one takes the road which passes the colossi, and at the edge of the desert one leaves the rest-house of the Department of Antiquities on the left, and takes the road which runs straight ahead into the desert. This road presently bends to the right, and passes round behind the hill known as Gurnet Murrai; and the little temple is then reached. From it a pathway leads over the hills to the south to the Tombs of the Queens.

The history of the temple.
Although the present building dates from Ptolemaic times, the site seems to have a much longer history. In the reign of Amenhotep IIIrd (B.C. 1411–1375) there lived a master builder named Amenhotep, the son of Hapu, who was famous for his religious and philosophical teaching. When he died he was buried somewhere in the necropolis of Thebes, and a chapel was erected for the benefit of his soul. In the year B.C. 1380 Amenhotep IIIrd called a meeting of various officials in this chapel, and issued a decree establishing services here for all time. Now the temple of Dêr el Medineh, which was founded by Ptolemy IVth Philopator, has often been thought to have been built upon the ruins of a chapel connected with this Amenhotep; for in the temple there is an inscription which states that the name of this wise man shall abide for ever, and that his sayings shall not perish. In spite of many arguments to the contrary, it is quite possible that the existing temple stands upon the ruins of this chapel which was dedicated to the soul of the old philosopher; and, moreover, it is possible that the tomb of Amenhotep was in the immediate

DÊR EL MEDINEH

neighbourhood. A tomb was recently found a few yards from the temple, which dated from the reign of Amenhotep IIIrd, and which belonged to a master builder; and thus there is no reason to suppose that the more famous master builder was not also buried here, in which case his chapel would be situated in the locality, and might well be the original of the temple which we are about to describe. In Ptolemaic times Amenhotep, son of Hapu, came to be regarded almost as a divinity, under the name Amenothes, son of Paapis; and he was ranked with another famous Egyptian master builder and sage, Imhotep, who had earlier received semi-divine honours. When the Ptolemies erected the existing temple they caused a representation of the figure of Amenhotep to be shown upon one of the pillars, and that of the figure of Imhotep on another. The reliefs in the sanctuaries are of a mortuary nature, as though the temple was actually a funerary chapel. It is said that the brick girdle wall dates from the earlier temple. In Christian times a monastery was built inside the enclosure, and portions of this building may be seen on the south side of the temple.

One enters through a stone gateway in the enclosing wall, and crosses an open court. On the outside wall of the temple there are many Greek and Coptic inscriptions, cut there after the building had fallen into disuse. One then enters the first court, the roof of which was supported by two columns. A partly destroyed screen wall shuts off the three chambers which lie beyond it. At either end of this screen wall there is a Hathor-headed pillar abutting the wall; and in the middle are two pillars with elaborate capitals. On these are the above-mentioned figures of the sages Amenhotep and Imhotep. Passing through the doorway in the middle of the screen, one sees on the left (1) a small window; and below it there was a stairway leading up to the roof, but this is destroyed. Let us first enter the chamber on the right or north side. On the right wall (2) Ptolemy IXth Physkon burns incense and pours out a libation to Osiris, Nut, Isis, Horus, Nephthys, and Anubis. At the end of the room (3) Ptolemy IVth Philopator makes an offering to Hathor and Maat. On the left wall (4) Ptolemy IXth Physkon offers a dish of food to Amen-Ra, Takat, Hathor, Amen-Ra again, Maat, and Isis.

We next pass into the middle chamber. Over the door outside, above the cornice, the heads of the seven Hathors are seen. Over the door inside (5) we see the scarab of the rising sun adored by the eight sacred apes, whose special duty it was, according to

The temple.

Northern chamber.

Middle chamber.

Egyptian mythology, to give praise to the sun as he rose above the eastern horizon (p. 566). On the left wall at the top (6) Ptolemy Physkon offers "Truth" to Amen-Ra, Mut, Khonsu; Hathor, and Shut. Below he offers to Min, Ament, Mentu, Maat, and Rataui. Farther along (7) at the top Ptolemy IVth and his wife Arsinoë offer to Amen-Ra in the form of Min; and still farther he offers to Osiris and Isis. Below this the king, with Hathor behind him, makes offering to Horus, and then to Osiris and Nephthys. On the right wall (8) at the top Ptolemy Physkon offers to Amen-Ra, Haka, Amen-Ra again, Shut, and Hathor; and below to Osiris, Isis, Nephthys, Horus, and Hathor. Farther along, Ptolemy IVth and Arsinoë offer a sacred eye to Min-Amen-Ra, and still farther along the king adores Hathor and Shut. Below this he and the goddess Maat offer to Mentu; and next the king presents two symbols of Hathor to Hathor and Maat. On the end wall (10) at the top the king worships Amen-Ra and Mut, and Amen-Ra and Khonsu. Below this he worships Hathor, Hathor with Horus upon her knee, and Maat.

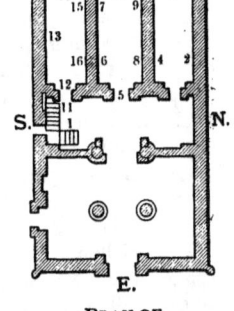

PLAN OF DER-EL-MEDÎNEH

Southern chamber.

We now pass on to the room on the left. On the outside wall, above the door (11), the cow of Hathor is seen standing in a shrine upon the sacred boat, and Ptolemy Physkon burns incense before it. Entering the room, we see over the doorway (12) the four-headed ram, typifying the four points of the compass, over which the goddess Nekheb, in the form of a vulture, hovers; while Hathor and Shut (behind) and Isis and Nephthys (in front) adore it. On the left wall (13) there is an interesting and impressive mortuary scene, representing the weighing of the heart of the deceased. The first figure is the goddess of Truth, Maat, and before her walks the soul of the deceased, who is about to enter the Hall of the Double Truth in order that his heart may be weighed. He is faced by a second figure of Maat as he enters the hall. We then see his heart weighed in the balances against the feather of truth. The god Horus holds the plumb of the scales, and Anubis assists. Next we see Thoth noting down the judgment of the scales. We then see the young Horus seated upon the

DÊR EL MEDINEH

crook, the symbol of dominion; and beside him there is a fearful monster. If the ordeal of the scales has been successfully passed, the soul of the deceased will be claimed by the youthful Horus, the mediator between man and his maker; but if he has failed in the trial he will be devoured by this creature. Next, presiding over the trial, sits Osiris; and before him are his four servants or genii, rising from out of the lotus-flower wherein they rest. At the top of the wall we see the forty-two judges of the dead. On the end wall of the room (14) Ptolemy IVth sacrifices to Osiris and Isis. On the right wall (15) the great sacred barque of Seker-Osiris is seen resting upon a pedestal. Before it are the two jackal standards of Wepwet, representing the frontiers of Egypt. Behind it are the three standards of the primitive tribes of Egypt (p. 36). Below is the plumed lotus-standard of the god Nefer-Tum, lying on another pedestal. At the far end of the wall (16) we see the god Min on a shrine, and a curious figure of Anubis clad in a red robe, and holding in his hand a disk. Before them Ptolemy Physkon burns incense in an elaborate censer.

To the south of the temple there are the remains of a town which dates from Pharaonic times. At the time of writing it has not been completely excavated; but sufficient has been found to indicate that it was a settlement of priests and necropolis workers. Behind these ruins there are several tombs, now numbered from 1 to 10, and some are of much interest. They are not open to the public. On the left of the hill pathway which leads from Dêr el Medineh to the Tombs of the Queens there is a group of Ramesside stelæ cut in the face of the rock. The first of these dates from the reign of Rameses IIIrd, and is dedicated to Ptah and Amen-Ra. The second is of the same date. At the top there is an interesting scene showing Rameses IIIrd suckled by the goddess Mersekert in the presence of Harmachis, and also receiving a sword from Amen-Ra. The third stela was made by Rameses IInd; and the fourth shows a king, whose names have been erased, between the gods. We next see two shrines, now destroyed, and near them there are more stelæ, including one which shows Rameses IIIrd and his father Setnekht. It would seem that the presence of the stelæ here is due to the fact that this hill was sacred.

Other remains at Dêr el Medineh.

THE TOMBS OF THE QUEENS AND PRINCES

The Valley of the Tombs of the Queens, the *Biban el Harim* of the natives, is decidedly worth a visit. It is situated in the hills at the back of the temple of Medinet Habu, and south of Dêr el Medineh. The tombs are lit only by candles, and visitors are earnestly requested to see that these are not held too close to the paintings. In the XVIIIth dynasty, when the Pharaohs were buried in the Royal Valley, it seems to have been the custom for their queens (not regnant) to be buried with them in their sepulchres, or perhaps near them in small pits. Thus in the tomb of Amenhotep IInd (p. 221) the female mummy which lies in a side chamber may be that of his queen. So far as we know, Amenhotep IIIrd was the first king who permitted his queen to lie in a large tomb of her own in the valley (p. 186); and he did this because he himself had decided to abandon the necropolis and to be buried in what is known as the Western Valley. The succeeding king, Akhnaton, was buried at El Amarna, and was later carried to Thebes; we do not know what became of his queen. The tomb of the next king, Tutankhamen, has not been found; and that of his successor, Ay, has been so much ransacked by early robbers that one cannot say whether the body of his queen lay with him or not. In the tomb of the next king, Horemheb, the bones of four persons were found, and one may suppose therefore that the queen was buried with him. Rameses Ist succeeded; and he decided to bury his queen, Setra (B.C. 1315), in a valley to the south of the necropolis, now known as the Valley of the Tombs of the Queens. It is just possible that this valley had already been used as a burying-place for a few of the members of the royal family of the XVIIIth dynasty. It is not known where the next queen, wife of Sety Ist, was buried. Rameses IInd interred his queen Nefertari in this new valley, and also his daughters Bantantha, Meretamen, and Nebtaui. The tomb o Merenptah's queen is not known. Tausert, wife of Septah and Sety IInd, being a queen regnant, was buried in the king's valley (p. 209). Prof. Petrie thinks that the wife of the next king, Setnekht, was buried in the Valley of the Queens in a certain tomb of which the name is now lost. Rameses IIIrd, the succeeding Pharaoh, buried his queen Ast (or Isis) in this Valley of the Queens; and he also here interred four sons and a daughter, all of whom died during his reign. The numerous uninscribed tombs in this

THE TOMBS OF THE QUEENS

valley probably belonged to the various princes and queens of the Ramesside age; but, like the Valley of the Tombs of the Kings, it probably ceased to be used as a royal necropolis at the fall of the XXth dynasty (B.C. 1090).

THE TOMB OF QUEEN NEFERTARI

Arriving at the valley, the visitor alights from his donkey at the donkey-stand, and turns to his right along the path which leads up the hill to the brick entrance of the beautiful and interesting tomb of Queen Nefertari, the wife of Rameses IInd. Queen Nefertari, "Beautiful companion," was already married to the king at his accession (B.C. 1292), but it is not known when she died. She was probably a daughter of the late king Sety Ist, and thus the sister or half-sister as well as the wife of Rameses IInd. She is very conspicuous in the reliefs at Abu Simbel (p. 574); and her figure will be remembered at the side of the colossi in the temple of Luxor (p. 81). She is known to have presented the king with at least two sons; but another queen, Astnefert, must have been somewhat of a rival to her, for she was the mother of the king's most famous sons.

We first enter a hall, on two sides of which is a high shelf upon which offerings might be placed. On the right of the entrance (1) the queen is seen adoring Osiris, the god of the underworld, who is seated in a shrine, the four genii who act as his agents being shown before him, and the god Anubis behind him. On the left of the entrance, from left to right at the top of the wall, we see (2) the *ka* or astral body of the queen sitting in the tomb playing draughts to pass the time; her soul, meanwhile, in the form of a human-headed bird, comes out of the tomb, and stands above the doorway; next, her *ka*, clad in flowing white robes, leaves the game of draughts, and, passing out of the tomb, kneels to adore the sun (3) rising between two lions; then we see her *khu*, or celestial spirit or intelligence, in the form of a pale blue crane, beautifully drawn; next is the mummy of Osiris lying on a bier watched by Isis and Nephthys in the form of hawks typifying the manner in which the queen's mummy will be guarded; and farther along, and continuing onto the next wall, we see various mythological figures who will be her protectors, ending over the door (5) with the four Osirian genii, the human-headed Amset, the ape-headed Hapi, the hawk-headed Duamutef, and the jackal-headed Khensenuf. Beyond the doorway (6) Osiris stands with

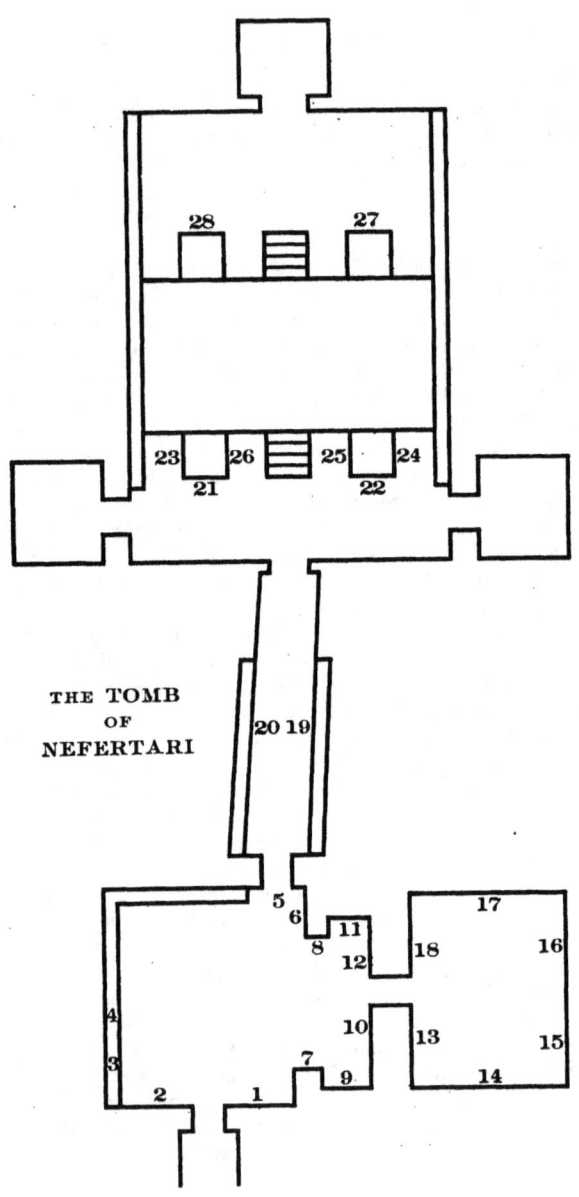

THE TOMBS OF THE QUEENS 283

the standards of Wepwet before and behind him. On the projecting walls at this side of the hall (7) Neith and (8) Selkis, both clad in fine red dresses, stand to receive the queen as she enters the side chamber. On the right (9) we see the queen led by Horus to (10) Harmachis and Hathor enthroned. The queen's charming profile, her reddened cheeks, her rich head-dress, and her flowing robes, combine to give this and other representations of her a grace and fascination which will not soon be forgotten by the visitor. On the left (11) Isis leads the queen forward to (12) Khepera, the beetle-headed god of the resurrection. We pass through the door leading into the side chamber, and observe on either side a figure of Maat, the goddess of Truth. On the right wall of this room (13) there is a ram-headed figure of the setting-sun supported, as Osiris was at his death, between Isis and Nephthys. Beyond this is a figure of the queen adoring various sacred cattle (14), which are depicted on the adjoining wall. On the next wall (15) she presents a great heap of offerings to a seated figure of Tum. On the other half of the wall (16) she presents offerings to Osiris in a similar manner. On the next wall (17) the queen stands in the presence of the ibis-headed Thoth, before whom are a palette upon which the god will write, and the frog Heket. On the next wall (18) she offers the symbol of fine linen to Ptah, who stands in a shrine, the window of which, in front of his face, is open.

We now return to the hall and pass down the steps to the lower chambers, observing on our left the goddess Selkis and on our right Neith. On the left wall (19) the queen makes an offering to Isis and Nephthys, behind whom is the winged goddess Maat. On the right side (20) she offers to Hathor and Selkis, and Maat is again seen behind them. Farther down we may notice on either side the jackal of the dead, and above it a winged cobra protecting the name of the queen as an inhabitant of the necropolis. Below it, on the left, is Isis again, and on the right Nephthys. One now passes into the lower hall, the roof of which is supported by four square columns. The area between the columns is sunk, and it was in this portion that the sarcophagus (now lost) was originally laid. The figures upon the columns may be noticed : on the left (21) is the fine figure of Horus-Supporter-of-his-Mother (see p. 199) ; on the right (22) is a similar figure ; on the far side of the left column (23) the queen is embraced by Hathor ; on the far side of the right column (24) she receives life from Isis ; on the near or inner side of the right column (25), and on the corresponding side of the opposite column (26), are imposing figures of Osiris. We descend three stairs into the middle of the hall. The scenes upon the walls are now much damaged by moisture, the rains of many winters having penetrated into these lower rooms. Here there are figures of the demi-gods of the underworld, who act as the protectors of the queen's body; and the four large *ded* signs, which are painted on the sides of the pillars facing this portion of the hall, and which are symbolic of the power and stability of Osiris, carry out this same idea of protection. The visitor may ascend the three stairs on the far side of the hall, and here, on the back of the pillars, he may notice on the right (27) the queen with Isis, and on the left (28) the queen with Hathor. The remaining scenes in this lower hall are too damaged to be of interest.

THE TOMB OF AMENKHEPESHEF

This tomb (No. 55) is reached by the path which leads farther into the valley from the tomb of Nefertari. It is one of the four tombs which the visitor to this valley should not fail to see. It was made for Prince Amenkhepeshef (or Amenherkhepeshef as it is sometimes written), one of the young sons of Rameses IIIrd (B.C. 1198–1167), who died in his childhood. Rameses IIIrd had the misfortune to lose at least four sons in their childhood. The mummies of the members of the royal family at this time show so much physical degeneracy, some having been deformed and others diseased, that this early mortality is not surprising. Nothing is known historically of this prince, except that he held the honorary title of Master of the King's Horse.

On the left as we enter (1) Rameses IIIrd, who has come to the tomb to introduce his son to the gods, is seen greeting Isis with a kiss, while behind him, Thoth, the god of Knowledge, holds pen and palette, as it were to take down the king's declaration of his son's virtues. Before them is the little prince clad in delicate robes of fine linen. He wears the side-lock indicating a royal prince, and holds an ostrich-plume standard. On the next wall (2) the king burns incense before a shrine in which stands the god Ptah. Next (3) the king introduces his son to another form of Ptah. Then (4) he presents him to the jackal-headed Duamutef, who leads them forward towards the inner chambers of the tomb. At the end of the wall (5) Amset meets them and conducts them

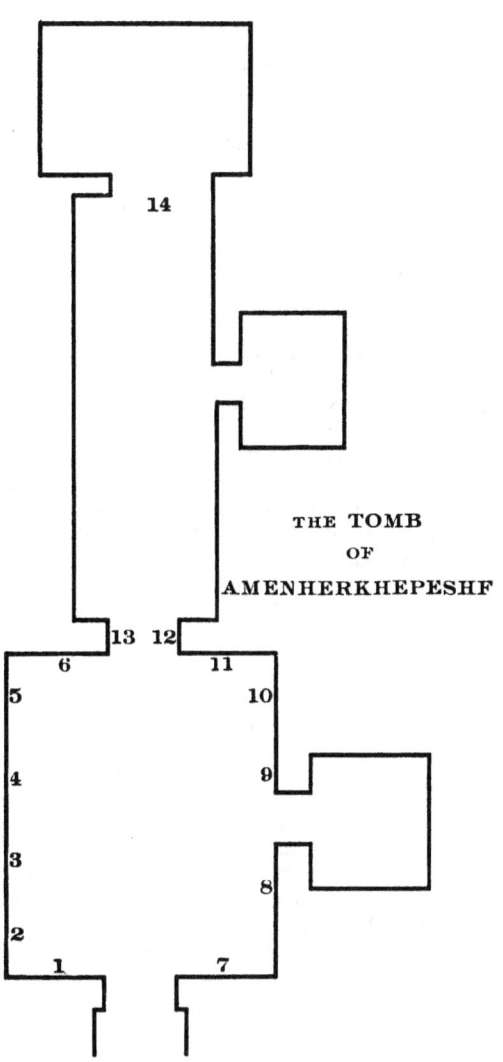

forward. On the adjoining wall (6) they are met by Isis, who leads them onwards. Returning to the right of the entrance (7), there is a damaged scene showing the king embracing a goddess (Isis?), and it is curious to notice how she affectionately strokes his chin with her finger. On the next wall (8) the king introduces his son to Shu. Beyond a doorway which leads into a blank room (9) Kebhsenuf (hawk-headed) leads the king forward, and (10) the ape-headed Hapi also conducts him onwards. On the next wall (11) the king and prince are met by Hathor. We see thus how the king, as mediator between earth and heaven, has presented his son to the gods : to Ptah the god of Memphis, in which city the prince, like so many other royal personages, probably lived ; to Shu the son of Ra ; to Isis and Hathor the great goddesses ; and to the four Osirian genii ; all of whom lead them onwards to the tomb and to the underworld. The visitor should particularly notice the elaborate costumes worn by the royal figures, and should compare them in his mind with the simpler dresses of earlier days, as they may be observed, for example, at the Tombs of the Kings.

Passing on into the inner chamber, the goddess Nephthys is seen on the right (12), and on the left (13) is Isis. The granite sarcophagus, in which the prince was buried, lies empty in this chamber. On the walls the king is shown presenting his son to various demons of the underworld, beside whom chapters of the funeral books are inscribed. Over the doorway into the final chamber (14) two winged serpents guard the cartouches of Rameses IIIrd.

THE TOMB OF THYTI

A short distance from the tomb of Amenkhepeshef is that of Thyti (No. 52), a queen of the Ramesside period, otherwise unknown. She is called a royal daughter, royal wife, and royal mother, that is to say, she was the daughter of a Pharaoh, married his successor, and was mother of the following sovereign. The tomb is not very impressive, and may be omitted by those who are pressed for time. The first corridor is much damaged, but we may still see the figures upon the walls. On the left is the goddess Maat with wings outspread, facing the doorway ; the queen worships before the shrine of Ptah ; she shakes two sistrums before Harmachis ; she worships Amset, Duamutef, and Isis. On the right wall Maat is seen as before ; the queen stands before Thoth ; she shakes sistrums before Tum ;

THE TOMBS OF THE QUEENS

and she worships Hapi, Kebhsenuf, and Nephthys. Entering the next room, we see on the left of the door the figure of Neith, and on the right that of Selkis, the scorpion goddess. On the walls to left and right of the chamber there are some remarkable figures of demi-gods. On the end walls of the room the queen worships the four genii again, two on either side, who this time all have human heads. The fine elaborate dress of the queen on the right should be noticed. In the chamber to the right there is an interesting representation of the queen adoring the Hathor cow, which comes forth from the western hills. Between the queen and the cow there stands a sycamore tree, from which the goddess Hathor appears in order to pour out the water of life for the queen to drink. In the room on the left is the burial-pit. In the innermost room we see Osiris enthroned. Behind him Isis and Thoth, and before him Neith and Selkis, are seen. On the side walls sixteen seated gods are worshipped by the queen.

THE TOMB OF ASET (ISIS)

Queen Isis, the wife of Rameses IIIrd, does not play an important part in history. Her full name seems to have been Aset-Amasereth, and as the second half of the name appears to be Syrian, it may be that she was of that nationality. The tomb (No. 51), which is situated on the left of the pathway leading to the higher southern group of sepulchres, is much damaged, and only a few scenes of a conventional kind remain. The fragments of a once fine sarcophagus are strewn over the floor.

THE TOMB OF SETYHERKHEPESHEF

This tomb (No. 43), a few yards from the last named, was made for another son of Rameses IIIrd who died in his childhood. It is blackened by smoke, and is not of particular interest. One passes through two long corridors in which the king is seen presenting his son to the gods as before. A room is then reached in which are representations of curious demons. On the left should be noticed the two mythological apes named Fu and Au. In the innermost chamber, on the end wall there are two seated figures of Osiris, and on the sides are a series of small figures of gods.

THE TOMB OF PARAHEREMEF

A few yards distant from the last tomb is No. 42, the tomb of Paraheremef, another member of the unfortunate family of Rameses IIIrd, who was perhaps the eldest son. In the first corridor the king introduces him to the gods as usual. A four-pillared hall is then reached, but the reliefs are so much damaged that they are of little interest.

THE TOMB OF KHAEMUAST

This tomb (No. 44) should certainly be visited. It is situated at the end of the pathway which leads off to the left from the donkey-stand to the south-east corner of the valley. It was made for Prince Khaemuast, another son of Rameses IIIrd, who died during his childhood; and here, as in the tombs of his other sons, the king is seen in the paintings introducing the young prince to the gods. The paintings are partly unfinished, and one may see the uncoloured white plaster here and there.

On the right as we enter (1) the king worships Ptah, and beyond this is the prince wearing the usual side-lock. Beyond a doorway (2) the king worships Seb; then (3) introduces his son to Shu; and next (4) advances with him to Tum, whose figure is destroyed. On the left wall (5) Ptah is seen in his shrine; (6) the king presents his son to Thoth; then (7) to Anubis; and lastly (8) to Harmachis. Entering the room on the right, we notice on the right of the doorway (9) Isis and Nephthys, and on the left (10) Neith and Selkis. On the side wall (left) we see (11) the prince standing alone adoring the demi-god Hapi, who by mistake has been given a jackal-head; (12) he adores Kebhsenuf; and (13) he adores two demi-gods. On the opposite wall (14) he worships Amset; (15) he worships Duamutef, who has been given an ape-head instead of that of a jackal; and (16) he worships two other demi-gods. On the end wall (17) Isis talks to a seated figure of Osiris on behalf of the prince; and (18) Nephthys likewise addresses another figure of Osiris. There is a similar room on the left of the corridor, and at the entrance are Isis, Nephthys, Neith, and Selkis, as in the case of the room just described. On the left wall (19) the prince stands alone before Anubis; and we then see him (20) before the four genii and Selkis. On the opposite wall (21) he stands before Anubis, and (22) again before

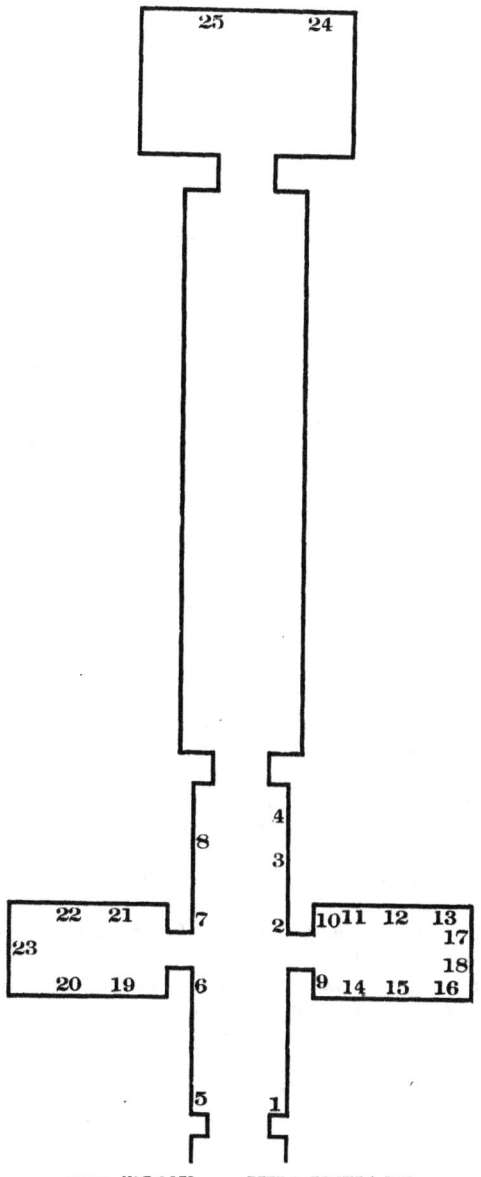

THE TOMB OF KHAEMUAST

the four genii, with whom is Neith. On the end wall (23) Isis and Nephthys address seated figures of Osiris on behalf of the prince.

We now enter a long corridor, the roof of which is vaulted. On the walls to right and left the king is seen presenting his son to demi-gods. In the final chamber, which is to be regarded as a kind of sanctuary, the king alone is seen worshipping the gods and interceding for his son. On the end wall, to the right (24), Selkis and Nephthys address Osiris; and to the left (25) Isis and Neith do likewise. In front of Osiris is the lotus-flower from which the four genii rise.

There are only two other tombs which call for remark in this valley. No. 38 is the burial-place of Queen Setra, the wife of Rameses Ist, and in it are a few figures drawn in outline only. No. 36 is the tomb of an unknown princess. The paintings are much damaged, but have once been good. It is curious to notice that, although the titles of the princess have been written in the inscriptions, her name has been left blank, as though the scribe knew only that he had to prepare a tomb for a princess, but did not know what she was called.

The Palace of Amenhotep IIIrd

The ruins of the palace of Amenhotep IIIrd are situated on the edge of the desert, some distance to the south of the temple of Medinet Habu. They are not sufficiently interesting to be visited by any but those who have ample time to spare. All that now remains of the palace is the ground-plan of portions of its area, outlined in crude brick walls a few inches in height. The palace was entirely built of brick; the walls, ceilings, and pavements being covered with plaster, upon which the most charming paintings were executed, judging by the few fragments which have been found. It is often asked why so many temples, but so few palaces, of the Pharaohs exist; and here the reader has the answer to the question. The palaces were not intended to be lived in by more than one generation, and therefore they were built lightly of brick; whereas the temples were erected for all time, and therefore were built of stone. In most cases they were placed on the cultivated land, in order that they might be surrounded by gardens, and hence the bricks have long-since disappeared into the soil,

THE PALACE OF AMENHOTEP IIIRD

and the ploughs of the natives have passed over their sites. Amenhotep IIIrd, however, decided to erect his palace upon the desert, and thus we are now able to trace the walls of the royal building. In order that there might be gardens near the palace in spite of the barren nature of the ground, he caused an enormous lake to be made on the east of the palace;[1] and the visitor may trace its limits by the mounds of rubbish which were thrown up during its excavation. These are specially to be noticed on the immediate east side of the palace. The lake, which is now called Birket Habu, was made by Amenhotep IIIrd in the eleventh year of his reign (B.C. 1400), and is said to have been designed for the entertainment of his much-loved queen, Thiy. One may suppose that the lake was surrounded by trees and flowers, and as our inscriptions tell us that here the royal couple sailed in their beautiful dahabiyeh, which was called "Aton-Gleams," we may reconstruct in the imagination a picture of great charm. It was probably in this palace that the heretic King Akhnaton was born (p. 161), and here Amenhotep IIIrd, who has been called "The Magnificent," and the beautiful Thiy held their brilliant court. Some of the halls in the palace were of considerable size, as the visitor may now perceive; and traces of the columns which supported the wooden roofs are to be seen here and there. In some of the rooms there are the remains of a raised daïs on which the king's throne was placed; and in some places there are traces of the paintings which covered the walls. The site was excavated incompletely by M. Grébaut, by M. Daressy, and by Mr. R. Tytus, but much still remains to be cleared.

The other ruins in this neighbourhood are not worthy of a visit. Some 700 feet south-west of the Pavilion of Medinet Habu is a small temple of Ptolemaic date, known as Kasr el 'Agûz, "the Old Man's Castle," which was dedicated to Thoth, but it is of little interest except from the fact that a series of Ptolemaic Pharaohs, important for the order in which the names appear, are mentioned as the ancestors of Ptolemy Euergetes IInd. Farther to the south there is a little Roman temple known as Dêr esh Shelwît, dedicated to Isis, Lady of Arment. In the desert to the west of this there is a cemetery in which the sacred apes were buried. It is now known as Gebânet el Kurûd.

---

[1] The cultivation had not encroached as far westwards in those days as at present.

Other Remains

There are, of course, several minor relics of the past which have not been recorded here. Of these perhaps the only site which will be of interest to the visitor is that of a little temple of King Seankhkara, of Dynasty XI., situated on the highest point of the great hill to the north-east of the entrance to the Valley of the Tombs of the Kings. It can be seen with the naked eye from the plain. Only a few bricks now remain. In a valley at the foot of this hill there are several watchmen's houses and some graffiti on the rocks, suggesting that there are tombs here. The surface of the upper desert has upon it many palæolithic flints.

CHAPTER XII

FROM THEBES TO ESNEH ON THE WEST BANK: ARMENT, RIZAKÂT, GEBELÊN, ASFUN — FROM THEBES TO ESNEH ON THE EAST BANK—TÛD, DABABIYEH—THE TEMPLE AND CEMETERIES OF ESNEH—FROM ESNEH TO EL KÂB ON THE EAST AND WEST BANKS

ARMENT

AFTER leaving the most southern of the antiquities of Thebes, there is no ancient site to be met with until the town of Arment is reached, which lies some nine miles up stream from Luxor. From the hills above the Tombs of the Queens one may look southwards over the wide, flat desert which sweeps round towards the south-east; and in the distance the trees of Arment can often be clearly seen. For visiting Arment the ordinary steamers do not allow the necessary time; but persons travelling by dahabiyeh will find the excursion to the ruins worth making, more for the sake of the beauty of the country at this point than of the interest of the antiquities. The dahabiyeh should be moored a mile or so below Arment, as the ruins lie in the village of Old Arment, which is about that distance north of the modern town, and rather less than a mile back from the river. The excursion may be made by train from Luxor, and in this case it will be found most comfortable to take donkeys with one from Luxor. At the station of Arment very miserable local donkeys may be hired, but these cannot be used except by active males. The train leaving Luxor at 10 A.M. or thereabouts reaches Arment in some forty minutes; and a ride of less than a mile brings one to the river. Here a native ferry will be found, which will convey oneself and one's donkey to the other side. A farther ride of half-an-hour then brings one to the ruins, which should thus be reached before noon. The return may be made in time to catch the train which brings

Methods of visiting the ruins of Arment.

one back to Luxor in time for five o'clock tea. Although the tourist very seldom visits these ruins, the excursion may be recommended to all those who have a desire to see Egypt thoroughly; and lovers of the picturesque will certainly appreciate the scenery.

The scenery of Arment.

The appearance of the country here is very different from that usually associated with Egypt. Along the bank of the river there is a splendid row of *lebbek* trees, and amidst these are the ruins of the ancient quay of Roman date, into which are built various blocks from a Ptolemaic temple. The main ruins are reached by a charming road running along the river's edge at first, and later passing a few yards farther inland. The path is deeply shaded by trees, through which the sun penetrates in broken patches of yellow light. On the west side there are wide fields of sugar-cane edged by European-looking bushes; and one catches a glimpse here and there of a running stream of water. In the autumn, when the cane is green, the fields present an extremely beautiful scene; but the winter visitor is likely to find them bare after the harvest.

The history of Arment.

In early times the name of Arment was An or On, sometimes called Southern On to distinguish it from Heliopolis, which was the Northern On. The hawk-headed war-god Menthu was here worshipped, and thus the town came to be known as An-Menthu, or Per-Menthu, "the Temple of Menthu," from which the Greek *Hermonthis* and the modern Arment seem to be derived. If the cemetery at Rizakât, six or eight miles to the south-west, is the ancient burial-place of this town, then there must have been a flourishing city here in the Middle Kingdom, of which date many graves have been found. In the XVIIIth dynasty temples of some size were erected here, but these are now all destroyed. The heretic Akhnaton built here; and of course the name of Rameses IInd is to be seen. The cartouche of Menkheperra, probably the second king of that name, the son of Painezem Ist, was observed here; but after that date no other records are found until the time of the famous Cleopatra, under whom a temple was built for herself and her son Cæsarion, whose father was Julius Cæsar. During this period Arment became an important city, and was the capital of the Hermonthite nome or province. In early Christian times it was still flourishing, and a large church was erected here. After this, however, it fell into insignificance, and remained an unimportant village until the modern sugar factories brought it again some degree of fame.

Arment the birth-place of Moses.

Amongst the modern inhabitants of Arment there is a firm belief that Moses was born at this spot. In the absence of any definite knowledge regarding this event, one may say that it is quite within the bounds of probability that the law-giver really was born here. Hidden amongst the rushes to the north of the town, his cradle would have been within a mile or so of the ordinary bathing-place of the princes and princesses living in the palaces near Medinet Habu. Indeed, one may go so far as to say that there is no more likely spot for a royal bathing-place than the west bank of the river, half-way between Luxor and Arment; and if the details of the Biblical account are to be accepted, one would naturally look in this direction for the place at which the baby was found by the princess.

During the days of the early modern travellers in Egypt, the temple of Cleopatra and Cæsarion was still to be seen, and appears to have been an elaborate construction, nearly 200 feet in length. Now, however, only a few fragments remain, for the temple was destroyed in order to provide stone for building the sugar factory. In different parts of the village, as one rides through it, masonry walls will be seen dating from Roman times, and several inscribed blocks of earlier date will be observed. In one place there is a chamber having a doorway upon which are reliefs representing one of the Roman Pharaohs worshipping the deities Min, Thoth, Horus-Menthu, Isis, and others. In the middle of the village there are the ruins of a Roman bath built of burnt bricks. The main chamber, in the corners of which are limestone pillars, seems to have contained the large plunge-bath, but this is now filled with rubbish. A small domed chamber stands at one corner, and other more ruined rooms near by were perhaps intended for the hot-air baths. At this part of the village there are extensive mounds of accumulated ruins and rubbish, and one obtains a good idea of the process of stratification. At the west end of the village there are a few remains of a Ptolemaic temple, and here in a wide and open space are the scanty remains of a Coptic church. Several granite pillars lie about, and one sees that the building was originally imposing. In the desert at the back of Arment there is a cemetery of the Roman period, from which a few antiquities have been obtained.

The ruins at Arment.

Amongst these antiquities there were a few tablets on which there was a representation of a sacred bull. Early writers speak at some length of this bull, which in Græco-Roman times was the chief glory of Arment. "In the city of Hermonthis," writes Macrobius, "they adore the bull Bacchis, which is consecrated to the sun, in the magnificent temple of Apollo. It is remarkable for certain extraordinary appearances, according with the nature of

The sacred bull of Arment.

the sun. For every hour it is reported to change its colour, and to have long hairs growing backwards, contrary to the nature of all other animals; whence it is thought to be an image of the sun shining on the opposite side of the world." Ælian mentions this wonderful bull, naming it Onuphis, and stating that "the name of the place where it is kept may be learnt from the books of the Egyptians, but it is too harsh both to mention and to hear." He adds that "its hair turns the contrary way from that of other animals, and it is the largest of all oxen." Strabo also writes of a sacred bull of Hermonthis, but he does nor mention its name. The coins of the Hermonthite province, too, bear the figure of a bull with lowered horns and waving tail. It may be that some day the tombs of these bulls will be found at Arment amongst the remains of the once "magnificent temple of Apollo."

RIZAKÂT

The road to Rizakât. To reach the cemetery of Rizakât, which is the next ancient site, one should follow the sugar railway, which runs at the back of the town towards the south. Just before reaching the village of Rizakât one must leave the line and bear off towards the west, crossing the canal, and finally reaching the edge of the desert near a group of small hamlets. The ride takes about two hours from Arment, and during the sugar harvests the fields through which one passes are extremely beautiful. The ride can be recommended to travellers who find themselves in this part of Egypt, for instance, those

The cemetery of Rizakât. who are moored here on dahabiyehs; but the cemetery, of course, has nothing of interest to show. It stretches for some considerable distance along the desert's edge. The tombs at the south end have been plundered several years ago, and those at the north end have been robbed until quite recently; so that now there remains little for the scientific excavator to do there. The tombs, of which there must have been several hundred, seem to have dated from the XIIth to XVIIIth dynasties, and mainly consist of mud-brick structures in the form of deep rectangular shafts, from the bottom of which a vaulted burial-chamber leads; wide rectangular pits lined with bricks, and entered by a sloping passage or stairway at one end; and other well-known forms. There is nothing interesting, either to the antiquarian or to the ordinary traveller, in wandering over a cemetery so wrecked and devastated by thieves, now stumbling into a half-filled grave, now treading underfoot the bleached bones of some worthy Egyptian; and one is glad to return to the rich, verdant fields, through which a path directly down to the river may be followed.

GEBELÊN

From Rizakât to Gebelên is a ride of some six or seven miles, but as there are no antiquities here, and no other objects of any particular interest, the ride cannot be recommended. Nor is Gebelên of sufficient interest to entice the ordinary traveller, though dahabiyeh-owners who are moored in this neighbourhood will find a climb up the hill in the early morning or late afternoon enjoyable. The two outcrops of rock which are known as Gebelên, "the two hills," form a very striking landmark as seen from the river. They each consist of a short and not very high range of limestone cliffs, and are on the western bank of the river, the south end of the first range running behind the north end of the second range. The first or northern range rises abruptly from the flat desert, and at its foot stands the small village of El Gherâreh. The ruins of an ancient town lie under the north-west end of the second range, but only a mound covered with fragments of pottery can now be seen.

In Egyptian times the two ranges were known as Anti, "the two rocks," though the name Aa-em-atur, "the island in the stream," seems also to have been used for Gebelên as a whole; and the town was called Per-Hathor, "the Abode of Hathor." From this the Greek name Pathoris was derived; and since Hathor was identified with Aphrodite, the name Aphroditopolis, which Strabo states to have been that of a city between Arment and Esneh, seems also to have been used. Close to Pathoris, and apparently at the foot of one of the two hills of Gebelên, stood the sister city of Crocodilopolis. Strabo places it on the west bank of the river not far south of Arment; and another writer[1] states that Asclepius, the inventor of medicine, was buried at a Crocodilopolis, and that on the Libyan hills in the vicinity there was a temple dedicated to him. Now, although there are several cities which were named Crocodilopolis, there is only one possible site near which there is a temple on the hills: namely here at Gebelên, where at the top of the southern range there are the ruins of a very ancient shrine, presently to be described. According to the Egyptians, the Greek god Asclepius was to be identified with the great Egyptian wise man Imhotep, who had lived in the reign of King Zeser; and if

The ancient name of Gebelên.

Gebelên the burial-place of Asclepius.

[1] Mercur, Trismegistus' dialogue with Asclepius.

298 ANTIQUITIES OF UPPER EGYPT

one is to give credence to the Greek legend, one must believe that this Imhotep was buried at Gebelên. It is more easy, however, to suppose that he was interred at Sakkâra, near the pyramid of his royal master; but, at the same time, the Greek story offers no improbabilities, since the temple and cemeteries of Gebelên date from very early times, and the activity of Imhotep in this part of the country is on record.[1] The figure of the wise man looms large in the dim history of the period at which he lived. Not only was he the inventor of many medicines and the author of medical works, but he was also a philosopher, a statesman, and an architect. To him are attributed the first buildings of hewn stone in Egypt; and to his genius the conditions which produced the rise of the great Pyramid Kings are due. If the hills of Gebelên contain his tomb, their interest to the visitor will be not less than that they hold the bones of the earliest philosopher and wise man known in the world's history.

The cemeteries of Gebelên.

Along the northern face of the first range there are many tombs dating from the Middle Empire, all thoroughly dug out, and more or less destroyed. Passing along the foot of the hills towards the south, there lies an almost continuous cemetery extending to the end of the range. This has been plundered again and again, and now presents a sadly chaotic appearance. The tombs date from early times down to the Roman period, but the majority are of the XIIth to XVIIIth dynasties. About half-way along the range are some grotto-like quarries, from which the stone for building the temple seems to have been procured.

The fortress at Gebelên.

On the top of the southern range, and on the western slope of the hill, an enormous quantity of large mud bricks will be seen tumbled in all directions. These form the ruins of a fortress built by Menkheperra, the royal high priest of Amen-Ra, who was the son of Painezem Ist of the XXIst dynasty. A rough pathway leads to the top of the hill from the west, but an easier ascent may be made on the eastern side, where, up a cleft in the rock, ran the original entrance path to the fortress. The main fort seems to have risen on the hill top, and the outbuildings stood lower down the western hillside. Many of the bricks are stamped with the cartouches of Menkheperra and of his wife Astemkheb. From the fortress a beautiful view may be obtained of the flat, open desert stretching westward for many miles. Across this wide expanse there runs a caravan road to the oasis of El Khârgeh; and the fortress is evidently connected with this

[1] Imhotep is said to have built a temple at Edfu.

route, being probably a defence against invasion from that direction.

During the troubled times in which Painezem Ist lived, it seems that a number of persons of high, and even royal, rank were banished to the Oasis; but under the rule of Menkheperra these exiles had obtained the sympathies of the Upper Egyptians, and there was good reason to suppose that they would enter the country again. The fortress thus appears to have been built to stop their entrance; but it ceased to be of use when, a few years later, Menkheperra issued a free pardon to the exiles, and obtained the sanction of the god Amen-Ra to a proclamation in which he vowed that never again should any one be banished "to the far distance of the Oasis, from this day for ever." *The object of the fortress at Gebelên.*

Amongst the ruins of the fortress a few pieces of broken limestone blocks mark the site of the ancient temple, dating from the Old Kingdom. No inscriptions now remain on the spot, but those removed from here show the names of the little known Pharaohs, Dudumes Dedneferra of the VIIth dynasty, Menthuḥotep Ist of the XIth dynasty, Senebmaan of the XIVth dynasty, Apepa Ist of the XVIth dynasty, and the well-known kings Horemheb of the XVIIIth dynasty, Sety Ist of the XIXth dynasty, and Ptolemy Euergetes IInd. Menthuhotep Ist speaks of himself as the vanquisher of the Libyans and Nubians, both of which peoples may have attempted to enter Egypt *viâ* El Khârgeh. Dudumes is represented as being led by the god Khonsu to Anubis. *The temple at Gebelên.*

One sees from the above-mentioned ruins that the city of Pathoris (Aphroditopolis) or Crocodilopolis dates from a very early period. Prehistoric and early dynastic cemeteries have been found in the neighbourhood, and it has been seen that there is a possibility that the great Imhotep of the IIIrd dynasty was closely connected with the city. Kings of the obscure VIIth, XIth, XIVth, XVIth dynasties built and restored the shrines here; and in the New Empire the place was still flourishing. The Ptolemies found it a worthy site for temple-building. Greek papyri of the IIIrd and IInd century B.C. have been discovered here, and there is an inscription dated in the twelfth year of Trajan. The Blemmyes, of whom the visitor will find so many traces in Lower Nubia, were settled here for some time. Thus, the traveller passing by on his dahabiyeh or steamer should at least give his attention for a few moments to the site of this most ancient city. *The history of Gebelên.*

Southwards from Gebelên the next ancient site lies under the modern village of Tofnîs. Here there was a small city, and in the desert behind there is a late cemetery, now entirely plundered.

ASFUN

We now reach the town of Asfun, the ancient Asphynis. The traveller will find, as at Arment, that the beauty of the country in this neighbourhood repays a visit to the town; but there are practically no antiquities to be seen. The site lies about a mile and a half back from the river, the road to it being shaded by beautiful trees. Very little is known of the history of Asfun. The town was certainly in existence as early as the XIIIth dynasty, for a statuette of that date was found there. At the west end of the town the remains of a temple were recently uncovered, and reliefs were found inscribed with the name of a King Psametik-se-neith Men-Kheper-ra. No such king exists, and M. Maspero has clearly shown that this inscription dated from Roman times and referred to earlier kings whose names were half forgotten. In the middle of the town there are very extensive mounds of ancient ruins, which are gradually being dug away by the peasants who use the old town-rubbish as manure. A stratum of red burnt material, running through these mounds at about the Roman level, shows that the town was once destroyed by fire. In the desert behind Asfun is a small cemetery of no importance. No other ancient remains are met with until the neighbourhood of Esneh is reached.

TÛD

The ancient remains between Luxor and Esneh on the east bank must now be recorded. The only site of interest is that of the ancient city of Tuphium which is to be identified with the modern town of Tûd. This town stands on the edge of the eastern desert opposite Arment, and may be approached along the embanked road leading east from the station. In Roman times it was called "the Great City of Ophiêon"; and in Pharaonic times there was a temple here dedicated to Ra. The high mound of debris upon which the modern village is built indicates that the site is very ancient. Fragments of a temple of Ptolemaic date are to be seen amidst the modern houses, and the cartouches of Ptolemy Physkon are to be seen. A temple, however, of much earlier date must have stood here, for there is a

FROM THEBES TO ESNEH

fragment of an obelisk of Senusert Ist built into a shêkh's tomb, while the cartouches of Nekhtnebef (XXXth dynasty) are also to be seen. Not far from here there are one or two cemeteries, now almost entirely plundered out.

DABABIYEH

The hills now draw in towards the river, and from the railway station of Chaghb to that of Matana they extend in a range of great beauty. About a mile and a half south of Chaghb station, just before reaching the village of Dababiyeh, a wide valley opens amidst the hills. Going up this and bearing to the north one comes upon some interesting quarries, which, though not of sufficient importance to attract the ordinary traveller, will be found to be worth a visit for the archæologist. The quarries consist of two wide, cave-like cuttings, the roof of which in each case is supported by rough pillars; and there are also some open quarries. In the northern cave there is a small stele cut in the rock, upon which King Sety Ist of the XIXth dynasty is seen offering to Amen-Ra. Below is an inscription relating to some quarry works, and at the bottom is the kneeling figure of the king's chief builder, named Huy. In the same quarry are some Greek graffiti written in red paint, one of which is dated in the reign of Caracalla, another in the first year of Elagabalus and Alexander Severus, and a third in the eleventh year of Alexander Severus. In the southern cave there is a large stele, part of which has been broken away, dating from the reign of Smendes, the first king of the XXIst dynasty. The inscription states that the king was sitting in the hall of his palace at Memphis, when messengers arrived informing him that a canal at Luxor had burst, and had flooded the Luxor temple. His majesty therefore despatched 3000 men and many builders to this quarry, to cut stone for the mending of the canal; and it was during this work that the stele was engraved. *Stele of Sety Ist.* *Stele of Smendes.*

In the neighbourhood of Maala and Matana, somewhat farther to the south, there are some extensive prehistoric cemeteries, now mostly dug out. It is evident that this stretch of country was thickly peopled in that early period. At one point there are also a few rock tombs of about the XIIth dynasty, but they are too damaged to be of much interest. In one of them there is a fragment of an inscription stating that the deceased was a Royal Registrar and Sole Companion, and traces of hunting scenes can *Maala, &c.*

be made out on the walls. At another point there is a cemetery of the New Empire, entirely plundered. Near the village of El Helleh there are the remains of a Ptolemaic or Roman town, now known as Kôm el Birbeh; and not far distant is a cemetery of the same date. The railway station of Esneh is a short distance south of this.

ESNEH TEMPLE

Methods of visiting Esneh.
The temple of Khonsu at Esneh should certainly be seen by all visitors to Upper Egypt. There are various ways of making the trip, those from the river being by far the most comfortable. All steamers stop sufficient time for the visit to the temple, which is only ten minutes' walk from the landing-stage, through the rather picturesque streets of the town. By railway it is best to take the train which leaves Luxor at sunrise, and arrives at Esneh station somewhere about 7 or 8 A.M. The visitor can walk to the river, and there his dragoman will have no difficulty in engaging a ferry. As one crosses the river one sees the town of Esneh standing imposingly on the mounds composed of the ruins of earlier cities. The ancient quay, composed of heavy blocks of sandstone, will be noticed, but the temple is buried out of sight amongst the houses. Originally it is probable that there was an open space between the river and the temple, the city lying mainly along the north and west of it. If the wind has been favourable the visitor will reach the temple by about 8 o'clock, and there he can remain until it is time to return to the station to catch either the 12 A.M. train to Assouan or the 11 A.M. train back to Luxor. It must be remembered, however, that the ordinary traveller can see the temple in half-an-hour, and there is thus a tedious wait to be endured before it is necessary to start back.

History of Esneh.
In Egyptian the name of this city was *Ta-Esna*, whence came the Coptic *'Snē*, and the Arabic *Esneh*. By the Greeks the city was called Latopolis, after the fish *Latus* which was here venerated; but this does not seem to have come into very common use, and there was soon a reversion to the older name. The early history of the city is unknown, and it is probable that it was of no great importance until the XVIIIth dynasty, when the trade with the Sudan began to open up. A good caravan road runs from Esneh, through the oasis of Kurkur, to Derr; and Esneh may have

FROM THEBES TO ESNEH

gained such importance as it had through being the terminus of this route. In modern times this trade was very considerable until the loss of the Sudan during the Mahdi's rebellion. It is probable that a temple was built here during the reign of Thothmes IIIrd. There is a record of the taxes imposed on the high officials of this city under Thothmes IIIrd. The Mayor had to pay each year a quantity of silver and gold, two oxen, some grain, and some linen. An official called the "Scribe of the Islands of Esneh" paid two *deben* of gold, half a *deben* of silver, a necklace, an ox, and some linen; while a third official paid two chests of linen, some grain, two oxen, and two calves.

At about this period a *Ha*-prince of El Kâb named Paheri was also *Ha*-prince of Esneh. In the XIXth dynasty the city was apparently flourishing. A block of stone near the river is inscribed with the name of Rameses IInd; and in the cemetery large tombs of about the same period have been found, among them being one of a certain Hui, who was overseer of the estates of Khonsu. Of the XXVIth dynasty tombs are found in the cemetery; and under the Ptolemies and Romans Esneh became of sufficient importance to justify the building of the great temple. At that time the city was the capital of the IIIrd nome of Upper Egypt, and in more modern times as capital of the province of Esneh it retained its importance. In 1889, however, it suffered a blow by the removal of the Government to Aswân. In the present day Esneh has no Sudan trade, and most of the inhabitants work with the loom.

The temple is for the main part unexcavated, and lies under the houses of the modern town. The pronaos, or first hall, however, is entirely cleared; but owing to the high level of the modern buildings, which are constructed upon the accumulated ruins of the ancient cities, the roof of this part of the temple is on a level with the house-tops, and to enter the pronaos one has to descend a steep flight of steps, as though the building were subterranean.

The temple as seen to-day is a rectangular building, 108 feet wide and 54 feet deep, facing to the east, or rather to the river. Originally there was probably an open space between the temple and the water. The roof is intact, and is supported by twenty-four pillars in six rows, each column being 37 feet high and $17\frac{3}{4}$ in circumference. The first row of six columns abut the front wall, or in other words the spaces between them, are walled in by balustrades, so that only one half of each is seen. The façade is 120 feet wide and about 50 feet high. The cornice is of the usual concave style.

In the back or west wall of this building there is a large gateway, now blocked, leading into the buried main temple. The general appearance of the construction leads one to suppose that this door was originally the front entrance of the temple, and that the pronaos which we now alone see was added at a later date. The decorations and inscriptions of the temple lead one to the same conclusion, for the gateway has the cartouches of Ptolemy VIth upon it, whereas on the wall around it, and on all the pronaos' walls and pillars, there are the cartouches of the later Roman emperors. It may be, however, that the whole temple, including the pronaos, was built under the Ptolemies, and that the pronaos was left undecorated until Roman times. This gateway in the west wall, as has been said, bears the cartouches of Ptolemy VIth (B.C. 181–140), and the king is seen before Khnum and other gods, as well as "King Ptolemy" and "Queen Cleopatra," probably his father and mother. The main temple, then, most probably dated from the reign of this king or from the time of his immediate predecessors. Nevertheless it is stated that Champollion, who managed to effect an entrance into the buried portion of the temple, found the name of Thothmes IIIrd there. If this is true, the Ptolemies must have rebuilt the temple on the site of an earlier sauctuary, as they so often did in the case of the other monuments.

The pronaos, it seems, was either built or was first decorated under the Emperor Claudius, whose cartouches were placed on the cornice outside. Under Vespasian the work was continued, and his name appears on the façade and in the decorations of the ceiling. The columns were decorated under Domitian, Trajan, and Hadrian, whose cartouches appear on them. The walls were then decorated under Antoninus Pius and Marcus Aurelius; and the blank pieces were finished under Commodus, Severus, Caracalla, and Geta. Geta's cartouche, however, wherever it occurs, was erased by Caracalla. It will be remembered that Caracalla made a boast of the fact that he had killed his brother Geta, and that he consecrated the sword which he had used for the purpose in the temple of Serapis at Alexandria. Caracalla cultivated the Egyptian religion to a considerable extent, and favoured the Egyptian natives to the exclusion of the Greek-Egyptians of Alexandria.

The last emperor who is mentioned in this temple is Decius, and the relief in which he figures is the latest dated representation of a Pharaoh. The work in the temple ceased about this time, and the decorations remain incomplete in places. The building thus, as it is seen to-day, dates from about B.C. 180 to A.D. 250.

FROM THEBES TO ESNEH 305

The points of interest in the temple are so apparent, and the possibility of overlooking anything of importance so remote, since there is but the one hall, that the visitor's attention requires little directing. The capitals of the pillars are extremely fine, and those two decorated with bunches of grapes (both pillars bearing the cartouches of Hadrian) are especially noticeable. Upon the south wall of the hall will be seen in bold relief the different emperors worshipping before the ram-headed Khnum; the hawk-headed Horus; the Horus in his form of a boy with the side-lock of hair, symbolic of youth; and the lion-headed Menhet. Upon the north wall these gods will again be noticed, though the eye will be mainly attracted by the large scene of the Pharaoh, with Horus and Khnum pulling in a netful of birds. Upon the ceiling are extraordinary mythological creatures, more familiar to, but no better understood by, the Egyptologist than the visitor. At the side of the entrance steps the doorkeeper's chamber will be seen.

The road back into the desert, where lies the ancient cemetery of Esneh, leads through the town and out into the fields at the north-west end. A bridge over the canal is presently crossed, after which the road bears to the north, then turns to the west; and finally a fairly straight path westward leads out into the desert a half-mile to the south of the small village of Hagar Esneh, the ride taking about three-quarters of an hour. Nothing of importance is here to be seen. Most of the tombs are of late dynastic date, though some are Ramesside. Such antiquities as have been found show a poorness of style not to be accounted for merely by the poverty of the inhabitants of Esneh, but rather suggesting that they were of a less cultured race, having a blood connection, no doubt, with the Sudanese with whom they traded. A large number of small pit tombs lie open, and the cemetery shows abundant signs of having been often plundered. *Esneh cemetery.*

Opposite the cemetery, but somewhat north of Esneh, are two mounds, known as Kôm ed Deir and Kôm es Sinûn, which stand in the cultivation. In 1830 temples were seen here, but now only a block or two is left, all the stones having been taken to build the factory which can be seen at the north extreme of Esneh. These stones were broken up, and no inscribed pieces are now to be found. *Neighbouring ruins.*

FROM ESNEH TO EL KÂB

West bank.   Between Esneh and Kôm el Ahmar on the west bank there are a few ancient sites which deserve a visit from the archæologist, but which have little to show to the ordinary traveller. A short way to the south of Esneh cemetery stands the Coptic monastery of Manaos (Ammonius) and Shenûdi (Senntios), a rectangular building of crude brick standing on the edge of the cultivation. The monastery now stands empty, but the Copts come there on certain festivals. It is said to have been founded by the Empress Helena. In it there are one or two early frescoes and several inscriptions. Near the village of Mesawiyeh there are prehistoric cemeteries of some extent. In the neighbourhood of Kôm el Mera (also called Kummir) are the remains of the ancient town of Pa-merà; and a few stone blocks from the temple can still be seen. In the desert there are cemeteries in which mummified gazelles were found, dating from the late dynastic period. A small cemetery lies near the village of Adem Agbeh, and another at El Kenân. Behind the town of Basaliyeh there stands a small stone pyramid, known as El Kulah. Its height is about 30 feet, and its base about 50 or 60 feet square. It is much ruined, and there is nothing to give a clue to its date. In the neighbourhood there are some prehistoric cemeteries. A ride of about an hour's duration now brings one to Kôm el Ahmar.

East bank.   On the east bank of the river one or two late cemeteries of no importance are the only ancient remains to be observed between Esneh and El Kâb. On the rocks not far from Esneh station there is an important inscription of the time of the "heretic" king Akhnaton, which relates to the quarrying works undertaken here early in his reign.

CHAPTER XIII

THE HISTORY OF EL KÂB (EILEITHYIAPOLIS) AND KÔM EL AHMAR (HIERACONPOLIS)—THE RUINS AT KÔM EL AHMAR AND AT EL KÂB—FROM EL KÂB TO EDFU

THE HISTORY OF EILEITHYIAPOLIS AND HIERACONPOLIS

THE ruins of the ancient cities of Eileithyiapolis and Hieraconpolis stand opposite to one another on the east and west banks of the Nile, the former close to the water, and the latter on the edge of the desert some distance back from the river. At the present time these two sites are known respectively as El Kâb and Kôm el Ahmar, "the Red Mound." In ancient times they were called Nekheb and Nekhen, and "El Kâb" may perhaps be a corruption of the former name. The city of Nekheb came to be named Eileithyiapolis by the Greeks owing to the fact that the goddess of the neighbourhood was identified with Eileithyia; while Nekhen was re-named Hieraconpolis, "the City of the Hawks," owing to the totem of that place being a hawk. The names of the two cities.

The large cemeteries of the pre-dynastic age which lie in the desert behind Kôm el Ahmar indicate that an extensive settlement of that period existed here ; and amidst the ruins of Hieraconpolis there have been found the remains of the first known kings of Egypt. The earliest of these kings, named Selk "the Scorpion" (who is probably to be identified with the King Ka buried at Abydos), seems to have been the ruler of Upper Egypt only; and Hieraconpolis appears to have been his capital. There is good reason to suppose that both he and his successors were originally chieftains of a hawk-worshipping tribe which came from Thinis, a city not far from Baliana ; that this tribe pushed southwards as far as Edfu, defeating the aborigines[1] ; and that its main capital was The archaic period.

[1] See the tradition of Horus and Set as interpreted in the chapter on the temple of Edfu.

fixed at Kôm el Ahmar, which continued to be the royal city of Upper Egypt even after Mena—the first king of a united Egypt, and probably the grandson of the Scorpion—had carried the government to Memphis. These early kings were buried at Abydos, near their ancestral home of Thinis, but they seem to have been crowned at Hieraconpolis; and the well-known hawk-name, or Horus-name, which every Egyptian Pharaoh possessed, was the name given to him as chief of the Hawk-tribe at Hieraconpolis at his coronation as king of Egypt.

A ceremonial mace-head belonging to King Selk was found by Mr. J. E. Quibell at Kôm el Ahmar, and on it are scenes representing that king performing the ceremony of breaking ground with a hoe at the time of sowing, and receiving a sheaf of corn at the harvest festival. Another mace-head belonging to Narmer, the next king, shows the monarch seated on his throne apparently at a festival in honour of his conquest of Lower Egypt; and a ceremonial palette also found here shows him at a city which is probably to be read Edfu, sacrificing his enemies before thè sacred barque of Horus. Many other antiquities found here by Mr. Quibell prove that a high state of civilisation existed at this early period at Hieraconpolis. The portraying of the figures of men and animals was as well executed as in many of the later periods of Egyptian history; while the workmanship displayed in the making of stone vases and of pottery has never been surpassed.

The early dynasties. When Mena, perhaps the son of Narmer, was made Pharaoh of a united Upper and Lower Egypt, and built himself a capital at Memphis, Hieraconpolis lost for a time something of its importance. In the IInd dynasty, however, Kings Khasekhem and Khasekhemui both associated themselves with the city. Of the former king there is a fine statue, found by Mr. Quibell at Hieraconpolis, the inscription on which states that in a war with a northern people he had slain or taken prisoners 42,209 persons; and on a ceremonial bowl also discovered here is the inscription: " The year of the smiting of the northerners; the *khent*, or ceremony of purification, at the city of Nekheb;" below which the Horus-name of Khasekhem and probably his cartouche-name, Besh, are written on either side of the symbol of the uniting of the two lands. Of King Khasekhemui there is an inscribed granite door-jamb from the Hieraconpolis temple.

The Old Kingdom. The history of this neighbourhood now passes from archaic times to the better known period of the Old Kingdom. A sealing of King Neter-Khet of the IIIrd dynasty, and a cylinder inscribed

EL KÂB AND KÔM EL AHMAR

with the name of King Sneferu of the IVth dynasty, have been found at Hieraconpolis. By this time Eileithyiapolis was also rising into prominence, and, judging by the elaborate burials, must have already contained many rich inhabitants. From this point a disused caravan road runs to various gold-mines in the eastern desert, and it is probable that the rise of this town was due to its importance as the terminus of this route. From the earliest period the Egyptians used gold for ornamental purposes; and even in prehistoric times gold-handled knives and gold-topped jars were employed, while in the Ist dynasty gold beads and other jewellery were also not uncommonly used. A prominent rock in the desert behind El Kâb has upon it many inscriptions, some of which might well have been written by persons coming from or going to the mines. While the god of Hieraconpolis was the hawk Horus, the deity of El Kâb was the vulture goddess Nekheb, who is sometimes called "the Lady of the Mouth of the Desert." Cylinders of Menkaura of the IVth dynasty and Userkaf of the Vth dynasty have been found at El Kâb, which show that the town was flourishing at that date; and we may imagine the place at this time as busily absorbed in the coming and going of the gold-caravans, possessing a market, a fort or camp, and no doubt a temple to the vulture goddess. Graffiti of Sahura and Asesa of the Vth dynasty are found on the rocks behind the town.

Meanwhile on the west of the river a road led up to the city of Hieraconpolis, which now possessed a fine temple, while in the desert stood the great fortress for the troops, which dates from very early times. Visitors came from far and near to worship at the shrine of Horus, where their kings had been crowned; and by the VIth dynasty the temple had become so important that it was now the repository for some of the artistic masterpieces of the time. Those who have seen the Cairo Museum will not have failed to admire the great bronze statues of King Pepy and his son which are exhibited there. These were discovered by Mr. Quibell at Hieraconpolis, where they once stood in the temple. The base of a limestone statue of Pepy IInd was also found here. Hidden below the floor of the Sanctuary, Mr. Quibell was fortunate enough to find the actual figure of the hawk which was worshipped at Hieraconpolis. The body was of bronze, but the head and head-dress were of pure gold, the eyes being inlaid with obsidian. This beautiful object is also to be seen in the Cairo Museum. Of the same dynasty the names of Kings Teta and Pepy are to be found on the rocks behind

The VIth dynasty.

El Kâb. The name of Dudumes, an obscure king of the middle period, whom we have noticed at Gebelên, is also found here.

The XIIth dynasty. In the XIIth dynasty Eileithyiapolis was the more important of the two cities. An altar of Senusert Ist, however, and a statue of Senusert IInd were found at Hieraconpolis, where they had been placed by these kings in the temple of Horus. At this time the negroes of Ethiopia had become unruly, and had penetrated more than once into the land of Lower Nubia. They were also wont to make incursions into Egyptian territory along the caravan routes of the eastern desert; and there was some possibility that they might attack Aswân and even El Kâb. A huge fortification was therefore erected along the east side of the cataract, which was already built in the third year of Senusert IInd; and soon afterwards the great brick wall, which to this day stands around the site of Eileithyiapolis, was erected. It was known as the "Wall of Seshemtaui," that being the hawk-name of Senusert IInd; and in the forty-fourth year of Amenemhat IIIrd a smaller wall inside the wall of Seshemtaui was built to enclose the temple area. A cylinder of this king was found at El Kâb, a statue representing him was discovered at Hieraconpolis, and a stele recording the building of the Eileithyiapolis wall is now in England.

The XIIIth dynasty. In the temple of Hieraconpolis the names of one of the Antef kings and of a Sebekhotep of the XIIIth dynasty were discovered. At Eileithyiapolis there are a few tombs of nobles of this date, one of whom, named Sebeknekht, lived in the reign of Sekhemra-seuaztaui Sebekhotep IInd, an obscure king of this dynasty. El Kâb is, indeed, one of the only cities in which there seems to have been a continuity of prosperity during the troubled XIIIth dynasty and the Hyksos rule which followed; and if proof were needed that the regime of the shepherd kings only obtained for a short period, one would have but to look at the rock sepulchres of El Kâb, where the tombs of the XIIIth dynasty and those of the XVIIth and early XVIIIth dynasties seem to run in unbroken sequence.

The XVIIIth dynasty. The noble family of which the above-mentioned Sebeknekht was a member managed to make itself extremely powerful during the Hyksos rule; and when the princes of Thebes, who were the descendants of the old line of Egyptian kings, began to struggle to recapture their throne from the foreigners, they had no more powerful supporters than these nobles of Eileithyiapolis. A certain Abana, the son of Raanet of this family, was a faithful servant of King Sekenenra IIIrd of the XVIIth dynasty; and his son Aahmes fought under King Aahmes Ist in his wars against the

Career of Aahmes son of Abana.

EL KÂB AND KÔM EL AHMAR

Hyksos, and covered himself with glory. He tells us in the inscriptions in his tomb at El Kâb how he was made captain of the king's fleet of ships in Lower Egypt, and how he was present at the siege of Avaris, the fall of which marked the end of the Hyksos rule in Egypt. Later he fought against the negroes of the south, and was much praised by the Pharaoh for his valour. During the reign of Amenhotep Ist, Aahmes still continued in active service, but his deeds are now somewhat eclipsed by those of another noble of El Kâb, known as Aahmes Pennekheb.

This personage was entitled *Erpa-ha*, Prince, Royal Registrar, Sole Companion, &c., and he begins his biography by stating that he fought against the Hyksos under Aahmes Ist, who heaped rewards upon him. He then fought in Ethiopia under Amenhotep Ist; and under Thothmes Ist he saw active service in Syria. Here also Aahmes son of Abana, was engaged in his old age. In the reign of Thothmes IInd, Aahmes Pennekheb was still active enough to fight against the Beduin; and in his old age he had the honour of acting as tutor to Princess Nefrura, the daughter of Thothmes IIIrd and Hatshepsut. Thus this noble, who, in his youth, had known Egypt in the hands of the Hyksos, lived to see it the greatest and most wealthy country in the world. [Career of Aahmes Pennekheb.]

In the temple at El Kâb King Amenhotep Ist seems to have undertaken some building operations. At Hieraconpolis there is a tomb of a certain Superintendent of the Sculptors, named Tehuti, who lived in the reign of Thothmes Ist. In the temple here there was found an architrave bearing the name of Thothmes IIIrd; and at El Kâb the cartouches of Thothmes IInd and IIIrd, and of Hatshepsut, are to be seen in the temple. One sees thus that in the early XVIIIth dynasty the two cities, especially Eileithyiapolis, received a considerable amount of attention. This was partly due to the richness of the local nobles and the importance attaching to El Kâb as a market and caravan terminus, but it was also partly due to the fact that the Pharaohs at this time were very ready to associate themselves with any relics of the old kingdom which they had restored, and were proud to point to the two cities as the home of their royal ancestors.

At about this period there lived at El Kâb a prince whose name was Paheri, and who was a grandson of Aahmes son of Abana. His father, who was named Atefrura, was tutor to Prince Uazmes the son of King Thothmes Ist, and in those days this office was one of the highest in the land. Paheri himself was tutor, it appears, to another young prince named Uazmes, and also held the titles of [Career of Paheri.]

Erpa-ha, Prince, Sole Companion, *Ha*-Prince of Eileithyiapolis, *Ha*-Prince of Esneh, and Superintendent of the Priests of Nekheb. He regulated the corn and grain accounts for the whole district from Arment to El Kâb, and registered the gold which came in from the mines. He was thus one of the most rich and important officials of this rich land; and he seems to have lived throughout the reign of Thothmes IIIrd, when, under the rule of that great king, Egypt rose to a height of prosperity never surpassed. The scenes depicted in his tomb give one a wonderful insight into the manners and customs of the period. A feast is there shown, in which one may detect the marks both of high civilisation and of luxurious dissoluteness, and one is led to suppose that in these days Eileithyiapolis was a wealthy and somewhat profligate city.

The Viceroys of Ethiopia.

A step had lately been taken by the government which had placed the city in an important administrative position. Some of the members of the family of Prince Aahmes Pennekheb are entitled "the First Royal Son of Eileithyiapolis," which seems to indicate that one of the sovereigns of about the time of Amenhotep Ist or Thothmes Ist had created them, in a manner, viceroys of this district. At about the same time we hear of a *Ha*-Prince of Hieraconpolis, who held office in the land of Wawat in Lower Nubia, and "attained old age" there. In the reign of Thothmes Ist a certain noble, named Thure, was given the title of "Royal Son, Governor of the Lands of the South." This title was held by other nobles in succession, and in the reign of Tutankhamen—nearly two centuries later—it was changed to "Royal Son of Kush," that is to say, "Viceroy of Ethiopia." There is evidence to show that these "Royal Sons" resided at El Kâb; and thus one may say, that from the time of Amenhotep Ist or Thothmes Ist to the late Ramesside times, when the office fell into disuse, El Kâb was the capital of Nubia, Ethiopia, and all the southern lands as far north as Esneh.

The city now continued in great prosperity, though we hear somewhat less of Hieraconpolis. In a list of taxes of the time of Thothmes IIIrd, one reads that the *Ha*-prince of Eileithyiapolis had to pay each year a personal tax of four *deben* of gold (a *deben* being 100 grammes), three *deben* of silver, and an ox; while another local official had to pay three *deben* of gold, one necklace, two oxen, and two chests of linen. On the rocks behind El Kâb there is an inscription bearing the name of Thothmes IVth, and that king is elsewhere stated to have paid a visit to Eileithyiapolis on his way to a war in the south. Amenhotep IIIrd erected a

EL KÂB AND KÔM EL AHMAR

charming little temple in the desert here, and dedicated it to the goddess Nekheb and to his father Thothmes IVth. He also restored, or added to, the temple in the town. The heretic King Akhnaton cut out the names of Amen in these temples, but they were later restored by Sety Ist. An altar of Akhnaton was discovered at Hieraconpolis, and there a statue of Sety Ist was also found. Rameses IInd built at both cities, the work in the town of El Kâb being carried out by the Vizir Nefer-renpit, which indicates that the viceroys of Ethiopia sometimes gave way to the vizirs in these matters; but on the other hand it was the viceroy Setau who built the little temple in the desert behind El Kâb for Rameses IInd. In the forty-first year of this king the jubilee of Rameses IInd was held in the temple here, under the direction of Prince Khaemuast. Mention is made of Rameses IIIrd in a tomb at Eileithyiapolis; and an inscription of Rameses VIth is found in the precincts of the later Ptolemaic temple in the desert behind El Kâb. A high priest of Nekheb under Rameses IXth is the owner of one of the El Kâb tombs; a block of stone bearing the name of Rameses Xth was unearthed in the temple of Hieraconpolis; and in a tomb behind that city the cartouches of Rameses XIIth occur. Thus one sees that the two cities continued to play an important part in the history of the Ramesside period, although they had lost much of their earlier wealth. *The XIXth and XXth dynasties.*

King Necho Uhemabra of the XXVIth dynasty placed a ceremonial vase in the temple of Hieraconpolis which was found there. King Hakar of the XXIXth dynasty undertook restorations at El Kâb on a large scale; and King Nectanebus Ist of the XXXth dynasty continued the work. In the Ptolemaic period a temple was erected at El Kâb by Ptolemy IXth Euergetes IInd, and was completed by Ptolemy Xth Soter IInd. A considerable amount of later pottery on the sites of both cities indicates that they still continued to flourish for some years yet; and in the Egyptian temples of Roman date one often reads of Horus of Hieraconpolis or of Nekheb of Eileithyiapolis as being still held in high honour. The goddess Nekheb is shown in the temple reliefs together with Uazet the goddess of Buto, the ancient capital of Lower Egypt, crowning the Pharaoh with the double crown of Upper and Lower Egypt. *The later periods.*

THE RUINS AT HIERACONPOLIS

Methods of visiting the site.
The ruins of Hieraconpolis stand on the west bank of the river near the village of El Mûssat, which forms part of the district of Basaliyeh. In the desert behind there are extensive cemeteries of the archaic period, some rock tombs, and a large fortress which is quite worth a visit. The excursion can be made from the river with ease, the ride from the Nile to the desert taking less than half-an-hour. Donkeys, however, have to be procured from the village, and the visitor should bring his own saddle. The tourist steamers do not stop to allow their passengers to see these ruins, but those who are travelling by dahabiyeh may find the excursion of interest. Should the visitor come by railway from Luxor, which is the best centre for so many excursions, he should take the early train from that town, which reaches Mahamid station at about 8 o'clock A.M. Here his dragoman should meet him with a donkey procured from the village, or better, from Edfu; and a ferry at the river's edge should be waiting. Kôm El Ahmar may be reached by 9 A.M., and a start on the return journey should be made about noon to catch the express back to Luxor. This, however, makes a long day, and the undertaking would hardly repay an ordinary traveller, though the interest of the ruins to an archæologist is considerable.

The city.
The chaos of small mounds and pits, overgrown with brambles and weeds, which marks the site of Hieraconpolis will be a sad shock to those who have hoped to find here a ruined city, through the deserted streets of which they might walk. Nevertheless these untidy, half-excavated heaps of mud and potsherds have yielded to the savant some of the most wonderful antiquities of the Cairo Museum. Here and there a trace of a wall will be observed, or an overturned stone from the temple buildings; but the visitor will no doubt prefer to pass quickly over the site, and to think only of the city as it was in the past, with its white temples towering above the crowded houses of the town, and with the noise of music and the savour of offerings rising continually to heaven.

The fort.
The first point to which the traveller's steps will be directed with interest is the fort, an imposing structure which forms a landmark for some distance around. The technical description given by Mr. Somers Clarke, F.S.A. in "Hieraconpolis II." (Quibell and

EL KÂB AND KÔM EL AHMAR 315

Green, 1902) may well be quoted here. "This building," he writes, "lies on the desert edge, but very little removed from the cultivated ground, and at the mouth of a valley which runs into the western desert. In plan it is rectangular, with the entrance towards the cultivated land. An outer wall has been built 2.34 m. thick, standing in advance of the inner and chief wall, which is 4.87 m. thick. There is a space of 2.23 m. between the walls. The outer wall was lower than the inner. The entrance is formed in a sort of bastion, or tower-like projection, and is sufficiently circuitous to make it impossible for any body of persons to rush through quickly. There is not evidence that any other entrance existed. The outer wall follows the plan of the projecting bastion. It is, however, so much ruined at this point that it is impossible to say definitely whether the doorway was in the long face towards the N.E., or in the short return face towards the N.W. There are indications which suggest that it may have been in the return face, and this arrangement would have made it most easy to defend. If there were stairs to ascend to the wall top, and we cannot suppose that there were not, these must have been of wood, and placed in the slits on either side of the entrance. All traces of them have now vanished. In the entrance can still be seen remains of panelling in the brickwork. Whilst the surface of the outer wall was plain, that of the inner wall, facing into the narrow space of 2.23 m., was built in panels. The walls are entirely of crude brick, and were plastered and whitened. The south-west wall remains unbroken, and stands to a height of some 8.0 m. or 9.0 m. above the plain. The walls near the gateway are also of about the same height, and it is probable that they have not lost more than 1.0 m." The area enclosed by the walls is covered with untidy heaps of rubbish and sand; but the visitor should not fail to enter the enclosure, for, shut in by the huge walls, and cut off from the sights and sounds outside, there is a wonderful impression of solemnity to be experienced. The fort probably dates, like that at Abydos, from the Ist or IInd dynasty.

Immediately to the west of the fort is a small mound or hillock, in the near side of which are many tombs, some cut into the rock and some made of crude brick. These tombs were excavated some years ago by Mr. Tyler, and recently by Mr. Garstang. Two rock tombs, opened by Mr. Tyler in 1893, are perhaps worth a visit, though they are partly filled with sand and not easily entered. The entrance of one faces us as we approach, and that

The rock tombs.

of the other is upon the right-hand side near by. The former tomb consists of a rectangular chamber, with a recess or shrine in the north-west corner. The decorations have been painted on stucco, and are now very faint. On either side of the doorway are figures in low relief representing the deceased, but these are much damaged. On the right as we enter is a figure of the owner, and before him are harvesting scenes, and a scene showing cows crossing the water. An inscription here shows him to have been a Sole Companion, Ritual-Priest, Treasurer of the Hawk, Sealer; and the cartouche of King Pepy is given. The north wall is destroyed, as is the shrine in it, which originally contained a stele and lists of offerings; but on the west wall is a figure of the deceased, and behind him scenes representing boats crossing the river helped by persons who stand in the water. The south wall is much damaged, but hunting scenes are traceable, and an inscription gives the titles quoted above with now some indication of the owner's name, which seems to be Pepy - - nen - - - ankh. The east wall—on the left as one entered the tomb—contains some scenes showing oxen being driven along, &c.

The other tomb is rectangular in shape, with a small burial chamber leading out of it, and is decorated in the same manner. On the west wall the owner stands with heaps of offerings piled before him, and an inscription here gives a prayer to Horus of Hieraconpolis. The north wall, from which the burial chamber leads, is much damaged, but a scene in which oxen are being led along is noticeable. On the east wall granaries are seen, and there is a painted stele, the inscription on which is mainly lost. The fine ceiling pattern should be noticed. The blue hieroglyphs down the middle of the design give the name and titles of the deceased, the former Horemkhauf-maa, "Hawk-with-his-Crowns is truthful," and the latter Overseer of the Priests, Superintendent of the Fields. Having seen these two tombs, a visit may be made to the terrace of tombs which can be seen in the face of a small hill about two kilometres westward along the wady. On the lower level there are four tomb entrances, and before these there is a wall constructed of limestone blocks which seems to have formed part of a courtyard. Of the two main tombs in this group, one is a rectangular, undecorated chamber with vaulted roof, and having a niche at the end in which are the broken and uninscribed statues of a man and woman. The other consists of an undecorated rectangular chamber with two rough chambers looking from it. From this group the pathway leads up the hill to the main terrace, from which a fine view can be obtained. The first two tombs have no inscriptions and are rough rectangular chambers. The third tomb has an inscription cut around the door. On the lintel the cartouche of Thothmes Ist is noticeable, while the name of the deceased, the Superintendent of the Sculptors, Tahuti, is also to be seen. The chamber inside is rectangular, and has a vaulted roof; and on the right side another chamber leads off. At the end of the main chamber is a niche in which are the seated figures of the deceased and his wife. On the right side of the niche is a little stele. From this one learns that Tahuti was "vigilant over the Public Works, dexterous in the exercise of art, gentle of heart towards his associates"; and that "there proceeded from his mouth nought perverse." The fourth tomb, of somewhat similar construction, has an inscription outside the door, but the name of the deceased is destroyed. The fifth tomb is a rectangular vaulted chamber, with six long niches or shelves in the walls, for the reception of mummies, these being probably of much later date than the tomb itself. The sixth tomb is similar. The seventh is a rectangular vaulted chamber with a niche in one wall in which are two statues much destroyed. On the sides of the door are figures of the owner almost obliterated. The roof has fallen in. The eighth tomb also lacks a roof. It is similar in construction, but has the later mummy-shelves cut in its sides. The path now goes round the corner to the ninth tomb, which consists of a rectangular hall with a chamber leading from it. Finally the tenth and last tomb is reached, this being perhaps the only one worthy of a visit. It consists of a long chamber from which another chamber leads off, having at the far end a shrine in which are two statues much broken. The front chamber has been well decorated, and traces of the scenes can still be made out, among these being an interesting representation of women dancing, carrying garlands of flowers and trailing vine-leaves. Upon the sides of the doorway leading into the inner room the name of the owner is seen. He was the "High Priest of Horus of Hieraconpolis," and was named Herames. Among his minor titles were those of "Divine Father," and "Washer of the [king's] hands." In the inner chamber is a marginal inscription giving the cartouches of Thothmes IIIrd, under whom Herames lived. The tomb, however, must have been re-used, for upon the walls of the inner chamber there appear the cartouches of Rameses XIIth.

The cemeteries at Kôm el Ahmar are very extensive, and date mainly from the prehistoric and early dynastic period. Over most

The cemeteries.

ANTIQUITIES OF UPPER EGYPT

of the desert to the north and south of the fort, both along the edge of the cultivation and also farther back in the desert, lie hundreds of archaic tombs, which have mostly been plundered, and now appear as sandy hollows surrounded by broken pottery. Some of these tombs were examined by Messrs. Quibell and Green in 1897–98, but robbers had ransacked the place for at least ten years previous to that. To the north of the fort are three small mounds of brickwork which were originally Old Empire mastaba-tombs. Beyond the XVIIIth dynasty rock tombs to the far west of the fort is a small prehistoric cemetery entirely plundered. Near the fort on the south side is a small group of late Middle Empire (?) tombs.

Other remains.
To the east of the fort are some mounds covered with red pottery, and one of these is especially known as the Kôm el Ahmar. Mr. Quibell dug here, and discovered that under the pottery there were a group of domed chambers which appear to have been granaries. The *sebakh*-diggers, however, had destroyed all but three of these chambers. Upon the large tracts of open desert to the south-west of the fort, that is to say, to the south of the rock tombs, quantities of archaic pottery were found scattered far and wide, and yet there were no tombs found to account for the phenomenon. Ashes and charcoal were encountered under the sand at different points. It is to be supposed that these open spaces were used as camping grounds by the large armies which in archaic times were garrisoned here. Little else remains to be seen of the remains of this most interesting and ancient city and its environs. The years have not dealt so lightly with it as with its twin city Eileithyiapolis, which has now to be described.

EL KÂB

Methods of visiting the ruins.
The visitor, travelling by railway from Luxor to Aswân, passes under the walls of the ancient town, soon after leaving the station of Mahamid, and a good view of them can thus be obtained. The excursion steamers do not often stop at El Kâb; but the ruins may be reached by railway from Luxor without discomfort. One leaves Luxor by the train which starts at dawn, arriving at Mahamid station somewhat over two hours later. One's dragoman should here be in waiting with village donkeys, for which saddles should have been brought by him from Luxor. A ride of half-an-hour brings one to El Kâb; and the return journey may be made by the express which reaches Mahamid on its way to

EL KÂB AND KÔM EL AHMAR

Luxor at about 2 P.M. Or one may go on to Aswân by the express which passes Mahamid at about 12.30 P.M. Sometimes, by a careful study of time-tables, one may find it possible to combine railway and steamer travelling, going to Mahamid by train, and being picked up a few hours later at El Kâb by a passing tourist-steamer by special arrangement, or *vice versa*.

THE CITY ENCLOSURE

The stout walls which surround the ruins of Eileithyiapolis are seen from a great distance, and it is surprising to think that although they have stood for nearly four thousand years they are still in parts almost perfectly preserved. The visitor should enter the enclosure from the west side, and in order to obtain a general view of it he should climb the west wall. From this point of vantage he will see that the area is divided into three distinct parts. Firstly, at his feet he will see a small walled enclosure, covered over with broken fragments of pottery, which was evidently the site of the town. Secondly, at the south-east corner of this enclosure, there are the temple ruins surrounded by another wall. And thirdly, there is the great area which lies between these two inner enclosures and the great outer wall, which was used for the camps of the troops and caravans. The city was, thus, not spread over the whole area, but was situated in a comparatively small space, and consisted evidently of nothing but a crowded mass of small houses, stores, and granaries. The dwelling-places of the nobility were probably built at the river's edge outside the walls. The water has eaten away the south-west corner of the enclosure, which originally was 360,000 square yards in area. The walls are some 37 feet in thickness, and are built of large mud bricks. There are gates at the north and south sides, but the main entrance, lined with masonry, is on the east side. Broad causeways lead to the top of the walls on this side, and the visitor will find it worth his while to ascend one of these, after seeing the town ruins.

The ancient city.

The remains of the temple which stood inside the enclosure are meagre. A mass of fallen walls, a granite altar, overturned blocks of stone, bases of pillars, and parts of the platform or pavement, alone remain to tell of the past magnificence of the building. The names of the various kings who built here, so far as they can now be seen, have been recorded above. The portion of the build-

The temple in the enclosure.

ing erected by Rameses IInd bears inscriptions stating that the work was carried out under the orders of the Vizir Nefer-renpit; and that the temple was of fine white sandstone, fitted with doors of cedar mounted in copper.

THE TOMBS OF THE NOBLES

The traveller should now visit the rock tombs which can be seen excavated in the side of a small hill just to the north-east of the town. The tombs have been made in an ascending line which follows the stratum of good rock, and in the following description the visitor is supposed to begin at the south-east or lower end of this line and to proceed to the north-west or upper end. Only four tombs, however, repay a visit: namely those of Paheri, Setau, Aahmes son of Abana, and Renni. The first tomb—not to mention a small, choked-up recess in an angle at the extreme end of the row—belonged to a sistrum-player in the temple of the goddess Nekheb named Thentas, dating from the late New Empire. It consists of a rectangular chamber from which an inner room leads, and in the walls there are five long niches for the reception of mummies of a much later date. Outside the doorway is a small stele giving the name of the deceased. Five tombs, entirely lacking inscriptions or decorations, are now passed, after which we reach the tomb of Prince Aahmes Pennekheb. From the inscriptions here we learn that this personage was entitled *Erpa-ha*-Prince, Sole Companion, Superintendent of the Sealings (*i.e.* one responsible for the sealing up and registering of all valuables), and Herald of the King. In the war against the Hyksos he fought under King Aahmes Ist, and at the siege of Zaha he captured one of the enemy and slew another apparently in single combat. Under Amenhotep Ist he fought in Ethiopia and there took another prisoner, while in a battle with the Libyans he slew three men. The king at various times presented him with two gold bracelets, two gold necklaces, a gold armlet, a gold dagger, a gold head-dress, and a fan ornamented with gold. In the reign of Thothmes Ist he again fought in Ethiopia, and captured five prisoners; and in Syria he slew twenty-one persons, and captured a horse and chariot. This king presented him with four gold necklaces, two gold bracelets, one gold armlet, six gold pendants in the form of flies, like those which the visitor may now see in the Cairo Museum, three gold ornaments in the form of lions, and two gold axes. Under Thothmes IInd he fought

Tomb of Aahmes Pennekheb.

EL KÂB AND KÔM EL AHMAR 321

against the Beduin, and captured so many prisoners that he tells us he did not count them. This king rewarded him with three gold bracelets, six gold necklaces, three gold armlets, and a silver axe. In his old age he was given charge of Princess Neferura, the young daughter of Thothmes IIIrd and Hatshepsut. In the tomb Aahmes is seen on the left side of the doorway with his son, "the Chief Royal Son of Eileithyiapolis," named Khaemuast; while on the right side there are the figures of other members of his family. The tomb, however, is much damaged, and the funeral statues lie broken at the far end of the chamber.

The next tomb is that of Paheri, whose titles were *Erpa-ha*-Prince, Sole Companion, *Ha*-Prince of Eileithyiapolis and of Esneh, Superintendent of the Priests of Nekheb, and Scribe of the Accounts of the Corn collected—perhaps for the use of the fortress and caravanserai—from all the country between Arment[1] and El Kâb. His father had been tutor to Prince Uazmes, the son of Thothmes Ist; and Paheri was made tutor to a second Prince Uazmes, who was probably the son of Thothmes IInd. He married a lady named Henut-erneheh, who was the daughter of a "chief of transport" named Ruru. Inside the tomb the walls are covered with highly coloured reliefs, executed with considerable artistic skill. The chamber is rectangular, and in a niche at the far end are three damaged statues, representing Paheri, his wife, and his mother. On the right or east wall the souls of Paheri and his wife are first shown standing before a number of offerings, and an inscription near by expresses the hope that in the underworld they may be allowed to come and go as living persons, and to leave the suffocating tomb in order to breathe the sweet breeze of the north wind. Paheri holds two five-wicked lamps; and beside the offerings stand women who each shake a sistrum, perhaps to attract the souls to their funeral meal. To the Egyptians, who believed that the soul of a dead man continued to inhabit his mummy, there was always the fear lest the bandages drawn across the face, and the plugging of the nostrils and mouth in the process of embalment, should suffocate the soul; while the dark and airless tomb should hold him stifling and starving in prison, unable to join in the pleasures of the outer world. The prayers, thus, were almost always for the sweet north wind, for coolness, for drink and food, and for liberty of movement. The long inscription which runs

Tomb of Paheri.

[1] In the inscriptions these limits are spoken of as "*An* to *Nekheb*" or "*Per-Hathor* to *Nekheb*." *An* is the name of Arment, and *Per-Hathor* is that of Gebelên, just near Arment.

above the scenes on the wall at which we are now looking, prays the gods of the underworld that they may allow Paheri "to eat bread, and to drink a cup of milk . . . to have water at hand, and to breathe the breeze of the north wind."

Paheri's feast. The remainder of the scenes on this wall represent a great feast prepared by the son of Paheri, at which his living relations celebrated him, and made merry for the edification of the souls of their ancestors. The souls of the grandparents of Paheri—the famous old sailor Aahmes son of Abana, and his wife; the souls of the parents—Atefrura and his wife; and the souls of Paheri himself and his wife are shown in large size seated before offerings. The pet monkey of Paheri scratches itself under his chair. The actual participants in the feast are shown in four rows, some receiving food or drink from the servants, some conversing, and some complacently smelling flowers. The inscriptions give specimens of the conversation, the nature of which suggests a very low tone of morals. A servant, pressing one of the guests to drink, says, "Order something, and I will let you alone," indicating that he will continue to pester as long as the guest continues to refuse to drink. A lady who does not wish to drink more is urged to do so by her companion, and the servant then says, "For your spirit, drink to drunkenness. Make holiday: O listen to what your friend is saying. Do not weary of taking." Her companion's words are: "Give me eighteen cups of wine, for I should love to drink to drunkenness. My stomach is as dry as straw!" Another servant urges a male guest to drink, saying, "Drink!—do not refuse. O, I am not going to leave you!" and his companion cries, "Drink!—do not spoil the entertainment; and let the cup come to me, for it is due to the soul of Paheri." In the bottom row one sees a female harper and piper, and other musicians. One can hardly believe that this drunken orgie is a funeral feast in honour of the dead.

The funeral of Paheri. On the west wall at the north end are scenes relating to the funeral of Paheri. In the top row one sees the sarcophagus dragged to the tomb by men and oxen, and behind it walk priests, one of which chants, "In peace, in peace, before the great God." In the next row a chest of funeral furniture is carried along, and behind this two men, called in the inscription "buffoons," dance apparently to amuse the crowds. Behind these again the funeral boats are floated across the temple (?) lake, in accordance with the ceremonial customs of the period. Below in the next row two men carrying long papyrus-topped staffs precede a sledge on which is

EL KÂB AND KÔM EL AHMAR

an oval object, now partly damaged. There is good reason to suppose that this object is a human being wrapped in a cow's skin, who is about to be sacrificed at the tomb. Professor Maspero has shown that these sacrifices are represented in several tombs; and Mr. F. Ll. Griffith points out that human sacrifices are stated by Plutarch to have been offered at Eileithyiapolis. In the lowest row we see the soul of Paheri adoring Osiris, the god of the dead, while behind him are mystical scenes from the underworld.

Farther along the wall Paheri and his wife are shown seated under a canopy, while servants bring them the products of the estate. Above them is a vineyard and wine-press, and below them are scenes of fishing with a net and bird catching. In the upper row Paheri is shown dandling Prince Uazmes on his knee, who is represented as a nude boy wearing the side-lock of hair. The scenes upon the upper part of the rest of the wall represent ploughing, sowing, harvesting, and threshing in the fields. Paheri stands at the far end watching the work. His chariot is shown in small size before him. The charioteer calls coaxingly to the horses, " Stand still !—do not be disobedient—you good horse whom your master loves, and of whom the prince boasts to everybody !" In the ploughing scenes, one of the labourers sings to himself, " It is a fine day, and I am cool. The oxen are pulling well, and the sky is as we would have it. Let us work for the prince." Another labourer calls to his comrade, " Friend, hurry the work: let us finish in good time"; to which he replies, " I am already doing more than is necessary. Be silent." In the harvesting scenes we see an old man combing off the seed-heads of the flax under a tree. He calls to the boy who brings him the sheaves, " If you bring me eleven thousand and nine sheaves I am the man to strip them all"; to which the youth replies, " Quick, do not chatter, you old fellow." Jars of water or wine are standing in the shade at one end of the field, and a servant keeps off the flies with a fan. In the top row oxen are shown threshing the corn, and here the famous song, so often quoted, is inscribed:—

> " Hie along oxen:
> Thresh the corn faster—
> The straw for yourselves :
> The corn for your master."

A man carrying back the pole of an empty basket exclaims, " Haven't I stuck to the pole all day like a man? That is what I like."

Paheri's estate.

324 ANTIQUITIES OF UPPER EGYPT

Lower down we see four boats, the two top ones being loaded with grain, and the other two having on board Paheri's chariots and horses. The labourers who bear the sacks of grain cry, "The granaries are full, and much is pouring over their edges. The barges are heavily laden, and corn is dropping out. But still the master urges us on. Well, we are men of iron!" Paheri is next shown watching the counting of the gold which has come in from the mines. Lastly, in the corner of the wall we see him registering the animals of his estate, oxen, donkeys, goats, swine, &c., being driven past him.

Paheri's virtues. Around the niche in which sit the statues at the end of the tomb there is a long inscription, which gives a prayer to Amen, Nekheb, Osiris, Hathor, Ptah-Seker, and Anubis, for the welfare of the soul of Paheri, whose virtues are here recorded. He is said to have been good and wise, walking upon the road which he had planned. He did not receive bribes; he did not lie; he obeyed his orders; he did not tell tales to those who were likely to repeat them; he recognised the divinity in men; his pen made him learned and caused him to be distinguished; but it was his own heart which guided him to the road of those who are praised by the king.

The tomb of Setau. An uninscribed tomb is now passed, after which one enters the tomb of Setau, the High Priest of Nekheb under Kings Rameses IIIrd to Rameses IXth of the XXth dynasty. Outside the doorway on the right there is a stele upon which the sacred boat of Harmachis is shown, while Setau is seen worshipping that god. Four steps lead down into the funeral chamber, from which three other chambers lead off. On the left wall there are badly damaged scenes, showing ploughing, harvesting, and also the funeral boats. Over these mention is made of the first *sed-heb* festival of Rameses IIIrd in his twenty-ninth year, which was performed by the Vizir Ta. On the right wall at the far end we see Setau and his wife seated, while their son-in-law, the "Holy Father" of Amen-Ra, offers to them. Numerous relatives are next shown, somewhat as in the tomb of Paheri, and Setau with his wife is then seen standing before a number of offerings. An inscription in this tomb states that it was made in the fourth year of Rameses IXth.

The tomb of Aahmes son of Abana. The next tomb is not inscribed. Then follows the tomb of the famous Aahmes son of Abana. This noble was the son of an official named Baba, who served under King Sekenenra IIIrd of the XVIIth dynasty; and his mother's name, which he generally adds to his own, was Abana. He tells us that he spent his youth

EL KÂB AND KÔM EL AHMAR

at El Kâb, and while still young served as captain of a warship named *The Offering*, under Aahmes Ist. After he had married he was transferred to the northern fleet, which at that time was engaged in fighting the Shepherd Kings. He was present at the siege of Avaris, and distinguished himself there by killing on two occasions an enemy in single combat, for which he was rewarded with gold by the king. At the fall of the city he captured a man and three women, who were given to him as slaves. In Upper Egypt he helped to suppress a rebellion, and took a prisoner there, for which he was again rewarded. He was then appointed to be captain of a warship named *Shining-in-Memphis*. He was present at the siege and fall of Sharuhen, and captured there two women, who were given to him as slaves. He also slew an enemy, for which he was rewarded. Next he fought in Nubia, there taking two men prisoners and killing three others. The king rewarded him with gold and with two female slaves. In another rebellion in Nubia he captured two archers, and was rewarded by a present of slaves and land. Under Amenhotep Ist he fought in Ethiopia with "incredible bravery," slaying two negroes in single combat and capturing a third. The king returned to Egypt on his vessel, which was rowed from the Second to the First Cataract in forty-eight hours, for which record journey he was rewarded with gold and with two female slaves. He was then appointed "Warrior of the King." Under Thothmes Ist he again fought in Nubia, and showed such daring in taking the ships up the Cataract that the king created him "Chief of the Sailors." In Syria Aahmes fought at the head of the troops, and captured a chariot and its occupant, for which he was rewarded in double measure. In his old age he settled down at El Kâb, where he made for himself this tomb.

The tomb consists of a chamber, from which the burial-room leads off. On the north or end wall one sees Aahmes and his wife Apu seated, while their relations make offerings to them. A pet monkey sits under its master's chair. This and the left walls were never finished, Aahmes having died before the paintings were completed; and one may see the red squares drawn by the artist to regulate his work. On the right wall we see a large figure of Aahmes, standing before the long inscription which records his biography.

The next two tombs contain nothing of interest. Then follows the tomb of Renni, who lived in the early XVIIIth dynasty, and who was entitled *Erpa-ha*-Prince and Superintendent of the

Tomb of Renni.

Priests. On the left wall are scenes showing a chariot and horses, a dog, soldiers, and huntsman; and near these are representations of harvesting and threshing. The figures of Renni and his wife are shown presiding over a feast at which many of his relations are present. On the right wall there are some very interesting funeral scenes. In the first row three figures are shown drawing along a sledge, on which is a seated man wrapped in a cow's skin. This again, like the somewhat similar representation in the tomb of Paheri, seems to suggest a human sacrifice. A chest is next carried on the shoulders of two men, after which come three dancing "buffoons." The sarcophagus is next dragged along by oxen and men, a priest walking in front. In the next row one sees Osiris and Anubis in the underworld; after which are representations of the ceremony of "opening the mouth" of the mummy. Then the mummy is seen lying on the bier, with weeping women beside it. A religious ceremony of pouring holy water over a priest is next shown; and finally we see the boats in which are the figures of the dead. In the third row various relations are represented, and offerings are shown; and lastly, we see the coffin carried to the tomb, while women weep and tear their hair. At the end of the tomb is a broken statue of Renni. Amongst the inscriptions in this tomb, mention is made of 1500 swine which belonged to the prince's estate; and in the tomb of Paheri it will be remembered that swine are also mentioned. This is somewhat curious, as the Egyptians, like the Jews, abhorred the flesh of these animals. Herodotus, however, states that swine were sacrificed to the goddess Selene, who is identified with Nekheb, the patron deity of El Kâb, and it may be that the swine were kept for this purpose.

Tomb of Beba, and others. The pathway now goes up the hill past some eight tombs, many of which lie exposed owing to the breaking away of the cliff. The tomb of Beba is then reached, a short flight of steps leading to the entrance. On the end wall of the tomb is a long inscription, above which are the figures of Beba and his wife. This personage was a "Secretary at the Princely Table," and his wife was a "Royal Handmaid," sometime during the obscure period, between the XIIIth and XVIIth dynasty. Amongst his possessions he names nine pigs, as though swine were in those days of considerable value. Passing two much damaged tombs, one reaches that of Sebek-nekht, an *Erpa-ha-*Prince and Superintendent of the Priests under Sebekhotep IInd Sekhemra-seuaztaui. The paintings here are practically all destroyed, but a few lines of inscription remain. Farther up the path there are a few other tombs, but these have no inscriptions.

EL KÂB AND KÔM EL AHMAR 327

There are a few tombs excavated in other hills to the north-east and north-west of those described above, but they do not contain anything of interest.

THE DESERT TEMPLES

As Eileithyiapolis was a city which derived its importance from its gold-mines, its general plan is suited to the needs of the caravans. Two or three miles back in the eastern desert there are three little temples, which were intended to be used by persons coming to or from the mines. The visitor should certainly ride out to see these shrines, as they are of considerable interest, and their isolated position gives them a certain charm. An ancient road led out to them from the great gate in the east wall of the city, but there are now two or three paths which may be taken. One first comes upon a small Ramesside temple, which stands at the roadside, and is only a few feet in size. The outside is quite plain, but entering by the doorway which faces the desert, one sees from the reliefs and inscriptions inside, that the temple was erected by the Viceroy of Ethiopia, Setau, for his master Rameses IInd. On the right and left side of the doorway as one enters there are figures of the Viceroy in an attitude of prayer, and just inside one again sees him holding the fan of office. On the south wall the king is shown worshipping a form of the goddess Nekheb, and other deities now much damaged. On the north wall he offers to Thoth and Horus. On the west wall Rameses offers to a seated figure of Horus; and in the corner two cynocephali are seen in attitudes of worship. There has been a small courtyard in front of the temple, but this is now destroyed. *The temple of Rameses IInd.*

A few yards to the north there is a temple built against the face of the rocks; and as one approaches it a number of ruined huts will be seen, which probably were the dwelling-places of the priests and custodians. This temple was built during the reigns of Ptolemy IXth Euergetes IInd, and Ptolemy Xth Soter IInd. A wide masonry stairway, with a balustrade on either side, leads up to the main court of the temple, which was entered through a now ruined doorway. Passing through a second ruined gateway one reaches the Sanctuary, which is excavated in the rock. On the outside of the much-damaged entrance there are figures of a Queen Cleopatra, but those of the king, her husband, are now destroyed. Inside the Sanctuary only the decoration on the upper part of the walls now remains. This decoration consists of a series of Hathor *The Ptolemaic temple.*

heads alternating with the cartouches of the king, each of which rests on the symbol of "gold," perhaps in reference to the gold-mines. At the far end the king is seen purified by Thoth and Horus. The temple was never finished, as can be seen from the uncompleted ceiling pattern of vultures with spread wings.

On the west of the court there has been an earlier platform constructed in front of a large rock-stele of Rameses VIth. On this stele one sees the king offering to Harmachis and Nekheb, but the monument was made by some official whose name is now lost, who prays that his *ka* may receive the usual benefits.

The temple of Amen-hotep IIIrd.
A rough pathway leads from this temple to the temple of Amenhotep IIIrd, which stands on a plateau of rock some distance farther eastward. It was dedicated to Nekheb, "Lady of the Mouth of the Desert," and evidently was used by the caravans as a place of prayer when setting out for or returning from the gold-mines. The building is quite small, and from the outside it appears to be unpretentious. A now ruined hall stood before the main building, which added much to its size. Above the doorway one sees Amenhotep IIIrd dancing before the gods. Entering the temple, we find ourselves in a rectangular chamber, the roof of which is supported by four sixteen-sided pillars with Hathor capitals. It was lighted by one window on the south side, but now there are two other openings on the north side. At the east end is a recess, which has later been converted into a doorway. The scenes on the walls still retain much of their colour, and their artistic merit is considerable. On the west wall, to right and left of the entrance, Amenhotep IIIrd is represented seated with his father, Thothmes IVth, before a number of offerings; while lower down on either side a conventional lion is represented. On the north wall the king is seen making offerings of oxen, gazelles, geese, ducks, bread, fruit, wine, and flowers to the sacred barque of Horus (?). Next, the king makes offering to Nekheb, who is represented in the form of a woman; and lastly, he is embraced by a seated figure of Amen-Ra, who gives him life. On the south wall the king is embraced by Horus of Hieraconpolis; he worships Nekheb; and he presents numerous offerings to the sacred barque. On the east wall, at either side of the recess, the king is seen worshipping Nekheb. Down each pillar is a perpendicular inscription giving the titles of the king, who is said to be beloved by Nekheb. A striking decoration, consisting of Hathor heads alternating with the king's cartouches, passes round the room.

EL KÂB AND KÔM EL AHMAR

On the façade of the temple there are a few later inscriptions and figures, the most important of which dates from the forty-first year of Rameses IInd, when the Prince Khaemuast[1] came to celebrate the king's jubilee here. Various crosses, footmarks, &c., which have been cut on the stones, date from early Christian times. Looking eastward from the temple, the visitor will see that the desert appears to open out into the distance beyond a natural doorway, formed by two hills. This is evidently the " Mouth of the Desert," of which Nekheb was patron goddess.

Returning towards the town, one passes some cliffs and an isolated hill, on the rocks of which there are numerous inscriptions, mostly dating from the early dynasties; while many drawings of boats, animals, and men were made in prehistoric times. The cartouches found here have already been mentioned, and the writers generally hold some priestly or official title. Across the valley to the north there is a natural spring, now choked with sand. A flight of steps has been cut in the rock leading down to the water. *Rock inscriptions, and a well.*

FROM EL KÂB TO EDFU

Between El Kâb or Kôm el Ahmar and Edfu there are few antiquities. On the east bank no ancient site is met with, except that of a late cemetery some two miles to the north of a point opposite Edfu temple. On the west bank there is a cemetery some six miles south of Hieraconpolis near the village of El Khirbeh, another at El Balalis, and a third just to the north of the Edfu cemetery; but these have all been pulled to pieces by the natives.

---

[1] See p. 363, Gebel Silsileh.

CHAPTER XIV

THE TEMPLE OF EDFU

Methods of visiting the temple.

ALL the tourist steamers stop at Edfu and give ample time for visiting the great temple, which stands in the town, some distance back from the river. To make the excursion by railway is quite comfortable, and can be recommended. One must leave Aswân or Luxor by the train which starts at daybreak, and which reaches Edfu—the half-way point between these two places—soon after 10 A.M. The native ferry across the river has to be taken, and donkeys will be required at the west bank. The trains back to Luxor or Aswân leave Edfu station at about 1.30 P.M., and bring one to either of those towns in time for tea. All visitors to Egypt should make an attempt to see this temple, for it is the most perfectly preserved of all the ancient buildings, and nowhere else can one obtain so clear an idea of the arrangement and plan of an Egyptian temple.

HISTORY OF EDFU

Early period.

Of the early history of Edfu very little is known. According to a tradition—which may have some germs of truth in it—the god Horus, with an army of men who are said to have understood the working of metal, here defeated his brother Set in a pitched battle, and was thenceforth worshipped in this town. In "Horus" one may perhaps see a conquering tribe of Hawk-worshippers, and in "Set" an aboriginal race of worshippers of the Set-monster. There is reason to suppose that the prehistoric tribes of Upper Egypt were largely devotees of Set; and a study of the archæology of the archaic period leads one to believe that these tribes were conquered by a more civilised race, perhaps using metal weapons instead of the primitive flint and stone implements. The Set-tribe which the Hawk-tribe thus defeated does not seem to have been settled at Edfu, but to have been pursued here from Den-

THE TEMPLE OF EDFU

dereh, where, according to the tradition, they had also been defeated. On a ceremonial object dating from the reign of Narmer, the predecessor of Mena the first Pharaoh of United Egypt, this archaic king is shown conducting a ceremony at a place which may be Edfu, according to the somewhat obscure hieroglyph. There are no archaic cemeteries, however, in the neighbourhood of Edfu, and the conquering Hawk-tribe does not seem to have risen to any importance until the IIIrd dynasty. At this epoch, however, Imhotep, the master-builder and wise man of the court of King Zeser, is said to have erected a temple at Edfu, built on a plan which "fell from heaven to the north of Memphis." This may mean that the plan was similar to that of some building in Lower Egypt. The temple was dedicated to the hawk Horus, the tribal totem; and in it, no doubt, were celebrated the festivals in commemoration of the archaic victory over the Set tribe. As time passed this Hawk-worship and these historical traditions began to be amalgamated and confused into the legend of the hawk Horus which did battle with its brother the Set-monster; and thus around the tribal totem there grew up a series of legends which gave to this god a high place in Egyptian mythology. These legends, it should be remarked, originally had nothing to do with the famous Lower Egyptian tradition of Horus, the son of Osiris and Isis, who defeated his uncle Set, the murderer of Osiris; but there is some reason to suppose that they are connected with the early Heliopolitan sun-worship.

An inscription was found recently near the temple of Edfu which was dated in the reign of Dudumes, the obscure king of the Middle Kingdom, whose name has already been noticed at Gebelên and El Kâb. King Amenemhat IIIrd of the XIIth dynasty seems to have shown some activity here;[1] and in the XIIIth dynasty a queen named Sebekemsaf was buried somewhere in this neighbourhood, perhaps owing to the fact that she was a native of Edfu. Queen Aah-hotep of the XVIIIth dynasty possessed lands here which were administered by an official named Auf, who lived on into the reign of Thothmes Ist. This personage restored the tomb of Queen Sebekemsaf, and carried out other good works here. During the reign of Queen Hatshepsut, the Superintendent of the Granaries of Amen, Senmut, left a statue in the temple here. Under Thothmes IIIrd the goddess Hathor of Dendereh is said to have been brought up the

[1] Breasted, "History," p. 196.

river in solemn procession to visit Horus in his temple at Edfu, and the king arranged that this festal journey should be instituted as a regular ceremony, which was to take place at the new moon of the month Epiphi. The goddess Hathor had now become the recognised consort of Horus in the Edfu ceremonial, and in the temple they were worshipped side by side. Perhaps as early as this a third god, who completes the trinity worshipped in the existing Ptolemaic temple, had taken his place at Edfu. This was "Horus the Uniter of the Two Lands," the son of Horus of Edfu and Hathor. He seems to typify the union of Upper and Lower Egypt under the archaic Kings Narmer and Mena, and thus was correctly termed the son of Horus (*i.e.* the hawk-tribes of Upper Egypt) and of Hathor, the primitive goddess of the south.

The gods of Edfu.

At this period Edfu seems to have been a fairly rich town. The yearly tax imposed on its mayor was eight *debens* of gold (a *deben* being about 100 grammes). The Recorder of the city had also to pay in some gold and an ox as a yearly tax. Thothmes IVth, on his way to a Nubian war, stopped at Edfu, and it is said that the god Horus was brought out to meet him, girded for war "like Set of Ombo" (Negada), a simile which is unexpected, since Horus and Set were enemies in later traditions.

The lower part of the pylon of a temple of Ramesside times has recently been uncovered at Edfu. The cartouches of Sety Ist or IInd, Rameses IIIrd and Rameses IVth, are here seen; while along one side runs an inscription dated in the fifteenth year of Rameses IIIrd, which states that there was an order from the king to purify the doors of the temples of all the towns of the south, to establish the treasuries and granaries, and to renew the temple offerings. In the confusion which preceded the accession of Rameses IIIrd, the temples had evidently been much neglected. Psametik Ist has left his name on a slab found near the present temple.

Darius Ist is the next Pharaoh whose name is found at Edfu; and Nectanebus Ist presented the granite shrine which still stands in the sanctuary of the existing temple. Nectanebus IInd also made gifts to the temple. The city had grown to such a size, and had become so wealthy, that it was now the capital of a nome or province, its southern frontier being situated probably at Gebel Silsileh, to which point the province of Elephantine extended. At the advent of the Ptolemaic dynasty it was felt that the old temple was no longer large enough for the requirements of the

THE TEMPLE OF EDFU

citizens and priests, and in the reign of Ptolemy IIIrd the building of a new temple was begun.

The foundations of this temple which we are about to visit were laid on August 23rd, B.C. 237, in the tenth year of the reign of Ptolemy IIIrd Euergetes Ist. Twenty-five years later the main building was completed, the last stone being laid on August 17th, B.C. 212, in the tenth year of Ptolemy IVth Philopator. The decoration of the walls with reliefs and inscriptions occupied six years, and was finished in B.C. 207. In the same year the great door was fixed in place. A revolution then broke out in Upper Egypt, which was not suppressed until the nineteenth year of Ptolemy Vth Epiphanes. When quiet was well restored the work continued, and by February 3rd, B.C. 176, in the fifth year of Ptolemy VIIth Philometor, doors and other fittings were fixed in place. The painting of the reliefs and inscriptions, the decoration of some of the walls with gold plates, and the furnishing of the temple, was completed during the next few years; and on September 10th, B.C. 142, in the twenty-eighth year of Ptolemy IXth Euergetes IInd, the opening ceremony took place amidst general rejoicings. The small Hypostyle Hall, however, was not finished till two years later, July 2nd, B.C. 140. Thus the building and decorating of the temple proper took about ninety-seven years to complete, which figure includes the long interruptions. The Hypostyle Hall, Forecourt, and Pylons were next commenced. The Hypostyle Hall was finished on September 5th, B.C. 122, in the forty-sixth year of Ptolemy IXth; the Forecourt was erected a few years later; and finally, the completion of the Pylons and the fixing of the great entrance door was accomplished by December 5th, B.C. 57, in the twenty-fifth year of Ptolemy XIIIth Neos Dionysos. The entire building and decorating of the temple, as we see it at the present day, was therefore accomplished in 180 years 3 months and 14 days. The temple was thus completed at the time when Julius Cæsar was setting out to conquer Britain, and when the Roman Imperial age was about to begin; and it had not been in use more than a score of years when the deaths of Antony and Cleopatra brought Egypt under the rule of Rome.

The building of the Ptolemaic temple.

In Roman times the temple continued to be used, and the wealth of the priesthood at this period was probably very great. An altar recently found at Edfu of this date has upon it representations of what are unquestionably scenes of human sacrifice; and it is more than probable that at this and at earlier periods also, human beings representing the Set worshippers who, accord-

Later history of Edfu temple.

ing to the tradition, were conquered by Horus, were slain before the shrine of the Hawk. The victims seem to have been those who were born with red hair, as in the case of other human sacrifices described by early writers; for red was the colour of Set. When Christianity took hold of the country, the devotees of the new religion hacked out with hammer and chisel the figures of most of the gods represented on the temple walls. In mediæval times the chambers were used as stables, storehouses, or dwelling-places; and gradually the rubbish accumulated until the interior was choked, and houses began to be built on the roof. Mariette found it almost entirely covered in 1860 when he commenced the work of excavating the temple. During the last few years the Department of Antiquities has carried out some large works here, under the able direction of M. Barsanti. Walls have been taken down and rebuilt, the ruined roof has been restored, the temple has been walled in, and so on. As one sees it now it seems almost incredible that, after two thousand years, the building should be in such a perfect state of preservation.

The names of Edfu. The ancient name of the town, from which the modern "Edfu" is derived, was *Dbu* or *Edbu*, which means "the Town of the Piercing," since it was here that Horus pierced Set. Its religious name was *Behudet*, and "Horus of Edfu" is generally called simply "Horus Behudet." Another name of the town was *Thes-Hor*, "the Raising of Horus," and this was also applied to the whole province. The Greeks and Romans, identifying Horus with Apollo, called the city Apollonopolis Magna, and the province the Apollinopolites Nome.

DESCRIPTION OF THE TEMPLE

The main axis of the temple, according to the inscriptions, lies from Orion in the south to the Great Bear in the north. Neither the rising nor the setting sun could be observed from the temple chambers, and thus the worship of the sun is not prominently *The entrance to the temple.* combined with that of Horus. The two front pylons, which are over 110 feet in height, look somewhat ungainly, as they have lost their cornices. Approaching the temple from the south, a large scene on either pylon shows King Ptolemy XIIIth Neos Dionysos smiting his enemies, in the presence of Horus of Edfu and Hathor of Denderch. The perpendicular recesses in these pylons were intended for the flagstaffs which always stood before Egyptian

THE TEMPLE OF EDFU

temples. These staffs were generally tipped with gold, and were clamped to the walls with shining bands of copper. Gay-coloured pennants fluttered from them in the wind, and these, together with the vivid painting of the reliefs on the pylons, the massive, highly decorated wooden door which was fixed at the entrance, and the two great statues of the hawk which were also strongly coloured, must have combined to form an effect very different to that which is now presented.

Passing through the great gateway in the pylons, the visitor finds himself in the large Forecourt. In front of him, at the far end, stands the main temple; while behind and on either side of him runs a colonnade, the thirty-two columns of which are embellished with reliefs showing the king worshipping various gods. The walls at the back of these colonnades are covered with reliefs, but it is obviously impossible for the traveller to examine them all closely. His attention need only be called to those in the colonnade to the right and left of the entrance. On the right or east side (1) the king, whose cartouches have been left blank, "comes forth from the palace," crowned with the crown of Upper Egypt, and preceded by a priest burning incense and by the four standards of the primitive tribes of Upper Egypt. These standards are the Jackal of the First Cataract,[1] the Ibis of Hermopolis, the Hawk of Edfu, and the emblem of Thebes; and they are found carried before the king from the days of Narmer, the first king of a United Egypt, down to the time of the late Roman Emperors. (2) The king is purified by Thoth and Horus of Edfu; (3) he is crowned with the double crown by Nekheb and Uazt; (4) he receives from Horus the wand of office in the presence of Tum, Safkhet, and Maat; (5) he is led by a god, who puts life into his nostrils, to Horus of Edfu; and (6) he stands in the presence of Horus of Edfu and Hathor of Dendereh. Below these scenes, at the bottom of the wall, are small but spirited representations of festival boats sailing up the Nile, towing the two sacred barques of Horus and Hathor. These are seen arriving at Edfu, and the two barques are carried by priests to the temple, where offerings are placed before them. These scenes represent the festival which has already been referred to, in which Hathor of Dendereh sailed up the Nile to Edfu at the new moon of the month Epiphi to meet her consort Horus.

On the left or west of the doorway one sees (7) the king, crowned with the crown of Lower Egypt, leaving the palace,

The Forecourt.

---

[1] He is called "the opener of the ways of the south."

preceded, as before, by the priest and the four standards. (8) He is purified by Thoth and Horus of Edfu; (9) he is crowned by Nekheb and Uazt; and (10) he is carried by three persons wearing hawk masks and representing "the glorious ones of the City of Pe" (a sacred city of the Delta), and by three other persons wearing jackal masks and representing "the glorious ones of the City of Hieraconpolis." Below these reliefs again are scenes of the festival of the sacred boats.

The ascent of the pylons may be made from here, a doorway leading into each of them from the Forecourt. The steps are dark, and the climb is long and somewhat exhausting. Standing in the middle of the Forecourt, one may look round at the scenes on the great pylons, where huge figures of Ptolemy XIIIth may be seen worshipping Horus and Hathor. This Forecourt was generally called "the Court of Offerings," probably from the fact that it was here that the common people made their offerings to the Hawk. An inscription states that sacrifices were made here by the priests three times a day. The court was also called "the Court of the Appearance of the Protecting Hawk," and there is reason to suppose that by this the Sun was meant. Approaching the main temple, one sees that there are six screen walls on which reliefs are cut, three on either side of the doorway. Those on the east represent (11) King Ptolemy IXth offering four jars of water to Horus of Edfu; (12) the king offering a sphinx to Hathor; and (13) the king in the presence of Horus. Those on the west side show (14) the king offering four vases of water to Horus; (15) the king offering a chaplet of electrum to Hathor; and (16) the king in the presence of Horus.

Great Hypostyle Hall.

One now passes into the Great Hypostyle Hall, the roof of which is supported by eighteen columns with variously formed capitals. Practically no colour is left on any of the walls or columns, and the original appearance of the place is therefore difficult to realise. At present the hall appears to be sombre and ponderous, and the great columns rather encumber and dwarf the building. Originally, when the capitals were vividly coloured, the eye no doubt would have been attracted upwards, and thus the proportions of the hall would have been more readily appreciated. The best method of obtaining an idea of the great size of this hall is to look at it from the doorway (28) at the east end. Some of the capitals are worthy of attention, their complicated forms being of considerable beauty. This hall was known to the Egyptians as *Khent*, "the Chief or First Hall." Turning to the left, one

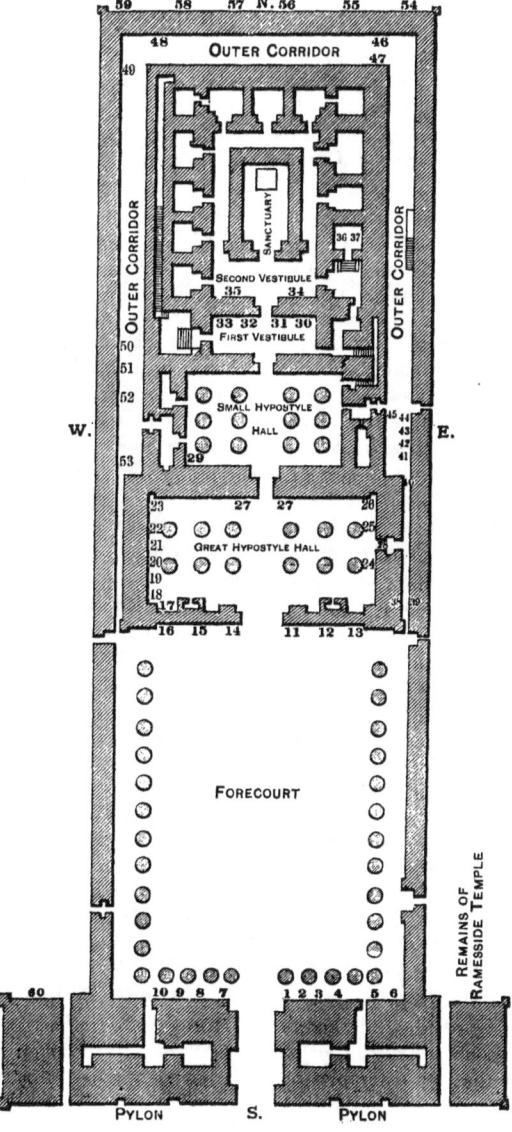

THE TEMPLE OF EDFU.

The Chamber of Consecration in the Great Hypostyle Hall. sees a small room built up against the wall, which was known as "the Chamber of Consecration." On its doorway is an inscription from which we learn that in this room were kept the golden vases used for the ceremony of purification, and particularly for that of purifying the King of Upper and Lower Egypt when he came here to celebrate the great festivals of Horus. In the room is a niche in the wall, in which these vases were kept. At the east side of the doorway of this Chamber of Consecration, the king in his war-helmet is seen approaching the door, preceded by three standards—the Jackal of the South, the Ibis of Hermopolis, and the Hawk of Edfu; and below this he is led into the chamber by a priest. On the west of the doorway, after the ceremony of purification has been finished, he is seen led by Harmachis towards the temple; and below this, crowned as King of Upper and Lower Egypt, he is led into the temple of Horus of Edfu. It is probable that all persons who were permitted to enter the temple were expected to purify themselves by touching the holy water which was kept in this chamber.

The library in the Great Hypostyle Hall. On the east of the main entrance there is another small chamber. This was the library in which the sacred books were kept. The two small niches in the wall acted as the necessary cupboards, but as these are quite small, not many rolls of papyrus could have been kept here, and probably only those which contained the ceremonial formulæ for the day were here preserved. The inscription over the doorway states that this was the chamber of the papyrus rolls of Horus and of Harmachis, arranged by the Chief Ritual-Priest for the twelve hours of the day. Immediately under the winged disk over the doorway is a damaged representation of the four senses—hearing, sight, taste, and reason—each in the form of a small human figure worshipping a scribe's palette. These four senses are again seen above the great doorway leading from this to the next hall.

Reliefs in the Great Hypostyle Hall. Just to the west of the Chamber of Consecration is a relief (17) in which the king is seen with Safkhet and Horus pegging out the limits of the temple before its foundation. This is the first of a series of scenes connected with the building of the temple, which continue along the west wall. One sees (18) Ptolemy IXth breaking ground with a hoe before Horus and Hathor; then (19) he throws sweet-smelling seed or incense into the broken ground, so that the future temple may not be contaminated by contact with dirt; (20) he raises with a crowbar (?) the first block of stone; (21) he encircles the temple, when it is built, with

THE TEMPLE OF EDFU

spices; (22) he presents the completed temple to Horus; and (23) he offers a symbol signifying "decoration," *i.e.* the reliefs and inscriptions of the temple walls, to Horus.

Returning to the east side of the hall, we see on the east wall (24) a large representation of the king carried forward by three hawk-headed and three jackal-headed men, who are called, as in the scene in the Forecourt (10), "the glorious ones of Pe and Hieraconpolis"; (25) he is led by Horus Uniter of the Two Lands to Horus of Edfu; and (26) he worships Horus and Hathor. Along the north wall of this hall, which is in reality the pylon of the Small Hypostyle Hall, the king is again seen performing ceremonies in connection with the founding of the temple. He is shown leaving his palace, pegging out the temple limits, breaking ground, offering oxen and stacks of grain; and (27) dancing before Horus at the foundation ceremony. On the columns and on the remainder of the walls the king is seen in the presence of numerous gods; but the visitor will probably have neither the time nor the inclination to examine these in detail. It will have been observed that the scenes in this hall, relating as they do to the building of the temple, are, as it were, an introduction to the shrines beyond, and are intended to remind those who are about to enter the holy place that every stone is sacred.

It will be admitted that the Small Hypostyle Hall into which one now passes, is of greater beauty, if of lesser size, than the hall which has just been described. At noon the sunlight falls in almost perpendicular shafts through the small apertures in the roof, and, shining on the floor, it is reflected against the walls, which are thus illuminated. This has the effect of lightening their weight, as it were, and of thus increasing the size and capacity of the hall. The columns are here somewhat more slender, and less crowded; and when the capitals were still bright with colour the hall must have been more brilliant and airy than is usually the case in Egyptian buildings. It was known as the "Festal Hall," and in it were celebrated the main festivals of the temple. The reliefs have greater merit from the artistic point of view than have those in the Great Hypostyle Hall. Their subjects are, however, more or less similar to those already described. We see King Ptolemy IVth Philopator leaving his palace; led by Hathor to Horus, pegging out the temple limits, breaking ground, offering (29) weights of gold to Horus, presenting the temple to that god, and so on. These scenes show us that we are still but on the threshold of the temple proper; though the two great reliefs on

The Small Hypostyle Hall.

the north wall admit us somewhat farther into the temple ceremonial. These two scenes show a priest (apparently not the king, though wearing the war-helmet), clad in the sacerdotal leopard-skin, walking beside the sacred barque of Horus in one case and of Hathor in the other, which is carried on the shoulders of the priests towards the King of Upper and Lower Egypt, who burns incense before it.

<small>Chambers, &c., leading from the Small Hypostyle Hall.</small> From the east side of this hall a doorway leads out into the outer corridor, while another leads to a stairway which ascends to the roof and which will be described later. On the west side of the hall there are again two doorways. The first leads into a chamber in which the holy water was kept. Upon the walls are reliefs showing the king, assisted by the Nile-god, Hapi, pouring libations or offering holy water to Horus and Hathor, and to the elemental gods Nu, Na, Hehu, Shu, and others. Through this room one may pass out into the outer corridor. The second door leads into a chamber in which the sacred amulets and utensils were kept, as may be seen from their representations on the walls.

<small>The First Vestibule.</small> One now enters the First Vestibule, a small transverse hall, the walls of which are covered with damaged reliefs showing the king in the presence of various gods. This vestibule was called "the Hall of the Altar of Offerings," and in it there probably stood an altar at which the ordinary sacrifices of the day were celebrated. At the east end of the north wall (30) the sacred bull Apis, in the form of a bull-headed man, makes offering with the king to Horus; and next to this (31) a ram, which was also sacred, does likewise. At the west end of the wall the corresponding scenes show two other sacred bulls (32 and 33). A doorway in the east wall of this vestibule, above which several sacred cows are shown, leads again to the stairway, also approached from the Small Hypostyle Hall; and another door at the west side leads into a chamber from which the western stairway ascends to the roof. On the walls of this chamber the king is shown in the presence of many of the more important gods of Egypt.

<small>The Second Vestibule.</small> The Second Vestibule, which lies immediately in front of the Sanctuary, and which was known as "the Hall of the Repose of the Gods," has upon its walls numerous scenes showing the king worshipping various gods. At the east end of the south wall the king (34) and his wife Arsinoë offer a scribe's palette to Horus and Hathor; and at the west end of the wall (35) he binds four kneeling captives before those gods. Perhaps this represents the

human sacrifice of which mention has been made above. Above this relief there is a scene in which the infant Horus is shown rising from amidst the reeds which symbolise the marshes in which the Lower Egyptian tradition states that he was born. At the west end of this vestibule a doorway leads into the chapel of Min, in which the king is shown worshipping that god on all the walls. It will be remembered that Min is the god of fertility, generation, and growth, and reigned both over the fields and over the family in his capacity as patron of the renewal of life. The main seat of his worship was at Koptos (Quft).

The doorway at the east of this Second Vestibule leads into a small court called " the Chamber of Offerings," in which stands a little chapel, approached by six steps. The reliefs in this chapel show the king and queen offering to Horus and Hathor. On the west wall, in the middle row of reliefs, the king and queen are seen (36) offering to King Ptolemy IIIrd and Queen Berenice, the royal parents; and on the east wall (37) the king enthroned, with his wife Arsinoë behind him, is adored by two blue-coloured figures of dead kings, who are called "the Fathers, the Hawks." A scene over the doorway of the little court shows the seven Hathors beating tambourines. These seven Hathors are the prototypes of the fairy god-mothers of more modern legends, and their particular vocation was the presiding at the birth of infants. One sees, thus, that in this part of the temple, which is immediately in front of the Sanctuary, the god Min the patron deity of reproduction, and the goddess Hathor the patron of childbirth, are particularly worshipped; while human sacrifice, which mystically signified the renewing of life, is here represented; the birth of Horus is shown; and the dead kings who live in the underworld are also displayed. Thus, the main idea is here that of Life in its most primitive aspect. None but the priests were admitted to this part of the temple; and these scenes, which the visitor may now so openly examine, represented the deepest mysteries of the cult of Horus of Edfu.

One now enters the Sanctuary, to which none but kings and chief priests were admitted. The reliefs on the walls of this chamber show the king worshipping Horus and his consort Hathor. In the middle of the room stands a low altar on which the sacred barque was placed. At the north end is a magnificent shrine of dark polished granite, in which stood the sacred figure of the Hawk. The inscription on this shrine states that it was made by King Nectanebus Ist, and thus it is older than the

The Sanctuary.

sanctuary in which it stands, having no doubt once stood in the earlier temple. As may be seen from the pivot-holes, it was fitted with double doors, which hid the holy image from sight. As one turns and looks down the middle aisle of the temple, through the many halls to the pylons, it will be realised how vast the building is. It must be remembered that there were stout double doors at each of the six doorways along this aisle, and none but the priests and high officials ever saw the inner vestibules and the sanctuary in which one now stands.

The chambers behind the Sanctuary. Behind this there are ten chambers which lead from a passage entered at the right and left of the Sanctuary. One passes into this passage from the right or east side, and the first door on the right leads into the "Chamber of the Spread-Wings." In it are reliefs chiefly representing the gods who protect Osiris, and take vengeance on his enemies. The next room is called the "Chamber of the Throne of the Sun," and in it one sees the hawk-headed sun-god accompanied by other deities. The third room is named the "Chamber of Khonsu," and in the reliefs that god, indistinguishable in form from Horus, is shown with accompanying deities. From this room another leads off, known as the "Chamber of Hathor," but the visitor will find it too dark to permit of an examination of the reliefs, which represent Hathor and various other gods. The next room, which lies immediately behind the Sanctuary, was called the "Chamber of the Victor." A small altar stands in the middle of the room, and this in the inscriptions is called the "Great Throne of the Dispenser of the Sun's Rays." On the walls various gods are shown, and the inscriptions state that their forms have been drawn accurately according to their prototypes. Then follow three chambers dedicated to the worship of Osiris. The first is called the "Chamber of the West," and on the walls Osiris, the god of the west, and his attendant demi-gods, are seen. The second room, leading from this, was known as the "Chamber of Osiris"; and the third room was called the "Chamber of the Tomb" of Osiris. The next room was named the "Chamber of the Throne of the Gods"; and finally, the last room seen before quitting the passage was called the "Chamber of the Linen."

The stairways to and from the roof. The visitor is strongly advised to ascend to the roof of the temple, as the reliefs on the stairways are interesting, and the view at the top is superb. Thanks to the admirably graded steps, the ascent is a matter of little exertion. One goes up by the stairway on the east side of the temple, which is entered either

THE TEMPLE OF EDFU 343

from the Small Hypostyle Hall or from the First Vestibule. One of the great ceremonies of the temple was the circumambulation or procession around the whole building, when the images of Horus and Hathor were taken in solemn state to see all their possessions. This ceremony seems to have taken place on New Year's Day. The procession was sometimes headed by the king if he was present in Edfu. Then followed a number of priests carrying the standards of the provinces of Egypt. Next came a priest chanting from a papyrus; then followed about a dozen priests, some shaking sistrums, some burning incense, and some carrying offerings. The queen and king sometimes walked next with the nobles of Edfu, and immediately behind them were carried the two caskets in which rested the figures of Horus and Hathor. Incense was burnt in front of and behind them; and following them came several priests carrying banners and all manner of paraphernalia enclosed in small caskets. It was believed that the whole company of the gods of Egypt were assembled at this ceremony, and marched with the procession of priests. Mounting the stairway, the visitor will first see on either side the figures of these gods; and at a turn in the passage he will presently notice the representations of the caskets of Horus and Hathor, each carefully held by the priests, while the king and queen look round anxiously to see that they are safe. Higher still the priests carrying the province-standards will be observed; and lastly, at a point where the passage is broken away and open, the king is seen at the head of the procession.

The gods were now carried to the north end of the temple; but as the passage is here interrupted by the collapse of part of the roof, the visitor must climb up by the small steps and so pass across the roof. The procession ascended the now damaged steps to the highest part of the roof above the Great Hypostyle Hall; and when the gods had feasted their eyes on the surrounding buildings and on the town which rose outside, they were conducted to the north-west corner of the temple, from which point another flight of steps leads down. On the walls of this stairway one now sees the procession descending. At the top of the steps, *i.e.* in the rear, are the priests bearing the paraphernalia. Then one sees again the two great caskets in which the sacred images rested. Lower down are the *Heq*-Prince of the Province, the *Ha*-Princes, the Superintendent of the Priests of Edfu, the Scribes of the Books, the *Sem*-Priest, a priest carrying boxes of fine linen, and others. The procession is met on the stairs by the king and queen, who offer incense and flowers; and lower down the priests carrying the province-standards are shown. One thus descends again to the First Vestibule.

The outer corridor. Around the main temple a high fender-wall is built, and between this and the outer wall of the temple space has been left for a corridor. It may be entered from various side doors, but the visitor who is following this guide should approach it from the north-east corner of the Forecourt. On one's left as one enters (38) is the usual large scene of the king smiting a group of kneeling captives, representing the foreign lands over which he ruled. He is in the presence of the Edfu trinity—Horus of Edfu; Hathor of Denderah; and Horus "Uniter of the Two Lands, the Child, Son of Hathor." Opposite this (39) is a scene showing the king with Khnum, Horus, and Thoth, dragging in from the marshes a net in which he has caught birds, animals, and men. Farther along on the same wall (40) the king is seen leaving his palace, preceded by five standards—the Jackal of the South, the Jackal of the North, the Ibis of Hermopolis, the Hawk of Edfu, and the emblem of Thebes. Next (41) he is purified by Thoth and Horus; (42) crowned by Nekheb and Uazt; (43) led by Horus Uniter of the Two Lands to Horus of Edfu; and lastly (44) he stands before Horus of Edfu. A group (45) which, in spite of the artist's exaggerations, has some decorative value, is to be observed opposite these last-named scenes, just to the south of the doorway into the Small Hypostyle Hall. Here the king is seen crowned by Nekheb and Uazt.

Presently we pass a subterranean passage which leads under the fender-wall out of the temple precincts. At the east end of the north part of the corridor, there is a large scene on one's right (46) showing a figure of Horus carried in a shrine by three hawk-headed and three jackal-headed figures. The king leads the way, holding a sistrum and a pot of incense, and conducts the shrine into the presence of the lion-headed goddess Sekhmet. Opposite this (47) the familiar scene of the king leaving his palace with his standards will be recognised. At the west end of this part of the corridor a large relief (48) shows the king, as in the above-mentioned scene (46), conducting the shrine of Horus to the goddess Mut. Turning the corner, we see on the west wall a number of curious scenes of figures standing in boats. These for the most part represent the god Horus spearing a hippopotamus, in miniature, or crocodile, which was the incarnation of Set, the evil one whom Horus overcame. Just after turning the corner,

THE TEMPLE OF EDFU

high up on the west wall (49), there is a fine representation of the sacred boat of Horus, standing on a sledge which is pulled by the king by means of a rope. Some distance along the wall there is (50) a spirited scene of a boat with its sail set. Horus stands in the boat, and the king on land, both spearing a hippopotamus; while Isis, kneeling, holds the monster by a rope. Above this, to the right, one sees Horus slaying one of the enemies of Osiris. Just to the left or south of this a sphinx is seen slaughtering two captives before Horus, Thoth, and Harmachis. Below is an interesting scene (51), in which Horus and Thoth stand in a boat, and Queen Cleopatra (not the famous queen of that name) and "the daughters of the women of the city of Pe" and "the daughters of the women of the city of Dedu" make music on sistrum and tambourine. The next scene (52) shows Horus standing on a chained hippopotamus, which he is spearing. At the point where the corridor narrows a remarkable relief (53) shows three figures, the first of which is killing a hippopotamus with a knife; the second, who represents the famous architect and magician Imhotep, reading from a magic roll; and the third, who represents the king, dropping food into the straining throat of a goose in order to fatten it for sacrifice. One now passes into the Forecourt once more; and those who wish to see the temple thoroughly may care to walk around the outside of the building, though there is not much of interest to be remarked there.

It is best to go out of the Forecourt through the main gateway and to turn to one's left, passing through a small passage in the pylon which leads one to the outside of the fender-wall of the temple. On the right, as one emerges from the passage, there are the ruins of the entrance pylons of a Ramesside temple, which evidently ran from east to west across the present Forecourt. As has been already said, the inscriptions here give the cartouches of Sety IInd (?), Rameses IIIrd, and Rameses IVth, and we learn that in the fifteenth year of Rameses IIIrd the king ordered the doorways of the temples of all the towns of the south, such as this, to be purified, and the temple revenues to be re-established. On the east side of the great fender-wall there are many reliefs showing King Ptolemy XIth Alexander Ist in the presence of various gods. At the north end of the temple there are six sets of large reliefs, which, from east to west, are as follows :—(54) the king offers the *kherp*, or baton of authority, to Horus; (65) he burns incense before Hathor and Horus Uniter of the Two Lands; (56) he presents a figure of Truth to Horus and Hathor; (57) he

The outside reliefs.

repeats this ceremony; (58) Queen Berenice offers a pot of incense and a pot of water to Hathor and Horus Uniter of the Two Lands; and (59) the king adores Horus. On the west wall numerous gods are represented, and on the north face of the west pylon (60) the king is seen before Horus, while between them is a representation of the two pylons and front gate of the temple, with the two great flagstaffs in position.

The Birth-House.
At the south-west corner of the space in front of the temple stands the ruined Birth-House. It consists of a sanctuary around which runs a pillared gallery, while in front there is an open court shut in by screen walls. This little temple was dedicated to Hathor, and in the reliefs one observes that goddess suckling the infant Horus and presenting him to Horus of Edfu. One here sees clearly that the elder Horus was the tribal hawk-god, while the infant Horus was the deified archaic king of that tribe who defeated Set, and united Upper and Lower Egypt. The seven Hathors are shown, in a relief on the north wall of the sanctuary, nursing the infant. At either side of the entrance to this sanctuary is a small chamber for the use of the priestly doorkeeper. On the pillars of the gallery and court Hathor is seen beating a tambourine, playing on a harp, or suckling Horus. The *motif* of all these reliefs is that of Maternal Love, Joy, and Thanksgiving; and as each king in succession came to the throne his divine birth was here celebrated.

The ancient town.
The mounds of the ancient town of Edfu are to be seen on the east, south, and west sides of the temple, rising to a considerable height. These cover over 45 *feddans* of land; but they are gradually being removed by the *sebakhîn*, or peasants who dig away old town-remains to be used as manure. In this work many antiquities are found, which are usually secured for the Cairo Museum, but large numbers of small objects are secreted by the diggers, who sell them to the tourists. It is probable, however, that the most important remains of the ancient city and temple lie under the present edifice. The great brick temenos or enclosing wall of the temple will be seen on the east and west sides, at the south end. In the cultivation between the temple and the western desert there is a low mound, known as *Kôm el Hedid*, "the Mound of the Iron," from the fact that a great deal of that metal was once found there. There seems once to have been a small temple and town here, dating, judging from the fragments of pottery, from late Ramesside to Ptolemaic times. The cemeteries of Edfu will be described in the next chapter.

CHAPTER XV

THE CEMETERIES OF EDFU — EDFU TO GEBEL SILSILEH ON THE WEST BANK — HASIYEH — SHUTT ER RIGÂL — THE TEMPLE OF REDESIYEH — EDFU TO GEBEL SILSILEH ON THE EAST BANK—BUEB

CEMETERIES OF EDFU

A PATHWAY running westward from the town of Edfu leads out to the desert and to the cemeteries situated there, which to the ordinary traveller will not repay a visit. Rising less than a hundred yards from the edge of the cultivation, a series of low hills here border the desert. At the foot of one of the northern hills stands the Coptic monastery of Mari Girgis. It is a rectangular building with fifteen domes forming its roof, on the four front ones of which are crosses. A fine sycamore rises on one side of it, and this, with the whitewashed walls of the building and the yellow sand around, forms a very picturesque scene. Permission to enter the monastery may be obtained from the Coptic authorities at Edfu, but there is little of interest to be seen inside. In the side of the hills behind the monastery, and extending to the north and south of it, there are a large number of rock tombs which were made for the richer inhabitants of Edfu. These tombs generally consist of a single chamber or sometimes two chambers of small dimensions opening immediately on to the slope of the hill; but they are often more elaborate, some having a kind of entrance shaft with steep steps leading down to the doorway, and others being made with a small court before them. In none of them is there any decoration or any inscriptions, and this fact is difficult to account for. Christian anchorites living in these tombs may have destroyed some of the original paintings, and natural decay may have caused the rest to disappear. But it is evident that though we have here the burial-places of the rich nobles of a rich city, these tombs are of the meanest description. There is certainly no undiscovered series of tombs of the Edfu princes: the authorised and unauthorised native and European diggers of the past twenty years have thoroughly searched the entire district. The only scientific excavations conducted here and in the cemeteries of poorer graves in the surrounding desert were those of Messrs. Garstang and Jones of the University of Liverpool in 1905.

FROM EDFU TO SILSILEH: WEST BANK

Between Edfu and Gebel Silsileh on the west bank of the river there are no points of sufficient importance to require a visit from the ordinary traveller, though those who are on a dahabiyeh may perhaps find a walk up the gorge known as Shutt er Rigâl to be of interest. The antiquarian will possibly care to visit the cemetery of El Hasiyeh, but this is somewhat difficult of access. After leaving Edfu the first antiquity met with is a small stone pyramid which stands in the open desert some three or four miles south-west of the town. Its area is about 18 or 20 square feet, and it appears to have been built in steps. It is possible that we have here the burial-place of some petty king of the VIIth-Xth dynasties, whose capital was at Edfu. There are kings of this period known whose influence was probably quite local, and who would be likely to be buried in a small pyramid. King Dudumes, for example, whose name is found at Gebelên, El Kâb, and Edfu, may very probably have been buried in this part of Egypt.

To the north of this pyramid the extensive, but entirely plundered, Nubian cemeteries of Genemieh are to be found; and some miles farther to the south lies the ransacked cemetery of El Hasiyeh, at the south side of a wide desert bay. The tombs here are of late dynastic and Ptolemaic times, and are mainly cut into the sandstone which underlies the sand at this point. Generally a short open stairway descends in a wedge form to a depth of about six feet, and at the bottom a low doorway leads into a rectangular chamber. In the hillside there are a series of rock-tombs, each consisting of two or three chambers, the doorways being ornamented with much damaged inscriptions written in badly formed hieroglyphs, and containing a number of faults in orthography. These tombs are partly choked with debris, and

El Hasiyeh.

are inhabited by hundreds of bats, while not a few snakes are to be found.

The various inscriptions show that the tombs were constructed for the princes of the province who lived somewhere about the XXVIth–XXXth dynasties. The family genealogy is as follows: A certain Petnef, who was Prince of Edfu and of Thebes and Priest of Horus, and his wife Aruiru, had a son Khonsurades who became *Erpa-Ha*-Prince, Prince of Thebes, Prince of Aswân, Superintendent of the Priests of Amen-Ra, of Hathor Lady of Esneh, of Nekheb, &c. The daughter of Khonsuardes, named Ary, married Prince Thothmes, who was Prince of Edfu and Superintendent of the Priests of Horus and Nekheb. The son of this union was Prince Pedeamen, whose titles were Prince of the Two Cities, Superintendent of the Priests of Amen-Ra, Priest of Horus, Superintendent of the Two Thrones (?) of Horus Uniter of the Two Lands, and Overseer of the Linen of the Temple of Horus. It will be seen that the titles held by this family are altogether out of proportion to the meanness of their burial-place. But it must be remembered that the Egyptians of this period had partly lost those beliefs regarding the next world which necessitated the burial of the dead body in surroundings as splendid as those enjoyed in life. A little paint and tinsel, a layer of plaster here and a dab of colour there, was all that was needed to make a showy funeral; and princely living was now too expensive a matter to permit of a fortune being spent upon "the eternal abode." On the other hand many of the titles held by these princes were as little intended for close scrutiny as the badly spelt inscriptions in which they were recorded. No doubt the weakness of the Pharaohs and their harassed governments at this period led the provincial nobles to assume titles to which they had no very real right.

Continuing the way southwards, cemeteries are passed at El Barasy; at Asab Allah there are many small rock tombs in the hillside, all uninscribed; at Zenigleh are extensive Nubian cemeteries; at Karableh are some large shaft tombs of late dynastic times; at Ghawalieh there are a few graffiti, one of which gives the name of Amenhotep Ist; and at Sheikh Said are a few undecorated rock-tombs and many graffiti. One now reaches the village of El Hosh ("The Courtyard"), so called from the large quarries which are to be found a few yards to the north of it, and which resemble great courts and open halls cut into the rock. A number of inscriptions are to be seen near here. The cartouche

Other cemeteries.

of Senusert Ist (?) occurs, and several nobles and officials of the Middle Kingdom. A commander of the troops of this date has left his name here, and in connection with this one may call attention to the Nubian cemeteries in the neighbourhood which may well be those of negro troops employed in Egypt. Several Greek inscriptions are also found, some dating from the eleventh year of Antoninus Pius, recording the quarrying operations of that time. A few ransacked graves of late date, and some small Nubian cemeteries, are passed as one proceeds southwards; and presently, about four miles north of Gebel Silsileh, the famous gorge of Shutt er Rigâl or Shutt es Sab'a Rigâl, "The Shore or Bank of the Seven Men," is reached. This narrow and sandy gorge winds westwards between the low hills of dark sandstone; and going up it for some distance one strikes the caravan road to Kurkur Oasis and the south, and to Aswân. At the east or river end of the pass, upon the left side, there is cut a group of four large figures with accompanying inscriptions. The largest crowned figure is that of King Neb-harpet-ra Menthuhotep IInd, and behind him stands "the royal mother," Aah. Facing the king stands "the Son of the Sun," Antef, whose name is written within a cartouche, but who neither holds the title of king nor wears a crown. Behind him again stands the chamberlain, Khety.

One may, perhaps, be permitted to hazard a guess as to the meaning of this important relief and the reason of its situation. After the turbulent feudal times between the VIIth and XIth dynasties, Menthuhotep IInd was the first Pharaoh to bring order once more into the country, and to consolidate the various petty states into a single kingdom again. Amongst the vassal princes now brought under the rule of the Pharaoh, the Antef shown in this scene seems to have been much favoured for his fidelity; and perhaps through the diplomacy of his chief counsellor, Khety, he managed to retain semi-regal control of his province. This province probably comprised the extreme southern regions of Egypt, and it may be that the pass of Gebel Silsileh, the frontier between the provinces of Elephantine and Edfu, was the northern boundary of his vassal kingdom. In this case the scene on the rocks celebrates Antef's crossing of the frontier by the desert road to do homage to Menthuhotep. On the rocks a short distance farther up the gorge there is another scene in which Khety alone does homage to Menthuhotep, when, likewise, he had crossed into Egypt proper. This same Khety is mentioned in a rock inscription at the First Cataract, where he was assisting Menthuhotep to

THE TEMPLE OF WÂDY ABÂD

transport an army into Nubia. On other parts of the rocks of Shutt er Rigâl are the cartouches of Senusert Ist of the XIIth dynasty, who may have used this road in one of his Nubian campaigns; a scene in which King Saankhkara of the XIth dynasty is represented enthroned in the presence of his nobles and servants, his pet dog being shown under his throne; the cartouches of Hatshepsut and Thothmes IIIrd of the XVIIIth dynasty; the name of a certain Penati who was an architect under Amenhotep Ist, Thothmes Ist, and Thothmes IInd; and various other inscriptions, all of which may have been written by persons using this road to and from the south.

A few quarries and rock inscriptions are passed as one proceeds northwards, and presently the larger quarries of Gebel Silsileh are reached.

THE TEMPLE OF WÂDY ABÂD

The temple of Sety Ist which stands in the Wâdy Abâd, some thirty-five miles east of Edfu, is generally known as the temple of Redesiyeh, owing to the fact that one of the early explorers set out to visit the building from the village of Redesiyeh which lies about five miles south of Edfu, on the east bank of the Nile. The name, however, is not a happy one; for the temple is now most generally approached from Edfu, and in ancient times the routes to it led from that city and from El Kâb. Redesiyeh is a place of no importance, and has no connection with the building other than that of having been by chance the starting-point of a journey once made to it long ago. By the natives the temple is known as *El Kaneis*, "the chapel"; and it would be best to speak of it as "the chapel, or temple, of Wâdy Abâd," for its connection with Redesiyeh is merely misleading.

The journey is a short one, and it is surprising that it is so rarely undertaken. Lepsius and Golenischeff are the only two Egyptologists who have visited the building. Leaving Edfu at dawn one reaches the Bir Abâd two hours later, without urging one's camel beyond a jog-trot. Half-an-hour later the Roman fortress of Abu Gehâd is passed; and after another two hours and a half one passes the Gebel Timsah, which is a well-known landmark. A ride of two hours and a quarter more brings one to the temple, which thus may be reached from Edfu in a little over seven hours. Good water is to be obtained at the well sunk by the Mines Department near the temple, and thus one's baggage for a stay of one or two nights need not be large. The baggage-camels cover the distance in under twelve hours, and if they start before dawn they will have arrived before sunset. Camels may be obtained at Edfu, the usual price being P.T. 10 per day for a baggage-camel and driver and P.T. 12 for a riding-camel.

The temple is built at the foot of the sandstone cliffs, and the main hall is excavated in the rock, in the manner of Abu Simbel. In front of this hall there is a masonry portico, the roof of which is supported on architraves resting on four lotus-bud columns. The roof consisted of twelve blocks of sandstone, but one has now fallen in. The preservation of this part of the building is bad. In ancient times one of the cracked architraves has been neatly supported by the building of a square pillar. A Greek inscription upon this shows that the restoration is not later than that date.

The façade was uninscribed and undecorated in the original design, but at a later date a large hawk has been carved at the east end, and a hieratic inscription records the coming of a certain scribe from Aswân. Upon entering the portico a number of interesting reliefs and inscriptions are seen. On the left, or east, wall one sees Sety grasping four negroes by the hair, being about to smite them with his mace. He wears the crown of Upper and Lower Egypt. Above him is the sun's disk, and the usual hovering vulture. Behind him is his *Ka* standard. The inscription states that the king is "smiting the chieftains of Ethiopia the Wretched." Facing the king stands Amen-Ra, Lord of the Earth, who presents a sickle-shaped sword to the Pharaoh. The god holds a rope which is attached to the ovals of ten captive lands.

On the right, or west, wall there is a somewhat similar scene, in which one sees the king, wearing the crown of Lower Egypt, smiting four crouching Asiatics who represent "the great ones of all lands." Before the king stands the hawk-headed Horus of Edfu, who presents a sword to the king. He holds a rope attached to the names of eight captive lands.

On the rear, or south, wall, to the left of the entrance to the hall, there is an unfinished scene representing the king offering a vase of incense to Harmachis "within *Ta-Khnumt*," which is evidently the name of the place. To the right of the entrance the king is seen offering the hieroglyphs which compose his name, *Ra-maa-men*, to Amen-Ra. Above him is the hovering hawk. The king is said to be "giving Truth to his father Amen-Ra, that he may make for him the gift of life." On either side of the entrance there is a recess in which is a colossal figure of the king

THE TEMPLE OF WÂDY ABÂD

in high relief, with the arms folded in the manner of Osiris. These figures are now much damaged, and the faces and details are erased.

On the architraves and pillars are inscribed the cartouches and titles of Sety. The ceiling pattern down the middle consists of winged vultures, between which are the king's titles and cartouches; and on either side the pattern is that of the usual yellow stars upon a blue ground.

The doorway into the inner hall is surmounted by a winged disk, above which is the usual concave cornice decorated with cartouches; and above this again there is an unfinished row of uraei carved in high relief. On the lintel the king is said to be beloved of Harmachis and Amen-Ra; and down either side is a perpendicular inscription, part of which shows traces of having been cut over an earlier and perhaps incorrect line of hieroglyphs.

One now enters the inner hall, excavated in the rock. The roof is supposed to be supported on two architraves each resting upon two square pillars, the whole being part of the living rock. On the left side of the doorway as one enters, a long inscription in five perpendicular lines is seen, which states how the soldiers of Sety make prayers to Amen on behalf of the king, because of his thoughtfulness in digging a well and building a temple at this point.

On the right wall of the hall as one enters (*i.e.* the north wall, west side) there is a long, somewhat damaged inscription in nineteen perpendicular lines; the main damage being due to the loss of a large irregular slab from the middle. The inscription tells how Sety built the temple, and pronounces blessings on those who maintain it, and curses on those who do not respect it. On the left wall (*i.e.* the north wall, east side) the king is seen standing facing a long inscription in fourteen perpendicular lines. Above him the vulture hovers over his cartouches. This inscription tells how Sety visited this part of the desert, and ordered the temple to be constructed, a well to be dug, and a town to be equipped here.

On the east wall of the hall there are three groups of figures, all somewhat damaged, though the colour is still good. Firstly, one sees the king offering a bunch of flowers to the ithyphallic Min-Amen-Ra, behind whom stands Isis; secondly, the king is seen offering wine to Horus of Edfu, a hawk-headed god seated upon a throne; thirdly, Sety is shown presenting a figure of Truth to Amen-Ra, who is seated upon a throne. On the west wall there are four groups of figures. Firstly, one sees the king lifting his hands in adoration to Amen-Ra; secondly, he worships Harmachis; thirdly, there is a much-damaged figure of the king offering to Ptah and Sekhmet; lastly, Sety is shown offering a figure of Truth to Osiris of Edfu, and to Isis.

At the south end of both this and the opposite wall there is an empty and undecorated recess. In the south wall of the hall there are three recesses, the middle one forming the axial sanctuary of the temple. At the back of that on the right or west side there are three seated statues carved from the living rock. They are now much damaged, but appear to have represented Horus of Edfu, Isis, and perhaps the king. In the left or east recess there are likewise three statues, representing Ptah, Osiris, and perhaps Sekhmet. The middle recess is approached by three steps. At the back are again three damaged statues, representing Harmachis, Amen-Ra, and Sety Ist. On either side of the entrance to this recess there is a figure of the king. On the left he wears the crown of Upper Egypt, and holds in his hand a mace and staff. On the right he wears the royal helmet, and burns incense and pours out a libation.

On the pillars there are smaller figures, in each case representing the king offering to some god. These gods are Amen-Ra, Horus of Edfu, Harmachis, Khonsu, Ptah, Osiris Unnefer, Tum, Mut, Isis, Hathor of Edfu, and Nekheb.

The ceiling in the middle aisle is decorated as before with winged vultures, and that of the side aisles with stars. The architraves bear inscriptions giving the titles and cartouches of the king. The floor of both the hall and the portico is covered with sand and loose stones; and amongst this in the hall there is a square block of grey granite, part of which lies in the portico. In the portico there is a square block of pink granite. Both these were perhaps used as altars. Outside the temple, lying on the sand which slopes up towards the entrance, there is a part of a round Greek altar of sandstone.

The temple seems to have been built towards the end of the reign of Sety, for it was left unfinished. It was open in Ramesside times, for on one of the columns the cartouche of Rameses IInd is written. No later king added to it; and the neatness of the Greek graffiti suggest that it was still regarded as a sacred place then.

The walls are much damaged by the writing of names, for every mining engineer or prospector has recorded the event of his coming, from Cailliaud, who discovered the temple in 1816, to the miners of 1908.

FROM EDFU TO GEBEL SILSILEH

The inscriptions state that the temple was built by Sety as a shrine at which the gold-miners might worship on their way to and from the mines. As Professor Breasted has pointed out, the gold was to be used for the upkeep of the king's great temple at Abydos ; and it is interesting to notice that just as that temple fell on evil days at the death of Sety Ist, as is there recorded by Rameses IInd, so also this temple was deserted and left unfinished when the king died. It may be asked why Sety selected this spot for his temple ; for, except that it lies on the route to the mines, the reason of its location is not apparent. The explanation is, however, not far to seek. On the great bluff of rock in which the temple is excavated there are many drawings of boats and animals which undoubtedly date from archaic times. Some of these boats are evidently sacred barques, for in some of them the shrines are shown, while in one case the god Min, with flail raised, stands before the shrine in the vessel. Thus it seems that already in archaic times this was a sacred spot, dedicated to Min. There are graffiti of the XVIIIth dynasty here, notably one which gives the cartouche of Amenhotep IIIrd ; and thus Sety was but carrying on the old tradition in constructing a shrine here. In Greek times many ex-votos dedicated to Pan, with whom Min was identified, were written on these rocks.

FROM EDFU TO GEBEL SILSILEH ON THE EAST BANK

Between Edfu and Serag there are no ancient sites of importance, though some stone tumuli at Ghretag are of interest. Behind the station of Serag there are the mounds of an old town, and near it are the remains of its cemeteries. The rocks now come close down to the river, and presently, about half-way between Edfu and Gebel Silsileh, one reaches the great Byzantine fortress of Bueb, built on the side of a hill which slopes rapidly to the river. It consists of a number of closely-built houses, surrounded by strong walls, at the corners of which are round towers. The church is the most conspicuous building in the enclosure, the walls still standing to a height of twenty feet or so. At the foot of the town there are some quarries dating from the XVIIIth dynasty. About half a mile to the north of this fortress there is another fortified town lying in a hollow on top of the hills; but it cannot well be seen from the passing trains or steamers, and is not of much interest. Between Bueb and Gebel Silsileh there are not many places of interest. A few quarries, a few graffiti, and one or two cemeteries are alone to be seen.

The fortress of Bueb.

CHAPTER XVI

GEBEL SILSILEH, WEST BANK — GEBEL SILSILEH, EAST BANK — FROM GEBEL SILSILEH TO KÔM OMBO

Method of visiting Gebel Silsileh.

TO visit the quarries and shrines of Gebel Silsileh the visitor, who is not travelling by steamer or dahabiyeh, should take the early train from Aswân, which arrives at Kagoug station before 9 A.M., returning to Aswân by the express in the early afternoon. There are no donkeys to be had at Kagoug, except by arrangement with the villagers, and a dragoman, therefore, should be sent to obtain them and also a ferry-boat, on the previous day. The ancient remains are about three miles or so from the station, a point of rocky hills to the south-west being one's objective. To the traveller the wonderful quarries on the east bank will not fail to be of interest, and the shrine of Horemheb on the west bank deserves a visit; while to the archæologist there are numerous small shrines, tombs, and rock steles which are worth visiting.

HISTORY OF SILSILEH

Early history of Gebel Silsileh.

Gebel Silsileh, "the Hills of the Chain," is the name given to the rocky defile through which the river passes on its way from Kôm Ombo to Edfu, and to the sandstone hills which come down to the water's edge here for about a mile on either side. Long before the dawn of history the Nile seems to have passed from Daraw to Silwah along the valley through which the railway line now runs; but, changing its course, it burst a way between the rocks, and at the beginning of Egyptian history it probably rushed down the present channel in a series of rapids, if not in a regular cataract. It thus formed something of an obstacle to shipping, and was a natural frontier between the territory under the sway of Elephantine (Aswân) and that belonging to Edfu. In some cases travellers of the Middle Kingdom seem to have preferred to avoid

GEBEL SILSILEH

the navigation of this part of the river, and to have gone overland to Aswân by way of the Shutt er Rigâl road, as the inscriptions there indicate. A town grew up on the west bank of the river between Shutt er Rigâl and Gebel Silsileh, which was named Khennui ; and here the Pharaohs of the XIIth dynasty are said to have had a residence.

It is not, however, until the XVIIIth dynasty that we obtain any information regarding this rocky pass. At that time there seems to have developed the custom of cutting small shrines in the rocks at certain points on the upper river, where the cliffs came down to the water's edge, and where the stream ran rapidly. It was a form of Nile-worship : an adoration of various gods, local and general, at the brink of the river, which was, in a way, the father of them all. Amenhotep IInd, Thothmes IIIrd, Hatshepsut, and a Viceroy of Ethiopia, excavated little shrines overlooking the water at Kasr Ibrim in Lower Nubia, where a magnificent head of rock falls almost sheer down to the water. Amenhotep IInd constructed a shrine overlooking the rushing waters of the cataract at Sehel, an island just above Aswân. King Ay, and a Viceroy of Ethiopia under Horemheb, caused somewhat similar rock shrines to be made at Gebel Addeh, not far from Abu Simbel, at a point where the cliffs in the same manner as at Kasr Ibrim boldly slope to the water. At Abahudeh, close to Abu Simbel, Horemheb made a more elaborate rock-cut temple, only able to be approached from the water. The temple of Abu Simbel, designed by Sety Ist and Rameses IInd, was a vast elaboration of the same idea. Under Rameses IInd another rock shrine was added to the group at Kasr Ibrim. At Gebel Silsileh, where the Nile seemed to pass through a gigantic gate of rock, and where, for the last time before entering Egypt proper, it was obstructed by natural barriers, it is not surprising to find that kings and nobles of the XVIIIth and XIXth dynasties cut these little chamber-like shrines into the rocks, as tokens of their reverence for the great river.

Gebel Silsileh in the New Empire.

The shrines at Gebel Silsileh.

Although but scanty remains of these monuments on the east bank of the river are preserved, on the west bank there are numerous shrines and steles to be seen. In the XVIIIth dynasty shrines were cut in the cliffs under Thothmes Ist, Hatshepsut, Thothmes IIIrd and Hatshepsut, Thothmes IIIrd, and Horemheb. The last-named king constructed a beautiful speos or small temple here, the decoration of which was never finished. Rameses IInd, Merenptah, Septah, Sety IInd, Rameses IIIrd, and Rameses Vth, all left steles of a religious nature on the rocks of the west bank; and there are many other inscriptions which attest to the veneration in which the place was held. The west bank was as usual the more holy side, but the east bank was, as has been said, also much venerated.

The forms of worship. From the various inscriptions one is able to discern something of the form that this worship took. The main deity of the place seems to have been the crocodile god Sebek, "Lord of Khennui"; but Hapi, the Nile, received a large share of the offerings. The great Cataract trinity—Khnum of Elephantine, Satet of Elephantine and Sehel, and Anuket of Sehel—were also venerated, and this is an indication that there was still, or was within the memory of history, a cataract or series of rapids here. "Seb and Nut who are in the Waters of Libation," are invoked, other gods are stated to be "within the Waters of Libation," and once a prayer to the "holy water" itself is made. Horuar, of the Sacred Eyes, and Sebek, the twin gods of Ombo, are often referred to. Taurt, the hippopotamus goddess, was held in much esteem here, and is one of the main deities of the speos of Horemheb. Sety Ist caused a hymn to the Nile to be inscribed on these rocks, and instituted two Nile festivals to be celebrated at this spot each year. Rameses IInd and Merenptah confirmed the endowments of these festivals. After this period, however, the gradual cessation of the rapids, and the turning of the neighbourhood into a huge quarry works, caused the religious aspect of Gebel Silsileh to be forgotten, and one hears no more of that side of its character.

The quarries. The quarrying of the sandstone commenced here in the XVIIIth dynasty, when the extensive use of that material for the building of temples first began. In the temples at the beginning of the XVIIIth dynasty, and at all times earlier, limestone and granite were the chief materials employed, and sandstone was used only in very small quantities. At about the time of Thothmes IIIrd its use became general; but the temple of Luxor, erected by Amenhotep IIIrd, is the first great building in which it was entirely employed. No point offered such facilities for quarrying sandstone as did Gebel Silsileh, where the blocks of stone had to be transported only a few yards to the boats; and moreover it was felt that the sacred nature of the rocks here gave an increased value to the stone. It was right that holy stone should be employed in the building of holy places. The quarrying seems to have begun on the east bank; and by the reign of Amenhotep IIIrd the cliffs and the town of Khennui were swarming with workmen,

GEBEL SILSILEH

and the river was crowded with boats. An inscription of that king states that blocks were quarried for a temple of Ptah, and the great temples of Amen also required vast quantities of stone. Amenhotep IVth, Akhnaton, states that he caused stone to be quarried here for the temple of Aton at Karnak. For the Ramesseum alone three thousand workmen were here employed; and under Rameses IIIrd mention is made of two thousand men who were being used for quarrying stone for Medinet Habu (?). As king after king came to the throne, and dynasty succeeded dynasty, the works continued unabated. Sheshonk Ist has left a memorial of his work here for his additions to the temple of Karnak; and other kings have had their names inscribed. In Ptolemaic times the huge temples at Dendereh, Thebes, Esneh, Edfu, and Kôm Ombo, not to mention the numerous small buildings, required an unprecedented amount of stone; and the pass must have echoed with the ring of thousands of hammers. In Roman days these vast works continued; but now the sanctity of the place was so far forgotten by the rough, hard-working crowds of Egyptian, Greek, Lydian, Carian, Phœnician, Jewish, and Syrian quarrymen who were now employed here (with those of many other lands), that little respect seems to have been paid to the ancient shrines. Those on the east bank were almost entirely quarried away, while those on the west bank have been partly destroyed for the obtaining of good stone. When the building of temples came to an end about A.D. 200, the work at Gebel Silsileh ceased, and from then until modern times the rocks have remained untouched.

The great quarries which the visitor will presently see have not their like in all the world; and both for their vast extent and on account of the care and the perfection of workmanship displayed in the cutting of the stone, they are to be considered as being amongst the greatest monuments of human labour known. We have admired the temples and tombs of Egypt as examples of the skill of the architect and of the builder; in the reliefs and paintings we have observed with wonder the art of the sculptor and painter; and in the inscriptions of the great Pharaohs we have read of splendid wars and wise administrations. But here we have an enormous record of the skilful handiwork of the Egyptian labourers; and it has been well said that "in comparison with this puissant and perfect quarrying our rough-and-ready blasting looks like the work of savages." "Some of the quarries," writes Mariette, "are cut in sharp edges to the height of fifty or sixty

Aspect of the great quarries.

feet; others are arranged in tiers of huge receding steps. The methodical care—we had almost said the extreme caution—with which the stone has been quarried is remarkable throughout. It would seem as though the mountain had been cut into blocks with as much regularity as planks would be cut by a skilful carpenter from the trunk of some valuable tree." Another great writer has said with equal truth that "the sandstone has been sliced out smooth and straight, like hay from a hayrick"; while yet another has likened the mountains to a cheese from which regular slices have been cut. The value of these quarries to the history of the world's crafts is enormous, and even those who take no interest in the past history of mankind will here find the abundant evidence of fine workmanship which they cannot fail to appreciate and admire.

The name "Silsileh." The town of Khennui was sometimes known to the later Egyptians as Khol-Khol, which means a barrier or frontier; and the Romans, who placed a garrison here in later times, corrupted the word into Sil-sil, or Silsili. The mediæval Arabs incorrectly identified the name with *Silsileh*, the Arabic word for "chain." Some story-teller, accounting for this name "chain," concocted a story to the effect that a great chain had here passed across the river in order to prevent the passage of boats; and two curiously formed rocks at either side of the river, which by chance had been quarried to the shape of posts, were identified as the posts to which the ends of the chain were attached. Thus the name Silsileh is but a misunderstanding of Khol-Khol, and the famous story of the chain seems to have no foundation of truth in it.

Modern quarrying. The last phase of the history of Gebel Silsileh has still to be written. In 1906 the construction of the Esneh barrage necessitated the quarrying of large quantities of sandstone, and it was felt that the best and most cheaply obtainable stone was to be found at Gebel Silsileh. In agreement with the Department of Antiquities certain of the ancient quarries were handed over to the contractors to be reworked. As the concessions required were large, and the available space for quarrying without doing damage to ancient records was small, there was some difficulty in effecting a compromise by which the very real interests both of the present day and of the past could be met. But, thanks to the magnanimity of the engineers concerned, it is to be hoped that no unnecessary damage has been done.

WEST BANK

Since the sanctity of Gebel Silsileh appears to be older than its fame as a quarry, the west bank of the river, on which are the sacred shrines, will be described before the east bank on which the main quarries are situated. At the extreme north end of this west bank there are some small quarries, and many of the rocks have inscriptions cut upon them, none of which are of much importance except two or three written in foreign letters by the non-Egyptian quarrymen. At the north end of the pass the speos of King Horemheb stands conspicuously; its five dark doorways forming a landmark to which the visitor from the east bank should direct his boat. It is cut in the rock, and consists of a transverse gallery with a vaulted roof; and in the back wall opposite the middle entrance a small sanctuary is excavated; while between the temple and the river there was, no doubt, originally a court and a flight of steps. The place was left unfinished by Horemheb, for mural decorations dating from his reign are only found at the sides of the middle entrance, at the south end of the gallery, and in the sanctuary. The bare walls were later covered with steles and inscriptions by kings and nobles of the following dynasties:— *The temple of Horemheb.*

Passing through the middle doorway one sees on the lintel and doorposts the cartouches of Horemheb, who is said to be beloved of Amen-Ra, Khnum of Kebu, Khnum of Elephantine, Anuket of Sehel, Harmachis, and Sebek of Silsileh. Inside the gallery the scene on one's right shows Horemheb offering flowers to Thoth of Hermopolis and to Hathor; and on one's left to Shepses and a goddess. Entering the sanctuary, on the right the king is represented burning incense and pouring a libation to Amen-Ra and Mut; and on the left he offers flowers and a vase to Harmachis and "the Lady of Heliopolis, the Lady of Heaven in the Temple of the Sun." At the back wall of the sanctuary sit seven much-damaged figures, which, from south to north, represented Sebek, Taurt, Mut, Amen-Ra, Khonsu, Horemheb, and Thoth. Of these the first two are the local gods; then follows the great Theban triad which the king mainly worshipped; and finally, Thoth is included as typifying the king's wisdom and heavenly guidance. Below these figures are prayers to Amen-Ra, Khonsu of Thebes, and Mut of Asher (Karnak). On the north wall twenty-three gods are represented; and on the *Horemheb's reliefs.*

south wall thirty-six gods and demi-gods are shown. On the east wall, south of the doorway, the gods Osiris of Abydos, Septu, Hermachis, and the scorpion-goddess Selket are shown; and on the north side are Khnum, Satet, and Anuket, while below them is a symbolical representation of the union of Upper and Lower Egypt, presided over by the goddess Taurt.

Returning into the gallery, the visitor will see on the south wall the king suckled by the hippopotamus-goddess Taurt, here shown in the form of a woman, in the presence of Amen-Ra, behind whom stands a damaged figure of Sebek of Khennui and Silsileh. Behind Taurt stands a damaged figure of Khnum. Although much damaged this relief is seen to have been executed by an artist of considerable skill; and the king, although wearing the martial war-helmet, is cleverly made to appear small and boyish in the presence of the great, motherly figure of the benevolent goddess. At right angles to this scene, on the west wall, are the famous festival reliefs of Horemheb. The figures are small and much damaged, and compared with other work of this reign they cannot be favourably criticised for their artistic merit. Yet there is a freedom of movement and grouping which is pleasing; and their historical value is considerable. At the corner of the wall Horemheb holding his battle-axe (for it will be remembered that this king was essentially a warrior, having risen to the kingship from the ranks of the army) is seen in the presence of Amen-Ra. Then he is shown seated in his sedan-chair, the arms of which are carved in the form of lions, carried by twelve plumed soldiers; while two fan-bearers protect his head from the sunshine. A priest burning incense walks in front of the king, and farther ahead are soldiers dragging along the negro captives which had been taken in a recent Ethiopian war. A trumpeter blows a fanfare, while the soldiers cry, "All health is with thee, O Lord of the Two Lands! The Sun-god is the protection of thy limbs." The inscriptions state that the king is all-powerful, and that these captives have been taken by his sword in Ethiopia. Some of the captives humbly cry, "Thy name is great in the land of Ethiopia, thy battle-cry is in their habitations"; but one at least has struggled to escape, and has been hurled to the ground by his guard. Except for a damaged figure of the king in his chariot shooting with a bow and arrows, these are the only reliefs of the time of Horemheb.

The later inscriptions and scenes may be briefly recorded. A damaged figure in high relief representing an official of Rameses

GEBEL SILSILEH

IInd named Khay. King Septah of the XXth dynasty, accompanied by the famous chancellor, Bey (who was buried in the Valley of the Tombs of the Kings), does homage to Amen-Ra. A stele dated in the second year of Merenptah, the so-called Pharaoh of the Exodus, upon which the king, his wife Astnefert, and his Vizir Panehesi, are seen adoring Amen-Ra and Mut. A figure in high relief representing Khaemuast, the eldest son and heir of Rameses IInd, who was famous for his priestly wisdom. The dedication is to Hapi and Sebek. A stele on which Rameses IInd and Khaemuast are shown adoring Ptah and Amen-Ra. Below is an inscription stating that jubilee celebrations were held in honour of the king in his 30th, 34th, 37th, and 40th years. The same, except that Sebek takes the place of Amen-Ra. A figure of Khaemuast. Khaemuast mentions that he is the son of the king and of Queen Astnefert; and he here gives a list of offerings dedicated to himself or to his father by the ritual priests. A further list of jubilees, the king being here shown in the presence of Amen-Ra, Harmachis, Maat, Sebek, and another god now damaged. Stele showing Rameses IInd in the presence of Amen-Ra, Mut, Khonsu, Harmachis, and Sebek. It is dated in the 45th year of the king's reign, and the inscription states that the Vizir Khay had come to celebrate another jubilee. Six figures, much damaged, cut in high relief. These represent the Vizir Panehesi, the goddess Maat, a male relation of Panehesi; a female relation, the god Ptah, and another female relation holding the title of "Songstress of the Sun." This is one of the rare instances where a private family group is augmented by the presence of gods. A large high-relief figure of the Vizir Khay; and a stele of Merenptah on which he is shown worshipping Amen-Ra, Mut, Sebek, and Hathor. A recess in which three damaged figures are seated, these probably representing the Vizir Paser and his son and wife. A stele on which Khaemuast, Rameses IInd, Queen Astnefert, and Princess Bantantha are shown before Ptah and Tum. An inscription stating that Khaemuast had come to celebrate the king's jubilee; and other Ramesside inscriptions. A stele made by certain commanders of the troops, showing Rameses IIIrd before Amen-Ra, Harmachis, and Sebek. Rameses IIIrd is seen offering to Sebek and Hathor of Khennui. Rameses IIIrd offers flowers to Ptah and Sekhmet. Stele of the second year of Sety IInd, a short-lived king who reigned in the troubled times between Merenptah and Rameses IIIrd. Merenptah accompanied by his wife, two

Later work in the temple of Horemheb.

princes, and some nobles, offers to Amen-Ra, Ptah, Harmachis, and Maāt. A recess, now much damaged, in which there have been three figures, probably those of Panehesi and his relations. Khaemuast celebrates the king's first jubilee in the 30th year of his reign. A figure of Khaemuast. Rameses IIIrd in the presence of a god. Rameses IInd, with the Vizir Nefer-renpit, worships Ptah and Sebek.

Khae- muast and the jubilees of Rameses IInd. In the above inscriptions reference is made so many times to Prince Khaemuast and to the jubilees which he celebrated, that a brief explanation is necessary. Khaemuast was the eldest son and heir of Rameses IInd, and in his early years he accompanied his father on his wars; but later in life he adopted a sacerdotal career, and became High Priest at Memphis. He was famed for his learning, and wonderful stories are told of his magic powers. It is to be presumed that he died in the interval between his celebration of the king's jubilee at El Kâb in the 41st year and the celebration in the 42nd year at Gebel Silsileh, which was conducted by the Vizir Khay. These jubilees, instituted by Khaemuast, were celebrated in the king's 30th, 33rd, 37th, 40th, 41st, 42nd, 44th, 47th (?), 50th (?), and 53rd (?) years. They seem to have taken the form of festivals of a religious nature performed, in Upper Egypt, at the First Cataract, Gebel Silsileh, El Kâb, and no doubt at Thebes. On the death of Khaemuast the festivals were placed in the charge of the Vizir Khay; but the king seems to have hesitated as to which of his sons he should cause to be named his heir, and it was not till his 55th year that Merenptah was declared to have succeeded Khaemuast as crown prince.

Three royal steles. After leaving the temple of Horemheb the visitor should walk southwards along the river's edge, by the rough path which passes beside the fallen boulders at the foot of the cliffs. A quarry is passed, and at about a hundred yards from the temple three large steles will be seen cut into the rock. The first of these shows Rameses Vth making an offering, consisting of the hieroglyphs which form his name, to Amen-Ra, Mut, Khonsu, and Sebek-Ra of Khennui. This king is very little known, and the present stele is the largest of his monuments. As, however, the inscription only contains boastful phrases without historical value, it is of no great importance. The second stele shows Sheshonk Ist being led by Mut to Amen-Ra, Harmachis of Heliopolis, and Ptah. Behind the king is the High Priest of Amen-Ra, Annapeta. The inscription states that Sheshonk opened quarries here for building works

GEBEL SILSILEH

at Karnak which he had undertaken in his 21st year. The third stele belongs to the reign of Rameses IIIrd, who is seen offering a figure of Truth to Amen-Ra, Mut, and Khonsu.

South of these steles there are more quarries, in one of which are two niches high up in the face of the rock. A small stone offering trough in front of one of these suggests that in the niches stood figures of the god worshipped by the quarrymen. A few yards farther to the south are three small shrines, much damaged, near the entrance of the second of which is a figure and inscription of the "Scribe of the Silver-House," named Thothmes. The third shrine was made by an *Erpa-ha*-prince named Min,[1] who lived under Thothmes IIIrd, and was nomarch of the south. Only an unfinished relief on the north wall, and a few damaged inscriptions above the door, remain. A short way farther on is a shrine of an official of the reign of Thothmes IIIrd. The half-finished ceiling pattern is noticeable. Below this shrine is a figure of the *Ha*-Prince of By named Aay. Near this is another shrine of an unknown official of the reign of Thothmes IIIrd and Hatshepsut. It will be observed that the cartouches of Hatshepsut are erased wherever they occur at Gebel Silsileh, and it seems that Thothmes IIIrd thus revenged himself upon the queen who had for so long prevented his enjoyment of full power. Three almost totally destroyed shrines are now passed, and a few yards farther to the south the small cartouche of Meryra of the VIth dynasty may be observed on the side of a rock.

Shrines.

Shrine of Min.

A roofless tomb is now reached, in which the lower parts of five statues can be seen. These and the scenes on the walls show that a certain Sennefer was buried here with his wife Hatshepsut, these names dating them to the XVIIIth dynasty. Sennefer was a libation priest of Amen attached to the palace at Thebes, and seems to have been the son of the "Royal Son, Governor of the Lands of the South," Usersatet and of Anun his wife. The lady Hatshepsut was the daughter of the chief nurse of the king, named Hemttaui, and of her husband Seninefer, a priest. Other relations were a High Priest of Horuar and Sebek of Ombo, a High Priest of Nekheb (at El Kâb), a Priest of Khnum, and others whose names and titles are now lost. On the north wall Sennefer and his wife are seen seated before a table of offerings, while before them a male harper plays upon a large harp and two nude women, one playing a stringed instrument, dance for the amusement of the souls of these dead persons. Three blind

Tomb of Sennefer.

---

[1] Not Min-nekht, as has been stated.

musicians clap their hands in unison, and chant a dirge. On the south wall five ritual priests perform a ceremony by which the souls receive food in the underworld. The inscription here reads: "May thy heart be cool, and mayest thou be remembered for bread in the Temple of the Sun and for incense in the Temple of Teh. Peace to thy heart every day. Mayest thou come forth from and go into (the underworld at pleasure); and mayest thou follow Aten and be strong like the lords of Eternity." Below the five figures at the west end of the tomb is written: "The king gives an offering to Osiris, Seb, Nut, and the gods who are in the Waters of Libation that they may give mortuary requisites to the *Ka* of the owners of this shrine who are seated (here) and who love the Prince (Osiris)."

A few yards to the south of this tomb there is a group of six shrines, three of which may be approached from the path, two must be entered by means of a difficult climb from the water's edge, and into the last one may descend from the rocks above the other shrines. The traveller can hardly be recommended to visit these monuments, which are all difficult of access. The first shrine of this group lacks its front and north wall. It belonged to Min-nekht, the "Royal Scribe, Superintendent of the Granaries of the North and South and of the Temple of Amen," in the reign of Thothmes IIIrd. On the walls one may still see the figures of Min-nekht and a relation seated before offerings. The tomb of Min-nekht is at Shêkh abd' el Gûrneh (Thebes). One passes through into the next shrine which belonged to Sennefera, "the Superintendent of the Sealing, and Royal Herald" of Thothmes IIIrd. The tomb of this noble also is at Shêkh abd' el Gûrneh. The third shrine, entered through the second, was made for Nehesi, a noble under Thothmes IIIrd and Hatshepsut. The king is here said to be beloved of Nu, the father of the gods, and Khnum of Elephantine, while the queen is beloved of Amen-Ra and Tum of On. The next shrine, approached from the water, was owned by Hapusenb, one of those nobles of the court of Hatshepsut who escaped disgrace on the accession of Thothmes IIIrd, her rival. Hapusenb was the son of a modest citizen named Hapu, who, in this shrine, is simply called an "official who pleased the god of his town." He entered the priesthood of Amen, and rose to be High Priest of that god, with which honour other titles, such as *Erpa-ha-Prince*, were given to him. He probably did not vigorously defend the legitimacy of Queen Hatshepsut, nor try, like other nobles, to prevent Thothmes IIIrd from coming to the throne;

GEBEL SILSILEH

and when Hatshepsut died or was murdered, and Thothmes IIIrd, by the express wish of that priesthood of which Hapusenb was the Chief, was elected Pharaoh, the wise noble quickly changed his allegiance, and the queen's name was struck out of the inscriptions in his shrine. On the north wall of the shrine Hapusenb and his wife are seen seated before a number of offerings, and below are the figures of his relatives. His son and daughter-in-law present these offerings: the former was High Priest and Chief Ritual Priest of the *Ka* of Thothmes Ist.[1] On the south wall two seated figures are shown, representing Hapusenb and his father Hapu, to whom his son and two daughters do homage. On the rest of this wall there is a long list of offerings, and here also a woman is shown dancing and playing the harp. In a niche in the west wall is a much-damaged figure of Hapusenb, at either side of which persons are shown bringing offerings of animals, &c., and over which are the erased cartouches of Hatshepsut. On either side of the entrance is a damaged figure of Hapusenb; and outside the doorway are the erased cartouches of the queen again.

The next shrine is that of Senmut, the famous statesman by whose power Hatshepsut was kept upon her throne. Senmut, believing that Hatshepsut was the only lawful sovereign, did his best to protect her against the very natural intrigues of Thothmes IInd and IIIrd. He was the architect who built the temple of Dêr el Bahri, and it was he who set up the famous obelisks of the queen at Karnak. His influence over the queen was unlimited, and his power in the land was very great. When Thothmes IIIrd obtained the power, Senmut was vigorously persecuted. His name was everywhere hacked out of inscriptions, and his figure erased from all paintings and reliefs. Here, in his shrine, it is only with difficulty that one can make out his name under the erasing chisel-marks of the agents of Thothmes IIIrd. On the east wall of the shrine, to the right on entering, is an erased figure of Senmut, before which a goose burns upon a table of offerings. Above are his erased titles "*Erpa-ha*-Prince, Steward of the Royal Daughter (probably Neferura the daughter of Hatshepsut)." On the north wall the erased figure of Senmut is shown worshipping various gods :—Amen-Ra, Tum of On, Nu, Sebek of Ombo, Khnum of Elephantine, Satet of Elephantine, Anuket of Lower

Shrine of Senmut.

---

[1] This shows that at the time when Hatshepsut was reigning alone, and having her cartouche alone inscribed on monuments such as this shrine, her father Thothmes Ist was dead, and a High Priest of his tomb was in office— an important fact in the complicated dates of the period.

Nubia, and Horuar, Chief of the Two Sacred Eyes in Ombo. On the south wall he worships Khnum of Elephantine, Satet of Elephantine, Anuket, and Sebek of Silsileh. In the west wall is a recess in which a damaged statue of Senmut is seated, above being the erased cartouches of Hatshepsut, and down the sides a damaged prayer for the *Ka* of the "Steward of the Queen," Senmut. On one side of the recess his erased figure is embraced by the goddess Nekheb, and on the other side by Sebek of Ombo. Outside the doorway are inscriptions containing the erased cartouche of "The Royal Daughter" Hatshepsut.

Shrine of Aamathu.

The next shrine is that of the Vizir Aamathu. It is roofless, and may best be approached from the rocks above. On the north wall is an intentionally erased figure of Aamathu seated before a heap of offerings. He is here called "Father of the God," *i.e.* father-in-law of the king, and is entitled *Erpa-ha*-Prince and Vizir. The offerings are presented by his son User, who is entitled *Erpa-ha*-Prince, Vizir, and High Priest of Amen. The rest of this wall is occupied with the figures of relations, of which one is "the Royal Son, Governor of the Lands of the South," named Thure. On the south wall the erased figure of Aamathu is shown seated before offerings presented by ritual priests. Various relations are also shown here. At the west end of the shrine are four seated statues representing, from south to north, Tuau (?), the daughter-in-law of Aamathu; User, his son; Aamathu himself; and Ta-amathu, his wife.

Just to the south of this there is another shrine which is most difficult of access. Over the doorway the cartouches of Amenhotep IInd are inscribed, but the name of the owner of the shrine is lost. On the right of the doorway is a stele inscribed with a prayer to Amen-Ra, Tum, Behudet, Sebek of Ombo, Sebek of Silsileh, Khnum, Satet, and Anuket, for the "soul of the Scribe of the Account of the grain in the granary of the divine offerings, the steward of the Vizir Amenemhat, the son of a certain Thothmes."

Shrine of Menkh.

After passing a shrine which is uninscribed, one next reaches that of a certain "Steward of the Queen," named Menkh, which name has been erased, but is still readable. The cartouches of Thothmes Ist occur, which indicate that the queen in question was either Aahmes or Mutnefert, one of the two wives of Thothmes Ist. The erasing of the steward's name looks like the work of Thothmes IIIrd, and we may suppose that Menkh lived on under Hatshepsut and assisted in her maintenance upon the throne, thereby exciting the wrath of Thothmes IIIrd. On the north wall

GEBEL SILSILEH 369

there is inscribed a prayer to Amen-Ra and Horuar, Chieftain of the Two Sacred Eyes in Ombo, for the *Ka* of Menkh. Below this he is shown seated with his wife, a fly-flap in his hands, and a dog under his chair. Before him is a table of offerings presented by five ritual priests; while near by other persons bring offerings, and a woman with head thrown back dances and plays upon the pipes. Below this Menkh is shown again, and behind him two servants carry his bows and other weapons. On the south wall Menkh is seated with his father Anena and his mother Thuau before offerings. It may be that this Anena is to be identified with the famous noble of that name whose wife was called Thuau, and whose tomb (No. 54) is at Shêkh abd' el Gûrneh. On the west wall, at the sides of the usual recess, are figures of Sebek of Khennui and an erased deity, and the cartouches of Thothmes Ist. Persons are here seen bringing offerings, amongst which may be noticed a standing statue of the king.

The next shrine is so much damaged that only the cartouches of Thothmes IIIrd and those of Hatshepsut, which have been erased, are visible. The following shrine belonged to Min-nekht. Shrine of Over the doorway are the erased cartouches of Hatshepsut and Min-nekht. those of Thothmes IIIrd. On the east wall Min-nekht and his father are represented seated, while relatives are shown near by. Three women clap their hands, one man plays a guitar and dances, and another woman plays a double pipe. Min-nekht is here called an *Erpa-ha*-Prince and Sole Companion, and his father is named Thothsen. On the west wall he sits with his mother before the offerings, while music is made to him as before. At the south end of the shrine are three much-damaged seated statues. The visitor, who in most cases will not trouble to climb up to these shrines, should pass through the quarry behind them, and so descend to the edge of the water farther south. Another shrine will now be Shrine of met with, which belonged to a certain Amenemhat, who was Amenem-*Erpa-ha*-Prince, Sole Companion, Superintendent of the Priests hat. of the South and North, and High Priest of Amen-Ra, under Amenhotep IInd. On the north wall Amenemhat and his wife Mimi are shown seated before offerings which have been brought by their son, a libation priest named Amenemusekht. Seated male and female relations are seen near by, and other persons are represented bringing more offerings. On the south wall we again see Amenemhat and Mimi seated before a table of offerings, behind which is a long list of supplies with which the shrine has been endowed. In the west wall is the usual recess containing a

24

damaged statue of the owner, and on either side of it servants are represented bringing offerings. The colour throughout is well preserved, and the ceiling decorations are still brilliant. In the floor are three coffin-shaped cuttings, which are evidently graves of a period long after the days of Amenemhat.

A few yards farther on there is another shrine much damaged, and beyond this two more have been partly quarried away. We now pass through quarries of considerable size, and so reach the mushroom-shaped rock to which the Arabs believe the traditional chain to have been attached. Twenty yards or so from this lies the picturesque group of shrines, which, after the temple of Horemheb, form the largest monuments of Gebel Silsileh. They stand amidst fallen boulders and ragged clumps of bush at the edge of the river; and, when visited at noon, they form a shady and beautiful resting-place. One first passes a large stele cut on a rock at right angles to the river. At the top Rameses IIIrd is shown in the presence of Amen-Ra, Harmachis, and Hapi. The inscription is dated in the king's sixth year. By the side of this stele is a small figure of an official named Horemheb, who adores the cartouches of Sety Ist.

Stele of Rameses IIIrd.

The first of the three great shrines was made by the orders of Merenptah. Each of these shrines consists of a wide and high recess cut in the rock, at the back of which is a large stele, and at the sides a series of gods. On either side of the entrance is a graceful pillar, and along the top runs the usual concave cornice. Traces of the once vivid colouring are still to be seen. At the top of the stele in the first shrine, Merenptah is seen worshipping the Theban trinity of Amen-Ra, Mut, and Khonsu, and another trinity, composed of Harmachis, Ptah, and Hapi. The inscription, dated in the king's first year, gives a hymn to the Nile, and refers to the institution of Nile festivals, for which a long list of offerings is decreed. On the north wall of the recess are four rows of figures. In the top row the king is shown offering to Osiris, Isis, and Rameses IInd; in the second row to Sebek of Ombo, a goddess, and Horus within the Waters of Libation; in the third row to Sebek of Silsileh, Hathor, and two other goddesses; and in the fourth row two figures of Hapi, the Nile, are seen. On the south wall, in the top row the king offers to Rameses IInd and two gods; in the second row to Anhur, Tefnut, and Seb within the Waters of Libation; in the third row the queen, Ast-nefert, offers to Taurt, Thoth, and Nut, all within the Waters of Libation; and in the fourth row two figures of Hapi are again seen.

Shrine of Merenptah.

GEBEL SILSILEH

Between this and the next shrine there is a small stele on which Merenptah is seen offering the figure of Truth to Amen-Ra; while behind the king are the figures of two nobles, one of whom is Panehesi, the well-known vizir. The next shrine, made by Rameses IInd in his first year, is very similar to that already described. The king worships the same gods upon the stele, and very similar inscriptions are there given. On the north side of the recess are four rows of figures, as before. In the top row the king is shown kneeling in the sacred tree, while Amen-Ra, Thoth, Ptah, and another god are grouped around; in the second row the king worships Osiris, Isis, and Min; in the third row Sebek of Silsileh, two obscure goddesses, and Hathor; and in the fourth row are two figures of Hapi. On the south wall, in the top row the king worships Menthu and two other deities; in the second row Anhur, Tefnut, and Seb; in the third row Queen Nefertari worships Taurt (whose dress, cape, and quaint hippopotamus body should be noticed), Thoth, and Nut; and in the fourth row the two Hapis again appear.

Shrine of Rameses IInd.

Beyond this shrine is a small stele of Merenptah's reign, on which the king and a famous high priest of Amen, named Roy, are seen worshipping Amen-Ra. By the side of this stele is a small figure of King Amenhotep Ist, probably dating from the XIXth dynasty.

The third shrine has been partly destroyed by a landslip. It was made by Sety Ist, and is thus the oldest of the group. It seems to have been almost precisely similar to the two shrines already described. Some distance farther to the south there is a small stele of the same king, now much damaged; and beyond this one soon reaches the point at which the rocks recede from the river.

Shrine of Sety Ist.

EAST BANK

At the north-east side of the rocks of Gebel Silsileh, some distance back from the river, there is a large tablet cut in the side of the cliff. This is the first monument which the visitor will observe when approaching Silsileh from the station of Kagoug. Upon the stele there is a much-damaged relief showing King Akhnaton (Amenhotep IVth) worshipping Amen; and below this is an inscription stating that a great muster of workmen was made in order to quarry stone for the Sanctuary of Aton in Karnak. This tablet is extremely important historically, as it

Stele of Akhnaton.

dates from the period when Akhnaton, the "heretic king," was first breaking away from the worship of Amen. It will be remembered that this king later on entirely broke away from all the old traditions, and founded for himself a new capital at Tell el Amarna. He persecuted the worshippers of Amen, and by his orders that god's name was cut out of all inscriptions throughout Egypt. On this tablet, however, he still worships Amen and still calls himself Amenhotep instead of the later Akhnaton; and yet he has already begun to build a temple in honour of Aton, and is called "high priest" of that god. To the visitor who has not studied Egyptian history this stele will not appear to be of interest, but those who have read any account of this period will find here a monument of very great importance. The lean, ascetic figure of Akhnaton, singing the exquisite hymns to the sun which he himself had composed; or, in his beautiful palace at Tell el Amarna, teaching a new art to his puzzled artists; or again preaching a doctrine of peace and goodwill to his people at home, while his empire in Asia tottered and fell, stamps its impression upon one's mind so forcibly that every monument of his is valuable.

The quarries.

The visitor who is pressed for time should make his way southwards along the river bank, and should only stop to examine the two great quarries, the entrances of which are closed by iron gates. The first of these is entered through a long and imposing passage which has been cut through the rock. The smooth walls, partly in deep shadow, tower above one on either side; and the vivid strip of blue sky seen above the yellow sandstone forms a scene of very considerable beauty. From the passage one emerges into a vast quarry, the walls of which rise to a great height on almost all sides. Greek and demotic inscriptions are found here and there, cut by the quarrymen. The remains of a causeway down which the stones were dragged are to be seen; and mounting this at the south end of the quarry one observes a second entrance passage which is now closed by a wall. The second great quarry is not quite so large, and its north end has been blasted away in the recent works for the Esneh barrage. The fine entrance passage, however, has been preserved by the Department of Antiquities, and the visitor is thus able to obtain sufficient idea of the original form of the quarry.

Those who have time, and who are interested in ancient works, should make a tour of the many other smaller quarries to the north, south, and east of these two described above. Some

GEBEL SILSILEH

distance back from the river lie three unfinished sandstone sphinxes; a hawk; and a naos, broken into two pieces, inscribed with the name of Amenhotep IIIrd. Those who have seen the quarries at Aswân will remember that there also are unfinished works of this king, which seem to have been left incomplete owing to the disgrace into which the chief sculptor fell. An inscription here records that the same king ordered stone to be quarried for a temple of Ptah. The name of Sety Ist is found in these quarries, and among other inscriptions may be noted a large tablet on the rocks overlooking the river, inscribed with the cartouches of Psametek II.

FROM GEBEL SILSILEH TO KÔM OMBO

Between Gebel Silsileh and Kôm Ombo on the east bank there do not seem to be any ancient remains except a few plundered cemeteries. On the west bank there are traces of a Ptolemaic or Roman temple, town, and cemetery at Faras, known to the natives as Ras-ras. One or two decorated and inscribed blocks of sandstone from the base of the walls are to be seen. A mile or so before arriving opposite Kôm Ombo there is again a late cemetery, and a block of stone upon which the god Sebek is figured.

CHAPTER XVII

THE TEMPLE OF KÔM OMBO—FROM KÔM OMBO TO ASWÂN

Situation, &c., of the temple.

THE temple of Kôm Ombo ("the Mound of Ombo") is beautifully situated on the east bank of the river, overlooking the water at a point where the Nile makes a wide bend from south to west. It stands upon a hill, partly composed of the ruins of an earlier temple and town, and on the north and west sides the mounds are covered with the debris of the contemporary and later houses. On the west side these are extensive, and are mainly composed of crude brick burnt red by some great town fire, amidst which gateways and isolated blocks of stone are to be seen. On the north side the *Kôm* is covered with sand, which, encroaching on the temple precincts, threatens to overwhelm the building as in former times, were the vigilance of the Department of Antiquities relaxed. On the south side the temple is continuously menaced by the water, which had already swallowed a large portion of the terrace and one side of the entrance pylon before it was held in check by the construction of a stone embankment in 1893. The temple did not always stand at the water's edge. In old days the Nile seems to have passed to the south and west of the island which now lies opposite Kôm Ombo, and its present eastern bed was probably a series of dry mud-flats, only covered by the water in flood time. A well at the front of the temple terrace indicates clearly that the water at that time was some distance away. The years have, however, dealt lightly with the temple in many respects; and much of it remains standing, while even the colour in some parts is brilliant. The buildings were cleared of sand, repaired, and walled in by this Department in 1893; and the visitor must now show his ticket of admission at the door before he is permitted to enter.

Methods of visiting the temple.

The visit to the temple is usually made from the river, as all the tourist steamers stop close to the ruins, and generally allow ample time for the traveller to obtain some idea of the place. From

THE TEMPLE OF KÔM OMBO

Aswân the excursion can also be made by railway. Taking the train which leaves Aswân at dawn, one arrives at Kôm Ombo station about a couple of hours later. Village donkeys with rough saddles can generally be obtained for the ride of three miles or so to the temple. The return journey can be made by the express which passes through about 3 o'clock, reaching Aswân in time for tea. At the coolest part of the year it is not uncomfortable to travel to Kôm Ombo by the express, reaching there just before noon, and, after a rapid view of the temple, returning to Aswân by the 3 o'clock train; but for this excursion good donkeys should be sent from Aswân by the early train—on which there is always a horse-box—to meet one at Kôm Ombo, so that there may be no delays. Another method is that by which both steamer and train are employed; as, for example, by going to Kôm Ombo in the express from Aswân, lunching and spending the afternoon in the ruins, and picking up Cook's post-boat on its way to Luxor, which touches at the temple just before sunset.

A traveller with whom the writer was acquainted found it possible to visit Kôm Ombo, Gebel Silsileh, Edfu, El Kâb, Esneh, and Luxor during the course of two days, by the following means. He left Aswân by the early train, arriving at Kôm Ombo about 8 A.M.; he left Kôm Ombo by the noon train, arriving at Gebel Silsileh (Kagoug station) an hour later; he then visited the ruins, and, by arrangement, the post-boat there picked him up in the evening, carrying him to Edfu, where it moors for the night at about 10 P.M. He visited Edfu temple at that hour by moonlight, and slept on board the steamer, which next morning dropped him, after an early breakfast, at El Kâb. From El Kâb he took the first train at about 11 A.M. to Esneh, where he arrived at noon, and after visiting the temple there he caught the express on to Luxor, arriving at 4.30 P.M. He then visited Luxor temple rapidly, and caught the evening express down to Cairo. The instance is here cited only as an example of what may be done by the combination of railway and steamer travelling.

An example of rapid travelling.

HISTORY OF KÔM OMBO

Unfortunately very little is known of the history of Kôm Ombo. The name *Ombo* is the modern rendering of the Coptic *Mbo*, which was derived from the Egyptian *Nbi* or *Nubi*. The Greeks called the place *Ombos*, by which name it is now sometimes known to

The early period.

Europeans. The holy name of the place was "the City of the Two Sacred Eyes," in reference to these symbols which were here worshipped. The town was certainly flourishing as early as the beginning of the XVIIIth dynasty, which means that it already existed in the XIIth dynasty. It derived such importance as it possessed from three causes. Firstly, it was built at a point where the cultivated land extended back from the Nile on the east bank for a greater distance than anywhere else in Egypt south of Thebes, and on the west bank also for some distance; and therefore a market town on the river became a necessity. Secondly, it was probably just opposite Kôm Ombo that the great caravan route—known as early as the VIth dynasty as the "Oasis Road"—started. This road runs direct to the oasis of Kurkur, and thence branches to Tomas in Lower Nubia, to Wady Halfa and the Sudan, and to the oasis of El Khârgeh. It was thus used by Libyans and Negroes: and in the VIth dynasty one hears of the great caravan-conductor, Herkhuf, whose tomb we shall see at Aswân, who, while travelling along it on his way to the land of Aam, met the army of that country passing through to invade El Khârgeh. Thirdly, on the east side a road ran from Kôm Ombo up to various gold-mines in the desert; and it is quite possible that the name of the town *Nbi*, which means "Gold," was derived from the fact that it was the terminus of the gold-caravans.[1] In the XVIIIth dynasty the town was surrounded by a great wall, something in the manner of El Kâb, and thus served as a fortress. As early as the reign of Amenhotep Ist a temple existed here, of which fragments were discovered a few years ago, although most of it had been swallowed up by the river. In the time of Thothmes IIIrd and Hatshepsut a gateway bearing these two names was let into the enclosing wall. Rameses IInd built here, and no doubt other kings also restored or added to the temple.

The worship of Sebek.
    There is an island, mainly consisting of sand-banks and mudflats, which lies opposite the temple. This island, which in ancient days was joined to the east bank, was, until recent times, infested by crocodiles, and, either for this reason or for some other cause, the first inhabitants of Nbi began to worship the god Sebek, whose form was that of a crocodile. There is always something in a manner mysterious in the habits of a crocodile, and here, where they caused the river to be unsafe, and where sometimes at nights they stole across the sand and carried away with them some

[1] *Nbi* is mentioned at Medinet Habu as one of the towns from which Rameses IIIrd obtained gold.

THE TEMPLE OF KÔM OMBO

human victim, one can well imagine how the townspeople first propitiated and finally worshipped them. Sebek, Lord of Nbi, is referred to several times at Gebel Silsileh in the XVIIIth dynasty, and the name of the temple is known to have been at that date *Per-Sebek*, "the House of Sebek"; but, at the same time, another and less malignant deity received great honour here also.

This deity was Horuar, "the Elder Horus," a form of the famous hawk-headed god whose worship was so common throughout Egypt. He was generally spoken of as "the Chieftain of the Two Sacred Eyes" and "the Lord of Nbi"; and in Greek times his name Horuar was converted into Haroeris or Arueris. As early as the beginning of the XVIIIth dynasty he is referred to at Gebel Silsileh under these titles. As the town grew in size and became more cosmopolitan in character, other gods were introduced, which gradually were formed into two great trinities. In the worship of Sebek was now included that of the goddess Hathor, who, being patron deity of the western desert, may have been brought in by the caravan-conductors of the "Oasis Road"; while Khonsu-Hor, a combination of the moon-god Khonsu of Thebes and Horus, formed the third member of the trinity. Likewise with Horuar there were associated Tasentnefert, "the Good Sister," a form of Hathor; and her son Penebtaui, "the Lord of the Two Lands," a form of Horus in his capacity as whilom Pharaoh of Egypt. Furthermore, perhaps in deference to the Sun-worshipping Nubians, the god Ra was associated with Sebek in the form Sebek-Ra.

<small>The worship of Horuar and the trinities.</small>

So important had these trinities become in Ptolemaic times, and so rich the town of Nbi—now the capital of a separate province—that under Ptolemy IVth Philometor the erection of the great dual temple, which we now see, was commenced, the east half being dedicated to Sebek and his trinity, and the west half to the Horuar trinity. A Greek inscription in the temple states that the troops at that time stationed in the district of Ombos had, at their expense, erected some portion of the buildings, in honour of Horuar, but apparently not of Sebek. During the reign of Ptolemy IXth Euergetes IInd the building and decoration was continued, and all but the decoration of the Hypostyle was completed by the reign of Ptolemy XIIIth Neos Dionysos. Under the Emperor Tiberius, at the beginning of the Christian era, the Forecourt was built and decorated; later touches were added to it under Domitian; and the last names found here are those of Geta, Caracalla, and Macrinus. Here and there, however, the decoration

<small>Later history of Kôm Ombo.</small>

of a chamber or the completion of a capital remains unfinished ; and the decline in the wealth of the priesthood which now ensued did not allow of the completion of the work. The time spent upon the temple was, thus, about four hundred years, a period of equal length to that between the reigns of Henry VIIth of England and Edward VIIth.

<small>Depopulation of the neighbourhood.</small>
The decline of Kôm Ombo may perhaps be traced to the abandoning of the trade with the Sudan along the " Oasis Road," the shutting down of the eastern gold-mines, and the depopulation, from some unknown cause, of the fields in the neighbourhood. Until recent years the great plain of Kôm Ombo, once so fertile, was covered with sand, and had assumed the appearance of the desert; but a few years ago a company was formed for the purpose of reclaiming these thousands of acres, and the work is now successfully proceeding. This abandoning of the land had already begun to take place in late Ptolemaic times, for a cemetery containing the mummies of the sacred crocodiles has been found near the temple, situated on arable ground. A native tradition of the present day, purporting to account for this desertion of such rich fields, runs as follows :—" There were once two brothers who reigned as princes of Ombo [in whom we may perhaps see the dual gods Sebek and Horuar]. The one [Horuar], who was in every way an estimable person, was expelled by his wicked brother [Sebek] from the castle [the temple], in which they had lived together all their lives. On the departure of the good prince, however, all the inhabitants of the neighbourhood followed after him, deserting their homes and fields for love of him. This exodus occurred just at the time of sowing, and the wicked prince was thus left with no man to sow the seed. Being a great magician, he therefore called upon the dead to do the work. This they did, but at the time of harvest not a blade was to be seen. The prince, hastening in dismay to the fields, discovered that the ground was already a barren wilderness, for the dead had sown sand instead of grain. Thereupon he returned to his castle, and presently, the building falling into ruins, he was buried amidst the debris." The town and temple of Ombo seem actually to have ended their history in the flames ; for the houses of the old town, the great enclosing wall, and those parts of the temple near it—for example, the chapel of Hathor—show unmistakable signs of some huge conflagration.

THE TEMPLE OF KÔM OMBO

DESCRIPTION OF THE TEMPLE

Persons who are using this guide are asked to study the plan of the temple here shown, before visiting the ruins. They will then observe that the building has been erected in duplicate; and that after hiding either one or the other side of the plan at the dotted line, there is still visible a more or less complete temple, consisting of a Forecourt, Hypostyle Halls, Vestibules, a Sanctuary, and several small chambers. The west half [the left side is considered as west and the right as east for convenience] is dedicated to Horuar and the east to Sebek, and when these gods are referred to on their wrong side, it is due, so to speak, to the courtesy of the priesthoods one to another. In the following description of the temple the visitor's attention is called to about fifty points of interest, numbered upon the plan, after observing which a general idea of the ruins may be said to have been obtained. *The duality of the temple.*

The temple is approached from the south-east corner. Here there was a double pylon, but that side of it which was nearest the river has fallen into the water, and only a few blocks of stone at the bottom of the embankment are still to be seen. On the east side of the pylon there are three scenes in relief. At the top the king, here Ptolemy XIIIth Neos Dionysos, is shown slaying an enemy; below this he is seen before Sebek and Hathor; and below this again he is shown offering to Horuar and Panebtaui. On the south or river side of the pylon there are scenes representing the king offering to various gods; and on the west side he again makes offerings to the different deities. Passing through the iron door one enters the front terrace of the temple, bounded on one's right by the ruined pylons which rose in front of the Forecourt. Some of the reliefs at the base of the east pylon are still to be seen. First (1) there are the figures of the three gods, Sebek, Hathor, and Khonsu, who formed the trinity to which this side of the temple was dedicated. Their praises are sung in fifty-two lines of hieroglyphic inscription (2). Next (3) the Pharaoh, here the Emperor Domitian, heads a procession of male and female deities, led by the Nile-god Hapi, and all bearing offerings. Just above this one sees the king in the act of leaving his palace, a *sem*-priest burning incense before him, while in front go seven standards, *i.e.* the four primitive standards of the archaic provinces of Upper Egypt, together with those of Thebes, and of *Entrance of temple.* *Terrace.*

380   ANTIQUITIES OF UPPER EGYPT

two other provinces. This scene has been more fully described in connection with its occurrence at Dendereh, but it may be repeated here that it represents the king performing the archaic ceremony of leaving his palace at Hieraconpolis or Thinis as King of Upper Egypt to take possession of the various cities and temples, and to be crowned King of Lower Egypt as well. Just round the corner of this pylon (4) there is a similar scene. On the south side of the terrace, rising from the modern embankment, are the remains of the circular temple well, which shows that the Nile was at that time some distance away. In ancient times one looked down from this terrace on to the mud-flats now covered by the Nile, and here there seems to have been the lake in which the sacred crocodiles were kept; for this sacred lake is referred to in the temple inscriptions, and it could not well have been situated elsewhere.

Forecourt.   One now enters the Forecourt, which, like all the other parts of the temple, has its east side dedicated to Sebek and its west to Horuar. A covered colonnade once passed along the sides of this court, but now only the lower parts of the columns and back walls remain. On the columns the Emperor Tiberius (his name is spelt *Tibariu*) is seen as Pharaoh worshipping the gods. On the column at the south-east corner (5) it should be observed that the eye and facial markings of the god Horus have been inlaid originally. Behind this column there is a doorway (6) which led to the stair mounting the pylon. Along the east wall of this court there is a long line of figures of Hapi (the Nile) led by the king, and each bearing offerings of holy water, bread, lotus flowers, &c. Similar scenes will be observed at the base of various walls in the temple. In the middle of the Forecourt is the base of the altar, on either side of which a small granite basin is let into the pavement, intended, perhaps, for holding water of purification, or the blood of the victims sacrificed on the altar. In some of the early temples a drain used to pass under the pavement from the altar to a distant basin, to which the blood was thus carried; and in one of the VIth dynasty temples at Abusir, near Gîzeh, this basin is situated outside the temple precincts, as though it were intended that the townspeople should be able to benefit by it.

The main building, from the Forecourt.   Standing in the Forecourt one looks up at the great temple towering before one, and it is hardly possible to fail in admiring its superb proportions. Some Egyptian temples are top-heavy, some crowded, some squat; but here the lines wonderfully com-

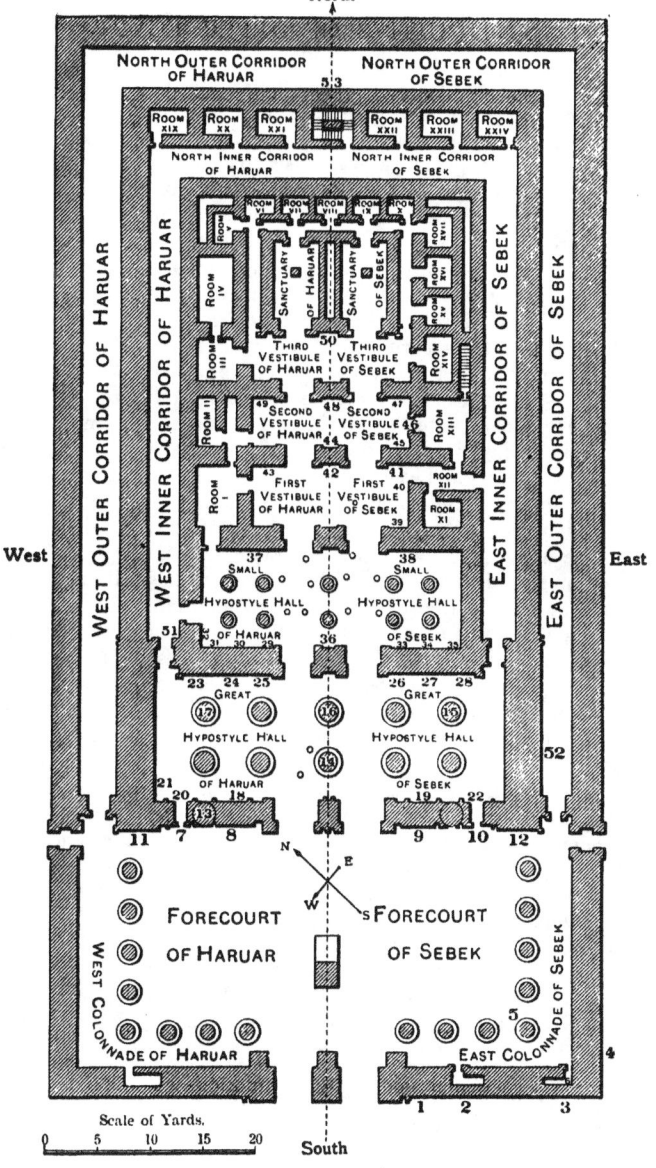

THE TEMPLE OF KÔM OMBO

bine the sense of stability with that of grace. Looking down either of the duplicate entrances, one's eye is carried through doorway after doorway, to the grey altar of the sanctuary at the end ; and once again one is conscious of the simple beauty of the Egyptian rectangular gateways, set off against the curves of cornice and capital. On either side of the double entrance to the temple proper there are two screen-walls decorated with reliefs and topped with a row of uraei : doorways pass through those at either end. From west to east the reliefs are as follows :—On the first screen (7) there is a great winged disk, beneath which are several lines of religious inscription ; on the next screen (8) Ptolemy XIIIth is purified with holy water poured over him by Thoth and Behudet in the presence of Horuar ; on the third screen (9) he is purified in the presence of Sebek, and here one should notice the finely preserved uraei ; and on the last screen (10) there is again a winged disk and an inscription. At the corner of the wall to the west and east of these screens (11 and 12) the king is again shown in the same archaic ceremony mentioned so often, in which he is preceded by the standards of seven provinces.

Great Hypostyle Hall.

One now enters the Great Hypostyle Hall, parts of which are well preserved. Into this hall the inscriptions tell us that the people and minor dignitaries of the town were admitted. The capitals of the columns will at once attract the visitor's attention by their beauty and their variety of forms. There is something particularly imposing in the elaborate capital at the south-west corner of the hall (13), the grouping of the design being masterly. That of the middle column (14), with its simpler lines, is splendidly balanced ; while the palm-leaf design on that of the north-east column (15) is very effective, though not uncommon. Two other capitals (16 and 17) are unique in form, but are unfinished. At this period the architect seems to have been at liberty to create whatever form of capital his fancy might choose, and he appears to have been restrained by few conventions. These capitals have been highly coloured, and even those which were unfinished have received their application of paint. Many of the roofing blocks are still in position, decorated with the well-known but always striking design of vultures with spread wings, holding in their talons the ostrich-feather fans which generally signify nobility. One's eye travels now to the architraves, upon which some comparatively small astronomical representations will be seen. These, like the two capitals, are unfinished, and one can still see the squares painted in red, without which the Egyptian artist, held down by

THE TEMPLE OF KÔM OMBO

the strictest rules of proportion, never attempted to draw. These squares here shown are of value as proving that the body was at this period divided into 21¼ parts, as Diodorus states, and not into 18 as formerly.

The visitor who has studied the temples already described will not require to be told that the proportions of the figures are not those of ancient times. He will now readily recognise the lines of a figure of this period. The old simplicity has gone : the delicate, tender muscles of the earlier rendering of the female figure has given place to an exaggerated valuation of the contours, which is wholly lacking in beauty; and the quiet strength of the male lines has been sacrificed to an attempt to obtain a certain fulness of form, which has, however, only produced an appearance of coarse fatness in the figures. As one of the best examples of the art of this period, the great scene on the screen-wall, just to one's left on entering the hall (18), is worthy of considerable attention. One sees Ptolemy XIIIth, in the presence of Horuar, receiving life from a cat-headed form of Isis, while both she and another goddess, Nut, place their arms around him. Behind these stand Thoth and Horus-son-of-Isis, with hands upraised. The grouping of the figures is carefully thought out; the modelling, although somewhat sketchy, does not show the exaggerations of the period to any absurd extent; and, though conventional in many ways, one sees in this scene a definite attempt to attain an ideal. An extraordinary piece of modelling is that just to the west of this scene, at right angles to it (21). The figures are headless, but one sees that the scene represented the king being led by two goddesses towards Horuar. The lines of the goddess behind the king convey the feeling of stilted motion, which, though quite unnatural, may have been the artist's conception of what a divinity's movements should be. The front goddess, who has turned the upper part of her body around, has given the artist a problem which conventionally he could not solve, and the muddle he has made of the figure is indeed painful. In the scene on the east side of the hall (19), corresponding to the fine group described above (18), one sees the king crowned by Nekheb and Uazt, the goddesses of the archaic capitals of Upper and Lower Egypt; but less care has been spent on this piece of work, and only the modelling of the faces has received close attention. The side doorway leading from the Forecourt to this Hypostyle Hall has above it a scene (21) representing Ptolemy XIIIth before Horuar, Sebek, and Tasentnefert. The inscription upon this doorway states that it is

Reliefs in the Great Hypostyle Hall.

"the door for entering the House of God by the chief libation priest at his (appointed) hour, after he has purified himself in the Lake of Pure Water." The corresponding scene over the door on the east side (22) has been partly erased. It showed the king in the presence of four mythological animals—a ram, a lion, a four-legged snake, and a hawk. The inscriptions giving the use of this door are damaged. The scenes on the back or north wall are of interest as examples of the low-relief modelling of the period. Along the lowest row of reliefs on the west end of the wall, from west to east, one sees (23) the king, now Ptolemy IXth, and Cleopatra before Horuar; (24) before Sebek and Hathor; and (25) before Horuar and a goddess whose figure is much damaged. At the east end of the hall (26) the king is shown before Sebek and Hathor; (27) he performs a foundation ceremony before Horuar and Tasentnefert; and (28) he worships Sebek, Hathor, and Penebtaui.

The Small Hypostyle Hall.

The Small Hypostyle Hall is now entered through one of the two great doorways. This hall is not so lofty as the Great Hypostyle, and the columns here, with uniform capitals, are much less imposing. The roof has almost entirely gone, and much of the walls has disappeared. Into this hall the public were not admitted, but only the "nobles of the great gate" and the priests were allowed to enter. On the south wall, just to one's left on entering, there is a scene (29) showing the Ptolemy IXth leaving his palace, preceded as usual by the *sem*-priest and by six standards, *i.e.* those of the archaic provinces, and of Thebes, and Kôm Ombo. In the next scene (30) he is purified by Thoth and Behudet; and lastly (31) he is crowned by Nekheb and Uazt in the presence of Horuar. The modelling of these two goddesses is in the usual exaggerated style, and their plump faces, with that also of the king, deserve notice. The king's round, smiling face, with the fat neck and chin, is remarkable; and one sees how entirely the artists of this period have lost the ability to hit off that serene, cold expression of earlier work, which is at once the admiration and the despair of the modern copyist. At right angles to this wall there is a fine scene (32), in which the king, accompanied by his sister Cleopatra and his wife of the same name, receives a curved symbolic wand from Horuar, who holds the symbol of Jubilees. The sharp, straight nose in each of the faces is curiously un-Egyptian. Crossing now to the east side of the hall, one observes the three scenes corresponding to the above. First (33) the king, whose figure is damaged, is led by two gods to

THE TEMPLE OF KÔM OMBO

Sebek; then (34) he is led by Nekheb and Uazt to Sebek; and lastly (35) he offers a symbol of festival to Horuar. The panel between the doorways (36) has upon it an interesting figure of a crocodile, symbolising Sebek, lying upon a shrine.

On the rear or north wall, at the west end, there is a noteworthy scene (37). The king makes offerings of all manner of food and furniture to Horuar and Tasentnefert. The offerings are drawn in small size in six horizontal lines, and it may be of interest to record some of them :—1st row: seven kinds of birds; 2nd row: incense, censers, palm branches, and a chaplet; 3rd row: jars of wine, flowers, fine linen, bags of eye-ointment; 4th row: round loaves of bread, trussed fowls; 5th row: vegetables, onions, bread, fruit, grapes; and 6th row: haunches of beef, heads of gazelles, ribs of meat, birds. At the east side corresponding to this (38) is a scene showing the king making somewhat similar offerings to Sebek and Hathor. A well-written Greek inscription will be observed along the edge of the cornice over the western gateway leading into the First Vestibule. It reads :—

"In honour of King Ptolemy and Queen Cleopatra, his sister, the god-like Philometores and their children, the infantry, cavalry, and other troops stationed in the Ombite district (erected) this temple to Aroeris, the great god, Apollo, and the gods worshipped with him in the same temple, in consequence of these gods goodwill towards them."

The visitor passes from the Small Hypostyle Hall into the First Vestibule, which is roofless, and entirely lacks its west wall. The priests of the city of Ombo were alone allowed to enter this hall. On the south wall the only relief which calls for special notice is that (39) at the east end. Here one sees Ptolemy IVth Philometor spilling grain (?) before Horuar and Tasentnefert. A relief on the east wall (40) shows the same king embraced by Sebek; while below is a scene representing the king and Queen Cleopatra offering vases of water and garlands of flowers to the gods. Turning to the north wall, one observes (41) a headless figure of the king pouring out a libation before Sebek, who is also headless, while between them are drawn all manner of offerings. Between the two doorways in this wall there is a scene (42) showing the king performing before Horuar some ceremony in connection with the founding of the temple. Lastly, one may notice the relief at the west end of this wall (45). It is partly destroyed, but one is still able to see Safkhet, the goddess of archives and writings, and

The First Vestibule.

Horuar, engaged in the ceremony of pegging out the limits of the temple. The dress of the goddess, a panther-skin over an ornamental robe, is noteworthy.

Second Vestibule.
The Second Vestibule is again much ruined, though some of the reliefs still retain their colour. Apparently no one except the officiating priests were allowed into this chamber and those behind it. On the south wall between the two doorways (44) a ram-headed deity, perhaps the sacred ram of Elephantine, offers with the king to the damaged figure of a god. Above this one sees the king making offering to Sebek and Penebtaui, and higher to Sebek and Isis. The east walls of the vestibule (45 and 46) contain a long but damaged list of festivals, each day of the year being assigned to some demi-god. On the left of the doorway leading into Room XIII there are representation of sacred bulls. At the east end of the north wall (47) there is a relief showing the sacred bull Hapi—or Apis—of Memphis (?), in the form of a bull-headed man, offering with the king to Horuar and Tasentnefert. Between the doorways (48) is a relief in which the sacred bull of Arment is seen offering with the king to Sebek and Hathor. At the west end of this wall (49) there is a damaged scene in which the king, now lost, has been offering to Sebek and Horuar together. Passing into Room XIII, where the colour on the reliefs is still good in parts, one should notice the sphinxes over the two small doorways; and, on the east wall, a figure of the king dancing may be observed.

The Third Vestibule.
The Third Vestibule, again much ruined, has a portion of the roof still intact, on which is a decoration of the usual flying vultures. The only scenes which call for particular attention are those on the north wall between the doorways (50). At the base of the wall are figures of Hapi, the Nile, of the North and South, bearing offerings. Above is a fine group in which the king is seen clad in a long white robe, the double crown upon his head, in the presence of the hawk-headed moon-god Khonsu-Hor, Horuar, and Sebek-Ra. Behind the king stands Queen Cleopatra. The god Khonsu-Hor marks the number of the king's jubilees upon a notched palm branch, as though ordaining for him a long reign. Above are scenes showing the king before Sebek and Horuar.

The Sanctuaries.
We now pass into the almost entirely ruined Sanctuaries, that on the west being dedicated to Horuar and that on the east to Sebek. In each sanctuary stands a much damaged altar of grey granite. A very interesting feature of this part of the temple is the

THE TEMPLE OF KÔM OMBO 387

secret passage which passed between the two sanctuaries, in the thickness of the wall. It was entered from one of the small chambers at the back, Room VIII, which, it must be remembered, was quite shut off by the high walls at the north end of the sanctuaries. Here a portion of the floor could be raised, admitting the priest to a dark passage, still intact, which passed between the sanctuaries below the level of the floor. A hole in its roof led to another passage on a level with the floor; and another hole in this roof communicated with a passage at a still higher level, of which only the south end can now be seen. The priest then passed northwards along that part of the passage which is now lost, until he stood immediately above the two altars. Whether from this point he chanted those decrees of the High Priest which were regarded as oracles spoken by the stone mouths of the statues of the gods below, or whether the passage was built that the priests might hear the confessions or supplications of the worshippers privileged to address the gods, one cannot now tell. It is almost a misfortune that this passage has survived the wreck of the sanctuaries, to add yet another simple explanation of those Egyptian mysteries which once so thrilled us.

Stepping over the remains of the small chambers at the back of the sanctuaries, the visitor finds himself in the Inner Corridor, from which, at this north part, seven intact doorways lead to six chambers and to a stairway mounting to the roof. From west to east these doors are numbered XIX to XXV; and the visitor who is interested in Egyptian low-relief work should certainly visit these chambers. The reliefs on their walls, which show the king before the gods, are unfinished, and one may here study the whole process of the work. It will be seen that after the walls had been dressed the scenes and inscriptions were outlined in red paint; the sculptor then blocked them into relief by chipping away the surrounding surfaces; he then rounded the edges of the figures and indicated the muscles; next he rubbed the surfaces smooth with sand(?), and cut in the ornamentation and other detail; and finally he applied himself to the inscriptions. These various stages may best be seen in the well-executed but unfinished relief on the east wall of Room XXI, the third from the west end. *The Inner Corridor.*

At the south end of the west side of the Inner Corridor there is a fine relief (51) showing the Pharaoh crowned as King of Lower Egypt leaving his palace, preceded by the seven standards mentioned before, and by the *sem*-priest, who burns incense. The king is said, in the accompanying inscription, to be going forth to the temple to subject the land of his father Horus, Lord of Nbi. The east side of the Inner Corridor is almost entirely ruined, and does not require to be visited.

The Outer Corridor. The Outer Corridor, which passed round between the temple proper and the outer wall, may now be noticed. Passing up the ruined west side, one reaches the northern length of the corridor, on the north side of which are reliefs showing the Emperors Antoninus (Caracalla), Geta (whose name Caracalla has erased), and Macrinus,[1] offering to the gods. Opposite, on the south wall, *i.e.* the back wall of the temple proper, there are some huge reliefs representing the Pharaoh before the two great trinities of Ombo. It will be observed that the eyes of these figures have been inlaid. In the middle of these reliefs, exactly in the axis of the temple, there is a remarkable mystic scene (53). One sees Horuar on the one side and Sebek on the other, standing before a shrine which contained a small seated figure, and which has on either side of it an eye, an ear, and other symbols. Above is an eight-headed and eight-winged cat, a sacred cow, an eight-winged hawk, and what was once a many-headed snake. Above this again are the two sacred eyes, and other mystical objects. Before Horuar is his sacred symbol—a human-footed reed leaf inscribed with an eye; and before Sebek, likewise, is his symbol—a lion-headed wand upon a naos, also inscribed with the eye. Farther along the wall to the east of this scene there is a small representation of a crocodile lying upon a four-wheeled cart; and it may be that either this animal itself, or its mummy or image, was wheeled around the temple at festivals.

At the south end of the east side of this outer corridor there has been a large scene (52) showing the king smiting his enemies. Only the king's feet and the bodies of the captives now remain, together with the figure of a ferocious lion, which runs at the king's side and bites the hand of one of his victims. The appearance of a lion in this well-known scene dates from the days of Rameses IInd, who is said to have had a tame lion at his side in battle; but since in certain reliefs, even of that date, the place of the ferocious monster is taken by a small pet dog, who sniffs at, or snaps, the feet of the victims, one may suppose that the creature here shown is only symbolic of might. Below this relief are the names of thirty-two captive lands, over each of which is the bust of a typical inhabitant; but the visitor who has seen those lists at

[1] The last relief at the east end.

THE TEMPLE OF KÔM OMBO

Thebes, Abu Simbel, and elsewhere, will at once see that these before us are but a meaningless copy. It will be observed that the face of each of these captives is carefully ground or scraped away to some depth—not merely erased; and one can only suppose that in mediæval times the powdered stone from the faces was used for some medicinal purpose by the ignorant peasants, who believed that demoniacal power was possessed by it. Instances of this grinding away of antiquities are not uncommon.

Returning to the terrace of the temple, a small ruined building will be seen at the south-west corner, overlooking the water. This seems to have been the Birth-House, and the reliefs show it to have been built by Ptolemy IXth. Only one scene is of interest namely, that on the west face of the highest portion of the walls. Here one sees the king standing in a boat, which floats amidst the papyrus reeds. In the boat with him are two Nile gods, and at the prow stands a tame bird. From the reeds the wild duck rise, and a little figure of a lion is shown climbing up one of the stems ! The king wears a closely-curled wig and a short skirt. Presiding over the scene is the god Min, the deity of life and vegetation. This relief is an example of the debased religion of the period ; for those who have seen the Theban tombs of the XVIIIth dynasty will at once perceive that here we have but a corrupt copy of a scene repeatedly depicted in those tombs, and representing the deceased noble hunting birds at the river's edge or in the swamps. The dress of the Ptolemaic king here is that of an XVIIIth dynasty noble ; the tame bird at the prow of the boat is the decoy-duck of the real scene ; the gods in the boat are the wife and other relatives always shown in the tomb scenes ; and the ridiculous lion is the tame cat or ichneumon trained to retrieve. The god Min is introduced owing to the fact that he appears in a somewhat similar scene in earlier temple reliefs (as at Luxor). The scene, thus, is here incorporated with the temple reliefs mainly owing to the priestly belief in the religious significance of a painting which had been observed in some open tombs at Thebes or elsewhere. The same misinterpretation of earlier tomb scenes, it will be remembered, was noticed at Esneh, where a Roman Pharaoh is shown snaring birds with a net. What religious significance was given to these purely human actions is not known ; but one sees that the priests were so imbued with a sense of the occult at this period that they were ready to find hidden meanings in almost anything.

The Birth-House.

Before leaving the temple, the little chapel of Hathor, which stands on the east side, not far from the entrance pylon, should be

The chapel of Hathor.

visited. It consists of two small chambers, one of which now contains a few mummified crocodiles discovered in the neighbouring cemeteries. Outside the doorway, amongst the crude reliefs, will be noticed one which shows a goddess of the north playing a harp before Hathor, who sits under a canopy. Inside the larger chamber the reliefs are much damaged, and have never been finished.

FROM KÔM OMBO TO ASWÂN

A few antiquities require to be recorded which lie between Kôm Ombo and Aswân, though it is unlikely that any but archæologists will care to visit them. On the east bank of the river the first place of interest to archæologists after leaving Kôm Ombo is Khanag, where there is the site of an old town, and traces of a temple and early church. Farther to the south there are some extensive quarries, from which sandstone was obtained for some of the Ptolemaic temples. High up on the rocks, about a mile north of the station of Khattarah, there is an inscription of the time of Thothmes IIIrd and Hatshepsut, written by an official apparently in charge of the neighbouring quarries. There are several other rock inscriptions, but little else on this bank of the river. On the west bank there are two or three cemeteries, notably opposite Daraw, and opposite Khattarah; but there are no antiquities of interest to the ordinary traveller.

East bank.

CHAPTER XVIII

THE HISTORY OF ASWÂN AND ELEPHANTINE

IT is not for the present writer to dilate upon the scenic beauties of Aswân and the neighbourhood : this guide is intended solely to furnish information regarding the ancient remains. In these Aswân is not very rich, though such antiquities as are to be found here are of very considerable interest. Only a fraction of the ancient buildings are still to be seen, even in ruins. The mounds of the town of Aswân certainly hide buildings of no small size ; and on Elephantine, besides the many temples still unexcavated, there stood, within the memory of living men, a magnificent and almost perfect temple. At Koubet el Howa there must still be many tombs undiscovered; while in the direction of the cataract, and on islands such as Sehel, there is every reason to suppose that there were shrines and temples in former days. The modern improvements in the town's appearance, the making of new roads, the laying out of gardens, the building of houses, the levelling and tidying of the disorderly mounds, all involve the destruction of ancient remains. But this is inevitable. The Egyptians of the New Empire in the same way destroyed the monuments of earlier days ; the Ptolemies ruthlessly pulled to pieces the temples of the XVIIIth dynasty to obtain stone for their own works ; the Romans, and later the Copts, levelled the Ptolemaic ruins to build their houses and their churches. At present a certain amount of care is taken to preserve antiquities when found during the course of such works, and the small antiquities are seldom destroyed, since the finder is always well aware of their value to a dealer. And thus one may say that, while the development and alteration of the neighbourhood is proceeding at a pace far greater than that of any former period, the loss of historical matter is, on the whole, less than it has ever been before. One must remember, of course, that the laying out and watering of a flower-bed may destroy a papyrus copy of the unknown sayings of Christ, or an unpublished Greek tragedy of

The destruction of ruins at Aswân.

enormous value, which may lie just below the surface. There are new gardens in Aswân which are actually known to be blooming above the libraries of the past; but in contemplating such catastrophes one can attach blame to no one, except perhaps to the archæologist and the archæologically interested public, who have failed to excavate these sites while there was yet time. The new buildings, the new roads, and these new gardens are healthy signs of modern progress and civilisation, which no sane person could wish to check, and no man could hope to regulate.

The archaic period.

The history of Aswân and the neighbourhood, owing to the paucity of remains, is not very detailed; but one is able to realise how full of incident it was in reality. The island of Elephantine in ancient times was named *Abu*, the Egyptian word for elephant. The Greeks translated *Abu* into *Elephantine*, and in modern times this latter name has been revived. The name of Aswân was written by the ancient Egyptians S-w-n, the vowels being now unknown, though one may suppose that the word was pronounced Swani, since the Greeks transliterated it Syene (the y being *upsilon*, that is to say *u* or *w*) and the Copts *Suan*.

The name Elephantine.

This word *Swn* has been interpreted in various ways, but there seems little doubt that it meant "market." In their names "Elephant" and "Market" lies the archaic history of these two towns. It seems that a tribe of conquering Egyptians, whose standard was an elephant, settled itself on the island, where it could not without difficulty be attacked by the aboriginal negro inhabitants of the district; and in times of peace the people of this tribe traded with the natives, and opened a regular market on the mainland at Aswân. It has been thought by some that the island was named "Elephant" owing to its shape being somewhat in the form of that animal, while others have suggested that it was at this point that the Egyptians first saw an elephant, or that the island, when first inhabited, was the home of a herd of elephants, who used to cross to the mainland at low water. Elephants, however, judging from the hundreds of rough drawings of them on rocks, were common enough in early times in this district; and there would be no reason to distinguish any one place by naming it after these animals. On prehistoric pottery, however, the elephant sometimes is drawn as the standard or sign of a tribe; and it is far more likely that the island derived its name from the fact that it was first inhabited by a branch of that tribe.

From these beginnings there grew up a fine fortified city on the

HISTORY OF ASWÂN AND ELEPHANTINE

island, and a trading town on the mainland, which already in the Ist and IInd dynasties must have formed an integral part of the united kingdom of Upper and Lower Egypt. King Semti of the Ist dynasty paved the floor of his tomb at Abydos with granite quarried from the Aswân rocks, and other monarchs of this early period employed the splendid stone in their monuments, as, for example, King Khasekhemui of the IInd dynasty in his temple at Hieraconpolis. Aswân must, therefore, have been a busy centre of industrial work at this date, and no doubt the chieftains of the Elephant people derived considerable importance from their position as guardians of the quarries and of the frontier of the Egyptian kingdom.

While the great kings of the IVth dynasty were reigning at Memphis, Aswân and Elephantine continued to be busy and prosperous towns, though they were no longer of great strategic value, since there is every reason to suppose that the kings of this and the previous dynasty had so chastised the negroes above the First Cataract that the territory for at least a hundred miles above Aswân was now under Egyptian rule. On a boulder at the south end of Elephantine a noble named Khufuankh has left his name as a record of his visit. The quarry works were at this time conducted on an enormous scale, and King Menkaura actually attempted to obtain sufficient granite to face the whole of his (the third) pyramid at Gîzeh, a work which his death left only half completed. One may thus think of the east bank of the river at Aswân at this date as literally swarming with quarrymen, while the great market which gave its name to the place must have formed a centre of continuous traffic; and in Elephantine, the busy town with its garrison of negro and Egyptian troops, one may already see the growing capital of a province which reached northwards perhaps as far as the pass of Gebel Silsileh.

The IVth dynasty.

Thus, with the advent of the Vth dynasty Elephantine had assumed the proportions of a city of the first magnitude, and its nobles, until now simply chieftains of the "Elephant" tribe, became great nomarchs, ranking with the princes of Egypt. There is a late tradition which states that the Pharaohs of the Vth dynasty were actually sprung from a family belonging to this island; but for various reasons this is improbable. Nevertheless it is true that the names of some of the kings of the dynasty are prominently connected with this neighbourhood. Sahura sent an expedition to the southern end of Lower Nubia, and an official of

The Vth dynasty.

this reign has inscribed his name [1] on the rocks of Sehel Island, between Elephantine and the First Cataract. Asesa, according to the story of a prince of Elephantine, despatched an officer up the river to bring him one of the pygmies who, he had been told, lived there in the Land of the Ghosts. Unas, the next king, has left his name largely inscribed upon a granite rock on Elephantine. Of course the mention of kings' names in this manner does not show that the neighbourhood had become a resort of these nomarchs; but still, with the exception of the Memphite necropolis, at no other place on the Nile are these names found.

The VIth dynasty.
The great market of Aswân, to which the negroes of Nubia, and perhaps even of the Sudan, brought their goods; the huge quarry works, and the consequent shipping of the enormous quantities of stone; the fortified city of Elephantine, from which the military administration of the Egyptian portion of Lower Nubia was conducted; and the various activities, industrial and otherwise, which could not fail to develop in so busy a place, all led to the enrichment and the extension of the power of the local princes. Under the kings of the VIth dynasty these nomarchs stand out clearly in the dim history of the period as the wealthy and important rulers of the upper country, whose organisation of their province brought them the favour of the Pharaoh, and whose adventures beyond the southern confines of their territory were the talk of all Egypt. The activity of the last dynasty in Nubia had continued unchecked. Teta, the first king of the VIth dynasty, organised expeditions which penetrated certainly so far as Tomâs, over 120 miles above the First Cataract; and under Pepy Ist an army was collected at Elephantine which consisted of contingents supplied by most of the negro tribes living between Aswân and Wâdy Halfa. In the reign of Merenra a great noble named Una, who had been instrumental in collecting the above-mentioned army, was appointed Governor of the South. In this capacity he was sent to Elephantine to superintend the quarrying and shipping of granite for the upper chamber of the king's pyramid at Sakkâra; and later on he was entrusted with the cutting of five canals down the lower part of the cataract, by which vessels laden with granite from the rocks amidst the rushing waters could pass to and fro safely. In all these works the powerful princes of Elephantine had rendered such assistance that, when Una died, a certain Herkhuf, the then reigning prince of the island, was appointed to

---

[1] Petrie, "History," i. 71, referring to de Morgan, *Monuments et Inscriptions*, i. 88. I have not been able to find this inscription at Sehel.

HISTORY OF ASWÂN AND ELEPHANTINE

the high office of Governor of all the Countries of the South, one of the greatest positions that the Egyptian Government could offer.

The adventures which befell Herkhuf in the south, how he brought a caravan of three hundred asses safely from the barbaric land of Aam, how he prevented a war between Aam and the Libyans of the oasis, and how he obtained a pygmy from the Land of the Ghosts and brought him safe to the king, have been recounted both in the portion of this guide which deals with Lower Nubia and in Chapter XX, and it is therefore not necessary here to repeat them. Herkhuf was buried in one of the great cliff-tombs opposite Elephantine, and seems to have been succeeded in his office of Governor of the South by Sabna, who was also a prince of Elephantine. The main adventure of the life of Sabna was the rescue of the body of his father Mekhu, who had been killed in Nubia during a rebellion. The tomb in which the mutilated body was laid when it reached Aswân may still be seen near those of Herkhuf and Sabna, in the cliffs of Koubet el Howa. Contemporary with Sabna was Prince Pepynekht, another noble of Elephantine, whose tomb may also be visited. Pepynekht conducted a campaign against the rebellious negroes, and also fought on the Red Sea coast.

Adventures of the nobles of Elephantine.

When Sabna died the high power of the princes of Elephantine came to an end, and they fell again into their condition of local celebrity. Pepy IInd appointed a certain Zau, who was Prince of the Province of the Snake Mountain (north of Assiut), to the office of "Keeper of the Door of the South"; and under the last kings of the dynasty another nomarch named Zauta, Prince of the Province of Min (Kasr es Sayâd) was appointed to succeed him in this office. Thus it seems that for some unknown reason the lords of the Elephant city lost their control of the affairs of the south, a loss, however, which in the chaotic period from the VIIth to XIth dynasties could hardly have been realised. Only once in this obscure era does one catch a glimpse of the Aswân neighbourhood, when one finds the people of Elephantine fighting with, and being defeated by, the prince of Assiut. Under the strong rule of Menthuhotep IIIrd of the XIth dynasty the place was again brought under control, and an inscription of this king is to be seen on the rocks near the cataract. The name of King Antefaa of this dynasty is also found here.

The end of the VIth to the XIth dynasty.

Amenemhat of the XIIth dynasty states that he visited Elephantine, a fact which is confirmed by an inscription on the island;

The XIIth dynasty.

and one is led to infer from the context that he reorganised the government there. The Pharaohs of this dynasty conducted countless campaigns in Nubia, directed against the incursions of the Ethiopians from above the Second Cataract; and Aswân was used as the military base of these operations. Serenpitu, the prince of Elephantine under Senusert Ist, was raised to the old rank of Governor of the Lands of the South, and his successor, named Serenpitu, under Amenemhat IInd held offices in connection with "the Door of the South." Elephantine once more boasted a princely court, and the cliffs of Koubet el Howa received the addition of new tombs.

The fleet of ships which carried the Egyptian armies to the south were probably at this period constructed above the cataract, at the modern Shellal; and it was generally necessary for the vessels which had brought the troops and their stores as far as Aswân, to unload at the lower end of the impassable cataract, the whole paraphernalia of war being transported by land to Shellal. Aswân was thus, during the whole of this dynasty, a military depôt of stores; and the eastern bank of the river, with its camps of soldiers, its multitudes of quarrymen, its celebrated market, and its busy quays, must have been a place of vast importance. Elephantine, too, filled to overflowing with the flower of the Egyptian soldiery, and now enriched by a fine temple, and boasting a wealthy priesthood dedicated to the service of the god Khnum, must have reached a degree of prosperity greater than all but that of the largest cities of Egypt. But amidst these activities, which culminated in the complete overthrow of the Ethiopians by Senusert IIIrd, there are no indications that the princes of Elephantine continued to wield any great power, though one may suppose that they lived in considerable prosperity.

<small>Senusert IIIrd and his Ethiopian campaigns.</small>

The campaigns of Senusert IIIrd relieved the inhabitants of Aswân of much anxiety, since for many years they had lived in the fear of a negro invasion. So serious had the outlook been, that many of the cities of Upper Egypt had been fortified, and the great wall, which may still be seen on the east bank between Aswân and Shellal, seems to date from this period; while it is known that building operations of a military nature were conducted on the island of Elephantine itself. In order to avoid the tedious overland transport of stores from Aswân to Shellal, a channel was cut through the cataract, apparently on the east side of the island of Sehel; and up this the warships of the Egyptians were dragged. The cataract having thus been made

HISTORY OF ASWÂN AND ELEPHANTINE 397

navigable, the land of Nubia as far as Wâdy Halfa having been entirely annexed, and the frontier having been fixed at the Second Cataract, Elephantine and Aswân ceased to be a basis for military operations in the south. There was no more reason for a Keeper of the Door of the South to be appointed at the First Cataract; and from now onwards the double city was famous mainly as a quarry station, and as a market and depôt for the goods coming in from the south either as merchandise or as tribute.

The cataract, however, although now navigated and conquered, still retained its grandeur, and still remained the wonder of the traveller. Of the many officials and visitors who came to Aswân, a large number felt it incumbent on them to sail up to the island of Sehel at the foot of the cataract, and there to look at the sacred rocks which for so long had formed the actual frontier of Egypt. The island was under the patronage of three deities. The first was Khnum, the ram-headed god of the cataract. He was very widely worshipped in Upper Egypt; and as he was closely connected with the origin of things, and especially with that of the Nile, he was supposed to dwell in the cataract, where, it seemed to the Egyptians, there must be some hidden fount of water. The second member of the trinity was Satet, or Sates as the Greeks called her, identifying her with Juno. She generally carries a bow and arrows, and her name is spelt with a hieroglyph representing the skin of an animal pierced by an arrow. Anuket, or, Anukis, the third member, is always distinguished by her lofty head-dress of feathers. This head-dress is so similar to that of the Philistines, that there is some reason to suppose that this goddess came, as they did, from Crete or the Syrian coast. Some early wanderers from the north may have brought her worship by chance to this neighbourhood some time before the Middle Kingdom, when she first appears. There are many inscriptions still to be seen on the rocks of Sehel, dating from this period, written by, or at the request of, distinguished visitors, and often dedicated to these gods.

The gods of the neighbourhood.

Elephantine was also under the protection of this trinity, but here Khnum was indisputably more important than his two colleagues. The ram was sacred to him, and it seems that even at this early date, before the religious tendencies of the Egyptians had developed their later exaggerations, there was a highly developed mythology and ceremonial surrounding him. Travellers were told how Khnum controlled the springs of the river; and famines, due to a low Nile, were attributed to the anger of this god, as we are told, for example, in a great inscription on the island of Sehel. By many he was thought to be the eldest of the gods, and thus the neighbourhood derived considerable importance from his worship.

The XIIIth to XVIIIth dynasties.

During the turbulent period between the XIIth and XVIIIth dynasties, one catches only fragmentary glimpses of this province, as, for instance, when King Neferhotep of the XIIIth dynasty had his name inscribed on various rocks near the cataract, always placing it close to that of Senusert IIIrd, his ideal, apparently, of what a king should be. In these troubled times the princely families of Elephantine seem to have been swept away; and when, under the XVIIIth dynasty, the government was firmly established once more over all Egypt, one hears little more of these nobles. There was now a military commander of the fortress, and the aristocracy was no doubt formed of this military class, and that of the rich merchants and caravan-conductors. The quarry works were renewed with unprecedented energy; once more the Egyptian armies passed through to the Ethiopian wars; and the market was again opened, no doubt. Thothmes IIIrd erected a fine temple on Elephantine, of which traces can still be seen; and that great king must have often passed through Aswân on his way to his Ethiopian wars. The canal which had been cut by Senusert IIIrd up the cataract was reopened by Thothmes IIIrd, who had found it choked. Under Amenhotep IInd, who also built at Elephantine, the inhabitants of Aswân must have been spectators of that gruesome procession when the king sailed up the cataract on his way to the Sudan with the body of a rebel Asiatic prince hanging head downwards from the prow of the royal galley. Thothmes IVth, the next king, has left on the rocks just above the cataract an account of his journey through Aswân to Nubia, where the negroes had revolted; and he seems to have added extensively to the temples of his fathers on Elephantine. Amenhotep IIIrd erected a superb little temple on the island, consisting of a sanctuary and other chambers surrounded by a covered colonnade, the whole standing on an elegant platform approached by a flight of steps. Statues of deities bearing his name have been found on the island; and it is evident that the priesthood at this period was wealthy and powerful. Its downfall, however, was no doubt brought about under the heretic King Akhnaton, indications of whose activity at Aswân are not wanting.

During this period, as has been said, the quarries had been

HISTORY OF ASWÂN AND ELEPHANTINE 399

worked vigorously, and the huge obelisks in the temples of Thebes and elsewhere tell of the almost unthinkable labours which Aswân witnessed. The administration of the southern countries was now no longer placed in the hands either of the nobles of Elephantine or of any of the princes of Upper Egypt. A specially chosen viceroy was appointed whose residence was at El Kâb, and who had under his orders the whole country from there to the Egyptian frontier in the Sudan. One of the main duties of this official was to see to the regular arrival of the gold which was now being mined in the Wâdy Alaki and elsewhere, and for which Nubia had already become famous. Gold was plentiful in Elephantine, where the mining officials came to spend it; and in the town taxes of the period a very large part of the Elephantine tax was paid in solid gold, instead of in cattle, cloth, grain, and so on, as was the custom in other cities. Under Thothmes IIIrd the commandant of the fortress paid into the treasury 40 *debens* of gold (a *deben* being about 100 grammes), and one chest of linen. The scribe of the Recording Office paid six *debens* of gold and some cloth; and two other officials paid two and one *debens* respectively, together with some linen, cloth, and two oxen. In the long list of taxes on the various towns which has been preserved to us in the tomb of Rekhmara at Thebes, only one to six *debens* of gold are required from the head officials of the other cities, the rest of the tax being paid in oxen, poultry, grain, honey, linen, cloth, &c.

Administration in the XVIIIth dynasty.

In the XIXth dynasty it goes without saying that the irrepressible Rameses IInd erected a temple here, parts of which are still to be seen; while on various rocks his figure and titles have been cut. His son Merenptah has left a statue of himself on the island of Elephantine; and the names of Septah and Rameses IIIrd, the succeeding kings, are found in the neighbourhood. From this time until the XXVIth dynasty one hears very little of the doings of Aswân, though the isolated names of one or two kings are found on the rocks. The quarries, however, continued to be worked on the mainland; and at Elephantine the development of the religious system brought considerable fame to the city. In all directions one now reads of high priests of Khnum, Satis, and Anukis. The tomb of one of these may be visited at Koubet el Howa, while on various rocks above and below the cataract the names of other high priests are cut. On the island of Elephantine there were now splendid temples built by Thothmes IIIrd, Amenhotep IIIrd, Rameses IInd, and other kings. The fame

The XIXth and XXth dynasties.

Development of the religion.

400   ANTIQUITIES OF UPPER EGYPT

of the cataract gods was widespread. In Nubia they were now generally worshipped, and northwards as far as Gebel Silsileh they held sway. Visitors to this neighbourhood went up to Sehel to see the cataract and to do homage to its gods; and on the rocks there and elsewhere many hundreds of inscriptions dating from this period have been written. There seems now to have been a sacred ram at Elephantine, which was thought to be an impersonation of Khnum, and which was kept in the temple. Throughout this long period the priesthood appears to have grown yearly richer; for the rise and fall of dynasties, the native rebellions, and foreign conquests affected this remote city but little. Not only were Elephantine, Sehel, and the other islands of the lower cataract now held as sacred, but Philæ also was beginning to be famous; while Bigeh and El Heseh, two islands at the head of the cataract which since the XVIIIth dynasty had been regarded with some piety, are now to be added to the list of highly sacred spots. In the XXVIth dynasty King Psametik Ist placed a Greek garrison at Elephantine to protect Egypt from the Nubians, who were now masters of almost all Lower Nubia. This garrison is said to have mutinied, and, together with other Greek troops, to have marched southwards in order to settle there. Psametik IInd visited Elephantine, and his name is to be seen on the rocks in several places. He seems to have sent a mercenary army to Nubia, for at Abu Simbel there is a Greek inscription which was written by these troops "when Psametik came to Elephantine."

The XXVIth dynasty to the Ptolemaic period.

King Nectanebus of the XXXth dynasty built a temple at Philæ which still stands; and shortly afterwards Alexander IInd erected a portal on the island of Elephantine. Under the Ptolemies Aswân and Elephantine may be said to have reached the zenith of their career. The fame of the temples of Philæ, which were daily growing in size and splendour, attracted many people to Aswân; and the priests of Elephantine seem to have made every effort to rival their younger colleagues. The temple of Amen-

Ptolemaic temples.

hotep IIIrd on the latter island was still in use, but those of Thothmes IIIrd and Rameses IInd had fallen into ruins, and were pulled to pieces to form the foundations of new buildings. Great quay walls were erected along the east side of the island, and splendid paved terraces overlooked the water. It was during this period that the famous Eratosthenes visited Aswân, and made discoveries there which led to his being able to measure the earth by the sun's shadows. The fame of the sacred rams of Khnum

HISTORY OF ASWÂN AND ELEPHANTINE

had now led to their increased honour, and as each died he was buried with much pomp in a sarcophagus prepared for him in a vault beneath the temple. A temple dedicated to Isis was now erected at Aswân, and others were built on the islands of Bigeh, el Heseh, and Sehel. Thus the traveller in this neighbourhood found himself in a very land of temples. The pillars and the pylons of the Elephantine edifices towered above him as he mounted the splendid steps of the quay to the terraces above ; he must needs visit the shrines of Sehel, where the waters of the cataract continuously thundered in his ears ; Isis required him to do homage in her new temple behind the town of Aswân ; and, going up to Philæ, he was there conducted through halls and courts, from sanctuary to sanctuary, the like of which the world did not possess.

The building of temples in no way ceased when the Romans took Egypt over ; and a temple at Elephantine, and many at and around Philæ, bear witness to the continued prosperity of the place at this time. But there was now never quite the same security that formerly left the inhabitants of Aswân so free to amass wealth. The Ethiopians were at almost continuous war with the Egypto-Roman armies, and, under their one-eyed Queen Kandake, they managed to capture Aswân in the year 23 B.C. They were, however, defeated by Petronius, the Prefect of Egypt, and were driven back to the Sudan. In the reign of Trajan a temple was erected at Elephantine, in the building of which the ruins of the earlier temples were largely used. *The Roman period.*

Probably during the reign of Domitian the famous satirist Juvenal was unwise enough to criticise severely the acting of Paris, a great favourite at the Roman theatre. He was therefore removed from Rome and sent, as Prefect of the Aswân garrison, to this the most remote frontier of the Empire. Here he led a sad and lonely life, cut off from those pleasures of Roman civilisation which he so well knew how to enjoy. He heartily disliked the Egyptians, and found their religion a matter for ridicule, as no doubt it rightly was at that period. A few Roman officers, a heterogeneous collection of so-called Roman troops, and half-a-dozen Roman houses were all that served to keep him in touch with his native land. To a European of the present day, stationed in Upper Egypt, the appalling loneliness of the long summer months will give a sympathy with, and a pity for, Juvenal, which perhaps may not be able to be felt by those visitors who only see Aswân in the winter, and under the favourable conditions of modern times. There are some *Juvenal at Aswân.*

lines in his satires written in Egypt which compel one to see behind the brilliant wit the miserable exile. Thus, for example, one may quote the lines : " That nature gave the noble man a feeling heart she proves herself by giving him tears ; this is the noblest part of all human nature." (15th Satire.)

As Prefect it must have been one of the duties of Juvenal to control the gathering of the tax. In this connection it is interesting to note that many tax receipts have been found at Elephantine dating from the reigns of various Roman emperors. The garrison was probably not kept busy at this period, and it remained for later Prefects to bear the brunt of frontier fighting. During the following centuries the warlike tribe of the Blemmyes caused constant trouble, and in A.D. 451 the Roman general Maximinus had to make an ignominious peace with them, which, however, was soon broken. Aswân seems to have become a continuous battlefield, and finally at the fall of the Roman power it was left in native hands. By this time the whole neighbourhood had become Christianised, and Philæ had been converted into a church, while another Coptic church was erected in the town of Aswân.[1]

In the year 640 A.D. the Mohammedan religion was forced upon many of the inhabitants, and it must have been at about this time that the great monastery of St. Simeon was built on the west bank of the river opposite Aswân. This monastery was destroyed in A.D. 1173, when a Mohammedan army penetrated to Nubia and attempted to convert the whole land to the doctrine of Islam. From now onwards the history of Aswân is very obscure, and such glimpses as one can obtain of its affairs show only a degradation and a chaos which appears in striking contrast to the wealth and prosperity of its earlier days. At one time a plague swept the country and carried off 20,000 persons from this province. In A.D. 1517, or somewhat later, a Turkish garrison was stationed here to check the incursions of the Arabs, and to this day there are persons here who claim to have Turkish blood in their veins. In 1821 Ismail Pasha conquered the whole of Nubia for his father Muhamed Ali ; and in 1822 the latter, desiring a palace in Aswân, ordered the complete destruction of the beautiful temple of Amenhotep IIIrd, which was still standing, almost perfect, on the island of Elephantine. The building was torn down by the local governor, the limestone was burnt to make lime for the mortar, and the great blocks of granite and sandstone were broken up to be used as material for building the walls.

[1] Remains of this were discovered near he railway station in 1907.

HISTORY OF ASWÂN AND ELEPHANTINE

After the British occupation of Egypt the Sudan wars brought Aswân into prominence as a military basis, and in 1895-6 Lord Kitchener's residence here, before his conquest of the Sudan, led to the modern improvements in the town. Hotels soon sprang up, streets were laid out, and good houses were built. Aswân is now one of the famous winter resorts of the world; and the buildings which have been, and are being, erected on top of the ruins of one of the oldest cities of Egypt are in many ways representative of the most modern phases of European civilisation.

CHAPTER XIX

THE TEMPLE OF ASWÂN—THE GRANITE QUARRIES—THE ROCK INSCRIPTIONS AND OTHER ANTIQUITIES ON THE EAST BANK OF THE RIVER—THE ISLAND OF ELEPHANTINE—THE ISLAND OF SEHEL

THE TEMPLE OF ASWÂN

Situation of the temple.

THE Temple of Isis at Aswân, which dates from the reigns of Ptolemy IIIrd and IVth, lies behind the town amongst the ruins of the ancient city. It will not be found to be of great interest to visitors, and only those who have ample time here should trouble to see it. To the archæologist it has some points of interest, the peculiarly plain and sombre style of its interior architecture being very striking. From the east side of the railway station a road leads up the hill, through the native town, and, bearing off somewhat to the north past a little iron foundry, brings one to the open ground after some ten minutes' walking. Before one lies the open desert, broken by clusters of rock. In the foreground are the ruins of the ancient town —a disorderly and unpleasing mess of sun-dried bricks and fragments of broken pottery, overlaid with modern rubbish. A few yards to the north a low wall with a small wooden gate marks the site of the temple. The building itself stands so low, or rather the town rubbish has heaped itself so high around, that the temple roof is on a level with the present road, and cannot be seen till the wall is reached. A watchman should be found at the gate, and to him the visitor must show his ticket of admission. A flight of steps leads down to the pavement level of the temple some six metres below the surface.

The façade.

The front wall is constructed of undecorated sandstone blocks. There are two entrances: the main portal in the middle, and the smaller portal at the side, both leading into the hall of the temple. The main portal through which the public were admitted

THE TEMPLE OF ASWÂN

into the temple is crowned with the usual concave cornice, below which is the winged disk. Upon the lintel are four panels, showing Ptolemy IIIrd Euergetes offering to different gods. The first panel at the north end gives a representation of Queen Berenice of Cyrene offering beside her husband the king.

One always looks with interest at any mention of this queen. It may be remembered that when her husband was conducting a war in Syria, Berenice vowed that if he were victorious she would cut off her hair, which was of exceptional beauty. The king was victorious, and the queen kept her word, for which she was much praised. The astronomer Conon, who was then conducting his studies at Alexandria, immortalised the act by naming a constellation *Coma Berenices*, "the hair of Berenice"; and Callimachus, the poet, gave birth in one of his verses to the fancy that the queen's hair had actually become deified, so to speak, in the form of these stars. Looking at this representation of the queen given here on the doorway, however, one would hardly believe that of her was written the epigram : Queen Berenice.

> "In Berenice's form and face
> Is all that gives the Graces grace."

Down either side of the portal are three panels again showing Ptolemy offering to the gods. As one enters the portal Ptolemy is seen on one's left side offering to Horus, and on the right to Thoth. Looking up as one stands inside the doorway, two pivot holes for the poles of a pair of swinging doors will be seen, one in each corner. The smaller doorway used by the priests has a similar cornice and winged disk. On the lintel are four small panels showing Ptolemy offering to the gods. On one's left the king is seen wearing the crown of Lower Egypt, and holding in his hand a mace and wand. A short inscription in front of him tells one to enter into this house twice purified ; and his arm is seen to be extended in a kind of gesture of salutation. On one's right is a corresponding scene partly destroyed, showing the king wearing the crown of Upper Egypt. Below these two panels are representations of Hapi (the Nile) of the North and South. The façade.

The Hall of the temple is remarkable, and is unlike that of any of the other temples in the country. In shape it is oblong, rectangular, and the roof, which is intact, is supported by two heavy, square pillars, with stiff, square capitals. There are four windows, one in the north and in the south wall, and one on either side of the entrance, these latter, however, being broken into The Hall.

shapeless apertures. In the walls there are several empty niches where once tablets were inserted. Two altars and the pedestal of a statue stand in the hall, the two former each having a short dedicatory inscription upon them. There is no decoration on the walls of the hall; and the plain, sombre surfaces are in depressing opposition to the decorations seen elsewhere. Sufficient pigment remains upon the walls of most of the temples of Upper Egypt to show that the colour scheme in these buildings was as brilliant as that of the sky and the hills and the trees outside. But here an intentional contrast seems to have been affected, and perhaps one may see in this sobriety the beginnings of the asceticism which was soon to take so fast a hold on Egypt.

Doorways leading to inner chambers.
In the back wall of the hall there are three doors. In the axial line is a large portal leading into the sanctuary, and on either side a door leads into a small chamber. The doorway leading into the sanctuary is surmounted by the usual cornice, below which is a winged disk, repeated again on the lintel. Down either side are four panels, of which the first three show the King offering to various gods, and the last on either side shows two figures of Hapi of the North and the South. As one passes through the doorway there is to be seen on either side an inscription in three perpendicular lines, giving a hymn to Isis-Sirius. This portal has, again, the pivot holes on which double doors swung.

The Sanctuary.
The Sanctuary is a sombre chamber lit by a small rectangular aperture in the roof. The back wall alone is inscribed. This wall is divided into two parts by a concave cornice, below which are two winged disks. Below this, again, are reliefs in four panels, now much damaged, showing Ptolemy IVth before groups of gods. The figures have been erased intentionally with a chisel, which suggests that the temple was used as a place of worship by early Christians. The south door in the back wall of the hall leads into a narrow chamber, lit by a small rectangular hole in the roof. This chamber communicates also with the sanctuary. It is devoid of decoration, but it is evident that it was used as a vestry or robing-room by the priests who entered the sanctuary from it, and who passed to and from it along the south side of the hall, and through the small south door in the front of the temple. On the north side of the sanctuary there is a similar chamber, entered only from the hall. It is lit by a small aperture at the top of the back wall, and was probably used for keeping some of the sacred utensils.

From the outside of the temple one sees that the masonry on

THE QUARRIES

the north side and the back or east side is very rough. The front and south sides, however, show more careful construction. From this it may be supposed that there were houses and rubbish mounds hiding the walls upon the north and east, but that an open court exposed the temple to the south and west. On the south wall two lions' heads projecting below the window ledge are noticeable. The sandstone roofing blocks appear rough from the outside, but originally, no doubt, they were shaped to the necessary rectangle by the addition of plaster. It should be remarked that the blocks which cover the sanctuary are of granite, as though it were thought that less durable material was not sufficient protection for the gods.

The outside of the temple.

In leaving the temple the visitor may walk northwards, turning to the left after a couple of hundred yards or so ; and, passing down one of the narrow native streets, he may reach the river front near the conspicuous building of the Grand Hotel.

THE QUARRIES

The ancient granite quarries lie in the eastern desert between Aswân and Shellal. They are of considerable interest, and should certainly be seen by the visitor to Aswân. For those who are much pressed for time, a morning visit to the quarries may be arranged, so that the visitors at the end find themselves at Shellal; and from thence they may go to Philæ, returning to Aswân in the afternoon. Others will prefer to ride over the quarries and back to their hotel in the morning. The most comfortable method, however, is to ride quietly around the points indicated below, starting from Aswân about 9.30 A.M., and arriving at Shellal in time to catch the noon train back to the town. For those starting from the town, the road to the temple may first be followed, and leaving that building behind one, the pathway to the south must be taken, which leads past the front of a small Christian cemetery enclosed by a whitewashed wall, and thence along the beaten track until the hills are reached. A short distance to the right or west of the path, the first quarry will be found situated amongst the high rocks.

Methods of visiting the quarries.

In this quarry there lies a huge unfinished obelisk, some thirty yards in length and over three in breadth.[1] It has never been detached

The obelisk.

---

[1] A second obelisk, to the south of Shellal station, is to be seen amidst the rocks.

from the parent rock, and its sides have not been fully trimmed. Looking at the obelisk as it lies here, one is able to realise what an enormous undertaking it must have been to remove a stone of this size to the river, to float it on rafts to its destination, and to set it up on end; and one can understand that to any but the most ingenious people the task would be quite impossible. It will be remembered that the obelisk at Karnak, which is of about an equal size to this, was quarried out, despatched, and erected in seven months from the time at which the order for it was given.

Method of quarrying the granite.
Near this obelisk are several indications of ancient quarrying. The method employed for breaking off the blocks was simple. A series of wedge-shaped holes were cut into the stone in a line, and into these were thrust wooden wedges, which were then wetted, and which, by their consequent expansion, cracked the stone. The visitor will notice numerous wedge marks upon the rocks around here. The blocks thus split from the hillside were then dressed with copper tools; and when they had approximately assumed the required shape a roughly paved causeway of stone was laid down, and over this they were dragged by ropes to the water's edge.

The causeway to the higher quarries.
A couple of hundred yards or so to the east of this quarry the traveller will find himself at the foot of a great embanked road, rising from the plain and sloping up towards the hills on the south. The path leads up this artificial incline, which was obviously constructed for the purpose of easing the removal of stone from the higher quarries; and at the top a fine view may be obtained. Away to the north behind one are the whitewashed cemeteries at the back of Aswân, and beyond one catches a beautiful glimpse of the Nile; while looking towards the west the eye wanders over an endless expanse of rough rocks and desolate wilderness. The pathway continues for some distance over the flat upper levels of the hills, and presently upon the left hand a wide, sandy valley comes into view; and to this, a little farther along, the pathway leads down by another embanked incline. It will be noticed that the road was here paved with sandstone, in order to prevent the heavy blocks of granite from fouling in the loose sand as they were dragged down the hillside. Having reached the valley, the visitor may choose his own path over the hard, sandy surface, keeping, however, well on the west of the valley, and leaving the telegraph poles and the railway line far on the left hand.

Sarcophagi and stela.
After a ride of over a mile a valley will be observed running up amidst the western rocks, and in it many traces of ancient quarrying will be found. Half-way up the rocky hill on the south side of the

THE QUARRIES

entrance to the valley there lies an unfinished sarcophagus of Ptolemaic or Roman date, roughly shaped, but not hollowed out, and a few paces higher up is another sarcophagus in a similar condition. A pathway bearing somewhat to the right from this point leads at once to a stela cut into a prominent face of rock. On this stela a male figure is seen in adoration before the cartouches of Amenhotep IIIrd, while below is an inscription reading "[Homage] to the Good God (*i.e.* the king) when there was made the great statue of his majesty [called] 'Sun of Rulers.'"[1] The male figure, which is that of the sculptor who was engaged on the statue, has been chiselled out, though the king's names are intact, and have not been touched by the agents of the heretic king, Akhnaton, who sought out and erased the word "Amen" wherever it was found. A suggested reason for this erasure will presently be given, when other remains bearing on the subject have been described.

The pathway to be followed now turns off to the south past the above-mentioned sarcophagi, and presently one comes upon a colossal seated statue, only the unfinished legs of which can be seen, the head and body being buried. One now passes up the hill, and so strikes a road running along the side of the hills some height above the valley. After a ride of some few minutes there is a bend in the path, and rounding this one comes into distant sight of Shellal with its palm-trees, and with Philæ rising from the blue water behind it. Just at the point where this view is first obtained, a granite colossus is seen lying half buried in sand on the left of the pathway. The figure is that of a king wearing the crown of Upper Egypt; but it is unfinished and uninscribed. *A colossus.*

A hundred yards farther along, on the left of the path and at a somewhat lower level, is another unfinished sarcophagus of Ptolemaic or Roman date. Returning again to the colossus and descending by a steep path behind it to the valley below, the railway line is at once encountered, and this should be followed towards the south until a distance of some four hundred yards separates one from the corrugated iron offices of Shellal station.[2] At this point a valley opens on the right, and amongst the rocks on the south side of the entrance there lies another colossal statue turned upon its side, and unfinished. *A sarcophagus and another colossus.*

---

[1] On the island of Sehel there is an inscription written by a scribe of the workmen engaged on this statue.
[2] The raising of the barrage will alter these landmarks.

ANTIQUITIES OF UPPER EGYPT

Explanation of presence of unfinished works.

As this completes the list of unfinished objects lying in these quarries, it may be as well to attempt an explanation of their presence. The obelisk and the three colossal statues may well belong to the reign of Amenhotep IIIrd, and the fact that they are unfinished may have been due to the sudden death of the king, and the cessation of the work under Akhnaton, his son, whose ideas on art and religion were so unique. But as the figure of the sculptor on the stele is erased, it is within the bounds of probability to suppose that this personage fell into disgrace, and that the king obliterated his name and figure, and abandoned his unfinished task. On the island of Sehel there is an inscription, partly obliterated, which gives the name of a certain Amenhotep who was in charge of the "builders of the two great obelisks," and who may be identical with the sculptor in question, the two obelisks being those to be seen in the quarries. It was probably the custom for sculptors to pay for their work, the money being refunded to them by the Government when the task was complete. Thus, when the sculptor was disgraced his works would be left lying in the quarries, the king refusing to pay for them. Had the Government paid in the first instance it would have made use of the statues under the direction of a new artist. The sarcophagi, which are of later date, were probably abandoned during one of the rebellions or invasions of the Græco-Roman period.

The main works from these quarries.

There is little else to see in these interesting quarries, and the visitor may now return by train or as he came. It may be of interest to mention some of the main works executed in granite obtained from here. Besides the great granite blocks employed in so many temples, there are the huge obelisks of the XVIIIth dynasty, especially those of Hatshepsut and Thothmes IIIrd; the colossal statues of Rameses IInd at the Ramesseum, at Memphis, and elsewhere; the sarcophagus of Merenptah in his tomb at Thebes; some of the Apis sarcophagi in the Serapeum at Sakkâra; a chapel mentioned by Herodotus, which was transported to Saïs, and which consisted of a single block of such size that its transport is said to have occupied 2000 men for three years; and a cubical shrine also mentioned by Herodotus as being at Buto, and which, from measurements given by him, must have weighed about 7000 tons.

THE WALL

The great wall of Aswân is of considerable interest to the antiquarian, and, although it does not present a very striking appearance to the tourist, it might well form the object of a desert ride to those who are spending some time in Aswân. On this excursion one sets out eastward from the Cataract Hotel, towards the mediæval cemetery; and presently one turns sharply to the right along a good road, passing the English cemetery on one's right hand. The wall passed along the side of this road, but it is now so much ruined that it is not until one has ridden about a mile that it becomes noticeable. From here onwards, however, it is quite clear, and in places it rises to a considerable height. It is built of sun-dried bricks, and originally seems to have been a very formidable fortification. One may follow it until it reaches the river some distance to the north of Shellal station.

The history of the wall seems fairly clear. Its object, since it runs in a single line from Aswân to Shellal, was evidently the protection of the Cataract shipping from the raids of the Negroes coming from the east and south-east. It seems to have been one of many fortifications erected during the reigns of Amenemhat IInd, Senusert IInd, and Senusert IIIrd, when the dangers of a negro invasion were very real. The wall was already built in the third year of Senusert IInd, for it was then inspected by a certain official named Hapi, who has left an inscription on one of the rocks behind the fortification, not far from its southern end, stating that he had come to visit the fortresses of Wawat. Wawat was the name of the north part of Lower Nubia, and the point at which the inscription is written, being south of the Egyptian frontier at Sehel, was actually in Wawat. Until the reign of Senusert IIIrd the wall must have been of considerable use in preventing these raids and the desultory sniping which the Egyptians had had to endure while hauling their boats up the Cataract. But when Senusert IIIrd had finally conquered the Ethiopians and had driven them behind the Second Cataract it fell into disuse, and it was probably not again garrisoned, unless the Romans in their wars with the Nubians and Blemmyes made use of it.

At various points along this road there are rock inscriptions of some interest. These have been numbered in white paint

412 ANTIQUITIES OF UPPER EGYPT

Inscriptions on the rocks near the wall.

by the present writer, in order that none should be destroyed during the quarrying necessitated by the barrage works, and there can also be seen the faint numerals painted by M. de Morgan, referring to his catalogue. Commencing from the Aswân end of the road, one may notice No. 314 (de M. 211), in which the 24th year of King Amenemhat IIIrd is given; No. 320 (de M. 205), showing a noble adoring the cartouches of Rameses IInd; and No. 322 (de M. 204), showing a noble likewise adoring the cartouches of Amenhotep IIIrd. Some distance farther on one comes to a knoll of rock on which are some valuable historical inscriptions. No. 474 (de M. 9) is a stele dated in the 1st year of Thothmes IInd, which states that a rebellion above the Second Cataract had been announced, that the Egyptian inhabitants were flying, that the king therefore had led an army thither; and that he had utterly defeated the Ethiopians. No. 476 (de M. 11) is dated in the 5th year of Amenhotep IIIrd, and again tells of a rebellion in Ethiopia crushed by the king. No. 477 (de M. 14) is dated in the 2nd year of Rameses IInd, and gives a bombastic account of his various conquests. A short distance to the east there is a stele of the time of Septah, numbered 471 (de M. 6). One sees Septah enthroned, while the chancellor Bey, who was the most important personage of the period, stands behind him; and before them the Viceroy of Ethiopia, Sety, bows.

ROCK INSCRIPTIONS

Inscriptions near the town.

Beside these inscriptions alongside of the great wall, there are very many others on the east bank of the river, in and around Aswân. A few will be observed in a small public garden just to the south of the railway station. No. 12 here shows Rameses IInd enthroned, welcoming Setau, the Viceroy of Ethiopia, who bows before him; and No. 13 gives the cartouche of Senusert Ist. Below this garden the rocks jut out into the water, and rounding this promontory by boat one sees numerous large inscriptions and figures, against each of which the number is conspicuous in white paint. No. 44 is dated in the third year of Thothmes Ist; No. 46 shows two figures adoring the cartouches of Rameses IIIrd; No. 49 probably shows Rameses IInd extending his hand to a bowing official; No. 48 represents Khnum adored by Rameses

ROCK INSCRIPTIONS

IInd, his wife Ast-nefert, his eldest son Prince Khaemuast, his son Prince Rameses, his daughter Princess Bant-antha, and his son Prince Merenptah, famous as the probable Pharaoh of the Exodus. No. 49 was inscribed by the famous Senmut in honour of Hatshepsut. No. 50 shows Amenhotep IIIrd and his queen, the famous Thiy, receiving the homage of an official; No. 54 represents Amenhotep IIIrd worshipping Khnum; No. 55 is an inscription recording that Prince Khaemuast celebrated the festival of the 37th anniversary of the accession of his father Rameses IInd. Opposite the Nilometer there is a niche cut in the rock, in which is a much-damaged crouching figure. No. 56, beside this niche, shows an official adoring Harmachis, and next to this is the cartouche of Amenhotep IIIrd and the figure of the Viceroy of Ethiopia, Merimes. Along the promenade at Aswân a few inscriptions of the Middle Kingdom are to be found, dedicated to Khnum, Satet, and Anuket by various officials. Perhaps the most interesting of these rock records is the large relief and inscription, numbered 23, which dates from the reign of Akhnaton, and which is to be found on a rock immediately under the south-east side of the house belonging to Dr. Leigh Canney, opposite the Cataract Hotel. It appears that Akhnaton, the famous king who renounced the worship of Amen and the other Egyptian gods in favour of that of Aton, the sun-god, sent his master-sculptor, Bek, to Aswân to see to the quarrying of some granite for one of his works. Bek improved the occasion by cutting this scene upon the rocks here, and inscribing a few laudatory sentences in honour of his extraordinary master. He here calls himself Chief of Works in the Red Mountain (*i.e.* the red granite hills of Aswân), and Chief of the Sculptors on the great and mighty monuments of the king in the Temple of Aton. He mentions the interesting fact that the king himself had taught him his art, for it will be remembered that Akhnaton originated an entirely new style of drawing and sculpture during his short reign. Bek states that his father, who was named Men, was Chief of Works in the Red Mountain under Amenhotep IIIrd. The scene represents Bek standing with flowers in his hand before Akhnaton, whose figure has been erased at a later date; and the characteristic sun's rays terminating in small hands, will be observed streaming down upon the two figures. The other half of the scene shows Men presenting a food-offering to a statue of Amenhotep IIIrd.

The stele of Akhnaton.

Several inscriptions are to be found on the rocks to the south of

414   ANTIQUITIES OF UPPER EGYPT

Inscriptions south of Aswân.

the Cataract Hotel. No. 28 mentions the 6th (?) year of Senusert IIIrd; No. 33 gives the cartouches of Senusert IInd; and No. 35 gives those of Queen Amenardes and Kashta of the XXVth dynasty (B.C. 700); farther to the south, along the river's edge, are numerous inscriptions, mainly of the Middle Kingdom. Opposite the southern extremity of the island of Sehel there is an inscription (No. 372) dated in the 41st year of Menthuhotep IIIrd, the king whose great temple at Dêr el Bahri has been recently discovered. Of the many hundreds of other inscriptions covering the rocks of the eastern bank of the river near the south end of Sehel, that is to say, overlooking the cataract, there are none which call for special mention here.

A few inscriptions in the desert to the west of Aswân are to be seen, but are not of great importance.

ELEPHANTINE

Situation, &c.

The island of Elephantine extends for about a mile and a half in front of the town of Aswân, the north end lying opposite the hospital and schools, and the south end opposite the Cataract Hotel. At the north end stands the Savoy Hotel surrounded by gardens; south-east of this is the village of El Ramleh, and beyond it are verdant fields extending to the village of El Kôm, which lies near the southern end of the island. To the south-east of this village, on the edge of the water opposite the railway station, stands the rest-house of the Public Works Department, beside which are the Nilometer and the temple terraces. The southern extremity of the island, behind the rest-house, is covered with the ruins of the ancient city, temples, and fortress of Elephantine. The visitor will find the Nilometer of some interest, but there is nothing else on the island which is likely to attract any but archæologists, although a walk over the mounds, from which there is a fine view to the south, will not be found amiss.

The Terraces.

In order to obtain a good view of the massive walls overhanging the river, in which the Nilometer is constructed, it will be best to approach this part of the island by boat. From the river one sees that above the granite boulders a masonry wall has been constructed to a great height, and extending for some considerable length along the water's edge. At the south end the mass of masonry juts out into a kind of lofty pier, while

ELEPHANTINE

at the north end a small opening in the wall leads to the Nilometer. This pier is built partly of blocks of stone taken from ruins of earlier date, and here and there inscribed pieces are to be seen. These include blocks with the names of Thothmes IVth and Rameses IInd upon them; and in the inner face of the south side—to be seen from the top of the pier—is a long and important inscription of Rameses IInd in two pieces. The pier is built upon a granite boulder on which is boldly cut the cartouches and Horus-name of Nefer-ab-Ra Psametik IInd (No. 60). A similar inscription occurs a few yards to the north of this.

The visitor should land at the Nilometer, the entrance to which stands clear of the water in the winter. A passage about three yards long leads into the masonry, and, turning to the south, a flight of steps running parallel with the river ascends to the top of the wall, at which level the ruins of the ancient temple lie. The roofing blocks of the passage are of granite, though the rest of the material used is sandstone; but only the lower part remains covered, the stairway being now open to the sunlight. Near the bottom of the steps is a casement by which the passage was lighted when the roof was intact. It seems that originally this stairway and passage were constructed as a means of exit from the temple above, or perhaps the steps were used for the ceremonies in which the priests descended to the water's edge to make offerings to the Nile gods. During the flood-time the water crept up the stairs day by day, and the priests found it useful to mark the levels upon the walls of the passage when the highest and lowest points were reached, and soon the place had become the official Nilometer. It was used mainly in the Roman period, and perhaps does not date earlier than that time. In 1822 it was re-discovered, and in 1870 Mahmud Bey, the eminent native astronomer, began to re-use it. On the walls the ancient markings may be seen with Greek and demotic inscriptions attached. The modern gauge is inscribed on marble tablets let into the wall. Strabo states that the levels of the water were published for the information of the people, and that taxes were raised or lowered in accordance with the extent of the flood as registered here.

The Nilometer.

Ascending the steps to the top of the passage the visitor finds himself upon what was once the courtyard of the temple. Turning to the south, past a modern water-wheel, a walk of fifty yards or so along the edge of the wall brings him to a point at which the side wall of a part of the temple is still standing. There are two recesses in the wall, with large protected windows or case-

The Terraces.

416 ANTIQUITIES OF UPPER EGYPT

ments, through which one may look sheer down on the rocks and water below. A few yards farther to the south is the promontory or pier of masonry which has just been mentioned, beyond which the wall does not extend for more than three or four yards.

The Temple of Trajan.
Turning now to the west, that is to say turning one's back on the river, heaps of potsherds, bricks, and debris are seen extending over all the southern part of the island—the only remains of the great city of Elephantine. A few paces to the west the ruins of the temple in connection with the river wall and Nilometer are partly exposed between two mounds of rubbish. Here one sees the base of a column, inscribed with the cartouche of Trajan, rising upon a platform of stone blocks taken from earlier ruins, this platform being built upon the drums of columns from earlier temples. These drums originally belonged to a temple of Thothmes IVth, but were reinscribed by Rameses IInd. The stones of the platform and those lying at random near by have upon them the cartouches of Thothmes IVth and of Rameses IIIrd.

Temple of Alexander IInd, &c.
A few yards to the west of these ruins stands a granite gateway inscribed with the names of Alexander IInd. Only the two sides of the gateway are standing, and on the east face of these there are reliefs in which the king is seen worshipping Khnum and other deities. West of the gateway are many fallen granite blocks, which seem to suggest that the gateway led into a small temple or shrine facing east. It will be remembered that when Alexander the Great died, his son, who was still a boy, was proclaimed king; but it was not long before the various generals revolted, each making himself king of the country he was governing. Ptolemy Soter loyally supported the young Alexander for some time, and this gateway was probably built for the king by his orders. But when Alexander was murdered, Ptolemy made himself Pharaoh of Egypt; and the visitor will notice amongst

Other temples.
the ruins here a few blocks bearing his cartouches, the name Ptolemy being written sometimes in its early form *Pthulmys*. At various parts of the mounds there are blocks of stones from the temples; one or two are seen to bear the cartouches of Amenhotep IInd, while others bear those of Thothmes IIIrd. Near the modern houses at the north of the mounds stands a granite seated statue of Merenptah, the so-called Pharaoh of the Exodus. The statue is of poor workmanship, and is hardly worth glancing at. It has already been stated in the last chapter that on this island there existed a beautiful temple of Amenhotep IIIrd,

ELEPHANTINE

and another of Thothmes IIIrd, both of which were ruthlessly destroyed in 1822; and it will be realised that in olden times this end of the island must have appeared very much as does Philæ, with buildings rising in all directions and with terraces overlooking the water.

The Department of Antiquities performed some excavations here some years ago, and recently M. Clermont Ganneau and Dr. Rubensohn have conducted works of importance on the island. Both these explorations have resulted in the uncovering of the houses of the Aramaic town, and of parts of the temple buildings.

One of the most interesting "finds" of recent years was made here by M. Clermont Ganneau's party in 1907. Immediately behind the rest-house a chamber was discovered in which were several small stone sarcophagi, and on opening these they were found to contain the mummies of the sacred rams of Khnum, of the Ptolemaic period. The bodies were enclosed in cartonnage cases, covered with gold-leaf, each being modelled in the form of a ram.

Much of the town debris has been dug out by the *sebakhîn*, i.e. the peasants who are authorised by the government to carry away the ancient rubbish to place upon their fields as manure. The destruction wrought by these peasants is enormous, but it is necessary that manure should be provided, and it has not been found practicable to place artificial fertilising matter at the disposal of the farmers. The *sebakhîn* have hacked their way through the ruins of the various towns of Elephantine, until they have reached, in some places, the levels of the early dynasties; and here they have from time to time found papyri, some of which contained the invaluable correspondence of those princes of Elephantine whose tombs will be described in the next chapter.[1] In the upper levels they have discovered papyri such as those Aramaic documents described above. The amount of historical records which has been destroyed under their picks is no doubt large; but where ancient and modern interests clash it will be readily understood that the former have often to be ignored. These excavations have in places exposed the ancient brick wall which enclosed the city, and this may be seen on the south-east and south-west of the island, where it still stands to some height.

On a granite boulder, over which this wall passes, is inscribed the name of a certain Khufu-ankh, an official who lived at the end of

[1] Some of these precious documents are now in the Berlin Museum.

the reign of the great King Khufu of the IVth dynasty. This is the oldest rock inscription in the Aswân neighbourhood. Another granite boulder lying to the south of the village of El Kôm and north of the rest-house (No. 61-63) bears the names of King Unas of the Vth dynasty, Pepy Ist and IInd of the VIIth dynasty, Antefaa of the XIth dynasty, and Amenemhat Ist of the XIIth dynasty. On the rocks on the east and west of the island a few other inscriptions are to be seen, but these are not of sufficient interest to call for mention here.

The well of Eratosthenes. One other antiquity remains to be recorded, and for some this may have a considerable interest. It is a deep well dating probably from Ptolemaic times; and it is to be found just to the north of the rest-house. The sides of the well are made of broken stones, and a footpath, some 20 inches wide, winds round at a sharp incline to the bottom, which is now choked. The well is still some 25 feet deep, and at the top the diameter is about 12 feet. As no other ancient well is known anywhere in the neighbourhood, it seems quite possible that this is the place where Eratosthenes obtained his first datum for the measuring of the earth. Eratosthenes, it may be remembered, was an Athenian scientist who lived 276-196 B.C., and was attached to the museum at Alexandria. While at Aswân he noticed that the noon sun at midsummer fell perpendicularly into a certain well, casting no shadow. At Alexandria at the same time he observed that the angle determined by the shadow of the sun-gnomon equalled one-fiftieth of a circle, and he reckoned from this that the distance from Alexandria to Aswân must equal the fiftieth part of a meridian circle. Thus he developed his famous theory of shadows from these data, and this method of measuring the earth is, of course, still employed. It cannot be said with certainty that this is the famous well, but it is situated near the temple precincts in which Eratosthenes most probably stayed, and by its large size it would at once attract the eye were there no shadow in it.

Krophi and Mophi. The high granite rocks which rise on the east side of Elephantine near the Nilometer, and opposite these on the mainland between the Cataract Hotel and the railway station, form a kind of pass which is conspicuous for its rugged beauty. These rocks seem to have been known in ancient times as the "*kerti*, or sources, of Elephantine." A certain official in Lower Egypt told Herodotus that between Elephantine and Syene (Aswân) there were two peaks of rock called Krophi and Mophi, from between which the Nile gushed, part of it flowing southwards to Ethiopia, and part

SEHEL

northwards through Egypt. This wild story indicates that the priests of Khnum at Elephantine claimed that one of that god's abodes lay here beneath the waters between Krophi and Mophi; this being, perhaps, in rivalry with the priests of Philæ, who believed that the god lived under the rocks of Bigeh Island, opposite the temple of Isis at Philæ. In very early times it is probable that the Egyptians considered that the source of the Nile was at the First Cataract, but when Lower Nubia began to be known, the source became a mystery which they believed would not be revealed to man until, after death, he had penetrated to the Twelfth Gate of the Underworld.

SEHEL

The island of Sehel, which lies some distance to the north of Aswân, at the foot of the cataract, may be visited by sailing boat. The scenery is rugged and picturesque, and the visitor who is interested in antiquities will find much there to interest him. With a favourable wind the excursion occupies about three hours; but some will find it pleasant to take their lunch with them, and to picnic on the splendid rocks of the island. Extensive quarrying goes on at present at the east side of the island, where the visitor lands, but passing these works and walking south-westward, an open plain will be reached which lies between three groups of rocks. These rocks are covered with over 250 inscriptions, some of which are of great historical importance. Monsieur de Morgan numbered and catalogued most of these, but the numerals had in many cases faded, and there was some danger that the inscriptions might be damaged unwittingly by the quarrymen. The present writer, therefore, renumbered all of them as conspicuously as possible. By the following list of these inscriptions the reader will be able to identify most of those which have historical value. No. 70 (de M. 1), Chief of the Builders in the Temple of Amen, Chief Sculptor in the Temple of Ptah, and Chief Vase-maker in the Palace, Amenemapt. No. 72 (de M. 3), Viceroy of Ethiopia, Hora. No. 75 (de M. 5), High Priest of Sebek and Anpu. No. 76 (de M. 8), Viceroy of Ethiopia, Huy, adoring the cartouches of Rameses IInd. No. 78 (de M. 11), Cartouches of King Neferhotep of the XIIIth dynasty. No. 79 (de M. 12), Cartouches of Senusert IIIrd of the XIIth dynasty. No. 80 (de M. 10), Car-

Situation, &c.

The inscriptions.

touches of Aahmes IInd of the XXVIth dynasty. No. 81 (de M. 21) is reserved for particular mention at the end of this list. No. 82 (de M. 22), Cartouches of Neferhotep. No. 83 (de M. 20) reserved for particular mention. No. 86 (de M. 13) also to be recorded later. No. 87 (de M. 14), Cartouches of Senusert IIIrd. Nos. 88 and 89 (de M. 15 and 16), Cartouches of Neferhotep. No. 91 (de M. 18) to be discussed later, as is also No. 92 (de M. 19). No. 96 (de M. 29), Viceroy of Ethiopia, Sety, adoring the cartouches of Septah in his third (?) year. No. 99 (de M. 30), A High Priest of Khnum, Satet, and Anuket. No. 101 (de M. 31), Viceroy of Ethiopia, Paser. No. 105 (de M. 44), The relatives of King Neferhotep. No. 111 (de M. 39), Neferhotep before the goddess Anuket. No. 112 (de M. 40) to be described later. No. 117 (de M. 48), High Priest of Khnum, Satet, and Anuket. No. 133, Royal Fan-bearer, Captain of the Archers, Governor of the gold-countries of Amen in Lower Nubia. No. 137 (de M. 63), The thirty-third year of Rameses IInd, when a jubilee was celebrated. No. 145, *Ha*-Prince, Scribe of the Nome of Elephantine, Accountant of the Gold of the City. No. 146, Cartouches of Amenhotep IIIrd, and figure of the Vizir Rames, whose tomb at Thebes is described on page 160. No. 150, High Priest of Amen, Amenhotep. No. 159 (de M. 89), Prince Usersatet, and Chief of the Builders of the North and South, Rera. No. 161 (de M. 84), Prince Thothmes. No. 164, Scribe of the account of the Gold, Aahmes. No. 165, Prince Merimes and the cartouche of Amenhotep IIIrd. No. 173 (de M. 93), Officials adoring cartouches of Merenptah. No. 177 (de M. 102), Captain of Pharaoh's archers. No. 183 (de M. 110), Chief Ritual Priest of Kubbân (near Dakkeh in Lower Nubia). No. 186 de M. 113), Scribe and overseer of the builders of "Sun of Rulers," Merira. This is the name of the unfinished colossus of Amenhotep IIIrd in the Aswân quarries. No. 198, Viceroy of Ethiopia, Amenhotep. No. 199 (de M. 132), Figures of Rameses IIIrd and gods. No. 203 (de M. 135), Captain of the archers of Thoth, Chief of the Builders, Chief Ritual Priest, Ptah-hotepu of Memphis. No. 206 (de M. 138), Royal Ambassador, Master of the King's Horse, Menkheper, an official of the court of Rameses IInd. No. 208 (de M. 140), Partly erased inscription of the Chief of the Builders in charge of the two Great Obelisks, Amenhotep. As the name is partly erased, this may be the sculptor who was disgraced, and who left his various works unfinished in the Aswân quarries. No. 213 (de M. 148), Cartouches of Amenhotep IInd. No. 215, Rameses IInd worshipping gods, and below him a figure of the

SEHEL

Viceroy of Ethiopia, Huy. No. 217, Cartouche of Rameses IIIrd, No. 221, Cartouches of Rameses IInd, and figure of the Chief of the Builders, Nekhtu. No. 232, Vizir Paser before cartouches of Rameses IInd. No. 237, Viceroy of Ethiopia, Setau, before Anuket, and cartouches of Rameses IInd. No. 245 (de M. 182), Figure of the Chief of the Goldsmiths of the Temple of Khnum, holding a statue of a ram, while near him are a pair of balances marked "gold." No. 254, Cartouches of Rameses IInd. No. 262 (de M. 197), Scribe of the Temple of Amen and Superintendent of the Seal of the Lands of the South, Khnum-em-heb, adoring Rameses IInd. No. 278 (de M. 218), Thothmes IIIrd worshipping Khnum, Satet, and Anuket. No. 282 (de M. 214), Guardian of the Temple of Khnum and Satet of Sehel, Nebmeh. No. 290, Guardian of the Temple of Anuket of Sehel, Mersu. No. 295 (de M. 204), High Priest and Divine Father of Khnum. No. 297 (de M. 203), Captain of the Archers, Chief of the Builders in the Temples of Ra, Amen, and Ptah, May. No. 303, Chief Sculptor of the Temple of Ra, &c., Amenemapt.

In the above list there are certain inscriptions which require a further explanation. No. 81 is a long inscription cut on the rocks at the north end of the island, high above the cataract. It was written in Ptolemaic times, but tells the story of a great famine which devastated Egypt in the reign of King Zeser of the IIIrd dynasty, 3000 B.C. It states that Zeser, being at a loss to know what to do, sent up to Elephantine, where he believed the source of the Nile to be located; and the priests there told him that the famine was due to the anger of the god Khnum. Zeser therefore dedicated to him the land between the Egyptian frontier and the island of Takompso, near Dakkeh, in Lower Nubia; and he restored his ruined temples at Elephantine. The fact that the inscription was placed at the southern extremity of Sehel, combined with the fact that at this point so many persons have inscribed their names, indicates that this point was actually the frontier of Egypt. *The Zeser inscriptions.*

Inscriptions Nos. 83, 86, 91, 92, and 112 all refer to a canal which was constructed by Senusert IIIrd of the XIIth dynasty during his great campaigns against the Ethiopians. An inscription on the west side of the island towards its south end states that the canal was made in the king's eighth year, and was 150 cubits in length, 20 in breadth, and 15 in depth. It was called "Beautiful are the ways of Senusert IIIrd." Another inscription of Senusert IIIrd referring to this canal is written at the south end of the island, and *The Cataract Canal.*

thus one may suppose that the canal passed along the west and south sides of Sehel. The first inscription overlooks the water at a narrow point of the river between the island and the village of Mahetta on the mainland. There are here many rocks rising from the water, and it is probable that the canal ran between one of these rocky islands and Sehel, thus avoiding the great rush of water which passed down under the rocks of the mainland. The canal, of course, was merely a passage so levelled and protected that a rapid but steady flow of water ran down it, against which the galleys could be pulled with relative ease. Thothmes Ist found the canal choked with stones, and ordered it to be cleared; and Thothmes IIIrd again caused it to be cleared of stones, giving instructions that the fishermen of Elephantine should each year remove all obstructions from it.

Temples at Sehel. From the various inscriptions on the rocks one sees at once that Khnum, Satet, and Anuket were the gods of the island; but it is perhaps to Anuket that the greatest honour is here paid. A small shrine, now almost entirely destroyed, was erected to her by Amenhotep IInd; and the name of a guardian of this temple has already been noticed amongst the rock inscriptions. On the west side of the island, near a modern village, there are a few blocks of stone, covered with reliefs, which formed part of a temple built by Ptolemy IVth Philopator, apparently in honour of the same gods. A few late inscriptions, some written in Greek, show that the island was still visited by many travellers and officials in late times.

CHAPTER XX

THE TOMBS OF THE PRINCES OF ELEPHANTINE
—THE MONASTERY OF ST. SIMEON — OTHER
TOMBS AND ROCK INSCRIPTIONS ON THE
WEST BANK—THE NUBIAN HIGHROAD

THE TOMBS

THE tombs of the princes of Elephantine, sometimes called Situation.
the Grenfell tombs, owing to the fact that some of them were
opened by Sir Francis Grenfell (assisted by Dr. Budge) in 1885,
should be visited by all those who take any interest in antiquities.
They are situated on the slope of the high sand-covered hills
which form the west bank of the river, at a point almost opposite
the northernmost end of the island of Elephantine. High above
the tombs stands the Mohammedan shrine known as Koubet Ali
el Howa, which is a landmark for many miles around, and after
which the tombs are now generally named. At the water's
edge there are tumbled granite rocks, half buried in golden sand,
from above which an ancient double stairway of about ninety steep
steps leads up to the terrace of the tombs. These monuments
should be visited in the afternoon, as the hillside is then in
shadow, and the ascent is thus less trying. Ample time should be
allowed for the excursion, as the small sailing boats have some
difficulty in rounding the island of Elephantine and reaching the
western shore, unless the wind is entirely favourable. Tickets of
admission should not be forgotten.

On reaching the summit of the stairway the visitor finds himself The tomb
in the courtyard of the joint tombs of Prince Mekhu, and his son, of Mekhu.
Prince Sabna. The doorway at the south end of this court is
entered, which brings one into the great and sombre tomb of the
former prince, numbered 25. As has already been stated in
Chapter XVIII, Prince Mekhu lost his life while travelling in Lower
Nubia, during the reign of Pepy IInd of the VIth dynasty. It

seems that Mekhu was murdered by the inhabitants of a district called Mether, in the province of Utheth, or Arthet, somewhere in the neighbourhood of the modern Tomâs, not far above Korosko. Two persons of Mekhu's company, a ship's captain named Antef, and an overseer named Behkesa, escaped to tell the news; and Sabna, the son of Mekhu, very pluckily organised an expedition for the purpose of finding the murdered prince's body. He succeeded in bringing the body back to Aswân, and it was buried with great state in this tomb. Mekhu's titles were *Ha*-Prince, Royal Registrar, Sole Companion (a title held by the king's intimates), and Ritual Priest. On the west side of the doorway, as one enters, Mekhu is seen clad in a panther skin and kilt, his wife with him, and persons are bringing him offerings. On the left side of the doorway Mekhu is shown together with a male relation named Baa. One now passes into a gloomy hall, the roof of which is supported by eighteen round and somewhat rough pillars, on some of which there are crude figures and inscriptions. A curious bench-like altar stands between the third and fourth pillars of the middle row. It is formed of a slab of stone resting on three upright slabs. In the back wall of the tomb behind this altar there is a recess screened on either side by high walls; and at the back of this recess, lit by a ray of light, is a false door or stele, inscribed with a prayer to Anubis and Osiris for the soul of Mekhu. The only part of the tomb walls which retains any decoration is that on the right as one enters. Here we see Mekhu leaning on his staff while persons sacrifice to him; and beyond are harvest scenes—ploughing, cutting the corn, and conveying it away on donkeys. The burial chamber is approached by an inclined passage, now filled up, which leads from the north-west corner of the hall.

Tomb of Sabna. The front entrance to the next tomb which belonged to Prince Sabna is now blocked, and one approaches it through the tomb of Mekhu, of which it is a continuation. It is numbered 26. Sabna held the titles of *Ha*-Prince, Royal Registrar, Sole Companion, Ritual Priest, and Governor of the Lands of the South. The rescue of his father's body was conducted by him in the following manner. Sabna took with him a troop of soldiers and a hundred asses bearing presents with which to pacify hostile chiefs; and, having sent information to the king to justify his absence, he set out for Arthet, probably along the caravan road which leads to the modern Tomâs. There he found the body, and having made a rough coffin for it, he loaded it upon an ass. Difficulties were now experienced owing to the hostility of the natives, and Sabna

THE TOMBS

therefore sent them presents of incense, clothing, and an elephant tusk, three cubits long; at the same time stating that he also had a tusk six cubits long, which might be given in return for assistance rendered. This had the desired effect, and Sabna started on the return journey with his precious burden. Just as he neared his home he was met by a shipload of embalmers, priests and mourners sent from Memphis by the king, who had been pleased and touched on hearing of Sabna's filial piety. The king also wrote a letter to Sabna, in which he said: "I will do for you every excellent thing as a reward for this great deed of bringing back your father." After the burial Sabna went down to Memphis, and was there presented to the Pharaoh, who lavished upon him all manner of gifts, from an ointment-box to a grant of land. Returning to Elephantine he lived in prosperity, and was at last buried in the tomb now to be described.

The hall of the tomb contains fourteen pillars in two rows. Above the blocked entrance there is a square window now closed with a grating—an unusual feature in a tomb, and intended, probably, as an exit for the soul of the deceased when he went to visit again the scenes of his lifetime. Some of the pillars are decorated with figures and inscriptions, one near the door showing a figure of Sabna. On the back wall of the hall there is a scene representing Sabna in a boat spearing fish, and amongst the reeds hunting birds with a boomerang. Just to the south of this are two rough steles cut in the rock, followed by the main stele which is inscribed with a prayer to Anubis for the soul of Sabna. Returning through the tomb of Mekhu to the courtyard outside, and looking at the entrance to the tomb of Sabna, it will be seen that figures of the deceased are cut on either side, while his son and other persons are represented offering to him.

A stairway leads from the north end of this courtyard to a pathway at a higher level, and walking along this one passes a small, uninscribed tomb; a blocked-up tomb numbered 27, also uninscribed, and so on to a tomb numbered 28. This is a small, low chamber, not much over three feet in height, and thus it is too small to enter, but it may be seen quite well from outside. A shaft, now filled up, led from this little room down to the burial chamber below. On the north wall the deceased, who is named Heqab, is represented as a negro, and he is shown shooting with a bow and arrows. On the south wall he is accompanied by male and female relatives. It is possible that this Heqab is the son of Prince Serenpitua who lived at the beginning of the XIIth

Tomb of Heqab.

dynasty, and whose tomb, in which a son of that name is mentioned, will presently be described.

Tomb of Serenpitu. The path now leads past three tomb entrances to a large tomb numbered 31, entered through a courtyard excavated in the face of the hill. This is perhaps the finest tomb here. It was built for Prince Serenpitu, who lived during or soon after the reign of Amenemhat IInd, and whose titles were *Erpa-ha*-Prince, Royal Registrar, Sole Companion, Superintendent of the Priests of Khnum and Satet,'and Captain of the Troops of the Door of the Southern Lands. Serenpitu was the son of a lady named Satet-hotep; and as the tomb of Serenpitua, a prince who lived during the reign of Senusert Ist, contains a reference to a daughter Satet-hotep, one may perhaps suppose that Serenpitu was the grandson of Serenpitua by this daughter Satet-hotep.

One enters a carefully excavated hall, the roof of which is supported by six square pillars. There are no inscriptions in this hall, but on the right side of the aisle stands a fine granite table of offerings inscribed with the name and titles of the deceased. A flight of nine steps ascends to a long, narrow passage which penetrates into the rock in the axial line of the tomb. There are three niches on either side of this passage, in each of which stands an Osirid figure sculptured from the living rock. On the left wall of this passage, near the entrance, there is a good painting representing Serenpitu, who stands holding a staff and bâton (called *kherp*), while behind him is his son. Visitors should be careful not to touch this painting, which, being quite exposed, is, so to speak, in their care. At the end of the passage there is a small chamber having four pillars, upon each of which a figure of the owner of the tomb is shown. At the west end of this chamber, catching the shaft of light which penetrates through the passage, is the carefully painted recess or shrine at which the soul of the deceased was worshipped. On the left or south wall Serenpitu is seen with his wife and son; on the west wall he is shown seated before offerings presented to him by his son; and on the north wall he is standing again, his mother being before the offerings. The elaborate and carefully painted hieroglyphs here are examples of the best work of the kind now known. The shaft leading down to the burial vault descends from the north side of this chamber.

Tombs of Aku and Khua. The next tomb, No. 32, is a poor copy of that of Serenpitu. A six-pillared hall is first entered, and from this a long passage leads back into the chamber containing the shrine. The owner was named Aku, who seems to have lived at about the same date as the former noble. An interesting little painting shows him seated with his wife in a grape arbour, while his son offers him food. After passing this tomb the main pathway ends, and one continues the way by a smaller path which leads just under the walls of a small Coptic monastery. At this point there is a tomb which is half-choked with sand. Four pillars support the roof, and at the end of the room is the shrine. The brief inscriptions state that the tomb belonged to a certain Khua, whose titles were *Ha*-Prince, Governor of the Palace, and Sole Companion. Khua is said to have made several expeditions to Punt, which was a considerable undertaking. This and the following tombs have all been used as dwelling-places by the monks of the monastery. A stairway has been cut from them up to their buildings on the rocks above. The little monastery is constructed of unbaked bricks, and several chambers can still be made out. It commands a magnificent view of the river, and is not without its interest to the visitor, in spite of its dilapidated condition. *[The Coptic monastery.]*

A few yards farther is a roughly cut tomb, the entrance of which has collapsed, leaving an eight-pillared hall exposed to the daylight. On the east wall representations of the deceased can still be seen seated before a table of offerings, and also hunting birds and spearing fish. On the south wall he and his wife stand or sit before offerings, and there are here some very damaged scenes showing cattle being led in, birds being trapped, pots being made; but these are very difficult to make out. The tomb was owned by a Ritual Priest named Maaa, his wife, the Royal Handmaiden and Priestess of Hathor, named Ankhsen, and his son the *Ha*-Prince Khunes, who probably lived at the end of the VIth dynasty. *[Tomb of Maaa and Khunes.]*

Three small entrances are now passed, and then a larger tomb is reached, around the door of which are lengthy inscriptions. Entering it one finds oneself in a small, low hall, the roof of which is supported by four square pillars. A sloping passage descends to the burial chamber, while a square shaft on the left of the door seems to have been a later burial-place. The pillars are inscribed with the name and titles of the members of a family here buried, while on the right of the sloping passage there is a stele also inscribed. The names on the pillars are those of Sabna, also called Pepy-ankh, who was a Royal Registrar, Sole Companion, Ritual Priest, Caravan Conductor, and Governor of all the Lands of the South ; a personage holding the same titles named Zema, also called Mesna ; and a lady named Depemnefert, also called Depa. The name on the outside inscriptions and upon the stele is *[Tombs of Sabna, Zema, and Herkhuf.]*

428　ANTIQUITIES OF UPPER EGYPT

that of the famous Herkhuf, whose titles were *Ha*-Prince, Sole Companion, Ritual Priest, Chamber-Attendant, Judge at Nekhen, Royal Registrar, Caravan Conductor, Privy Councillor of all the Affairs of the South, and Governor of the South.

Life of Herkhuf. Unfortunately nothing is known of Sabna and Zema, but of Herkhuf much has been told. He lived during the reigns of Merenra and Pepy IInd of the VIth dynasty, and was one of the great nobles of Elephantine. He is said to have been a man who gave bread to the hungry and clothing to the naked; who ferried him who had no boat; who never spoke evil against any man, nor deprived a son of his inheritance; who set the fear of the king in the heart of the foreigners; and who performed journeys of exploration never before undertaken. While still a young man he accompanied his father, the Sole Companion and Ritual Priest Ara, on an expedition to the land of Aam, to the north of the Second Cataract. He was away seven months, and returned laden with gifts from the natives. Later in life he made a second expedition to Aam, and visited several other native states lying between Wâdy Halfa and Korosko. Still another of these dangerous expeditions was made to the land of Aam. Herkhuf set out on "the Oasis road," *i.e.* the road which leads to the Oasis of Kurkur, and thence branches westwards to the Oasis of El Khârgeh and southwards to Tomâs. At the junction he met some natives of Aam on their way to invade El Khârgeh, the chief and his army having already passed through. Herkhuf did not consider it conducive to Egyptian interests to allow the people of Aam to conquer the Oasis, and therefore he hurried after the chief, and, by means of fair words, induced him to turn back. This accomplished, Herkhuf seems to have accompanied the chief to Aam, and to have returned later with a caravan of 300 asses, laden with the presents which he had there obtained. While passing through other states, in the neighbourhood of the modern Derr, he met with considerable hostility; and had it not been for the fact that he had with him some of the much-feared soldiers of Aam it might have fared ill with him. A display of force resulted in the complete submission of these tribes, and he was conducted back to the desert roads in safety. Herkhuf, on his return, set out to visit the king at Memphis, and on his way down stream he was met by one of the king's galleys which had brought him a royal present of cakes, bread, wine, beer, and other provisions.

In the second year of Pepy IInd, who was then still a boy, Herkhuf made a fourth journey to Aam, and there he was fortunate

THE TOMBS

enough to procure one of the pygmies which some trader had captured in the lands farther south. Having brought the pygmy safely to Aswân, he informed the king, and in reply received the following letter :—

"Royal seal ; year 2, third month of the first season, day 15. The king's letter to Herkhuf.

"The Royal decree to the Sole Companion, the Ritual Priest, the Caravan Conductor, Herkhuf.

"I have noted the matter of this your letter, which you have sent to me, the king, to the palace, in order that I might know that you have returned in safety from Aam with the army which was with you. You say in your letter that you have brought all manner of gifts which Hathor has given to the Ka of the king, myself. You say also in your letter that you have brought a holy dancing dwarf from the Land of the Ghosts, like the dwarf which the Treasurer Baurded brought from Somaliland in the time of King Asesa. You say to my majesty, 'Never before has one like him been brought by any one who has visited Aam.'

"Each year I hear that you are doing that which your lord desires and praises ; you spend day and night with the caravans doing that which your lord desires, praises, and commands. My majesty will give you many excellent honours which will be an ornament for the son of your son forever, so that all the people will say when they hear what my majesty has done for you, ' Is there anything like this which was done for the Sole Companion, Herkhuf, when he descended the river from Aam, because of the vigilance which he showed in doing that which his lord desired, praised, and commanded !'

"Come northwards to the court immediately, and you shall bring this dwarf with you, which you have brought living, prosperous, and healthy from the Land of the Ghosts, to perform the dances of the god, and to gladden the heart of the king. When he goes down with thee into the vessel, appoint trustworthy people who shall be beside him on each side of the vessel. Take care that he does not fall into the water. When he sleeps at night appoint trustworthy people who shall sleep beside him in his cabin. Inspect them ten times a night. My majesty desires to see this dwarf more than the gifts of Sinai or of Somaliland. If you arrive at court this dwarf being with you alive, prosperous, and healthy, my majesty will do for you greater things than those which were done for the Treasurer Baurded in the time of King Asesa, according to the heart's desire of my majesty to see this dwarf. Commands have been sent to the Chief of the New Towns, the Companion, and Chief Priest, to command that sustenance be taken from him in every store, city, and every temple without stint."

In this letter one can see the excitement of the boy-Pharaoh, and one can only hope that the pygmy proved as amusing to him as he had expected. Herkhuf does not seem to have made any more expeditions after this, nor does the smallness of his tomb, shared with other members of his family, suggest that he amassed great wealth. In leaving the tomb the visitor should look once more at the inscriptions around the doorway, which relate so much concerning the life of Herkhuf; and it is not without its pathos that one reads there a prayer to all of us "living ones on earth who shall pass by this tomb" to say that formula which shall bring comfort to the soul of the old traveller. He reminds us that he is a Ritual Priest, and therefore knows the secrets by which he can in turn do us some small favour in the underworld.

Tomb of Pepy-nekht.

The next tomb, No. 35, is partly filled up. It consists of a small chamber, the roof of which is supported by two pillars; and here and there are traces of figures and inscriptions. Around the doorway on the outside are long inscriptions, which give the name, titles, and part of the biography of the noble here buried. This personage was named Pepynekht, and held the titles *Ha*-Prince, Sole Companion, Chamber-Attendant, Judge at Nekhen, Custodian of the Domain and Scribe of the Phyle of the Pyramid of Neferkara, Chief of the Phyle of the Pyramid of Merenra, Governor of the Pyramid-city of Pepy, Royal Registrar, and Governor of Foreign Countries. He lived during the reign of Pepy IInd of the VIIth dynasty, by whom he was much favoured. Like Herkhuf, he is said to have been a man of high moral character, who fed the hungry and clothed the naked, and only spoke that which was good. It will be remembered that Prince Mekhu, who lived during this reign, lost his life in the province of Arthet in Lower Nubia, and that Herkhuf had difficulties with this same tribe on his return from Aam. Pepynekht was ordered by the king to take an army into the troubled district, and to chastise the people there. This he did with much success, making a great slaughter of their captains and chieftains, and bringing others captive to Egypt, together with much spoil. Pepynekht was now sent to the Arabian or Sinaitic coast to rescue the body of a Commander of the Sailors and Caravan Conductor named Anankhet, who had been murdered together with all his men by the Beduin, while he was engaged in building a ship there for a journey to

THE TOMBS

Punt or Somaliland. The inscription here breaks off, but one may presume that the expedition was successful in recovering the body.

A few yards farther on is a tomb, the entrance of which is in the form of a two-pillared portico; and on the side of the left hand pillar there is an inscription in six horizontal lines, reading: " Hail, living ones . . . all you who are upon earth, who are happy . . . you who make to flourish your professions for your children. . . . Say a prayer for the soul of Senmes." Inside the tomb there is a four-columned hall, of good workmanship, and at one end is a stele which gives the name of Senmes again, who seems to have lived in the XIIIth dynasty. After this we pass two small, uninscribed tombs, and so reach the large tomb, numbered 36, which was the burial-place of Prince Serenpitua, a noble of Elephantine under Senusert Ist of the XIIth dynasty. One first enters a large and imposing courtyard, the doorway being built of fine white limestone, quarried probably at Toura (near Cairo). On either side of this doorway Serenpitua is seen seated, and holding a staff and bâton. Entering the courtyard, one sees that the tomb has had a portico consisting of a roof of thin slabs of stone supported upon seven square pillars. The roof has now disappeared, but the groove in the façade of the tomb into which it fitted can still be seen. On these pillars are figures of Serenpitua, and inscriptions giving his titles, which are :—*Erpa-Ha*-Prince, Superintendent of the Priests of Khnum and Satet, Prince (*Heridep aa*) of Lower Nubia (*Ta-Kens*), Governor of the Lands of the South, Royal Registrar, and Sole Companion. Little is known of the biography of this noble, but no doubt he participated in the activity of his master in Nubia.

At either end of the portico is a recess in which figures of Serenpitua and his wife are shown; while at the north end of the portico there is a square wall, which may be the burial pit. The scenes on the façade of the tomb are of considerable interest. Commencing from the south end one sees a large representation of Serenpitua standing in a boat and spearing fish in the water, which is quaintly drawn as though it had risen up to meet his spear. His wife sits in the boat and holds his legs to prevent him falling. On the prow of the boat a tame duck is perched, which has probably been trained as a decoy. His son, represented below his arm, is intended to be standing upon the bank. Above this scene is an inscription reading: " Catching fish and geese: by Prince Serenpitua." Above this scene are some spirited drawings of his oxen, and one sees some of these animals

Tomb of Senmes, &c.

Tomb of Serenpitua.

The façade.

brought to Serenpitua, who leans upon his staff and is said to be inspecting the cattle for a festival of the gods of Elephantine. Beside this scene there is a large figure of Serenpitua, and behind him a small figure carrying a staff and sandals, followed by a hound of the *slugie* breed and a bitch of another and smaller breed. On the north of the doorway is a corresponding large figure of Serenpitua, immediately behind which are the figures of a man carrying a staff and bow, and a *slugie* hound. Next, on the upper part of the wall one sees Serenpitua seated on a throne in a hall, the roof of which is supported by three delicate columns. Four women, each holding a flower, stand before him. The first is his wife, "his dear one, who is enthroned in his heart," Set-thena; the next figure is that of his mother, Set-then; following her is his daughter, Satet-hotep; and lastly comes his second daughter, Set-then. Below this scene three men are shown: the first is "his eldest son, his beloved one, the possessor of his properties, possessor of his inheritance, the excellent one of his house, the Prince Heqab, born of the lady Set-then"; the second figure is his son Heqab-herab; and the third figure is his son Heqabur. Lastly there is a curious scene representing a girl and two boys seated upon the ground, each holding one hand to the ear, and extending the other with one finger pointing. They are probably chanting a funeral song, as these attitudes are often connected with musicians in other tomb paintings and reliefs. Around the doorway are long inscriptions in which the titles of Serenpitua are given at length.

Interior of the tomb of Serenpitua.

Entering the tomb the visitor finds himself in a four-pillared hall, which has once been decorated with scenes painted on plaster; but these are now nearly all lost. On the south side of the doorway one can still make out a scene representing fishermen pulling at the two ends of a net which is being dragged through the water, in which many fish are shown. The other scenes are too much damaged to describe, but one may discern fragmentary boats and various figures; while on the north side of the doorway parts of an elaborately painted inscription remain. From this hall a long passage, with a slightly vaulted roof, leads to an inner chamber, the roof of which is supported by two pillars; and at the end of this chamber is a recess and shrine. The whole tomb shows that considerable care and skill was expended upon its execution; and it is evident that Serenpitua was able to command the services of the best artists of the day.

The pathway now passes northwards, descending slightly and

THE TOMBS

leading to a small tomb, enclosed by a wall, which is situated on a spur of the hills about a hundred yards distant. This is the tomb of Kagem-em-ahu, the High Priest of Khnum, Satet, and Anuket, which, by the style of the paintings, may be put down to the late New Empire. It was discovered by Lady William Cecil and Mr. Howard Carter in 1902. One first enters a courtyard, which had a pillared gallery on either side, now almost entirely destroyed. The walls of the courtyard have been covered with paintings executed on plaster, but these were never finished, and now are for the most part destroyed. On the west side of the south wall there is a damaged scene showing the deceased High Priest standing between two red-robed goddesses, of which one is the goddess of Amenta, who stands amidst the western rocks. At the south end of the west wall the funeral boats are shown crossing the river from Elephantine and arriving at the western shore, where offerings have been heaped up, and where two servants stand weeping. The largest of the vessels is furnished with an elaborately decorated shrine, and, drawn in outline, there are two figures of Isis and Nephthys weeping on either side of it. At the north end of this wall one sees the soul of Kagem-em-ahu kneeling before the cow of Hathor which emerges from the western rocks in which it was thought to dwell. Above this there is a faint scene of the weighing of the heart of the deceased. At the west end of the north wall Kagem-em-ahu prays before Khnum, and at the east end he stands before other deities now too damaged to be recognised. On the east wall the mummy of the High Priest is seen standing upright, supported by a priest. Before the mummy kneels his wife, whose tears are seen streaming down her face as she casts dust upon her hair. The little figure is very well drawn, and the breast and drapery are executed with an unusual freedom of touch. Behind the mummy is a stele on which his titles are inscribed, and behind this again is the representation of a pyramid-shaped tomb built at the side of the rocks. It may be that this is an actual picture of this tomb, in which case a masonry or brick pyramid rose above it.

Entering the tomb, which is very low, the visitor finds himself in a hall with four pillars supporting the roof. Persons wearing hats should be careful not to let them touch the ceiling, which is covered with delicate paintings. Near the door this ceiling decoration shows a great blue scarabæus supporting the sun's disk upon its head, which is adored by green-coloured baboons. Down the middle aisle are beautiful flights of blue and white pigeons and

Tomb of Kagem-em-ahu.

wild duck against a background of yellow; while on other parts of the ceiling are elaborate geometrical patterns. These patterns are divided by bands of inscription, which give prayers to Ptah-Seker-Osiris, Nefer Tum, Isis, Anubis, and other gods, for the soul of Kagem-em-ahu. The walls of the hall are not decorated, but on one of the pillars are representations of the deceased in the presence of Osiris and Isis. A recess at the end of the chamber probably contained the statue or stele of the High Priest. The burial chamber is entered by a sloping passage at the west side of the hall.

This completes the series of tombs which are to be seen here, and the visitor can now descend to the river at this point, to which the boatman should have been told to proceed.

THE MONASTERY

Situation, &c.

The monastery of St. Simeon should most certainly be visited by all those who have any interest in Christian history, and even those to whom the past does not appeal will find it the goal of a very pleasant excursion. The monastery stands about a mile and a half south of the "Grenfell" tombs, and less than half a mile back from the river. The excursion should be made by boats in the early afternoon. The afternoon lights are far more beautiful than those of the morning as they fall upon the ruins and the surrounding desert, but for the visitor who has not much time at his disposal it may be better to visit the "Grenfell" tombs and the monastery in one long morning. The point to which the boat should be directed is a little bay in the western bank just to the south of the granite rocks rising from the water at the southern end of "Kitchener's" Island, and nearly opposite the south end of Elephantine Island. This bay lies at the mouth of a valley full of blown sand, which runs up between the hills for a short distance. In the hills, at the south side of the bay, a few rock tombs of a late period are to be seen, but these lack inscriptions or decoration, and are not worth visiting. The boat passes into the still waters of the little bay, and moors against the yellow sand, where grow a few green rushes. As one commences to walk up the valley the ruins of the monastery come clearly into sight, standing boldly on the edge of a promontory on the south side of the valley. A short climb brings one to the outer east wall, and the

THE MONASTERY

entrance will be found through a domed portal halfway along the length of this.

The monastery was founded in very early times, the date being unknown, and it was destroyed by the expedition sent into Nubia by Saladin, commanded by his brother Shems-ed-Dulah, in 1173, when Theodorus was bishop of Aswân. Shems-ed-Dulah routed out the Christian communities wherever he found them. In some cases he slaughtered the monks, but more generally he was content with destroying their property, and imposing a tax upon all those who professed Christianity. As one enters the portal there will come to the mind of the more imaginative a picture of the holy men as they fled before the Arabs, and it will not be without a kind of reverence that the visitor will notice the different indications of the faith which cost the monks so much. The monastery is surrounded by a high wall of rough stones, topped by a smaller brick wall, and the area thus enclosed must be some 7000 square yards in size. At intervals along this enclosure wall there are towers, and this, with the stone and brick construction, gives to the fortifications so much the appearance of a Roman building that one is inclined to suppose that the monks built their monastery within some deserted fortress of that period, perhaps that of Contra Syene, which is known to have existed, and may well have been situated here.

The enclosed area is divided into an upper and a lower level by a low face of cliff, which cuts through it from north to south. The portal in the eastern wall leads directly on to the lower level, where was the main chapel and some buildings constructed in connection with a row of caves cut into the cliff's side. A stairway leads to the upper level, upon the north end of which rises the two-storied main building. The north wall of this is built above the enclosure wall, and the north windows thus look out over a steep precipice descending into the valley. To the south of this building is an open courtyard, while numerous other buildings stand farther back, and also on the east side. To describe the monastery now in more detail we may commence at the main entrance again. Opposite this is a domed and whitewashed chamber with Coptic inscriptions upon the walls. Passing through this the visitor finds himself in the large church, the roof of which (originally a series of domes) has fallen in. The lower part of some square pillars and walls are to be seen amidst the debris. In the east end is the domed altar-recess, upon which is a fairly well-preserved painting of Christ seated, clad

History of the monastery.

The buildings.

The church.

in gorgeous robes, and raising His hand in the sign of benediction. The face is much damaged, but otherwise the painting is not in bad preservation. On either side of this figure stand two angels, the two main angels being winged, long-haired, and robed in elaborate garments. On either side of the recess are seven seated figures. There is a small vaulted chamber to right and left. At the west end of the church is a small recess with damaged paintings. Leading from the north-west corner of the chapel is a highly decorated cave, with an elaborate ceiling pattern. There have been paintings of saints all around the walls, but in each case the faces are intentionally damaged. This cave was evidently considered to be of great importance, and one may suppose that it was here where the patron saint originally dwelt as a hermit amidst the ruins of the Roman fortress before founding the monastery. There are several other caves farther along, some filled up, but none are decorated. It is possible that originally they were tombs of the Pharaonic age.

<small>St. Simeon's cave.</small>

The visitor should now ascend to the upper level by the steps on the north side of the church. Entering the main building through a small chamber, and turning to the right, he will find himself in a long and wide corridor, with vaulted roof partly fallen in. This corridor was lighted by windows at the north end. On either side small chambers lead off, and one perceives that this was the monks' dormitory. The third room from the south on the left-hand side of the passage should be selected for examination, as being the best-preserved example of the series. In this room mud brick benches are built around the walls, capable of resting about six persons lying in a somewhat cramped attitude. Six little cupboards are let into the walls, each with a small shelf in it. Three narrow windows, or slits, light the room. The walls are whitewashed, and are decorated with ornamental bands of colour, and with geometrical designs. The decoration has evidently been left unfinished, as though the painter had been interrupted in his work by the news of the approach of Shems-ed-Dulah's army. On one of the walls of the corridor is a painting of Christ, an angel, and six apostles; but the faces are all damaged. A passage leading from the west side takes one into a large hall, originally roofed by a series of domes. This was probably the refectory or common-room.

<small>The main building.</small>

Returning now to the entrance and ascending a further flight of steps, another corridor is reached, which ran immediately above the lower one. This, however, is inaccessible owing to the

THE MONASTERY

damaged state of the floor. The steps now continue to the top of the building—a somewhat dangerous climb, but well worth undertaking for the sake of the view from the roof. Looking down the valley up which the visitor has come, he will see the river in the distance; and he will here obtain a comprehensive view of the intricate buildings of the monastery. Descending the stairs again and walking to the west end of the enclosure, the battlements should now be climbed by way of the steps at the north-west corner. From here a fine view may be obtained of the rugged and desolate wilderness in which the monks lived. The wide, sweeping sand-drifts are particularly striking in the afternoon light; and the soft blue shadows, contrasting with the billowy, sunlit surfaces, form a scene of almost mystic beauty. The main building, looked at from this side, is imposing. The tower-like walls rise to a height of thirty feet or more, the plastered surface being relieved here and there by narrow windows. It is unfortunate that nothing is being done for the preservation of this interesting building, with its fine paintings and well-preserved fittings. The Coptic monasteries are not under the charge of the Department of Antiquities, and they do not interest the present heads of the Coptic Church; but private enterprise might do much.

The west of the enclosure.

TOMBS AND INSCRIPTIONS

In returning to the river the path along the top of the cliffs on the south side of the valley should be followed; and presently the visitor arrives at a point where the rock tombs, mentioned above as being near the river, are overlooked. Here there is a cemetery mainly consisting of rock chambers approached by sloping passages and of deep shaft-tombs. Lady William Cecil and Mr. Howard Carter conducted a small excavation here in 1901, but nothing of importance was found. The date of the cemetery is late dynastic and Ptolemaic. A wonderful view of the river and of the town can be obtained at various points along this road from the monastery. The path now descends to the valley at the point where the boat has been moored; and the return journey to Aswân or Elephantine, with a favourable wind, is performed in a few minutes.

A few inscriptions are to be found on the rocks overlooking the water not far to the north and south of the valley leading to the monastery. Some of these have been written by priests of Khnum, Salet, and Anuket, and most of them date from the New Empire.

THE NUBIAN HIGHROAD

The Prince of Elephantine, Herkhuf, whose tomb has been described in this chapter, states that on his second journey to the land of Aam he set out by the "Elephantine road," and descended at Arthet, which is, as will be seen in the next chapter, the district around Tomâs in Lower Nubia. Large numbers of inscriptions written by caravan conductors are found on the rocks at Tomâs, and it is obvious that these persons had come thither along the great highroad which still runs from Egypt to this part of Lower Nubia along the western desert. Now if the visitor will climb the hills on the south side of the valley leading to the monastery of St. Simeon, and will make his way southwards towards a prominent Shêkh's tomb and a conspicuous boulder just west of it, he will soon come upon an ancient road which sweeps up from the valley and mounts the hill by a well-built causeway. Following this road he will find that it passes about thirty yards to the west of the above-mentioned rock, bends to the right, and so runs over a ridge. This road, starting as it does from a point immediately opposite Elephantine, and leading up to a point where it meets the caravan road to Tomâs (*i.e.* Arthet) which is still used, is evidently the "Elephantine road" referred to by Herkhuf. The visitor should now examine this conspicuous rock more closely, and he will find that upon it many inscriptions have been cut, most of which date from the XVIIIth to the XXVth dynasties. The following are amongst the persons who have left their names here: An *Erpa-ha* Prince, Superintendent of the Priests of Khnum, Salet, and Anuket, named Thoth-hotep; a High Priest of the same gods; a Second Priest, and an official of the temple of these gods; a Scribe of the Province of Elephantine and of the Account of the Gold of the Province; a Scribe of the Gold of Wawat; a Scribe of the Account of the Gold of Amen; another Scribe of the Gold of Wawat; a Chief Builder of Amen; a Chief Builder in the Temple of Amen; a Chief Builder and Sculptor of Amen; another Chief Sculptor; a Captain of the Archers; and various Libation-Priests. A wall of rough stones has been erected around the rock, and one sees that it has been used as a kind of shrine marking the beginning of the road. To the west of

Inscriptions on the boulder.

the rock for a wide area on either side of the route the ground bristles with little heaps of stone, some surmounted by a block set upright. Both in this area and around the rock there are many fragments of broken pots. It is thus clear that we have here the terminus of a much-used roadway, the travellers along which were wont to leave a small heap of stones and a pot of water (?) as an offering to the gods when setting out from or returning to Elephantine, while it became customary for some of the more important officials in the New Empire to inscribe their names here.

As the visitor stands here and looks down at these indications of ancient travel and adventure he will not fail to be stirred by the thoughts which they arouse. Here Prince Sabna marched on his way to rescue the body of his father; here Prince Herkhuf set out on his adventurous expeditions to Aam; and here countless other Egyptians have passed, some bent on exploration, some to make war on the negroes, some to trade with the merchants in the Land of the Ghosts, and some, as one sees in their rock inscriptions, to collect the gold from the Nubian mines. The road, here paved with stones, passes over the ridge and down into the boundless hills and valleys of the desert; and there will be a few at least of the readers of this guide who will follow into the country to which it leads.

CHAPTER XXI

THE HISTORY OF LOWER NUBIA

The extent of the country.
IN ancient times the country of Lower Nubia extended northwards as far as the neighbourhood of El Kâb. It is at about this point that the aspect of the country changes, and instead of the wide fields of Middle Egypt there are only narrow strips of cultivated land at the water's edge, alternating with stretches of rock and desert. In the XVIIIth dynasty and onwards the Viceroy of Kush, or Ethiopia, ruled from El Kâb southwards, but as the title of this official is always "Viceroy of Kush and Governor of the Southern Lands" it is not necessary to suppose that the country called Kush extended any farther north than the Second Cataract. From Wâdy Halfa to Aswân the territory was known as *Ta-kens*, "The Bend-Land," or "The Land of the Bow"; and, as will be seen, there were three or four principalities included in this district, while between Aswân and El Kâb there was the nome of Edfu. The Egyptians were always at war with "Kush the Vile," but seldom in dynastic history is a war recorded with Lower Nubia. In the viceroy's title the country north of the Second Cataract was included in the "Southern Lands," and is quite distinct from Kush. When, therefore, in the following history one reads of the king smiting Kush, one must remember that it was above Wâdy Halfa that the war took place, unless the people of Kush had invaded Lower Nubia. Throughout almost the entire history of the Nile Valley the people of Lower Nubia were the faithful allies of the Egyptians, and assisted the Pharaoh to keep the Kushites under control and in their own territory. When Senusert IIIrd drove these Kushites back from the land north of the cataract, which they had invaded, the people of Lower Nubia celebrated his victories and converted him into a national hero, worshipping him in a deified form for several hundreds of years afterwards. In the following account of the history and antiquities of Lower Nubia, therefore, one has nothing

THE HISTORY OF LOWER NUBIA 441

to do with Kush, except in so far as it affects some question in Lower Nubian affairs.

Perhaps the earliest historical evidence of Egyptian influence in Lower Nubia is to be found in the drawing of an archaic king on a rock near Gerf Husen. In Ptolemaic times the priests of Philæ stated that King Zeser, the first sovereign of the IIIrd dynasty, ruled Lower Nubia as far south as Takompso, *i.e.* the Island of Derâr, near Dakkeh; and there is no reason why one should doubt this. The people of Lower Nubia at this early age were in part the close relations of the archaic Egyptians, and the people buried in the great prehistoric cemeteries of Egypt had similar utensils and similar funeral customs to those found in the early cemeteries of Lower Nubia. On the rocks at Toshkeh one of the archaic inhabitants of the country is drawn, and from this one sees that the custom of wearing a feather in the hair, which is so often depicted in later Nubian scenes, was already in existence. This figure carries a bow and arrow, and as there is considerable later evidence to show that this weapon was in very general use amongst the natives here, it may be that the country's name *Ta-kens* owes its origin to the habit. The early inhabitants were good draughtsmen and delighted in covering the rocks with drawings of the gazelles, oxen, giraffes, elephants, and other animals which they saw around them, as well as with drawings of boats and sometimes of themselves. ^{The archaic period.}

It is in the IVth dynasty that one obtains the first insight into Nubian affairs. King Sneferu conducted a campaign against Lower Nubia or Kush, and records the fact that he captured seven thousand prisoners and two hundred thousand cattle. This must have practically ruined the country, and one hears nothing more of it until a century and a half later, when Userkaf, the founder of the Vth dynasty, visited Aswân, and most probably organised the government of the region above that town, thereby making it possible for his successor, Sahura, to send his officials up as far as Tomâs, where the name of that king is found. During the reign of King Asesa, at the end of the Vth dynasty, a naval officer named Khnumhotep wrote his name on the rocks at Tomâs; while three officials of the time of Teta, of the VIth dynasty, also recorded their names on these rocks. In the reign of Pepy Ist war was made on the Beduin of the Eastern Delta, and a great noble of the period, named Una, was commanded to collect an army of negroes from Nubia. This he did, taking the men from the tribes of Arthet, Mazoi, Aam, Wawat, Kaw, and Temeh. ^{The IVth to VIth dynasties.}

ANTIQUITIES OF UPPER EGYPT

The tribes of Lower Nubia.

In the present writer's opinion the country between the First and Second Cataracts in the VIth dynasty is to be divided amongst these tribes in the following manner. The rugged country between the First Cataract and the Bâb el Kalâbsheh or thereabouts belonged to the tribes of Kaw. At this time there was a cataract rushing down the Bâb, and a natural frontier would thus be formed. Between this and Koshtâmneh lived the Sethu. Just south of Koshtâmneh the country on the west bank completely changes in aspect, the sandy desert taking the place of the shelving rocks. Along this bank, as far south perhaps as Derr, lived the Mazoi; while on the east bank opposite them, and in the rocky valleys running back towards the eastern desert, lived the people of Wawat. At about Tomâs on the west bank and Ibrîm on the east began the territory of Arthet. Probably there were rapids at this point, and thus there was a natural frontier as before. Arthet extended southwards to just above Abu Simbel, where again there were probably rapids. Above Abu Simbel the aspect of the country entirely changes once more, and becomes more open and sandy; and here one may place the people of Aam, whose southern frontier was perhaps the Second Cataract. Each of these tribes thus occupied an area quite as large as most of the nomes or provinces of Egypt, and there is, therefore, no need to consider them as extending beyond the Second Cataract, and the above arrangement cannot be said to cramp them into an unnaturally small space.

Under Pepy's successor, Merenra, Una was appointed Governor of the South, his province extending as far south as the First Cataract only. This cataract and the neighbouring district was now known as "the Door or Frontier of the South," of which some high official was always "the Keeper." The fact that Una was able to collect troops above "the Door" shows that the Lower Nubian tribes were friendly; though, as the frontier was so clearly marked and so well guarded, the Egyptian control there must have been loose.

Career of Una in Lower Nubia.

Una was now sent to the First Cataract to dig five canals at the most difficult points for the transport of boats. He was then ordered to build three cargo boats and four ordinary boats, in order to bring down from the quarries at the south end of the cataract the granite blocks destined for the king's pyramid. For the building of these boats Una invited the negro chiefs of Arthet, Wawat, Aam, and Mazoi, to cut the timber, which they did with such promptitude that Una is able to state that the whole undertaking, including

THE HISTORY OF LOWER NUBIA 443

the making of the canals and the building of the boats, was completed in one year. Now the building of the boats must have taken at least three months, for in the present day one vessel of a thousand *ardebs* takes from six weeks to three months to build if the work is carried out quickly. The cutting down of the trees must have taken three months at least, for between five hundred and a thousand acacia trees would have been required to build the seven large vessels; and their floating down the river must have required another month. To complete the whole undertaking in a year, therefore, shows that these works in the extreme south of Egypt must have been well organised.

At about this same time another noble, the Herkhuf whose tomb we have seen near Aswân, was commanded by King Merenra to make an expedition to Aam in order to discover the best means of opening up communications with that country. The expedition occupied seven months, and brought back with it "all manner of gifts" from the Aamites. Soon after this Herkhuf made a second expedition, which he describes in the following words: "I set out upon the Elephantine road, and I descended [to the river] at Arthet, Makher, Tereres, and Artheth, being an affair of eight months. When I returned I brought gifts from this country in very great quantity. . . . I descended to the dwelling of the chief of Sethu and Arthet, after I had explored these countries. Never before had any noble or caravan-conductor who went forth to Aam done this." The Elephantine road, upon which Herkhuf started, is probably the great road which runs on the west bank south of the Grenfell tombs, and which is approached from the valley which leads to the monastery of St. Simeon. This road runs southward at no great distance from the river, except where it cuts inland to avoid the bends, and for that reason it is much used by persons who are in no hurry and who do not wish to carry much provision along with them. Herkhuf descended to the river perhaps at Arthet and Makher on his way up, and at Tereres and Arthet again on his way down, afterwards being entertained by the chief of Arthet and of Sethu. Tomâs is the point at which most persons who now use the road descend to the river for the first time after leaving Aswân, and the rocks here are covered with inscriptions of the VIth dynasty. There is thus some likelihood that the principality of Arthet may have included Tomâs; and, as will be seen presently, there are other facts which point to the same conclusion. The second descent is generally made just above Abu Simbel, a district which in Ramesside times was called Maha.

Career of Herkhuf in Lower Nubia.

This name is not altogether unlike Makher, when one remembers that a thousand years would separate the two readings. The third descent is usually made at the Second Cataract, and in this neighbourhood one must look for Aam. If it was on his return journey that Herkhuf visited Tereres, one may perhaps identify this place with Taray, a town which is to be identified with Anâybeh, as will be pointed out later. He may have next descended into the principality of Arthet somewhere about Amada, which was one of the usual resting-places, as the many graffiti on the rocks prove. Herkhuf then visited Sethu, a district which is known to have been below Arthet; and he boasts that this route was one which had not been followed before. This probably indicates that he returned by way of the great Korosko bend : a route which the complete lack of graffiti along its course shows to have been rarely used. Herkhuf was again sent on an expedition to Aam in later years, and this expedition he describes as follows : " His Majesty sent me a third time to Aam. I set out on the *What* road, and I found the chief of Aam going to the land of Temeh to smite Temeh as far as the western corner of heaven. I went after him to the land of Temeh, and I pacified him, until he praised all the gods for the king's sake. . . . Now when I had pacified that chief of Aam [I descended to the river] below Arthet and above Sethu, and [there] I found the chief of Arthet, Sethu, and Wawat. I descended with 300 asses laden with incense, ebony, grain, panther-[skins], ivory, boomerangs, and every good product. Now when the chief of Arthet, Sethu, and Wawat saw how strong and numerous were the soldiers of Aam which descended with me . . . this chief brought and gave me bulls and small cattle, and conducted me to the roads of the highlands of Arthet."

To understand this expedition it must first be pointed out that the Temeh are the same as the later Temehu, the semi-Libyan inhabitants of the Oases, who cannot have been in any great numbers farther south than El Khârgeh. The chief of Aam was therefore probably invading the Oasis of El Khârgeh. Now the only road to El Khârgeh which runs from the region of the Second Cataract meets the road from Tomâs near that place, and runs to the Oasis of Kurkur. Here there is a junction, and one road runs towards the Nile which it meets at Daraw, while the other road runs to El Khârgeh. The word *what* is to be identified with *wahet*, " oasis," and the " *what* road " spoken of by Herkhuf must therefore be this Daraw-Kurkur road. This route from Egypt to

THE HISTORY OF LOWER NUBIA 445

the Second Cataract *viâ* the Kurkur oasis is the best one to be taken, and is generally used by express caravans at the present day. It seems that when Herkhuf arrived at Kurkur he found that the chief of Aam had passed through this junction shortly before him, on his way to drive the Temehu westward. Herkhuf, remembering that Una, as has been seen, recruited troops from these Temehu, thought it very necessary to prevent their extermination; and he therefore hurried along the Kurkur-Khârgeh road to catch the chief up. This he succeeded in doing, and with him he returned to Kurkur, and thence to the river at a point below Arthet and above Sethu, where he found the chief of these two tribes and of the tribe of Wawat. Arthet probably did not extend northwards much beyond Amada, and Herkhuf may have descended to the river at some point such as Medik, to which place a road leads from the Kurkur-Tomâs road, and on the rocks of which there are many VIth dynasty graffiti like those at Tomâs. Herkhuf was now conducted by the chief to some road such as that on which he had travelled on his first expedition, and thus he returned to Aswân.

After the death of Merenra Herkhuf made a fourth expedition to Aam, and on his return he wrote to the young King Pepy IInd, dating his letter in the second year of his reign, and informing him that he had brought back a pigmy from Aam. The king was immensely pleased, and wrote to Herkhuf, saying, "Come northward to the court immediately, and bring with you the pigmy which you have brought living, in good condition, and healthy, from the land of ghosts, for the amusement of the king, to rejoice and gladden his heart." It is probable that Herkhuf had heard of these pigmies while he was in Aam, and had managed to obtain this one, through the agency of the Aamite chief, from the far south.

These expeditions of the VIth dynasty had opened up the country, and had brought it under Egyptian rule. To the new régime the various tribes objected, and a revolt soon followed. The official Mekhu, while on an expedition somewhere above "the land of Wawat and Utheth" [probably Arthet], was murdered; and as soon as the news was brought to his son Sabna an expedition was fitted out, and every effort was made to recover the body. It seems to have been Sabna's first consideration to find his father's body and give it decent burial, and the punishment of the culprits was postponed. Sabna actually took presents to the chief of Wawat and Utheth, and made friendly overtures to him. Later in life Sabna, as we have seen, *Expeditions in the VIth dynasty.*

was made "Governor of the South," but the Lower Nubians seem to have been still in a rebellious state; and the General Pepynekht had to be despatched to teach them a lesson. Pepynekht states that his orders were "to hack up Wawat and Arthet," and that he slew large numbers of the enemy, including the chief's children and the nobles, while others were taken prisoners. On his return he was sent again to these countries to arrange for their future government; and he brought back to the king the two chiefs of Wawat and Arthet, together with their children and some of the nobles. A period of absolute peace followed, and a certain Khnumhotep states that he accompanied a great personage named Khuy to Punt, and another noble named Thethy to Kush, on eleven expeditions. This is the first mention of the name Kush, and here, as in later times, it no doubt designates the country above the Second Cataract. During the obscure period which followed one may perhaps place the King Hor-nefer-hen whose cartouche is found three times on the rocks at Tomâs. In one of these three inscriptions reference is made to the land of Arthet, which is a further indication that that tribe is to be located near Tomâs.

The XIth dynasty. The next reference which one finds to Lower Nubia dates from the reign of Menthuhotep IInd of the XIth dynasty, when, in the forty-first year of that king, an official, named Kheti, refers to Wawat in vague terms. During all this period, from the VIth to the XIth dynasties, Egyptian officials seem to have travelled very considerably in the country, for, as will be seen in the following pages, they have left numerous graffiti on the rocks. But towards the end of the XIth dynasty, the feeble rule of the Egyptian Pharaohs left the chieftains of the different tribes free to manage their own affairs; and when Amenemhat Ist,

The XIIth dynasty. founder of the XIIth dynasty, reasserted his rights, the Lower Nubians were at first unmanageable. In the well-known "Teachings" of Amenemhat Ist, he says, "I seized the people of Wawat, I captured the people of Mazoi"; and on a stele at Korôsko, dated in the king's twenty-ninth year, there are the words, "We came to overthrow Wawat . . .," the end of the inscription being lost. This was the second and last revolt of the Lower Nubians until Ptolemaic times.

Senusert Ist. Senusert Ist, the next king, made the now peaceful Lower Nubia the basis of a campaign against Kush, and in his eighteenth year he was able to set up a tablet at Wâdy Halfa stating that he had conquered ten of the tribes who lived above that town and prob-

THE HISTORY OF LOWER NUBIA 447

ably above the Second Cataract. In the forty-third year of Senusert Ist the Prince of the Oryx Nome, named Ameny [Amenemhat] records that at some time previous to this date he sailed up with the king to conquer the Kushites, taking with him a contingent of the troops from his nome ; and on a rock at Amada he seems to have recorded his name. In the forty-fifth year, Senusert Ist inscribed his name on the same rock ; but it is a question whether he was here on a tour of inspection or was returning from another campaign in Kush. On this rock the next king, Amenemhat IInd, records his fifth year ; and at Dehmêd his third year is recorded. During his reign an official named Sehathor states that he visited Lower Nubia, and went round the islands of Ha. The name *Ha* is referred to in the New Empire at Abu Simbel, and it may have been situated in that neighbourhood. There are islands opposite Gebel Addeh, but, on the other hand, the largest groups of islands are to be found in the reach between Ermenneh and Tomâs.

At this period the Kushites began to get out of hand, and it is probable that they invaded Lower Nubia. The new king, Senusert IInd, was much agitated by this southern danger, and he seems to have regarded an invasion of Upper Egypt as imminent. He therefore constructed the huge brick wall around El Kâb, which to this day encloses the ruined city. To him the great wall along the cataract road at Aswân may be attributed ; and as the first mention of the Lower Nubian fortresses is made in this reign, it is probable that he built these also. An official named Hapu has recorded at Aswân the fact that he made "an inspection of the fortresses of Wawat." The great fortresses of Lower Nubia, not including those at the Second Cataract which were built by Senusert IIIrd, are three in number. The most northerly stands at Koshtâmneh, the next at Kubbân, and the third at Anâybeh, the last two being named Baki and Taray respectively. In the New Empire the land of Wawat had practically absorbed all the other tribes of Lower Nubia, and the beginnings of this development are here seen, since Anâybeh fortress seems to have been included under the general term "fortresses of Wawat." There was now no question of disaffection amongst the Lower Nubians ; the energies of all were combined in the attempt to meet the negroes from Kush, and to drive them back to their own land. The fact that no fortress was built higher up stream than Anâybeh perhaps shows that the country to this point was already in the hands of the enemy.

Senusert IInd.

448　ANTIQUITIES OF UPPER EGYPT

About this time Senusert IInd died, and was succeeded by Senusert IIIrd. This king was now called on to face one of the greatest crises in Upper Egyptian history. The war against Kush which had to be undertaken was this time no amusement for a dull year; but there would have to be a long series of campaigns, and the negroes would have to be slowly rolled back beyond the Second Cataract.

Senusert IIIrd. Senusert IIIrd, at the very beginning of his reign, cut a canal at the First Cataract, in order to allow his fleet to sail up on to higher water; and in his eighth year he had it enlarged and improved. Its length was 150 cubits, its width 20, and its depth 15. In this same year he passed through the canal to commence his campaign. By this time the people of Kush must have threatened the frontier at Aswân, for Senusert gave orders to have the fortress at Elephantine strengthened. The war was apparently a series of successes for the Egyptians, and before the close of the eighth year the king had driven the Kushites back beyond the Second Cataract. The invasion of these southern negroes had been such a serious menace to Egypt that Senusert IIIrd now made the strictest laws regarding the frontier, and on the great stele set up at Semneh, near the cataract, he states that this boundary stone was placed here "in order to prevent any negro from crossing it by water or by land, with a ship or leading herds; except a negro who shall come to trade . . . or who has a commission. Every good thing shall be done to these, but a ship of the negroes shall not be allowed to pass by Semneh, going down stream, for ever."

Eight years later the Kushites had become so restless again that the king was obliged to conduct another campaign against them, and to re-establish his frontier at Semneh. This time he engraved a very remarkable inscription on the boundary stone, in which he states that it is his nature to do what he says and to act promptly. He jeers at the Kushites for being conquered upon their own borders, and he says of them that "they are not a strong people, but are poor and broken in heart." He states that he captured their women, slaughtered their herds, reaped their grain, or fired their crops. His scorn of his enemies, however, was by no means sincere, for he made every effort to prevent them again invading Lower Nubia, and he even erected a statue of himself at the frontier "in order that ye [the troops] may fight for it," and prevent it being taken. The huge fortresses around the Second Cataract were now built, but the king was obliged to visit the country once again during his reign. Great rejoicings followed on the conquest of the invaders, and the Lower Nubians were so sincerely grateful to the king that they established annual feasts in his honour, and presently began to regard him as a god; while by the New Empire Senusert IIIrd had taken his place as one of the great gods of Lower Nubia. The frontier was still maintained in the reign of Amenemhat IVth, for that king records the height of the Nile at Kummeh (near the cataract) in his fifth year.

In the XIIIth dynasty, under Sekhemra-Khutawi, a commander of the Semneh fortress records the Nile level; while another king of this obscure period, Neferkara-Sebekhotep, left a small statue of himself which was afterwards carried to Arko. In the troubled times of the XIIIth-XVIIth dynasty the throne of Egypt fell to the strongest man, and there were few who managed to hold it above a year or so. One Pharaoh puts the word *nehsi*, "the negro," in his cartouche; and as will be seen presently there were other Nubian Pharaohs.

The XIIIth dynasty.

The inscriptions on the rocks throw considerable light on this period. In several places in Lower Nubia the present writer found the names and titles of two kings who certainly are to be dated to this time, and who seem to have reigned successively. The names of these kings are Kakara and Seanra, and, judging from the fact that their most elaborate inscriptions are to be found between Tomâs and Tôshkeh, the largest being at Ibrîm, one may suppose that they were originally princes of that district. After the VIth dynasty one does not hear again of the tribes of Arthet and Sethu. The land of Wawat seems now to have absorbed Sethu, and Aam appears to have pushed northwards over the territory of Arthet. In the XVIIIth dynasty one finds the principality of Maam extending from Derr to Ermenneh, and it is well within the bounds of probability that Aam and Maam are to be identified. It must be remembered that these names were foreign to the Egyptians, and in early times there were certainly many discrepancies in the spelling of them. Thus Arthet is sometimes called Artheth, sometimes Wtheth, and apparently sometimes Wthek. Wawat is called Wawaw, and sometimes Waat. Aam itself is sometimes called Amam and Amemaaw in the VIth dynasty inscriptions, and the former is practically the same word as Maam or Emaam. The princes of Maam in the New Empire are the most important nobles of Lower Nubia, and their territory was recognised as late as Græco-Roman times.

It is not, then, pushing one's conclusions too far to see in these kings, Kakara and Seanra, two princes of Maam or Aam, who had taken this opportunity of calling themselves Pharaoh. Their rule extended northwards well into the territory of Wawat, for the cartouche of Kakara is found on the rocks at Gerf Husen. At another time during this obscure period a king who called himself Iabkhentra arose. His cartouche is found at Medîk and Abû Hôr, which, perhaps, indicates that he was a prince of Wawat, whose capital was in the neighbourhood of Sebûa. On the rocks at Dehmîd another king of this period is mentioned. His cartouche reads Hakara or Wazkara, and the accompanying inscriptions name one of his nobles.

The XVIIIth dynasty. Towards the end of the XVIIth dynasty the princes of Thebes began to assert themselves; and, preparatory to their attempt to overthrow the Hyksos, they made an effort to consolidate their power by obtaining control of Lower Nubia. An inscription found by the present writer at Tôshkeh gives the cartouches of Kames and of Aahmes Ist; and it is thus evident that these kings' dominions extended to the Second Cataract. It was this fact which allowed Aahmes to conduct his wars in Lower Egypt without distractions from the south; and it was not till his twenty-second year that he found it necessary to turn his attention to Nubia, and even then it was only to punish the nomads perhaps above the Second Cataract. Shortly after this a rebellion, led by a prince called Teta, broke out at a place called Tanttaamu, "She of the land of the water-supply," by which is probably meant Aswân, though it may be that it refers to some place in Lower Nubia. The inscription from Tôshkeh mentions a Prince Teta, who may have been the son of Aahmes Ist, and it is just within the bounds of possibility that he may be identified with the rebel. Amenhotep Ist conducted a campaign against Kush, and seems to have made great havoc amongst the negroes, no doubt much to the delight of the Lower Nubians. At about this period one reads of an official named Hermana, whose duties lay both in El Kâb and in Wawat, which indicates that Wawat now extended northwards to the Egyptian frontier without other tribes between. Thus Wawat and Maam now divided Lower Nubia between them; in a scene painted in the tomb of a certain Huy at Thebes two lines of negroes are shown, the first being "chiefs of Kush, &c.," and the second "the chief of Maam, the good ruler, and the chiefs of Wawat." In Wawat there was the military district of Baki, which centred in the fortresses of Kubbân and Koshtâmneh; and in Maam there was the district of Tarey, the fortress of that name

THE HISTORY OF LOWER NUBIA 451

being situated at Anâybeh. In the neighbourhood of Abu Simbel there was the civil district of Maha, and at Wâdy Halfa was the district of Beheni. These last were probably independent of Maam. At the Second Cataract the great fortresses formed a third military district.

On the death of Amenhotep Ist a decree announcing the accession of Thothmes Ist was set up at Kubbân, and another at Wâdy Halfa ; and almost immediately the king made war on Kush, and set the Egyptian frontier at or above the Third Cataract. On his return to the First Cataract he had the canal of Senusert IIIrd cleaned and restored ; and his dahabiyeh sailed through on its way to Thebes with the dead body of the chief of his enemies hanging head downwards from the prow, to be jeered at by all the people of Lower Nubia as he passed. The king now appointed a governor of this district, whose title was " Royal Son [*i.e.* Viceroy] of Kush, Governor of the Southern Lands," and whose province extended from El Kâb in the north to Napata in the far south ; and for several centuries afterwards this viceroyalty was maintained.

On the death of Thothmes Ist the people of Kush again rebelled, and had to be subdued by Thothmes IInd. This king seems to have built a temple at Dakkeh, for his name has been observed there. Early in the reign of Thothmes IIIrd a temple at the Second Cataract was built, and offerings were established for the god Dedun, a deity who must have been of Kushite origin, as he is hardly ever mentioned in Lower Nubian temples. Amongst the offerings "the water of Wawat is referred to." It has been seen that the name Wawat now designated the country as far north as the First Cataract. In later times the Nile was thought to have one of its sources at the island of Bîgeh near Philæ, and on this island is a statue of Thothmes IIIrd. Thus one may perhaps suppose that the sacred "water of Wawat" came from the Bîgeh neighbourhood. This king built considerably in Lower Nubia. A statue of his was seen at Kalâbsheh ; blocks inscribed with his name are found at Dakkeh ; a stele of his comes from Kubbân ; he seems to have built the temple of Kûrteh ; he commenced to build the temple of Amada in his old age ; at Ellesîyeh a shrine was made by him in his forty-third or fiftieth year ; and at Kasr Ibrîm he also excavated a shrine in the face of the cliff in his fifty-second year. It was during these last years of the king that his attention was turned to Nubia, and he conducted the usual campaigns against Kush. His Viceroy Nehi

Thothmes IIIrd.

had governed the country meanwhile, and in the Annals of the King one reads of the impost of Wawat each year. In the thirty-first year this consists of 31 oxen and calves, 61 bulls, and one of the harvests. In the thirty-third year it consists of 20 slaves, 44 oxen and calves, 60 bulls, and a harvest. In the thirty-fourth year there were 254 *deben* of gold (a *deben* weighing from 80 to 100 grammes), 10 slaves, and an unknown number of oxen. In the thirty-fifth year there were 34 slaves, 94 oxen, calves, and bulls, and one of the harvests. In the thirty-eighth year the tribute consisted of 2844 *deben* of gold, 16 slaves, and 77 oxen and calves. In the thirty-ninth year there were 89 head of cattle, and some ebony, ivory, and other merchandise. In the forty-first year 3144 *deben* of gold, 79 head of cattle, and some ivory, &c., were brought in. In the forty-second year there were 2374 *deben* of gold, and one of the harvests. Unfortunately the tribute of other years is not preserved, but from the above one can see that the king's hand was not particularly heavy on the country. There were two or sometimes three harvests in the year, but the government does not seem to have taken more than one of them, and the number of cattle and slaves is very small. The gold seems to have come from the Wâdy Alâki, probably by way of Kubbân and Tôshkeh, and the fact that nearly 300,000 grammes were produced each year shows that the mines were vigorously worked.

It is interesting to notice that the tribute of Lower Nubia is now called that of "Wawat." In some of the yearly lists the tribute of Kush is also given; and, as there is no mention of Maam, one must suppose that Wawat was now recognised as the main principality of Lower Nubia. Yet, at about this date, various graffiti make mention of princes of Maam, and priests and officials of that country; while the god "Horus, Lord of Maam," is invoked over as large a region as was at any time under the influence of this principality. It may be that Maam was exempt from taxation; but, on the other hand, this general use of the name Wawat to denote the whole of Lower Nubia is indicated by other evidence. Graffiti at Gebel Addeh, above Abu Simbel, mention officials of Wawat; and one official who there calls himself "Scribe of the Offerings of all the gods of Wawat" inscribes his name at Dendûr, where he refers to Horus of Maam. Even at Ellesîyeh, which is close to the site of the capital of Maam, an official of Wawat inscribes his name amidst those of the priests, scribes, and the Prince of Maam. One sees, thus, that the name Wawat was now the usual term for Lower Nubia, although the

THE HISTORY OF LOWER NUBIA 453

principality of Maam and the less important districts of Maha, Beheni, and Baki still retained their individuality.

Another interesting record of taxation occurs in the tomb of Rekhmara, where the government is said to receive as a tax from the commandant of the fortress of Bîgeh 20 *deben* of gold, 5 good hides, apes, 10 bows, 20 large staves of cedar wood ; and from the commandant of the fortress at Elephantine 40 *deben* of gold and one chest of linen. The taxation of the officials of the other towns and settlements as far north as Assiût is given, but two or three *debens* are all that are asked of them in gold. The importance of Lower Nubia as a gold-bearing region is seen from these records of the tribute and taxation. The mines of Wâdy Alâki, as has been said, were certainly approached from Kubbân, and perhaps from Tôshkeh also. An inscription of a high official at Tôshkeh gives him the title of "Superintendent of the Gold of . . ."; and the importance and prosperity of the east bank of the river in this region is perhaps due to the influx of gold. It is almost certain that Korôsko was never used as a starting-point for the mines, as it is so often thought to have been, for there is hardly a single inscription or graffito between Medîk and Amada on either side of the river, and the east bank continues without traces of ancient activity as far north as Kubbân.

Amenhotep IInd, the next king, was also an energetic ruler of Lower Nubia. Early in his reign he completed the temple of Amada begun by his father; and it is on a tablet here that he tells how he carried one of his captive Asiatic princes up to Napata and hanged him on the walls of that town. The reliefs in the temple of Kalâbsheh show Amenhotep IInd amongst the gods, and it is probable that he was the builder of a temple here. At Anâybeh he seems to have erected a temple, and at Kasr Ibrîm he excavated a shrine near that of his father. At Bîgeh his name has also been found. His wars in Kush resulted in the establishing of the frontier permanently at the Fourth Cataract. Thothmes IVth was the next king, and during his somewhat weak rule the Nubians "from above Wawat" revolted, and were reconquered. In the king's mortuary temple at Thebes a tablet marks the quarter where the "colony of Kush the Vile, which his Majesty brought back from his victories," was located. The rebels "from above Wawat" thus seem to have been Kushites living above the Second Cataract, and thus one has here another indication of the use of the name Wawat at this period to signify all Lower Nubia. This king's only monument here is the hall of the temple of

Amen-
hotep
IInd.

Amada, which was added by him to the building of Thothmes IIIrd and Amenhotep IInd.

Amenhotep IIIrd.

Under Amenhotep IIIrd the tribes of Kush again rebelled, and the viceroy Merimes was obliged to collect an army in friendly Lower Nubia. An inscription recording the muster runs : " He collected troops, commanded by captains, each man with his village, from the fortress of Baki to the fortress of Taray, which is 52 *aters* of sailing." Baki is, of course, Kubbân ; and, taking an *ater* to be about 2.22 kilometres, Taray would be situated 115.38 kilometres above Kubbân—that is to say, in the neighbourhood of Anáybeh, at which town the present writer found the ruins of a great fortress. The army was thus collected from the land which seems to have been occupied by the fighting Mazoi. During the reign of Akhnaton these Mazoi seem to have been used as police in the king's new city. Under the next king, Tutankhamen, the Viceroy of Kush was a certain Huy, in whose tomb at Gûrneh are the scenes representing the chief of Maam and the chiefs of Wawat, which have been mentioned already. At Gebel Addeh a damaged cartouche may give the name of the next king, Ay. Under King Horemheb the rock temple of Abahûdeh was excavated, and at Kubbân his name has been found. It was, no doubt, a considerable undertaking for this soldier-king to reorganise these southern provinces after the slack rule of his predecessors, but the Kushites do not seem to have given him much trouble.

The XIXth dynasty.

Rameses Ist of the XIXth dynasty has left a record at Amada of some event which occurred in his first year, and the mutilated inscription refers to a viceroy of Kush, while in the next year he left inscriptions at Wâdy Halfa. Sety Ist seems to have built at Dakkeh and Amada, and together with his father he appears at Wâdy Halfa in a temple inscription. In his third year Rameses IInd undertook some mining operations in Wâdy Alâki district, and he records on a stele found at Kubbân how he found water in an abandoned well of the time of Sety Ist after sinking it for a few cubits farther. He here refers to Wâdy Alâki as the district of Akaata. This king built or completed several temples in Lower Nubia. These are at Kalâbsheh, Gerf Husen, Sebua, Derr, Abu Simbel, and Ashkeh. Various shrines and stelæ are also found, as will be seen in the following pages. In these temples he executed reliefs representing his conquests in Asia, Libya, Ethiopia, and especially his so-called victory over the Hittites. His wars in Kush, however, are shown in a very sketchy manner, and it is not possible to follow their course. Nowhere is

Rameses IInd.

THE HISTORY OF LOWER NUBIA 455

Lower Nubia referred to as an enemy, and one must regard this country as still enjoying the friendship and protection of Egypt. But now most of the high officials and princes were Egyptianised, and one sees from the various inscriptions that they had ordinary Egyptian names. Thus at Abu Simbel one reads of "the Scribe of the Treasury, the Commander of the Troops in the Country, the Deputy, Mery, *of Wawat*," and these last words, on the analogy of another inscription of a viceroy of Kush named Any, who calls himself "*of Heracleopolis*," refer to his nationality. At Ermenneh a prince of Maam inscribes his name, which is Rahotep; while at Ellesîyeh and Tonkâleh princes of Maam with the names Mes and Thothmes are recorded. The next king, Merenptah, does not seem to have had much trouble in Lower Nubia; but the political importance of the country as a gold-bearing and a military district is shown by the fact that the next king, Septah, made every effort to obtain its support. He bribed the Viceroy of Kush with rich gifts, and arranged that the gold mines should be placed in his hands, thus making as much as possible of this source of wealth. Many inscriptions of his reign are found in the Wâdy Halfa neighbourhood, and at Amada his cartouches and those of his queen are inscribed. The viceroys ever since the XVIIIth-XIXth dynasties had been called "Superintendents of the Gold-country of Amen," and this title is held by the above-mentioned Viceroy of Septah. The power of the Amen priesthood is thus seen, and Septah, by obtaining the fidelity of the officials at this point, could command the resources, and hence the support, of this priesthood.

Rameses IIIrd conducted the usual wars in Kush, but it is not until the reign of Rameses VIth that one obtains the next insight into Lower Nubian conditions. Of this date there is a tomb at Anâybeh belonging to a certain Pennut, who held the offices of deputy of Wawat, chief of the quarry service, and superintendent of the Temple of Horus of Maam. This temple is one of the many shrines of the Horus of this principality, and it is probable that a temple of which the present writer found traces at Anâybeh is here referred to. Pennut was a man of considerable wealth, and he erected a statue of Rameses VIth in the temple, and endowed it with the income derived from parts of his estate. In return the king presented him with two silver vases, sending the viceroy to him to make the gift, who said in doing so that the king was pleased with that which Pennut did in the countries of the negroes and in the land of Akata. Akata, as has been seen above, is the

The later Ramesside Pharaohs.

Wâdy Alâki region, and Pennut's title of "chief of the quarry service" may refer to the mining operations. Certainly there are no quarries of any size in this part of Lower Nubia. The fact that Pennut lived at Anâybeh is a further indication that Wâdy Alâki was reached from the Tôshkeh-Ibrîm neighbourhood, as has been suggested above. Pennut, in describing the limits of his endowments, refers to the estate of Queen Nefertari and to the flax-fields of the king, thus showing that much of the land hereabouts was the private property of the royal house.

In the reign of Rameses XIIth an important alteration was made in the administration of Lower Nubia. It has been seen that in the new kingdom the gold-mining operations were regarded as being under the jurisdiction of the viceroy on behalf of the priesthood of Amen. This, no doubt, led to many difficulties between the Church and the State; and finally Herhor, the high priest of Amen, who afterwards seized the throne, took the extraordinary measure of combining the offices of high priest and viceroy of Kush. Upper Nubia had ceased to be a menace to Egypt as a military power, and Lower Nubia was now regarded solely as a gold-producing district which did not require a military administration. Egypt, as far south as the First Cataract, was more or less consolidated into one kingdom, and thus a viceroy resident at El Kâb was of little use. The duties on the frontier at or above the Second Cataract seemed no longer to call for special energy on the part of any official, and therefore the high priest of Amen found an excuse for obtaining from the weak king the supreme authority over these southern regions, which authority meant nothing to him but the control of the gold supply. Rameses XIIth signed not only the death warrant of his house in thus handing over the mines to Herhor, but he made the supremacy of Ethiopia over Egypt a possibility. For now that there was no proper administration of Lower Nubia, the people of Kush were able to make their influence felt there, and it was not long before they turned most of the incoming gold in the direction of Napata. In Egypt the title of Viceroy of Kush soon became purely nominal, and was in one case given to a princess. In Ethiopia the new wealth brought prosperity and a line of more or less civilised kings, who called themselves Pharaohs of Egypt. In the eighth century B.C. a king of this line, named Piankhi, took possession first of Lower Nubia and then of all Egypt; and thus the despised Ethiopians, always known as "Kush the Vile" or "Kush the Wretched," became masters of their former conquerors.

THE HISTORY OF LOWER NUBIA

Lower Nubia was during this period very much neglected, and there are very few contemporaneous inscriptions or buildings. Even the gold mines seem to have been but feebly worked, and most of the caravans set out from points in Upper Nubia. The temples were more or less deserted, and half a century later the foreign soldiers of Psametik IInd were able to cut their names over the legs of the colossi at Abu Simbel with impunity.

The Ethiopian Pharaohs.

Piankhi's successor, Shabaka, was followed by another Ethiopian named Shabataka, who after a short reign was murdered by Shabaka's nephew, Taharka, who then seized the throne. Napata was still the real capital of these kings, but Tanis in Lower Egypt seems now to have been made their northern residence. Taharka reigned unmolested for several years, but at last was utterly defeated by the Assyrians, and was forced to retire to his southern capital. After a few years, however, he managed to regain possession of Upper Egypt, and even in Lower Egypt his name was sometimes used in the dating of documents. An inscription of his eighteenth year is found on the road from Kalâbsheh to Tâfeh, and it may be that this was written at the time when he made his first movements towards regaining his Egyptian kingdom after his defeat. Taharka has left his name on an altar at Philæ, and on a block of stone at Kasr Ibrîm, and his Egyptian monuments are quite numerous. The next king, Tanutamen, made a desperate attempt to drive out the Assyrians, and at first his arms were attended with success; but the inevitable defeat followed, Thebes and the Upper Egyptian cities were sacked, and Tanutamen fled to Napata. With him ended the Ethiopian supremacy in Egypt, and henceforth the negro kingdom extended to the First Cataract only.

A few years later, about B.C. 625, a king of Nubia named Aspelta, who was probably a descendant of Tanutamen, erected a stele at Napata, from which one learns that at this time the kings of Nubia were elected by six nobles, their choice being ratified by the priesthood of Amen. Contemporary with Aahmes IInd of Egypt reigned the Nubian king Horseatef, and a long list of his conquests in the Sudan is preserved. Amongst the holy shrines mentioned by him is that of Ra of Mehe, which may perhaps be *Maha* or Abu Simbel. Another Nubian sovereign, named Nastasen, seems to have been the king who defeated the expedition sent by Cambyses to Nubia in B.C. 525. The names of several other kings are known, but their reigns cannot be dated, and can only be said to have been before the Greek supremacy in B.C. 332. It is

458 ANTIQUITIES OF UPPER EGYPT

probable that these kings did not exert much control over Lower Nubia, nor, on the other hand, did the kings of Egypt. The names of neither sovereigns are found between Philæ and the Second Cataract. At the former place Nectanebus IInd built a shrine, and there are inscriptions on the rocks which indicate that the sacred islands were regarded as Egyptian property. The shrines and temples of Lower Nubia at this time fell into ruins, and remained unrepaired. At Dendûr two chieftains, named Petisis and Pehorus, rose into momentary fame, and were later worshipped as demigods; and it is possible that Mandulis of Kalâbsheh was also one of the heroes of this period. The Nubians at this time had almost lost the civilisation which they had derived from the Egyptians, and had passed into a state of splendid barbarity. Tales of their wealth and of their strength began to drift into Egypt, and soon Ethiopia became a land where giants and demigods lived. When Cambyses, for example, sent some gifts, including a bow, to the King of Nubia, that sovereign sent back an enormous Ethiopian bow, with a message stating that Cambyses must not attempt to invade his country until his troops could draw a bow of that size. Cambyses' envoys told wonderful tales of the physical strength of the Nubians, and of their wealth. The gold mines were, no doubt, worked by them, and this must have been a constant source of riches. They were said to reach the age of one hundred and twenty years, and it is quite possible that they actually were very long-lived. In Lower Nubia the petty princes no doubt held the power, and recognised the authority of the government at Napata.

The Ptolemies. On the accession of the Ptolemaic dynasty Lower Nubia soon began to claim the attention of Egypt. Although the Ethiopian power extended in its full force only as far north as the Second Cataract, the most of the gold which came in by the Lower Nubian mine-roads was now sent to Napata, and the district round Dakkeh and Kubbân was one of the busy centres from which it was despatched. Contemporary with Ptolemy IInd of Egypt there was reigning in Ethiopia a young king whom the Greeks called Ergamenes, and whose Egyptian name was Arkamen. He had been educated at the Ptolemaic court, and he had there learned to think as did the Western world of the time. Consequently he very soon offended the priesthood of his country, and they, acting on some ancient barbaric custom, ordered him to put himself to death. Ergamenes, however, did not stand in awe of the priests as did his ancestors, and he immediately marched a body of troops to the

THE HISTORY OF LOWER NUBIA 459

temple and cut the throats of the whole priestly community. This act seems to have rendered his position dangerous in Upper Nubia, and very soon afterwards he is found reigning as king of Lower Nubia, his southern frontier being the island of Takômpso, the modern Derar, near Maharaka, and his northern being at the First Cataract. Dakkeh was his capital, and thus he had command of the caravan routes to the mines. Philæ and the neighbourhood appears to have been neutral ground, and here Ptolemy and Ergamenes could meet in friendship. This little kingdom was known as the land of the Twelve Schoinoi, a schoinos being usually reckoned as $7\frac{1}{2}$ miles. It was the same district which, according to tradition, King Zeser of the IIIrd dynasty had given to the priests of Philæ. It was less than half of Lower Nubia; and in an inscription at Kalâbsheh the territory of Isis is reckoned at one stage during this period as extending from the First to the Second Cataract. It was, however, a rich country, and included some of the largest towns in Lower Nubia.

Ergamenes at once commenced to beautify his new capital, and he built on the site of the ruined temple of the XVIIIth dynasty a shrine dedicated to Thoth of *Penubs*, *i.e.* "the Place of the Sycamore," a name which he had given to that part of his capital where now stand the ruins of the temple of Maharaka. It is possible that the place had been so named in memory of the Penubs of Upper Nubia, over which he had reigned. By this time Ptolemy IInd and his successor, Ptolemy IIIrd, were both dead, and the throne of Egypt was occupied by Ptolemy IVth. This king now paid Ergamenes the compliment of building on to the temple of Dakkeh; and after a few years Ergamenes returned the kindness by restoring the buildings of Ptolemy IVth at Philæ. The two kings, who may well have been comrades, are thus seen to have worked hand in hand for the good of their country; but when they both grew old there seems to have been much friction. Ptolemy Vth, the next king, is found to have mutilated the cartouches of Ergamenes at Philæ, and it is probable that he claimed the temple as Egyptian property. The next Nubian king, Azkheramen, was, at all events, obliged to build his temple at Dabôd, which is a short distance from Philæ. At this time Upper Egypt was in a very troubled condition, and it was not till well on in the reign of Ptolemy Vth that matters again became settled. At Philæ an inscription of Ptolemy VIth states that that king, in his twenty-fourth year, presented the land of the Twelve Schoinoi to Isis of Philæ, and from this it is seen that, when the Nubian troubles had come to an end and the Nubian king Azkheramen was dead, the little kingdom was handed over to the administration of the Philæ priesthood and ceased to be an independent state. Ptolemy VIIth found everything quite peaceful, and was able to add an inscription to the temple at Dabôd. He also left his mark on the island of Heseh, just above Philæ. Ptolemy IXth dedicated a shrine at Dabôd, and he also built at Dakkeh. Ptolemy Xth undertook a little building at Kalâbsheh; but by this time the Ethiopians were again becoming aggressive on the southern frontier, and there does not seem any longer to have been an energetic administration of the Twelve Schoinoi between this and Philæ.

The Roman occupation.

With the advent of the Romans Lower Nubia came in for considerable attention. Under Augustus the great temple of Kalâbsheh was built, and the temples of Dabôd, Dendur, and Dakkeh were added to. Cornelius Gallus, the Roman prefect of Egypt, invited Ethiopian ambassadors to meet him, and it was arranged that the "Land of the Thirty Schoinoi," *i.e.* from the First to the Second Cataract, should remain Ethiopian, but should be under Roman protection. It was probably about this period that the inscription was written on the rocks in the Bâb el Kalâbsheh stating that Isis owned these Thirty Schoinoi. Very shortly after this, however, the Ethiopians, under their one-eyed queen, Kandake, decided that the Roman protectorate was not conducive to their happiness; and, while the Egyptian prefect, Ælius Gallus, was otherwise engaged, they collected an army of 30,000 men, captured all the Nubian outposts, and established themselves at Aswân itself. Gaius Petronius, the new prefect, with a force of 10,000 infantry and 800 cavalry, defeated them and drove them back to Dakkeh, where in a pitched battle he utterly routed them. Many of the flying negroes ran through the town of Kôrteh, and clinging to rafts and pieces of wood, made their way across the river to the island of Derar. The remainder retreated to Kasr Ibrîm, and when Petronius had driven them out of that fortress they retired to Napata, were they finally capitulated. No sooner was his back turned, however, than Kandake again resumed the offensive, and had to be defeated once more. Petronius then organised the district from the First Cataract to Derar as a military province, and returned to Egypt. For a short time he also kept a garrison of 400 men at Kasr Ibrîm, building a fortress on the hill-top, and supplying it with provisions for two years.

For many years Lower Nubia now remained unharassed, and there is every indication that the country enjoyed the greatest

THE HISTORY OF LOWER NUBIA

prosperity. The names of various emperors are found in the temples, and considerable building works were undertaken. According to the Itinerary of Antoninus the Roman military stations were now listed as follows :—

				Roman Miles.
West Bank.	From Contra Syene to	Parembole	16
	,, Parembole	,, Tzitzi	2
	,, Tzitzi	,, Taphis	14
	,, Taphis	,, Talmis	8
	,, Talmis	,, Tutzis	20
	,, Tutzis	,, Pselcis	12
	,, Pselcis	,, Corte	4
	,, Corte	,, Hierasycaminos	4
East Bank.	,, Syene	,, Philæ	3
	,, Philæ	,, Contra Taphis	24
	,, Contra Taphis	,, Contra Talmis	10
	,, Contra Talmis	,, Contra Pselcis	24

The most important strategic point was the Bâb or Pass of Kalâbsheh. At Kalâbsheh was the station of Talmis commanding the south end of the pass; and at Tâfeh were the stations of Taphis and Contra Taphis guarding its north end. Here large bodies of troops were collected, and one sees at the modern Tâfeh how the officers attempted to make themselves comfortable in this distant land, forcing the natives to build them houses of hewn stone for the sake of coolness, and erecting pavilions on the top of the cliffs at the point where the view is finest and the wind blows most freshly.

This state of security, however, could not last. For some time the wild tribes of the eastern desert, known as the Blemmyes, had begun to intrude themselves into the northern part of Lower Nubia, and by the reign of Probus in A.D. 276 they had extended their influence over the whole of Lower Nubia and the Thebaid. The Roman force in this part of the country had now been reduced in numbers, and when Diocletian became emperor he was obliged to vacate the whole of Lower Nubia, and to fix his frontier at Aswân. The Blemmyes made Kalâbsheh their capital, and many of their tombs are to be seen on the hills around. Meanwhile Diocletian invited the Nobadae, a wandering tribe of the western desert, perhaps related to the ancient Mazoi, to settle between Kalâbsheh and Thebes, and he offered them an annual subsidy on condition that they kept the Blemmyes in check. This arrangement seems to have worked well until the days of Marcianus, A.D 450, when the Blemmyes are again found raiding the Thebaid. The general Maximinus, however, thoroughly defeated them, and they were glad to make the best terms they could. It was agreed that there should be peace for a period of one hundred years, that all Roman prisoners should be released, that an indemnity should be paid, and that hostages should be handed over. The Blemmyes, on their part, were allowed to visit the temple of Philæ, and on certain occasions to take the statue of Isis into their own country, returning it undamaged at the end of the fixed period.

This peace, however, was not kept for long, and they were defeated once more, this time by the Roman prefect Florus. When Justinianus Ist (A.D. 527) came to the throne he ordered the temple of Isis at Philæ to be destroyed, the Blemmyes' adoration of that goddess being offensive to his religious ideas. The priests were imprisoned, the statues were carried to Constantinople, and, of course, the Blemmyes revolted. A short time later the Romans evacuated Egypt, and the Blemmyes and Nobadae were left supreme in Lower Nubia.

During this and the following periods large numbers of Christian monks had erected monasteries in various parts of Lower Nubia, and most of the temples were converted into churches. There had even been Christian kings of Nubia, and one of these, named Silko, records how he defeated the Blemmyes, and penetrated as far as Tâfeh and Kalâbsheh. Another king, named Eīspanōme, sent a certain Abraham to found a Christian church at Dendûr. These Christians had a difficult time in 640 when the Muhammedans conquered Egypt, and many were converted to the doctrine of Islam. In their monasteries many of them lived most rigorous lives, and at Medîk one may still see traces of one of their settlements in which the huts of the monks are barely big enough to permit of them lying down. Some of the ruins, however, are situated at points where the scenery is finest, and the buildings are large and comfortable. In 1173 the brother of Saladin penetrated to Nubia and massacred the Christians, or turned them out of their monasteries. He forced the survivors to pay a poll-tax, and he took from them the provinces at the north end of Lower Nubia. Some of the Christian communities now sought refuge in the south, joining themselves to the Abyssinian Church which had been founded many centuries before. Lower Nubia became more or less Muhammedan, and seems generally to have acknowledged the rule of Egypt. The Mamelukes at the beginning of the nineteenth century fortified themselves in various parts of Lower Nubia, but were driven southwards by Ibrahîm Pasha. During the next half century Lower Nubia was ruled by a native prince, who lived at Derr. In the 'eighties the country became prominent as the basis of the Anglo-Egyptian operations against the Sudan, and on 19th January 1899 it was placed under the jurisdiction of the Mudir, or Governor of Aswân, its southern frontier being fixed at the village of Adendan, some 40 kilometres north of Wâdy Halfa, the capital of the northernmost province of the Sudan.

CHAPTER XXII

FROM SEHEL TO PHILÆ

THE BARRAGE

THE antiquities in the neighbourhood of Aswân as far south as the island of Sehel have already been described. Not far above this stands the great Barrage which was built for the purpose of storing water in Lower Nubia during the winter in order to use it when the Nile is low in the early summer. Unfortunately the construction of this reservoir necessitated the submersion of the island of Philæ, and at the present time the winter visitor to Egypt may sail in a boat through the temple there. It has now been decided to raise the barrage considerably, and in about the year 1912 the temple will be almost wholly submerged, and many other ruins will meet with the same fate. Very elaborate works are now being undertaken by the Egyptian Government to prevent any damage being done to these buildings by the water; and extensive excavations are being carried out over the threatened territory. The visitor to Lower Nubia, after 1912, will find the following sites flooded during the winter:—

> The Temples of Philæ.
> The Temple of Bîgeh.
> The Temple of Dabôd.
> The Fortress and Quarries of Kertassi.
> The Temple of Wâdy Hedîd.
> The Temple of Tâfeh.
> The Temple of Kalâbsheh.
> Part of the Temple of Dendur.
> The Fortress of Koshtamneh.
> The Temple of Dakkeh.
> Part of the Fortress of Kubbân.
> The Temple of Kûrteh.
> The Temple of Maharaka.

In the summer and autumn, however, the ruins will be out of water.

KONOSSO ISLAND

The numerous inscriptions on this little island, which lies just to the north of the direct route from Shellal station to Philæ, need not be described here at length, as they are unlikely to be visited. There are here to be seen the great inscription of Thothmes IVth relating to his Nubian war, the cartouches of Neferabra Psametik and Apries, and the names of various persons of the XIIIth-XVIIIth dynasties, and later. The well-known inscriptions of Neferhotep are found here; and also a stele of Amenhotep IIIrd.

BÎGEH ISLAND

The large and rocky island of Bîgeh lies just to the west of Philæ. On the north-west side of the island, opposite the island of Salîb, there is a rock on which are cut ten small figures, apparently representing a family of persons worshipping a group of gods. On the same rock there are the figures of three gods, of which two seem to be Khnum and Isis. Beside them there is a rough and much-damaged Greek inscription (2 B). Opposite the north end of the temple of Isis at Philæ is an inscription (3 B) giving the cartouches of Aahmes IInd, and his Horus-name, beloved of Khnum of Senem. Above this (4 B) are the cartouches of Psametik Neferabra, and his Horus-name. On the same rock, immediately under these cartouches, is an inscription (5 B) stating that Prince Khaemuast celebrated the jubilee of Rameses IInd for the first time in the thirtieth year, for the second time in the thirty-fourth year, and for the third time in the thirty-seventh year. A space has been left for the recording of later jubilees, but these have never been added. Farther to the south, opposite the colonnade of the temple of Philæ are the cartouches of Apries, beloved of Hathor of Senem (6 B). The following nine inscriptions form part of the same group. The cartouche of Nebmaara [Amenhotep IIIrd], together with a figure of a man with an inscription stating that the Vizir Rames came to make offerings to all the gods of Senem (7 B). The figure of a priest with the inscription, "The priest of Anuket, Khnumhotep" (8 B). An inscription reading, "The Viceroy of Kush Messuy" (9 B). The cartouche of Usermaara-setepnra (Rameses IInd) followed by the words, "The *Sem*-priest Prince Khaemuast" (10 B and 11 B). A

The inscriptions at Bîgeh.

30

well-executed figure of a priest in low relief with the inscription, "The High Priest of Anuket Amenhotep" (12 B). An inscription, reading as before, "The *Sem*-priest Prince Khaemuast (13 B). The figure of a man holding a wand of office accompanied by the cartouche of Nebmaara and the inscription "The Viceroy of Kush Merimes" (14 B). A line of small, damaged hieroglyphs giving the name of an official which is very difficult to read (15 B).

On the rocks above this group of inscriptions there is a small mediæval monastery built of crude brick. There are three rooms with vaulted roofs, more or less intact; and a stairway, under which is a closet, leads to an upper storey, now ruined. The ruins of what may have been the church stand on the north side of this building. Descending to a point below the group of inscriptions, one finds a few other inscriptions just behind the walls of the modern houses, and half buried in refuse. The first of this group reads "The *wab*-priest May, made by the *wab*-priest Usersatet (16 B). Next there are ten small figures, accompanied by quite unreadable inscriptions, and probably representing a New Empire family (17 B). Near this is a large inscription of "The Viceroy of Kush Huy," and a figure of a man is shown holding a crook and wand of office (18 B). Near this is a figure with hands raised, and an inscription reading "The Priest of Khnum, User (19 B). Upside down, and built into the wall of a house, is a stele, on which a XIXth dynasty figure stands with hands raised, accompanied by an inscription giving a prayer to Khnum for the *Ka* of the "Commander of the Archers of Kush, Nekht-Min," and for "The Commander of the Archers, the Superintendent of the Lands of the South, Pen-nesutawi (20 B). Another inscription built into the wall refers to a high priest of Amen, but it is impossible to see it properly. Ascending the rocks again to a point just behind 15 B, one finds an inscription (21 B) reading, "The priest of Khnum, Thothmes," and beside it is a figure of that personage. Near this is a large figure with an unreadable inscription beside it (22 B). Farther to the south, opposite the south end of the Island of Philæ, and at the north side of a valley, is an interesting inscription giving the cartouches of Amenhotep IIIrd, and the words: "The Royal Scribe, the Truth of his Lord, the Commander of the Troops of the Lord of the Two Lands, Amenhotep," and "the Superintendent of the Great Palace in Memphis, Amenhotep." Two figures are shown with hands raised (23 B). Near this is the figure of the Vizir Rames (?) and the cartouche of Nebmaara (24 B).

The temple of Bîgeh is situated on the east of the island, The temple of Bîgeh. opposite the colonnade of the temple of Philæ. It consists of a quay at the water's edge, a doorway some distance back, an open court, and a pronaos, the rest of the temple being now lost. A pink granite altar lies half buried on the terrace. The reliefs on the first doorway show "Autocrator Cæsar" before Harendotes of Abaton, Isis of the Southern Lands, Horus, Nephthys of Abaton, Khnum of Senem, Neith, Thoth of Senem, Sekhmet of Senem, Horus of Edfu, Hathor of On, and other deities now destroyed. A Roman masonry arch has been built into the doorway. In the court which is now entered there are modern houses, and built into one of the walls there is a pink granite altar, having upon it a dedicatory inscription of a Ptolemy, whose cartouche is not clear, and his queen. The pronaos is entered by a doorway, on each side of which rises a pillar with an elaborate capital. These pillars are connected with two others by screen walls, partly built into the houses. On the east side of these walls Ptolemy XIIIth Neos Dionysos is represented before Unnefer, Khnum of Senem, Isis, and other gods. On the doorway some smaller reliefs show him before Isis and other deities. On the west face of the walls the king is seen leaving his palace, wearing, on the north side, the crown of Lower Egypt, and, on the south side, the crown of Upper Egypt. Before him are the four usual standards. Farther on he is blessed by Hathor of Senem. The houses cover the area on which the rest of the temple stood. On the north side of the temple is a broken seated statue in pink granite inscribed with the cartouches and titles of Menkheperra Thothmes IIIrd. A statue bearing the cartouches of Amenhotep IInd used to lie at the back of the temple, but the present writer did not find any trace of it.

As will be seen from the inscriptions and the remains of statues of Amenhotep IInd and Thothmes IInd, the island was already sacred in the XVIIIth dynasty. There is, however, nothing to show that it was regarded with particular reverence before that date. In the tomb of Rekhmara at Thebes mention is made of the commandant of the fortress of Bîgeh, but no trace of the fortress remains. In ancient times it was called Senem, or Senmet; and at Philæ and elsewhere constant mention is made of the gods of Senem. Khnum and Hathor were the chief of these, but Isis and the other favourite gods of Philæ are often described as being of Senem. At Philæ Nectanebus dedicated a temple to "all the gods of Senem." The scenes in Hadrian's Gateway at Philæ show that in the Roman age Bîgeh was

History of Bîgeh.

regarded as one of the sources of the Nile. In a cave under the rocks the Nile god was thought to live, guarded by a serpent which encircled the chamber. The sanctity of Philæ is of much later date than is that of Bîgeh; and thus the latter island has an interest which one must not overlook.

PHILÆ

Situation and condition of Philæ.

The island of Philæ is situated at the head of the First Cataract, some two miles above the barrage. It is about 500 yards long from north to south, and 160 yards from east to west. It is formed by a mass of crystalline rock, of which the main part is hornblendic granite; and a deep deposit of Nile mud has been collected above this. At only two points does the granite rise in any great quantity above the mud, namely, at the south-east corner, where there is a high mound of rock, and at the Temple of Isis, where it pushes up under the second pylon, and breaks through the pavement of the hall. The island is almost covered with temples, courts, and ancient constructions of one kind and another; and the banks of the river are largely built up with quay-walls and high terraces. The foundations of these buildings partly rest upon the rocks, and partly upon the mud; but for the most part they are well built and deeply laid. When it was decided to turn this part of the river into a reservoir, Captain Lyons (afterwards Director-General, Survey Department) undertook the work of examining the buildings, and of ascertaining the strength of the foundations. The works then carried out by him have placed the buildings in a condition to resist the force of the water at their yearly flooding, and at present there is no likelihood of a collapse of any part of the actual temples.

The temples are flooded each year from December to about April, and during part of this time one may visit them by boat, passing through the Kiosk and into the court of the Temple of Isis. From May to December the island stands quite out of water, and when the river is at its lowest the temples have much of their original appearance, except that the palms and brick ruins are gone. Viewed as a whole, the place does not then show much sign of its submersion. Between the east side of the main temple and the Kiosk a lawn of grass and green herbage stretches; and

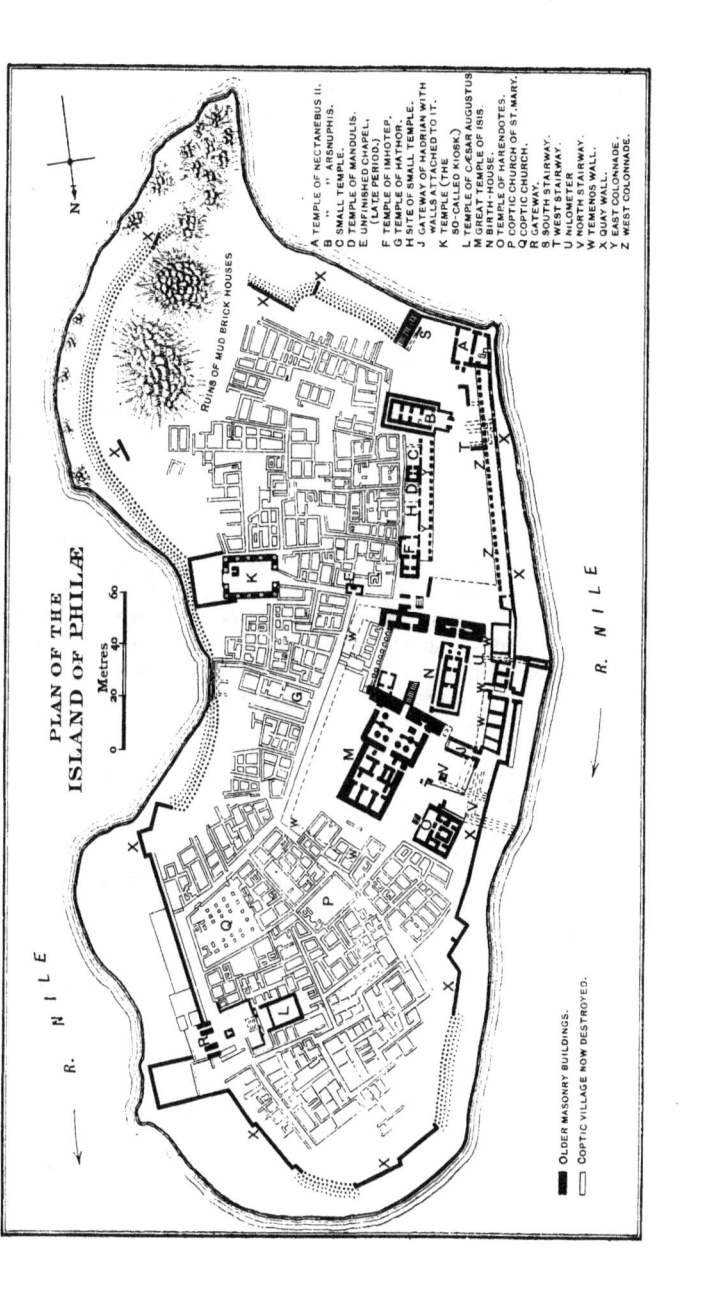

various grasses, reeds, water-melons, creepers, and so on, grow in profusion amidst the ruins.

THE HISTORY OF PHILÆ

The known history of Philæ does not carry one back to a period earlier than the Ethiopian dynasty, an altar of Taharka being the oldest monument on the island. The frontier of Egypt during late dynastic times seems to have been placed at the southern end of the island of Sehel, which rises at the north end of the cataract. The large island of Bîgeh and the desert mainland around Shellal were important Egyptian military outposts at all times; but they were seldom regarded as anything but Lower Nubian territory. The island of Philæ, however, does not seem to have been fortified, or to have been regarded as a place of any importance until late dynastic times; but when at last it began to be built upon, it was classed as a Lower Nubian settlement, having no connection with Aswân, the southernmost town of Egypt. Its ancient name was *Alek* or *Pe-alek*, and the word *alek* has been sometimes considered as meaning "the end," the name thus being rendered "The Island of the End." This, however, is improbable, as Philæ was essentially part of the *beginning* of Lower Nubia and not the *end* of Egypt; while it is unlikely that the *end* of Lower Nubia—as viewed from south to north—could have been meant, since there are other islands of Lower Nubia still farther to the north. The name is more probably purely Nubian.

The earliest standing building at Philæ was erected by Nectanebus IInd, though the name of Aahmes IInd on a block of stone and the above-mentioned inscription of Taharka show that earlier buildings stood here. The priests of Philæ, however, believed that their island had a far longer history than this, and at the Egyptian frontier at Sehel there is an inscription written by them, stating that as early as the IIIrd dynasty King Zeser gave them the country from the First Cataract to the island of Takômpso (*i.e.* Derâr, near Maharaka). It may well be that Zeser sent expeditions into Lower Nubia, and left this territory in charge of the military commanders of the fortresses at the head of the cataract; but it is extremely improbable that there were any priests at Philæ at that early date, for no very ancient remains were found in Captain Lyons' excavations. The Isis worship which grew up here in Ptolemaic times, and for which the

FROM SEHEL TO PHILÆ

Ptolemies and Roman Pharaohs erected such splendid temples, brought Philæ into great prominence at this period; and the priests obtained a power unequalled at that date in Upper Egypt. This may have been due in part to their holding, perhaps, the gold mines of Wâdy Alâki, the terminus of the caravan route at Kubbân being within their sphere of administration. In the reign of Ptolemy IInd or IIIrd, the territory from the First Cataract to Takômpso, known as the Dodekaschoinoi, or the Land of the Twelve *Aru* or *Schoinoi* (a schoinos being about $7\frac{1}{2}$ miles) was formed into a kingdom under the native king Ergamenes; and Philæ perhaps was partly in this kingdom. But under Ptolemy Vth the kingdom of the Dodekaschoinoi was abolished, and Philæ again came under Egyptian rule. In the twenty-fourth year of Ptolemy VIth Philometor, this territory was handed over to the priests of Philæ to administer and rule on behalf of the king; but an inscription near Kalâbsheh dating from late times seems to show that at some time after this the priests acquired the whole of Lower Nubia as far south as the Second Cataract. In late Roman times the Blemmyes became ardent worshippers of Isis of Philæ, and at one period when the island had passed out of their sphere of influence, an arrangement was made by which they were allowed to visit the temple at fixed periods, and to take the statue of the goddess into their own land for a short time. The old Egyptian religion died very hard, and at Philæ the worship of Isis continued for a long period after Christianity had become the only legal religion of Egypt. Bishop Theodorus, about 577 A.D., converted part of the temple into a place of Christian worship, dedicating it to Saint Stephen. A large Coptic town grew up around the old temples, and this was excavated and planned in 1895. Sufficient has been said regarding Philæ in the History of Lower Nubia to render further remarks here unnecessary.

The goddess Isis was by no means the only deity worshipped on the island, although she held the position of patroness. She was generally worshipped as Isis of Philæ, Isis of Abaton, Isis of Senem, Isis of Elephantine, Isis of the Southern Countries, Isis of Coptos, and Isis of Memphis. The trinities of which she was the chief member were:—Unnefer, Isis, and Harendotes; Isis, Hathor, and Harpocrates; Unnefer, Isis, and Nephthys; Isis, Horus, and Hathor; Isis, Neith, and Maat; Isis, Horus, and Nephthys; and Unnefer, Isis, and Harpocrates. A very large number of gods appear in the reliefs, but those connected with the myth of Osiris, Isis, and Horus predominate. It is now impossible

The religion of Philæ.

to state what was the original religion of the island; but the earliest of the standing temples—that of Nectanebus IInd—is dedicated to Hathor, Isis, and to all the gods of Senem (Bîgeh). It has just been seen that Bîgeh was sacred a long time before Philæ had attracted the attention of the priesthood, and it is therefore not surprising to find the gods of Senem worshipped on the latter island. Isis, however, does not seem to have been a patron deity of Bîgeh; and one may suppose that her worship was newly introduced at Philæ. The reader will be familiar with the myth which relates how Osiris was murdered by his brother Set, and how his widow, Isis, gave birth to a son, Horus, in the marshes of Lower Egypt, who, when he grew up, avenged his father's death. This legend seems to have taken hold of the inhabitants of this neighbourhood during the Greek era, and the main events related in the story were soon thought by them to have taken place here. The god Horus had been introduced into Lower Nubia by the Egyptians in early days. There was a Horus of the military districts of Maam (Anâybeh), of Beheni (Halfa), of Baki (Kubbân), and of Senem (Bîgeh), who in each case was a fighting god; and it was natural that the traditions relating to the wars of the original Horus with Set should be identified with the history of the wars of these military districts with the negroes. It followed that Isis and Osiris, who are essential to the story of the traditional wars of Horus, should come to be closely related to Horus in the temple ceremonies, just as they were at the main Egyptian seats of that god's worship.

At Philæ Osiris, Isis, and Horus were regarded essentially as deified mortals, or as gods who for a space had been mortal. Osiris is here the first Pharaoh of Egypt who taught the arts of civilisation to the Egyptians. His name, Unnefer, is often written in a cartouche, with the words indicating "deceased" written after it; the name Isis is also written within a cartouche; while Horus has the mortal titles of *Ser*-Prince of Beheni, *Ser*-Prince of Maam, Pharaoh of Senem, and so on. The tendency, however, amongst the natives of this neighbourhood, as indicated by that of the later Blemmyes, was towards goddess-worship rather than god-worship; and gradually Isis assumed a more important position than that of either the original Horus or of Osiris. Strange to say, this worship so prospered that Philæ, at the southern extremity of Egypt, became the chief seat of the worship of Isis, who was originally a Lower Egyptian goddess. It will be seen, then, that the original god of Philæ was the military Horus of Senem or Bîgeh and of

FROM SEHEL TO PHILÆ

other districts, and with him were associated the gods of Bigeh; that in accordance with the requirements of the adopted tradition Osiris and Isis were introduced; and that finally Isis assumed the position of the greatest importance here, and Horus became a secondary god.

DESCRIPTION OF THE TEMPLES

The temples which are still standing may now be described, but it must be understood that from December to May a large part of the buildings are flooded, and cannot be seen. We may begin at the south end of the island, which is submerged during these months. The Temple, or Vestibule as it is sometimes called, of Nectanebus IInd stands immediately over the water when the river is low, and from its south side the quay wall drops sheer down to the Nile. There are six pillars on the west side and seven on the east, between which are low screen walls. The pillars are destroyed on the east side, but are nearly perfect on the west, and are seen to have lotus capitals, above which are Hathor heads supporting the architrave. The vestibule was entered by a main door on the north side, and by side doors on the east and west sides. At the south end there was probably only a window, as there are no traces of steps leading up the quay, by which the temple could be reached. Two sandstone obelisks stood at the south end of the temple, one of which is now lost. On the other are Greek and Arabic inscriptions. On the east side of the temple there is an open court, forming the top of the quay, and from it down to the water run two flights of steps, one being subterranean. Inside the temple the reliefs on the screen walls show Nectanebus before various gods. On the east side he stands before Isis, Nephthys, and Hathor; Isis of Elephantine, Isis of Coptos, and Harseisis; and various other gods now more or less destroyed. On the west side he is seen before Osiris-Unnefer, Isis, and Harseisis; before Nekheb and Buto; he is led by Khnum and Horus of Edfu towards Isis; and he is purified by Horus of Edfu and Ta-kens, and by Thoth of Hermopolis. At the east end of the north wall he is seen wearing the crown of Upper Egypt, leaving his palace, while before him go the standards of the shell and jackal, and a *sem*-priest burns incense. On the sides of the main doorway are figures of Thoth and Horus of Edfu pouring out the holy water. Outside the temple on the east face of the screen walls, the king is seen before Khnum and Satis, Osiris-

The temple of Nectanebus IInd.

474 ANTIQUITIES OF UPPER EGYPT

Unnefer and Isis, and other gods now destroyed. On the west face of the screen walls the king is shown before Amen-Ra and Mut; Isis and Anukis; Khnum and Buto; Isis and Harpocrates. On either side of the doorway in this wall a figure of the king is shown with the usual inscriptions relating to the double purification necessary when entering this "temple of Isis." The temple is approached on the north side by a short flight of steps, and on the wall to the left of the entrance the king is seen before Hathor, while on the right there seems originally to have been a figure of Isis.

The temple of Arsnuphis. The temple of Arsnuphis stands just to the north-east of the temple of Nectanebus. It consists of a small shrine made up of a pronaos, vestibule, adytum, and sanctuary, this building being surrounded by a high enclosure wall. The shrine is for the most part destroyed; but the main part of the enclosure wall stands on the north and east sides, though on the west side it has fallen and lies scattered on the ground. There has here been a Coptic church which was constructed of the fallen blocks. Inside the sanctuary are fragments of a granite altar. Only the base of the pronaos walls remains, and one sees here the decorations of Nile figures which went around the chamber. The vestibule is almost in the same condition, but reliefs can be seen showing Ptolemy Vth Epiphanes before Isis, and other gods, while around the doorway into the adytum are small reliefs showing the king in the presence of Amen-Ra, Shu, Khnum, and Horus. Of the adytum the south walls are standing, and one sees the king, now Ptolemy IVth Philopator, before Isis, Horus, Unnefer, and other gods whose names are now lost. In the sanctuary only the bases of the walls with decorations of Nile figures are now left. This decoration is also found on the outside walls of the shrine. The enclosure walls are covered with reliefs. On the north wall there are four rows of scenes. In the top row the Pharaoh, who is here Tiberius, is represented before Osiris, Isis, and Harseisis; Harseisis, Nephthys, and Isis; Khnum, Satis, and Anukis; Arsnuphis and Tefnut. In the second row he stands before Isis, Hathor, Harpocrates, Arsnuphis, Thoth, and Dedun. In the third row he is shown leaving his palace, while before him are the four standards which so often precede the king and a figure burning incense. Next he is purified by Thoth and Horus of Edfu, and crowned by Nekheb and Buto. Then he is led by Horus and Menthu of On towards Arsnuphis; he stands in the presence of Arsnuphis and Isis; and he offers to other gods now damaged.

The fourth row consists of a line of forty-eight gods and goddesses all facing towards three figures representing Unnefer, Isis, and Harseisis. The fallen blocks of the south wall show Ergamenes, the king of the Land of the Twelve Schoinoi, Ptolemy IVth Philopator, Ptolemy VIIth Philometor, and Tiberius, before various gods. The cartouches of Ergamenes seem to show signs of having been erased, and this was probably due to the enmity of Ptolemy Vth Epiphanes towards the Nubians after their revolt (p. 459).

The east colonnade, still partly roofed, leading from the temple of Arsnuphis to the Great Pylon, has never been finished. Of the seventeen columns only six have their capitals completed, and the outer wall has no relief upon it. Seven doorways are cut through this wall. The first five from the south end lead out on to the court in which stood a now ruined chapel of Mandulis; and the sixth leads into the small temple of Imhotep (Asclepius). Passing through this door one finds oneself in a little court, on the north side of which is the doorway into the temple. On the left side of the doorway King Ptolemy Vth Epiphanes is seen before Imhotep; and on the right side he is shown before Khnum, Satis, and Anukis; and before Unnefer, Isis, and Imhotep. On the lintel is a Greek inscription which dates from the reign of Ptolemy Vth Epiphanes, and refers to his wife and son. Through this doorway one passes into two chambers, both of which are undecorated. *The east colonnade.*

Between the temple of Imhotep and the Great Pylon stands the imposing gateway built by Ptolemy IInd Philadelphus, which probably formed the eastern entrance of a dromos, now lost, which stood on the site of the present colonnade. On the west face of the doorway the reliefs on the lintel show the king dancing before Khnum and Hathor, and before Unnefer and Isis. Inside the doorway there is a large relief showing the king being led forward by Isis; and small damaged reliefs showing Tiberius before Unnefer, Isis, Anubis, and other gods. On the east face of the doorway King Ptolemy is seen in the presence of Unnefer, Isis, Satis, Anukis, Hathor, and other deities. *The gateway of Philadelphus.*

Returning now to the temple of Nectanebus at the south end of the island, the west colonnade which lies between that point and the Great Pylon must be described. The thirty-one columns here, with fine capitals, still support parts of the roof, decorated with vultures with spread wings and stars; while the outer wall, decorated with numerous reliefs, is mainly intact. At intervals in *The west colonnade.*

ANTIQUITIES OF UPPER EGYPT

this wall are windows overlooking the water and the island of Bigeh. This colonnade rises immediately above the high quay-wall, so that at low water there is a sheer drop of several metres below the windows. The reliefs show the Pharaohs Claudius, Tiberius, and Germanicus before various gods, including Sebek of Ombos, Tasentnefer of Ombos, Penebtawi, and the others already so frequently named. The most common groups here are those consisting of Osiris, Unnefer, Isis, and a form of Horus; or Osiris, Hathor, and Harpocrates, while Arsnuphis is several times represented. Towards the north end of the colonnade there is a well-preserved Greek inscription on the wall, which states that a certain Ammonius fulfilled a vow made to Isis, Serapis, and other gods, by presenting to them the worship of his brother and children, in the thirty-first year of Cæsar Augustus. Beneath the colonnade, and running at right angles to it, is a passage descending to the water, which was used as a Nilometer.

The Great Pylon.
The Great Pylon is now reached. In front of it are two fallen Roman lions of pink granite, which stood on pedestals, of which only one still remains. The large reliefs upon the pylon must now be described. On the south or front face of the west pylon King Ptolemy XIIIth Neos Dionysos is seen with mace upraised, slaying a group of enemies whom he grasps by the hair. A large figure of Isis and small figures of Hathor and Horus of Edfu are before him. Above this the king is seen in the presence of Unnefer and Isis, Isis and Harseisis. The reliefs have been damaged intentionally in Christian times. On the east pylon the king is shown slaying his enemies as before in the presence of Isis, Horus, and Hathor; while higher up he stands before Horus and Nephthys, Isis and Harpocrates. The scenes here are interfered with by the Gateway of Philadelphus, but it is obvious from the masonry that the pylon and the gateway were built at the same time. Along the whole length of the base of this face of the pylon are reliefs showing small Nile figures bringing offerings. In the west pylon a doorway is constructed, leading into the Birth-House. At the foot of the wall on either side is a representation of a sacred boat. The reliefs on the inner sides of the doorway will be described later in connection with the Birth-House.

The main gateway in the Great Pylon.
The main gateway through the pylon was built by King Nectanebus IInd at the same time as his temple at the south end of the island. On the south face of this gateway the reliefs on the lintel show Nectanebus dancing before Osiris-Unnefer and Isis; Khnum and Hathor. A Coptic cross has been inserted on either side of

FROM SEHEL TO PHILÆ 477

the doorway. As one passes through the doorway one sees on either side a number of reliefs showing Nectanebus in the presence of various gods ; and there is a large relief showing him before Isis. Around the base of the walls are figures of Nile gods bearing offerings. On the east wall is a French inscription dated in the seventh year of the Republic, and recording the presence of officers of the French army which had recently defeated the Mamelukes. One now finds oneself in the forecourt of the temple of Isis, and, turning round, one may examine the reliefs on the north side of the Great Pylon. On the east pylon Ptolemy XIIIth is represented offering to Amen-Ra and Mut ; Khnum and Hathor ; Unnefer and Isis. On the west pylon Ptolemy XIIIth is shown before Unnefer and Isis ; Horus and Hathor; Hathor and Harpocrates ; Unnefer and Isis ; and Isis. Below this a number of priests are shown carrying two sacred boats. In the east pylon there is a small doorway in the north side leading into a guard-room. Passing through this doorway one sees on the left side reliefs showing King Ptolemy Xth Soter IInd, before Isis, Hathor, and Horus ; and, accompanied by Queen and Princess Cleopatra, before Isis. The chamber into which one now passes has reliefs on the south wall showing the king before Osiris, Isis, Horus, and Harpocrates. Four niches have been cut in the walls in later times in order to form cupboards. From this room another small chamber leads off, but this is entirely undecorated. Another doorway in this pylon is to be found in the east corner under the colonnade. Above it are reliefs showing Ptolemy XIIIth leaving his palace, with the four standards (the jackal, ibis, hawk, and another) before him. Passing through the doorway one ascends a flight of steps which leads to the roof. A chamber opens off the steps a few metres from the ground, and farther up a second chamber leads on to the top of the doorway of Nectanebus. From here the steps ascend up each of the pylons to the top. On different parts of the walls of the Great Pylon there are Greek and demotic inscriptions, the former being particularly numerous. *[The small east gateway in the Great Pylon.]*

The Birth-House, which is built between the Great Pylon and the Second Pylon, forms the west side of the forecourt. It was intended to be approached through the doorway in the west pylon, the south side of which has already been described. Passing into this doorway one sees on either side of the doorposts a series of small reliefs showing Ptolemy VIIth Philometor before Harmachis, Khonsu of Thebes, Anukis, Isis, Harpocrates, Ptah, Min, Unnefer, and other deities. Beyond this, on either side, there are reliefs *[The entrance to the Birth-House.]*

representing scenes introductory to the story of the birth of Horus, which is related in the reliefs in the Birth-House. On the west wall, above a small doorway which leads into an undecorated guard-room, the king stands before Harpocrates, who is suckled by Isis; and he offers to Isis and to other deities now damaged. Beyond this there is an elaborate group of scenes. At the top the king is shown in the presence of Isis of Abaton and other gods. Below this he worships Hathor, Harpocrates, and Arsnuphis; kneeling hawk-, jackal-, and human-headed figures being in front of him. Below this the seven Hathors, who attend women in childbirth and act the part of the fairy godmother, are shown beating tambourines in the presence of Unnefer and Isis, who are called Lord and Lady of the Birth-House. Under this again a goddess plays a harp, and the king, with his Queen Cleopatra, makes offerings to Isis and other deities now partly destroyed. On the west wall of the passage there is also a doorway leading into a small guard-room, and the reliefs beside it are again elaborate. In the top row one sees the king offering to Isis, Harpocrates, Neith, Bast, Hathor, Khnum, and other deities. Below this the king, with eight cynocephali, adores Isis, Harpocrates, and Arsnuphis. The lowest row of reliefs on either wall shows the king and queen leading a procession of Nubian districts:—Senem or Bîgeh, Het-Khent, Baki or Kubbân, Maa(m) or Ibrîm, Mehy or Abu Simbel, Tawazet, Penubs, Petenhor, Napata, Meroe, and three others which are unreadable. Tawazet and the following names are districts of Upper Nubia. Around the north face of the doorway is a series of reliefs showing Ptolemy XIIIth before Horus, Hathor, Harpocrates, Isis, Unnefer, and Harsemtawi.

The portico of the Birth-House.

The main building consists of a portico, the roof of which is supported by four columns with varying capitals, a vestibule, an adytum, and a sanctuary. On the west, north, and east sides of this building runs a colonnade which is entered by a doorway on the west side of the portico. On the doorway leading to the portico Ptolemy VIIth is seen on either side, with the crown of Upper and Lower Egypt on his head, and holding a mace and sceptre in his hands. On the west wall are eight reliefs showing Tiberius before Osiris, Isis, and Horus; Shu and Tefnut; Horus, Hathor, and another deity; Satis and Anukis; Isis, Osiris, and Horus; Hathor suckling a child, and Shu; Unnefer, Isis, and Horus; and Harpocrates and Hathor. On the east wall the eight reliefs show Tiberius before Osiris, Isis, and Horus; Thoth and a goddess whose name is not clear; Amen-Ra, Mut, and Khonsu; Isis suckling a child, and Shu; Isis, Osiris, and Horus; and Isis suckling Harpocrates. On the north wall Ptolemy VIth Philometor is seen before Isis and Hathor; Khnum, Satis, and Anukis; Osiris-Unnefer and Isis; Isis and Hathor; Shu and two other deities; and Isis and Horus. On the architraves are small figures of deities, most of which represent Taurt. The ceiling decoration is in the usual form of vultures with wings spread. The walls of the vestibule are not decorated with reliefs, but many demotic inscriptions have been written here. Entering the adytum, the reliefs on this side of the doorway are seen to represent eight (*sic*) figures of Hathor, each holding a tambourine, while a king and queen whose cartouches have not been filled in worship Isis. Around the lower part of the walls of this chamber are a series of curious reliefs, representing various deities standing amidst the papyrus swamps in which Isis gave birth to Horus. Here there are hawk- and snake-headed figures holding spears, snakes, hippopotami-gods with cows' and hawks' heads, a cynocephalus enthroned, and so on. At the top of the wall Amen-Ra addresses Khnum; Khnum models a figure of the king; Thoth speaks with the queen-mother; and the queen is led forward by Khnum and another god. On the east wall the scenes are much damaged, but one can make out a child being presented to various gods, and Hathor addressing Amen. These scenes are intended to indicate the divine birth of the king by showing the various gods interesting themselves in the child's creation. We have seen similar scenes at Luxor (p. 75) and Dêr el Bahri (p. 266).

The vestibule and adytum of the Birth-House.

Around the doorway leading into the sanctuary Ptolemy VIth Philometor, is shown before Isis and other gods. The reliefs on the west, east, and south walls of the sanctuary show Ptolemy VIth before various gods. On the north wall the central scene shows a hawk, crowned with the crown of Upper and Lower Egypt, standing amidst a clump of papyrus reeds; and below this Isis is seen with the baby to whom she has just given birth in her arms. Beside her stand Thoth, Wazet, Amen-Ra, Nekheb, and Behudet. Above these scenes the king is shown before the trinities of Khnum, Hathor, and Horus; and Osiris, Isis, and Horus.

The sanctuary of the Birth-House.

Passing now into the colonnade around the temple, the reliefs on the west side must be recorded. These are in four rows. In the top row the Pharaoh Tiberius is seen worshipping Osiris-Unnefer and Isis; Isis, Hathor, and Horus; Khnum and Hathor; Min; the Pharaoh of Senem; Horus and Hathor; Seb, Nut, and Horus; Hathor and Horus; Isis suckling the young Harpocrates,

The colonnades of the Birth-House.

and Horus ; and Isis. In the second row the king offers to Horus, who is carried in a chest on a lion's back, and Isis; he offers to Hathor and Horus, while a goddess with a bunch of papyri on her head plays a harp ; he offers to Ptah and Sekhmet ; Thoth ; Arsnuphis and Tefnut ; Amen-Ra, Mut, and Khonsu; Isis suckling Horus; Neith and Maat ; and Horus and Hathor. In the third row the king worships various gods. The bottom row consists of a group, many times repeated, made up of an ibis standing on a shrine, and a hawk perched on a clump of papyrus. It is perhaps worthy of note that the representation of an ibis upon a shrine occurs as early as the Ist dynasty, and is to be observed on the mace-head of King Narmer found at Hieraconpolis. The reliefs on the north wall are in four rows. In the first two rows the king is shown before Khnum and Hathor ; Hathor suckling Horus, and Wepwat ; Osiris and Isis ; and other deities as before. In the third row Isis, nursing Horus, is seated between Amen-Ra and Wazet, while Thoth, Neith, another goddess, and the king stand by them; and next to this Hathor nurses Horus, while Nekheb sits behind her, and Khnum models a figure before her, Thoth, two goddesses, and the king standing behind. In the lowest row the king and various demi-gods bring offerings to Isis nursing Horus in the papyrus swamps. The reliefs on the east wall are damaged in part. They repeat more or less closely the scenes on the west wall, and do not mention any different gods. The east walls of this temple, outside the colonnade, are also decorated with reliefs. At the south end the king, Neos Dionysos, is seen before Min, Arsnuphis, Khnum, and other gods ; and seven Hathors beating tambourines stand before Isis and Hathor. Along the lower line the king is seen leaving the palace with seven standards before him, and a priest who burns incense. He is then purified by Thoth and Behudet ; is crowned by Nekheb and Wazet ; is led to Isis by Horus ; and worships Osiris-Unnefer, Isis, and Horus, and other gods now damaged. At the north end various mythological figures are represented. The architrave inscription on the east face of the east part of the colonnade around the temple states that Ptolemy IXth Euergetes, built it. Under the reliefs of Neos Dionysos at the south end of the wall are demotic and hieroglyphic decrees dated in the twenty-first year of Ptolemy Vth Epiphanes, one of which relates to the suppression of what seems to be the revolt of Ergamenes, king of the Dodekaschoinos, or of his successor Azkheramen.

The east side of the forecourt between the two pylons is formed

The outside of east colonnade of the Birth-House.

FROM SEHEL TO PHILÆ

by a colonnade, from the back of which six doorways lead. The reliefs on this wall from south to north show King Neos Dionysos before Thoth; slaying a form of Set before Horus of Edfu; offering to Unnefer and Isis; burning incense before six standards— the jackals, the ibis, the hawk, the Theban emblem, and the disk and feathers; dragging a sleigh on which is the boat of Sokaris in the presence of Sokaris and Isis; worshipping Isis; kneeling before Hathor; and worshipping Osiris and Isis. Lower down the king is seen before Isis, Unnefer, Horus, Neith, while along the bottom of the wall is a procession of the nomes. On the columns the king is shown in the presence of the same gods as usual. The inscription on the architrave states that Ptolemy IXth Euergetes IInd, built the colonnade, and it is thus seen that Neos Dionysos only added the reliefs. The southernmost of the six doorways leads through a chamber onto the terrace. There is also a stairway here leading to the roof. On the doorway are long inscriptions giving the receipt for making the temple incense, and it is to be presumed that this was the room in which it was made. The second and third doorways admit one to uninscribed chambers. The fourth doorway leads into a small chamber, upon the walls of which are the four following reliefs in large size—a cow-headed goddess offers two vases to Unnefer, Isis, and Horus; the Pharaoh (Augustus?) makes offering to Isis; Maat offers a paint-box and brushes to Thoth, Tefnut, and Safkhet; and the Pharaoh offers to Ptah. There is a niche in the north wall over which is a figure of an ibis, and under it a figure of an ape writing upon a palette. This room, as one sees from the inscription outside the doorway, was the chamber in which the sacred books were kept, and it was probably actually in this niche that they lay. The wooden door-pivot at the entrance is noteworthy. The fifth and largest door leads through a vestibule and a second doorway to the terrace outside. On the east side of the doorway Neos Dionysos is seen worshipping the two trinities—Khnum, Hathor, and Horus; and Osiris, Isis, and Horus; and other gods. On the second doorway leading from this vestibule to the terrace Tiberius is seen with his queen, whose cartouche is blank, before Osiris, Isis, and Horus, and other deities. Coptic crosses have been cut on the east side of the doorway. The sixth doorway leads to the north. Above it on the inside the king is seen worshipping Osiris and Isis, and below is a lion. On the right side of the doorway, as one passes through, the king is seen slaying a captive before Horus. At the sides of the

The east side of the Forecourt of the temple of Isis.

doorway are inscriptions addressed to the mythical Keeper of the Portal.

<small>The Fore-court of the temple of Isis.</small>
Returning now to the forecourt, in the south-east corner there stands a granite altar dedicated to Amen-Ra by Taharka. Protruding from the east side of the smaller pylon there is a large block of the natural granite, which has been trimmed down and has had reliefs and inscriptions cut upon it in the manner of a stele. In front of it a small chapel, now almost totally lost, was erected by one of the emperors. The reliefs on the stele show Ptolemy VIIth Philometor and his queen standing before Isis and Horus, and Osiris and Isis, while Horus in another form stands near. The inscription, dated in the twenty-fourth year, refers to the presenting to Isis of the country from Takômpso (or Derar) to Aswân, making twelve *aru* or *schoinoi* on the east bank, and twelve *schoinoi* on the west bank.

<small>The Second Pylon.</small>
The east side of the second or smaller pylon, which is built over this natural rock, has on it a large relief showing King Neos Dionysos worshipping Horus and Hathor; and above this he is shown in smaller size offering to Horus and Isis; and to Osiris, Isis, and Horus. Below are figures of the king and the Nile-gods offering to Unnefer, Nephthys, and Horus. On the west pylon the king is shown in large size before Unnefer and Isis, and in smaller size before Horus and Isis, and Unnefer, Isis, and Horus. Lower down the king is seen at the head of a procession of Nile-figures, making offering to Unnefer, Isis, and Horus. The five standards of the jackal, ibis, hawk, Theban emblem, and feathers and disk are shown near the king. These scenes are interrupted by the doorway which joins the Birth-House to the pylon. A flight of steps leads up to the main doorway between the pylons. The reliefs on the east side of the east pylon show Neos Dionysos before Horus, Ptah, and three other forms of Horus.

<small>The Hypostyle Hall of the temple of Isis.</small>
Ascending the stairs from the forecourt one passes through the great doorway. On the two jambs are reliefs showing the king offering to various gods. On the east side is an inscription of Bishop Theodorus. On the main inner wall of the doorway is a Coptic painting of Christ (?) with adoring angels. On the west side Ptolemy IXth offers before Unnefer, Isis, and Horus. Passing through the doorway one finds oneself in a rectangular hall, having ten columns, and in the middle a restored semi-portal. The beautiful capitals of the columns excite one's profound admiration for the work of this period. The roof is intact but only covers half the hall, a large part having been left open in the

FROM SEHEL TO PHILÆ   483

original design. From the north end a gateway leads into the vestibule and sanctuary. On the east and west sides are small doorways, and in the west side of the pylon another doorway leads to a staircase by which one may ascend to the roof. The walls and columns of the hall are covered with reliefs, some of which are much damaged by bird-droppings, while others have been quite chiselled out by Christians. The water when the reservoir is full floods this hall to the depth of about a foot or so; but when the height of the barrage is raised the hall will be about entirely submerged. The reliefs show Ptolemy IXth and other Pharaohs before the gods. On the north wall of the hall Ptolemy IIIrd and Berenice are seen in attitudes of worship. These figures were introduced by Ptolemy IXth. On the east side of the hall part of the wall decorations have been removed, and a small Christian altar has been erected. The reliefs have also been erased on the lower part of the other walls. The floor at this side of the hall shows the rough granite protruding through the pavement in several places, while it actually forms part of the wall in one place. Considering the care with which the temple is built, one can only suppose that this natural rock has been left untouched owing to the objection which the priests felt to cutting it away, all the rocks of the island being regarded as sacred.

One now passes from the hall into an inner court, and on either side of the doorway is an inscription relating to Bishop Theodorus. High up over the doorway is a large modern inscription dated in 1841 under Gregory XVIth. The small court which one now enters was originally divided into two parts by a doorway now destroyed. The west portion formed a hall in front of the main chambers of the Isis Temple; and the east part was partly roofed, and through it one passed into a passage which led round into the adytum again. As one enters the court a series of reliefs will be seen on its south wall. To the west of the doorway King Ptolemy IInd is represented, having the crown of Lower Egypt on his head, leaving his palace censed by a *sem*-priest, and preceded by the two jackal standards. Above this he offers to Isis. On the east doorway he leaves the palace crowned with the Upper Egyptian crown, and is preceded by the jackal, shell, ibis, and standards. Above this he is seen dancing before Isis, and performing an unknown ceremony before Isis and Nephthys. At the bottom on the east side the goddess Safkhet writes the *Ka*-name of the king, while on the west side Thoth does likewise. One sees, then, from these reliefs that

The Inner Court of the temple of Isis.

the king has left his palace; and in the presence of various gods has come to worship Isis. The inscription here tells one that these gods are giving to the king many jubilees in which he is crowned as King of Upper and Lower Egypt on the throne of Horus-Menthu. On the west wall the king is now seen to be purified by Horus and Thoth. Above this he offers to the Pharaoh of Senem, who is crowned with the war-helmet; and still higher he offers to Amen-Ra and Isis. On the north wall, *i.e.* on the sides of the door into the inner chambers, he is crowned, on the west side, by Menthu of Thebes and Tum of On, and is given many years and jubilees. Above this he worships Seb and Horus. On the east side he is led forward by Khnum and Isis; and above he worships Isis, and Isis suckling Harpocrates, and Wazet. This scene is much damaged, and cannot be easily distinguished. Over the doorway he worships Osiris and Isis; and down either side he offers to Hathor, Sekhmet, Isis, and Tefnut.

<small>The vestibule and adytum of the temple of Isis.</small>

One may now enter from this court into the main building consisting of the vestibule, adytum, and sanctuary. In the west wall of the vestibule there is a doorway leading into an inner chamber which is quite dark, and the reliefs of which are much damaged. On this west wall there is a relief showing the king offering to Osiris. The east wall is much damaged, but it can be seen that the king has been shown offering to Isis. The adytum is somewhat dark, and as there is generally a foot or so of water in it in winter, it is seldom visited. On the west end of the south wall Ptolemy IInd is seen before Osiris and Isis, and before Harmachis and Tefnut. On the east end of the south wall he stands before Unnefer, Isis, and other deities. On the east wall he worships Isis, and on the west wall Isis, Hathor, &c. On the north wall he is seen worshipping Isis of Philæ and Arsinoë. From this room a doorway in the west wall leads into a chamber in which there are reliefs showing the king in the presence of Sekhmet, Hathor, and Nephthys. There is an additional inscription added by Ptolemy IIIrd (?). In the north wall of the adytum is a door leading into a dark chamber in which are large reliefs showing Ptolemy IInd before Hathor, Anukis, and Isis in various forms. There is again an additional inscription by Ptolemy IIIrd.

<small>The sanctuary of the temple of Isis.</small>

The sanctuary is lighter, and most of the reliefs can be easily seen. The walls are covered with scenes showing Ptolemy IInd before the gods. Isis predominates here of course, and on the north wall which forms the main wall of the sanctuary she is shown six times, no other deities being with her. In this chamber

FROM SEHEL TO PHILÆ

there is a pink granite altar or pedestal of a statue, inscribed with the cartouches of Ptolemy IIIrd and Berenice.

Returning to the small court or hall before the vestibule, one should now visit the eastern portion of the building. On the south wall there is a damaged relief of the king offering to Horus. On the east wall the king worships Isis, who says that she gives him the sovereignty of Horus ; he offers to Isis; and, in large size, he presents a large heap of offerings of all kinds to the temple. The north wall is covered with scenes which have been damaged by the Christians. The king is here seen offering to Isis and Unnefer. On the west wall he worships Osiris, Isis, Nephthys, Hathor, Khnum, Satis, Anukis, and Horus. The king throughout these reliefs is Ptolemy IInd, but Ptolemy IIIrd has added his name here and there. A door in the north wall leads into a passage which turns into the adytum. In this passage, on the east wall, the king is seen carrying a miniature barque, while two priests bear its case behind him. He offers it to Isis and Horus. On the west wall he offers a similar barque to Osiris-Unnefer and Isis. Returning once more to the court in front of the vestibule, one may now pass out by the doorway on the west side, which brings one into an antechamber from which two passages lead, that in the west wall taking one outside the temple, and that in the north wall taking one up a straight flight of steps to the roof. In the anteroom there are three big reliefs showing the king before Isis.

The eastern chambers of the temple of Isis.

Ascending the steps the roof is found to be constructed in the form of a platform, at each of the four corners of which is an open chamber sunk some eight feet. The stairway by which one has ascended has led through the first of these. That at the northeast corner has a small room leading off it, but there are no inscriptions or reliefs on the walls. That at the south-east corner has lost its flooring, and thus one looks down on to the hall below. That at the south-west corner is the most interesting. On the north wall Isis, Nephthys, Horus, and Anubis are shown making offerings to Unnefer, and Isis and Nephthys spread their wings around him. On the north wall Isis weeps by the bier of Osiris, beside which stands Anubis, while above it hovers a hawk. The gods Harmachis, Seb, Thoth, Tefnut, Nut, Hathor, Sekhmet, and others stand near bewailing. On the east wall various gods worship before Unnefer, Isis, and Nephthys. In the south wall is a door leading into a second chamber, and on either side of it is a relief showing the king, here called simply "Pharaoh," slaying his enemies. In this chamber, which one now enters, the reliefs

The roof of the temple of Isis.

are very curious. On the north wall one sees in the top row the king, whose cartouches are blank, worshipping Min; and Unnefer is worshipped by Isis, Nephthys, Anubis, Horus, Wazet, and Nekheb. In the second row a sacred boat in which is the bier of Osiris is worshipped by the four genii of Anubis—Amset, Hapu, Duamutef, and Khebsen. In the third row a shrine is shown in which is a sacred tree. On the west wall in the top row the king worships before Ptah, Harmachis, Shu, Tefnut, a god whose name is not clear, Nut, Unnefer, Isis, Khnum, Satis, Horus, Nephthys, Hathor, Harpocrates, and Wazet. In the second row Khnum is seen fashioning a pot; behind him are Hapi, a hawk-headed lion, the frog Heket, Osiris, Isis (?), Horus, a lion-headed god, Osiris, Isis, Horus, Remtet in the form of a human-headed snake, Sekhmet, a form of Khepera, Wazet of the fields, Anhur-Shu, Osiris, and Isis. In the third row are the nome standards. On the south wall, in the top row, Osiris and Isis stand beside the sacred head of Osiris on a pole; Horus and two goddesses stand before a large *ded;* and Satis, Anukis, Sokaris, and a ram-headed god are shown before another sacred symbol. In the second row Osiris-Unnefer in the form of a mummified hawk lies on a bier supported by four figures; Isis and Nephthys kneel by the legs of Osiris, which are in a chest; and Isis and Nephthys lean over the bier on which the resurrection of Osiris in the form of Horus is taking place. In the third row Anubis, Isis, and Nephthys are seen tending the body of Osiris; the body of Osiris lies on a bier, while Horus sprinkles water over it, thus causing lotus-flowers to grow from it; the body of Osiris lying on its bier is worshipped by Horus and Heket. On the east wall, in the top row, is the king before the gods Amen-Ra, Nun and Nunt, Hehu and Hehut, Kekui and Kekuit, Nuy and Nuyt, Tum, Thoth, &c. In the second row the king offers to Ptah who fashions a vase, Hapi, Horus, Osiris, Isis, Neith, Selket, Osiris, Urthekau snake-formed, Horus, Nekheb, Horus of Edfu, Sokaris protected by a goddess, and a shrine in which is the head of Isis protected by a goddess. In the third row are the nome signs. One may now ascend to the pylon by means of a stairway.

The outside walls of the temple of Isis.   The outside walls of the temple of Isis are decorated with reliefs dating mainly from the reign of Tiberius. At the south end of the west wall the king is shown slaying his enemies in the presence of Osiris, Isis, Horus, and Hathor. Above this he is shown slaying a captive before the Pharaoh of Senem. In the other reliefs he is shown worshipping Unnefer and Isis; Amen-Ra, Mut, and Khonsu;

Khnum and Hathor; Horus, Isis, and Nephthys; Thoth; Min; Hathor and Horus; Nut; Shu and Tefnut; Nephthys; and others; he is crowned by Nekheb and Wazet in the presence of Isis; and he slays a captive before Horus and Hathor. On the north side, or back, of the temple four large reliefs show him before Isis and Horus; Unnefer and Isis; Isis and Nephthys; and Hathor and Horus; while other smaller reliefs represent other gods. On the east side of the temple at the south end he is seen slaying his enemies before Isis, Hathor, and Horus; he makes offering to Unnefer and Isis; Khnum, Hathor, and Horus; Isis, Hathor, and Horus; Horus, Nephthys, and the Pharaoh of Senem; and Unnefer, Isis, and Nephthys. Along the north end of this side the Pharaoh is seen leaving his palace, with the jackal-, ibis-, and hawk-standards before him; he is purified by Behudet and Thoth; he is crowned by Nekheb and Wazet; he is led by Menthu of On and Harmachis to Isis; and he worships Isis, Unnefer and Isis, Horus and Isis, and Isis and Horus. Higher up he stands before Isis, Horus, and others. On the west of the temple, near the second pylon, stands a gateway and passage built by Hadrian. The flight of steps by which it led to the water is now lost, though the quay and much construction stands. On the lintel of the doorway the king is seen before Osiris, Isis, and Harpocrates; and on the sides of the doorway are the wig of Osiris resting on a pole, and the spine of Osiris in the form of a *ded*, these two relics belonging to Abydos and Busiris respectively. On the south wall of the passage the reliefs have never been finished, and all are much damaged. In the top row Horus is seated between Isis and Nephthys, while Neith and Thoth number his years; and Osiris, Anubis, Shu, Tefnut, and a goddess playing a harp are shown near by. In the second row, near a small side door, there is a very interesting relief. It shows the king bearing a chest upon his shoulder, and walking with Thoth and Isis towards a temple, on the west side of which are two doorways, probably representing this actual building. Beyond these doorways is the river, across which a crocodile swims with Osiris on its back towards some steep rocks, probably representing the rocks of Bîgeh, which can be seen in reality on one's right. Above the river are the sun, moon, and stars, and amidst the blue sky are Harpocrates and Osiris. Other reliefs show Horus slaying a monster, Osiris standing in the sacred tree, and the king worshipping various gods. On the north wall the king offers to Isis and Hathor, Osiris-Sokaris, Isis, Nephthys, and Horus. Lower down Isis, Nephthys, Horus,

The gateway of Hadrian.

Amen, and the cow-headed Isis worship the hawk which rises above the reeds of the river at the foot of the rocks of Bigeh, on which a vulture perches, and under which is a cave surrounded by a serpent and containing a figure of Hapi. This is intended to represent the source of the Nile. On the front of this building is a Demotic inscription in red letters mentioning Aurelius Antoninus Pius and Lucius Verus, and giving them titles derived from conquered provinces. Just to the north of this gateway there are traces of a temple, of which the platform and a few scattered blocks from the walls alone remain. There are here no traces of gods' names or kings' cartouches by which to name the place; but formerly some inscriptions were found which showed that it was built by Claudius and was partly dedicated to Harendotes; while other inscribed blocks built into the Coptic church which stands just to the north also named Claudius as the builder. To the south of Hadrian's gateway is the Nilometer, on the walls of which are Demotic, Hieratic, and Coptic inscriptions. Farther to the north is a ruined temple of Augustus, built in the eighteenth year of his reign. A paved court fronts the temple, and pink granite pillars lie fallen on the ground, and on an architrave there is a Greek inscription. Here Capt. Lyons found the trilingual inscription of Cornelius Gallus, which is now in the Cairo Museum. Beyond this, at the extreme north of the island, stands the Roman Town Gate, built with three arches, the side arches being lower than the middle arch. A domical stone vault is to be seen in the west arch, but that of the east arch has fallen. It is probable that this gateway was erected by Diocletian. A flight of steps leads up from the water to the gateway. Walking now towards the south-east one passes another large ruined Coptic church, and presently the Temple of Hathor is reached, which stands immediately to the east of the second pylon. It consists of a hall and a pronaos, the other chambers being now destroyed. The hall had six pillars on either side, and screen walls joined them; but the pillars are now only standing in part. Entering the hall one sees on the south end of the west wall a damaged relief showing the king worshipping Mut and Hathor, and on the opposite side Hathor is again seen. On the south wall, passing along the lower row from west to east, the following reliefs are seen: a figure standing by some reeds plays a double reed pipe; the king offers a festal coronet to Isis; a figure plays upon a harp; the king offers flowers to Nephthys; a small figure of Bes beats a tambourine; the king offers sistra to Sekhmet; a full-faced figure of Bes plays upon a harp; the king offers a coronet to Hathor; an

ape plays upon a guitar; and the king offers wine to Isis. On the
north wall a figure plays on a double pipe; another figure plays
on a harp; a man carries a gazelle decorated with flowers on his
shoulder; the king offers an ape amulet to Satis; he offers an
ornamental sphinx to Tefnut; a full-faced figure of Bes plays a
harp and dances; an ape plays a guitar; and the king offers wine
to Hathor. The festive nature of these scenes will at once be
observed. Hathor was the goddess of beauty and joy, and these
scenes are intended to inspire the worshipper with those feelings
of gaiety which were pleasing to the goddess. Other reliefs in the
hall show the king in the presence of Horus, Arsnuphis, and Hathor.
There is a doorway on either side of the hall; and at the east end
a semi-portal decorated with Hathor-heads leads into the pronaos,
the roof of which is supported by two pillars. The reliefs in this
chamber are unfinished, but show the king before the usual gods.
A doorway led into the farther chambers, but only the pavement
of these now remains. Outside the pronaos, on the north side, the
king is seen leaving his palace with the Upper Egyptian crown on
his head, and with the four standards before him: the jackal, ibis,
hawk, and Theban emblem; and he burns incense before Unnefer
and Isis. On the south, the king with the crown of Lower Egypt
on his head and with the standards before him, leaves the palace;
and he worships Hathor and Horus, and Khnum and Horus. A
doorway on this side admits to the pronaos, and around it are small
figures of the king worshipping some nearly obliterated gods;
while at the foot of each jamb is a lion holding a knife. The
pronaos of this temple was dedicated to Hathor by Ptolemy VIIth
Philometor and Ptolemy IXth Euergetes; but the hall in the front
and the lost sanctuary were added by Augustus. A Greek inscription reading " Hiertia directed a prayer to Aphrodite " proves that
the temple was dedicated to Hathor.

Just to the south-east of this temple is the famous Kiosk, some- *The
times called "Pharaoh's Bed." Fourteen pillars with floral capitals Kiosk.*
support the architrave, which on the outside is decorated with a
concave cornice. Screen walls rise between the columns on which
reliefs were intended to be sculptured; but only two of them have
been decorated. Wide doorways at the east and west ends admit one
to the Kiosk, and there is a smaller door on the north side. The
pavement of the Kiosk does not now exist, and perhaps it was never
laid down. The only two reliefs show Trajan burning incense before
Unnefer and Isis, and offering wine to Isis and Horus. On the east
side of the Kiosk the terrace or quay still exists, and originally this
seems to have been walled in, thus forming another chamber.

CHAPTER XXIII

FROM PHILÆ TO KALÀBSHEH

DABÔD

<small>The history of Dabôd.</small>

THE village of Dabôd lies about ten miles above the barrage. The temple stood originally a short distance back from the river, with a strip of cultivated land in front of it. The barrage, however, has raised the water in the winter so that it covers the main part of the temple. To the north of the temple there is a fair-sized village rising on the hillside, and to the south there are a few houses. Behind it the scenery is very magnificent; jagged points of dark rock protrude from smooth drifts of vividly yellow sand, while in the distance the hills gather together into a series of ranges. The palms still stand in the water in front of the temple, but these will not last for long.

The ancient Egyptian name for Dabôd is not known with any certainty, but one is tempted to see in it the Abaton, which occurs so frequently in the inscriptions at Philæ and elsewhere. This word in Egyptian reads 'Et-u'byt, and Dabôd might well be the modern rendering. In Greek times 'Et-u'byt was named Abaton, and it is generally identified with Philæ; but this is not certain. A stele of Amenemhat IInd, now at Berlin, was found here, which shows that the town was in existence as early as the XIIth dynasty. It was then probably a military outpost in connection with the garrison at Aswân. The King of Nubia who is responsible for the building of the temple is named "The King of Upper and Lower Egypt, Rantaa-Setepenneteru, Son of the Sun Azkharamen, Living for ever, beloved of Isis." Ptolemy VIIth, who seems to have lived just after Azkharamen's reign, added a Greek inscription on one of the temple walls. The temple was embellished by Ptolemy Euergetes IInd, and in later times Augustus and Tiberius added some reliefs. Diocletian ceded Dabôd with the main part of Lower Nubia to the Nubae, whom he brought from the Oasis of El Khârgeh to act as a

FROM PHILÆ TO KALÂBSHEH

buffer state between Egypt and Ethiopia, and more especially to defend the lower Nile from the attacks of the Blemmyes. The temple was still unfinished at that date, and the introduction of Christianity into the country prevented its completion. In 1868 an earthquake shattered the vestibule and other parts of the building, and since then there have been other falls of masonry. The temple, however, has now been repaired and restored.

The most important deity to the inhabitants of Dabôd was, of course, Isis; and in the temple she is represented generally in connection with Osiris-Unnefer and Harpocrates. Other deities were worshipped in the temple, including Khnum, Amen-Ra, Mut, and Hathor. Amen-Ra is, in one place, called "Lord of the Throne of the Two Lands in Bîgeh, Bull finding his place in Abaton."

The temple buildings were made up as follows :—On the edge of the river there was a terrace or quay, from which a paved way led to the front gate, which was built into the enclosing wall of the courtyard. Beyond this gate a second and a third were passed through, though these seem to have had only an ornamental value. The main building was then reached. Along its face there was a portico, the roof of which was supported by four columns connected by screen walls. A doorway in the middle led into the hall, and from this another door opened into an antechamber, in the back wall of which a third door led into the sanctuary. From the antechamber a door on either side opened into a long narrow chamber, that on the north side being intended for the keeping of the sacred utensils, and that on the south side for a vestry. The priests could approach the latter by way of a narrow passage which ran along the south side of the building, and they would thus avoid passing through the public parts of the temple. From this side of the temple a stairway ascended to the roof. On the south of the portico a wing was added at a later date, but it is now much ruined. The quay is now under water in winter; in summer ten tiers of masonry blocks sometimes can be seen, and one is able to make out the stairway which was built into the stonework. The pavement around the temple has all been dug away by the natives during the last century, and the thresholds of the doorways and floors of the chambers are high above the level of the ground outside, the foundations thus being entirely exposed. The first gateway is ornamented with the usual cornice and disk. The granite pivot on which the door swung is still *in situ*. The threshold of the second gateway is of granite.

_{The temple.}

On the upper part of this building there is a much-damaged Greek inscription giving the name of Ptolemy VIIth and Queen Cleopatra. The third doorway has lately collapsed, and lies in a confused heap on the ground. The portico of the temple has also fallen, and fragments of the capitals of the columns, never finished by the sculptor, are to be seen on the ground. On the standing front wall of the temple "Autocrator Cæsar" is represented worshipping Isis, Osiris-Unnefer, Khnum, and a lion-headed god whose name is not readable. As one enters the roofless pronaos the reliefs on the inner sides of the doorway are seen to represent Horus and Thoth pouring a vessel of holy water over the approaching worshipper, while behind them "the Chief Reader-priest, the Chief Scribe of the North and South," the demi-god Imhotep, sees that the necessary ritual is said. The walls of the hall are covered with reliefs, some of them much damaged, showing the Nubian King Azkheramen adoring the gods of Dabôd. Passing into the antechamber one finds there a large naos of pink granite, lately restored to its place. It is inscribed with what appear to be the names of Ptolemy Euergetes IInd, but the inscription is very hard to read. The remainder of the temple is uninscribed, but these innermost rooms are the best preserved, the walls and roof being more or less intact, whereas in the front rooms the outer walls used to lean in all directions. In the room on the north side of the antechamber, *i.e.* that in which the ceremonial objects of value were kept, there is a man-hole in the floor, opening into a narrow passage, which leads up a flight of steps into a secret chamber constructed in the thickness of the wall. It was evidently the treasure-room of the temple, in which the more valuable objects were hidden.

The quarries and cemeteries.

The quarries from which the stone for the building of the temple was cut are situated about a mile to the west, amongst the rocky hillocks and smooth sand-drifts of the desert. They are not extensive, and they have no inscriptions of any kind upon them. A walk up to them, however, repays the visitor, as the view is extremely fine from the higher ground.

In the high ground to the north-west of the temple there are a few tombs cut into the hillside, but now covered again with sand. They are said not to be inscribed, and one, into which the writer penetrated, was quite devoid of decoration. To the south of the temple, beyond a sandy valley, there are a number of tombs of a very poor kind, mostly untouched. They are marked by small mounds of stone; while here and there some broken pottery of

FROM PHILÆ TO KALÂBSHEH

Roman date and a few white bones show where the inquisitive native has ransacked one of the graves. Some of these tombs are somewhat curious in form. Three or four coffin-shaped basins have been neatly cut into a flat-surfaced outcrop of rock, and, when the body was placed inside, each was covered by a heap of rough stones.

FROM DABÔD TO TÂFEH

A short distance above Dabôd lies the village of Dimri, situated amidst the rugged granite rocks. In summer and autumn, when the water is low, there is to be seen something of the remains of an ancient temple and town. Fragments of a column of sandstone and its capital, a block of granite, and a masonry wall projecting into the river still exist. These ruins probably mark the site of the Roman Parembole, which is stated to be sixteen Roman miles above Syene, that place being reckoned as beginning three Roman miles below Philæ. Thus Parembole is thirteen Roman miles above Philæ, which would place it somewhere about here, or a little farther south. _{Dimri.}

The antiquities on the west side of the river are few in number. In the village of Dimri there are traces of a quay wall, and the substructure of a small temple of Roman date; but very little of it now remains. One large block of hewn stone has a curious legend attached to it. During the Mameluke occupation of this country there lived a woman named Gamr ("Moon"), who acquired great wealth, which she buried before she died. It is the opinion of some that the treasure is to be found in a valley named after her Wâdy Gamar. But others consider that the treasure lies inside or under this stone. They say that the stone gives out such peculiar noises during the night that the people who live near it are sometimes unable to sleep; and they regard this as an indication of the existence of the treasure. The noises are variously described as being like the grinding of a mill, like a *sakiyeh* or water-wheel, and like a cock crowing!

On the island of Morgos, some way above Dimri, there are some ruins of crude brick, which are probably the remains of a Christian monastery of the name, it may be supposed, of Markos. A main building can be discerned rising amidst the granite boulders, and there are outbuildings at the southern end of the island. Much Roman and Coptic pottery lies about. _{Morgos.}

A mile or so south of Morgos there are a number of groups of

Dehmîd. tumbled granite rocks, which in winter become islands, but at low water are joined to the main land. On one of these rocks the present writer found a fine Greek inscription, dating from the reign of Hadrian. The houses on the rocks above it form the north end of the hamlet of Wesîyeh, which is part of the village of Dehmîd. Somewhere in this neighbourhood was the Roman station of Tzitzi, which was fourteen Roman miles north of Tâfeh. About 500 yards south of this inscription the granite rocks abruptly cease, and the sandstone reappears. Some 200 yards south of the point at which the change takes place, and near the southern houses of Wesîyeh, a group of hieroglyphical inscriptions of considerable size was also found. The inscriptions are of some length, and are cut on the sides of the shelving sandstone rocks. They relate to early wars in Lower Nubia; and are of great historical value.

Near the southernmost end of Dehmîd there stands the hamlet of Sheymeh, and on the south side of the mouth of a rocky valley which lies just to the south of this hamlet there is another group of inscriptions. The most important of these gives the third year of a king who seems to be Amenemhat IInd. The cartouche of Senusert Ist is also inscribed here, and there are various names of officials.

On the east bank the village of Dehmîd is separated from the following village, named Umberakab, by a wide valley in which there is a small plundered cemetery. On the rocks at the south side of the mouth of this valley there are two long inscriptions cut in large size. The second of these gives the cartouche of an unknown king, probably of the XIIIth–XVIIth dynasty, whose name seems to read Hakara or Wazkara, and it refers to one of his nobles. The other inscription calls on persons who read it to offer a prayer for this same noble. Near here the writer obtained from a native's house a stele which gives the cartouche of Amenemhat IInd. At Umberakab there is a modern pottery manufactory, which supplies a large part of Nubia.

WÂDY HEDÎD AND KERTASSI

Situation. The group of ancient sites which seems to have connected the ancient Tzitzi with Taphis, commences at the village of Wâdy Hedîd and extends to the village of Kertassi, some two miles farther to the south. In winter the houses of Wâdy Hedîd, built

FROM PHILÆ TO KALÂBSHEH

on the low sandstone rocks, are lapped by the river; and the wâdys are filled with water for some distance back, having thus the appearance of tributary streams. The village stands at the mouth of one of these wâdys, and another larger creek separates this neighbourhood from that of Kertassi. The temple of Kertassi stands on a plateau of rock, fortunately above the highest level of the water. It overlooks the river, and is a landmark for some miles in either direction. The ruin outlined against the sky, with its delicate columns rising from the rocks, forms a picture of the greatest charm. The fortress, which is some distance farther to the south, stands in water in winter; and when the barrage is raised it will disappear during that season.

Unfortunately there is no mention of the original name of this site in the inscriptions. The name Tzitzi may perhaps correspond to the *-tassi* in the word Kertassi, the *ker-* being a prefix. There are no antiquities of any kind which can be dated to a period earlier than that of the Ptolemies, and it does not seem to have been a place of any importance until the quarries were first worked here. These quarries were extensive, and from them the stone for building Philæ temple was mainly obtained. The tombs at Wâdy Hedîd are Ptolemaic in character, but now that the water has flooded all but the plundered graves on the higher levels, one is unable to say at what date the town was founded. In Roman times there was a garrison here, and the place was largely peopled by Greek quarrymen. *History.*

Amongst the houses towards the north end of this village, just at the mouth of a narrow valley, there stands a column of sandstone with an unpretentious fluted capital, and near it are the bases of three other columns. This evidently is the ruin of a small temple, and between it and the water there is a large quantity of broken stones which seems to form the remains of the ancient town. The site stands low and will be lost when the water is raised. *Wâdy Hedîd.*

The temple of Kertassi, though much ruined and of very small size, is one of the gems of the country, and one is grateful to the original architect for having placed it on ground high enough to be out of reach of the water-levels of the present age. The temple is built in the form of a single small chamber, not unlike the Kiosk at Philæ. There are four upright columns, and their well-executed floral capitals are of the greatest beauty. The screen walls connecting the columns are preserved on the east, north, and west sides, but that on the south is destroyed. On the *Temple of Kertassi.*

north there is the entrance door, on either side of which is a Hathor-headed column; and on the west there is a small door. The columns still support one of the cross beams, but the rest of the roof has fallen. On one column there is a relief showing the figure of the king before Isis and Horus, but there are no inscriptions, and the temple is otherwise undecorated.

The quarries of Kertassi. The quarries lie to the north, west, and south of the temple, the last being the most extensive. These extend along the river's edge and also back on the high levels of the rocks for nearly a mile. The inscriptions and graffiti, however, are confined to a fine quarry which lies about half-way between the temple and the fortress. This quarry is entered by a narrow passage cut through the rock just as in the case of the quarries at Gebel Silsileh. On the sides of the passage there are some votive stelæ, two of which are dedicated to Osiris. A hawk is also engraved on the stone here. On the west wall of this quarry there are a large number of Greek inscriptions, Egypto-Roman figures, &c. There is here a shrine or niche in which the statue of a deity may have been placed; the front is worked in the form of an Egyptian doorway, with uræi and the sun's disk above, and pillars up either side. To the right and left of this there is a Roman bust cut in high relief, the face being in each case damaged. The togas and hands, however, are well preserved. These busts probably represented a certain Gaius Dioscuros Julius Macrinus, who records, in a Greek inscription, that he held the office of Priest of the Carrying of the Stones (*Gomos*) under Severus, Caracalla, Maximinus, and Philippus Arabus, for a total period of about fifty years, in which he had spent about £300 sterling from his own pocket. The main part of the quarry wall is covered with upwards of fifty Greek inscriptions, each having some six or eight lines of well-cut Greek letters, and each being enclosed in a rectangle with a triangular tag at either end. There is also one inscription in demotic. These inscriptions are *ex votos*, of the time of Antoninus Pius, Marcus Aurelius, Severus, Caracalla, and Gordian, and are addressed to Isis, Sruptikhis, and Pursepmunis. They were mostly engraved by the priests presiding over the carriage of the stones, and one of them mentions that 110 stones were cut by a certain Orses. Philæ is referred to as being the temple for which the stones were intended. The gods Sruptikhis and Pursepmunis are of Nubian origin, and seem to have been patrons of Kertassi, the latter being identified also with Osiris. On the lower part of the wall there are several

FROM PHILÆ TO KALÂBSHEH

figures of Isis, &c., cut in relief, some being represented full face.

The fortress of Kertassi is situated on the edge of the river, nearly a mile south of the temple. It is a large rectangular enclosure surrounded by a strong masonry wall, still rising in parts to a height of some twenty feet. The main gateway is on the north side, and there are other entrances on the south and west. The former has the usual concave cornice, and on the sides are a few scratchings, including one of the figure of Isis. The enclosure wall is constructed of two skins of masonry with a space between formerly filled with rough stones, and is a valuable specimen of this type of building. Inside the wall, against its north side there is a solid mass of masonry, which may have formed some kind of tower; and at about the centre of the enclosure there is another solid construction, which in all probability was the main tower or citadel. In 1812 Legh saw, in the south-east corner of the enclosure, a small "temple of Isis," possessing "six beautiful columns of 3 feet diameter"; but this has now vanished. On the west side of the fort one may trace the line of the ancient moat. Within this enclosure the village of Kertassi was built, but when the barrage was made the place was flooded, and the village was reconstructed at a higher level. In summer, when the site is dry, the enclosure is found to be full of broken stones, ruins of houses, and fragments of the original construction; but in winter only the walls and gateway are to be seen.

The fortress of Kertassi.

TÂFEH

Tâfeh is one of the most beautifully situated villages on the Nile. At this point the hills fall back somewhat, leaving a bay about a mile and a half across. To the south the magnificent granite rocks of the Bâb el Kalâbsheh shut in the view, and to the north and west the lower sandstone rocks confine the scene. Along the ridges at the back of the bay the houses of the village rise, and here a whitewashed mosque stands out conspicuously against the blue sky. On the lower level there is a profusion of palms and sycamore trees, which in winter rise from the water, but in summer and autumn stand amidst crops of beans and other vegetables. The various ruins stand at different parts of the bay, and on the hills around; and they are therefore partly flooded when the water is high. The best time to see the place

Situation.

is in early November, when the reservoir is still empty and the weather already cool. Tâfeh is about thirty-one miles above the barrage, and it is therefore by no means difficult of access.

History of Tâfeh.

The ancient name of the place was Taphis, but this is not found in hieroglyphical form. Its position is of considerable strategical importance, as it lies just at the mouth of the Bâb or Pass, where originally there were rapids. On the east bank there was the Roman fort of Contra Taphis, which is given in the Itinerary of Antoninus as ten Roman miles below Talmis or Kalâbsheh; and on the west bank the same list calls Taphis itself eight Roman miles below Talmis. There are no ruins here which are to be dated earlier than the Roman occupation, and all the existing buildings seem to have been built at about the same time as the temples of Kertassi and Kalâbsheh. In A.D. 300 Taphis became part of the Kingdom of the Blemmyes, who had conquered the Romans; but in the sixth century the Christian Nubian king Silko penetrated as far as this town, defeating the Blemmyes who were still living here. In later times the various ruins were turned into monasteries and churches, and an early Arabic MS. gives the general name as the Monastery of Ansoun, and refers to the solid construction of the walls.

The houses of Tâfeh.

The ruins at Tâfeh consist of two temples, one of which has almost entirely disappeared, and a large number of dwelling-houses constructed of heavy masonry blocks. It will be best to describe first the latter buildings. At the north-west end of the bay there is a group of six of these houses. They each consist of a powerful enclosure wall forming a rectangle, of which the sides are generally some 55 feet in length; and a number of internal chambers now ruined and more or less indistinguishable. The height of these walls is still in parts 15 to 18 feet, and originally all the walls must have been at least 18 feet high. The roofs, now fallen in, were partly constructed of stone, and, as will be seen later, were perhaps partly built of vaulted brickwork. Fragments of ornamented doorways, &c., are lying about, the usual decoration being the winged disk and row of uræi. This group of buildings is perhaps to be regarded as the quarters of the governor of the place, since it consists of the largest and best situated of the houses. Between here and the temple there are four or five enclosures, of which the most northerly is the best preserved of all the buildings. Entering by the doorway at the south-east corner one passes into a long entrance hall, at the end of which another doorway leads into a small anteroom. A passage

FROM PHILÆ TO KALÂBSHEH

on the left-hand side leads to a second anteroom, which again gives on to a chamber which may have been the sleeping- or living-room. From the passage a doorway on the left side leads up to the raised hall which occupies the middle of the building, and was probably the reception-room. Perhaps this was also approached from the entrance hall by a short flight of steps. The roofing was mainly of stone, but the reception-room may have had a vaulted brick roof. It will be realised that these stone-built rooms must have been very cool in summer, and it is probably for this reason that they were built in such a solid manner. The isolated position of each building, and the lack of loop-holes or turrets, shows that they were not constructed of such fine masonry for defensive purposes. In time of war they would have been nothing else but traps for the defenders. To the west of the temple two small enclosures stand, and near to it there is another which may have been occupied by the chief priest. Only the outer walls stand, and in one case there seems to have been a cornice topping the wall about eight feet from the ground. Here it is quite certain that the roofing must have been of brick.

The temple stands not far from the river, and early travellers speak of a flight of steps which led to it from a quay, but this has entirely disappeared. The little building is almost perfect, and only a part of the west wall has fallen. It consists of a single chamber, the roof of which is supported by six columns with floral capitals. On the north side is a recess for the altar; while the main entrance is on the south side, and is ornamented with an elaborate cornice. Originally there was probably a portico on the south side, and the whole temple stood on a platform which, under the main building, consists of six tiers of masonry, making a height of ten feet from the ground. But these foundations were, of course, not exposed. There are no decorations on the temple walls. Another temple, still standing at the south-west side of the bay in 1870, has now almost totally disappeared; and the natives still speak casually of how it was broken up to supply stone for their houses. Regarding this building they have a curious story to tell, which relates how travellers returning to Tâfeh from the north see the temple standing as it used to do, but as they approach nearer it vanishes.

The temple of Tâfeh.

Between the standing temple and the next ruins to the south there is a wide space over which the ancient town probably spread. Just under the towering granite rocks at the south of the bay there are three more enclosures. The internal walls are ruined and pulled to pieces. From behind these ruins a rough, and now almost entirely demolished, stairway led to the summit of the rocks. Here, commanding perhaps the finest view in Egypt, stand the well-preserved ruins of three buildings. The northern building consists of a rectangular wall of good masonry, enclosing a space which was apparently filled with earth and stones, thus forming a platform some 10 or 12 feet in height. Upon this basis rises a large chamber, the walls of which are made of crude brick, the roof being vaulted. Set in the brick wall at the south end there was a masonry doorway, which is now broken and has fallen. The ornamentation on the fragments shows a mixture of Roman and Egyptian architectural designs, and is a beautiful piece of work. A smaller doorway in the east wall led into an anteroom also with a vaulted roof. The southern building has its lower part also constructed of well-laid masonry blocks; but here these rise higher than the floor-level of the chamber which is built above. This chamber is of crude brick, and its roof was flat, being supported by cross-beams. Around the walls runs a brick bench which seems to have been faced with stone. The doorway in the north wall is now destroyed, but fragments of its ornamental cornice can be seen. Between these two buildings there is a smaller brick chamber which has had a vaulted roof. The broken ground upon which the group of buildings stands has been levelled into a kind of platform, on which there are traces of smaller buildings. The view from here is indeed superb. To the north the town and temple of Tâfeh is overlooked, and beyond this the Nile is seen flowing towards the distant hills. To the south and west the tumbled granite boulders and ragged hills extend as far as the eye can see. To the east one looks sheer down on the river as it winds between the sombre cliffs, and here and there one catches a glimpse of a little bay in which stand a few palms or other trees, looking wonderfully green against the purple-brown of the rocks. Up here all the coolness of the north wind is felt; and it does not require much effort of imagination to suppose that these buildings formed the pleasure-house of the Roman governor of Tâfeh—a copy, in idea, perhaps, of the palace of Tiberius on the cliffs of Capri. The buildings were certainly not used as a fortress or even as watch-towers, for they have no defensive walls, and do not command the view towards the south which would be necessary.

Looking again at the remains of the Roman town, one now sees how the natives of Lower Nubia were enslaved and driven to

FROM PHILÆ TO KALÂBSHEH 501

quarry the necessary stone for the building of these cool houses in the plain, and this pavilion on the cliffs. Gardens, no doubt, surrounded the houses; and the Roman officers seem to have made every effort to render their life comfortable in this distant post. Everywhere traces of elegant ornamentation are found; and there must be many remains still unexcavated. For the best part of the Roman occupation there was little danger of attack at Taphis, the frontier being many miles to the south, and there being several Roman stations between them. Thus the officers could amuse themselves here as well as they were able so far from Rome.

The quarries from which the stone was obtained for the building of the houses and temples lie at the west of the bay, but no inscriptions were found there. Not far from this there is a mediæval cemetery in which are many Cufic inscriptions. On the rocks at the south of the village there are two short inscriptions of the Middle Kingdom. On a rock some distance inland there is an inscription of Taharka's reign.

FROM TÂFEH TO KALÂBSHEH

Immediately after leaving Tâfeh one enters the pass known as Bâb el Kalâbsheh, and the scenery for the next few miles is magnificent. At the mouth of the pass there are some inscriptions on the rocks, but these are mostly unreadable, having been lightly scratched on the scaling surface of the granite. *The Bâb el Kalâbsheh.*

A number of islands are presently passed, upon the largest of which there are some ruined houses of modern times. About half a mile south of these ruins, the village of Khartum lies at the mouth of a valley on the west bank. A number of rocks forming islands in winter, but being connected with the mainland in summer, lie some distance in front of the village. On the largest of these groups there are a few inscriptions. The most important of these states that Isis of Philæ owns the country for the thirty *schoinoi* between the two *wepwat*, which in this case means "frontiers." A *schoinos* is usually reckoned about $7\frac{1}{2}$ miles, and thus the thirty *schoinoi* give the exact distance between the First and Second Cataracts. It would be interesting to know at what date this statement was made: the inscription is certainly Ptolemaic or Roman, of course.

Behind the village of Khartum runs the road from Tâfeh to

502 ANTIQUITIES OF UPPER EGYPT

The Tâfeh-Kalâbsheh road. Kalâbsheh, where there are some matters of interest for the archæologist. One passes through the village and over the sandy slope, turning, after less than a mile, to the north and entering a rocky valley along which the pathway runs. On a rock on the left side of the pathway there is a small inscription dated in the eighteenth year of Taharka. Passing on up this path one reaches, after about a mile and a half, an open space in which stands a small Christian ruin known as the church of *Sitteh Kasmar*. The walls of the church are constructed of rough stones, and the roof was supported by four small pillars, of which the capitals are Egyptian, and may have been taken from Tâfeh. There is a recess for the altar at the west end. Behind the church are four living rooms for the priest in charge. The nearest road to the river is directly to the east, but the road to Khartum is more easily followed.

KALÂBSHEH

Situation. The town of Kalâbsheh comprises a large number of villages, and spreads itself over a considerable tract of country on either side of the river. The temple is a magnificent building standing at the foot of the hills, and can be seen for some distance before it is reached. The water at its present winter level covers a part of the pier or terrace of the temple, but the whole edifice will stand in deep water when the barrage is raised. The temple of Bêt el Wâli stands higher up on the hill-side to the north of Kalâbsheh, at a point where there is a wide wâdy running up into the desert. The space between the two temples is covered by the ruins of the ancient town. The country is desolate here, but the view from the hills above the temple is wonderful. On one side the Nile is seen winding between the rugged hills, and on the other the desert stretches away to the western horizon in a series of barren hills and valleys.

History. The ancient Egyptian name for Kalâbsheh was Thelmes, and from this the Roman name of Thalmis, or Talmis, was derived. From the fact that King Amenhotep IInd is shown in one part of the mural reliefs of the large temple, it may be supposed that he was the builder of the original temple; and the great activity of that king elsewhere in Nubia gives colour to the supposition. A statue, bearing the name of Thothmes IIIrd, was seen some years ago lying near the quay. At Bêt el Wâli Rameses IInd records his victories over the people of Upper Nubia. Ptolemy Xth

FROM PHILÆ TO KALÂBSHEH

records his name in one of the buildings near the great temple. This latter building was erected in the reign of Augustus, and was continued under the rule of Caligula, Trajan, Severus, and others. A decree of Aurelius Besarion, military governor of Ombos and Elephantine, A.D. 249, is inscribed on one of the walls, and orders owners of swine to remove these animals from Talmis; which suggests that the temple had fallen into disuse just previous to that reform. There is a cursive Latin inscription in the temple dated in the twelfth year of Nerva. The Roman withdrawal from Lower Nubia about A.D. 300 left Talmis in the hands of the Blemmyes, who made it their capital, remaining there until Silko, the Nubian king, conquered them. Shortly afterwards the place became Christianised, and both Kalâbsheh temple and Bêt el Wâli were used as churches. It remained thus until the end of the twelfth century, when the Christians were converted to Muhammedanism at the point of the sword. Bêt el Wâli, as is indicated by its name, "the house of the saint," was probably used as a dwelling-place by some "saint" of modern times.

The inhabitants of Kalâbsheh are stated by the travellers of fifty years ago to have been quarrelsome and riotous. They never permitted a tax-gatherer or conscript-catcher to enter the neighbourhood, and travellers were greeted by them with curses or with angry demands for money. They carried spears, shields, daggers, and other weapons, with which they threatened their visitors on some occasions. Nowadays they sometimes carry spears or daggers, but the custom is fast dying out, as is also their turbulence ; and visitors will find them as docile as the inhabitants of the other Nubian towns. *Modern inhabitants.*

The great god of Talmis was *Merul* or *Melul*, the Mandulis or Malulis of the Greeks. He belonged entirely to Kalâbsheh, and is never called anything else but "of Talmis." He is represented in various forms, but he is mainly regarded either as a form of Osiris or as Harpocrates. In most cases he is associated with the goddess Wazet, or Buto, Lady of Pe and Dep, the two sacred cities of the Delta. He is always represented in a human form, and he may be a deified hero, just as is Petisis of Dendûr. A Neo-Platonic hymn in the temple refers to his twin brother Breith. The human sign is written at the end of his name, and not that of divine beings. He does not seem to have been in existence as early as the XIXth dynasty, for he is not mentioned in the Bêt el Wâli temple. In this temple many other deities are mentioned, such as Amen-Ra, Khnum, Min, Ptah, Horus, Isis, &c. In the

504 ANTIQUITIES OF UPPER EGYPT

Kalâbsheh temple the deities, besides Melul, are Osiris-Unnefer, Isis, Horus, Hathor, Menthu-Harmachis, Amen-Ra, Mut, Min, Khnum, and many others. Unnefer is perhaps the most important of these gods; he is sometimes called "Prince of the Hawks." Isis and Horus are the next most important deities. It is to be observed that Amenhotep IInd is represented, in the single scene in which his name occurs, as worshipping Min; and it may be that that god was of local importance in the XVIIIth dynasty.

The original plan of the temple. The temple is intended to be approached from the river. Originally one's vessel would draw up at a quay, some twenty feet high, constructed of solid masonry. Mounting this one would find oneself on a broad terrace extending to right and left along the river's edge. This has a breadth of some sixty yards, and leads back to a second terrace or platform, and upon this the front pylon of the temple rises, being slightly deflected from the axis. Between the upper and lower terrace there is a causeway six and a half yards wide and fifty-three yards long, running out towards the river in the axis of the temple, and ending in a rectangular platform, while at the west end a flight of steps leads up to the temple. Passing through the pylon one enters the great hall, which originally was embellished with a colonnade on the north, east, and south sides. From this hall one passes through a doorway into the Hypostyle Hall, from which a doorway on the north and south sides leads into a court, enclosed by a high wall, two metres thick, which shuts in the western end of the temple. This may also be entered from the west side of the great hall. From the Hypostyle Hall one enters the vestibule, and passes on into the adytum, and finally into the sanctuary, the doors of these three chambers being in the main axis of the temple. A stairway leads from the south side of the vestibule to the roof. The whole temple is enclosed by an enormous girdle wall, starting from either side of the front pylon, and enclosing a large area. This wall is twelve feet thick, and is constructed like that of the fortress at Kertassi, *i.e.* with two skins of masonry, having a space between filled with loose stones. It rises at an average distance of thirty feet from the inner wall. At the south-west corner of the space thus enclosed there is a rock chapel, which may have been intended as a "Birth-house." There was a portico in front of the door of this chapel. At the north-east corner of the temple there was again a chapel.

As seen at the present day, the temple is found to be in a state of great dilapidation, although the main walls are not ruined, and

FROM PHILÆ TO KALÂBSHEH

the works recently carried on there have rendered the building safe and tidy. The reliefs on the walls, however, are not badly damaged, and still show much of their original colouring. The stairway ascending to the roof from the vestibule is well preserved, though the chambers to which it leads are much damaged. The quay and terraces are all fairly perfect and are most imposing. It has been thought that an earthquake is responsible for the falling of the roof and columns, and if this is so it is a matter for surprise that the walls of the temple are not more damaged also.

The present condition of the temple.

From the river the visitor ascends through the front gateway into the great hall, the walls of which are not decorated with reliefs, except in the case of the western screen-walls which separate this hall from the next. On one of these to the south of the doorway there is an unfinished scene of the Pharaoh in the presence of Horus, being purified by Thoth. On another of the screen-walls to the north of the doorway there is a Greek inscription in twenty-one lines, inscribed in the sixth century A.D., by the orders of Silko, a Christian king of Nubia, who had descended the river as far as Kalâbsheh and Tâfeh in a successful expedition against the Blemmyes. The first part of the inscription reads :—

The Great Hall.

> I, Silko, puissant king of the Nubians and all the Ethiopians,
> I came twice as far as Talmis and Taphis.
> I fought against the Blemmyes, and God granted me the victory.
> I vanquished them a second time three to one ; and the first time
> I fortified myself there with my troops.
> I vanquished them, and they supplicated me.
> I made peace with them, and they swore to me by their idols.
> I trusted them, because they are a people of good faith.
> Then I returned to my dominions in the Upper Country.
> For I am a king.
> Not only am I no follower in the train of other kings,
> But I go before them.

Near this inscription is a small picture of a man in Roman dress seated on a horse, and receiving a wreath from a winged victory. Perhaps this is intended to represent Silko. The inscription is written in very bad Greek, but it is of great historical importance. Not far from this inscription is one in Meroitic or Ethiopian Demotic. On the screen-wall, next to that on which the Silko inscription occurs, is written the decree of Aurelius Besarion, also called Amonius, referred to above. On a door in the south wall there is a Neo-Platonic hymn in thirty-four Sotadaic verses, referring to Mandulis and his twin brother Breith.

The Hypostyle Hall.
In the Hypostyle Hall the reliefs are unfinished, and many of the scenes lack their accompanying inscriptions. On the screen-wall at the south-east side of the hall there is a fairly well-preserved Christian painting of three Hebrew figures in the fiery furnace, while an angel in the form of a child offers the central figure a sword.

The inner chambers.
On the walls of the vestibule the Roman Emperors are seen making offerings to the various gods. One may mount the stairs to the roof which leads from the small chamber on the south-east of this room. At their summit there is another short flight of steps descending again into a chamber overlooking the vestibule. A further, though somewhat dangerous, flight of steps, leads up to the top of the gateway above the Hypostyle Hall. On returning to the lower level, the adytum is entered, and here again the walls are covered with scenes representing the Roman Pharaohs worshipping the gods. Down either side of the gateway leading into the sanctuary there are inscriptions dedicated to Osiris of Abaton and Melul of Talmis. The sanctuary is decorated with mural reliefs in much the same manner as in the previous two rooms. The reliefs in these chambers are in many ways interesting. The colouring is well preserved, and originally must have been painfully crude. The figures are ill-formed, and the faces quite negroid in character. The costumes of the Pharaohs and gods are elaborate, and their head-dresses multiform. The gods are often painted black as though they were negroes, and it is with some surprise that one sees the youthful Horus with skin of ebony.

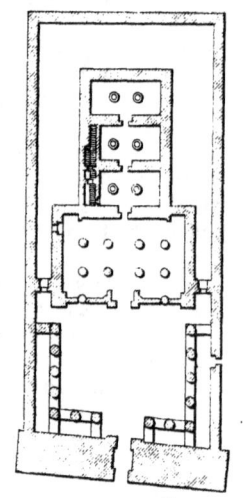

TEMPLE OF KALÂBSHEH.

The rock chapel and other outbuildings are hardly worth a visit, having nothing of particular interest, and requiring something of a climb over the fallen stones before they can be reached. When the barrage is raised the visitor will be able to sail at his ease through the different halls and chambers of the temple. Most of

FROM PHILÆ TO KALÂBSHEH

the temple stands on the rock, and now that it has been strengthened it will bear the strain of the water safely.

THE TEMPLE OF BÊT EL WÂLI

The temple of Bêt el Wâli, which was constructed by Rameses IInd, is situated on the hillside to the north-west of Kalâbsheh. It is a rock-cut shrine consisting of an outer court, a vestibule cut in the rock, and a sanctuary. A pathway leads up to it through the north end of Kalâbsheh village, but the original dromos is lost. The visitor first finds himself in the open court, only the two side walls of which remain, and on these are the well-known historical scenes from the life of Rameses IInd. Turning to the south wall the first scene at the east end shows the king in his chariot furiously charging down on the flying host of Ethiopians, and shooting arrows from his bow into their midst. Behind him in two chariots are the king's sons Amenherunamf and Khaemuast, the latter being described as "the water of the god coming forth in strength." Each of the princes has a driver in the chariot with him, and the drawing of these is most spirited. The negroes, who carry bows and arrows, dash back towards their camp amongst the dôm-palms; two warriors lead along a wounded comrade; the women and children run hither and thither in panic; and one woman looks up, terrified, from her cooking. The scene at the west end of the wall shows the king seated under a canopy, while the nobles and princes of Egypt bring the tribute of the Ethiopians to him. Amongst these nobles is Amenemapt, son of Paser, who was also viceroy. The tribute is shown in two lines. In the upper line are gold rings, bags of precious objects, fruit, bows, leopard skins, shields, chairs, fans, feathers, tusks, a lion, a gazelle, oxen, and finally a group of negro soldiers with spears. In the lower line are prisoners, monkeys, a leopard, a giraffe, bulls, one of which has its horns ornamented with a head and hands, women with their children, one carrying two babies in a basket on her back, a gazelle, an ostrich, and a leopard.

The above scenes refer to one of the expeditions conducted by Rameses IInd against the Ethiopians, after his long wars in Asia Minor had been brought to a satisfactory close. The tribute which he received from the unfortunate negroes is most interesting, and such objects as the ornamented chairs show that these tribes were not so uncivilised as one might suppose. The Viceroy

The open court.

508 ANTIQUITIES OF UPPER EGYPT

Amenemapt no doubt carried out all the arrangements for the expedition; and with the superior arms and organisation of the Egyptian troops there was probably small chance of defeat. The negro soldiers represented here before Rameses show that the Lower Nubians were as usual employed to fight their ancient enemies from Kush. On the north wall of the court the scenes refer to the wars of the king in Asia Minor and Libya, and their representation here was intended to show the natives that the Pharaoh was as powerful at one end of the earth as at another. The first scene at the east end of the wall shows the king, with axe raised, holding a group of Syrian captives by the hair; while the Egyptian princes lead in other prisoners, who are drawn in attitudes of the utmost despair and exhaustion. In the next scene the king is attacking a Syrian fortress, and is slaughtering a figure who appears at the top of the tower, holding a broken bow; while one of the king's sons bursts in the door with an axe. Dead warriors fall from the battlements, while other figures supplicate the conqueror, making offerings to him as though he were a god. The following scene shows the king bending forward from his chariot, which is being whirled along by a pair of galloping horses. He is in the act of striking down his Syrian enemies, who are flying before his onslaught. Then follows a scene in which Rameses is represented putting to death a kneeling figure of a Libyan, while, as an indication of the prisoner's utter humiliation, the king's pet dog is shown biting him as he kneels. At a respectful distance various princes and nobles of Egypt bow before the king. In the next portion the king, seated under a canopy, with his tame lion at his feet, receives the princes who bring in prisoners. Three forlorn old men are dragged forward, walking on tiptoe, as though from fright. Below these are other nobles bowing before the conqueror.

The vestibule. Through the west wall of this court three doorways lead into the vestibule, and on the east face of this wall, over the middle door, the king is seen dancing before Amen-Ra, while at the sides he stands before Min, Khonsu, Horus, &c. The vestibule is a rock-cut chamber, the roof of which is supported by two stout fluted columns, each having four perpendicular bands of inscription down it, giving the titles of the king. The middle doorway of the three is the largest, and there is reason to suppose that the other two were added somewhat later. On either side of the doorway into the sanctuary there is a niche in which sit three figures, those on the south side perhaps being the king between

FROM PHILÆ TO KALÂBSHEH

Isis and Horus, and those on the north the king between Khnum and Anukis, but all the figures are much damaged. On the sides of the central door as one enters the vestibule the king is seen being embraced by Amen-Ra and Mut (?). There is also the small figure of a kneeling man who is the Viceroy of Ethiopia, Messuy. At the side of the north door is the figure of the king entering the chamber, wearing the crown of Lower Egypt; and at the side of the south door the king enters wearing the double crown. Inside the vestibule the scene on the south side of the east wall shows the king smiting a negro, representing his conquest of Nubia. On the south wall the king offers incense and libations to Horus and Selkis, the scorpion-goddess, while behind the king is another goddess, whose name is erased, holding the symbols of the years of the king's life. On the west wall, south of the doorway into the sanctuary, is the niche mentioned above, and a scene showing the king offering the symbol of Truth to Amen-Ra of Takens. North of the doorway is a similar niche and a scene showing the king worshipping Amen-Ra. On the north wall the king is seen offering to Khnum and Satis, while behind him stands Anukis with the symbols of years. On the north end of the east wall the king smites a Syrian from "the Lands of the North."

From the vestibule a door leads into the sanctuary, a rock-cut chamber at the west end of which was a niche in which three statues sat. These are now quite destroyed, but no doubt originally represented Rameses seated between two gods. The colouring in this chamber is fairly well preserved, and is a contrast to the crude painting in the Kalâbsheh temple. On the south side of the doorway Rameses is seen embraced by Satis, and on the north side is a defaced figure of the king embraced by Maket, who says to him, "I am thy mother Maket, the Great Lady, Lady of Heaven, wife of all the gods." On the south side of the east wall the king is suckled by Isis, Lady of Takens; and on the north side of the east wall he is suckled by Anukis, Lady of Elephantine. The south wall shows the king offering to Horus and to Amen-Ra. On the north wall he is given "life" by Khnum, and is supported by Satis; and in the second scene he worships Amen-Ra. On the sides of the niche in the west wall there are figures of Min and Ptah, but the accompanying inscriptions are gone. *The sanctuary.*

The historical reliefs of this temple have been brought to public notice by the casts which were taken from them by Bonomi at the expense of Mr. Hay, and which were finally set up on the walls of the Fourth Egyptian Room in the British Museum, being coloured from notes made by Bonomi. The remains of the brick domes which roofed the Christian church may be noticed above the walls of the court.

The town and quarries.

The ancient town lay mainly to the north of the temple of Kalâbsheh, on the hillside between that and Bêt el Wâli, and to the west of the former temple on the steep slope of the hill. The houses were made of broken sandstone blocks, and the remains consist only of large masses of these blocks intermixed with broken pottery. There is a fortified wall of broken stones which encloses the whole hillside behind this temple, and this may have bounded the town on the west side. There are also indications of late settlements on the top of the hills. The modern village is clustered around the great temple, but the rising of the water will oblige the inhabitants to transfer their houses to higher ground. To the north-west of the temple there are some quarries in which are two Christian epitaphs, with the Pagan ending "Grieve not : no one is immortal."

The cemeteries.

There seem to have been some tombs of a late date cut into the rock at the back of Kalâbsheh temple on the hillside. At various points on the hilltops some distance back from the river there are groups of very curious tombs, which, from the pottery fragments in and around them, appear to date from late Roman times. The tombs are constructed in the form of circular tumuli, having a diameter of from six to ten feet. They stand about from one to two metres high, and their sides in some cases slope sharply. They are neatly built of broken stones tightly packed, and the outside surface is remarkably smooth. In the centre of each tumulus there is a small chamber, either rectangular or roughly circular, the sides and roof of which are formed of larger slabs of unshaped stone. The body inside must have been contracted. Stones seem to have been piled on top of this chamber, bringing the top surface of the tumulus to a flat level. All these graves have been plundered, and only a few broken bones and fragments of Roman pottery remain. Sometimes a number of these tumuli are built so close to each other that one tomb overlaps another, and loses a segment of its circle thereby. Tombs somewhat similar to these have been found in the eastern desert, and it is quite possible that these in question are to be attributed to the Blemmyes, who inhabited Kalâbsheh, as has already been said, during the late Roman period.

CHAPTER XXIV

FROM KALÂBSHEH TO MAHÂRAKA

RUINS ON THE WEST BANK

THREE miles south of Kalâbsheh on the west bank, above the hamlet of Dîb, there are the ruins of a Roman village; and a small building, which was perhaps a monastery, stands on the hilltop in ruins. Built into a wall of a modern house here there is a block of stone upon which a row of uræi are sculptured, as though the block had formed part of a temple cornice. About a mile farther on, behind the hamlet of Abu Târfeh, which forms part of the village of Abu Hôr, there is a ruin on the hilltop by the side of a rocky valley. The small, well-cut blocks of stone, and a door-cornice with a well-sculptured winged disk, lead one to suppose that the building was a Roman temple. But there is a semicircular recess in the east wall, and a Coptic cross is cut on one of the blocks; and this indicates that the place was a Christian church. A brick chamber with a vaulted roof stands near by.

Along the east bank there is only one point at which the attention of the archæologist is arrested. About half-way between Kalâbsheh and Dendûr, in the district of Abu Hôr, there are the ruins of a Ptolemaic and Roman temple. At the water's edge, and therefore only to be seen in summer, there is an imposing terrace or quay, some 180 feet in length and over 3 feet in height, being constructed of well-cut and large blocks of stone. A broad stairway runs up from the water, and 80 feet back there is a heap of fallen stones which is all that is left of the temple. Some of these stones are covered with reliefs, and one sees "Pharaoh" (no other name is given) dancing before a god; and several times worshipping Mandulis of Talmis. The upper part of a stele of one of the Ptolemys shows the king worshipping three gods: Mandulis of Talmis, Wazt, and another god, perhaps Khnum. Two fragmentary Greek inscriptions were also seen. It would be interesting to know how it is that a temple is found at this barren

The temple of Abu Hôr.

point of the river. The cliffs rise precipitously immediately behind the ruins, and there could have been little room for a town. It is between this temple and Kalâbsheh that King Iabkhentra of the XIII–XVIIth dynasty inscribed his name ; and thus the neighbourhood may be considered to have had some political or religious importance from early times. The river here flows at a great speed, and originally there were rapids in this region.

Some distance up a rugged watercourse just to the north of the temple, there is a ledge of rock upon which the figures of a man leading a cow are depicted in red paint. The cow has a bunch of rope or ribbons around its neck, and from between its horns projects a branch of a tree, or stem of a flower. The little painting is well executed, and is probably the work of one of the priests of the temple.

INSCRIPTIONS ON THE EAST BANK

Some five miles south of Kalâbsheh, on the east bank, the present writer found a large and interesting inscription giving the titles and cartouche of a king whose date is certainly XIIIth–XVIIth dynasty, and whose name seems to read Iabkhentra. Another inscription of his was found at Mendik in which the cartouche reads somewhat differently. As has been said in the chapter on the history of Nubia, there is reason to suppose that this king was originally a chief of Wawat who, during these turbulent times, had taken the opportunity of calling himself Pharaoh. This important group of inscriptions is to be found on a large boulder at the north side of the mouth of a small valley.

Some two miles north of the temple of Dendûr, above the hamlet of Inkerêk, which forms part of the village of Morwâw, there is a rock on which is the following inscription : " The Scribe of the offerings of all the gods Merapt, son of the Superintendent of the Granary Pamerkaw, son of Thothmes of (?) the land of Horus, Lord of Maa[m]." This official, who here connects himself with Maam, although he was at the time in Wawat, has also written his name at Gebel Addeh, where he refers to Wawat, although then travelling in the sphere of influence of Maam. On a rock near by there is a drawing of a XIXth dynasty priest, clad in a panther skin. There are several uninscribed tombs excavated in the hillside at this point, one of which has two chambers of some size.

DENDÛR

The imposing little temple of Dendûr stands on the side of the rocks close to the river's edge, about twelve miles south of Kalâbsheh, and fifty above the First Cataract. To the north and south of it, and in its courtyard, there are the remains of an ancient town, consisting of large quantities of broken stones and a certain amount of late pottery.

The temple is peculiarly interesting, owing to the fact that it is dedicated to two deified Nubian heroes, Petisis and Pehorus, who seem by their names to have lived some time not earlier than the XXVIth dynasty, when those names first come into use. On the temple walls one sees these two heroes in the form of gods. They are called Chieftains of "The court of the Divine Brother[s]." On the east side of the first gateway, in the lowest panel on the right side, and on the west side in two panels, Petisis is called "The serpent [or perhaps a Nubian word for 'chief'] of Hethu or Hethhor," this being perhaps an ancient name of the district. The full names of the two brothers are "The Osirian Favoured One, Great in the City of the Court of the Divine Brother[s], Petisis, son of Kuper, true-voiced," and "The Osirian Favoured One, Great Divine Brother, Pehorus, son of Kuper, true-voiced." Nothing else is known of the two heroes, and one must suppose them to have been chieftains or warriors who lived and died at Dendûr. In one part of the temple the brothers are shown in the act of offering to Isis; and it seems, therefore, that that goddess was recognised to be their superior. Petisis is shown in one place with a goddess or woman beside him, but her name is left blank, as though there were some doubt as to who his consort was. As gods the two brothers are worshipped in the temple reliefs by the Pharaoh, and since these reliefs are probably of about the time of Augustus, one here has the strange spectacle of a great Cæsar humbling himself before two obscure nigger heroes!

The religion.

The temple buildings are made up as follows: There is a well-built and imposing terrace overlooking the water. From this a short causeway leads to the main gateway, from which a wall originally projected to right and left. A short way farther to the west is the main building, consisting of a vestibule, having an intact roof supported by two columns with floral capitals; an antechamber also with an intact roof; and finally the sanctuary, the roof of which has fallen in.

The temple.

514   ANTIQUITIES OF UPPER EGYPT

The main gateway.

The main gateway has upon it a few reliefs. On the east face there are reliefs in small panels showing the Pharaoh before Osiris, Isis, Tefnut, Petisis, Pehorus, Khnum, Horus, &c. The reliefs inside the doorway are damaged, but on the south side (1) the king is shown in a large relief before Isis, and, in smaller scenes, before Horus, Osiris, Isis, and others whose names are erased. On the west face of the doorway there are scenes showing the king before Osiris, Isis, Horus, Hathor, Amen (with a ram's head), Petisis, Pehorus, Satis, and Nephthys. Passing now to the main temple, the reliefs in the vestibule are seen to be as follows: On the eastern face of the front wall, on its south side (2), Horus, Thoth, and Isis are worshipped by the king; while on its north side (3)

The vestibules and sanctuary.

the gods are Petisis, Amen-Ra, and Arsnuphis. On the south wall of the vestibule the scenes are much damaged, but Isis, Petisis, Pehorus, Osiris, Harpocrates, &c., can be seen. On the north wall the king offers to Horus, Thoth, Tefnut, Isis, Petisis, and Pehorus. The doorway in this wall was cut at a later date, perhaps by the Christians. On the west wall, to the south of the doorway into the antechamber (4), the king is seen offering to Khnum and Isis; and on the north of the doorway (5), to Arsnuphis and Petisis. In the south wall of this chamber there is a doorway leading out into the courtyard, and on the east wall of its porch (6) there is a long Coptic inscription stating that the Presbyter Abraham set up the cross in this temple at the command of the Nubian king Eīspanome, when Joseph was exarch of Kalâbsheh and Theodorus bishop of Philæ, *i.e.* in A.D. 577. At Kalâbsheh it has already been seen that the Christian king Silko invaded this country, and here one finds King Eīspanome, who was probably of the same family, sending a Christian monk to convert the inhabitants. The doorway leading into the antechamber has upon it the figures of the gods Arsnuphis, Horus, Hathor, &c., worshipped by the king; and on either side one sees a lion holding a reed and guarding the doorway. The antechamber and sanctuary are undecorated, except for a small panel (7) at the west end of the latter, on which the local gods Petisis and Pehorus are shown worshipping Isis of Abaton and Philæ. The outside walls of the temple have some larger reliefs sculptured upon them. On the south wall, in the top row, are Arsnuphis and Isis, Petisis, Mandulis of Kalâbsheh and Uazet, and Amen-Ra and Mut, Lady of Asher [Karnak]. In the bottom row are Unnefer and Isis, Petisis and his unnamed wife, and Horus and Hathor. The doorway into the temple is beautifully ornamented on this side (8): a winged disk and winged

The outside walls.

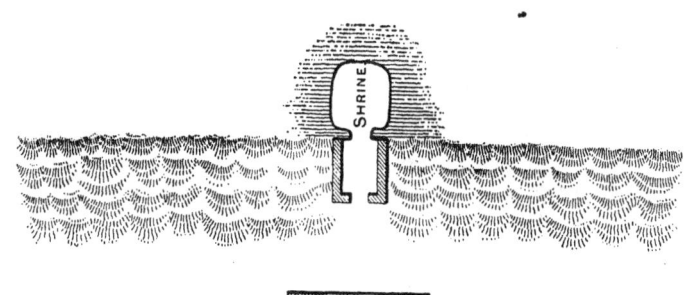

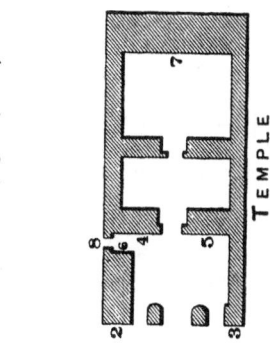

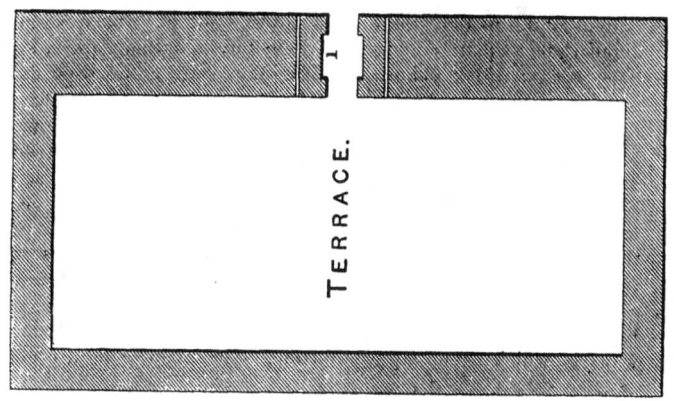

THE TEMPLE OF DENDÛR

516 ANTIQUITIES OF UPPER EGYPT

scarab are represented above the door, while down either side is a papyrus flower and stem, around which an elaborate snake twines itself. On the north wall of the temple, in the upper row, there are representations of Arsnuphis, Petisis, Khnum, and a goddess whose name is lost. In the lower row there are Isis and Horus, Pehorus, Hathor and Harmachis, and Thoth of Penubs and Tefnut.

The rock chamber. In the hillside at the back of the temple, and approximately in its axial line, there is a one-chambered rock tomb, the door of which has been restored when the temple was built, and strengthened by blocks of stone. A kind of small court has been built in front of it, and evidently considerable care has been expended upon it. It is quite possible that this is the tomb of Petisis and Pehorus, though the place may be only the original shrine in which the brothers were worshipped. On the above-mentioned stele in the sanctuary, however, Petisis and Pehorus are said to be entombed in the Holy Hill, and this may mean that they were really buried here. In this case the whole temple would have to be regarded as a funerary chapel.

FROM DENDÛR TO GERF HUSÊN

West bank. About three miles south of Dendûr temple on the west bank, just to the south of a hamlet named Derâysh, and forming part of the village of Merîeh, there is a graffito naming a "scribe of the treasury of the temple (?) of Anuket." It appears to date from the late period. Four miles to the south, high on the cliffs above the hamlet of Farâkaleh, there is a tower built of broken stones, about 13 feet square and 10 high. On top of it there appears to have been a brick chamber. The place was either used as a watch-tower or as a shrine. The latter is the more probable, as there are numerous footmarks of visitors cut in the stones around, while the Greek inscription, "Hail, Zeus Serapis," occurs twice. There are many drawings, including horses, dogs, camels, scorpions, boats, men, men leading cattle, a man standing on a tower, shrines, &c. About three-quarters of a mile south of this there is a valley, on the south side of which are several inscriptions and drawings which date from the XIth–XIIIth dynasties.

East bank. About three-quarters of a mile north of Gerf Husên, on the east bank, stand the ruins of the Byzantine fortress of Sabagura, the walls of which stretch up the hillside. The main walls are con-

FROM KALÂBSHEH TO MAHÂRAKA

structed of broken stone, but the buildings inside the enclosure are mainly of brick. A walk over the hill at the back of the fortress is well worth taking, as the view is superb. A path leads up on the south side of the buildings.

GERF HUSÊN

The temple of Gerf Husên stands on the hill-slope on the western bank, about eight or nine miles south of Dendûr and sixty miles above the First Cataract. It is excavated in the rock, and is a poor and smaller copy of the great temple of Abu Simbel. A portion of the village of Gerf Husên stands between the temple and the river, but when the barrage is raised the water will come up to the edge of the rocks.

From the earliest times the cliffs of the western bank at this spot seem to have been sacred. On a group of rocks to the south of the temple there are a large number of prehistoric drawings, as well as some of the Middle and New Empire. Persons of the Middle Empire inscribed their names here, and in the XIXth dynasty Rameses IInd selected this site for his temple. The town was situated on the east bank, opposite these sacred cliffs, and in later times it was known as Tutzis, from which the Coptic Thosh and the modern Kirsh are derived. Mr. Legh, in 1813, found a Coptic papyrus at Kirsh in which the name Thosh is given. Rameses IInd called his temple *Per Ptah*, "The Temple of Ptah," and it seems that this district was sacred to that god. A rough drawing of Ptah occurs on the rocks near the temple, together with some inscriptions and drawings which are earlier than Ramesside times. The official who was responsible for the work of building the temple was Setau, the Viceroy of Ethiopia. In Roman times no temple seems to have been erected here, and one must suppose that Tutzis was no longer a place of any importance. In Christian times the temple was used as a church, and a monastery was erected near by, which was probably destroyed in the persecutions of 1173 A.D. *History.*

The temple of Rameses IInd was dedicated primarily to Ptah of Memphis, and secondarily to Amen-Ra, Horus of Baki, Horus Beheni, Horus of Maam, Harmachis of Wawat, Khnum, Nefertem, Min, Wepwat of the South, Mut, Hathor, Sekhmet, Maat (?), Satet, Anuket, Ewsos of Heliopolis, and Isis.

The temple is entered through an open court, originally sur- *The court.*

rounded on three sides by a covered colonnade, the eastern columns of which were lotus-formed, while the northern and southern were rectangular, and were each faced by a colossal figure of Rameses IInd. Most of these have now fallen, and at present only five remain standing. The walls of the court are cut out of the natural rock, and have reliefs upon them, now practically indistinguishable. On the west wall Rameses can just be seen smiting his enemies. The north and south walls of the court, also cut out of the natural rock, each have a niche or recess cut in them, in which three mutilated figures sit, representing Rameses between two gods. A doorway at the west end of the court leads into the hall, excavated in the rock, the roof being supported by six rectangular pillars faced with colossal statues of the king. One walks up the hall between the two rows of these figures, and in the gloomy half-light their ill-shaped and heavy forms appeal rather to one's sense of the grotesque than to one's reverence. Their size, nevertheless, tells to a certain extent, and makes them impressive.

<small>The first hall.</small>

These colossi represent the king in Osirian form, with the crown on his head, and in his hand the crook and flail. He wears a skirt ornamented with a lion's head; and on the belt in some cases a little colour is left. On the north and south sides of the hall, behind the colossi, there are four recesses, in each of which are three figures carved from the rock, and representing the Pharaoh between two gods. In the northern recesses these deities are the Heliopolitan goddess Ewsos and Horus, Isis and Horus of Maam, Satis and Nefertem, and Anukis and Khnum. In the southern ones they are Amen-Ra and Mut, Horus of Baki and Horus of Beheni, Ptah-Taenen and Hathor, and Ptah and Sekhmet. The much damaged reliefs on the walls and on the pillars show Rameses in the presence of the various gods already mentioned. The only scene of any interest is that on the east wall at the north side of the doorway. Here the king is seen offering to Horus and Maat (?), while between these two sits Rameses himself. The height of the vanity of this great egoist may be said to have been reached when, at the summit of his career, he is here seen to have turned in adoration to himself as a god amongst the gods.

<small>The Adytum and Sanctuary.</small>

From the hall one enters the adytum, a dim chamber in which are some almost indistinguishable reliefs representing the king offering to the gods and to himself. The roof is supported by two square pillars, and, behind these, small doorways on the north, south, and west sides lead to unornamented chambers, in which

FROM KALÂBSHEH TO MAHÂRAKA

are countless numbers of bats. The main doorway in this chamber leads on into the sanctuary, in the middle of which stands a small pedestal or altar, intended, probably, to support the boats of Ptah and Harmachis during the ceremonies. These boats are seen in the reliefs on either side of the chamber, that on the south wall being of Ptah, and that on the north wall of Harmachis. At the west end of the chamber there is a recess in which four large figures are seated, clumsily executed and somewhat damaged. From north to south the figures represent Hathor, Ptah-Tatenen, Rameses, and Ptah. Over the recess is a representation again of the sacred boat.

Originally the temple appears to have been brilliantly coloured; and this, no doubt, removed from it that gloominess which is now its characteristic feature. The walls, now blackened by smoke and dirt, show little of the ancient paint. The real magnificence of the temple can only be appreciated when one thinks of it as it was in Ramesside times. There was then a pylon near the water; an avenue of sphinxes led from this to the foot of the hill; a flight of steps stretched up the hillside; a gateway stood at the head of the stairs; the court with its colonnades followed; and finally the main temple was reached.

At the same level as the temple, and a few minutes' walk to the south, there is a group of large boulders on which a large number of drawings and a few inscriptions are to be seen. Most of the drawings are prehistoric, and take the usual forms of that period. There are many-oared boats, giraffes, oxen, gazelles, ostriches, a lizard, and an elephant. The most interesting drawing is that of two horses, which one would be inclined to call Old Kingdom, were it possible that the horse could have been known here as early as this. The cartouche of the Nubian Pharaoh Kakara is here inscribed. *Rock inscriptions, &c.*

Three or four hundred yards to the north of the temple there stands the ruin of a crude brick building, which was probably a Christian monastery. The walls are still some sixteen feet high, and are solidly built. The roof was formed of a series of domes, but these have fallen in. The remains of a stairway leading up to a tower at the north-west corner of the building should be noticed.

KOSHTÂMNEH

The fortress.

The next ancient site of interest is the fortress of Koshtâmneh, which stands on the west bank of the river. The actual village of Koshtâmneh stands for the most part on the east bank of the river, and near the fortress there are no houses. The desert here is low and undulating, and is more open than it has previously been south of the Cataract. The fortress is about eight miles above Gerf Husên temple, and sixty above the Cataract. In all probability the building dates from the Old Kingdom, and one may perhaps attribute it to the actual archaic period, as will have been seen in the chapter on the history of Lower Nubia. A peculiar architectural feature of the fortress is its serpentine walls, and similar walls have been found in the "false" tomb of Senusert IIIrd at Abydos, and in the temple of Nebharpetra at Dêr el Bahri; and it may be that that king restored the building. Koshtâmneh is the first of the three great fortresses below Wâdy Halfa, the other two being at Kubbân and at Anâybeh.

The crude brick walls of the building are much damaged, those on the north, east, and west sides having alone withstood the siege of the years. Within the main enclosure wall there is a second wall, along the length of which round towers are constructed at intervals. This seems to have enclosed the main tower or citadel, but the fortress requires to be excavated before a description of its design can be made. On the west side, outside the main walls, there is a fender-wall built in the curious serpentine style mentioned above. The bricks throughout the building are of the large size commonly found in the XIIth dynasty.

Byzantine fortress.

On the east bank about half-way been Gerf Husên and Kubbân there are the ruins of a small Byzantine fortress on the hillside, but the place is too ruined to be worth a visit.

DAKKEH

Situation.

The temple of Dakkeh is situated on the west bank of the river, ten miles from Gerf Husên and seventy from the First Cataract. The country here is open and sandy, and the hills rise in isolated groups some considerable distance back from the river. In early times it seems that the larger part of the wide area between the hills and the water was under cultivation, but now the sand lies

FROM KALÂBSHEH TO MAHÂRAKA

over the whole surface, except in a few small patches where the natives have been sufficiently enterprising to attempt the reclaiming of the ground.

Dakkeh marks the site of the ancient *Pa-Selk*, "The Abode of the Scorpion," which name in Greek was written *Pselkis*, and by Strabo is called Pselche. There are indications of early cemeteries in the neighbourhood, and one may suppose that the town already existed in archaic times. In the desert behind Dakkeh there are extensive cemeteries of the Middle Kingdom, and near the temple a stone bearing the name of Amenemhat of the XIIth dynasty was found. The names of Thothmes IInd and IIIrd and Sety Ist have also been observed on stones unearthed here, and one may therefore regard the history of the town as being continuous throughout dynastic times. The temple as it now stands was built by the Lower Nubian King who calls himself "The King of Upper and Lower Egypt Amendet Anhtaara, Son of the Sun Argamen Living for ever, beloved of Isis," commonly called Ergamenes, a contemporary of Ptolemy IInd, IIIrd, and IVth, a king who has already been discussed with reference to his work at Philæ. Ptolemy IVth Philopator himself added some of the reliefs, and he records the cartouches of Ptolemy IIIrd, his father, Berenice, his mother, Arsinoë IIIrd, his sister and wife, and Arsinoë IVth, his daughter. The vestibule was added by Ptolemy IXth Euergetes IInd. There are a number of Greek inscriptions in different parts of the temple, one of which mentions that in the

History of Dakkeh.

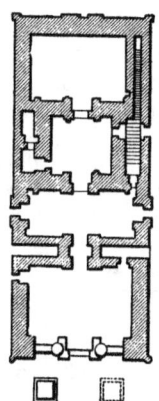

THE TEMPLE OF DAKKEH

thirty-fifth year of Ptolemy IXth the pronaos was built and dedicated to Hermes Paotnuphis. The sanctuary was built by an unidentified Roman Pharaoh. An inscription here records the fact that Saturninus Veteranus Aquila executed the gilding of parts of the temple. Dakkeh was the scene of a great battle between the Romans and Ethiopians in the year 24 B.C. While Aelius Gallus, the third Prefect of Egypt, was engaged in a badly managed and unsuccessful war in Arabia, the Ethiopians, under their queen Kandake, revolted, and, with 30,000 ill-armed men, successfully besieged Aswân, Elephantine, and Philæ, defeating the three Roman cohorts which were stationed there. Gaius Petronius, the successor of the disgraced Aelius Gallus, hurried southwards with an army of 10,000 infantry and 800 cavalry, and pushed the Ethiopians back to Dakkeh, where, after three days of useless negotiations, he defeated them, following them to Napata, their southern capital. Strabo mentions an island near here to which the Ethiopians fled. This may have been the island of Derâr, which lies a few miles to the south of Dakkeh.

In Christian times the temple was used as a church by the inhabitants of Dakkeh.

The gods of Dakkeh. One would imagine from the name of the town, "The Abode of the Scorpion," that the scorpion-goddess Selket was here worshipped, and her appearance amongst the reliefs in the temple of Bêt el Wâli, which is not so very far away, might favour this view. But the goddess is only found in one instance in the reliefs which are standing at Dakkeh, and it is to be presumed that the name has some other origin. The temple was dedicated to Thoth of *Penubs*, also written without the initial *P*, which stood for *Per* "The abode of." The word *Nubs*, it should be added, means the "sycamore tree." This city is perhaps to be identified with Kôrteh and Ofendîneh, though Ptolemy mentions one Panubs in Upper Nubia. Thoth is called Lord of Penubs in Takens (Lower Nubia), Lord of Dakkeh, Twice Great of Hermopolis, Lord of Biggeh, Lord of the Lands of the South. Many other gods were also worshipped here, whose figures will be seen in the reliefs.

The pylon. The main feature of the temple is its pylon, which is practically undamaged. In front of the pylon there is an avenue of approach, 170 feet in length, and nearly 15 in breadth, bordered on either side by a wall of masonry, and ending, to the north, in a rectangular platform or terrace. Both the avenue and the terrace are so much damaged that they are only just discernible. It is said that many blocks used in this terrace bear the cartouche of

FROM KALÂBSHEH TO MAHÂRAKA 523

Thothmes IIIrd. The walls and cornice of the pylon still retain their original smoothness of surface, and although the natives had exposed six feet of the foundation on every side, they were still standing when the present repairs were effected. The height of the pylon is forty feet, or nearly fifty feet when the foundations are included. The gateway in the pylon is surmounted by a concave cornice on which is the usual winged disk. The threshold is made of two heavy grey granite blocks. Inside the doorway there have been some unfinished reliefs on both sides, but those on the east side are alone remaining, and represent an unnamed Pharaoh offering to Thoth, Tefnut, and Isis. In the north side of the pylon there are two niches which have been intended for the usual flagstaffs. In the south side there are two doorways leading to flights of stairs which ascend to the guard-rooms and to the top of the pylon. The ascent is well worth undertaking, as the view from the top is a fine one. Upon the pylon there are a few isolated and unfinished reliefs and numerous Greek inscriptions.

Between the pylon and the main temple there is an open space of some thirty feet, in which originally there was some construction. The main building consisted of a series of four chambers lying in the axis and leading from one to the other. First there was the pronaos, then the vestibule, next the adytum, and finally the sanctuary. The pronaos, vestibule, and part of the adytum were overthrown quite recently, owing to the digging away of the foundations by the natives, but they have now been rebuilt and rendered quite secure. On the north-west corner one sees Ptolemy Euergetes IInd making offerings to Horus, Isis, Osiris, and Osiris-Unnefer. Some Christian paintings have been superimposed on the original decorations, but these can only be seen now in scattered fragments. They are said to have represented God the Father enthroned, the Crucifixion, and some other scenes. Inside the doorway into the vestibule, on the east, there is a damaged relief showing the king offering a figure of Truth to Thoth of Penubs and Lower Nubia, and to Tefnut. On the south side of the doorway King Ptolemy Philopator Ist worships Anuket, Satet, Isis, and Hathor; while on the lintel there are the cartouches of his family. The first three names are those of the king himself; the next is that of his wife, the " Royal Wife, Sister, and Daughter Arsinoë," then the " Royal Father of Ptolemy," the " Royal Mother Berenice," and finally the " Daughter of Amen Arsinoë."

The pronaos.

Passing through the vestibule one enters the adytum. A portion of the roof still remains in position, and this has preserved the

The vestibule and adytum.

reliefs to a certain extent from damage. From this chamber a doorway, probably hidden by blocks of stone, leads off to the north into a chamber below a stairway ascending to the roof. The reliefs in the adytum show the Nubian king Ergamenes before various gods, amongst which the Pharaoh of Senem, wearing the war-helmet, may be noticed. On the east side of the doorway into the sanctuary there is a scene showing King Ergamenes offering to Isis, and an inscription, in four and a half perpendicular lines, states that Isis has given to him the Land of *Ta-kens*, or Lower Nubia, from Aswân to Takhômpso—namely, the *Twelve Ar*. The territory of the Twelve Ar in Greek was called the Dodekaschoinos, a Greek schoinos being equal to the Egyptian Ar, and corresponding to $7\frac{1}{2}$ English miles. On either jamb of the doorway Ergamenes is shown making a prayer to Thoth of [P]nubs and Selket and to Isis of Philæ.

The sanctuary.
Passing now into the sanctuary, one sees that the reliefs have been added in Roman times by an emperor who is simply named "Pharaoh." A block of pink granite lying on the floor forms the top of a shrine, the other portions of which lie broken outside the temple, not far away. As a dado around this chamber there are a series of figures of Hapi, the Nile, alternating with garlands of lotus-flowers. The figures carry vases of water, and lead cattle, geese, &c., these being symbolic of plenty. On the east side of the doorway the design is extended by the addition of a cedar tree, under which an ape, symbolising Thoth, stands; while the figure of Hapi pours a vase of water amongst the leaves. The main scenes on the walls, commencing from the east side of the doorway and going round the room, are as follows: The king before Isis and Harseisis; the king kneeling before Thoth and Tefnut; offering a sphinx to Arsnuphis and Tefnut; offering to Arsnuphis alone; to Thoth (damaged); to Osiris-Unnefer and Isis; to Isis; to Hathor and Harpocrates; to Isis and Horus of Behudet; and finally offering to Thoth and Tefnut. Above these main reliefs are others in which many of the gods mentioned above are found. Miss Edwards, in her "Thousand Miles," speaks of the "dumpy, smirking goddesses, and . . . clownish kings" which are seen in these reliefs; but compared with other work of the Ptolemaic period the figures here are by no means inferior.

The chamber on the east of the vestibule.
Returning now to the vestibule, a small chamber will be found built on to the east side of the adytum. Here there has been a crypt, which is now choked. The reliefs on the south wall show two ibises seated

FROM KALÂBSHEH TO MAHÂRAKA 525

on shrines, a lion before which an ape raises its arms in worship; two hawks guarding the cartouches of the Pharaoh, and two seated lions. On the east wall the king is seen worshipping Arsnuphis and Tefnut, and Osiris and Isis; and on the west wall he worships Horus and Hathor, and Thoth and Tefnut. On the west of the adytum there is a stairway ascending to the roof. Originally there was an enclosure wall running around the temple, but this is now destroyed. There is much evidence that a temple of Thothmes IIIrd existed on this site, and Gau believed that it was to the right of the present edifice.

The remains of the ancient town lie around the temple, a large quantity of potsherds being all that is left of the once important Pselchis. The main portion of the town seems to have been 500 yards to the north of the temple. In Murray's Handbook it is stated that there was a Roman custom-house near the temple, and that many ostraka have been found on its site.

The town.

KUBBÂN

The town, fortress, and temple of Kubbân stand on the east bank of the river a short distance south of Dakkeh, and sixty-five miles above the barrage. No one in this part of the country should fail to pay a visit to the ruined fortress, which is one of the most impressive sights in Nubia. It has been said that this ruin brings the lost ages before the imagination in a way that no temple could ever bring them, and this is indeed so. The gaunt, ruined walls, still towering to a considerable height, the crumbling scarp and counterscarp, the moat, and the covered way, all suggest to one's mind thoughts of the activities of ancient Egypt. The temples have told so often and so persistently of the solemnities of the past, that it is with reawakened interest that one turns to this memorial of human energy.

In ancient times Kubbân was named *Baka* or *Baki*, and it will be remembered that Horus of Baki is one of the great gods worshipped throughout Lower Nubia. A stele of Amenemhat IIIrd of the XIIth dynasty was found here, which shows that the place was already in existence at that date. The fortress was probably built at the same time as were those of El Kâb, Aswân, Kummeh, and Semneh—that is to say, about the time of Senusert IInd or IIIrd. There seems little doubt that the defences here were intended as a safeguard to the caravans which set out

History of Kubbân.

ANTIQUITIES OF UPPER EGYPT

from this point for the gold mines of Wâdy Alâki. From these mines it is probable that the Egyptians obtained their gold in the early stages of their history, just as they certainly did in the New Empire and in Roman times. The Nile above Kubbân was not always in the hands of the Pharaohs, and there were several periods in which the "vile Ethiopians" extended their influence northwards as far as this point. The busy terminus of the caravans, therefore, with its granaries and store-houses, its market and its ready gold, must have been the objective of many a raid. A stele of the time of Thothmes IIIrd was found here, and the names of Horemheb and Rameses IInd have been also observed, thus showing that the gold-mining operations were steadily carried on from dynasty to dynasty. A most important inscription, dated in the third year of Rameses IInd, was found in the desert near Kubbân. It states that the king, after holding a council regarding the working of these mines, decided to attempt to obtain water by increasing the depth of a well dug by Seti Ist, which had been given up as useless after a depth of 120 cubits had been reached. Engineers were despatched to the spot, and, by boring in the old well for only twelve more cubits, water was reached, and the mines were able to be reopened. In this inscription the king speaks of Horus of Baki, the god of the district, and we are told that Wâdy Alâki was then called the county of Akaata.

The fortress.
The fortress as it now appears is in a very ruinous condition, and the enclosure is so heaped with fallen bricks and broken pottery that it is no easy matter to make out any of the details of the original buildings inside the main walls. The north wall stands nearly complete; of the south wall the east end is standing; only the middle of the east wall remains; and the west wall is entirely gone. These walls, which are constructed of large-sized bricks, are six metres thick at their base, and rise in places to eight metres in height. Outside the walls there is a moat, cut in the rock, surrounding the fortress, and having a scarp on the one side and a counterscarp on the other. As in most Egyptian fortresses there are gateways in the walls which lie at right angles to the Nile, *i.e.* on the north and south sides. The gateways are flanked by towers which project inwards, and leave a narrow outlet, about three metres wide and ten metres long. At intervals around the walls there are other towers, rectangular in form and built on to the inner face of the wall. From the south-west corner a covered way ran down to the river, lined and roofed with stone,

and covered with a thick skin of brickwork. Within the enclosure there seems to have been a second wall surrounding the mounds which form the ruins of the main tower or citadel, and leaving a clear space between it and the first line of defences.

About half a mile to the south of the fortress there are the remains of a small temple, which was perhaps dedicated to the Horus of Baki, and which appears to have been erected in the Middle or early New Empire. Very little of it is now to be seen, and the ordinary visitor will not find it worth looking at. Originally it consisted of a small hall, having six columns with "clustered" capitals; a sanctuary; and a courtyard excavated in the rock enclosing the whole building. *The temple.*

A short distance to the south-east of the fortress there is a cemetery of the Middle Empire, consisting of shaft-tombs sunk in the rock, and of rock chambers in front of which are brick constructions. Of the other antiquities of Kubbân mention may be made of a large cistern hewn in the rock near the temple, and twenty feet in diameter; and of the remains of another demolished temple, at the north of the village. Part of a large stele was seen by the writer outside the south-east corner of the fortress. A temple in the south-east angle of the fortress is also mentioned in Baedeker.

The village of Kubbân is one of the cleanest villages in Nubia. The walls of the houses are smoothly plastered, and in many cases whitewashed; the courtyards are sprinkled with fresh sand; the refuse is carefully removed to a distance; and the little streets are as clean as one could wish. Over the doorways of many of the houses there are curious designs painted in whitewash, which may perhaps be a deterioration of the bulls' skulls with which the ancient inhabitants used to decorate their doorways. A picturesque little mosque stands amidst the houses, and this, like all else here, is wonderfully clean. Looking northwards from the village the dark walls of the fortress tower above the modern dwellings, and at the edge of the river clusters of palms add colour to a scene which one leaves behind with regret.

KÛRTEH

On the west bank of the river, south of Kubbân, there lie the remains of an ancient city, known to the ancient Egyptians as *Karte*, and to the Copts as *Korte*. The modern village, which lies near the old site, is called Kûrteh, and thus carries on the ancient name. There are cemeteries of the Middle Empire near the town, which indicate that, like Dakkeh, the place was in existence at an early date. Modern travellers of fifty years ago state that there was here a gateway standing, inscribed with the name of Thothmes IIIrd; and the name of that king was more recently observed on a block of stone near the remains of the temple of Ptolemaic or Roman date. One may thus say that the history of the town was continuous. Kûrteh is not more than four miles south of Dakkeh, and at different points along the intervening country there are indications of Roman settlements. It is therefore likely that Pselkis and Karte, although originally separate townships, were in late times amalgamated into one city. Strabo speaks of the island of Takhômpso as being opposite Pselkis, and for this reason Kubbân has been identified with Takhômpso, although that site lies on the mainland. Now opposite Kûrteh there is the large island of Derâr, and here with far more probability Takhômpso may be placed. The Ethiopians, defeated by Petronius at Dakkeh, fled to Takhômpso; but it is not likely that they would have done so had the island been less than four miles from the scene of the battle.

The remains of the ancient site consist of the temple, the town ruins, and the cemeteries. The temple lies to the north of the modern village, but little of it now exists. A rectangular space outlined by masonry walls only one block in height is all that is to be seen; and there are no traces of inscriptions to name the deity worshipped here, or the date of the temple's foundation. The mounds of the town site are somewhat farther westward, and are of very considerable extent. The cemeteries are still farther to the west. In the rocks there are several shallow trenches which have served as tombs, and bones lie around them. Near here there are the remains of the quarries from which the stone for the temple was procured.

Like Kubbân, the village of Kûrteh is a model of cleanliness and neatness. It stands on the edge of the river behind thick groves of palm-trees, and to the westward the sandy desert stretches back in a gradual rise until the low hills are reached. Much of the land at the back of the village seems to have been cultivated at one time, and to have been converted into a part of the desert by the inroads of the sand.

DERÂR

The island of Derâr lies opposite the south end of the village of Kûrteh. In summer, when the water is low, it appears to be a place of some size, but in winter its main feature is its abundance of palms and other trees. The channel of the river runs on its eastern side, and in summer the water is so shallow between the island and the western bank that the natives dispense with a ferry, wading across with their clothes upon their heads. It has been pointed out that this island is probably to be identified with the ancient Takhômpso, or Metakhômpso, as it is sometimes called. This name is derived from the hieroglyphic *Takemtsa*. In the temple of Dakkeh it will be remembered that Ergamenes states that he ruled the land from Aswân to Takemtsa, and it seems that this island was, at various periods, the limit of the Egyptian or Lower Nubian dominions.

MAHÂRAKA

The ruins which are usually known as those of Mahâraka are often called after the village of Ofeduîneh, which lies just to the north of the temple, whereas the village of Mahâraka is on the opposite bank of the river, some distance away. The ruins stand on the west bank, about seven miles above Dakkeh, and seventy-seven south of the barrage. The western bank here is low and sandy, and the ruins of the temple rise abruptly from a slightly elevated plateau, and stand out sharply against the sky. A few trees stand between the temple and the water; but the country is bare and desolate at this point, though the hamlet of Ofeduîneh is well provided with palms.

The temple was built in late Roman times, though the exact date is not known. The town was then named Hierasykaminos, and was the limit of the Dodekaschoinos, the "Land of the Twelve Schonoi," *i.e.* the territory which lay northwards as far as the First Cataract. In Ptolemaic times, as has been said above, the frontier was placed at Takhômpso, but the Romans seem to have pushed it forward to this point. At Dakkeh it has been seen that the chief god of the temple was Thoth of Penubs. The word *Penubs* means the "Place of the Sycamore"; and, in the dado of

History of Mahâraka.

the sanctuary at Dakkeh, an ape, symbolising Thoth, was seen standing under the sacred sycamore. Now Hierasykaminos also means "the Place of the Sycamore," and on one of the walls of its temple Isis is seen seated under a sycamore, while Thoth stands near by. One may, therefore, identify this site with the Penubs of the hieroglyphs.

<small>The temple.</small>
The temple consists of a small hall, around the sides of which were pillars joined by screen-walls. There were six pillars on the north and south sides and three on the east and west, but only five of these remain standing. Presumably the main entrance was on the east side. The hall seems to have been enclosed by a girdle wall, but this has fallen on all sides, except on the north. At the north-east angle of the hall there has been a spiral staircase, parts of which can still be seen. This is a unique feature in an Egyptian temple. Another feature which makes this temple quite peculiar must now be described. Between the main temple and the water there is another construction, the plan of which is not easy to determine. It stands somewhat to the south of the axis of the hall, and its north wall seems to have formed the side of an entrance passage leading to the main temple. On the north face of this wall there is a most remarkable relief, executed partly in the Roman and partly in the Egyptian style. It represents a full-faced figure of Isis, seated under the sacred sycamore tree, and clad in Roman costume. Above her a hawk hovers, while another rests in the branches of the tree. She stretches out her arm to an approaching figure of a boy clad in a toga and representing Horus, who brings a vessel of wine to her. Above him are three small figures representing Min, Isis, and Serapis, these again being portrayed in Roman style. To the left of this scene Thoth is shown in the Egyptian conventional style, and to the right is Isis, also portrayed in the Egyptian manner. There are no readable inscriptions.[1] There is little else of interest in the temple, and indeed its ruined condition makes any description difficult. Miss Edwards notes a Greek inscription which was observed on one of the fallen stones, and which reads : "The vow of Verecundus the soldier, and his most pious parents, and Gaius his little brother, and the rest of his brethren." Another Greek inscription on one of the columns says that the temple was dedicated to Isis and Serapis. There are some Coptic inscriptions to be seen on the

---

[1] This entire wall has now been removed to the Cairo Museum, where it is to be seen in the gallery to the right of the central hall.

walls of the hall, and from these one may find that the Coptic name of the town was Mauraqe, which is almost similar to the modern Mahâraka.

To the south-west of the temple there are cemeteries. Much Roman broken pottery lies about in all directions. The main mounds of the ancient town run southwards from the temple along the edge of the river.

CHAPTER XXV

FROM MAHÂRAKA TO KASR IBRÎM

MEHÊNDI

A SHORT way south of the temple of Mahâraka the hills close in towards the river, and on a flat-topped hill on the west bank, overlooking the water, stands the fortified Byzantine town of Mehêndi. The enclosing walls of the town are built of uncemented blocks of sandstone, like those already noticed at Sabagura, Kalâbsheh, and elsewhere. A rough pathway leads up the hill on the north and south, and on both these sides there is a gateway into the enclosure. Hewn blocks of sandstone from some Egyptian temple in the neighbourhood have been used in the building of these gateways, and the figure of Amen-Ra can still be seen on one of them. Within the enclosure, a chaos of ruined walls of brick and stone meets the eye, which, after careful examination, resolves itself into a labyrinth of houses and streets. On the high ground near the middle of the town stands the church, in which the recess for the altar at the east end can be distinguished. Many of the houses in the town have vaulted roofs which have not yet fallen in; and it is with something of a feeling of romance that one picks a way through the narrow streets, glancing to right and left into the darkness of the empty chambers which seem to have been deserted only yesterday. The view from the town is very fine. To the east is a wide desert bay, on the north of which are the picturesque hills of Gebel Mahâraka; to the west the desert stretches back in rugged grandeur as far as the eye can see.

A much-ruined Coptic building is to be observed nearly opposite Sayaleh Post Office, and on the walls there are some Coptic texts. Below it there is an extensive cemetery of the same period.

MEDÎK

The village of Medîk is now reached, and on some high rocks which come down to the water, two early Christian buildings stand. On ascending the hill at the north side one first finds a large area entirely covered with broken stones and fragments of pottery. On close observation it is seen that these stones are the ruins of a large number of little huts, not more than one or two yards square, and usually built over a crevice in the rocks, in order that the walls might not require to be raised very high. These hovels, where a man could never stand upright, and where the ground area was nothing more than a coffin-like cleft in the rock, seem to have served the monks for shelter from the summer sun and from the winter winds. When the writer visited the place in the autumn the rocks were still too hot to be touched by the hand, and in the height of summer the bare plateau must be literally scorched. In many of these clefts in the rock, under the fallen walls, lie the bones of the monks; and it thus seems either that it was the custom in this brotherhood for the dead to be buried where they had lived, or else that the monks were massacred at some time in their huts. A few yards to the south rises the little church, built of broken stones, topped with mud-bricks. Over the body of the building rises a dome now in ruins, and the rest of the roofing was supported on brick arches. At the east end is a recess for the altar, with a niche in the south wall for holding the sacred utensils. On either side of this recess there is a small chamber, and a passage runs behind the altar from one to the other. In the wall of the north chamber there is a niche, and in the corner a projecting slab of stone forms a rough shelf. A few yards farther to the south there is another small ruined building, which seems to have been divided into a few small chambers; and, as the quarters of the monks have been already observed, this building is perhaps to be regarded as a guest-house. From this point the road leading to Tomâs, cutting off the bend of the river, runs back into the desert; and there must have been many travellers who passed the monastery, and would be glad to claim its shelter. This point being the terminus of the shortest road to the south, it is not surprising that a number of Egyptian graffiti are found on the rocks. Here the writer found a large inscription of the unknown king, Iabkhentra, who may be attributed to the XIVth-XVIIth dynasty.

ES SEBÛA

The XIXth dynasty temple of Es Sebûa, or Wâdy es Sebûa (" the lions "), stands on the west bank of the river, about six or eight miles above Mehêndi, ninety-seven above the barrage, and twelve below Korosko. Its pylons, though small, can be seen for some distance, for they stand in open ground a short way back from the river. The village of Es Sebûa stands, for the main part, on the opposite bank of the river, near the mouth of a rocky valley, up which a caravan road runs to meet the main road to Abu Hamîd.

<small>History of Es Sebûa.</small> The mounds which mark the site of the ancient town are to be seen at the river's edge in front of the temple, the surface pottery being mainly late. The cemeteries of that date lie to the north of the temple. The town of the XIXth dynasty seems to have continued down to Roman times. A rock shrine of Amenhotep IIIrd, which will be described presently, stands near the temple; and two hundred yards to the north there are two graffiti, inscribed upon a rock, which show that the early XVIIIth dynasty and the late Ramesside period saw Egyptian officials and priests visiting the town. Several fragments of pottery of the Middle Kingdom, or early XVIIIth dynasty, were picked up near the temple. The temple was built by Rameses IInd, and was called " The Temple of Amen." It was dedicated to Amen-Ra, and in the second place to Harmachis and Ptah. The shrine of Amenhotep IIIrd was dedicated to Amen-Ra. The ancient name of the town is lost; but perhaps a full study of the inscriptions in the temple would reveal it. Unfortunately almost the whole temple, except the pylons, is covered by the sand which has partly blown in and partly has been placed there purposely to protect the place owing to the behaviour of some travellers many years ago.[1] Persons who visited the temple while it was still accessible, however, have stated that the preservation of the interior is good. The whole temple is badly built, and the joints between the stones are wide and gaping. Originally they were filled with cement to make the surface appear smooth, but this has now dropped out and can only be seen deeper in the wall.

<small>The temple.</small> A description of the temple must be very inadequate at present, as so little of it can be seen. In front of the pylon there runs a dromos of sphinxes, only three or four of which can be seen above

[1] The temple is now being cleared.

the sand. At the east end of the dromos stand two statues of the king, in a fair state of preservation. Down the plinth are his cartouches and titles, and he is said to be beloved of Amen-Ra, Ptah, and Harmachis. On either side of the gateway in the pylon is a fallen colossus of Rameses the Great. Upon the east face of the pylons the king is seen slaying his enemies before Harmachis on the one side, and before Amen-Ra on the other. Around the doorway the king is seen in the presence of various gods, who cannot now be recognised. Inside the doorway are the king's cartouches, beloved of Ptah and Amen-Ra, and there have been figures of him standing before Amen-Ra and other gods. Passing through the gateway one enters an open court, along either side of which are five square pillars having headless and much broken colossi against them. The space between these pillars and the wall was roofed, and thus a gallery was formed on either side of the court. Some of the roofing blocks still remain in position. On the north wall of the court the only relief which can now be seen shows the king before a god; and on the south wall he is seen before a deified form of himself, before Horus of Maam, and before another Horus. On the west face of the pylon, at the north side, there is a large relief showing the king before Harmachis and Sekhmet (?), and a smaller scene in which he is led by Nekheb and another deity into the presence of a third god. Below this there is a long procession of the daughters of Rameses. At the south side there is a large relief showing the king before Amen-Ra and Mut; and a smaller relief showing him worshipping Amen-Ra, Mut, and Khonsu. Below is a procession of the king's daughters as before. On the west face of the doorway are panels showing the king before Amen-Ra, Osiris, and other gods; and over the doorway he is seen in the presence of Amen-Ra and " Rameses in the Temple of Amen."

Nothing more can now be seen, but from the descriptions of early archæologists one may gather the following notes. Around the walls of the court the procession of the king's daughters continues, and there is also a series of sons. Altogether 111 sons and 67 daughters are shown here, which is not by any means an impossible number to be produced by an oriental potentate with an unlimited *harêm*. Augustus the Strong is said to have had a thousand children. Behind the court are the great hall, adytum, sanctuary, and antechambers, all excavated in the rock. On the walls are reliefs showing the king in the presence of Amen-Ra, Harmachis, Ptah, Hathor, Khnum Ra, &c. These inner chambers have been used as a church by the Copts, and some of their paintings still remain on the walls. In one case the combination of the ancient reliefs and Coptic paintings produces the curious spectacle of Rameses IInd offering flowers to St. Peter, who is shown with a large key in his hand. At the end of the sanctuary there are three much-damaged statues, representing Amen, Harmachis, and Rameses.

AMÂDA

Between Es Sebûa and Amâda there are no antiquities of any interest to the traveller. A short distance below Amâda lies the town of Korôsko, once famous as the headquarters of the British troops in Lower Nubia, but now a place of no size. The river here makes a bend, and runs due south for some miles. The British cemetery, in which there are some forty tombstones, lies a short distance up the great valley behind the town. Before the Sudan wars a large number of caravans passed along the road to and from the Sudan, and at present a certain amount of traffic continues. It has generally been considered by Egyptologists that this was the road used by the Pharaohs in their wars against Kush; but this is most certainly not the case. A fairly thorough search over the neighbouring hills and valleys, and for some five miles along the caravan road, did not reveal a single inscription or graffito. The writer was even unable to find the one known inscription from this neighbourhood, which gives the twenty-ninth year of Amenemhat Ist, but which is now perhaps destroyed. If Korôsko had been the starting-point of the Pharaonic expeditions into Ethiopia, there would certainly be graffiti and steles on the rocks. Dahabiyehs generally stop for a short time at Korôsko, and the ascent of the conical hill behind the village will be found pleasant, as the view from the summit is very fine.

Korôsko.

The name Amâda is not that of any village, but is applied to the temple only. In this description, however, it has been found convenient to apply the name to the whole region within sight of the temple. About three miles to the south of it there lies near the river, and just to the north of a group of houses, a large boulder, some twelve feet in height and perhaps forty in circumference. This rock is covered with inscriptions dating from the XIIth dynasty, and it seems to have escaped the observation of all travellers in Nubia. They seem to have been written by members of the expeditions to Nubia under Senusert Ist, Amenemhat IIIrd,

The Amâda Rock.

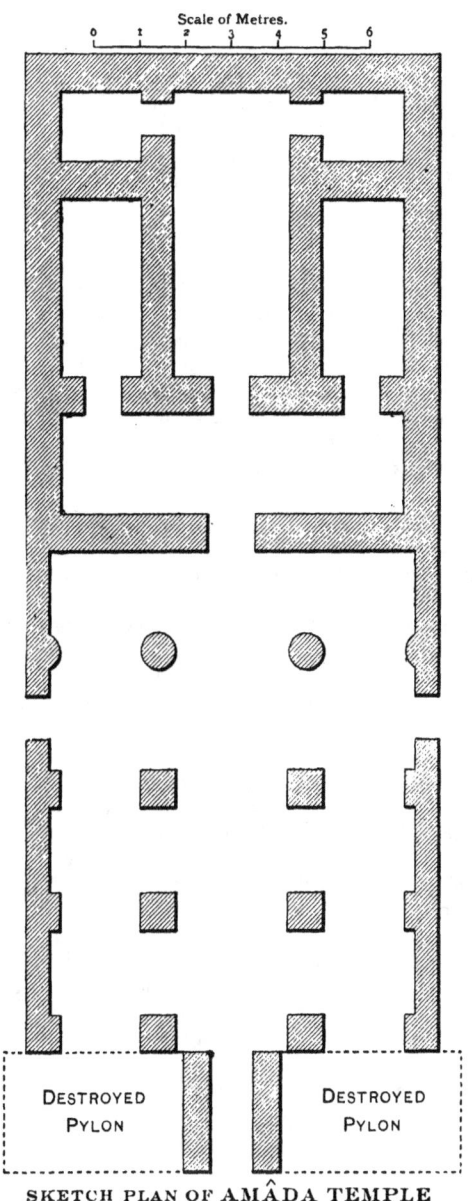

SKETCH PLAN OF AMÂDA TEMPLE

and Senusert IIIrd; and the Nubian king Seanra has also left his name here. A short way to the north of this rock are some Nubian cemeteries, now plundered; and Dr. D. Randall MacIver here discovered in 1907 a kind of city of refuge or garrison-town of the XVIIIth dynasty. Several stone circles and enclosures are to be seen in the neighbourhood. Between here and the temple there are other cemeteries, mostly robbed.

<small>The temple of Amâda.</small>
The temple of Amâda stands a short way back from the river, at the top of a gentle slope. Half buried in sand, there is little in its outward appearance to impress the visitor; and as one trudges over the soft desert towards its doorway, the heavy walls and pillars of the hall look squat and uninviting. The building stands amidst the most desolate scenery, this bank of the river being here quite uninhabited. The hills have receded into the distance, and the undulating desert stretches uninterrupted for many miles. The sandy bank of the Nile is edged with small trees, but nothing else grows, and if there was ever any cultivated land here, it is now deep under the sand. The opposite bank of the river, however, is here lined with a thick growth of palms and other trees, while good crops are grown around them. A splendid range of dark, many-peaked hills rises behind these trees, and as seen from Amâda, with the morning light upon them, or the sun setting behind them, they form one of the grandest scenes upon the Nile.

<small>History of Amâda.</small>
In ancient times the district around Amâda seems to have been thickly populated by those tribes whose cemeteries have just been mentioned. These people maintained themselves by their herds of cattle or goats, as is evidenced by the remains of stockades, and probably made no attempt to grow any crops, even if the land had permitted. Evidence was noticed which shows that they had settled here during the Old Kingdom, but their numbers were increased during the XIIth dynasty, and when the expeditions of that dynasty visited the Amâda rock, they probably found the place to be very populous. Senusert IIIrd seems to have had some definite connection with the place, for his name is particularly mentioned in the temple. The existing building, dedicated to Ra-Harmachis, was begun by Thothmes IIIrd, but the reliefs were not executed until the first years of the reign of his son Amenhotep IInd. All over the temple the names of these two kings occur side by side. If, on the north wall, the cartouche of Thothmes is above that of Amenhotep, then, on the south wall, the cartouche of Amenhotep will be above that of Thothmes. And if the cartouche of the former is written on the left doorpost,

FROM MAHÂRAKA TO KASR IBRÎM

the cartouche of the latter will be found on the right doorpost. It is certain, then, that Amenhotep IInd is responsible for the decoration of the temple, and the fact that he placed his father's cartouches side by side with his own shows both that filial piety was not absent from his character, and also that he was very well aware of his father's great reputation, and realised that his name was one to juggle with. Amenhotep IInd had not been on the throne more than two years when he completed this temple, and he must have been doubtful of the potency of his own as yet unknown name to strike terror into the hearts of the rebellious. The Hypostyle Hall was added in the front of the main building by Thothmes IVth, whose cartouches may here be observed. One scene shows the king as a boy, with the side-lock of hair which is characteristic of Egyptian youths. It will be remembered that this king was still a young man when he died. Amenhotep IVth sent his agents here to erase the name of Amen from the temple inscriptions; and later on Sety Ist built a temple here, restored the obliterated name wherever it occurred in the older temple, and had his cartouches inscribed here and there on the walls. At a later date the sign *Set* in his own name was erased, as that god had fallen into disrepute, and was well on his way to becoming the *Satan* of the present day. King Septah's cartouches are inscribed on the doorposts of the vestibule, together with figures of Queen Tawsret and the great chancellor Bey. The temple's history now passes to Coptic times when the building was turned into a church, and the reliefs covered with plaster. This plaster has now peeled off, and the fine reliefs beneath still retain their colour as a consequence of this Christian obliteration.

In other respects also the temple proper is well preserved, and the roofing is more or less complete. The Hypostyle Hall, however, is more ruined, and the side walls are much broken. Formerly there were two pylons at the main entrance, but these have disappeared, and the doorway thus appears isolated.

The temple is entered through a doorway upon the west side, facing the river. On the left doorpost King Thothmes IIIrd is represented, embraced by Harmachis, the patron god of the temple; and on the right Amenhotep IInd is shown embraced by the same god. Below these scenes there are Ramesside inscriptions of a Viceroy of Ethiopia. Entering the doorway one sees on either side of the doorposts the cartouches of Sety Ist, beloved of Harmachis-Tum. On the left wall Amenhotep IInd is seen being led up to Harmachis by Horus. Below is an inscription in

The doorway.

thirteen lines, referring to Merenptah's campaign in Ethiopia. On the right wall is an inscription referring to the inspection of the temple by Setau, Viceroy of Ethiopia, on behalf of Rameses IInd. On the inner left wall of the doorway occurs the cartouche of Amenhotep IInd, which has been erased by Amenhotep IVth, altered to Ra-aa-Kheperu, the first name of the king, and then re-written as Amenhotep, probably by Sety Ist. On the inner right wall is a similar inscription of Thothmes IIIrd.

The Hypostyle Hall. The visitor now finds himself in the Hypostyle Hall, erected mainly by Thothmes IVth. The roof, which is intact for the most part, is supported by twelve square and four proto-Doric columns, the latter being part of the original building. Walls, built between the pillars of the outer row on either side, enclose the hall. On the pillars on either side of the entrance a figure of a Governor of Ethiopia named Nekhtu (?) worships the cartouches of Rameses IInd. On the pillars up the middle of the hall the cartouches of Thothmes IVth occur, and the king is seen embraced by Anuket of Elephantine, Harmachis, Amen-Ra, and Ptah. On the pillars and walls of the north side of the hall there is firstly an inscription of Thothmes IVth, in which he is said to be beloved of Senusert IIIrd, the great king who first conquered Upper Nubia. The king is next represented as being presented to Harmachis by Satet; after which he is seen being led to Amen-Ra by Horus; and lastly he is embraced by Isis. On the south side, the first scene shows the king as a youth, presented to Harmachis by a goddess whose name is lost. Next, Thoth is shown recording the years of the king; after this there is a broken scene representing the king kneeling before a sacred tree; and finally, the king is embraced by Hathor of Abu Simbel. The end wall of the hall is, of course, the front wall of the temple proper, and through a doorway lying in the axial line of the building one passes into the vestibule. On the north side of this wall there is a representation of the king being led forward by Horus and another god; while next to this he is shown with Harmachis and Anuket. On the south side King Thothmes IIIrd is led forward by Khnum, worships Harmachis, and is embraced by Amen-Ra. On the sides of the doorway leading into the vestibule are figures of Thothmes IIIrd and Amenhotep IInd, and below them there are two very interesting inscriptions of the time of King Septah. On the south side there is the figure of Queen Tawsret, and on the north side is the figure of the chancellor Bey, and near him the cartouches of Septah, but no figure of the king. The inscriptions

FROM MAHÂRAKA TO KASR IBRÎM 541

state that these figures, &c., were carved by order of the Commander of the Troops of Kush, Piaay. Septah's connections with Nubia are recorded in various inscriptions, and in his brief reign he seems to have obtained full control of this part of his kingdom. As one passes through the doorway the cartouches of Sety Ist will be seen on either side.

The vestibule is a transverse chamber from which three door- *The vestibule.* ways lead into three inner chambers, the middle one being the sanctuary. On the inside, or east face of the doorway leading from the hall to the vestibule, there are the names of Thothmes and Amenhotep. On the west wall of the vestibule, Amenhotep is seen with the water of life poured over him by Horus of Edfu and Thoth ; Thothmes is embraced and kissed by Isis; and Amenhotep makes an offering to Amen-Ra. On the north wall Amenhotep dances before Amen-Ra. On the south wall Thothmes is embraced by Horus of Maam and Harmachis. On the east wall are the three doorways leading into the inner chambers. That on the north is inscribed with the name of Amenhotep, beloved of Ra and Amen-Ra ; that on the south has the cartouches of Thothmes ; and the doorway into the sanctuary is inscribed with the cartouches of Thothmes. On the north side of this last-mentioned doorway Amenhotep is represented embraced by Harmachis, and on the south side Thothmes is embraced by Amen-Ra.

The chamber on the north side of the sanctuary should now be *Chamber on north of sanctuary.* visited. In the upper row on the north wall Amenhotep offers three times to Amen-Ra ; and in the lower row he offers to Harmachis three times. In the upper row of the south wall Thothmes offers to Harmachis and Amen-Ra ; and in the lower row he offers to Ra and Harmachis, while Hathor stands beside him. In the east wall a doorway has been cut into a small chamber, which should really be entered from the sanctuary. The doorway cuts through scenes in which Thothmes worships Hathor, Amen-Ra, and Harmachis. The chamber on the south side of *Chamber on south of sanctuary.* the sanctuary should now be examined, and the scenes in it will be found to be of considerable interest. They represent the ceremonies performed at the foundation of the temple, and they show that Thothmes founded the building, and Amenhotep performed the first sacrifices there. In the upper row of the north wall Thothmes worships Amen-Ra ; Safkhet and Amen-Ra drive in the posts which mark the limits of the new temple ; the king stands before Amen-Ra ; and lastly, the king is embraced by

Amen-Ra. In the lower row the king dances before Harmachis; "stretches the cord," for planning the temple, before Harmachis; and makes offerings to Ra. In the upper row of the south wall Amenhotep brings cattle to sacrifice before Amen-Ra; and offers the same when slain to Harmachis and Amen-Ra. In the lower row Amenhotep is led forward by Horus and Harmachis; he uplifts the bâton before Harmachis; and dances before that god. In the east wall the doorway has been cut, as before, and the scenes are obliterated.

The sanctuary. Returning and entering the sanctuary, the cartouches of Thothmes are seen on the inside face of the doorway, and he is said to be beloved of Ra. On the north wall Amenhotep is represented standing between Hathor and Harmachis; and the king is also shown offering to Amen-Ra. At the end of this wall is a doorway leading into the small chamber mentioned above. On the south wall the king is given life by Amen-Ra; he is saluted by Satet'; and offers to Harmachis. The doorway at the end of this wall, which leads into the corresponding small chamber, is surmounted by the cartouches of Amenhotep. On the east wall Amenhotep is seen in the sacred boat of the sun, offering to Harmachis and Amen-Ra. Below this scene there is an inscription in twenty horizontal lines, which is of great historical importance. It is dated in the third year of Amenhotep IInd, and states that that king was a great warrior, and could draw a bow which no man in his army could use; that he was also a great builder of temples, and established the laws relative to divine offerings; that he decorated this temple which had been begun by his father; that it was built of stone; that he surrounded it with a brick wall, made the doorways of sandstone and the doors themselves of cedar, erected pylons of stone, and placed vessels of silver and bronze, altars, fire-pans, tables, &c., in the temple; that on his return from a war in Asia he had this tablet erected and engraved with his great name; that he brought from Asia seven captive princes, six of whom he slew with his own hand in Thebes, and the seventh he hanged on the wall of Napata (in the Sudan), in order to strike terror into the hearts of the inhabitants.

Chambers behind the sanctuary. Passing now through the door in the north wall into the small chamber, one finds the name of Thothmes on the inner face of the doorway, and above it the cartouche of Amenhotep. On the east wall Thothmes is twice shown before Harmachis, and Amenhotep twice before Amen-Ra. On the north wall Amenhotep offers to Amen-Ra, while Hathor stands behind him; and to Harmachis,

FROM MAHÂRAKA TO KASR IBRÎM 543

while Horus of Edfu stands behind him. On the west wall the doorway has been cut through scenes representing Thothmes offering to Amen-Ra and Amenhotep to Harmachis. Returning and entering the corresponding little chamber on the south side of the sanctuary, the cartouches of Amenhotep, beloved of Ra and Amen-Ra, are seen on the doorway, while above them are those of Thothmes. On the east wall Amenhotep and Thothmes offer to Amen-Ra and Harmachis. On the south wall Amenhotep offers to Amen-Ra, and Thothmes to Harmachis. On the west wall Amenhotep is embraced by Amen-Ra, and Thothmes pours water over the figure of Amen-Ra, the other scenes being lost.

On the roof of the temple there are a few Coptic inscriptions of no interest. There is here an interesting forgery probably dating from the last century. It is a Greek inscription reading "Herodotus of Halicarnassus beheld and admired"; and near it in a later style and writing is "No he did not." Herodotus, of course, did not go nearly as far up the Nile as this. On the outside of the Hypostyle Hall, south side, there is an inscription of a viceroy of Ethiopia adoring Harmachis. In the Hypostyle Hall there is a small pyramidion of 'the Viceroy of Ethiopia, Mesu; and a fragment of an inscription, giving the date "Year I" under Rameses Ist, and referring to a viceroy of Ethiopia; but unfortunately the main part of the inscription is lost. This is one of the only two dated inscriptions of this reign. *The roof, and outside of the temple, &c.*

Between the temple and the river there is a square platform of hewn stone, which seems to have been the pavement of a temple. There are remains of fluted columns, and in two places the cartouche of Sety Ist was seen. There are steps mounting between stone balustrades to the platform on its west side. The place requires to be excavated before more can be said.

DÊRR

After one or two miles have been covered one comes into sight of Dêrr, the white buildings of which can be seen on the opposite bank under the tall palms. Exactly opposite the police station there are one or two inscriptions on the rocks, of no particular importance; and some prehistoric drawings of cattle are to be seen. One large inscription gives the name of a certain Dema, an official of the Middle Kingdom. The town of Dêrr is situated about thirteen miles above Korôsko, about four above Amâda temple, and 120 above the barrage. It stands amidst a forest of palms, and the steep cliffs rising behind it are more than half a mile from the river. There is here a Post Office, a small store, and the police station, from which the whole district from Dehmîd in the north to Adendân in the south is administered.

The temple. The temple is excavated in the cliffs at the back of the town; its preservation is not good. The open hall has been much damaged, and all the pillars have disappeared, except for their bases. The colossi on the pillars of the portico have been intentionally destroyed, perhaps by the Early Christians, and only their feet remain. Parts of the roof of the interior have fallen in, and rocks from above the main entrance now completely block the passage. At present a side door, cut in later times, admits the visitor to the temple. The main reason for the ruined condition of the temple is that it was excavated in faulty rock. No masonry was used, but every wall, pillar, architrave, roofing block, and statue was cut from the natural rock; except, perhaps, at the northern extremity of the outer hall, where the architraves and wall-tops may have been finished off with stone construction. The poor quality of the stone has not always allowed the walls to be cut in straight lines, and here and there a sweeping curve has had to be made.

History of the temple. On the west bank it has been seen that there are no antiquities after Sebûa and Amâda, and on the east bank Dêrr is the first met with. From these points towards the south there is a continuous series of ancient remains on both banks as far as Ermenneh, where the next break comes. This temple of Rameses was, thus, on the northern frontier of the populous district, and not in the midst of it, as one might have expected. As has been pointed out in the chapter on the history, this district formed the principality of Maam; and Rameses IInd must, therefore, have been influenced rather by religious than by political motives in placing his temple here, where there does not seem to have been an important town of which any remains have been left nearer than Amâda or Ibrîm. The temple, however, is half-way between the shrine of Thothmes IIIrd at Ellesîyeh and that king's temple at Amâda, and the site thus seems to have been held in religious esteem. Rameses IInd called his temple "The Temple of Ra," and, according to the inscriptions, dedicated it to Ra, Harmachis, and Amen-Ra, while Ptah also takes a prominent place, one of the four statues in the sanctuary representing him.

There is no mention of the restoration of the temple by any later

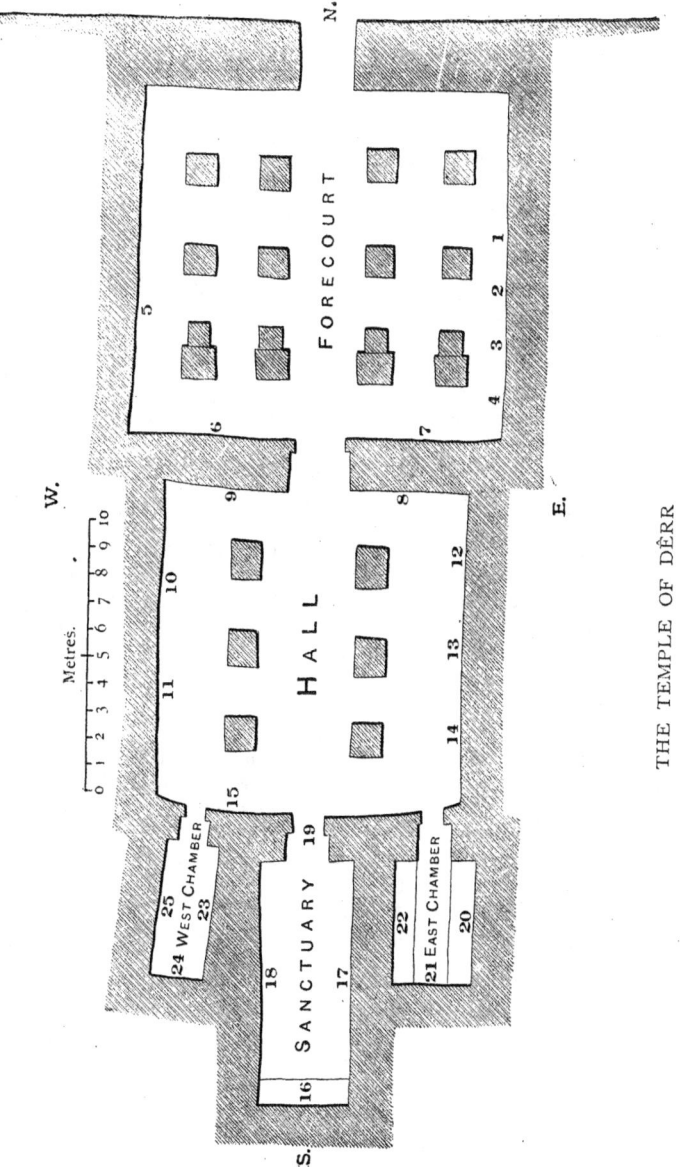

THE TEMPLE OF DÊRR

king, nor of any visit to it; and one must therefore suppose that it gradually fell into ruin, and did not survive the fame of Rameses IInd.

The outer hall. The pillared forecourt in front of the temple has upon its walls some scenes of considerable interest. On the east end of the north wall a battle-scene has been represented, but only parts of some figures and a chariot now remain. On the east wall (1) prisoners are led to the king, but this scene has almost disappeared; next (2) the king, in his chariot, drawn by galloping horses, goes into battle, and the enemy fly before him or are trampled under his horses' hoofs; then (3) the king, having alighted from his chariot, seizes four of the enemy by the hair; and finally (4) he leads a row of prisoners to Ra-Harmachis. Above these scenes the king has been shown before the gods, but only the representation in which he stands before Tum of On is left. On the west wall the main, and only easily understandable, scene (5) shows the king in his chariot shooting arrows at the enemy who fly from him. Negroes with bows and arrows are seen hastening back to their encampment amongst the hills and trees. Some are carrying away a wounded comrade upon their shoulders, while others break the news to the women. A child flies to its mother, a calf runs towards a cow; the goats and oxen belonging to the negroes wander unattended. Some Egyptian princes or officers bring in the prisoners whom they have captured, but the Pharaoh, galloping after the defeated enemy, does not seem to heed them. Above this scene the king is represented worshipping Amen-Ra. On the south wall, at the west side of the entrance, the king is shown (6) in the act of slaying four Asiatic prisoners in the presence of Amen-Ra, while beside the king is his pet lion. The king is also shown here before Ptah and before Thoth of Hermopolis. Below these scenes nine daughters of Rameses are shown. These are Bakmut, Nefertari, Nebtawi, Isis-nefert, Hemttawi, Wernure, Nezemmut, and two others whose names are obliterated. On the east side of the doorway the king is represented (7) slaying four Asiatics again, in the presence of Harmachis, while the pet lion seizes one of the victims—a fact which shows that this lion's actions, as seen in these reliefs, are to be regarded symbolically, for no lion which was allowed to taste blood in this indiscriminate manner could be kept under any sort of control. On this wall the king is also shown before Khnum, but the rest of the scenes are lost. On the lower part of the wall eight of the king's sons are shown, these being Amenherkhepshef,

Rameses, Paraherunemef, Khaemuast, Menthuherkhepshef, and three others whose names are lost. On the pillars the king is seen before the following gods : Horus of Beheni, Horus of Baki, two other forms of Horus now unreadable, Harmachis, Ptah, Tum, Khonsu, Thoth, Mut, Isis, Werthekaw, and Sekhmet.

On entering the interior of the temple one finds oneself in a square hall, the roof of which is supported by six square pillars. At the far end there are three doors leading to three chambers, of which the middle one is the sanctuary. The reliefs in the hall are purely of a religious nature. On the north wall, to the east of the entrance (8), the king, between Harseïsis and another god, is led up to Harmachis and a goddess. On the west side of the entrance (9) he offers to Neith, and is anointed by Harseïsis and a god who seems to be Thoth. On the west wall (10) the king offers incense and a libation to the boat of Harmachis carried on the shoulders of priests ; and (11) farther on he kneels upon a *heb* sign before Amen-Ra, who blesses him. Behind Amen-Ra stands Mut, and behind the king are Thoth of Hermopolis, Menthu of Thebes, and Harseïsis, each carrying a jubilee sign. On the east wall the king (12) offers again to a sacred boat carried on the shoulders of the priests ; he (13) worships the ithyphallic Amen-Ra and Isis ; and (14) he stands beside a sacred tree, while Ptah and Sekhmet are before him, and Thoth behind him. On the east end of the south wall the king worships Harmachis and Hathor of On. Above the small doorway leading into the side chamber here the figures of gods can just be discerned. On the west end of the south wall (15) the king is represented before Amen-Ra, Rameses deified, and Mut. Upon the architraves the king states that he made the temple for Amen-Ra, Ra, and Harmachis. The roof is painted with the usual decoration of vultures and cartouches, but little of this now remains.

The interior of the temple.

Passing into the sanctuary four almost completely destroyed statues will be found at the south end (16). These represented Ptah, Amen-Ra, the king, and Harmachis. On the east wall (17) the king worships the sacred boat, behind which is the deified figure of himself ; and he stands before Ptah. On the west wall (18) he worships the sacred boat, and offers to Harmachis. Inside the doorway (19) the king is seen before Harmachis and Amen-Ra. The chamber on the east side of the sanctuary is dark and partly filled with stones. Inside the doorway the king is shown before Harmachis. On the east wall (20) he stands before Tum, before Amen-Ra, and before a hawk-headed deification of himself.

The sanctuary.

On the south wall (21) he stands before Harmachis and Amen-Ra (?). On the west wall (22) he stands before Thoth, before Mut, and dances before a deified form of himself "in the sacred boat in the temple of Ra." The chamber on the west side of the sanctuary is also very dark, and the floor is much broken up by stones. In the doorway the king is seen before Harmachis. On the east wall (23) he stands before Ptah, before Amen-Ra, and before Harmachis. On the south wall (24) he stands twice before Rameses "in the sacred boat in the Temple of Ra." On the west wall (25) he dances before Osiris, Isis, and Horus; and worships Harmachis.

Neighbouring antiquities.
About two hundred yards north of the temple there is a Ramesside stele now almost obliterated. It is peculiar in the fact that it is enclosed in a kind of frame, consisting, on either side, of a miniature lotus pillar in high relief; at the top, of the architrave; and, at the bottom, of the pavement. Near it is another stele having upon it a figure adoring Horus of Maam. This figure represented a Viceroy of Ethiopia (?) named Amenemheb. Above the stele is the cartouche of Rameses IInd. On the rocks near by there are some drawings of giraffes and gazelles. The writer was unable to find the tomb, mentioned by Murray, in which two dogs facing one another are said to be represented, but at Ellesîyeh there is a tomb, at the door of which two rams facing one another are seen.

TOMÂS

The Nile now turns again, and the left bank of the stream becomes the north-west bank. A short distance beyond Dêrr on this bank there is a fine head of rock coming down to the water's edge, with trees at the foot of it. Beyond this the hills recede and the large village of Tomâs commences, and extends for the next three miles or so. There are here broad fields in front of the houses, and steep rocks behind them. On these rocks there are several inscriptions. Just behind the west end of the village there is the ruin of a Byzantine fortress, or monastery, on the side of a head of rock, and higher up there is a ruined tomb, having an arched doorway of good masonry. This is known as Shêkh Daud, and the name Daud (David) may perhaps refer to the ancient building rather than to a more modern Shêkh's tomb in the neighbourhood. On the south side of the head of rock there are some quarries, which may have supplied the stone for Amada temple.

FROM MAHÂRAKA TO KASR IBRÎM 549

There are several inscriptions of different dates here, amongst which is a large one of the Governor of Ethiopia, Setau, with the cartouche of Rameses IInd. A few yards farther along there are some inscriptions, two of which give the cartouches of the unknown kings, Kakara and Seanra. At the south end of Tomâs there is another bluff of rock, on the north side of which is a fine valley known as the Khor Bet er Risk. On one side of this there is a plundered cemetery of Ptolemaic times. On the south face of the rock there is a large inscription of Kakara, and beneath it a large number of prehistoric drawings of giraffes. Farther along there is cut a praying figure of Setau worshipping the cartouche of Rameses IInd. A few yards more and one comes to a spirited drawing of a man on a camel, with the Greek inscription, "Paulou Michael." This is probably a piece of work of the last century. Beyond this again there are numerous inscriptions of the Old and Middle Kingdom. One shows the cartouches of Pepy and Teta of the VIth dynasty; another gives the cartouche of Sahura; another seems to give the cartouche of Assa; and another the sixth year of an unnamed king, probably of the VIth dynasty. The three most important inscriptions, however, are those which give the cartouches of Hor-nefer-hen, a king whose name has so far only been known on a fragment of alabaster belonging to Professor Petrie. From here a great caravan road runs back into the desert, leading to Khârgeh Oasis, Aswân, and finally to Lower Egypt, and southwards to the Sudan; and it is probable that these inscriptions were written by members of expeditions into Nubia, who were camping at this point where the road and the river meet. The road leading to Medîk, and cutting off the bend of the river, also starts from here, and these inscriptions may have a close relation to those found at Medîk of the same period. Beyond this the hills recede, and the village soon comes to an end. An island off this end of the village is able to be cultivated by the natives, and the crops and trees rising from the water form a scene of considerable beauty. The desert now comes down to the water's edge in a gentle slope until it is interrupted by the recommencement of palm groves belonging to the village of Ajieh. Half-way between the palms of Tomâs Ajieh. and those of Ajieh there is a sand mound covered with Ptolemaic or earlier pottery, and showing signs of being the remains of a good-sized town. The cemetery is just to the west of the mound, behind the first houses of the village, but the tombs are entirely robbed. The village extends for some distance, with the palms in front of it, and behind it a short strip of sandy desert bordered by low rocks, the higher hills being far back in the distance.

On the east bank exactly opposite the strip of sand which lies between the villages of Tomâs and Ajieh there is a remarkable cistern hewn in the rock. It consists of two basins, the one being higher than the other and connected with it by a drain. The sides of the basins are cemented. For some distance the hills have come down to the water's edge, but now they recede, and there is again room for a narrow strip of arable land. Farther to the south the writer found a stele, at the top of which there is a seated figure of Horus of Maam, before whom a figure of Rameses IInd offers two vases. The inscription in four horizontal lines refers to offerings given to the statue of Rameses IInd by Thothmes, Prince of Maam, in what may have been the sixty-third year of his reign. At the bottom of the stele there is a praying figure of Setau, Viceroy of Ethiopia, stating that he made the stele.

A mile to the south, at the north end of the village of Sheîmeh, there is an inscription on the rocks reading, "Made by the High Priest of Horus Lord of Maa[m] Dua . . . kha, beloved of Ra." Near this there is a rock tomb of two chambers, without inscriptions. The village of Katteh is now reached, and, near the hamlet of Naga Oglan, there is a graffito reading, "The Retainer of Maam, Herhora."

KARÂNKO

Beyond Ajieh, on the west bank, the palms give out, and the bank becomes sandy again. The large and richly cultivated island, known as Gezîret Ibrîm, or Gezîret Abu Râs, is now reached; and on the low rocks of the desert, opposite its northeast end, there stands a fortified building known as Karânko. The building is three stories in height, and is of crude brick for the main part, but the base of the walls is of masonry. The roofing is mainly vaulted, and most of it has fallen in; but there is one chamber quite intact in all respects, while many of the walls in other parts of the building rise to a considerable height. To the west of the monastery there are the remains of a town in which the walls of many of the houses can be detected without excavation. Beyond Karânko there is little of interest except one late cemetery until the outskirts of the village of Anâybeh are reached.

ELLESÎYEH

About three or four miles to the south stands the small rock temple of Ellesîyeh. At this point the hills rise precipitously behind the palms at a distance of about half a mile from the river, and the little temple is cut in the side of the cliff. It consists only of a transverse chamber with a small recess leading from it. It was excavated by Thothmes IIIrd, and a large stele outside the doorway gives a date which has been read as "Year 43," but which, in the opinion of the writer, is more probably "Year 50." On the façade of the temple many inscriptions have been cut.

The temple of Ellesiyeh.

These give the names of a high priest of Horus of Maam, a priest of Horus of Maam, a Prince of Maam, and an official of Wawat, which go to show the general locality in which the temple stands. There is here a stele also, showing Rameses IInd offering to Amen-Ra and Horus of Maam, while below there is a kneeling figure of Setau, Viceroy of Ethiopia. Another stele shows a figure offering to Amen-Ra and Horus of Maam, but the inscription is obliterated. The dated stele of Thothmes IIIrd, mentioned above, has upon it a representation of that king worshipping Horus of Maam and Satet. The stele is cut on the south side of the doorway, and on the north side, opposite it, there is another stele which is much damaged, the date being quite unreadable. Along the whole length of the temple façade, above these inscriptions, there is a line of small rectangular holes apparently intended for supporting the beams of a wooden roof which may have formed a kind of portico to the temple. The ground level was also raised in order to make the floor for the portico.

The inscriptions on the façade.

Over the doorway is the cartouche of Thothmes IIIrd. Entering the little temple the visitor finds himself in a chamber once beautified by reliefs executed in the best style of the XVIIIth dynasty, but now made filthy and evil-smelling by bats, and by the habits of the natives. The roof of the chamber is slightly vaulted, but a great part of it has fallen in. The reliefs are so covered with the grime of ages that they are hard to decipher. On the south end of the west wall the king is seen offering to Horus of Hieraconpolis, embraced by Dedun of Takens, and standing before the deified Khakaura Senusert IIIrd. On the north end of the west wall he stands before a Horus, and is embraced by Anuket of Takens and Satet. On the south wall the king offers to Hathor of Abshek; is given life by Horus of Beheni (Halfa); is embraced by two

The interior of the temple.

goddesses; offers to Horus of Maam; and finally stands before a goddess whose name cannot easily be made out. On the north wall he worships Khnum; makes an offering to Amen-Ra; worships Min of Koptos; and is embraced by Menthu of On. On the south end of the east wall the king is kissed by Satet, and presents offerings to Horus of Maam. On the north end of the same wall he is kissed by a goddess, and offers to Amen-Ra.

One now enters the recess, at the end of which there are three much damaged statues, probably representing the king between Horus of Maam and another deity. On the north wall the king is represented before Horus of Maam, before Amen-Ra, and before Satet of Elephantine. On the south wall he stands before Horus "Bull of Takens," before Horus of Maam, and before Thoth. On both these walls there is a small praying figure, and an obliterated inscription added in later Ramesside times.

Neighbouring antiquities. High up on the rocks, about 200 yards to the south of the temple, there is a small, low chamber cut in the rocks, and outside the doorway there is a well-executed ram in relief on either side. The chamber is only about 6 feet square, and has a shaft in it, now filled up.

About two miles south of the temple stands the Post Office of Ibrîm, and on the rocks immediately behind it were found the large inscriptions of the unplaced kings, Karkara and Seanra, accompanied by the figure of a Pharaoh wearing the crown of Upper and Lower Egypt. This is the largest inscription of these kings which the writer found in Lower Nubia. A short distance farther on is an obliterated stele of Ramesside times. Two miles north of Kasr Ibrîm there are traces of a small quarry, and on a rock near by there is a small stele of Ptolemaic or Roman date, having upon it the figure of a king, whose cartouche is quite unreadable, worshipping a goddess who is Lady of Elephantine. Below is an almost obliterated inscription giving a prayer for the *Ka* of the dedicator. Beside the stele are the inscriptions, "Made by the libation-priest of Horus Lord of Maa[m] Pera" and "the libation-priest . . . Hor-hat."

ANÂYBEH

The village of Anâybeh stands on the west bank of the river, some twelve miles above Dêrr, 132 miles above the First Cataract, and about four miles below Kasr Ibrîm. Along the edge of the river, in front of the houses, there is the usual palm grove, and behind the village are the mounds which mark the site of the ancient town and fortress. Behind this, again, the desert slopes up towards the low shelving rocks, and in this space lie many extensive cemeteries for the most part of the Middle Kingdom, and Egyptian cemeteries of Græco-Roman times. On the higher levels behind this the desert stretches in a flat plain, and here there are several brick pyramids, which now stand in ruins. Nearly one and a half miles farther back the dark hills rise abruptly from the plain, and in one of these a fine tomb of the XXth dynasty is cut. It will be seen, then, that there is much of interest in Anâybeh. The ruins and remains show that an important city existed here.

The ancient name of Anâybeh seems to have been Maam, and it may have formed, with Ibrîm, the capital of the province of that name. Pennut, whose tomb is to be seen here, was Superintendent of the Temple of Horus, Lord of Maam, and his wife was a songstress of that god. In the brick pyramid tombs here Dr. D. Randall MacIver has recently found inscriptions of other nobles who call themselves "*deceased*," *in Maam*. There is no question that the Province of Maam, in the New Empire, was centred at about this point, for there are more references to it in graffiti and other inscriptions at Anâybeh and Ibrîm than anywhere else. At Anâybeh, as will be seen presently, there was a large town dating from the XVIIIth dynasty, or earlier, and having a great fortress, a temple in which Amenhotep IInd left his name, and a series of cemeteries more extensive than any others in Lower Nubia.

History of Anâybeh.

Anâybeh occupied a position of considerably strategic importance. It is probable that there were rapids at Kasr Ibrîm, and a fortress was therefore necessary there both to defend the shipping going south and to attack the enemy coming north. The fortress at Anâybeh appears to date from the XIIth dynasty, and it was probably in use at the same time as were those of Koshtâmneh and Kubbân, which have been already described. Much of the pottery lying on the mounds of the ancient town belongs to the XIIth dynasty, but there are also very large quantities of Nubian pottery found here, which showed that these people occupied the place in great numbers. There is a block of stone lying near the temple bearing the name of Amenhotep IInd, which indicates that he built or restored this temple of Horus. Under Rameses VIth Pennut is said, in his tomb inscriptions, to have been superintendent of this temple. In Ptolemaic times the town was generally beyond the frontiers of Egypt, but under the Romans it was for some time within them.

<small>The town and fortress.</small>
The mounds which mark the site of the ancient town lie behind the houses of the modern village. They are very extensive, and the broken pottery lying on them dates from the XIIth, XVIIIth, and XIXth dynasties, and from the Ptolemaic and Græco-Roman periods. The intermediate periods are no doubt represented also, though, while walking over the mounds, the writer did not happen to notice any but fragments of the above dates. Towards the north end of the mounds there is an enclosure over a hundred yards square which may mark the site of a fortress. To the south of this there is a mound upon which are a few weathered blocks of stone, and near by there lies the slab of limestone inscribed with the cartouche of Ra-aa-Kheperu (Amenhotep IInd). This is all that can be seen of the temple, but no doubt an excavation would reveal much. To the south of the temple there is a great rectangular space, having high mounds around it which are obviously the remains of the walls. On closer examination it is seen that these walls are constructed of brick, and on the east side one may even observe the remains of the turrets which projected from the wall at regular intervals along its whole length. One of the features observed in this fortress may give a clue to its date. Near the east corners there seem to have been serpentine walls, like those of Koshtâmneh, and which, in the description of that place, were shown to belong to the reign of Senusert IIIrd.

The cemeteries lie in the desert behind the town, and consist for the most part of plundered Nubian graves.

Somewhat farther back in the desert, on the ledges of sandstone which rise above the sand, there are to be seen a few shaft tombs of ambiguous date. About a dozen ruined brick pyramids are here to be observed which formed the burial-places of members of the family of Pennut, as Dr. Randall MacIver's excavations of 1907 have shown.

<small>The tomb of Pennut.</small>
The most important monument at Anâybeh is the tomb of Pennut, which is cut in the side of a hill fifteen minutes' walk back from the cemeteries just described. It consists of a rectangular chamber, from which a small niche, opposite the entrance, is excavated, having in it three much broken statues cut from the natural rock. In the middle of the chamber, between the entrance and the niche, is a shaft about ten feet deep, and from it the burial chamber leads off. The shaft was originally hidden by a

FROM MAHÂRAKA TO KASR IBRÎM

slab of stone, and the groove for its reception can still be seen. The walls of the main chamber are covered with fairly well-executed scenes, the colour of which has remained. These scenes are not broken at all, except in the south-east corner, where a part of the surface has fallen away. The tomb at present stands open. The personage who was buried here was named Pennut, and held the office of Superintendent of the Temple of Horus, Lord of Maam. He presented lands and temple furniture for the worship of his master, Rameses VIth, and in return he received honours and presents from that king. His wife, named Takha, was a singer in the temple of Anâybeh. The other members of his family held various appointments, such as Superintendent of the King's Treasury in Lower Nubia, Scribe of the Treasury, High Priest of Isis, Prince of Maam. The last-named official was also called Pennut, and seems to have been the elder Pennut's grandson. He married the lady Baksatet.

On entering the tomb one sees upon the left side of the doorway the figures of Pennut and his wife, with an inscription above them. On the north end of the west wall there is an inscription, in twenty horizontal lines, which gives a record of the lands presented to the king for the maintenance of the priests and sacrifices in honour of the statue of the king which stood in the temple of Maam. On either side of this inscription are the figures of the gods Ptah, Thoth, Amen-Ra, Mut of Asher, and Khonsu of Thebes. In the upper row on the north wall the Governor of Ethiopia is seen bowing to Rameses VIth, who sits under a canopy and announces to him the presentations made by Pennut; the Governor then inspects a small statue of the king which stands upon a wooden pedestal; and Pennut, robed by two servants, holds two silver (?) vessels presented to him by the king. In the lower room there is a family gathering, in which seven men and seven women are shown, attended by women servants. On the east wall, to the north of the niche, Pennut and his wife, with their six sons behind them, stand before Ra-Harmachis, who is seated upon a throne. On the south side of the recess, in the upper row, Pennut and his wife stand before Ra-Khepera. Pennut kneels before Hathor, who is represented as a cow issuing from the mountain, at the foot of which stands the usual shrine with pyramidical roof; and near by the goddess Taurt is seen holding a scarab in one hand and a staff in the other. In the lower row Pennut and his wife stand before Ptah-Sokaris; Ra-Harmachis is shown beneath a canopy; and Anubis and Thoth pour the water of life over Pennut, who is clothed in a linen robe and wears a scarab at his neck. Pennut and his wife are also shown here before Unnefer. On the south wall, in the upper row, Anubis stands by the coffin of the deceased Pennut; while Isis, clothed in white, and Nephthys in red, lament for him with arms raised; and next, Harseïsis leads Pennut and his wife to the throne of Osiris, behind whom are Isis and Nephthys and the four Genii of the Dead issuing from a lotus-flower. In the lower row the Fields of the Blessed are shown, and Pennut and his wife are seen in a boat upon one of the celestial canals. He is also shown worshipping Ra-Harmachis, Tum, and Khepera. Below are scenes representing harvest time in the celestial fields. On the south half of the west wall, in the upper row, Anubis and Thoth officiate at the weighing of the heart of Pennut, while the monster who devours the hearts of the evil-doers sits by; Pennut and his wife are next seen in an attitude of prayer, and standing before a sacred shrine. In the lower row the funeral of Pennut is shown. The mummy stands before the door of the tomb, while women weep before it, and priests and friends perform the last ceremonies.

CHAPTER XXVI

KASR IBRÎM—ABU SIMBEL—FROM ABU SIMBEL TO ADENDÂN

KASR IBRÎM

FOR many miles in either direction the fortress of Kasr Ibrîm forms an imposing landmark. Approaching from the north one sees three heads of rock projecting into the water, and on the flat top of the middle hill stand the ruined houses and walls of the fortress. At Dakkeh, it will be remembered, the Ethiopians were defeated by the Roman general Petronius in B.C. 25, who then followed them to Napata, their southern capital. It was during this campaign that the fortress played its first part in history. The Ethiopians had placed a garrison on the hill to resist the Roman advance, and Petronius had to take the place by storm. He then fortified it on an elaborate scale, and left a garrison of 400 men there with provisions for two years. After the decline of the Roman power in Egypt the fortress must have changed hands more than once; but in the sixteenth century the Sultan Selim placed a garrison of Bosnians here, who, being more or less forgotten by their Government, lived on here from generation to generation until the beginning of the nineteenth century. In 1811 the Mamelukes, retreating from the north towards Shendy, drove out the Bosnians, but were themselves driven out by Ibrahim Pasha. When he returned to Egypt the fortress was vacated, and has remained uninhabited ever since. In Roman times the place seems to have been called Primis Parva or Premis; and in more ancient days it seems to have formed part of the district of Maam. There were perhaps rapids at this point, and the hill upon which the fortress was built seems to have been sacred in the New Empire.

It is best to ascend the hill on the south-west side, where the ancient road may still be followed, with its rock-cut steps at the steeper parts. The battlements on the south and west sides are

History of the fortress.

The fortress.

very formidable, and those on the east side are also strong. One sees here and there parts of the well-built Roman walls enclosed within the rougher walls of later times. On the east side, at the point where the battlements reach the lowest level, there is a small doorway crowned with a disk and Egyptian cornice. In Roman times there was an internal rock passage leading up from this doorway to the fortress above; but now this is blocked. The main Roman entrance stands on the north-east side of the hill-top, and consists of a well-built Egyptian doorway, ornamented with the usual cornice, and having pylon-like buildings on either side of it, in which the recess for the flagstaff, so common in Egyptian pylons, is found. This building is solidly constructed of large, well-cut blocks of sandstone, some of which are thought to have been taken from an Egyptian temple. The name of Taharka is said to have been seen on one of these blocks, but the writer could not find this. The Bosnian town is now entered, and the jumble of roughly built houses makes it difficult to picture the place as it was in Roman times. The main building of that date, however, to which one now comes, indicates that an attempt had been made to render the place civilised and habitable. This building is the church, which occupied the centre of the hill-top, and towards which the streets seem to converge. It is solidly built of masonry, and on three of its sides the walls are still standing. At the north-east end there is a semicircular recess for the altar; while down the south-east side, and originally down the opposite side also, there runs a series of three masonry arches with granite pillars standing before them. The arches are light and delicate, but the pillars are clumsy. At three points in each arch there is a small decorative cross or other symbol, and on the side of the pillars a cross is fashioned. The south-east wall is plastered and was probably painted; and a recess in it is built of flat red bricks of purely Roman origin. A short staircase here seems to have led to a kind of pulpit. A slab of grey granite lying in the middle of the building may have been an altar; and at the west foot of the hill near the water there is a large block of pink granite, which may have come from here. Around this church the more modern buildings cluster, and one sees here and there a granite pillar used as a doorstep, or a block of masonry as a corner stone to a rough wall. The Governor's quarters seem to have been situated on the west side of the fortress, where the spaces are more open and the Bosnian houses are larger. The water for the garrison seems to have been carried up from the river on the

KASR IBRÎM

precipitous side of the hill, and some steps have been cut here to render the climb more easy. Tanks cut in the rock seem to have held the water, and these are seen to be very numerous. On either side of the fortress, a mile back in the desert, there are numerous small tumuli. In the bay to the north of the fortress there are some brick tombs with domed roofs, such as are also found at Gebel Addeh. It is a question whether these are Christian or Muhammedan, but they are certainly mediæval. There are here the ruins of a Coptic church, around which much Coptic pottery is found; but there is no foundation for the statement which is sometimes made that the remains of the town of Maam are to be seen here, though there are the remains of a small late town.

Immediately below the fortress, in the west face of the cliffs at the edge of the water, five shrines are cut, dating from the XVIIIth and XIXth dynasties. The first shrine was made in the reign of Thothmes IIIrd, the second shrine dates from the reign of Rameses IInd, the third from the reign of Thothmes IIIrd, the fourth from that of Amenhotep IInd, and the fifth is unfinished, and has no inscription. The shrines are not easy to enter, as they are several feet from the ground, and some have practically no footholes or steps by which an ordinary European could climb up to them. The Arab sailors, however, are able to reach them, and when a rope has been let down there will be no difficulty to an active person in swarming up hand over hand. To the archæologist the interior of the shrines is worth visiting, as the scenes and inscriptions are of great interest.

The shrines.

The inscriptions outside the doorway of the first or southernmost shrine give the cartouches of Thothmes IIIrd, beloved of Satet of Takens, and Horus of Maam; and originally they also gave the titles of the Viceroy of Ethiopia Nehi, who made the shrine. Three damaged statues are seated at the end of the shrine, and probably represented the king between Satet and Horus. On the south wall the king is seen with Min of Koptos behind him, and before him are some damaged figures near which is an inscription in two horizontal lines giving the titles of Nehi. Near by an inscription states that Nehi brings the tribute of the south in gold, ivory, and ebony, in the fifty-second year of the king's reign. On the north wall are Anuket, Satet of Elephantine, Horus of Baki, Hathor, Horus of Beheni, Horus of Maam, and Amen-Ra. The name of Amen has been erased and rewritten. The second shrine has three broken statues in the rear wall, which represent Rameses

ANTIQUITIES OF UPPER EGYPT

IInd between two gods. On the north and south walls several officials are shown doing homage to Rameses, who is seated on a throne. The names of some of these figures can be made out: the Viceroy of Ethiopia Setau, the scribe Horemheb, the scribe of the Troops Amenemapt, the scribe Hornekht, the scribe Paser, the scribe of the Granaries, Horhotep; but the rest are now more or less unreadable. The third shrine has few inscriptions, but the colour is well preserved, and the pattern of red, yellow, and white on the ceiling is quite distinct. In the recess at the end of the chamber there are four squat figures seated, representing the king, with Horus of Maam and with Satet of Elephantine. Over the recess there is a well-executed winged disk, while down one side is the name of Thothmes IIIrd, beloved of Horus of Maam, and down the other side is an obliterated cartouche, which was probably that of Hatshepsut, beloved of Satet of Takens. On the side walls there are no inscriptions, except, unfortunately, those written by modern travellers.

The fourth shrine is the most important of the group. In the rear wall are three damaged figures, representing King Amenhotep IInd with a god and a goddess. On either side of the recess in which these statues sit is a painted figure of the king, now almost faded. On the south wall King Amenhotep is seen seated under a canopy, while behind him stands a fan-bearer, and near by stands Satet of Elephantine. Before him two officials holding fans bow before him. A long, much-damaged, inscription here refers to the tribute of leopards (?), oxen, ostriches, &c., some of which are also pictured on the wall. On the north wall the king, with Horus of Beheni behind him, worships Khnum, Satet of Elephantine, Anuket of Elephantine, Sept, Hathor of Elephantine, and Nekheb. Then there is a damaged figure of the king before Horus of Maam. On the north side of the doorway the king is represented with a goddess. Over the doorway, on the outside, there are the cartouches of Amenhotep IInd, and down the sides are damaged inscriptions referring to the Royal Son User-Satet.

Other antiquities. A few yards to the south of the shrines, on a rock near the water, there is an inscription in Greek characters but in an unknown language, called by Lepsius "Christian Ethiopic." Another example of this is found in the temple of Abahûdeh. In the bay to the south of Kasr Ibrîm there are the ruins of a Coptic town of no particular interest. The third great head of rock now comes down to the water, and on a smooth part of the cliff there is cut a great stele of Sety Ist, recording his victories. At the top the king is

FROM KASR IBRÎM TO ABU SIMBEL

seen slaying an enemy in the presence of a god, and near him stands his chariot; but only the lower part of this scene is left. Below this there are twelve horizontal and three perpendicular lines of inscription, and a small figure of the Viceroy of Ethiopia, Amenemapt. A short distance farther on there is a graffito reading "The Chief 'Reader' of Khnum, Aakheperkara, called Hor," and by it is the figure of a man with hands raised. Persons who visit the Sety stele should walk along the rocks from the north, where there is quite a good pathway. To approach it from the south requires a somewhat dangerous climb, which should not be attempted, unless, as in the case of the writer, the visitor happens to be walking from south to north and has no time to make a detour.

FROM KASR IBRÎM TO ABU SIMBEL

About 4½ miles south of Anâybeh, and exactly opposite Kasr Ibrîm, there stands a small fortress, the brick walls of which are in places still 10 feet high. Perhaps it was built in connection with the fort of Kasr Ibrîm. Near it are the remains of a Roman town, which probably formed part of the ancient Primis. The mounds stand amidst a castor plantation.

After passing the southernmost of the three heads of rock which have been described under the name of Kasr Ibrîm, the hills recede again, but along this east bank there are shelving rocks and great boulders. About eight miles to the south, and some three below Tôshkeh Post Office, there are two hills which rise from a high plateau of rock, the west side of which slopes precipitously to the water. These two hills are surrounded on three sides by a stout wall of broken stones, which thus enclose altogether an area of a square mile or more. The fourth side is protected by the cliffs. No pottery is found within the enclosure except a few fragments of Roman date, and one or two of Nubian form, the latter being on the hill. It is possible that the place is a Roman stronghold, or again it is perhaps a Nubian fortress of dynastic times. High up on the south-west side of the hill there is a ledge of rock to which a rough and disused pathway leads. A portion of the surface of the rock at the back of the ledge has been smoothed and a small figure of a king slaying a negro has been cut in and coloured. Beside the king is the cartouche of Senusert IIIrd, and the workmanship leads one to suppose that it dates from the reign of that king and is not a later instance of the king's worship. His figure

The rock shrine.

is coloured red, his cartouche and the upraised weapon are yellow, and the negro's skirt is red. Near by there is a very neatly executed series of figures and inscriptions dating probably from the XVIIIth dynasty. At one end of the scene there are three seated gods, Horus of Maam, Senusert IIIrd, and Reshep. Horus wears the double crown and holds the usual wand in his hand; and the inscription states that "a thousand of all good and pure things' are offered to his *Ka*. Senusert IIIrd is called "The King, the Mighty One, living for ever," and wears the crown of Upper Egypt. He holds the crook and flail, and before him a single long-stemmed lotus rises. Reshep wears the crown of Upper Egypt, and holds a mace upraised in one hand and a shield in the other. Before these interesting gods five equally interesting persons worship. The first figure is that of a man who offers incense, and pours a libation on to a table upon which lies a palm-branch. He is called Nebsey. Behind him is "his wife who loves him" Thabau. Next comes Nebsey's son, "the hunter of the king," holding in one hand a bow and arrows and in the other a gazelle which he has shot. Behind him is another of Nebsey's sons carrying a pair of sandals and a bird, and called "the watchman of the cattle of Horus, Lord of Maam, Sennefer." Finally, there is a man carrying two boomerangs, and called "the retainer of the king, the watchman of the royal horns (?)," but his name does not seem to have been given. Below this row of figures there is the figure of the sacred ram feeding from an altar, and having a disk and horns upon its head. The inscription states that a thousand of all good and pure things are offered by the above-mentioned hunter. A longer inscription makes an offering to all the gods of Lower Nubia, but the sense is not clear. Below this again there is the figure of a man offering a vase, and an inscription. There is an interest in this shrine which is as rare as it is pleasing. One sees here a native herdsman or farmer offering to an Egyptian and an Asiatic war-god and to a deified hero in a rude rock shrine on a hilltop; one sees his hunter son bringing as a sacrifice the gazelle which he has shot in the desert; and one reads of the herdsman of the sacred cattle, and the watchman whose care it was to collect the horns which formed part of the Nubian tribute. To this day one may here still see the gazelles wandering over the rocks; and, with this shrine before one, the imagination is able to recreate the pastoral scenes in which Nebsey and his sons lived.

A mile or so to the south, about 500 yards back from the river, there is a low mound of rocks, on one of the boulders of which are

FROM KASR IBRÎM TO ABU SIMBEL 563

several inscriptions and drawings. Judging by the discoloration of the stone, the most ancient drawing here is one representing a negro with a bow and arrows. The man seems to have a feather in his hair, a necklace round his neck, and perhaps a beard. There are also some drawings of ships and animals of the same date. Rather less discoloured, and therefore less ancient, are some giraffes and gazelles; and cut right over these there is the interesting inscription which gives the full titles of the king, or the two kings, Kakara and Seanra. The rough inscriptions by the side of this seem to be of the same date. *Rock inscriptions.*

A mile or so south of this a somewhat important neighbourhood is reached, which probably formed one of the chief centres of the district of Maam. The site lies behind the Post Office of Tôshkeh, and consists of rock tombs, rock inscriptions, and the remains of the town. The tombs are three in number, and are to be found at the north end of the desert bay, in the west side of an isolated mound of rock. The first consists of a chamber from which an arched doorway leads into a six-pillared hall. Parts of the roof and three of the pillars have fallen in. The second tomb has a four-pillared hall from which a long arched passage leads into an inner chamber, in which is the burial shaft. The third tomb has only two simple chambers, each about 12 feet square. In each case the workmanship is rough, and there are no inscriptions on the inner walls, though there are traces of plaster which may have been decorated with paintings. The first tomb has had an inscription outside the doorway, but not much of it can now be read, except a dedication to Osiris and Harmachis by a steward. The town remains lie to the west of these tombs, and have been dug over by the *sebakhîn*. A certain amount of Nubian pottery is to be observed here, and some fragments of Ramesside and Roman shapes. The tombs may be attributed to the Ramesside period. A Copt has written the name Jesu on a rock near here. *Tôshkeh.*

Towards the south end of the bay there is a rocky valley leading up from behind a modern cemetery. On a rock on the south side of this valley, about a hundred yards from its mouth, there is a large, well-cut inscription of about the XVIIIth or XIXth dynasty, reading "The Chieftain of Maam, Rahotep, endowed with life; Hatawy caused [this] to be made." Another graffito here reads, "The Scribe Aahmes-seuser; [made] by his son, causing his name to live." A third inscription reads, "Made by the Scribe Thase." A scarab with the disk upon its head is cut on these rocks in two places.

The inscription of Aahmes and Kames, &c. Some three miles south of this site, at a point between Tôshkeh and Ermênneh, the writer was fortunate enough to find an important inscription of the XVIIth–XVIIIth dynasty. It is inscribed on a rock at the side of the pathway, about 50 feet back from the river, but being inside a little shady nook of rocks it cannot be seen from the path. This seems to read, " The King of Upper and Lower Egypt, Wazet Kheperra, Son of the Sun Kames, given life. The King of Upper and Lower Egypt Nebpehtira, Son of the Sun Aahmes, given life . . . Teta. The Royal Son. . . ." The fact that the two kings are named together perhaps shows that, like the sovereigns of the XIIth dynasty, the kings of the XVIIth–XVIIIth dynasties sometimes associated their sons upon the throne with them. It is interesting to find the name of King Kames so far up the Nile, and it is evident that he was not the petty prince of Thebes which he was thought to be, but was king of most of Upper Egypt, and of all Lower Nubia. It will be remembered that Aahmes, the son of Kames, drove out the shepherd kings, and founded the XVIIIth dynasty.

About half a mile south of this, at a point opposite the north end of a range of hills, on the western side of the river, which runs southwards from Tôshkeh and Ermênneh, there is a stele dating from about the XIXth dynasty. It is cut on some overhanging rocks, a few yards back from the river. Upon it one sees a male figure offering a libation to Horus of Maam, while behind the man stand his wife and a small male figure. The inscription commences, " Hail to thee, shining like gold, O Horus Lord of Maam, King of the gods, Bull of the Cycle of the gods ; " and, after further laudatory phrases, a prayer is asked for the *Ka* of " the Commandant of the country, the Superintendent of the gold of . . ., the Royal Son of a Royal Son, the Superintendent of the Land of the south. . . ." The name of this personage is unfortunately lost.

Opposite the island known as Gheziret Ermênneh there is an ancient well which is still in use, and near it there is a cemetery of Roman date. On the west bank the ruins of Græco-Roman buildings may be seen at intervals. Just before reaching Abu Simbel on this bank there is a fine desert bay, enclosed by low hills, and having mounds of sand along the river's edge, overgrown with bushes on which the Beduin camels feed.

ABU SIMBEL

The great temple of Abu Simbel is situated on the east side ofا fine head of sandstone rock, which comes down to the water on the west bank of the river opposite the village of Farêk. The smaller temple stands a few yards to the north, and faces the south-east. The temples are 35 miles above Anâybeh, 166 above the barrage, and some 40 below Wâdy Halfa. In ancient times the town of Maha seems to have stood on the site now occupied by Farêk, and thus the Abu Simbel hills were to this town what the Kubet el Howa hills were to Aswân, or the Theban hills to Luxor. There was a small town near the temple, called Abshek, and the goddess Hathor, who presided over the hills here, was known as "Hathor of Abshek." The selection of this site for the great temple was not a matter of chance, nor yet was it altogether due to the fact that no such suitable hills for a rock temple were to be found in the neighbourhood. Certainly as early as the XIIIth dynasty these rocks were considered of importance, for they had been selected by King Kakara as one of the few places where he should inscribe his cartouche; and several officials of that date had taken the trouble to write their names there. In the temple inscriptions the site is called "the hill of libations," and in the XVIIIth dynasty temple of Horemheb at Abahûdeh the same expression is used. It is possible that there was a minor cataract at this point, which would account for the temples and shrines in the neighbourhood.

The great temple is the work of Rameses IInd. An inscription, certainly placed in the temple after the completion of the internal decorations, is dated in the king's thirty-fifth year. The marriage of Rameses IInd with the Hittite princess, afterwards known as Mutneferura, which took place at about this date, had to be recorded outside the temple, as there was no vacant place for the stele inside. The temple, thus, was completed before the year 1359 B.C. During the reign of Sety IInd the colossus on the north side of the façade of the great temple was restored; but from that time until the Greek age nothing is heard of the temple. The Greek mercenary army of Psametik IInd left a record of its visit to the temple in the XXVIth dynasty, and other Greek, Carian, and Phœnician travellers cut inscriptions on the legs of the colossi. In 1817 Belzoni entered the temple; in 1844 Lepsius copied the reliefs; and in 1869 Mariette opened up the place.

History of the temple.

The gods.

The great temple, like so many temples in Nubia, was dedicated to the worship of Ra-Harmachis. A fine statue of that god stands above the entrance, and at early morning the sun's rays strike full upon it, so that the figure appears to be stepping forward to greet the sunrise. Along the cornice a row of baboons, nearly always associated with the sun, sit in attitudes of worship. As the temple faces towards the east, it is only at sunrise that the light penetrates into the sanctuary, and only then can the reliefs on the walls be distinctly seen. Thus the whole temple is designed for the one hour of sunrise. Those who visit it at dawn and pass into the vestibule and sanctuary will be amazed at the irresistible solemnity of that moment when the sun passes above the hills, and the dim halls are suddenly transformed into a brilliantly lighted temple; and though one has sickened of the eulogies of the literary traveller in Egypt, one may in this case adopt his language, and describe the hour of sunrise here as one of profound and stirring grandeur. At no other time and in no other place in Egypt does one feel the same capacity for appreciating the ancient Egyptian spirit of worship. The smaller temple was dedicated to Hathor Lady of Abshek, but Harmachis takes a prominent place here also. Besides these the gods worshipped in the temples were very numerous, and included many of the more important deities of Egypt. Rameses himself was also worshipped here.

THE GREAT TEMPLE

The façade of the great temple. The main feature of the great temple is of course the four seated colossi, hewn out of the rock. Despite their immense size, these figures have been executed with considerable artistic skill, and do not at once exhibit any glaring faults of proportion. One's eye turns to the faces of the figures, and these are of such real beauty that the malformations of the lower parts remain quite unobserved. The expression of the faces is serene and thoughtful; the hands are laid upon the knees without extreme stiffness; and the whole motionless pose produces an effect of placid solemnity, which no figure where movement is shown could excel. On either side of the legs of each colossus there is a smaller female figure, and between the legs a male or female figure in each case is represented. On the southernmost colossus these figures represent Princess Nebt-tawi, Princess Batha-antha, and an unnamed princess. On the next colossus the figures are Queen Nefertari,

ABU SIMBEL

Prince Amenherkhepshef, and the queen again. On the third colossus the figures represent the queen, Prince Rameses, and the queen again. The figures on the fourth colossus are buried in the sand. The pedestals of the two southern colossi have the king's

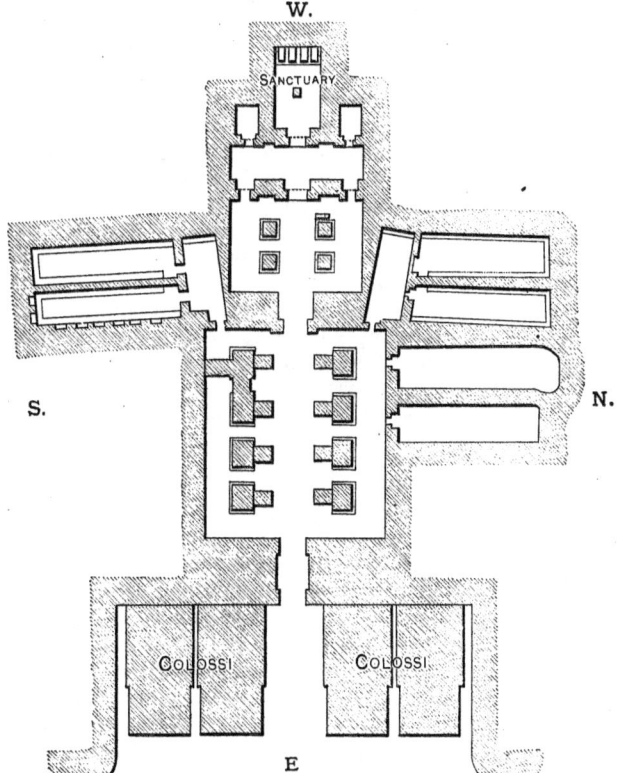

THE GREAT TEMPLE OF ABU SIMBEL

cartouches inscribed upon their eastern sides, while on the other sides lines of negro captives are shown. These are drawn conventionally, and show no individual characteristics. On the southern pedestals figures of Asiatics of different racial types are shown. The main entrance to the temple is reached between the pedestals of the two middle colossi, and thus one passes between a row of negroes and Asiatics. On the sides of the thrones of the colossi, which one also sees while going towards the temple doorway, there are conventional representations of the uniting of Upper and Lower Egypt. Around the doorway there are the king's cartouches, figures of numerous gods, all unnamed, and representations of the king dancing before Amen-Ra and Mut, and before Harmachis and Werthekau. High above the doorway, and forming one of the principal features of the façade, there is a fine full-faced statue of the hawk-headed Harmachis, stepping forward from a shallow recess. On the one side of him is the jackal-headed staff, *user*, and on the other a damaged figure of *maat*; and thus, taking the figure of Harmachis to represent Ra, one obtains the king's name Ra-user-maat in statuary. Reliefs on either side of the recess show the king worshipping Harmachis. The façade is topped by a row of twenty-two cynocephali, or baboons, some of which are destroyed; and below these there is a decoration made up of the king's cartouches and uræi.

<small>The main doorway.</small>

Before entering the temple it will be best to describe the steles which are found on the south side of the façade. The space between the southern colossus and the end wall has been partitioned off by a stone wall, and at the end of the enclosure so formed there is a large stele with twenty-three lines of horizontal inscription. At the top of the stele King Rameses IInd is represented worshipping Amen-Ra, Harmachis, and Horus. The inscription relates to the king's conquests in Asia and Kush. A small stele in the south wall of the enclosure shows the figure of Amen worshipped by the Viceroy of Ethiopia, Sety, who states that he was the king's envoy into all foreign lands. Just outside this little enclosure, on the south wall of the façade, there is the great stele recording the marriage of Rameses IInd with the Hittite princess in the thirty-fourth year of his reign. The inscription is written in forty horizontal lines, and above it the king is shown seated beneath a canopy between two gods, while King Khetasar of the Hittites, accompanied by the King of Kode, brings his daughter forward.

<small>Steles at the south side of the façade.</small>

On the left leg of the headless colossus there is a Greek inscription of considerable interest. It reads, "When King Psammetichus came to Elephantine the companions of Psammetichus, son of Theokles, wrote this. They came by ship *viâ* Kerkis to where the river rises, Potasimto leading the foreigners and Amasis the Egyptians. Demerarchon son of Amoibichos, and Pelekos

<small>Greek inscriptions.</small>

ABU SIMBEL

son of Udamos, wrote." Kerkis is perhaps to be identified with the modern Kirsh, opposite Gerf Husên. The name Potasimto has been thought to be the Egyptian Pedesamtawi ; but the whole reading of this sentence is questionable. In a Phœnician inscription near by one of the mercenaries mentions a general named Horus. There are several other Greek graffiti, a Teian, a Kolophonian, and an Ialysian from Rhodes being amongst the writers of the earlier period.

The great hall of the temple is now entered. On the sides of the doorway, as one passes in, the cartouches of the king are seen. On the south side the king is represented offering to Amen-Ra. The hall has for its main feature two rows of four pillars, against the front sides of which stand colossal figures of the king. The most perfect of these figures is the last on the north side, the face of which as seen in profile is the most striking feature of the whole temple interior. On the pillars at the back of these colossi are reliefs showing the king in the presence of Amen-Ra, Harmachis, Ptah, Horus, Tum of On, Thoth of Hermopolis, Anhur, Menthu of Thebes, Sebek-Ra, Khnum of Elephantine, Min-Amen, Hathor of Abshek, Hathor of On, Hathor of Thebes, Anuket, Satet, Isis, and other deities.

The great hall.

On the north end of the east wall the king is seen smiting a group of Asiatics, in the presence of Harmachis. The vulture hovers over the king's head, and behind him there is the standard giving his Ka-names. Below this scene nine of the king's daughters are shown : Batha-anthat, Bakmut, Nefertari, Amenmeri, Nebttawi, Isis-nefert, Hemttawi, Wernure, and Nezemmut. In the corner, below the reliefs, there is an isolated inscription stating that this inscription, or perhaps the whole series of reliefs, was "made by the sculptor of Rameses-Meriamen Piaay son of Khanefer." On the south end of the east wall the king is again seen smiting a group of prisoners, this time in the presence of Amen-Ra. Below are eight of the king's sons : Amenherkhepshef, Rameses, Paraherunemef, Khaemuast, Menthuherkhepshef, Nebenkhar, Meriamen, and Amenemwa. The north wall of the hall is covered with historical scenes of considerable interest, though one has become familiar with the main incidents in the temples at Thebes. The scenes represent the great battle of Kadesh, and the stirring incidents which led to the Egyptians' ultimate defeat of the Hittites. The battle took place at the end of April in the year 1388 B.C., *i.e.* the fifth year of the king's reign, when he was still a young man. Rameses had invaded the Hittite country and

The historical scenes on the north wall of the great hall.

was advancing with his army to lay siege to Kadesh when the battle took place. When still some miles from the city the Egyptians had captured two spies, who said they were deserters from the Hittite army, and stated that the enemy had retreated behind Kadesh. Rameses, therefore, very rashly pushed on to attack the city at once; and the first scene in the lower half of this wall shows his line of march. Meanwhile the Hittite king was in ambush; and, as soon as Rameses had got out of touch with the main Egyptian army, he made a detour and pushed in between the two Egyptian divisions, thus completely isolating Rameses, who had now pitched his camp. The scene represented on the wall, between the two doors, shows the camp, surrounded by a stockade, formed of the soldiers' shields. Horses are being fed, soldiers are seen resting, and the whole appearance of the camp shows how entirely unaware of their danger were the Egyptians. Rameses now re-questioned the captured spies, and ordered them to be flogged—an incident here represented. He then learnt his true position, and the reliefs show the council of war which was then held, the king seated upon his throne surrounded by his officers. Soon after this the Hittites attacked the camp, and Rameses was obliged to cut his way through them almost single-handed. This scene is in the upper half of the reliefs, and is drawn with much spirit. It was not long after this that the main Egyptian army arrived, and the Hittites were driven off, some being drowned in crossing the river to Kadesh. In these reliefs one sees the town of Kadesh situated on the hill, with the Orontes running round it, and the Hittites are shown retreating on to it. The final scene shows Rameses with his officers counting the prisoners, and the hands cut from the dead.

At the north end of the west wall the king is seen leading prisoners to Harmachis, and to his deified self; and on the south end of this wall the king leads his prisoners before Amen-Ra, Rameses, and Mut. At the sides of the doorway in this wall leading to the vestibule the king is seen in the presence of Ptah, Harmachis, Amen-Ra, and Min. Above the door the king dances before Amen-Ra and Mut, and before Harmachis and Sekhmet (?). The south wall is divided into two rows. In the upper row the king is seen before the ram-headed Mermutef and a lion-headed goddess; he offers sacks of grain to Amen-Ra; he burns incense before Ptah; Safkhet numbers his years; he kneels beneath the sacred tree while Thoth and Horus are by him; and finally he worships Amen-Ra from whose throne a large uræus rises. In

ABU SIMBEL

the lower row Rameses is seen in his chariot shooting arrows at the defenders of a fortress which stands on a hill. From the walls the slain are seen falling, while others kneel in supplication, and one man is shown driving the cattle to a place of safety. Behind the king are chariots containing his three sons, Amenherkhepshef, Rameses, and thirdly Paraherunemef. The inscription here praises the king's bravery and strength, and describes how he overthrows the rebels on their hills and in their valleys. The king is next seen leaping over a fallen Asiatic, and thrusting his spear through another. The inscription states that the king destroys the tribes of the Nine Bows; devastates the lands of the north; transports the negroes to the north and the northerners to Nubia, the people of the Shasu to . . . and the people of Tehen to the mountains; and that he brings for the temple the plunder from Syria and Retennu. A third relief shows the king driving slowly in his chariot, with his lion by his side; while one of the officers leads two lines of captives before him, the upper line consisting of black negroes and the lower line of brown Nubians. The horse which draws the chariot is named "Victorious in Thebes." The inscription accompanying this scene speaks of the king as overawing the people of Wawat and of Retennu. On the architraves in this hall the king is said to have made this temple for his father "Harmachis the great god Lord of Ta-Kens"; and for his father "Amen-Ra, king of the gods." Between the third and fourth colossus on the south side of the hall a large stele has been set up, the inscription on which, dated in the thirty-fifth year of the king's reign, refers to the building of a temple at Memphis dedicated to Ptah. The ceiling of the hall is decorated with the usual design of vultures and cartouches.

From the north side of the hall two chambers lead off. In the first room only the west wall is decorated with reliefs, and here one sees in the presence of Amen-Ra, Harmachis, Rameses, Horus of Beheni, Horus of Maam, and Horus of Baki. In the second room, on the west side of the south wall, the king stands before Hathor of Abshek. On the west wall he stands before Thoth, Rameses human-headed, Rameses hawk-headed, Khonsu, Ptah, Rameses ram-headed, and Harmachis. On the north wall he is seen before Amen-Ra twice. On the east wall he stands before Harmachis, Horus of Maam, Horus of Baki, Horus of Beheni, Tum, Shepses-in-Hermopolis, and Thoth. On the east end of the south wall the king is in the presence of a god whose name is lost.

Chambers leading from the great hall.

572   ANTIQUITIES OF UPPER EGYPT

From the north side of the west wall a chamber leads off. On its south wall the king is seen before the ithyphallic Amen-Ra and Isis; before Amen-Ra, Mut, and Khonsu; and before Tum of On. On the west wall he stands before Harmachis and Amen-Ra. On the north wall he is in the presence of Menthu of Thebes, the hawk-headed Rameses, and a Rameses with the head now destroyed. Two doors lead through this wall into two further chambers. In the first of these chambers, on the west wall, is a figure of Isis; after which the king is seen offering cattle to Mut; and standing before Khepera, Khonsu, Wepwat, and Amen-Ra. On the north wall he is twice shown before Harmachis. On the east wall he is seen before Ptah, Thoth, Menthu, Mut, Harmachis, and Thoth. On the south wall the scene is lost. In the second room the king is seen, on the south wall, before Rameses. On the west wall he is shown before Harmachis, Ptah, Sekhmet, Anubis, and Rameses. On the north wall he stands before Harmachis and Amen-Ra. On the east wall he is seen before Menthu, Rameses, Amen-Ra, Isis, and Thoth.

From the south side of the west wall of the hall a corresponding set of rooms is entered. On the east wall of the room first entered the king is seen before Amen-Ra. On the north wall he stands before Rameses, Min-Amen, Isis, and Ptah. On the west wall the king is presented by Thoth to Harmachis, and by another god to Amen-Ra. On the south wall the king is seen before Rameses. Two doors in this wall lead into the other two chambers. In the first of these, on the north wall, the king stands before Rameses. In the east wall there are six niches between which are the king's cartouches, while above them is an inscription stating that the king constructed "this monument for his father Amen in Takens, and made for him great treasuries, and colossi in the court, of good white stone." In the south wall are two more niches. On the west wall the king is seen before Ptah, Menthu of Thebes and On, Thoth, Amen-Ra, Amen, Min-Amen, and Harmachis. In the second room, on the east wall, the king is shown in the presence of Tum-Ra-Horus-Khepera, Isis, Amen-Ra, and Harmachis. On the south wall he is before Harmachis and Rameses. On the west wall he is represented before Amen-Ra, Ra, Thoth, Harmachis, and two other gods whose names are now obliterated. On the north wall he is seen before Amen-Ra.

The vestibule.   Passing up the axis of the great hall and through the doorway in the west wall one enters the vestibule, the roof of which is supported by four square pillars. On these pillars the reliefs show

ABU SIMBEL

the king in the presence of or embraced by the gods. On the north end of the east wall the king is seen offering to Min-Amen, Rameses, and Isis. On the north wall the king with the queen behind him offers to the sacred boat borne on the shoulders of priests. On the north end of the west wall the king is seen with Harmachis. On the south end of the west wall the king worships Amen-Ra. On the south wall the king and queen offer to the sacred boat carried by priests. On the south end of the east wall the king worships Amen-Ra, Rameses, and Mut. On the south side of the doorway leading from the hall to the vestibule the king is shown before Harmachis, and below this scene there is a much-damaged inscription, dated in the first year of Rameses IInd; but only the beginning of five of the lines can be made out. Down the sides of the doorway leading into the adytum there are four small panels showing the king worshipping Thoth, Khonsu, Harmachis, and Ptah. Above the doorway there are the figures of Amen-Ra, Mut, and Khonsu and another Trinity which is difficult to make out.

The adytum is now entered. On the north end of the east wall the king is represented offering to Tum of On; and on the south end of this wall he offers to Min Amen. On the north wall he worships Thoth; and, on the south wall, Amen-Ra. On the north end of the west wall he offers to Ptah; and, on the south end of this wall, to Amen-Ra. On the sides of the doorways leading from the vestibule to the adytum the king is seen with Thoth, Horus, Amen-Ra, and Ra. From the west wall of the adytum three doorways lead, those on either side opening into small uninscribed chambers, and that in the middle passing into the sanctuary. *The adytum.*

The main feature of the sanctuary is the row of four seated statues at its west end. These figures represent Ptah, Amen, Rameses, and Harmachis. They are badly executed, and one of the shoulders of the figure of Rameses is higher than the other; but when, at sunrise, the shaft of light strikes full upon them, even these statues become impressive and fraught with dignity. On either side of the doorway there is a figure of the king with arm extended. On the north wall the king burns incense and offers a libation before the sacred boat; and here he is also seen adoring Ra. On the south wall he is seen before the sacred boat, and worshipping Min-Maat-Amen. In the centre of the room there is a broken and uninscribed altar. It should be mentioned that the pedestal of the statue standing in the vestibule was made by Paser. *The sanctuary.*

THE SMALLER TEMPLE

The façade of the smaller temple.

A pathway leads from the great temple to the smaller temple along the water's edge. In summer, when the water is high, it passes under the trees and one is obliged to break one's way through the thorny branches; but in winter it lies nearer the water in open ground. The temple is not easily entered, for the doorway is high above the path, and the original stairway leading up to it is lost. The façade of the temple, although not so large as that of the great temple, is imposing. Three standing colossi on either side of the doorway form the main feature. These rise from recesses divided from one another by projecting buttresses. Four of the colossi represent the king and two the Queen Nefertari; and at the sides of each are two small figures, those in the case of the king's colossi being sons, and those in the case of the queen's being daughters. Down each of the buttresses runs an inscription. The three on the south side of the doorway give the cartouches of the king and queen. The first on the north side states that the king "made this temple in [the form of] an excavation in the hill as an eternal work in the land of Ta-Kens." The second inscription gives the cartouches of the king and queen; and the third states that " His Majesty commanded a temple to be made in the land of Ta-Kens in [the form of] an excavation in the hill: nothing like it had been made before."

The interior of the smaller temple.

Entering the temple one sees on the south side of the doorway, the king before Hathor of Abshek; and on the north the queen before Isis. On each side of the doorway are the cartouches of the king and queen, the latter being called " beloved of Hathor and Isis," and the former " beloved of Thoth and Amen-Ra." One now stands in a large low hall, the roof being supported by six columns, down the front of which are Hathor totems. On the north end of the west wall a relief shows the king slaying a captive before Harmachis of Maha, while behind the king is the queen. On the south end of the west wall the king slays a negro before Amen-Ra; while the queen again appears behind. On the north wall the king is seen before Ptah; he worships the ram-headed Hershef of Heracleopolis; the queen stands before Hathor of On; and the king adores Ra-Harmachis. On the south wall the king stands before Hathor of Abshek; he stands between Set of Nubt and Horus of Maha; the queen worships Anuket; and the king adores Amen-Ra. On the west wall the queen is shown before

ABU SIMBEL

Hathor of Abshek, and before Mut. In the west wall there are three doorways leading into the vestibule. The south and north doors have above them the king's and queen's cartouches, while down the sides are the king's cartouches alone. The middle door, to which three steps lead, has the king's cartouches above it, while a figure of him is represented on either side. The Hathor pillars have on their front sides the cartouches of the king and queen. On the other sides of the pillars are figures of the king, the queen, Horus of Beheni, Horus of Maam, Horus of Baki, Thoth, Khonsu, Khnum, Hathor, Satet, Isis, and Werthekau. The figures of the queen are represented on the east side of the first two pillars, as well as elsewhere, and she thus has the most prominent position. On the architrave the queen is said to have "made the temple in the hill of Libations." This inscription, together with the queen's colossi and prominent reliefs, show that this temple was dedicated by her to Hathor just as the great temple was dedicated by the king to Harmachis.

The vestibule is now entered. On the north end of the east wall the king and queen are seen before Hathor; and the doorway here is inscribed with the queen's cartouches. On the south end of the east wall the queen is shown between Hathor of Abshek and Isis; and the doorway here also has the queen's cartouches upon it. On the north and south walls the king worships the Hathor cow, which stands in a boat amidst the reeds. There is a doorway in each of these walls leading into a small uninscribed chamber; and around the doorway are the king's cartouches. On the north end of the west wall there is a large relief of the king before Harmachis, and a smaller relief of the queen before Khnum, Satis, and Anukis. On the south end of the west wall the large relief represents the king before Amen-Ra, and the smaller one shows the king in the presence of Horus of Maam, Horus of Baki, and Horus of Beheni. In the middle of this wall is a doorway leading into the Sanctuary, and on either is a figure of the king, while above it are small figures of the king and queen before Hathor. *The vestibule.*

The sanctuary is a small chamber having in the west wall a full-faced cow in high relief, and under its head the figure of a man, probably the king. On either side is a Hathor totem, and on the south side of this the king is seen worshipping. The cow and figure are much damaged. On the south wall the queen is represented in the presence of Mut and Hathor. On the north wall the king stands before the seated figures of himself and the *The sanctuary.*

576   ANTIQUITIES OF UPPER EGYPT

queen. On either side of the doorway is a figure of Hapi, and over the door are the cartouches of the queen.

NEIGHBOURING ANTIQUITIES

The chapel south of the great temple. A few paces to the south of the great temple there is a small rock chamber which was probably used as a chapel for the lesser ceremonies. On either side of the doorway there is a figure of the king with the accompanying inscription, stating that to enter the temple one must be four times purified. On the north wall the king is seen burning incense before the sacred boat of Amen-Ra ; and on the south wall before the sacred boat of " Thoth Lord of Hermopolis within Amenheriab." On the west wall the king stands before Ra-Harmachis-Tum-Horus-Kheper in the form of one god, and before Amen-Ra of Napata. Above these scenes there is a frieze of cartouches alternating with small seated figures of the gods. The roof is decorated with the usual vultures and cartouches. The colour is good in this chamber, as it has not been so long open to the air, it having been discovered in 1874 by Miss Amelia Edwards and her party. In front of this rock chamber there was originally a pronaos constructed of brick or stone which has now disappeared, though the plan is given in Miss Edwards' *Thousand Miles up the Nile.*

Rock inscriptions. North of the smaller temple there are various inscriptions and steles. One first sees a figure of a viceroy of Ethiopia bowing to Rameses IInd, with the inscription, " Made by the Viceroy of Kush, Any, of the People of Heracleopolis." Farther on is a large stele of an official bowing to Rameses IInd, but this is inaccessible without a ladder. Farther northwards there is a damaged stele showing a man bowing before Amen-Ra, Rameses, Harmachis, and Horus ; and near it another figure bows before Horus. High up on the rocks is a large well-cut inscription reading, " Made by the Scribe of the Temple, the Father-in-law of the king, Superintendent of the Cattle, Prince, High Priest, Ahmose, called Ture." Three other small graffiti on the rocks are of the Middle Empire, and give the characteristic names Sebekhotep and Menthuhotep. South of the great temple is a group of three large steles. The first shows a viceroy of Ethiopia worshipping Rameses IInd ; the second shows the king before Thoth, Harmachis, and Shepses, while below is a figure of an official ; and the third shows Rameses and the queen before

Amen-Ra, Rameses, and Harmachis, while below is a figure of a certain Nekhtu before the queen. Beyond these, and only to be seen from the water, are three large steles of Rameses IInd. Near this is the inscription, " Made by the Scribe of the Treasury, Superintendent of the Troops in the country, the governor, Mery, of the Land of Wawat." Two small steles are next seen. Just round the corner of the rock, at the point where the next bay of land commences, there is an almost obliterated inscription of the unplaced King Kakara.

The great head of rock in the east side of which the temple of Abu Simbel is excavated, is followed immediately by a second head, a small sandy bay lying between them. On the south side of this second hill a small tomb is excavated, consisting of a rough chamber with a shaft in the floor leading down into the burial chamber. Outside the entrance there is a small stele, upon which two figures are shown before Osiris, but the inscription is too much damaged to read. The tomb probably dates from the late Ramesside period. In the valley which lies to the south there is a plundered cemetery of Græco-Roman date.

Opposite the temples of Abu Simbel stands the village of Farêk, which extends for some distance along the edge of the river. In an open bay about half a mile south of the temples there is an extensive cemetery of Nubian graves. South of this there is a figure of Horus cut on the rocks. In the hillside here and there some tombs without inscriptions will be found. Two of these consist of two chambers, and two others have wells leading down to the sepulchral chambers; but they are all rough, and of no interest.

ABAHÛDEH

The rocks now come quite down to the water, and on their precipitous sides a few graffiti may be found. Going southwards the first inscription met with reads, "The Scribe of the Divine offerings of all the gods of Wawat, Merapt, son of Pe-merkaw." Farther to the south is the inscription, "Superintendent of the Granaries in the Hill (?) of Horus Lord of Beheni (Hâlfa) Merapt, son of the Superintendent of the Granaries Pemerkaw, deceased." Near this are two inscriptions reading "The Scribes of the Temple Tewre and Hormes."

Rock inscriptions.

578   ANTIQUITIES OF UPPER EGYPT

<small>The temple.</small>

A few yards farther southward, in a head of rock which rises from the water, there is excavated a small temple which dates from the reign of King Horemheb of the XVIIIth dynasty. From the outside nothing can be seen of the temple except the narrow slit in the hillside which is its doorway. The steps which originally led up to the doorway have now crumbled away, and it is something of a climb to reach the entrance. The temple is excavated in the west face of the rock, and consists of a hall, the roof of which is supported by four pillars with clustered capitals; two chambers leading off the hall; and a sanctuary, in the floor of which a shaft leads down into a crypt. Around the hall a bench or step runs, less than half a yard high. The reliefs are executed in good style, but have been entirely covered by Coptic paintings of mediæval date, which have fallen off only in parts. These paintings are extremely interesting. Much of them seems to have been intentionally scraped off by early antiquarians in order to expose the reliefs below; but fortunately the archæologists who destroy the less ancient remains in their search for the work of earlier periods have become more rare now that archæology has been placed on a scientific basis.

In this neighbourhood the reader will have seen that there are tombs probably dating from the New Empire, cemeteries of Nubian graves of the Middle Kingdom, graffiti of the XIIIth dynasty and of the New Empire, the cartouche of the Middle Kingdom king Kakara; and presently he will find stelæ of the XVIIIth dynasty, and inscriptions of the Ramesside period. It seems certain, thus, that there was a large town near here of sufficient importance to induce Horemheb to honour it with his only Nubian shrine and Rameses with his greatest temple. The name of this town cannot be stated with certainty, but it was probably *Amenheri-ab*.

<small>The reliefs in the temple.</small>

In describing this temple it will be best to record the original reliefs on the walls, and afterwards to give some account of the Coptic paintings. On the north side of the doorway there is a damaged figure of Horemheb with six lines of almost unreadable inscription by his side. On the south end of the west wall the king is seen before Thoth; and on the north end of this wall he is shown suckled by Anuket in Amenheriab, in the presence of Khnum in Peduabi. On the south wall most of the reliefs are hidden, but at the east end there is a figure of the king before Amen. In this wall is a doorway leading into an uninscribed chamber, and around it are the cartouches of Horemheb, beloved

ABAHÛDEH

of Amen, Amen-Ra, and Thoth. On the north wall at the west end the king is seen adoring Thoth, Horus of Maam, Horus of Beheni, and Horus of Maha; while at the east end the king is shown between Set of Nubt (Nekâdeh) who is called Lord of the South Land, and Horus. Around the doorway in this wall, which leads into another uninscribed chamber, are the cartouches of the king. On the north end of the east wall the king is represented before Amen-Ra, and on the south end before Harmachis. The

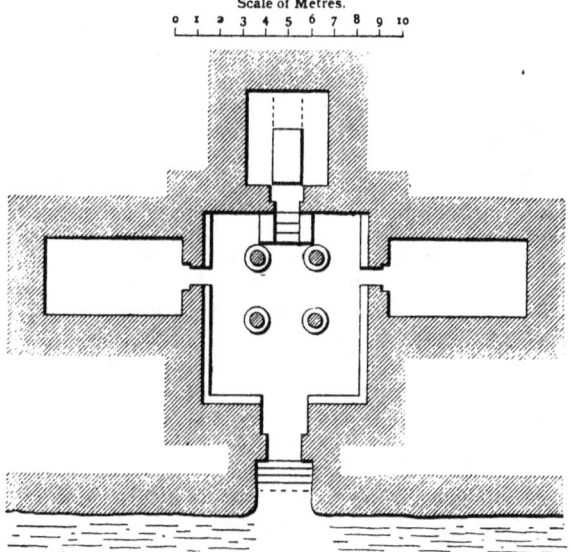

ABAHÛDEH TEMPLE.

steps lead up to the door into the sanctuary. On the inner sides of the doorway there are figures of Hapi. On the north wall the king is seen worshipping the sacred boat; but on the south and east walls the reliefs are hidden. The shaft in the floor is some ten feet in depth, and at the bottom a chamber leads off to the east; but this is now filled with debris. In the north and south walls of the sanctuary the Copts have cut a small niche.

The Coptic paintings are extremely fresh as to their colour, but are much damaged by intentional scraping and cutting, and some

The Coptic paintings.

of the following descriptions may be incorrect. Over the doorway is a head of Christ or a saint enclosed in a circle ornamented with flowers. On the ceiling of the hall there is the figure of a saint wearing a white garment, over which is a red robe, and holding in his left hand a staff tipped with a cross. The right hand is raised above his head, holding a crown studded with jewels. On this ceiling there is also a figure of Christ, clothed in a brown or dark red robe. His hair is brown and His beard red-brown. His right hand is raised in benediction, the two first fingers being raised, and the thumb, the third, and the fourth finger being bent. The architraves and pillars are decorated with various Coptic patterns. On either side of the doorway there is an angel holding a staff and globe or musical instrument, and clothed in brown and yellow. On the north end of the west wall there is a much-damaged figure of an angel, with long yellow wings, clothed in a red and white garment. On the west end of the north wall there is a large painting of a prancing horse, with an almost invisible rider, and near by there is a standing figure. Another horse is then seen, upon which is a rider, and having rich trappings. A tall seated figure with a red and yellow crown is next represented. On the west end of the wall there was evidently a picture of some importance, but it is almost entirely lost. On the north side of the east wall there are two large figures of saints or apostles clad in purple robes; and on the south half there are again two large standing figures, one clad in yellow, the other in red. On the west end of the south wall there is a large figure of an angel with widely spread wings; and a large horse with rich trappings, and having upon it a rider—depicted with much flying drapery, and wearing a crown studded with blue stones—who is thrusting downwards with a long spear at a dragon. Above the horse's head there is a circle enclosing the head of God or an angel. On the east end of the south wall there is a horse and rider, much damaged. On the south end of the west wall there is again a figure mounted on a horse, and spearing a dragon. On the south wall of the sanctuary there is an inscription written in Greek characters, in an unknown language. A similar inscription at Kasr Ibrîm has already been recorded.

GÊBEL ADDEH

The fortress. Three or four miles to the south of the Temple of Abahûdeh there rises an isolated hill, the northern and western sides of which

GÊBEL ADDEH

descend precipitously to the water. Upon this hill stand the ruins of a mediæval fortress, the ascent to which is best made on the southern side. The buildings cover all the top and part of the sides of the hill, and portions of the walls of defence can be seen, especially on the north side. There are many rooms and passages to be discerned, the walls being built either of crude brick or of broken stones. The hill is littered with fragments of pottery, all of which are to be dated to a period after the Roman occupation. The ware is coarse, and is not unlike that used at the present day in Nubia. There are few fragments that can be called Roman, and in this the fortress is unlike those at Sabagura and elsewhere, where Byzantine-Roman forms are common.

The view from the hill is very fine. In the river below lies the island of Shatani; to the north one obtains a wonderful prospect of the Nile; and to the south the neighbouring hills rise in a series of rugged peaks. The nearest hill, with a curious double peak, is not more than half a mile distant, and its western side slopes precipitously down to the river. The hill is called Gêbel Es-Shemsh, "The hill of the sun," perhaps a translation. A few yards above the water a small shrine and some inscriptions will be observed, but they are somewhat difficult of access, and the traveller who is not accustomed to climbing might find his attempt to reach them terminated by a fall into the river. The shrine is a small chamber about 5 feet deep and 6 broad, a large part of which is occupied by a damaged statue of a divinity which has had a disk and horns upon the head. Around the walls are reliefs and inscriptions referring to Prince Paser, who is here entitled Governor of Ethiopia, and "Superintendent of Country of the Gold of Amen." On the south side of the doorway appears the unreadable cartouche of the king. On the north and south walls, Paser is seated while his relatives pay him homage; and on the east wall he worships the above-mentioned statue. Just to the north of this shrine there is a little stele, upon which two figures are shown worshipping Anuket of Amenheriab, dedicated by an official of Wawat named Hor. To the north of this again there is a stele showing in the top register a king adoring Amen-Ra, Harmachis, Ptah, Satet, and two forms of Horus. The cartouche of this king is now practically unreadable, but some copyists have read it as that of king Ay of the XVIIIth dynasty. In the lower register the Governor of Ethiopia, Paser, kneels before Anubis, Sebek-Ra, King Senusert IIIrd, and Anuket. In the inscriptions Horus of *Maha* is invoked. South of the shrine of Paser there is

The shrines.

an inscription made by "the Scribe of the Treasury of the Lord of the Two Lands in Ta-kens, the Superintendent of the Granary of Wawat, Kaza, son of Thothmes," and referring to the goddesses Werthekawi and Anuket of Amenheriab.

FROM GÊBEL ADDEH TO ADENDÂN

In the bay between the fortress and this hill there stand a large number of small domed tombs constructed of crude brick, and dating from the Middle Ages, though whether they are Christian or Muhammedan is a matter of doubt. The road to Hâlfa runs inland here behind the hill on which the inscriptions are cut, and, amidst the rocky valleys and promontories around it, one expected to find more graffiti; but a prolonged search proved fruitless in this respect. Shortly after this the hills recede from the river, and the bank becomes flat and uninteresting.

The country on the west bank now becomes un-Egyptian, and reminds one more of the desert borderlands in North Africa. Behind the palms at the river's edge, amidst which the houses of Ballânyeh stand, the surface of the desert is covered with blown sand in which clumps of desert plants grow. Here and there are humps and ridges of sand covered with scrub, while between them small forests of *sunt*-trees or groups of tamarisks give pleasant shade to the traveller. Behind the village of Ballânyeh there are some traces of ruined buildings of the Ptolemaic age. Farther southward the desert becomes flatter, and after a few miles the low hills come down to the water again. To the archæologist the country here is uninteresting, and the writer found no traces of any ancient sites, except where a few Roman or mediæval fragments of pottery indicated the existence of villages of that time. Presently the large island of Adendân is passed, with the village of that name upon it; and less than a mile to the south a ridge of sand, upon which stands a wooden signboard, marks the frontier between Egypt and the Sudan. Wâdy Halfa, with its ruins of Beheni, lies about twenty-five miles to the south, but these ruins are not under the jurisdiction of the Department which the present writer serves.

INDEX

AAH-HOTEP, 137, 331, 350
Aahmes I., 6, 25, 63, 86, 310, 324
—— II., 9, 49, 108, 465
—— Abana, 310, 320, 324
——- mortuary chapel of, 131, 155
—— Queen, 268, 273, 368
—— Pennekheb, 311, 320
Aahmeshenttameh, 166
Aahmes-nefertari, 166, 177, 181, 220, 230, 244, 280
Aahmes-seuser, 563
Aahset, 220
Aakheperkara, 561
Aam, 395, 428, 444
Aamathu, shrine of, 368
Aay, 365
Aba, mortuary chapel of, 173
Abahùdeh, 357, 454, 577
Abana, 310
Abaton, 490
Abdu, 3, 4, 6
Abraham, 462, 514
Abshek, 565
Abu Gehâd, 351
Abû Hôr, 450, 511
Abu'l Haggâg, 81
Abu Simbel, 281, 357, 400, 454, 565
Abusir, 380
Abydos, 1, 25, 487
Adem Agbeh, 306
Adendân, 463, 582
Adon, 78
Adu, Prince, 29
Aelian quoted, 50, 296
Ælius Gallus, 460, 522
Ajieh, 549
Aha, 272
Ahmose, 576
Ahy, 62
Aimadua, mortuary chapel of, 152
Akata, 454
Akhnaton, 7, 14, 49, 51, 65, 71, 87, 99, 122, 160, 164, 184, 218, 228, 273, 280, 291, 294, 313, 359, 371, 398, 410, 413, 539
Aku, tomb of, 426
Alexander the Great, 72, 76
—— II., 400; temple of, 416
—— Severus, 301
Amâda, 447, 451, 453; temple of, 536
Amelineau quoted, 25
Amenardes, 414
Amenartas, 231; mortuary temple of, 245
Amendet Ankhtaara. *See* Ergamenes
Amenemapt, mortuary chapel of, 170; 507, 560; tomb of, 227
Amenemhat I., 34, 48, 63, 86, 418, 446, 536
—— II., 447, 490
—— III., 5, 310, 331, 525, 536
—— IV., 449
—— mortuary chapels of, 131, 166, 170; shrine of, 369
Amenemheb, mortuary chapel of, 126, 149, 548
Amenemusekht, mortuary chapel of, 154, 369
Amenemwa, 569
Amenherkhepshef, 19, 546, 567
Amenherunamf, 507
Amenhotep I., 6, 166, 177, 181, 186, 188, 191, 256, 311, 325, 343, 351, 376, 451; tomb of, 223; mortuary temple of, 230
—— II., 55, 59, 63, 83, 90, 109, 115, 117, 120, 128, 148, 158, 191, 196, 202, 204, 210, 225, 227, 262, 280, 357, 368, 398, 416, 422, 453, 502, 538, 553, 559; tomb of, 221; mortuary temple of, 255
—— III., 7, 14, 62, 65, 70, 87, 97, 112, 124, 154, 156, 169, 170, 186, 204, 264, 276, 280, 355, 398, 409, 454, 465, 534; tomb of, 217, 230; mor-

tuary temple of, 245; palace of, 290, 312; temple of, 328
Amenhotep IV. *See* Akhnaton
—— (High Priest), 86, 109, 162, 466, 541; mortuary chapel of, 156
—— (Builder), 276
Amenhotepsase, mortuary chapel of, 143, 172
Amenkhepeshef, tomb of, 284
Amenmeri, 569
Amenmerib, 181
Amenmes, mortuary chapel of, 170, 177
Amenmeses, 188; tomb of, 206
Amenneb, mortuary chapel of, 122, 179
Amenothes, 277
Amen, Feast of, 78
Amen-Ra, 51, 58, 68, 70, 87, 90, 106, 109, 112, 145, 153, 163, 172, 192, 199, 217, 232, 244, 250, 258, 266, 271, 277, 299, 301, 324, 328, 352, 359, 474, 479, 482, 491, 508, 517, 532, 534, 540, 546, 551, 555, 568, 576, 581; temple of, 84, 92
Ament, 91, 106, 259
Amenta, 433
Amentet-Hapet, 14
Amenysenb, 6
Amnefer, 120
Amonius, 476, 505
Amset, 217, 281, 284, 286, 288, 486
Amunezeh, mortuary chapel of, 129
Anâybeh, 444, 447, 453, 552
Anba Musas, 25
Anena, 86, 223; mortuary chapel of, 133, 186, 369
Anhapu, 201
Anhur, 3, 15, 23, 208, 232, 370
Ankh-hor, 73, 176
Ankhnes-neferabra, 108
Ankhsen, 427
Annapeta, 364
Ant, 31
Antef, 4, 7, 62, 310, 350
Antefaa, 395, 418
Antefakr, 63; mortuary chapel of, 155
Antoninus, Emperor, 46, 388
—— Pius, 59, 243, 304, 350, 496
Anubis, 17, 24, 105, 121, 166, 168, 180, 202, 208, 210, 211, 213, 214, 227, 245, 265, 277, 281, 288, 299, 324, 424, 434, 555, 581
Anuket or Anukis, 358, 438, 474, 484, 509, 516, 523, 540, 551, 578, 581

Anun, 365
Any, 455, 576
Apepa I., 49, 299
Aphrodite, 35
Apis, 340, 386, 410
Apollinopolis Parva, 57
Apollo, 385; temple of, 295
Apophis, 197, 212
Apries, 465
Apts, the two, 60; festival of, 78
Apuaa, 162
Ara, 428
Archer, mortuary chapel of a chief, 121
Arkamen. *See* Ergamenes
Arko, 449
Arment, 62, 293
Arsinoë I., 49, 106, 278, 340
—— III., 521
—— IV., 521
Arsnuphis, 514, 524; temple of, 474
Arthet, 424, 438, 442
Arueris, 57
Aruiru, 349
Ary, 349
Asaballah, 349
Asclepius, 297
Asesa, 309, 394, 441
Aset, 220, 280; tomb of, 287
Asfun, 300
Ashurbanipal, 67
Asklepiodotus, 248
Aspelta, 457
Assa, 549
Astemkheb, 298
Astnefert, 281, 363, 370
Aswân, 48, 53, 303, 391, 400; temple of, 404; siege of, 522
Atefrura, 311
Aton, 51, 71, 87, 161, 163, 359, 371, 413
Atum, 197, 208, 254
Au, 287
Auf, 331
Augustus, Emperor, 36, 51, 490, 503, 513
—— the Strong, 535
Aurelius Antoninus Pius, 488
—— Besarion, 503
Avaris, siege of, 311, 325
Ay, 188; tomb of, 218, 280, 357, 454
Azkheramen, 459, 480, 492

Baa, 424
Baba, 324
Bâb el Kalâbsheh, 460, 497, 501

INDEX

Bak, mortuary chapel of, 178
Bakenkhonsu, 72
Baki, 450, 525
Bakmut, 546, 569
Baksatet, 555
Bakt, 132
Balianeh, 1
Ballânyeh, 582
Ballas, 53
Bantantha, 280, 363, 413, 566, 569
Banutanath, 81
Barrage, the, 464, 497
Barsanti, M., 334
Bast, 217, 478
Beba, tomb of, 326
Beduins, the, 101
Beheni, 451, 517
Behudet, 44, 368, 382, 480
Bek, 413
Belzoni, 213, 565
Berenice, 89, 341, 405, 483, 521
Berlin Museum, 417
Bes, 76, 112, 488
Besh. *See* Khasekhem
Bet el Wâli, 502, 507
Bey, 9, 188, 363, 540; tomb of, 209
Bibân el Molûk, 184
Bibliothèque Nationale, Paris, 105
Blgeh, 419, 453, 465
Birket Habu, 291
Birth-House, explanation of, 45; at Kôm Ombo, 389; at Philæ, 477
Blemmyes, the, 299, 461, 471, 510
Bonomi, 509
Bopos, 28
Breasted, Professor, 161, 331, 355
British Museum, relics at, 509
Budge, Dr., 423
Bueb, fortress of, 355
Busiris, 67, 487
Buto, 2, 36, 239, 410, 474, 503

" CÆSAR, Autocrator," 467, 492
—— Augustus, 476
—— Claudius, 36, 51, 304, 475, 488
—— Julius, 44, 294, 333
Cailliaud, 354
Cairo Museum, 51, 55, 164, 191, 202, 213, 223, 226, 262, 270, 275, 309, 320, 530
Caligula, 36, 503
Cambyses, 67, 457
Caracalla, 301, 304, 377, 388, 496
Carchemish, battle of, 126
Carter, Howard, 433, 437
Cataract Canal of Senusert III., 421
Cecil, Lady William, 433, 437

Champollion, 250, 304
Christianity, relics of, 50, 59, 72, 104, 245, 265, 294, 329, 334, 347, 377, 391, 402, 406, 435, 462, 471, 482, 491, 502, 510, 511, 514, 517, 522, 532, 536, 559, 563, 580,
Clarke, Somers, 314
Cleopatra, 44, 294, 327, 384, 477, 492
Colossi, the, 245
Commodus, 304
Conon, 405
Contra Syene, 435
Coptic remains, 59, 83, 104, 242, 295, 306, 347, 391, 402, 427, 435, 471, 482, 488, 511, 517, 530, 532, 536, 543, 559, 560, 578
Cornelius Gallus, 460, 488
Crocodile worship, 50, 55, 380
Crocodilopolis, 297

DABABIYEH, 301
Dabôd, 459, 490
Dakkeh, 27, 45, 557; temple of, 520
Daressy, M., 291
Darius I., 332
Davis, T. M., 195, 210
Decius, 304
Dedneferra, 299
Dedun, 247, 451, 474, 551
Dehmêd, 447, 450
Dema, 543
Demerarchon, 568
Dendereh, 31
Dendûr, 458, 462; temple of, 513
Depemnefert (or Depa), 427
Dêr, 53
Dêr el Bahri, 62, 176; temples of, 184, 191, 202, 206, 212, 213, 216, 217, 219, 223, 225, 261, 367
—— el Medineh, 64, 182, 384; temple of, 276
—— el Melak, 59
—— el Salib, 59
—— es Shelwît, 291
—— Mari Bokli, 59
—— Mari Girgis, 59
Derâr, 459, 522, 529
Dêrr, 428, 463, 543
Deshneh, 30
Dinri, 493
Diocletian, 50, 461, 488, 490
Diodorus quoted, 61, 67, 191, 250
Diospolis Parva, 26, 53
Dodekaschoinci, 471, 524
Domitian, 35, 304, 377
Dra Abu'l Neggar, 62, 114, 176, 186

Duamutef, 217, 281, 284, 286, 288, 486
Dudumes, 262, 299, 310, 331, 348

EBERS, 162
Edfu, 5, 36, 55; temple of, 330; cemeteries of, 347
Edwards, Miss, referred to, 524, 530, 576
Egypt, union of Upper and Lower, 2; emblems of unity, 32, 81, 274, 313, 332
Eileithyiapolis, 23, 27, 36, 48, 53, 171, 307, 318, 399, 447
Eïspanöme, 462, 514
El Amarna, 184
El Amrah, cemetery of, 25
El Arâbat el Madfûneh, 2
El Assasif, 114, 169, 172
El Balalis, 329
El Barasy, 349
El Gherâreh, 297
El Hasiyeh, 348
El Heseh, 400
El Hosh, 349
El Kâb. *See* Eileithyiapolis
El Kanawieh, 31
El Kenân, 306
El Khârgeh, 27, 299, 444
El Khirbeh, 329
El Kòm, 414
El Kulah, 306
El Ramleh, 414
Elagabalus, 301
Elephantine, 27, 53, 391, 414; siege of, 522
Ellesiyeh, 451, 548, 551
Eos, 247
Eratosthenes, 400, 418
Ergamenes, 458, 480, 521, 529
Ermenneh, 455
Esneh, 97; temple of, 302
Es Sebûa, 534
Ewsos, 517

FARAS, 373
Farêk, 577
Fitzwilliam Museum, relics at, 206
Florus, 462
Fou, 28
Fu, 287

GAIUS, 530
Gaius Dioscuros Julius Macrinus, 496
Gamr, 493
Ganneau, Clermont, 417
Garstang referred to, 315, 348

Gau referred to, 525
Gebânet el Kurûd, 291
Gêbel Addeh, 357, 452, 580
—— Dukhan, 50
—— es Shemsh, 581
—— Silselah, 356
—— Timsah, 351
Gebelên, 33, 297
Genemieh, 348
Gerf Husên, 450, 517
Germanicus, 476
Geta, 304, 377, 388
Geziret Ibrîm, 550
Ghawalieh, 349
Ghretag, 355
Gizeh, pyramid of, 32
Golenischeff referred to, 351
Gordian, 496
Grébaut, M., 291
Green referred to, 314
Gregory XVI., 483
Grenfell, Sir Francis, 423
Griffith, F. Ll., 323
Gûrneh, temple of, 256
Gurnet el Murrai, 114, 170, 276

HAABRA, 9
Hadrian, 27, 248, 304, 494
Hagar Esneh, 305
Hakar, 72, 92, 244, 313
Hakara, 450, 494
Hall, H. R., 262
Hapi, 105, 217, 258, 274, 281, 286, 288, 340, 358, 379, 386, 405, 524, 579
Hapi, 411
Hapu, 276; shrine of, 367, 447
—— of Annubis, 486
Hapusenb, mortuary chapel of, 152, 367
Harendotes, 13, 467, 471
Harmachis, 12, 90, 168, 172-3, 195, 196, 198-9, 204, 207, 210-11, 213, 227, 237, 266, 279, 283, 286, 288, 324, 328, 338, 352, 361, 413, 477, 514, 517, 534, 539, 546, 555, 563, 566, 575, 579
Harseisis, 13, 473, 524, 547
Harsemtawi, 478
Hathor, 13, 23, 24, 26, 32, 61, 69, 87, 105, 106, 112, 115, 121, 124, 132, 143, 147, 158, 164, 172, 178, 180, 214, 218, 244, 259, 262, 277, 283, 286, 324, 327, 331, 354, 370, 377, 433, 465, 467, 471, 491, 514, 517, 541, 555, 560, 565, 574
Hathor Chapel, 272

INDEX

Hatshepent, 63
Hatshepsut (wife of Sennefer), 365
—— Queen, 49, 70, 86, 98, 106, 110, 112, 148, 152, 223, 230, 268, 311, 331, 351, 357, 376, 410; tomb of, 217; mortuary temple of, 263
Hay, Mr., referred to, 509
Hehu, 340
Heket, 18, 24, 268, 283
Hehut, 486
Helena, Empress, 306
Heliopolis, 6, 69
Hemtaui, 365, 546, 569
Henut-erneheh, 321
Heqab, tomb of, 425, 432
Heqab-herab, 432
Heqabur, 452
Heqerheh, mortuary chapel of, 153
Heqhet, 29
Herames, 317
Herhor, 66, 88-9, 201, 456
Herkhuf, 376, 395, 428, 438, 443
Hermachis, 362
Hermana, 450
Hermes Paotnuphis, 522
Hermopolis, 15, 36
Herodotus, 326, 410, 418, 543
Heseh, 460
Het-Sekhem, 26
Heturt-Amenemhat, 27
Hieraconpolis, 5, 27, 36, 53, 307, 314
Hierasycaminos, 27, 529
Hittites. *See under* Syria
Homer quoted, 61, 67
Hor, 581
Horemheb, 14, 66, 71, 87, 97, 111, 169, 188-9, 243, 299, 357, 454, 526, 560, 565, 578; mortuary chapel of, 140; tomb of, 228
Hor-nefer-hen, 446, 549
Hornekht, 560
Horseatef, 457
Horseosiris, 13
Horsmataui, 32, 36
Horua, mortuary chapel of, 173
Hor-uar, 57, 358, 377
Horus, 8, 12, 23, 32, 50, 54, 58, 77, 86, 90, 193, 195, 199, 203, 210, 211-12, 239, 259, 277, 283, 295, 305, 309, 317, 327-8, 330, 332, 353, 370, 377, 405, 452, 467, 471, 492, 496, 504, 508, 514, 517, 535, 547, 550-1, 560, 562, 574, 579
Hou, 26
Hui, 303
Huy, 301, 450, 466; mortuary chapel of, 165, 170

IABKHENTRA, 450, 512, 533
Ibrahim Pasha, 557
Ibrim, 171
Imhotep, 106, 277, 297, 331, 475, 492
Isis. *See* Aset
Isis, 8, 12, 36, 50, 55, 58, 75, 121, 154, 163, 199, 202, 210, 214, 227, 259, 277, 281, 284, 286, 288, 295, 331, 354, 370, 386, 401, 404, 419, 433, 462, 465, 470, 491, 496, 501, 504, 513, 523, 530, 540, 556, 574
Isis-nefert, 546

JONES, Mr., referred to, 348
Joseph, 514
Justinianus I., 462
Juvenal quoted, 55, 248, 401

KA, 2
Kadesh, battle of, 83, 102, 126, 250, 569
Kagem-em-ahu, tomb of, 433
Kagoug, 366
Kainepolis, 31
Kakara, 449, 519, 549, 551, 565, 577
Kalâbsheh, temple of, 453, 459, 502, 514
Kaleh, 52
Kames, King, 63, 450, 564
Kamuleh, 59
Kandake, 401, 522
Karableh, 349
Karanko, 550
Karnak, 48, 60, 70, 84, 165, 265, 514
Kashta, 245
Kasr el 'Agûz, 291
Kasr es Sayâd, 26
Kasr Ibrim, 257, 451, 453, 553, 557
Kauit, 262
Kaza, 582
Kebh, 217
Kebhsenuf, 287, 288
Kekuit, 486
Ken, mortuary chapel of, 156
Ken-Amen, mortuary chapel of, 120
Keneh, 31, 57
Kenure, mortuary chapel of, 165
Kerkis, 569
Kertassi, 494
Keshy, 162
Keskes, 57
Khaemhat, mortuary chapel of, 156, 163
Khaemuast, 321, 329, 363, 413, 465, 507, 547, 569; tomb of, 288
Khanag, 390
Khaneferra Sebekhotep III., 34

Khartum, 501
Khasekhem, 308
Khasekhemui, 2, 308, 393
Khay, 363
Khebsen, 486
Khennui, 358
Khenoboskion, 27-8, 53
Khensenuf, 281, 286
Khentamenta, 3, 8
Khenzer, 6
Khepera, 17, 212, 283, 556, 564
Khetasar, 568
Kheti, 350, 446
Khnum, 12, 75, 201, 217, 268, 304, 344, 358, 396, 412, 438, 491, 509, 511, 514, 517, 540, 546, 552, 560
Khnumhotep, 446, 465
Khonsu, 13, 58, 68, 70, 84, 88, 92, 107, 109, 153, 176, 200, 217, 239, 253, 258, 278, 299, 354, 361, 377, 422, 426, 465, 473, 508, 535, 555
Khonsuardes, 349
Khonsumes, mortuary chapel of, 17; 176
Khor Bet er Risk, 549
Khua, tomb of, 427
Khufu, 3, 32, 48, 418
Khufu-ankh, 393, 417
Khunes, tomb of, 427
Khuy, 446
Kode, 568
Kôm el Ahmar, 2, 32, 306. See Hierancopolis
Kôm el Birbeh, 302
Kôm el Deir, 305
Kôm el Mera, 306
Kôm el Sinûn, 305
Kôm Ombo, 53, 76; temple of, 374
Konosso Island, 465
Koptos, 47
Korôsko, stele at, 446; mines at, 453; town of, 536
Kôrteh, 522
Koshtamneh, 442, 447, 450; fortress of, 520
Koubet el Howa, 391, 395, 423
Krophi, 418
Kubbân, 53, 447, 450; fortress of, 525
Kuft, 47
Kurkur, 444
Kûrteh, temple of, 451; town of, 527
Kus, 50, 53, 56
Kush, 440, 446, 453, 541, 569

LEGH, Mr., referred to, 517
Legrain, M., referred to, 88, 108

Lepsius referred to, 351, 565
Loret, M., referred to, 195
Louvre Museum, relics at, 206
Lucius Verus, 488
Luxor, 60, 70, 86
Lyons, Captain, referred to, 468, 488
Lysimachus, 49

MAAA, tomb of, 427
Maala, 301
Maam, 449, 450
Maat, 14, 102, 153, 164, 200, 211, 212, 227, 241, 259, 277, 283, 286, 335, 363, 471, 517
MacIver, Dr. D. R., referred to, 25, 538, 553
Macrinus, 377, 388
Macrobius quoted, 295
Maha, 443, 451, 565
Mahâraka, 529
Maherpra, tomb of, 223
Mahetta, 422
Mahmud Bey, 415
Mahui, 124
Makher, 443
Mameluke invasion, 557
Manaos, 306
Mandulis, 458, 503, 511
Marcianus, 462
Marcus Aurelius, 304, 496
Mari Girgis, monastery at, 347
Mariette referred to, 10, 265, 334, 359, 565
Markos, 493
Ma'sara, 86
Maspero referred to, 300, 323
Matana, 301
Maximianopolis, 59
Maximinus, 462, 496
May, 162, 466
Maya, 225
Mazoi troops, 122, 126
Medamût, 59
Medik, 450, 462
Medinet Habu, 62, 66, 173, 190; mortuary temples of, 229, 230, 243, 250, 359
Mehe, 457
Mehêndi, 532
Mehtenusekht, 245
Mekhu, 395; tomb of, 423
Memnon, 68, 248; tomb of, 204, 247
Memphis, 21
Mena, 2, 19, 308
Mendik, 512
Menes, 56
Menhet, 305

INDEX 589

Menkaura, 3, 309, 393
Menkh, shrine of, 368
Menkheperra, 34, 72, 294, 298, 467; mortuary chapel of, 139
Menkheperrasenb, 49
Menna, mortuary chapel of, 149
Menthu, 36, 59, 68, 81, 108, 253, 278, 294, 371, 474, 547
Mentuemhat, 9, 88, 176
Mentuherkhepshef, 547
Mentuhotep I., 33, 299
—— II., 4, 62, 350, 446, 520; mortuary chapel of, 261
—— III., 4, 62, 186, 189, 395, 414
Mentuhotep Sankhkara, 4, 48
Merapet, 512, 577
Merenptah, 8, 19, 49, 55, 71, 104, 109, 250, 258, 265, 357, 399, 410, 413, 416, 455, 540; tomb of, 202; mortuary temple of, 248; shrine of, 370
Merenra, 4, 394, 443
Meretamen, 280
Meriamen, 569
Merieh, 516
Merimes, 466
Merra, 33
Mersekert or Mersergert, 198, 199, 217, 279
Mery, 577
Meryra, 365
Meryt, 118
Mes, 455
Mesawiyeh, 306
Mesna. *See* Zema
Mesu, 543
Meskhent, 269
Metakhómpso, 529
Mether, 424
Mimi, 369
Min, 13, 23, 48, 58, 76, 90, 94, 111, 239, 253, 258, 265, 278, 295, 341, 353, 389, 466, 480, 508, 517, 530, 552; shrine of, 365
Minmes, 8
Min-nekht, 125; shrine of, 366, 369
Mitanni, 71
Mohammedan invasion of Nubia, 402, 462
Mophi, 418
Morgan, M. de, referred to, 56, 419
Morgos, 493
Mortuary chapels, list of, 182, 229
Moses, supposed birthplace of, 294
Mut, 12, 58, 68, 70, 84, 90, 92, 106, 110, 153, 163, 236, 245, 253, 258, 266, 278, 344, 354, 361, 474, 491, 509, 517, 535, 555, 568, 574; temple of, 87, 111
Mutemua, 34, 71, 246
Mutnefert, 368
Mut-Nefertari, 81
Mutneferura, 565

Na, 340
Nag'-Hamâdi, 26
Naharin, 83, 123, 126
Namlot, 9
Napata, 171, 457, 522
Narmer, 2, 36, 308, 331, 480
Nastasen, 457
Naville, Professor, 262, 265
Nbi, 376
Nebenkhar, 569
Nebhapetra. *See* Mentuhotep II.
Nebhotep, 33, 261
Nebsenuy, 179
Nebsey, 562
Nebtkheru, 220
Nebuana, 6, 7
Neby, 162, 451
Necho Uhemabra, 313
Nectanebo I., 9, 49, 90, 105, 313, 332, 400
—— II., 9, 72, 458, 470, 472; temple of, 473, 475
Neferabra Psametik, 465
Neferarkara, 4
Neferhotep, 8, 200, 398; mortuary chapel of, 169
Neferkara-Sebekhotep, 449
Nefer-renpit, 320, 364
Nefertari, 371, 546, 566, 569, 574; tomb of, 281
Nefertiti, 165
Nefertum, 211, 212, 279, 434, 517
Neferura, 311, 321
Neferusi, 121
Nehesi, 366
Nehi, 559
Neitakert, 108, 173, 245
Neith, 16, 75, 212, 283, 287, 288, 467, 471, 547
Nekâdeh, 56
Nekheb, 23, 36, 239, 266, 278, 309, 313, 320, 327-8, 335, 474, 480, 535
Nekhen, 16, 175, 212
Nekht, 466; mortuary chapel of, 167
Nekhtnebef, 243, 301
Nekhtu, 540
Nephthys, 14, 38, 121, 163, 202, 208,

227, 259, 277, 281, 287, 288, 354, 383, 433, 467, 471, 514, 556, 560
Nerferukayt, 34
Nero, 36
Nerva. *See* Trajan
Nesert, 213
Nesikhonsu, 216
Nespaneferher, mortuary chapel of, 152
Netakret, 173
Neter-Khet, 308
Nezemmut, 546, 569
Nezerra, 6
Nilometer, the, 413, 488
Nobadae, the, 461
Nu, 17, 340, 366
Nubians, the, 22, 27, 86, 325, 393; history of Lower, 440; districts of, depicted on tomb, 478
Nubkheperura Antef, 49
Nunt, 487
Nut, 38, 196-7, 205, 211, 218, 277, 358, 383
Nuyt, 486

OFENDÛINEH, 522, 529
Ombos, 47, 53
Onuphis, 296
Orses, 496
Osiris, 2-10, 12, 20, 38, 50, 55, 91, 111, 119, 121, 128, 142, 146, 150, 153, 158-9, 166, 168, 172, 180, 181, 193, 195, 199, 203-4, 208, 210, 212, 214, 217-18, 227, 240, 259, 266, 277, 281, 287-8, 323, 331, 354, 362, 424, 434, 472, 491, 496, 506, 513, 535, 556, 563
Osorkon I., 49
—— II., 72
Osymandyas, statue of, 252

PAAPIS, 277
Paheri, 303, 311, 320
Painezem I., 49, 72, 243, 298
—— II., 9, 112
Pa-mera, 306
Pan, 355
Panebtaui, 379
Panehesi, 363; mortuary chapel of, 180
Papyrus, Abbot, 224
Paraheremef, tomb of, 288, 547, 569
Parahotep, 8
Parahu, 270
Parembole, the Roman, 493
Paser, 507, 581
Pathoris, 297

"Paulou Michael," 549
Pausanias, 248
Paynezem. *See* Painezem
Pe, 16, 23, 175, 212, 336
Pedeamen, 349
Pedeamenapt, 243
Peduamenemapt, 176
Peduneit, 108
Pefnefdeneit, 9
Pehorus, 458, 513
Pehsukher, mortuary chapel of, 124
Pelekos, 568
Penati, 351
Penebtaui, 377, 384, 476
Pen-nesutawi, 466
Pennut, 455, 553
Penthen, 6
Pepy I., 4, 48, 309, 316, 394, 418, 441
—— II., 4, 33, 42, 48, 309, 395, 428, 445, 549
Pepy-ankh. *See* Sahna
Pepy-nekht, 395; tomb of, 430, 446
Perabsen, 2
Petisis, 458, 513
Petnef, 349
Petrie, Professor Flinders, referred to, 25, 28, 33, 48, 53, 56, 249, 250, 255, 280, 394, 549
Petronius, 401, 460, 522, 528, 557
"Pharach's Bed," 489
Philæ, 401, 459, 468, 496; siege of, 522
Philip, King, 72
—— Aridaeus, 86, 99
Philippus Arabus, 496
Philometer I., 27
—— II., 27
Piaay, 541, 569
Piankhi I., 112, 456
—— II., 245
Pisentius, Bishop, 68
Pliny quoted, 50, 248
Potasimeto, 568
Primis, 561
Probus, 460
Psametichus, 568
Psametik-se-neith Men-Kheper-ra, 300
Psammetik or Psamtek I., 49, 173, 332, 400
—— II., 94, 373, 400, 415, 565
Pselchis. *See* Dakkeh
Ptah, 12, 39, 87, 91, 200, 208, 210-11, 216-17, 232, 259, 279, 283-4, 286, 288, 324, 354, 359, 434, 477, 517, 534, 540, 546, 555, 571, 581; temple of, 106

INDEX

Ptahmeryt, 162
Ptahmes, 142
Ptah-Seker-Ausar, 195
Ptah-Tatenen, 518
Ptolemy I., Soter I., 112
—— II., Philadelphus, 49, 57, 108, 475, 485
—— III., Euergetes I., 59, 89, 106, 333, 341, 405, 483, 521
—— IV., Philopater, 51, 94, 276, 333, 377, 406, 422, 459, 474, 521
—— V., Epiphanes, 67, 333, 459, 471, 474
—— VI., Philometor, 27, 304, 333, 459, 471, 475, 477, 479
—— VII., Eupator, 27, 460, 482, 489, 490
—— IX., Euergetes II., 59, 291, 299, 313, 327, 333, 377, 450, 460, 483, 489, 490, 521, 523
—— X., Soter II., 27, 34, 313, 320, 416, 460, 477, 502
—— XI., Alexander I., 34, 106, 345
—— XII., Alexander II.,
—— XIII., Neos Dionysos, 34, 51, 106, 333, 377, 467, 476, 480
—— XVI., Cæsarion, 34, 44
—— Auletes, 59, 243
—— Lathyros, 59, 243, 265
—— Physkon, 244, 265, 277, 300, 384
Puamra, mortuary chapel of, 172
Punt, 49; colonnade, 269, 446
Pursepmunis, 496

QUARRIES, at Gebel Silsileh, 358, 372; at Aswân, 399, 407; at Sehel, 419; at Dabôd, 492; at Kertassi, 496; at Tâfeh, 501
Quibell, J. E., referred to, 308, 314

RA, 69, 84, 196, 211–12; mortuary chapel of, 147
Ra-aakhepersenb, 168
Raanet, 310
Ra-horakhti. *See* Aton
Ra-hotep, 49, 455, 563
Ramenkheper-Senb, mortuary chapel of, 125, 139
Ramery, 220
Rames, 113, 119, 164, 170, 465; mortuary chapel of, 160
Rameses I., 7, 66, 87, 95, 303, 313, 320, 329, 354, 376, 388, 399, 410, 412, 415, 454, 465, 502, 507, 517, 526, 534, 544, 549, 559, 565; tomb of, 212; mortuary temple of, 256; temple of, 327, 454

Rameses II., 8, 11, 20, 34, 49, 55, 59, 66, 70, 87, 92, 108–9, 112, 188, **258,** 265, 280, 294, 357; tomb of, 20; mortuary temple of, 249, 256; shrine of, 371
—— III., 9, 34, 49, 55, 66, 71, 88, 94, 106, 109, 112, 192, 194, 230, 244, 250, 279, 284, 287–8, 313, 332, 357, 399, 412, 455, 547; tomb of, 198, 206; mortuary pavilion of, 231; mortuary temple of, 234
—— IV., 9, 49, 71, 90, 112, 332; tomb of, 196
—— V., 195; tomb of, 204, 245, 357
—— VI., 49, 71, 97, 195, 316, 328, 455, 553; tomb of, 204
—— VII., 9; tomb of, 195
—— VIII., 184
—— IX., 86, 109, 184, 263; tomb of, 198
—— X., 190; tomb of, 198
—— XI., tomb of, 216
—— XII., 66, 90, 186, 456; tomb of, 198
Ramesseum, 190, 410
Raneferu, 275
Rantaa-Setepenneteru, 490
Razeserkasenb, 145; mortuary chapel of, 172
Redesiyeh, 351
Rekhmara, mortuary chapel of, 115, 453, 467
Remtet, 486
Renni, 320, 325
Rennut, 156, 172
Renpet, 14
Reshep, 562
Retennu, 571
Rey, mortuary chapel of, 142
Rizakât, 294, 296
Robberies from tombs, 188, 190, 198, 201, 280
Romans in Nubia, 460
Rubensohn, Dr., 417
Ruru, 321

SAANKHUKARA, 351
Sabagura, 516
Sabina, 248
Sabna, 395, 423, 439, 445; tomb of, 427
Safkhet, 13, 20, 36, 232, 254, 269, 335, 541
Sahura, 309, 393, 441, 549
St. Simeon, monastery at, 434
Saïs, 410
Sakkâra, 121

Saladin, 435
Satet, 438
Satet-hotep, 426, 432
Satis, 474, 509, 514
Saturna, 83
Saturninus Veteranus Aquila, 522
Sayaleh, 532
Schoinoi, the, 459
Seankhkara, temple of, 292
Seanra, 538
Seb, 288, 358, 370, 479
Sebek, 51, 358, 376, 476
Sebekemsaf, King, 6
—— Queen, 331
Sebekhotep II., 70, 310, 326
—— III., 5, 6, 49, 55, 63
—— mortuary chapel of, 154
Sebeknekt, 310, 326
Sebûa, 450
Sehathor, 447
Sehel, 357, 391, 396, 409, 419
Sekenenra I., 63
—— II., 63
—— III., 63, 310
Seker, 13, 211, 266, 324, 434
Sekhemra-Khutawi, 449
Sekhmet, 13, 102, 112, 217, 232, 254, 354, 467, 517, 535, 547
Selene, 326
Selk, 1, 24, 307
Selket or Selkis, 75, 283, 287-8, 362, 468, 509
Semti, 393
Senebmaan, 299
Seninefer, 365
Senmes, tomb of, 431
Senmut, 70, 112, 265, 331, 413; mortuary chapel of, 148; shrine of, 367
Sennefer, mortuary chapel of, 117; remains found, 225, 365, 562
Senseneb, 273
Sentnefert, 118
Senusert I., 4, 34, 48, 55, 63, 86, 301, 310, 350, 411, 446, 494, 536
—— II., 310, 447
—— III., 4-6, 25, 48, 55, 63, 396, 411, 421, 430, 447, 520, 538, 551, 561, 581
Senzara, battle of, 126
Septah, 9, 258, 263, 357, 363, 399, 412, 455, 539; tomb of, 209, 226; mortuary temple of, 255
Septimius Severus, 247
Septu, 362
Serag, 355
Serapis, temple of, 304, 476, 530
Serenpitu, tomb of, 426, 431

Set, 8, 39, 54, 193, 211, 330, 481, 574
Setau, tomb of, 320, 324, 517, 549, 560
Sethu, 444
Setnekht, 112, 188, 194, 202, 206; tomb of, 209, 279, 280
Setra, 280, 290
Set-then, 432
Set-thena, 432
Sety I., 1, 7, 20, 49, 55, 59, 66, 71, 87, 90, 189, 201, 243, 250, 280, 299, 301, 313, 332, 351, 357, 454, 539, 560, 565; tomb of, 213; mortuary temple of, 256
—— II., 55, 71, 87, 92, 109, 112, 190, 195, 209, 227, 345, 357; tomb of, 211
Setyherkhepeshef, tomb of, 287
Severus, 496, 503
Shabaka, 49, 72, 243
Shabataka, 72, 457
Sharuhen, siege of, 325
Shatani, 581
Sheikh Said, 349
Shêkh abd' el Gûrneh, 63, 86, 112, 114, 191, 366
—— Daud, 548
Shellal, 396
Shelley quoted, 252
Shems-ed-Dulah, 435
Shenet Debhib, 25
Shenhûr, 56
Shentait, 18
Shenûdi, 306
Shepenapt, 173, 245
Shepses, 361, 576
Shepseskaf, 4
Sheshemtaui, wall of, 310
Sheshonk I., 95, 112, 359
—— Prince, 108
Sheymeh, 494
Shu, 17, 124, 200, 208, 286, 288, 340, 474
Shunet es Zebib, 2, 25
Shut, 278
Shutt er Rigâl, 350
Silks, 462, 505
Sitteh Kasmar, church of, 502
Smendes, 72, 301
Smenkhkara, 184
Sneferu, 309, 441
Soane Museum, relics at, 213
Sokaris, 195, 208, 486, 555
Sruptikhis, 496
Strabo qucted, 10, 50, 67, 191, 248, 296-7, 415, 521
Stuart, Villiers, referred to, 162

INDEX

Sudanese wars, 403
Sumnut, mortuary chapel of, 120
Surere, mortuary chapel of, 170
Sutekh, 55
Syene, 27
Syria, war with, 64, 83, 102, 251, 320, 325

TA, Vizir, 324
Taa, 222
Ta-amarthu, 368
Taari, 173
Tabenna, 46
Tâfeh, 461, 497
Taharka, 9, 94, 108, 111–12, 243, 457, 470, 482, 502
Tahuti, 317
Takeloth, 9
Takens, 574, 582
Takha, 555
Takhat, 137, 277
Takômpso, 421, 459, 528-9
Tantarer, 31
Tantatamu, 450
Tanutamen, 111, 457
Taphis. *See* Tâfeh
Taray, 447
Tasentnefert, 377, 383, 476
Taurt, 18, 76, 91, 358, 479, 555
Tausert, 188, 194, 206; tomb of, 209, 227-8; mortuary temple of, 249, 280, 540
Taxes at Abydos-Thinis, 7; at Hou, 27; of geese at Khenoboskion, 27–8; at Dendereh, 34; at Koptos, 49; at Eileithyiapolis, 312; at Elephantine, 398; at Wawat, 452; at Bîgeh and Lower Nubia, 453
Tefnut, 370, 478, 514, 523
Tehuti, 170, 311
Tehutiemheb, 170
Tehutinefer, mortuary chapel of, 137
Tell el Amarna, 65, 165, 188
Temeh, 444
Temenos of Osiris, 2, 24
Tentkareu, tomb of, 226
Tereres, 443
Teta, King, 4, 49, 309, 394, 441, 549
—— Prince, 450, 560
Tetashera, 60
Thaa, 154
Thabau, 562
Tharu, 101
Thase, 563
Thebes, 12, 39, 60, 86, 186
Thelmes. *See* Kalâbsheh
Thentas, 320

Thenuna, mortuary chapel of, 142
Theodorus, Bishop, 471, 482, 514
Thethy, 446
Thinis, 1-4, 307
This, city of, 24
Thiy, 65, 71, 186, 226-7, 246, 264, 291
Thoth, 12, 20, 36, 58, 75, 81, 90, 110, 142, 146, 151, 168, 201, 208, 217, 232, 239, 245, 253, 268, 284, 286, 288, 291, 295, 327-8, 344, 361, 382, 459, 467, 473, 492, 505, 522, 541, 547, 555, 576, 578
Thothmes I., 6, 55, 63, 86, 97,168, 188, 217, 230, 264, 317, 320, 351, 357, 368, 422, 451; tomb of, 223; mortuary temple of, 243
—— II., 6, 49, 63, 86, 230, 264, 320, 451; tomb of, 224
—— III., 6, 34, 51, 63, 70, 82, 86, 91, 106, 109, 112, 115, 117, 124, 126, 147-8, 152, 177, 190, 192, 230, 243, 264, 271, 303, 311, 317, 331, 351, 357, 376, 398, 410, 416, 422, 502, 525, 528, 538, 551, 559; tomb of, 219; mortuary temple of, 255
—— IV., 7, 14, 34, 49, 55, 65, 71, 87, 141, 145, 146, 192, 212, 312, 328, 332, 398, 415, 453, 465, 539; tomb of, 225; mortuary temple of, 249
Thothmes, mortuary chapel of, 176
—— Prince, 349
Thure, 312
Thyti, tomb of, 286
Tuau, 136, 164, 186; tomb of, 226, 368-9
Tiberius, 35, 59, 377, 474, 490
Tikhsi, 65
Tofnis, 300
Tomâs, 394, 424, 438, 443, 548
Tombs, Valley of the, 280
Tôshkeh, 441, 450, 563
Tossoun, Djemil Pasha, 255
Trajan, Nerva, 27, 35, 50, 58, 299, 304, 416, 489, 503
Tûd, 300
Tum, 36, 91, 195, 212, 232, 244, 253, 283, 288, 335, 354, 363, 546
Tunip, 83
Ture, 576
Tutankhamen,14,71,171,184,280,454
Tutzis. *See* Gerf Husên
Tyitzi, 494
Tyler, Mr., referred to, 315
Tytus, R., 291

UAZET, 16, 36, 77, 239, 266, 313, 335, 383, 514

Uazmes, 249, 311
Umberakab, 494
Una, 394, 441
Unas, 394, 418
Unnefer, 7-8, 15, 20, 91, 128, 138, 196, 354, 467, 471, 491, 504, 523, 556
Urethekau cr Urthekaw, 272, 486, 547, 568, 575, 582
Urnure, 162
User, 131; mortuary chapel of, 155, 388, 466
Userenra, 4
Userhat, mortuary chapel of, 158, 170; tomb of, 226
Userkaf, 4, 309, 441
Usersatet, 365, 466, 560

VENUS, 35
Verecundus, 530
Vespasian, 304

WÂDY ABAD, temple of, 351
—— Alâki, 452, 471, 526
—— Fowakhieh, 48
—— Gamr, 493
—— Halfa, 446, 451, 582
—— Hammamat, 48
—— Hêdid, 494

Wahast, 31
Wakf, 31
Wawat, 22, 171, 411, 444, 450, 512, 571
Wazet, 480, 503, 511, 564
Wazkara. *See* Hakara
Wealth of Abydos and Thinis. *See* Taxes
Wepwat, 2, 8, 12, 36, 81, 216, 259, 266, 279, 283, 480, 517
Wernure, 546, 569
Werthekaw. *See* Urthekaw
Wesiyeh, 494

YUAA, 78, 164, 186; tomb of, 226

ZAHA, siege of, 320
Zapur, siege of, 254
Zau, 395
Zauta, 29-30, 395
Zema, tomb of, 427
Zenigleh, 349
Zenoam, 101
Zenuni, mortuary chapel of, 146
Zesr, 297, 421, 441, 459, 470
Zesret, 261, 264
Zet, 2-3
Zeus, 61

BOOKS ON EGYPT

BY

W. M. FLINDERS PETRIE, D.C.L., LL.D.

Professor of Egyptology at University College.

A HISTORY OF EGYPT. Fully Illustrated. In six volumes. Crown 8vo, 6s. each.

This history aims at being a student's reference book, which shall suffice for all ordinary purposes, while the information is given in such a way that the general reader may readily grasp it. Every fact and object has an authority stated for it.

Vol. I. FROM THE EARLIEST KINGS TO XVITH DYNASTY. Sixth Edition.
Vol. II. THE XVIITH AND XVIIITH DYNASTIES. Fourth Edition.
Vol. III. XIXTH TO XXXTH DYNASTIES.
Vol. IV. EGYPT UNDER THE PTOLEMAIC DYNASTY. J. P. MAHAFFY, Litt.D.
Vol. V. EGYPT UNDER ROMAN RULE. G. J. MILNE, M.A.
Vol. VI. EGYPT IN THE MIDDLE AGES. STANLEY LANE-POOLE, M.A.

RELIGION AND CONSCIENCE IN ANCIENT EGYPT. Lectures delivered at University College, London. Illustrated. Crown 8vo, 2s. 6d.

Deals mainly with the historical growth of the Egyptian religion and the arrangement of all the moral sayings into something like a handbook. But far larger interests are discussed, as the origin of Intolerance, the fusions of Religions, and the nature of Conscience.

SYRIA AND EGYPT, FROM THE TELL EL AMARNA LETTERS. Crown 8vo, 2s. 6d.

This book contains the results of the most recent research, so far as it bears on the earlier history of Egypt. The volume thus forms an appendix to the first and second volumes of Professor Petrie's "History of Egypt," and a considerable amount of new light is thrown upon this period.

EGYPTIAN TALES. Translated from the Papyri. First Series, IVth to XIIth Dynasty. Edited by W. M. FLINDERS PETRIE. With 23 Illustrations by TRISTRAM ELLIS. Second Edition. Crown 8vo, 3s. 6d.

EGYPTIAN TALES. Translated from the Papyri. Second Series, XVIIIth to XIXth Dynasty. Edited by W. M. FLINDERS PETRIE. With 34 Illustrations by TRISTRAM ELLIS. Crown 8vo, 3s. 6d.
A collection of short Egyptian tales.

EGYPTIAN DECORATIVE ART. A Course of Lectures delivered at the Royal Institution. Illustrated. Crown 8vo, 3s. 6d.

This book describes the Egyptian taste for decorative hieroglyphics, the origin of patterns, geometrical, natural, structural, and symbolic ornaments.

METHUEN & CO., LTD., 36 ESSEX STREET, LONDON, W.C.

A SELECTION OF BOOKS PUBLISHED BY METHUEN AND COMPANY: LONDON 36 ESSEX STREET W.C.

CONTENTS

	PAGE		PAGE
General Literature	2	Little Library	20
Ancient Cities	15	Little Quarto Shakespeare	21
Antiquary's Books	15	Miniature Library	21
Arden Shakespeare	15	New Library of Medicine	21
Classics of Art	16	New Library of Music	22
"Complete" Series	16	Oxford Biographies	22
Connoisseur's Library	16	Romantic History	22
Handbooks of English Church History	17	Handbooks of Theology	22
		Westminster Commentaries	23
Illustrated Pocket Library of Plain and Coloured Books	17		
Leaders of Religion	18		
Library of Devotion	18	Fiction	23
Little Books on Art	19	Books for Boys and Girls	28
Little Galleries	19	Novels of Alexandre Dumas	29
Little Guides	19	Methuen's Sixpenny Books	29

FEBRUARY 1910

A SELECTION OF

MESSRS. METHUEN'S
PUBLICATIONS

In this Catalogue the order is according to authors. An asterisk denotes that the book is in the press.
Colonial Editions are published of all Messrs. METHUEN'S Novels issued at a price above 2s. 6d., and similar editions are published of some works of General Literature. Colonial editions are only for circulation in the British Colonies and India.
All books marked net are not subject to discount, and cannot be bought at less than the published price. Books not marked net are subject to the discount which the bookseller allows.
Messrs. METHUEN'S books are kept in stock by all good booksellers. If there is any difficulty in seeing copies, Messrs. Methuen will be very glad to have early information, and specimen copies of any books will be sent on receipt of the published price *plus* postage for net books, and of the published price for ordinary books.
This Catalogue contains only a selection of the more important books published by Messrs. Methuen. A complete and illustrated catalogue of their publications may be obtained on application.

Addleshaw (Percy). SIR PHILIP SIDNEY. Illustrated. *Second Edition. Demy 8vo.* 10s. 6d. *net.*

Adeney (W. F.), M.A. See Bennett (W.H.).

Ady (Cecilia M.). A HISTORY OF MILAN UNDER THE SFORZA. Illustrated. *Demy 8vo.* 10s. 6d. *net.*

Aldis (Janet). THE QUEEN OF LETTER WRITERS, MARQUISE DE SÉVIGNÉ, DAME DE BOURBILLY, 1626-96. Illustrated. *Second Edition. Demy 8vo.* 12s. 6d. *net.*

Alexander (William), D. D., Archbishop of Armagh. THOUGHTS AND COUNSELS OF MANY YEARS. *Demy 16mo.* 2s. 6d.

*****Allen (M.).** A HISTORY OF VERONA. Illustrated. *Demy 8vo.* 12s. 6d. *net.*

Amherst (Lady). A SKETCH OF EGYPTIAN HISTORY FROM THE EARLIEST TIMES TO THE PRESENT DAY. Illustrated. *A New and Cheaper Issue. Demy 8vo.* 7s. 6d. *net.*

Andrewes (Bishop). PRECES PRIVATAE. Translated and edited, with Notes, by F. E. BRIGHTMAN, M.A., of Pusey House, Oxford. *Cr. 8vo.* 6s.

Anon. THE WESTMINSTER PROBLEMS BOOK. Prose and Verse. Compiled from *The Saturday Westminster Gazette* Competitions, 1904-1907. *Cr. 8vo.* 3s. 6d. *net.*
VENICE AND HER TREASURES. Illustrated. *Round corners. Fcap. 8vo.* 5s. *net.*

Aristotle. THE ETHICS OF. Edited, with an Introduction and Notes, by JOHN BURNET, M.A. *Cheaper issue. Demy 8vo.* 10s. 6d. net.

Atkinson (C. T.), M.A., Fellow of Exeter College, Oxford, sometime Demy of Magdalen College. A HISTORY OF GERMANY, from 1715-1815. Illustrated. *Demy 8vo.* 12s. 6d. *net.*

Atkinson (T. D.). ENGLISH ARCHITECTURE. Illustrated. *Fcap. 8vo.* 3s. 6d *net.*
A GLOSSARY OF TERMS USED IN ENGLISH ARCHITECTURE. Illustrated. *Second Edition. Fcap. 8vo.* 3s. 6d. *net.*

Atteridge (A. H.). NAPOLEON'S BROTHERS. Illustrated. *Demy 8vo.* 18s. *net.*

Aves (Ernest). CO-OPERATIVE INDUSTRY. *Cr. 8vo.* 5s. *net.*

Bagot (Richard). THE LAKES OF NORTHERN ITALY. Illustrated. *Fcap. 8vo.* 5s. *net.*

General Literature

Bain (R. Nisbet). THE LAST KING OF POLAND AND HIS CONTEMPORARIES. Illustrated. *Demy 8vo. 10s. 6d. net.*

Balfour (Graham). THE LIFE OF ROBERT LOUIS STEVENSON. Illustrated. *Fourth Edition in one Volume. Cr. 8vo. Buckram, 6s.*

Baring (The Hon. Maurice). WITH THE RUSSIANS IN MANCHURIA. *Third Edition. Demy 8vo. 7s. 6d. net.*
A YEAR IN RUSSIA. *Second Edition. Demy 8vo. 10s. 6d. net.*
RUSSIAN ESSAYS AND STORIES. *Second Edition. Cr. 8vo. 5s. net.*
LANDMARKS IN RUSSIAN LITERATURE. *Cr. 8vo. 6s. net.*

Baring-Gould (S.). THE LIFE OF NAPOLEON BONAPARTE. Illustrated. *Second Edition. Wide Royal 8vo. 10s. 6d. net.*
THE TRAGEDY OF THE CÆSARS: A STUDY OF THE CHARACTERS OF THE CÆSARS OF THE JULIAN AND CLAUDIAN HOUSES. Illustrated. *Seventh Edition. Royal 8vo. 10s. 6d. net.*
A BOOK OF FAIRY TALES. Illustrated. *Second Edition. Cr. 8vo. Buckram. 6s.* Also *Medium 8vo. 6d.*
OLD ENGLISH FAIRY TALES. Illustrated. *Third Edition. Cr. 8vo. Buckram. 6s.*
THE VICAR OF MORWENSTOW. Revised Edition. With a Portrait. *Third Edition. Cr. 8vo. 3s. 6d.*
OLD COUNTRY LIFE. Illustrated. *Fifth Edition. Large Cr. 8vo. 6s.*
A GARLAND OF COUNTRY SONG: English Folk Songs with their Traditional Melodies. Collected and arranged by S. BARING-GOULD and H. F. SHEPPARD. *Demy 4to. 6s.*
SONGS OF THE WEST: Folk Songs of Devon and Cornwall. Collected from the Mouths of the People. By S. BARING-GOULD, M.A., and H. FLEETWOOD SHEPPARD, M.A. New and Revised Edition, under the musical editorship of CECIL J. SHARP. *Large Imperial 8vo. 5s. net.*
STRANGE SURVIVALS: SOME CHAPTERS IN THE HISTORY OF MAN. Illustrated. *Third Edition. Cr. 8vo. 2s. 6d. net.*
YORKSHIRE ODDITIES: INCIDENTS AND STRANGE EVENTS. *Fifth Edition. Cr. 8vo. 2s. 6d. net.*
A BOOK OF CORNWALL. Illustrated. *Second Edition. Cr. 8vo. 6s.*
A BOOK OF DARTMOOR. Illustrated. *Second Edition. Cr. 8vo. 6s.*
A BOOK OF DEVON. Illustrated. *Third Edition. Cr. 8vo. 6s.*
A BOOK OF NORTH WALES. Illustrated. *Cr. 8vo. 6s.*
A BOOK OF SOUTH WALES. Illustrated. *Cr. 8vo. 6s.*

A BOOK OF BRITTANY. Illustrated. *Second Edition. Cr. 8vo. 6s.*
A BOOK OF THE RHINE: From Cleve to Mainz. Illustrated. *Second Edition. Cr. 8vo. 6s.*
A BOOK OF THE RIVIERA. Illustrated. *Second Edition. Cr. 8vo. 6s.*
A BOOK OF THE PYRENEES. Illustrated. *Cr. 8vo. 6s.*

Barker (E.), M.A., (Late) Fellow of Merton College, Oxford. THE POLITICAL THOUGHT OF PLATO AND ARISTOTLE. *Demy 8vo. 10s. 6d. net.*

Baron (R. R. N.), M.A. FRENCH PROSE COMPOSITION. *Fourth Edition. Cr. 8vo. 2s. 6d. Key, 3s. net.*

Bartholomew (J. G.), F.R.S.E. See Robertson (C. G.).

Bastable (C. F.), LL.D. THE COMMERCE OF NATIONS. *Fourth Edition. Cr. 8vo. 2s. 6d.*

Bastian (H. Charlton), M.A., M.D., F.R.S. THE EVOLUTION OF LIFE. Illustrated. *Demy 8vo. 7s. 6d. net.*

Batson (Mrs. Stephen). A CONCISE HANDBOOK OF GARDEN FLOWERS. *Fcap. 8vo. 3s. 6d. net.*
THE SUMMER GARDEN OF PLEASURE. Illustrated. *Wide Demy 8vo. 15s. net.*

Beckett (Arthur). THE SPIRIT OF THE DOWNS: Impressions and Reminiscences of the Sussex Downs. Illustrated. *Second Edition. Demy 8vo. 10s. 6d. net.*

Beckford (Peter). THOUGHTS ON HUNTING. Edited by J. OTHO PAGET. Illustrated. *Second Edition. Demy 8vo. 6s.*

Begbie (Harold). MASTER WORKERS. Illustrated. *Demy 8vo. 7s. 6d. net.*

Behmen (Jacob). DIALOGUES ON THE SUPERSENSUAL LIFE. Edited by BERNARD HOLLAND. *Fcap. 8vo. 3s. 6d.*

Bell (Mrs. Arthur G.). THE SKIRTS OF THE GREAT CITY. Illustrated. *Second Edition. Cr. 8vo. 6s.*

Belloc (H.), M.P. PARIS. Illustrated. *Second Edition, Revised. Cr. 8vo. 6s.*
HILLS AND THE SEA. *Second Edition. Cr. 8vo. 6s.*
ON NOTHING AND KINDRED SUBJECTS. *Third Edition. Fcap. 8vo. 5s.*
ON EVERYTHING. *Second Edition. Fcap. 8vo. 5s.*
MARIE ANTOINETTE. Illustrated. *Second Edition. Demy 8vo. 15s. net.*
THE PYRENEES. Illustrated. *Second Edition. Demy 8vo. 7s. 6d. net.*

Bellot (H. H. L.), M.A. See Jones (L. A. A.)

Bennett (Joseph). FORTY YEARS OF MUSIC, 1865-1905. Illustrated. *Demy 8vo.* 16s. net.

Bennett (W. H.), M.A. A PRIMER OF THE BIBLE. *Fifth Edition. Cr. 8vo.* 2s. 6d.

Bennett (W. H.) and Adeney. (W. F.). A BIBLICAL INTRODUCTION. With a concise Bibliography. *Fifth Edition. Cr. 8vo.* 7s. 6d.

Benson (Archbishop). GOD'S BOARD. Communion Addresses. *Second Edition. Fcap. 8vo.* 3s. 6d. net.

Benson (R. M.). THE WAY OF HOLINESS. An Exposition of Psalm cxix. Analytical and Devotional. *Cr. 8vo.* 5s.

*****Bensusan (Samuel L.).** HOME LIFE IN SPAIN. Illustrated. *Demy 8vo.* 10s. 6d. net.

Berry (W. Grinton), M.A. FRANCE SINCE WATERLOO. Illustrated. *Cr. 8vo.* 6s.

Betham-Edwards (Miss). HOME LIFE IN FRANCE. Illustrated. *Fifth Edition. Cr. 8vo.* 6s.

Bindley (T. Herbert), B.D. THE OECUMENICAL DOCUMENTS OF THE FAITH. With Introductions and Notes. *Second Edition. Cr. 8vo.* 6s. net.

Binyon (Laurence). See Blake (William).

Blake (William). ILLUSTRATIONS OF THE BOOK OF JOB. With General Introduction by LAURENCE BINYON. Illustrated. *Quarto.* 21s. net.

Body (George), D.D. THE SOUL'S PILGRIMAGE: Devotional Readings from the Published and Unpublished writings of George Body, D.D. Selected and arranged by J. H. BURN, D.D., F.R.S.E. *Demy 16mo.* 2s. 6d.

Boulting (W.). TASSO AND HIS TIMES. Illustrated. *Demy 8vo.* 10s. 6d. net.

Bovill (W. B. Forster). HUNGARY AND THE HUNGARIANS. Illustrated. *Demy 8vo.* 7s. 6d. net.

Bowden (E. M.). THE IMITATION OF BUDDHA: Being Quotations from Buddhist Literature for each Day in the Year. *Fifth Edition. Cr. 16mo.* 2s. 6d.

Brabant (F. G.), M.A. RAMBLES IN SUSSEX. Illustrated. *Cr. 8vo.* 6s.

Bradley (A. G.). ROUND ABOUT WILTSHIRE. Illustrated. *Second Edition. Cr. 8vo.* 6s.
THE ROMANCE OF NORTHUMBERLAND. Illustrated. *Second Edition. Demy 8vo.* 7s. 6d. net.

Braid (James), Open Champion, 1901, 1905 and 1906. ADVANCED GOLF. Illustrated. *Fifth Edition. Demy 8vo.* 10s. 6d. net.

Braid (James) and Others. GREAT GOLFERS IN THE MAKING. Edited by HENRY LEACH. Illustrated. *Second Edition. Demy 8vo.* 7s. 6d. net.

Brailsford (H. N.). MACEDONIA: ITS RACES AND THEIR FUTURE. Illustrated. *Demy 8vo.* 12s. 6d. net.

Brodrick (Mary) and Morton (A. Anderson). A CONCISE DICTIONARY OF EGYPTIAN ARCHÆOLOGY. A Handbook for Students and Travellers. Illustrated. *Cr. 8vo.* 3s. 6d.

Brown (J. Wood), M.A. THE BUILDERS OF FLORENCE. Illustrated. *Demy 4to.* 18s. net.

Browning (Robert). PARACELSUS. Edited with Introduction, Notes, and Bibliography by MARGARET L. LEE and KATHARINE B. LOCOCK. *Fcap. 8vo.* 3s. 6d. net.

Buckton (A. M.). EAGER HEART: A Mystery Play. *Eighth Edition. Cr. 8vo.* 1s. net.

Budge (E. A. Wallis). THE GODS OF THE EGYPTIANS. Illustrated. *Two Volumes. Royal 8vo.* £3 3s. net.

Bull (Paul), Army Chaplain. GOD AND OUR SOLDIERS. *Second Edition. Cr. 8vo.* 6s.

Bulley (Miss). See Dilke (Lady).

Burns (Robert), THE POEMS. Edited by ANDREW LANG and W. A. CRAIGIE. With Portrait. *Third Edition. Wide Demy 8vo, gilt top.* 6s.

Bussell (F. W.), D.D. CHRISTIAN THEOLOGY AND SOCIAL PROGRESS (The Bampton Lectures of 1905). *Demy 8vo.* 10s. 6d. net.

Butler (Sir William), Lieut.-General, G.C.B. THE LIGHT OF THE WEST. With some other Wayside Thoughts, 1865-1908. *Cr. 8vo.* 5s. net.

Butlin (F. M.). AMONG THE DANES. Illustrated. *Demy 8vo.* 7s. 6d. net.

Cain (Georges), Curator of the Carnavalet Museum, Paris. WALKS IN PARIS. Translated by A. R. ALLINSON, M.A. Illustrated. *Demy 8vo.* 7s. 6d. net.

Cameron (Mary Lovett). OLD ETRURIA AND MODERN TUSCANY. Illustrated. *Second Edition. Cr. 8vo.* 6s. net.

Carden (Robert W.). THE CITY OF GENOA. Illustrated. *Demy 8vo.* 10s. 6d. net.

General Literature 5

Carlyle (Thomas). THE FRENCH REVOLUTION. Edited by C. R. L. FLETCHER, Fellow of Magdalen College, Oxford. *Three Volumes. Cr. 8vo. 18s.*
THE LETTERS AND SPEECHES OF OLIVER CROMWELL. With an Introduction by C. H. FIRTH, M.A., and Notes and Appendices by Mrs. S. C. LOMAS. *Three Volumes. Demy 8vo. 18s. net.*

Celano (Brother Thomas of). THE LIVES OF FRANCIS OF ASSISI. Translated by A. G. FERRERS HOWELL. Illustrated. *Cr. 8vo. 5s. net.*

Chambers (Mrs. Lambert). Lawn Tennis for Ladies. Illustrated. *Crown 8vo. 2s. 6d. net.*

Chandler (Arthur), Bishop of Bloemfontein. ARA CŒLI: AN ESSAY IN MYSTICAL THEOLOGY. *Third Edition. Cr. 8vo. 3s. 6d. net.*

Chesterfield (Lord). THE LETTERS OF THE EARL OF CHESTERFIELD TO HIS SON. Edited, with an Introduction by C. STRACHEY, with Notes by A. CALTHROP. *Two Volumes. Cr. 8vo. 12s.*

Chesterton (G.K.). CHARLES DICKENS. With two Portraits in Photogravure. *Sixth Edition. Cr. 8vo. 6s.*
ALL THINGS CONSIDERED. *Fifth Edition. Fcap. 8vo. 5s.*
TREMENDOUS TRIFLES. *Fourth Edition. Fcap. 8vo. 5s.*

Clausen (George), A.R.A., R.W.S. SIX LECTURES ON PAINTING. Illustrated. *Third Edition. Large Post. 8vo. 3s. 6d. net.*
AIMS AND IDEALS IN ART. Eight Lectures delivered to the Students of the Royal Academy of Arts. Illustrated. *Second Edition. Large Post 8vo. 5s. net.*

Clutton-Brock (A.) SHELLEY: THE MAN AND THE POET. Illustrated. *Demy 8vo. 7s. 6d. net.*

Cobb (W. F.), M.A. THE BOOK OF PSALMS: with an Introduction and Notes. *Demy 8vo. 10s. 6d. net.*

Cockshott (Winifred), St. Hilda's Hall, Oxford. THE PILGRIM FATHERS, THEIR CHURCH AND COLONY. Illustrated. *Demy 8vo. 7s. 6d. net.*

Collingwood (W. G.), M.A. THE LIFE OF JOHN RUSKIN. With Portrait. *Sixth Edition. Cr. 8vo. 2s. 6d. net.*

Colvill (Helen H.). ST. TERESA OF SPAIN. Illustrated. *Second Edition. Demy 8vo. 7s. 6d. net.*

*****Condamine (Robert de la).** THE UPPER GARDEN. *Fcap. 8vo. 5s. net.*

Conrad (Joseph). THE MIRROR OF THE SEA: Memories and Impressions. *Third Edition. Cr. 8vo. 6s.*

Coolidge (W. A. B.), M.A. THE ALPS. Illustrated. *Demy 8vo. 7s. 6d. net.*

Cooper (C. S.), F.R.H.S. See Westell (W.P.)

Coulton (G. G.). CHAUCER AND HIS ENGLAND. Illustrated. *Second Edition. Demy 8vo. 10s. 6d. net.*

Cowper (William). THE POEMS. Edited with an Introduction and Notes by J. C. BAILEY, M.A. Illustrated. *Demy 8vo. 10s. 6d. net.*

Crane (Walter), R.W.S. AN ARTIST'S REMINISCENCES. Illustrated. *Second Edition. Demy 8vo. 18s. net.*
INDIA IMPRESSIONS. Illustrated. *Second Edition. Demy 8vo. 7s. 6d. net.*

Crispe (T. E.). REMINISCENCES OF A K.C. With 2 Portraits. *Second Edition. Demy 8vo. 10s. 6d. net.*

Crowley (Ralph H.). THE HYGIENE OF SCHOOL LIFE. Illustrated. *Cr. 8vo. 3s. 6d. net.*

Dante (Alighieri). LA COMMEDIA DI DANTE. The Italian Text edited by PAGET TOYNBEE, M.A., D.Litt. *Cr. 8vo. 6s.*

Davey (Richard). THE PAGEANT OF LONDON. Illustrated. *In Two Volumes. Demy 8vo. 15s. net.*

Davis (H. W. C.), M.A., Fellow and Tutor of Balliol College. ENGLAND UNDER THE NORMANS AND ANGEVINS: 1066-1272. Illustrated. *Demy 8vo. 10s. 6d. net.*

Deans (R. Storry). THE TRIALS OF FIVE QUEENS: KATHARINE OF ARAGON, ANNE BOLEYN, MARY QUEEN OF SCOTS, MARIE ANTOINETTE and CAROLINE OF BRUNSWICK. Illustrated. *Second Edition. Demy 8vo. 10s. 6d. net.*

Dearmer (Mabel). A CHILD'S LIFE OF CHRIST. Illustrated. *Large Cr. 8vo. 6s.*

D'Este (Margaret). IN THE CANARIES WITH A CAMERA. Illustrated. *Cr. 8vo. 7s. 6d. net.*

Dickinson (G. L.), M.A., Fellow of King's College, Cambridge. THE GREEK VIEW OF LIFE. *Seventh and Revised Edition. Crown 8vo. 2s. 6d. net.*

Ditchfield (P. H.). M.A., F.S.A. THE PARISH CLERK. Illustrated. *Third Edition. Demy 8vo. 7s. 6d. net.*
THE OLD-TIME PARSON. Illustrated. *Second Edition. Demy 8vo. 7s. 6d. net.*

Douglas (Hugh A.). VENICE ON FOOT. With the Itinerary of the Grand Canal. Illustrated. *Fcap. 8vo. 5s. net.*

Douglas (James). THE MAN IN THE PULPIT. *Cr. 8vo.* 2s. 6d. *net.*

Dowden (J.), D.D., Late Lord Bishop of Edinburgh. FURTHER STUDIES IN THE PRAYER BOOK. *Cr. 8vo.* 6s.

Driver (S. R.), D.D., D.C.L., Regius Professor of Hebrew in the University of Oxford. SERMONS ON SUBJECTS CONNECTED WITH THE OLD TESTAMENT. *Cr. 8vo.* 6s.

Duff (Nora). MATILDA OF TUSCANY. Illustrated. *Demy 8vo.* 10s. 6d. *net.*

Dumas (Alexandre). THE CRIMES OF THE BORGIAS AND OTHERS. With an Introduction by R. S. GARNETT. Illustrated. *Cr. 8vo.* 6s.
THE CRIMES OF URBAIN GRANDIER AND OTHERS. Illustrated. *Cr. 8vo.* 6s.
THE CRIMES OF THE MARQUISE DE BRINVILLIERS AND OTHERS. Illustrated. *Cr. 8vo.* 6s.
THE CRIMES OF ALI PACHA AND OTHERS. Illustrated. *Cr. 8vo.* 6s.
MY MEMOIRS. Translated by E. M. WALLER. With an Introduction by ANDREW LANG. With Frontispieces in Photogravure. In six Volumes. *Cr. 8vo.* 6s. *each volume.*
VOL. I. 1802-1821. VOL. IV. 1830-1831.
VOL. II. 1822-1825. VOL. V. 1831-1832.
VOL. III. 1826-1830. VOL. VI. 1832-1833.
MY PETS. Newly translated by A. R. ALLINSON, M.A. Illustrated. *Cr. 8vo.* 6s.

Duncan (David), D.Sc., LL.D. THE LIFE AND LETTERS OF HERBERT SPENCER. Illustrated. *Demy 8vo.* 15s.

Dunn-Pattison (R. P.) NAPOLEON'S MARSHALS. Illustrated. *Demy 8vo. Second Edition.* 12s. 6d. *net.*
*EDWARD THE BLACK PRINCE. Illustrated. *Demy 8vo.* 7s. 6d. *net.*

Durham (The Earl of) A REPORT ON CANADA. With an Introductory Note. *Demy 8vo.* 4s. 6d. *net.*

Dutt (W. A.) THE NORFOLK BROADS. Illustrated. *Second Edition. Cr. 8vo.* 6s.
WILD LIFE IN EAST ANGLIA. Illustrated. *Second Edition. Demy 8vo.* 7s. 6d. *net.*
SOME LITERARY ASSOCIATIONS OF EAST ANGLIA. Illustrated. *Demy 8vo.* 10s. 6d. *net.*

Edmonds (Major J. E.), R.E. ; D. A. Q.-M, G, See Wood (W. Birkbeck).

Edwardes (Tickner). THE LORE OF THE HONEY BEE. Illustrated. *Cr. 8vo.* 6s.
*LIFT-LUCK ON SOUTHERN ROADS. Illustrated. *Cr. 8vo.* 6s.

Egerton (H. E.), M.A. A HISTORY OF BRITISH COLONIAL POLICY. *Second Edition, Revised. Demy 8vo.* 7s. 6d. *net.*

Everett-Green (Mary Anne). ELIZABETH; ELECTRESS PALATINE AND QUEEN OF BOHEMIA. Revised by her Niece S. C. LOMAS. With a Prefatory Note by A. W. WARD, Litt.D. *Demy 8vo.* 10s. 6d. *net.*

Fairbrother (W. H.), M.A. THE PHILOSOPHY OF T. H. GREEN. *Second Edition. Cr. 8vo,* 3s. 6d.

Fea (Allan). THE FLIGHT OF THE KING. Illustrated. *New and Revised Edition. Demy 8vo.* 7s. 6d. *net.*
SECRET CHAMBERS AND HIDING-PLACES. Illustrated. *New and Revised Edition. Demy 8vo.* 7s. 6d. *net.*
JAMES II. AND HIS WIVES. Illustrated. *Demy 8vo.* 10s. 6d. *net.*

Fell (E. F. B.). THE FOUNDATIONS OF LIBERTY. *Cr. 8vo.* 5s. *net.*

Firth (C. H.), M.A., Regius Professor of Modern History at Oxford. CROMWELL'S ARMY: A History of the English Soldier during the Civil Wars, the Commonwealth, and the Protectorate. *Cr. 8vo.* 6s.

FitzGerald (Edward). THE RUBÁIYÁT OF OMAR KHAYYÁM. Printed from the Fifth and last Edition. With a Commentary by Mrs. STEPHEN BATSON, and a Biography of Omar by E. D. ROSS. *Cr. 8vo.* 6s.

*Fletcher (B. F. and H. P.). THE ENGLISH HOME. Illustrated. *Demy 8vo.* 12s. 6d. *net.*

Fletcher (J. S.). A BOOK OF YORKSHIRE. Illustrated. *Demy 8vo.* 7s. 6d. *net.*

Flux (A. W.), M.A., William Dow Professor of Political Economy in M'Gill University, Montreal. ECONOMIC PRINCIPLES. *Demy 8vo.* 7s. 6d. *net.*

Foot (Constance M.). INSECT WONDERLAND. Illustrated. *Cr. 8vo.* 3s. 6d. *net.*

Forel (A.). THE SENSES OF INSECTS. Translated by MACLEOD YEARSLEY. Illustrated. *Demy 8vo.* 10s. 6d. *net.*

Fouqué (La Motte). SINTRAM AND HIS COMPANIONS. Translated by A. C. FARQUHARSON. Illustrated. *Demy 8vo.* 7s. 6d. *net. Half White Vellum,* 10s. 6d. *net.*

Fraser (J. F.). ROUND THE WORLD ON A WHEEL. Illustrated. *Fifth Edition. Cr. 8vo.* 6s.

GENERAL LITERATURE

Galton (Sir Francis), F.R.S.; D.C.L., Oxf.; Hon. Sc.D., Camb.; Hon. Fellow Trinity College, Cambridge. MEMORIES OF MY LIFE. Illustrated. *Third Edition. Demy 8vo. 10s. 6d. net.*

Garnett (Lucy M. J.). THE TURKISH PEOPLE; THEIR SOCIAL LIFE, RELIGIOUS BELIEFS AND INSTITUTIONS, AND DOMESTIC LIFE. Illustrated. *Demy 8vo. 10s. 6d. net.*

Gibbins (H. de B.), Litt.D., M.A. INDUSTRY IN ENGLAND: HISTORICAL OUTLINES. With 5 Maps. *Fifth Edition. Demy 8vo. 10s. 6d.*
THE INDUSTRIAL HISTORY OF ENGLAND. Illustrated. *Fifteenth Edition Revised. Cr. 8vo. 3s.*
ENGLISH SOCIAL REFORMERS. *Second Edition. Cr. 8vo. 2s. 6d.*
See also Hadfield, R.A.

Gibbon (Edward). MEMOIRS OF THE LIFE OF EDWARD GIBBON. Edited by G. BIRKBECK HILL, LL.D. *Cr. 8vo. 6s.*
*THE DECLINE AND FALL OF THE ROMAN EMPIRE. Edited, with Notes, Appendices, and Maps, by J. B. BURY, M.A., Litt.D., Regius Professor of Modern History at Cambridge. Illustrated. *In Seven Volumes. Demy 8vo. Gilt Top. Each 10s. 6d. net.*

Gibbs (Philip.) THE ROMANCE OF GEORGE VILLIERS: FIRST DUKE OF BUCKINGHAM, AND SOME MEN AND WOMEN OF THE STUART COURT. Illustrated. *Second Edition. Demy 8vo. 15s. net.*

Gloag (M. R.) and Wyatt (Kate M.). A BOOK OF ENGLISH GARDENS. Illustrated. *Demy 8vo. 10s. 6d. net.*

Glover (T. R.), M.A., Fellow and Classical Lecturer of St. John's College, Cambridge. THE CONFLICT OF RELIGIONS IN THE EARLY ROMAN EMPIRE. *Third Edition. Demy 8vo. 7s. 6d. net.*

Godfrey (Elizabeth). A BOOK OF REMEMBRANCE. Being Lyrical Selections for every day in the Year. Arranged by E. Godfrey. *Second Edition. Fcap. 8vo. 2s. 6d. net.*
ENGLISH CHILDREN IN THE OLDEN TIME. Illustrated. *Second Edition. Demy 8vo. 7s. 6d. net.*

Godley (A. D.), M.A., Fellow of Magdalen College, Oxford. OXFORD IN THE EIGHTEENTH CENTURY. Illustrated. *Second Edition. Demy 8vo. 7s. 6d. net.*
LYRA FRIVOLA. *Fourth Edition. Fcap. 8vo. 2s. 6d.*
VERSES TO ORDER. *Second Edition. Fcap. 8vo. 2s. 6d.*
SECOND STRINGS. *Fcap. 8vo. 2s. 6d.*

Goll (August). CRIMINAL TYPES IN SHAKESPEARE. Authorised Translation from the Danish by Mrs. CHARLES WEEKES. *Cr. 8vo. 5s. net.*

Gordon (Lina Duff) (Mrs. Aubrey Waterfield). HOME LIFE IN ITALY: LETTERS FROM THE APENNINES. Illustrated. *Second Edition. Demy 8vo. 10s. 6d. net.*

Gostling (Frances M.). THE BRETONS AT HOME. Illustrated. *Second Edition. Demy 8vo. 10s. 6d. net.*

Graham (Harry). A GROUP OF SCOTTISH WOMEN. Illustrated. *Second Edition. Demy 8vo. 10s. 6d. net.*

Grahame (Kenneth). THE WIND IN THE WILLOWS. Illustrated. *Fourth Edition. Cr. 8vo. 6s.*

Gwynn (Stephen), M.P. A HOLIDAY IN CONNEMARA. Illustrated. *Demy 8vo. 10s 6d. net.*

Hall (Cyril). THE YOUNG CARPENTER. Illustrated. *Cr. 8vo. 5s.*

Hall (Hammond). THE YOUNG ENGINEER; or MODERN ENGINES AND THEIR MODELS. Illustrated. *Second Edition. Cr. 8vo. 5s.*

Hall (Mary). A WOMAN'S TREK FROM THE CAPE TO CAIRO. Illustrated. *Second Edition. Demy 8vo. 16s. net.*

Hamel (Frank). FAMOUS FRENCH SALONS. Illustrated. *Third Edition. Demy 8vo. 12s. 6d. net.*

Hannay (D.). A SHORT HISTORY OF THE ROYAL NAVY. Vol. I., 1217-1688. Vol. II., 1689-1815. *Demy 8vo. Each 7s. 6d. net.*

Hannay (James O.), M.A. THE SPIRIT AND ORIGIN OF CHRISTIAN MONASTICISM. *Cr. 8vo. 6s.*
THE WISDOM OF THE DESERT. *Fcap. 8vo. 3s. 6d. net.*

Harper (Charles G.). THE AUTOCAR ROAD-BOOK. Four Volumes with Maps. *Cr. 8vo. Each 7s. 6d. net.*
Vol. I.—SOUTH OF THE THAMES.
Vol. II.—NORTH AND SOUTH WALES AND WEST MIDLANDS.

Headley (F. W.). DARWINISM AND MODERN SOCIALISM. *Second Edition. Cr. 8vo. 5s. net.*

Henderson (B. W.), Fellow of Exeter, College, Oxford. THE LIFE AND PRINCIPATE OF THE EMPEROR NERO. Illustrated. *New and cheaper issue. Demy 8vo. 7s. 6d. net.*

Henderson (M. Sturge). GEORGE MEREDITH; NOVELIST, POET, REFORMER. Illustrated. *Second Edition. Cr. 8vo. 6s.*

Henderson (T. F.) and Watt (Francis). SCOTLAND OF TO-DAY. Illustrated. *Second Edition. Cr. 8vo. 6s.*

Henley (W. E.). ENGLISH LYRICS. CHAUCER TO POE, 1340-1849. *Second Edition. Cr. 8vo. 2s. 6d. net.*

*****Heywood (W.).** A HISTORY OF PERUGIA. Illustrated. *Demy 8vo. 12s. 6d. net.*

*****Hill (George Francis).** ONE HUNDRED MASTERPIECES OF SCULPTURE. Illustrated. *Demy 8vo. 10s. 6d. net.*

Hind (C. Lewis). DAYS IN CORNWALL. Illustrated. *Second Edition. Cr. 8vo. 6s.*

Hobhouse (L. T.), late Fellow of C.C.C., Oxford. THE THEORY OF KNOWLEDGE. *Demy 8vo. 10s. 6d. net.*

Hodgetts (E. A. Brayley). THE COURT OF RUSSIA IN THE NINETEENTH CENTURY. Illustrated. *Two volumes. Demy 8vo. 24s. net.*

Hodgson (Mrs. W.). HOW TO IDENTIFY OLD CHINESE PORCELAIN. Illustrated. *Second Edition. Post 8vo. 6s.*

Holdich (Sir T. H.), K.C.I.E., C.B., F.S.A. THE INDIAN BORDERLAND, 1880-1900. Illustrated. *Second Edition. Demy 8vo. 10s. 6d. net.*

Holdsworth (W. S.), D.C.L. A HISTORY OF ENGLISH LAW. *In Four Volumes. Vols. I., II., III. Demy 8vo. Each 10s. 6d. net.*

Holland (Clive). TYROL AND ITS PEOPLE. Illustrated. *Demy 8vo. 10s. 6d. net.*

Hollway-Calthrop (H. C.), late of Balliol College, Oxford; Bursar of Eton College. PETRARCH: HIS LIFE, WORK, AND TIMES. Illustrated. *Demy 8vo. 12s. 6d. net.*

Horsburgh (E. L. S.), M.A. LORENZO THE MAGNIFICENT: AND FLORENCE IN HER GOLDEN AGE. Illustrated. *Second Edition. Demy 8vo. 15s. net.*
WATERLOO: with Plans. *Second Edition. Cr. 8vo. 5s.*

Hosie (Alexander). MANCHURIA. Illustrated. *Second Edition. Demy 8vo. 7s. 6d. net.*

Hulton (Samuel F.). THE CLERK OF OXFORD IN FICTION. Illustrated. *Demy 8vo. 10s. 6d. net.*

*****Humphreys (John H.).** PROPORTIONAL REPRESENTATION. *Cr. 8vo. 3s. 6d. net.*

Hutchinson (Horace G.). THE NEW FOREST. Illustrated. *Fourth Edition. Cr. 8vo. 6s.*

Hutton (Edward). THE CITIES OF UMBRIA. Illustrated. *Third Edition. Cr. 8vo. 6s.*
THE CITIES OF SPAIN. Illustrated. *Third Edition. Cr. 8vo. 6s.*
FLORENCE AND THE CITIES OF NORTHERN TUSCANY, WITH GENOA. Illustrated. *Second Edition. Crown 8vo. 6s.*
ENGLISH LOVE POEMS. Edited with an Introduction. *Fcap. 8vo. 3s. 6d. net.*
COUNTRY WALKS ABOUT FLORENCE. Illustrated. *Fcap. 8vo. 5s. net.*
IN UNKNOWN TUSCANY. With an Appendix by WILLIAM HEYWOOD. Illustrated. *Second Edition. Demy 8vo. 7s. 6d. net.*
ROME. Illustrated. *Cr. 8vo. 6s.*

Hyett (F. A.) FLORENCE: HER HISTORY AND ART TO THE FALL OF THE REPUBLIC. *Demy 8vo. 7s. 6d. net.*

Ibsen (Henrik). BRAND. A Drama. Translated by WILLIAM WILSON. *Third Edition. Cr. 8vo. 3s. 6d.*

Inge (W. R.), M.A., Fellow and Tutor of Hertford College, Oxford. CHRISTIAN MYSTICISM. (The Bampton Lectures of 1899.) *Demy 8vo. 12s. 6d. net.*

Innes (A. D.), M.A. A HISTORY OF THE BRITISH IN INDIA. With Maps and Plans. *Cr. 8vo. 6s.*
ENGLAND UNDER THE TUDORS. With Maps. *Second Edition. Demy 8vo. 10s. 6d. net.*

*****Innes (Mary).** SCHOOLS OF PAINTING. Illustrated. *Cr. 8vo. 5s. net.*

James (Norman G. B.). THE CHARM OF SWITZERLAND. *Cr. 8vo. 5s. net.*

Jebb (Camilla). A STAR OF THE SALONS: JULIE DE LESPINASSE. Illustrated. *Demy 8vo. 10s. 6d. net.*

Jeffery (Reginald W.), M.A. THE HISTORY OF THE THIRTEEN COLONIES OF NORTH AMERICA, 1497-1763. Illustrated. *Demy 8vo. 7s. 6d. net.*

Jenks (E.), M.A., B.C.L. AN OUTLINE OF ENGLISH LOCAL GOVERNMENT. *Second Edition.* Revised by R. C. K. ENSOR, M.A. *Cr. 8vo. 2s. 6d.*

Jennings (Oscar), M.D. EARLY WOODCUT INITIALS. Illustrated. *Demy 4to. 21s. net.*

Jerningham (Charles Edward). THE MAXIMS OF MARMADUKE. *Second Edition. Cr. 8vo. 5s.*

Johnston (Sir H. H.), K.C.B. BRITISH CENTRAL AFRICA. Illustrated. *Third Edition. Cr. 4to. 18s. net.*

General Literature 9

*THE NEGRO IN THE NEW WORLD. Illustrated. *Demy 8vo.* 16s. *net.*

Jones (R. Crompton), M.A. POEMS OF THE INNER LIFE. Selected by R. C. JONES. *Thirteenth Edition. Fcap 8vo.* 2s. 6d. net.

Julian (Lady) of Norwich. REVELATIONS OF DIVINE LOVE. Edited by GRACE WARRACK. *Third Edition. Cr. 8vo.* 3s. 6d.

'Kappa.' LET YOUTH BUT KNOW: A Plea for Reason in Education. *Second Edition. Cr. 8vo.* 3s. 6d. net.

Keats (John). THE POEMS. Edited with Introduction and Notes by E. de SÉLINCOURT, M.A. With a Frontispiece in Photogravure. *Second Edition Revised. Demy 8vo.* 7s. 6d. net.

Keble (John). THE CHRISTIAN YEAR. With an Introduction and Notes by W. LOCK, D.D., Warden of Keble College. Illustrated. *Third Edition. Fcap. 8vo.* 3s. 6d.; *padded morocco.* 5s.

Kempis (Thomas à). THE IMITATION OF CHRIST. With an Introduction by DEAN FARRAR. Illustrated. *Third Edition. Fcap 8vo.* 3s. 6d.; *padded morocco,* 5s.
Also translated by C. BIGG, D.D. *Cr. 8vo.* 3s. 6d.

Kerr (S. Parnell). GEORGE SELWYN AND THE WITS. Illustrated. *Demy 8vo.* 12s. 6d. net.

Kipling (Rudyard). BARRACK-ROOM BALLADS. 94th *Thousand. Twenty-seventh Edition. Cr. 8vo.* 6s. Also *Fcap. 8vo, Leather.* 5s. net.
THE SEVEN SEAS. 79th *Thousand. Fifteenth Edition. Cr. 8vo.* 6s. Also *Fcap. 8vo, Leather.* 5s. net.
THE FIVE NATIONS. 66th *Thousand. Sixth Edition. Cr. 8vo.* 6s. Also *Fcap. 8vo, Leather.* 5s. net.
DEPARTMENTAL DITTIES. *Eighteenth Edition. Cr. 8vo.* 6s. Also *Fcap. 8vo, Leather.* 5s. net.

Knox (Winifred F.). THE COURT OF A SAINT. Illustrated. *Demy 8vo.* 10s. 6d. net.

Lamb (Charles and Mary), THE WORKS. Edited by E. V. LUCAS. Illustrated. *In Seven Volumes. Demy 8vo.* 7s. 6d. *each.*

Lane-Poole (Stanley). A HISTORY OF EGYPT IN THE MIDDLE AGES. Illustrated. *Cr. 8vo.* 6s.

*****Lankester (Sir Ray),** K.C.B., F.R.S. SCIENCE FROM AN EASY CHAIR. Illustrated. *Cr. 8vo.* 6s.

Leach (Henry). THE SPIRIT OF THE LINKS. *Cr. 8vo.* 6s.

Le Braz (Anatole). THE LAND OF PARDONS. Translated by FRANCES M. GOSTLING. Illustrated. *Third Edition. Cr. 8vo.* 6s.

Lees (Frederick). A SUMMER IN TOURAINE. Illustrated. *Second Edition. Demy 8vo.* 10s. 6d. net.

Lindsay (Lady Mabel). ANNI DOMINI : A GOSPEL STUDY. With Maps. *Two Volumes. Super Royal 8vo.* 10s. net.

Llewellyn (Owen) and Raven-Hill (L.). THE SOUTH-BOUND CAR. Illustrated. *Cr. 8vo.* 6s.

Lock (Walter), D.D., Warden of Keble College. ST. PAUL, THE MASTER-BUILDER. *Second Edition. Cr. 8vo.* 3s. 6d.
THE BIBLE AND CHRISTIAN LIFE. *Cr. 8vo.* 6s.

Lodge (Sir Oliver), F.R.S. THE SUBSTANCE OF FAITH, ALLIED WITH SCIENCE: A Catechism for Parents and Teachers. *Tenth Edition. Cr. 8vo.* 2s. net.
MAN AND THE UNIVERSE : A STUDY OF THE INFLUENCE OF THE ADVANCE IN SCIENTIFIC KNOWLEDGE UPON OUR UNDERSTANDING OF CHRISTIANITY. *Seventh Edition. Demy 8vo.* 7s. 6d. net.
THE SURVIVAL OF MAN. A STUDY IN UNRECOGNISED HUMAN FACULTY. *Third Edition. Demy 8vo.* 7s. 6d. net.

Lofthouse (W. F.), M.A. ETHICS AND ATONEMENT. With a Frontispiece. *Demy 8vo.* 5s. net.

Lorimer (George Horace). LETTERS FROM A SELF-MADE MERCHANT TO HIS SON. Illustrated. *Seventeenth Edition. Cr. 8vo.* 3s. 6d.
OLD GORGON GRAHAM. Illustrated. *Second Edition. Cr. 8vo.* 6s.

Lorimer (Norma). BY THE WATERS OF EGYPT. Illustrated. *Demy 8vo.* 16s. net.

"Loyal Serviteur." THE STORY OF BAYARD. Adapted by AMY G. ANDREWES. *Cr. 8vo.* 2s. 6d.

Lucas (E. V.). THE LIFE OF CHARLES LAMB. Illustrated. *Fifth and Revised Edition in One Volume. Demy 8vo.* 7s. 6d. net.
A WANDERER IN HOLLAND. Illustrated. *Tenth Edition. Cr. 8vo.* 6s.
A WANDERER IN LONDON. Illustrated. *Eighth Edition. Cr. 8vo.* 6s.
A WANDERER IN PARIS. Illustrated. *Fourth Edition. Cr. 8vo.* 6s.

THE OPEN ROAD: A Little Book for Wayfarers. *Fifteenth Edition. Fcp. 8vo.* 5s.; *India Paper,* 7s. 6d.
THE FRIENDLY TOWN: a Little Book for the Urbane. *Fifth Edition. Fcap. 8vo.* 5s.; *India Paper,* 7s. 6d.
FIRESIDE AND SUNSHINE. *Fifth Edition. Fcap. 8vo.* 5s.
CHARACTER AND COMEDY. *Fifth Edition. Fcap. 8vo.* 5s.
THE GENTLEST ART. A Choice of Letters by Entertaining Hands. *Fifth Edition. Fcap 8vo.* 5s.
A SWAN AND HER FRIENDS. Illustrated. *Demy 8vo.* 12s. 6d. net.
HER INFINITE VARIETY: A FEMININE PORTRAIT GALLERY. *Fourth Edition. Fcap. 8vo.* 5s.
LISTENER'S LURE: AN OBLIQUE NARRATION. *Sixth Edition. Fcap. 8vo.* 5s.
GOOD COMPANY: A RALLY OF MEN. *Second Edition. Fcap. 8vo.* 5s.
ONE DAY AND ANOTHER. *Third Edition. Fcap. 8vo.* 5s.
OVER BEMERTON'S: AN EASY-GOING CHRONICLE. *Seventh Edition. Fcap. 8vo.* 5s. *net.*

M. (R.). THE THOUGHTS OF LUCIA HALLIDAY. With some of her Letters. Edited by R. M. *Fcap. 8vo.* 2s. 6d. net.

Macaulay (Lord). CRITICAL AND HISTORICAL ESSAYS. Edited by F. C. MONTAGUE, M.A. *Three Volumes. Cr. 8vo.* 18s.

McCabe (Joseph) (formerly Very Rev. F. ANTONY, O.S.F.). THE DECAY OF THE CHURCH OF ROME. *Second Edition. Demy 8vo.* 7s. 6d. net.

McCullagh (Francis). The Fall of Abd-ul-Hamid. Illustrated. *Demy 8vo.* 10s. 6d. net.

MacCunn (Florence A.). MARY STUART. Illustrated. *New and Cheaper Edition. Large Cr. 8vo.* 6s.

McDougall (William), M.A. (Oxon., M.B. (Cantab.). AN INTRODUCTION TO SOCIAL PSYCHOLOGY. *Second Edition. Cr. 8vo.* 5s. net.

'Mdlle. Mori' (Author of). ST. CATHERINE OF SIENA AND HER TIMES. Illustrated. *Second Edition. Demy 8vo.* 7s. 6d. net.

Maeterlinck (Maurice). THE BLUE BIRD: A FAIRY PLAY IN FIVE ACTS. Translated by ALEXANDER TEIXEIRA DE MATTOS. *Eighth Edition. Fcap. 8vo.* Deckle Edges. 3s. 6d. net. Also *Fcap. 8vo.* Paper covers, 1s. net.

Mahaffy (J. P.), Litt.D. A HISTORY OF THE EGYPT OF THE PTOLEMIES. Illustrated. *Cr. 8vo.* 6s.

Maitland (F. W.), M.A., LL.D. ROMAN CANON LAW IN THE CHURCH OF ENGLAND. *Royal 8vo.* 7s. 6d.

Marett (R. R.), M.A., Fellow and Tutor of Exeter College, Oxford. THE THRESHOLD OF RELIGION. *Cr. 8vo.* 3s. 6d. net.

Marriott (Charles). A SPANISH HOLIDAY. Illustrated. *Demy 8vo.* 7s. 6d. net.

Marriott (J. A. R.), M.A. THE LIFE AND TIMES OF LORD FALKLAND. Illustrated. *Second Edition. Demy 8vo.* 7s. 6d. net.

Masefield (John). SEA LIFE IN NELSON'S TIME. Illustrated. *Cr. 8vo.* 3s. 6d. net.
A SAILOR'S GARLAND. Selected and Edited. *Second Edition. Cr. 8vo.* 3s. 6d. net.
AN ENGLISH PROSE MISCELLANY. Selected and Edited. *Cr. 8vo.* 6s.

Masterman (C. F. G.), M.A., M.P. TENNYSON AS A RELIGIOUS TEACHER. *Cr. 8vo.* 6s.
THE CONDITION OF ENGLAND. *Third Edition. Cr. 8vo.* 6s.

Mayne (Ethel Colburn). ENCHANTERS OF MEN. Illustrated. *Demy 8vo.* 10s. 6d. net.

Meakin (Annette M. B.), Fellow of the Anthropological Institute. WOMAN IN TRANSITION. *Cr. 8vo.* 6s.
GALICIA: THE SWITZERLAND OF SPAIN. Illustrated. *Demy 8vo.* 12s. 6d. net.

Medley (D. J.), M.A., Professor of History in the University of Glasgow. ORIGINAL ILLUSTRATIONS OF ENGLISH CONSTITUTIONAL HISTORY, COMPRISING A SELECTED NUMBER OF THE CHIEF CHARTERS AND STATUTES. *Cr. 8vo.* 7s. 6d. net.

Methuen (A. M. S.), M.A. THE TRAGEDY OF SOUTH AFRICA. *Cr. 8vo.* 2s. net.
ENGLAND'S RUIN: DISCUSSED IN FOURTEEN LETTERS TO A PROTECTIONIST. *Ninth Edition. Cr. 8vo.* 3d. net.

Meynell (Everard). COROT AND HIS FRIENDS. Illustrated. *Demy 8vo.* 10s. 6d. net.

Miles (Eustace), M.A. LIFE AFTER LIFE: OR, THE THEORY OF REINCARNATION. *Cr. 8vo.* 2s. 6d. net.
THE POWER OF CONCENTRATION: HOW TO ACQUIRE IT. *Third Edition. Cr. 8vo.* 3s. 6d. net.

Millais (J. G.). THE LIFE AND LETTERS OF SIR JOHN EVERETT MILLAIS, President of the Royal Academy. Illustrated. *New Edition. Demy 8vo.* 7s. 6d. net.

Milne (J. G.), M.A. A HISTORY OF EGYPT UNDER ROMAN RULE. Illustrated. *Cr. 8vo.* 6s.

GENERAL LITERATURE 11

Mitton (G. E.). JANE AUSTEN AND HER TIMES. Illustrated. *Second and Cheaper Edition. Large Cr. 8vo. 6s.*

Moffat (Mary M.). QUEEN LOUISA OF PRUSSIA. Illustrated. *Fourth Edition. Cr. 8vo. 6s.*

Money (L. G. Chiozza). RICHES AND POVERTY. *Ninth Edition. Demy 8vo. 5s. net.* Also *Cr. 8vo. 1s. net.*
MONEY'S FISCAL DICTIONARY, 1910. *Demy 8vo. 5s. net.*

Moore (T. Sturge). ART AND LIFE. Illustrated. *Cr. 8vo. 5s. net.*

Moorhouse (E. Hallam). NELSON'S LADY HAMILTON. Illustrated. *Second Edition. Demy 8vo. 7s. 6d. net.*

Morgan (J. H.), M.A. THE HOUSE OF LORDS AND THE CONSTITUTION. With an Introduction by the LORD CHANCELLOR. *Cr. 8vo. 1s. net.*

Morton (A. Anderson). See Brodrick (M.).

Norway (A. H.). NAPLES. PAST AND PRESENT. Illustrated. *Third Edition. Cr. 8vo. 6s.*

Oman (C. W. C.), M.A., Fellow of All Souls', Oxford. A HISTORY OF THE ART OF WAR IN THE MIDDLE AGES. Illustrated. *Demy 8vo. 10s. 6d. net.*
*ENGLAND BEFORE THE CONQUEST. With Maps. *Demy 8vo. 10s. 6d. net.*

Oxford (M. N.), of Guy's Hospital. A HANDBOOK OF NURSING. *Fifth Edition. Cr. 8vo. 3s. 6d.*

Pakes (W. C. C.). THE SCIENCE OF HYGIENE. Illustrated. *Demy 8vo. 15s.*

Parker (Eric). THE BOOK OF THE ZOO; BY DAY AND NIGHT. Illustrated. *Second Edition. Cr. 8vo. 6s.*

Parsons (Mrs. C.). THE INCOMPARABLE SIDDONS. Illustrated. *Demy 8vo. 12s. 6d. net.*

Patmore (K. A.). THE COURT OF LOUIS XIII. Illustrated. *Third Edition. Demy 8vo. 10s. 6d. net.*

Patterson (A. H.). MAN AND NATURE ON TIDAL WATERS. Illustrated. *Cr. 8vo. 6s.*

Peel (Robert), and Minchin (H. C.), M.A. OXFORD. Illustrated. *Cr. 8vo. 6s.*

Petrie (W. M. Flinders), D.C.L., LL.D., Professor of Egyptology at University College. A HISTORY OF EGYPT. Illustrated. *In Six Volumes. Cr. 8vo. 6s. each.*

VOL. I. FROM THE EARLIEST KINGS TO XVITH DYNASTY. *Sixth Edition.*
VOL. II. THE XVIITH AND XVIIITH DYNASTIES. *Fourth Edition.*
VOL. III. XIXTH TO XXXTH DYNASTIES.
VOL IV. EGYPT UNDER THE PTOLEMAIC DYNASTY. J. P. MAHAFFY, Litt.D.
VOL. V. EGYPT UNDER ROMAN RULE. J. G. MILNE, M.A.
VOL. VI. EGYPT IN THE MIDDLE AGES. STANLEY LANE-POOLE, M.A.
RELIGION AND CONSCIENCE IN ANCIENT EGYPT. Lectures delivered at University College, London. Illustrated. *Cr. 8vo. 2s. 6d.*
SYRIA AND EGYPT, FROM THE TELL EL AMARNA LETTERS. *Cr. 8vo. 2s. 6d.*
EGYPTIAN TALES. Translated from the Papyri. First Series, ivth to xiith Dynasty. Edited by W. M. FLINDERS PETRIE. Illustrated. *Second Edition. Cr. 8vo. 3s. 6d.*
EGYPTIAN TALES. Translated from the Papyri. Second Series, xviiith to xixth Dynasty. Illustrated. *Cr. 8vo. 3s. 6d.*
EGYPTIAN DECORATIVE ART. A Course of Lectures delivered at the Royal Institution. Illustrated. *Cr. 8vo. 3s. 6d.*

***Phelps (Ruth S.).** SKIES ITALIAN: A LITTLE BREVIARY FOR TRAVELLERS IN ITALY. *Fcap. 8vo. 5s. net.*

Phythian (J. Ernest). TREES IN NATURE, MYTH, AND ART. Illustrated. *Cr. 8vo. 6s.*

Podmore (Frank). MODERN SPIRITUALISM. *Two Volumes. Demy 8vo. 21s. net.*
MESMERISM AND CHRISTIAN SCIENCE: A Short History of Mental Healing. *Second Edition. Demy 8vo. 10s. 6d. net.*

Pollard (Alfred W.). SHAKESPEARE FOLIOS AND QUARTOS. A Study in the Bibliography of Shakespeare's Plays, 1594-1685. Illustrated. *Folio. 21s. net.*

Powell (Arthur E.). FOOD AND HEALTH. *Cr. 8vo. 3s. 6d. net.*

Power (J. O'Connor). THE MAKING OF AN ORATOR. *Cr. 8vo. 6s.*

Price (L. L.), M.A., Fellow of Oriel College, Oxon. A HISTORY OF ENGLISH POLITICAL ECONOMY FROM ADAM SMITH TO ARNOLD TOYNBEE. *Sixth Edition. Cr. 8vo. 2s. 6d.*

Pullen-Burry (B.). IN A GERMAN COLONY; or, FOUR WEEKS IN NEW BRITAIN. Illustrated. *Cr. 8vo. 5s. net.*

Pycraft (W. P.). BIRD LIFE. Illustrated. *Demy 8vo. 10s. 6d. net.*

Ragg (Lonsdale), B.D. Oxon. DANTE AND HIS ITALY. Illustrated. *Demy 8vo. 12s. 6d. net.*

*****Rappoport (Angelo S.)**. HOME LIFE IN RUSSIA. Illustrated. *Demy 8vo. 10s. 6d. net.*

Raven-Hill (L.). See Llewellyn (Owen).

Rawlings (Gertrude). COINS AND HOW TO KNOW THEM. Illustrated. *Second Edition. Cr. 8vo. 5s. net.*

Rea (Lilian). THE LIFE AND TIMES OF MARIE MADELEINE COUNTESS OF LA FAYETTE. Illustrated. *Demy 8vo. 10s. 6d. net.*

Read (C. Stanford), M.B. (Lond.), M.R.C.S., L.R.C.P. FADS AND FEEDING. *Cr. 8vo. 2s. 6d. net.*

Rees (J. D.), C.I.E., M.P. THE REAL INDIA. *Second Edition. Demy 8vo. 10s. 6d. net.*

Reich (Emil), Doctor Juris. WOMAN THROUGH THE AGES. Illustrated. *Two Volumes. Demy 8vo. 21s. net.*

Reid (Archdall), M.B. The Laws of Heredity. *Demy 8vo. 21s. net.*

Richmond (Wilfrid), Chaplain of Lincoln's Inn. THE CREED IN THE EPISTLES. *Cr. 8vo. 2s. 6d. net.*

Roberts (M. E.). See Channer (C.C.).

Robertson (A.), D.D., Lord Bishop of Exeter. REGNUM DEI. (The Bampton Lectures of 1901.) *A New and Cheaper Edition. Demy 8vo. 7s. 6d. net.*

Robertson (C. Grant), M.A., Fellow of All Souls' College, Oxford. SELECT STATUTES, CASES, AND CONSTITUTIONAL DOCUMENTS, 1660-1832. *Demy 8vo. 10s. 6d. net.*

Robertson (Sir G. S.), K.C.S.I. CHITRAL: THE STORY OF A MINOR SIEGE. Illustrated. *Third Edition. Demy 8vo. 10s. 6d. net.*

Roe (Fred). OLD OAK FURNITURE. Illustrated. *Second Edition. Demy 8vo. 10s. 6d. net.*

Royde-Smith (N. G.). THE PILLOW BOOK: A GARNER OF MANY MOODS. Collected. *Second Edition. Cr. 8vo. 4s. 6d. net.*
POETS OF OUR DAY. Selected, with an Introduction. *Fcap. 8vo. 5s.*

Rumbold (The Right Hon. Sir Horace), Bart., G. C. B., G. C. M. G. THE AUSTRIAN COURT IN THE NINETEENTH CENTURY. Illustrated. *Second Edition. Demy 8vo. 18s. net.*

Russell (W. Clark). THE LIFE OF ADMIRAL LORD COLLINGWOOD. Illustrated. *Fourth Edition. Cr. 8vo. 6s.*

Ryley (M. Beresford). QUEENS OF THE RENAISSANCE. Illustrated. *Demy 8vo. 10s. 6d. net.*

St. Francis of Assisi. THE LITTLE FLOWERS OF THE GLORIOUS MESSER, AND OF HIS FRIARS. Done into English, with Notes by WILLIAM HEYWOOD. Illustrated. *Demy 8vo. 5s. net.*

'Saki' (H. Munro). REGINALD. *Second Edition. Fcap. 8vo. 2s. 6d. net.*
REGINALD IN RUSSIA. *Fcap. 8vo. 2s. 6d. net.*

Sanders (Lloyd). THE HOLLAND HOUSE CIRCLE. Illustrated. *Second Edition. Demy 8vo. 12s. 6d. net.*

*****Scott (Ernest)**. TERRE NAPOLÉON, AND THE EXPEDITION OF DISCOVERY DESPATCHED TO AUSTRALIA BY ORDER OF BONAPARTE, 1800-1804. Illustrated. *Demy 8vo. 10s. 6d. net.*

Sélincourt (Hugh de). GREAT RALEGH. Illustrated. *Demy 8vo. 10s. 6d. net.*

Selous (Edmund). TOMMY SMITH'S ANIMALS. Illustrated. *Eleventh Edition. Fcap. 8vo. 2s. 6d.*
TOMMY SMITH'S OTHER ANIMALS. Illustrated. *Fifth Edition. Fcap. 8vo. 2s. 6d.*

*****Shafer (Sara A.)**. A WHITE PAPER GARDEN. Illustrated. *Demy 8vo. 7s. 6d. net.*

Shakespeare (William).
THE FOUR FOLIOS, 1623; 1632; 1664; 1685. Each £4 4s. net, or a complete set, £12 12s. net.
Folios 2, 3 and 4 are ready.
THE POEMS OF WILLIAM SHAKESPEARE. With an Introduction and Notes by GEORGE WYNDHAM. *Demy 8vo. Buckram, gilt top. 10s. 6d.*

Sharp (A.). VICTORIAN POETS. *Cr. 8vo. 2s. 6d.*

Sidgwick (Mrs. Alfred). HOME LIFE IN GERMANY. Illustrated. *Second Edition. Demy 8vo. 10s. 6d. net.*

Sime (John). See Little Books on Art.

Sladen (Douglas). SICILY: The New Winter Resort. Illustrated. *Second Edition. Cr. 8vo. 5s. net.*

Smith (Adam). THE WEALTH OF NATIONS. Edited with an Introduction and numerous Notes by EDWIN CANNAN, M.A. *Two Volumes. Demy 8vo. 21s. net.*

Smith (Sophia S.). DEAN SWIFT. Illustrated. *Demy 8vo. 10s. 6d. net.*

Snell (F. J.). A BOOK OF EXMOOR. Illustrated. *Cr. 8vo. 6s.*

'Stancliffe' GOLF DO'S AND DONT'S. *Second Edition. Fcap. 8vo. 1s.*

General Literature 13

Stead (Francis H.), M.A. HOW OLD AGE PENSIONS BEGAN TO BE. Illustrated. *Demy 8vo. 2s. 6d. net.*

Stevenson (R. L.). THE LETTERS OF ROBERT LOUIS STEVENSON TO HIS FAMILY AND FRIENDS. Selected and Edited by Sidney Colvin. *Eighth Edition. Two Volumes. Cr. 8vo. 12s.*
VAILIMA LETTERS. With an Etched Portrait by William Strang. *Seventh Edition. Cr. 8vo. Buckram. 6s.*
THE LIFE OF R. L. STEVENSON. See Balfour (G.).

Stevenson (M. I.). FROM SARANAC TO THE MARQUESAS. Being Letters written by Mrs. M. I. Stevenson during 1887–88. *Cr. 8vo. 6s. net.*
LETTERS FROM SAMOA, 1891–95. Edited and arranged by M. C. Balfour. Illustrated. *Second Edition. Cr. 8vo. 6s. net.*

Storr (Vernon F.), M.A., Canon of Winchester. DEVELOPMENT AND DIVINE PURPOSE. *Cr. 8vo. 5s. net.*

Streatfeild (R. A.). MODERN MUSIC AND MUSICIANS. Illustrated. *Second Edition. Demy 8vo. 7s. 6d. net.*

Swanton (E. W.). FUNGI AND HOW TO KNOW THEM. Illustrated. *Cr. 8vo. 6s. net.*

*****Sykes (Ella C.).** PERSIA AND ITS PEOPLE. Illustrated. *Demy 8vo. 10s. 6d. net.*

Symes (J. E.), M.A. THE FRENCH REVOLUTION. *Second Edition. Cr. 8vo. 2s. 6d.*

Tabor (Margaret E.). THE SAINTS IN ART. Illustrated. *Fcap. 8vo. 3s. 6d. net.*

Taylor (A. E.). THE ELEMENTS OF METAPHYSICS. *Second Edition. Demy 8vo. 10s. 6d. net.*

Taylor (John W.). THE COMING OF THE SAINTS. Illustrated. *Demy 8vo. 7s. 6d. net.*

Thibaudeau (A. C.). BONAPARTE AND THE CONSULATE. Translated and Edited by G. K. Fortescue, LL.D. Illustrated. *Demy 8vo. 10s. 6d. net.*

Thompson (Francis). SELECTED POEMS OF FRANCIS THOMPSON. With a Biographical Note by Wilfrid Meynell. With a Portrait in Photogravure. *Second Edition. Fcap. 8vo. 5s. net.*

Tileston (Mary W.). DAILY STRENGTH FOR DAILY NEEDS. *Sixteenth Edition. Medium 16mo. 2s. 6d. net.* Also an edition in superior binding, 6s.

Toynbee (Paget), M.A., D. Litt. DANTE IN ENGLISH LITERATURE: FROM CHAUCER TO CARY. *Two Volumes. Demy 8vo. 21s. net.*
See also Oxford Biographies.

Tozer (Basil). THE HORSE IN HISTORY. Illustrated. *Cr. 8vo. 6s.*

Trench (Herbert). DEIRDRE WEDDED, and Other Poems. *Second and Revised Edition. Large Post 8vo. 6s.*
NEW POEMS. *Second Edition. Large Post 8vo. 6s.*
APOLLO AND THE SEAMAN. *Large Post 8vo. Paper, 1s. 6d. net; cloth, 2s. 6d. net.*

Trevelyan (G. M.), Fellow of Trinity College, Cambridge. ENGLAND UNDER THE STUARTS. With Maps and Plans. *Third Edition. Demy 8vo. 10s. 6d. net.*

Triggs (Inigo H.), A.R.I.B.A. TOWN PLANNING: Past, Present, and Possible. Illustrated. *Wide Royal 8vo. 15s. net.*

Vaughan (Herbert M.), B.A.(Oxon). THE LAST OF THE ROYAL STUARTS, HENRY STUART, CARDINAL, DUKE OF YORK. Illustrated. *Second Edition. Demy 8vo. 10s. 6d. net.*
THE MEDICI POPES (LEO X. and Clement VII.). Illustrated. *Demy 8vo. 15s. net.*
THE NAPLES RIVIERA. Illustrated. *Second Edition. Cr. 8vo. 6s.*
*FLORENCE AND HER TREASURES. Illustrated. *Fcap. 8vo. 5s. net.*

Vernon (Hon. W. Warren), M.A. READINGS ON THE INFERNO OF DANTE. With an Introduction by the Rev. Dr. Moore. *Two Volumes. Second Edition. Cr. 8vo. 15s. net.*
READINGS ON THE PURGATORIO OF DANTE. With an Introduction by the late Dean Church. *Two Volumes. Third Edition. Cr. 8vo. 15s. net.*
READINGS ON THE PARADISO OF DANTE. With an Introduction by the Bishop of Ripon. *Two Volumes. Second Edition. Cr. 8vo. 15s. net.*

Vincent (J. E.). THROUGH EAST ANGLIA IN A MOTOR CAR. Illustrated. *Cr. 8vo. 6s.*

Waddell (Col. L. A.), LL.D., C.B. LHASA AND ITS MYSTERIES. With a Record of the Expedition of 1903-1904. Illustrated. *Third and Cheaper Edition. Medium 8vo. 7s. 6d. net.*

Wagner (Richard). RICHARD WAGNER'S MUSIC DRAMAS: Interpretations, embodying Wagner's own explanations. By Alice Leighton Cleather and Basil Crump. *In Three Volumes. Fcap. 8vo. 2s. 6d. each.*
Vol. I.—The Ring of the Nibelung. *Third Edition.*

VOL. II.—PARSIFAL, LOHENGRIN, and THE HOLY GRAIL.
VOL. III.—TRISTAN AND ISOLDE.

Waineman (Paul). A SUMMER TOUR IN FINLAND. Illustrated. *Demy 8vo.* 10s. 6d. net.

Walkley (A. B.). DRAMA AND LIFE. *Cr. 8vo.* 6s.

Waterhouse (Elizabeth). WITH THE SIMPLE-HEARTED: Little Homilies to Women in Country Places. *Second Edition. Small Pott 8vo.* 2s. net.
COMPANIONS OF THE WAY. Being Selections for Morning and Evening Reading. Chosen and arranged by ELIZABETH WATERHOUSE. *Large Cr. 8vo.* 5s. net.
THOUGHTS OF A TERTIARY. *Second Edition. Small Pott 8vo.* 1s. net.

Watt (Francis). See Henderson (T. F.).

Weigall (Arthur E. P.). A GUIDE TO THE ANTIQUITIES OF UPPER EGYPT: From Abydos to the Sudan Frontier. Illustrated. *Cr. 8vo.* 7s. 6d. net.

Welch (Catharine). THE LITTLE DAUPHIN. Illustrated. *Cr. 8vo.* 6s.

Wells (J.), M.A., Fellow and Tutor of Wadham College. OXFORD AND OXFORD LIFE. *Third Edition. Cr. 8vo.* 3s. 6d.
A SHORT HISTORY OF ROME. *Ninth Edition.* With 3 Maps. *Cr. 8vo.* 3s. 6d.

Westell (W. Percival). THE YOUNG NATURALIST. Illustrated. *Cr. 8vo.* 6s.

Westell (W. Percival), F.L.S., M.B.O.U., and Cooper (C. S.), F.R.H.S. THE YOUNG BOTANIST. Illustrated. *Cr. 8vo.* 3s. 6d. net.

*****Wheeler (Ethel R.).** FAMOUS BLUE STOCKINGS. Illustrated. *Demy 8vo.* 10s. 6d. net.

Whibley (C.). See Henley (W. E.).

White (George F.), Lieut.-Col. A CENTURY OF SPAIN AND PORTUGAL, 1788-1898. *Demy 8vo.* 12s. 6d. net.

Whitley (Miss). See Dilke (Lady).

Wilde (Oscar). DE PROFUNDIS. *Twelfth Edition. Cr. 8vo.* 5s. net.

THE WORKS OF OSCAR WILDE. *In Twelve Volumes. Fcap. 8vo.* 5s. net each volume.
I. LORD ARTHUR SAVILE'S CRIME AND THE PORTRAIT OF MR. W. H. II. THE DUCHESS OF PADUA. III. POEMS. IV. LADY WINDERMERE'S FAN. V. A WOMAN OF NO IMPORTANCE. VI. AN IDEAL HUSBAND. VII. THE IMPORTANCE OF BEING EARNEST. VIII. A HOUSE OF POMEGRANATES. IX. INTENTIONS. X. DE PROFUNDIS AND PRISON LETTERS. XI. ESSAYS. XII. SALOMÉ, A FLORENTINE TRAGEDY, and LA SAINTE COURTISANE.

Williams (H. Noel). THE WOMEN BONAPARTES. The Mother and three Sisters of Napoleon. Illustrated. *In Two Volumes. Demy 8vo.* 24s. net.
A ROSE OF SAVOY: MARIE ADELÉIDE OF SAVOY, DUCHESSE DE BOURGOGNE, MOTHER OF LOUIS XV. Illustrated. *Second Edition. Demy 8vo.* 15s. net.
*THE FASCINATING DUC DE RICHELIEU: LOUIS FRANÇOIS ARMAND DU PLESSIS, MARÉCHAL DUC DE RICHELIEU. Illustrated. *Demy 8vo.* 15s. net.

Wood (Sir Evelyn), F.M., V.C., G.C.B., G.C.M.G. FROM MIDSHIPMAN TO FIELD-MARSHAL. Illustrated. *Fifth and Cheaper Edition. Demy 8vo.* 7s. 6d. net.
THE REVOLT IN HINDUSTAN. 1857-59. Illustrated. *Second Edition. Cr. 8vo.* 6s.

Wood (W. Birkbeck), M.A., late Scholar of Worcester College, Oxford, and **Edmonds (Major J. E.), R.E., D.A.Q.-M.G.** A HISTORY OF THE CIVIL WAR IN THE UNITED STATES. With an Introduction by H. SPENSER WILKINSON. With 24 Maps and Plans. *Second Edition. Demy 8vo.* 12s. 6d. net.

Wordsworth (W.). THE POEMS. With an Introduction and Notes by NOWELL C. SMITH, late Fellow of New College, Oxford. *In Three Volumes. Demy 8vo.* 15s. net.
POEMS BY WILLIAM WORDSWORTH. Selected with an Introduction by STOPFORD A. BROOKE. Illustrated. *Cr. 8vo.* 7s. 6d. net.

Wyatt (Kate M.). See Gloag (M. R.).

Wyllie (M. A.). NORWAY AND ITS FJORDS. Illustrated. *Second Edition. Cr. 8vo.* 6s.

Yeats (W. B.). A BOOK OF IRISH VERSE. *Revised and Enlarged Edition. Cr. 8vo.* 3s. 6d.

Young (Filson). See The Complete Series.

GENERAL LITERATURE

PART II.—A SELECTION OF SERIES.

Ancient Cities.

General Editor, B. C. A. WINDLE, D.Sc., F.R.S.

Cr. 8vo. 4s. 6d. net.

With Illustrations by E. H. NEW, and other Artists.

BRISTOL. By Alfred Harvey, M.B.
CANTERBURY. By J. C. Cox, LL.D., F.S.A.
CHESTER. By B. C. A. Windle, D.Sc., F.R.S.
DUBLIN. By S. A. O. Fitzpatrick.

EDINBURGH. By M. G. Williamson, M.A.
LINCOLN. By E. Mansel Sympson, M.A.
SHREWSBURY. By T. Auden, M.A., F.S.A.
WELLS and GLASTONBURY. By T. S. Holmes.

The Antiquary's Books.

General Editor, J. CHARLES COX, LL.D., F.S.A.

Demy 8vo. 7s. 6d. net.

With Numerous Illustrations.

ARCHÆOLOGY AND FALSE ANTIQUITIES. By R. Munro.
BELLS OF ENGLAND, THE. By Canon J. J. Raven. *Second Edition.*
BRASSES OF ENGLAND, THE. By Herbert W. Macklin. *Second Edition.*
CELTIC ART IN PAGAN AND CHRISTIAN TIMES. By J. Romilly Allen.
DOMESDAY INQUEST, THE. By Adolphus Ballard.
ENGLISH CHURCH FURNITURE. By J. C. Cox and A. Harvey. *Second Edition.*
ENGLISH COSTUME. From Prehistoric Times to the End of the Eighteenth Century. By George Clinch.
ENGLISH MONASTIC LIFE. By the Right Rev. Abbot Gasquet. *Fourth Edition.*
ENGLISH SEALS. By J. Harvey Bloom.
FOLK-LORE AS AN HISTORICAL SCIENCE. By G. L. Gomme.

GILDS AND COMPANIES OF LONDON, THE. By George Unwin.
MANOR AND MANORIAL RECORDS, THE. By Nathaniel J. Hone.
MEDIÆVAL HOSPITALS OF ENGLAND, THE. By Rotha Mary Clay.
OLD SERVICE BOOKS OF THE ENGLISH CHURCH. By Christopher Wordsworth, M.A., and Henry Littlehales.
PARISH LIFE IN MEDIÆVAL ENGLAND. By the Right Rev. Abbott Gasquet. *Second Edition.*
*PARISH REGISTERS OF ENGLAND, THE. By J. C. Cox.
REMAINS OF THE PREHISTORIC AGE IN ENGLAND. By B. C. A. Windle. *Second Edition.*
ROYAL FORESTS OF ENGLAND, THE. By J. C. Cox, LL.D.
SHRINES OF BRITISH SAINTS. By J. C. Wall.

The Arden Shakespeare.

Demy 8vo. 2s. 6d. net each volume.

An edition of Shakespeare in single Plays. Edited with a full Introduction, Textual Notes, and a Commentary at the foot of the page.

ALL'S WELL THAT ENDS WELL.
ANTONY AND CLEOPATRA.
CYMBELINE.
COMEDY OF ERRORS, THE.
HAMLET. *Second Edition.*
JULIUS CAESAR.
KING HENRY V.
KING HENRY VI. PT. I.
KING HENRY VI. PT. II.
KING HENRY VI. PT. III.
KING LEAR.
KING RICHARD III.
LIFE AND DEATH OF KING JOHN, THE.
LOVE'S LABOUR'S LOST.
MACBETH.

MEASURE FOR MEASURE.
MERCHANT OF VENICE, THE.
MERRY WIVES OF WINDSOR, THE.
MIDSUMMER NIGHT'S DREAM, A.
OTHELLO.
PERICLES.
ROMEO AND JULIET.
TAMING OF THE SHREW, THE.
TEMPEST, THE.
TIMON OF ATHENS.
TITUS ANDRONICUS.
TROILUS AND CRESSIDA.
TWO GENTLEMEN OF VERONA, THE.
TWELFTH NIGHT.

Classics of Art.

Edited by Dr. J. H. W. LAING.

With numerous Illustrations. Wide Royal 8vo. Gilt top.

THE ART OF THE GREEKS. By H. B. Walters. 12s. 6d. net.
FLORENTINE SCULPTORS OF THE RENAISSANCE. Wilhelm Bode, Ph.D. Translated by Jessie Haynes. 12s. 6d. net.
*GEORGE ROMNEY. By Arthur B. Chamberlain. 12s. 6d. net.
GHIRLANDAIO. Gerald S. Davies. *Second Edition*. 10s. 6d.

MICHELANGELO. By Gerald S. Davies. 12s. 6d. net.
RUBENS. By Edward Dillon, M.A. 25s. net.
RAPHAEL. By A. P. Oppé. 12s. 6d. net.
*TITIAN. By Charles Ricketts. 12s. 6d. net.
*TURNER'S SKETCHES AND DRAWINGS. By A. J. FINBERG. 12s. 6d. net.
VELAZQUEZ. By A. de Beruete. 10s. 6d. net.

The "Complete" Series.

Fully Illustrated. Demy 8vo.

THE COMPLETE COOK. By Lilian Whitling. 7s. 6d. net.
THE COMPLETE CRICKETER. By Albert E. Knight. 7s. 6d. net.
THE COMPLETE FOXHUNTER. By Charles Richardson. 12s. 6d. net. *Second Edition*.
THE COMPLETE GOLFER. By Harry Vardon. 10s. 6d. net. *Tenth Edition*.
THE COMPLETE HOCKEY-PLAYER. By Eustace E. White. 5s. net. *Second Edition*.
THE COMPLETE LAWN TENNIS PLAYER. By A. Wallace Myers. 10s. 6d. net. *Second Edition*.

THE COMPLETE MOTORIST. By Filson Young. 12s. 6d. net. *New Edition (Seventh)*.
THE COMPLETE MOUNTAINEER. By G. D. Abraham. 15s. net. *Second Edition*.
THE COMPLETE OARSMAN. By R. C. Lehmann, M.P. 10s. 6d. net.
THE COMPLETE PHOTOGRAPHER. By R. Child Bayley. 10s. 6d. net. *Fourth Edition*.
THE COMPLETE RUGBY FOOTBALLER, ON THE NEW ZEALAND SYSTEM. By D. Gallaher and W. J. Stead. 10s. 6d. net. *Second Edition*.
THE COMPLETE SHOT. By G. T. Teasdale Buckell. 12s. 6d. net. *Third Edition*.

The Connoisseur's Library.

With numerous Illustrations. Wide Royal 8vo. 25s. net.

ENGLISH FURNITURE. By F. S. Robinson. *Second Edition*.
ENGLISH COLOURED BOOKS. By Martin Hardie.
EUROPEAN ENAMELS. By Henry H. Cunynghame, C.B.
GLASS. By Edward Dillon.
GOLDSMITHS' AND SILVERSMITHS' WORK. By Nelson Dawson. *Second Edition*.

*ILLUMINATED MANUSCRIPTS. By J. A. Herbert.
IVORIES. By A. Maskell.
JEWELLERY. By H. Clifford Smith. *Second Edition*.
MEZZOTINTS. By Cyril Davenport.
MINIATURES. By Dudley Heath.
PORCELAIN. By Edward Dillon.
SEALS. By Walter de Gray Birch.

Handbooks of English Church History.

Edited by J. H. BURN, B.D. *Crown 8vo. 2s. 6d. net.*

THE FOUNDATIONS OF THE ENGLISH CHURCH. By J. H. Maude.
THE SAXON CHURCH AND THE NORMAN CONQUEST. By C. T. Cruttwell.
THE MEDIÆVAL CHURCH AND THE PAPACY. By A. C. Jennings.

THE REFORMATION PERIOD. By Henry Gee.
THE STRUGGLE WITH PURITANISM. By Bruce Blaxland.
THE CHURCH OF ENGLAND IN THE EIGHTEENTH CENTURY. By Alfred Plummer.

The Illustrated Pocket Library of Plain and Coloured Books.

Fcap. 8vo. 3s. 6d. net each volume.

WITH COLOURED ILLUSTRATIONS.

OLD COLOURED BOOKS. By George Paston. *2s. net.*
THE LIFE AND DEATH OF JOHN MYTTON, ESQ. By Nimrod. *Fifth Edition.*
THE LIFE OF A SPORTSMAN. By Nimrod.
HANDLEY CROSS. By R. S. Surtees. *Third Edition.*
MR. SPONGE'S SPORTING TOUR. By R. S. Surtees.
JORROCKS' JAUNTS AND JOLLITIES. By R. S. Surtees. *Second Edition.*
ASK MAMMA. By R. S. Surtees.
THE ANALYSIS OF THE HUNTING FIELD. By R. S. Surtees.
THE TOUR OF DR. SYNTAX IN SEARCH OF THE PICTURESQUE. By William Combe.
THE TOUR OF DR. SYNTAX IN SEARCH OF CONSOLATION. By William Combe.
THE THIRD TOUR OF DR. SYNTAX IN SEARCH OF A WIFE. By William Combe.
THE HISTORY OF JOHNNY QUAE GENUS. By the Author of 'The Three Tours.'
THE ENGLISH DANCE OF DEATH, from the Designs of T. Rowlandson, with Metrical Illustrations by the Author of 'Doctor Syntax.' *Two Volumes.*

THE DANCE OF LIFE: A Poem. By the Author of 'Dr. Syntax.'
LIFE IN LONDON. By Pierce Egan.
REAL LIFE IN LONDON. By an Amateur (Pierce Egan). *Two Volumes.*
THE LIFE OF AN ACTOR. By Pierce Egan.
THE VICAR OF WAKEFIELD. By Oliver Goldsmith.
THE MILITARY ADVENTURES OF JOHNNY NEWCOMBE. By an Officer.
THE NATIONAL SPORTS OF GREAT BRITAIN. With Descriptions and 50 Coloured Plates by Henry Alken.
THE ADVENTURES OF A POST CAPTAIN. By a Naval Officer.
GAMONIA. By Lawrence Rawstone, Esq.
AN ACADEMY FOR GROWN HORSEMEN. By Geoffrey Gambado, Esq.
REAL LIFE IN IRELAND. By a Real Paddy.
THE ADVENTURES OF JOHNNY NEWCOMBE IN THE NAVY. By Alfred Burton.
THE OLD ENGLISH SQUIRE. By John Careless, Esq.
THE ENGLISH SPY. By Bernard Blackmantle. *Two Volumes. 7s. net.*

WITH PLAIN ILLUSTRATIONS.

THE GRAVE: A Poem. By Robert Blair.
ILLUSTRATIONS OF THE BOOK OF JOB. Invented and engraved by William Blake.
WINDSOR CASTLE. By W. Harrison Ainsworth.
THE TOWER OF LONDON. By W. Harrison Ainsworth.

FRANK FAIRLEGH. By F. E. Smedley.
HANDY ANDY. By Samuel Lover.
THE COMPLEAT ANGLER. By Izaak Walton and Charles Cotton.
THE PICKWICK PAPERS. By Charles Dickens.

Leaders of Religion.

Edited by H. C. BEECHING, M.A., Canon of Westminster. *With Portraits.*

Crown 8vo. 2s. net.

CARDINAL NEWMAN. By R. H. Hutton.
JOHN WESLEY. By J. H. Overton, M.A.
BISHOP WILBERFORCE. By G. W. Daniell, M.A.
CARDINAL MANNING. By A. W. Hutton, M.A.
CHARLES SIMEON. By H. C. G. Moule, D.D.
JOHN KNOX. By F. MacCunn. *Second Edition.*
JOHN HOWE. By R. F. Horton, D.D.
THOMAS KEN. By F. A. Clarke, M.A.
GEORGE FOX, THE QUAKER. By T. Hodgkin, D.C.L. *Third Edition.*

JOHN KEBLE. By Walter Lock, D.D.
THOMAS CHALMERS. By Mrs. Oliphant.
LANCELOT ANDREWES. By R. L. Ottley, D.D. *Second Edition.*
AUGUSTINE OF CANTERBURY. By E. L. Cutts, D.D.
WILLIAM LAUD. By W. H. Hutton, M.A. *Third Edition.*
JOHN DONNE. By Augustus Jessop, D.D.
THOMAS CRANMER. By A. J. Mason, D.D.
BISHOP LATIMER. By R. M. Carlyle and A. J. Carlyle, M.A.
BISHOP BUTLER. By W. A. Spooner, M.A.

The Library of Devotion.

With Introductions and (where necessary) Notes.

Small Pott 8vo, cloth, 2s. ; leather, 2s. 6d. net.

THE CONFESSIONS OF ST. AUGUSTINE. *Seventh Edition.*
THE IMITATION OF CHRIST. *Fifth Edition.*
THE CHRISTIAN YEAR. *Fourth Edition.*
LYRA INNOCENTIUM. *Second Edition.*
THE TEMPLE. *Second Edition.*
A BOOK OF DEVOTIONS. *Second Edition.*
A SERIOUS CALL TO A DEVOUT AND HOLY LIFE. *Fourth Edition.*
A GUIDE TO ETERNITY.
THE INNER WAY. *Second Edition.*
ON THE LOVE OF GOD.
THE PSALMS OF DAVID.
LYRA APOSTOLICA.
THE SONG OF SONGS.
THE THOUGHTS OF PASCAL. *Second Edition.*
A MANUAL OF CONSOLATION FROM THE SAINTS AND FATHERS.
DEVOTIONS FROM THE APOCRYPHA.
THE SPIRITUAL COMBAT.
THE DEVOTIONS OF ST. ANSELM.
BISHOP WILSON'S SACRA PRIVATA.

GRACE ABOUNDING TO THE CHIEF OF SINNERS.
LYRA SACRA: A Book of Sacred Verse. *Second Edition.*
A DAY BOOK FROM THE SAINTS AND FATHERS.
A LITTLE BOOK OF HEAVENLY WISDOM. A Selection from the English Mystics.
LIGHT, LIFE, and LOVE. A Selection from the German Mystics.
AN INTRODUCTION TO THE DEVOUT LIFE.
THE LITTLE FLOWERS OF THE GLORIOUS MESSER ST. FRANCIS AND OF HIS FRIARS.
DEATH AND IMMORTALITY.
THE SPIRITUAL GUIDE.
DEVOTIONS FOR EVERY DAY IN THE WEEK AND THE GREAT FESTIVALS.
PRECES PRIVATÆ.
HORÆ MYSTICÆ: A Day Book from the Writings of Mystics of Many Nations.

GENERAL LITERATURE 19

Little Books on Art.

With many Illustrations. Demy 16mo. 2s. 6d. net.

Each volume consists of about 200 pages, and contains from 30 to 40 Illustrations, including a Frontispiece in Photogravure.

ALBRECHT DURER. J. Allen.
ARTS OF JAPAN, THE. E. Dillon.
BOOKPLATES. E. Almack.
BOTTICELLI. Mary L. Bloomer.
BURNE-JONES. F. de Lisle.
*CHRISTIAN SYMBOLISM. Mrs. H. Jenner.
CHRIST IN ART. Mrs. H. Jenner.
CLAUDE. E. Dillon.
CONSTABLE. H. W. Tompkins.
COROT. A. Pollard and E. Birnstingl.
ENAMELS. Mrs. N. Dawson.
FREDERIC LEIGHTON. A. Corkran.
GEORGE ROMNEY. G. Paston.
GREEK ART. H. B. Walters.
GREUZE AND BOUCHER. E. F. Pollard.
HOLBEIN. Mrs. G. Fortescue.
ILLUMINATED MANUSCRIPTS. J. W. Bradley.
JEWELLERY. C. Davenport.
JOHN HOPPNER. H. P. K. Skipton.
SIR JOSHUA REYNOLDS. J. Sime.
MILLET. N. Peacock.
MINIATURES. C. Davenport.
OUR LADY IN ART. Mrs. H. Jenner.
RAPHAEL. A. R. Dryhurst. *Second Edition*.
REMBRANDT. Mrs. E. A. Sharp.
TURNER. F. Tyrrell-Gill.
VANDYCK. M. G. Smallwood.
VELASQUEZ. W. Wilberforce and A. R. Gilbert.
WATTS. R. E. D. Sketchley.

The Little Galleries.

Demy 16mo. 2s. 6d. net.

Each volume contains 20 plates in Photogravure, together with a short outline of the life and work of the master to whom the book is devoted.

A LITTLE GALLERY OF REYNOLDS.
A LITTLE GALLERY OF ROMNEY.
A LITTLE GALLERY OF HOPPNER.
A LITTLE GALLERY OF MILLAIS.
A LITTLE GALLERY OF ENGLISH POETS.

The Little Guides.

With many Illustrations by E. H. NEW and other artists, and from photographs.

Small Pott 8vo, cloth, 2s. 6d. net; leather, 3s. 6d. net.

The main features of these Guides are (1) a handy and charming form; (2) illustrations from photographs and by well-known artists; (3) good plans and maps; (4) an adequate but compact presentation of everything that is interesting in the natural features, history, archæology, and architecture of the town or district treated.

CAMBRIDGE AND ITS COLLEGES. A. H. Thompson. *Second Edition*.
ENGLISH LAKES, THE. F. G. Brabant.
ISLE OF WIGHT, THE. G. Clinch.
MALVERN COUNTRY, THE. B. C. A. Windle.
NORTH WALES. A. T. Story.
OXFORD AND ITS COLLEGES. J. Wells. *Eighth Edition*.
SHAKESPEARE'S COUNTRY. B. C. A. Windle. *Third Edition*.
ST. PAUL'S CATHEDRAL. G. Clinch.
WESTMINSTER ABBEY. G. E. Troutbeck. *Second Edition*.

BUCKINGHAMSHIRE. E. S. Roscoe.
CHESHIRE. W. M. Gallichan.

THE LITTLE GUIDES—*continued.*

CORNWALL. A. L. Salmon.
DERBYSHIRE. J. C. Cox.
DEVON. S. Baring-Gould.
DORSET. F. R. Heath. *Second Edition.*
ESSEX. J. C. Cox.
HAMPSHIRE. J. C. Cox.
HERTFORDSHIRE. H. W. Tompkins.
KENT. G. Clinch.
KERRY. C. P. Crane.
MIDDLESEX. J. B. Firth.
MONMOUTHSHIRE. G. W. Wade and J. H. Wade.
NORFOLK. W. A. Dutt.
NORTHAMPTONSHIRE. W. Dry.
*NORTHUMBERLAND. J. E. Morris.
NOTTINGHAMSHIRE. L. Guilford.

OXFORDSHIRE. F. G. Brabant.
SOMERSET. G. W. and J. H. Wade.
*STAFFORDSHIRE. C. E. Masefield.
SUFFOLK. W. A. Dutt.
SURREY. F. A. H. Lambert.
SUSSEX. F. G. Brabant. *Second Edition.*
*WILTSHIRE. F. R. Heath.
YORKSHIRE, THE EAST RIDING. J. E. Morris.
YORKSHIRE, THE NORTH RIDING. J. E. Morris.

BRITTANY. S. Baring-Gould.
NORMANDY. C. Scudamore.
ROME. C. G. Ellaby.
SICILY. F. H. Jackson.

The Little Library.

With Introductions, Notes, and Photogravure Frontispieces.

Small Pott 8vo. Each Volume, cloth, 1s. 6d. net; leather, 2s. 6d. net.

Anon. A LITTLE BOOK OF ENGLISH LYRICS. *Second Edition.*

Austen (Jane). PRIDE AND PREJUDICE. *Two Volumes.*
NORTHANGER ABBEY.

Bacon (Francis). THE ESSAYS OF LORD BACON.

Barham (R. H.). THE INGOLDSBY LEGENDS. *Two Volumes.*

Barnet (Mrs. P. A.). A LITTLE BOOK OF ENGLISH PROSE.

Beckford (William). THE HISTORY OF THE CALIPH VATHEK.

Blake (William). SELECTIONS FROM WILLIAM BLAKE.

Borrow (George). LAVENGRO. *Two Volumes.*
THE ROMANY RYE.

Browning (Robert). SELECTIONS FROM THE EARLY POEMS OF ROBERT BROWNING.

Canning (George). SELECTIONS FROM THE ANTI-JACOBIN: with GEORGE CANNING'S additional Poems.

Cowley (Abraham). THE ESSAYS OF ABRAHAM COWLEY.

Crabbe (George). SELECTIONS FROM GEORGE CRABBE.

Craik (Mrs.). JOHN HALIFAX, GENTLEMAN. *Two Volumes.*

Crashaw (Richard). THE ENGLISH POEMS OF RICHARD CRASHAW.

Dante (Alighieri). THE INFERNO OF DANTE. Translated by H. F. CARY.
THE PURGATORIO OF DANTE. Translated by H. F. CARY.
THE PARADISO OF DANTE. Translated by H. F. CARY.

Darley (George). SELECTIONS FROM THE POEMS OF GEORGE DARLEY.

Deane (A. C.). A LITTLE BOOK OF LIGHT VERSE.

Dickens (Charles). CHRISTMAS BOOKS. *Two Volumes.*

Ferrier (Susan). MARRIAGE. *Two Volumes.*
THE INHERITANCE. *Two Volumes.*

Gaskell (Mrs.). CRANFORD.

Hawthorne (Nathaniel). THE SCARLET LETTER.

Henderson (T. F.). A LITTLE BOOK OF SCOTTISH VERSE.

Keats (John). POEMS.

Kinglake (A. W.). EOTHEN. *Second Edition.*

Lamb (Charles). ELIA, AND THE LAST ESSAYS OF ELIA.

Locker (F.). LONDON LYRICS.

Longfellow (H. W.). SELECTIONS FROM LONGFELLOW.

General Literature 21

The Little Library—*continued.*

Marvell (Andrew). THE POEMS OF ANDREW MARVELL.
Milton (John). THE MINOR POEMS OF JOHN MILTON.
Moir (D. M.). MANSIE WAUCH.
Nichols (J. B. B.). A LITTLE BOOK OF ENGLISH SONNETS.
Rochefoucauld (La). THE MAXIMS OF LA ROCHEFOUCAULD.
Smith (Horace and James). REJECTED ADDRESSES.
Sterne (Laurence). A SENTIMENTAL JOURNEY.
Tennyson (Alfred, Lord). THE EARLY POEMS OF ALFRED, LORD TENNYSON.
IN MEMORIAM.
THE PRINCESS.

Maud.
Thackeray (W. M.). VANITY FAIR. *Three Volumes.*
PENDENNIS. *Three Volumes.*
ESMOND.
CHRISTMAS BOOKS.
Vaughan (Henry). THE POEMS OF HENRY VAUGHAN.
Walton (Izaak). THE COMPLEAT ANGLER.
Waterhouse (Elizabeth). A LITTLE BOOK OF LIFE AND DEATH. *Twelfth Edition.*
Wordsworth (W.). SELECTIONS FROM WORDSWORTH.
Wordsworth (W.) and **Coleridge (S. T.)** LYRICAL BALLADS.

The Little Quarto Shakespeare.

Edited by W. J. CRAIG. With Introductions and Notes.

Pott 16mo. In 40 Volumes. Leather, price 1s. net each volume.

Mahogany Revolving Book Case. 10s. net.

Miniature Library.

EUPHRANOR: A Dialogue on Youth. By Edward FitzGerald. *Demy 32mo. Leather, 2s. net.*
THE LIFE OF EDWARD, LORD HERBERT OF CHERBURY. Written by himself. *Demy 32mo. Leather, 2s. net.*

POLONIUS: or Wise Saws and Modern Instances. By Edward FitzGerald. *Demy 32mo. Leather, 2s. net.*
THE RUBÁIYÁT OF OMAR KHAYYÁM. By Edward FitzGerald. *Fourth Edition. Leather, 1s. net.*

The New Library of Medicine.

Edited by C. W. SALEEBY, M.D.; F.R.S.Edin. *Demy 8vo.*

CARE OF THE BODY, THE. By F. Cavanagh. *Second Edition.* 7s. 6d. net.
CHILDREN OF THE NATION, THE. By the Right Hon. Sir John Gorst. *Second Edition.* 7s. 6d. net.
CONTROL OF A SCOURGE, THE; or, How Cancer is Curable. By Chas. P. Childe. 7s. 6d. net.
DISEASES OF OCCUPATION. By Sir Thomas Oliver. 10s. 6d. net.
DRINK PROBLEM, THE, in its Medico-Sociological Aspects. Edited by T. N. Kelynack. 7s. 6d. net.
DRUGS AND THE DRUG HABIT. By H. Sainsbury.

FUNCTIONAL NERVE DISEASES. By A. T. Schofield. 7s. 6d. net.
*HEREDITY, THE LAWS OF. By Archdall Reid. 21s. net.
HYGIENE OF MIND, THE. By T. S. Clouston. *Fifth Edition.* 7s. 6d. net.
INFANT MORTALITY. By George Newman. 7s. 6d. net.
PREVENTION OF TUBERCULOSIS (CONSUMPTION), THE. By Arthur Newsholme. 10s. 6d. net.
AIR AND HEALTH. By Ronald C. Macfie. 7s. 6d. net. *Second Edition.*

The New Library of Music.

Edited by ERNEST NEWMAN. *Illustrated. Demy 8vo. 7s. 6d. net.*

HUGO WOLF. By Ernest Newman. Illustrated.

HANDEL. By R. A. Streatfeild. Illustrated. *Second Edition.*

Oxford Biographies.

Illustrated. Fcap. 8vo. Each volume, cloth, 2s. 6d. net; leather, 3s. 6d. net.

DANTE ALIGHIERI. By Paget Tonybee, M.A., D. Litt. *Third Edition.*
GIROLAMO SAVONAROLA By E. L. S. Horsburgh, M.A. *Second Edition.*
JOHN HOWARD. By E. C. S. Gibson, D.D., Bishop of Gloucester.
ALFRED TENNYSON. By A. C. Benson, M.A. *Second Edition.*
SIR WALTER RALEIGH. By I. A. Taylor.
ERASMUS. By E. F. H. Capey.

THE YOUNG PRETENDER. By C. S. Terry.
ROBERT BURNS. By T. F. Henderson.
CHATHAM. By A. S. M'Dowall.
FRANCIS OF ASSISI. By Anna M. Stoddart.
CANNING. By W. Alison Phillips.
BEACONSFIELD. By Walter Sichel.
JOHANN WOLFGANG GOETHE. By H. G. Atkins.
FRANÇOIS FENELON. By Viscount St. Cyres.

Romantic History

Edited by MARTIN HUME, M.A. *Illustrated. Demy 8vo.*

A series of attractive volumes in which the periods and personalities selected are such as afford romantic human interest, in addition to their historical importance.

THE FIRST GOVERNESS OF THE NETHERLANDS, MARGARET OF AUSTRIA. Eleanor E. Tremayne. 10s. 6d. *net.*
TWO ENGLISH QUEENS AND PHILIP. Martin Hume, M.A. 15s. *net.*
THE NINE DAYS' QUEEN. Richard Davey. With a Preface by Martin Hume, M.A. 10s. 6d. *net.*

Handbooks of Theology.

THE DOCTRINE OF THE INCARNATION. By R. L. Ottley, D.D. *Fourth Edition revised. Demy 8vo.* 12s. 6d.
A HISTORY OF EARLY CHRISTIAN DOCTRINE. By J. F. Bethune-Baker, M.A. *Demy 8vo.* 10s. 6d.
AN INTRODUCTION TO THE HISTORY OF RELIGION. By F. B. Jevons. M.A. Litt. D. *Fourth Edition. Demy 8vo.* 10s. 6d.

AN INTRODUCTION TO THE HISTORY OF THE CREEDS. By A. E. Burn, D.D. *Demy 8vo.* 10s. 6d.
THE PHILOSOPHY OF RELIGION IN ENGLAND AND AMERICA. By Alfred Caldecott, D.D. *Demy 8vo.* 10s. 6d.
THE XXXIX. ARTICLES OF THE CHURCH OF ENGLAND. Edited by E. C. S. Gibson, D.D. *Sixth Edition. Demy 8vo.* 12s. 6d.

FICTION 23

The Westminster Commentaries.

General Editor, WALTER LOCK, D.D., Warden of Keble College.

Dean Ireland's Professor of Exegesis in the University of Oxford.

THE ACTS OF THE APOSTLES. Edited by R. B. Rackham, M.A. *Demy 8vo. Fourth Edition.* 10s. 6d.

THE FIRST EPISTLE OF PAUL THE APOSTLE TO THE CORINTHIANS. Edited by H. L. Goudge, M.A. *Second Ed. Demy 8vo.* 6s.

THE BOOK OF EXODUS. Edited by A. H. M'Neile, B.D. With a Map and 3 Plans. *Demy 8vo.* 10s. 6d.

THE BOOK OF EZEKIEL. Edited by H. A. Redpath, M.A., D.Litt. *Demy 8vo.* 10s. 6d.

THE BOOK OF GENESIS. Edited with Introduction and Notes by S. R. Driver, D.D. *Seventh Edition. Demy 8vo.* 10s. 6d.

ADDITIONS AND CORRECTIONS IN THE SEVENTH EDITION OF THE BOOK OF GENESIS. By S. R. Driver, D.D. *Demy 8vo.* 1s.

THE BOOK OF JOB. Edited by E. C. S. Gibson, D.D. *Second Edition. Demy 8vo.* 6s.

THE EPISTLE OF ST. JAMES. Edited with Introduction and Notes by R. J. Knowling, D.D. *Demy 8vo.* 6s.

PART III.—A SELECTION OF WORKS OF FICTION

Albanesi (E. Maria). SUSANNAH AND ONE OTHER. *Fourth Edition. Cr. 8vo.* 6s.
LOVE AND LOUISA. *Second Edition. Cr. 8vo.* 6s.
THE BROWN EYES OF MARY. *Third Edition. Cr. 8vo.* 6s.
I KNOW A MAIDEN. *Third Edition. Cr. 8vo.* 6s.
THE INVINCIBLE AMELIA: OR, THE POLITE ADVENTURESS. *Third Edition. Cr. 8vo.* 3s. 6d.
*THE GLAD HEART. *Cr. 8vo.* 6s.

Allerton (Mark). SUCH AND SUCH THINGS. *Cr. 8vo.* 6s.

Annesley (Maude). THIS DAY'S MADNESS. *Second Edition. Cr. 8vo.* 6s.

Bagot (Richard). A ROMAN MYSTERY. *Third Edition. Cr. 8vo.* 6s.
THE PASSPORT. *Fourth Edition. Cr. 8vo.* 6s.
TEMPTATION. *Fifth Edition. Cr. 8vo.* 6s.
ANTHONY CUTHBERT. *Fourth Edition. Cr. 8vo.* 6s.
LOVE'S PROXY. *Cr. 8vo.* 6s.
DONNA DIANA. *Second Edition. Cr. 8vo.* 6s.
CASTING OF NETS. *Twelfth Edition. Cr. 8vo.* 6s.

Bailey (H. C.). STORM AND TREASURE. *Cr. 8vo.* 6s.

Ball (Oona H.) (Barbara Burke). THEIR OXFORD YEAR. Illustrated. *Cr. 8vo.* 6s.
BARBARA GOES TO OXFORD. Illustrated. *Third Edition. Cr. 8vo.* 6s.

Baring-Gould (S.). ARMINELL. *Fifth Edition. Cr. 8vo.* 6s.
URITH. *Fifth Edition. Cr. 8vo.* 6s.
IN THE ROAR OF THE SEA. *Seventh Edition. Cr. 8vo.* 6s.
MARGERY OF QUETHER. *Third Edition. Cr. 8vo.* 6s.
THE QUEEN OF LOVE. *Fifth Edition. Cr. 8vo.* 6s.
JACQUETTA. *Third Edition. Cr. 8vo.* 6s.
KITTY ALONE. *Fifth Edition. Cr. 8vo.* 6s.
NOÉMI. Illustrated. *Fourth Edition. Cr. 8vo.* 6s.
THE BROOM-SQUIRE. Illustrated. *Fifth Edition. Cr. 8vo.* 6s.
DARTMOOR IDYLLS. *Cr. 8vo.* 6s.
GUAVAS THE TINNER. Illustrated. *Second Edition. Cr. 8vo.* 6s.
BLADYS OF THE STEWPONEY. Illustrated. *Second Edition. Cr. 8vo.* 6s.
PABO THE PRIEST. *Cr. 8vo.* 6s.
WINEFRED. Illustrated. *Second Edition. Cr. 8vo.* 6s.
ROYAL GEORGIE. Illustrated. *Cr. 8vo.* 6s.
CHRIS OF ALL SORTS. *Cr. 8vo.* 6s.
IN DEWISLAND. *Second Edition. Cr. 8vo.* 6s.
THE FROBISHERS. *Cr. 8vo.* 6s.
DOMITIA. Illustrated. *Second Edition. Cr. 8vo.* 6s.
MRS. CURGENVEN OF CURGENVEN. *Cr. 8vo.* 6s.

Barr (Robert). IN THE MIDST OF ALARMS. *Third Edition. Cr. 8vo.* 6s.
THE COUNTESS TEKLA. *Fifth Edition. Cr. 8vo.* 6s.

THE MUTABLE MANY. *Third Edition.* Cr. 8vo. 6s.

Begbie (Harold). THE CURIOUS AND DIVERTING ADVENTURES OF SIR JOHN SPARROW; OR, THE PROGRESS OF AN OPEN MIND. *Second Edition.* Cr. 8vo. 6s.

Belloc (H.). EMMANUEL BURDEN, MERCHANT. Illustrated. *Second Edition.* Cr. 8vo. 6s.
A CHANGE IN THE CABINET. *Third Edition.* Cr. 8vo. 6s.

Benson (E. F.). DODO: A DETAIL OF THE DAY. *Fifteenth Edition.* Cr. 8vo. 6s.

Birmingham (George A.). THE BAD TIMES. *Second Edition.* Cr. 8vo. 6s.
SPANISH GOLD. *Fourth Edition.* Cr. 8vo. 6s.
THE SEARCH PARTY. *Fourth Edition.* Cr. 8vo. 6s.

Bowen (Marjorie). I WILL MAINTAIN. Cr. 8vo. 6s.

Bretherton (Ralph Harold). AN HONEST MAN. *Second Edition.* Cr. 8vo. 6s.

Capes (Bernard). WHY DID HE DO IT? *Second Edition.* Cr. 8vo. 6s.

Castle (Agnes and Egerton). FLOWER O' THE ORANGE, and Other Tales. *Third Edition.* Cr. 8vo. 6s.

Clifford (Mrs. W. K.). THE GETTING WELL OF DOROTHY. Illustrated. *Second Edition.* Cr. 8vo. 3s. 6d.

Conrad (Joseph). THE SECRET AGENT: A Simple Tale. *Fourth Ed.* Cr. 8vo. 6s.
A SET OF SIX. *Fourth Edition.* Cr. 8vo. 6s.

Corelli (Marie). A ROMANCE OF TWO WORLDS. *Twenty-Ninth Ed.* Cr. 8vo. 6s.
VENDETTA. *Twenty-Seventh Edition.* Cr. 8vo. 6s.
THELMA. *Fortieth Ed.* Cr. 8vo. 6s.
ARDATH: THE STORY OF A DEAD SELF. *Nineteenth Edition.* Cr. 8vo. 6s.
THE SOUL OF LILITH. *Sixteenth Edition.* Cr. 8vo. 6s.
WORMWOOD. *Seventeenth Ed.* Cr. 8vo. 6s.
BARABBAS: A DREAM OF THE WORLD'S TRAGEDY. *Forty-Fourth Edition.* Cr. 8vo. 6s.
THE SORROWS OF SATAN. *Fifty-Fifth Edition.* Cr. 8vo. 6s.
THE MASTER CHRISTIAN. *Twelfth Edition.* 177th Thousand. Cr. 8vo. 6s.
TEMPORAL POWER: A STUDY IN SUPREMACY. *Second Edition.* 150th Thousand. Cr. 8vo. 6s.
GOD'S GOOD MAN; A SIMPLE LOVE STORY. *Thirteenth Edition.* 150th Thousand. Cr. 8vo. 6s.
HOLY ORDERS: THE TRAGEDY OF A QUIET LIFE. *Second Edition.* 120th Thousand. Crown 8vo. 6s.
THE MIGHTY ATOM. *Twenty-eighth Edition.* Cr. 8vo. 6s.
BOY: a Sketch. *Eleventh Edition.* Cr. 8vo. 6s.
CAMEOS. *Thirteenth Edition.* Cr. 8vo. 6s.

Cotes (Mrs. Everard). See Duncan (Sara Jeannette).

Crockett (S. R.). LOCHINVAR. Illustrated. *Third Edition.* Cr. 8vo. 6s.
THE STANDARD BEARER. *Second Edition.* Cr. 8vo. 6s.

Croker (Mrs. B. M.). THE OLD CANTONMENT. Cr. 8vo. 6s.
JOHANNA. *Second Edition.* Cr. 8vo. 6s.
THE HAPPY VALLEY. *Fourth Edition.* Cr. 8vo. 6s.
A NINE DAYS' WONDER. *Third Edition.* Cr. 8vo. 6s.
PEGGY OF THE BARTONS. *Seventh Edition.* Cr. 8vo. 6s.
ANGEL. *Fifth Edition.* Cr. 8vo. 6s.
A STATE SECRET. *Third Edition.* Cr. 8vo. 3s. 6d.
KATHERINE THE ARROGANT. *Sixth Edition.* Cr. 8vo. 6s.

Cuthell (Edith E.). ONLY A GUARDROOM DOG. Illustrated. Cr. 8vo. 3s. 6d.

Dawson (Warrington). THE SCAR. *Second Edition.* Cr. 8vo. 6s.
THE SCOURGE. Cr. 8vo. 6s.

Douglas (Theo.). COUSIN HUGH. Cr. 8vo. 6s.

Doyle (A. Conan). ROUND THE RED LAMP. *Eleventh Edition.* Cr. 8vo. 6s.

Duncan (Sara Jeannette) (Mrs. Everard Cotes).
A VOYAGE OF CONSOLATION. Illustrated. *Third Edition.* Cr. 8vo. 6s.
COUSIN CINDERELLA. *Second Edition.* Cr. 8vo. 6s.
THE BURNT OFFERING. *Second Edition.* Cr. 8vo. 6s.

*****Elliott (Robert).** THE IMMORTAL CHARLATAN. *Crown 8vo.* 6s.

Fenn (G. Manville). SYD BELTON; or, The Boy who would not go to Sea. Illustrated. *Second Ed.* Cr. 8vo. 3s. 6d.

Findlater (J. H.). THE GREEN GRAVES OF BALGOWRIE. *Fifth Edition.* Cr. 8vo. 6s.
THE LADDER TO THE STARS. *Second Edition.* Cr. 8vo. 6s.

Findlater (Mary). A NARROW WAY. *Third Edition.* Cr. 8vo. 6s.
OVER THE HILLS. *Second Edition.* Cr. 8vo. 6s.
THE ROSE OF JOY. *Third Edition.* Cr. 8vo. 6s.
A BLIND BIRD'S NEST. Illustrated. *Second Edition.* Cr. 8vo. 6s.

Francis (M. E.). (Mrs. Francis Blundell). STEPPING WESTWARD. *Second Edition.* Cr. 8vo. 6s.

Fiction

MARGERY O' THE MILL. *Third Edition. Cr. 8vo. 6s.*
HARDY-ON-THE-HILL. *Third Edition. Cr. 8vo. 6s.*
GALATEA OF THE WHEATFIELD. *Second Edition. Cr. 8vo. 6s.*

Fraser (Mrs. Hugh). THE SLAKING OF THE SWORD. *Second Edition. Cr. 8vo. 6s.*
GIANNELLA. *Second Edition. Cr. 8vo. 6s.*
IN THE SHADOW OF THE LORD. *Third Edition. Cr. 8vo. 6s.*

Fry (B. and C. B.). A MOTHER'S SON. *Fifth Edition. Cr. 8vo. 6s.*

Gerard (Louise). THE GOLDEN CENTIPEDE. *Cr. 8vo. 6s.*

Gibbs (Philip). THE SPIRIT OF REVOLT. *Second Edition. Cr. 8vo. 6s.*

Gissing (George). THE CROWN OF LIFE. *Cr. 8vo. 6s.*

*****Glendon (George).** THE EMPEROR OF THE AIR. Illustrated. *Cr. 8vo. 6s.*

Hamilton (Cosmo). MRS. SKEFFINGTON. *Cr. 8vo. 6s.*

Harraden (Beatrice). IN VARYING MOODS. *Fourteenth Edition. Cr. 8vo. 6s.*
THE SCHOLAR'S DAUGHTER. *Fourth Edition. Cr. 8vo. 6s.*
HILDA STRAFFORD and THE REMITTANCE MAN. *Twelfth Ed. Cr. 8vo. 6s.*
INTERPLAY. *Fifth Edition. Cr. 8vo. 6s.*

Hichens (Robert). THE PROPHET OF BERKELEY SQUARE. *Second Edition. Cr. 8vo. 6s.*
TONGUES OF CONSCIENCE. *Third Edition. Cr. 8vo. 6s.*
FELIX. *Sixth Edition. Cr. 8vo. 6s.*
THE WOMAN WITH THE FAN. *Seventh Edition. Cr. 8vo. 6s.*
BYEWAYS. *Cr. 8vo. 6s.*
THE GARDEN OF ALLAH. *Eighteenth Edition. Cr. 8vo. 6s.*
THE BLACK SPANIEL. *Cr. 8vo. 6s.*
THE CALL OF THE BLOOD. *Seventh Edition. Cr. 8vo. 6s.*
BARBARY SHEEP. *Second Edition. Cr. 8vo. 6s.*

*****Hilliers (Ashton).** THE MASTER-GIRL. Illustrated. *Cr. 8vo. 6s.*

Hope (Anthony). THE GOD IN THE CAR. *Eleventh Edition. Cr. 8vo. 6s.*
A CHANGE OF AIR. *Sixth Edition. Cr. 8vo. 6s.*
A MAN OF MARK. *Sixth Ed. Cr. 8vo. 6s.*
THE CHRONICLES OF COUNT ANTONIO. *Sixth Edition. Cr. 8vo. 6s.*
PHROSO. Illustrated. *Eighth Edition. Cr. 8vo. 6s.*
SIMON DALE. Illustrated. *Eighth Edition. Cr. 8vo. 6s.*
THE KING'S MIRROR. *Fourth Edition. Cr. 8vo. 6s.*

QUISANTE. *Fourth Edition. Cr. 8vo. 6s.*
THE DOLLY DIALOGUES. *Cr. 8vo. 6s.*
A SERVANT OF THE PUBLIC. Illustrated. *Fourth Edition. Cr. 8vo. 6s.*
TALES OF TWO PEOPLE. *Third Edition. Cr. 8vo. 6s.*
THE GREAT MISS DRIVER. *Fourth Edition. Cr. 8vo. 6s.*

Hueffer (Ford Maddox). AN ENGLISH GIRL: A ROMANCE. *Second Edition. Cr. 8vo. 6s.*
MR. APOLLO: A JUST POSSIBLE STORY. *Second Edition. Cr. 8vo. 6s.*

Hutten (Baroness von). THE HALO. *Fifth Edition. Cr. 8vo. 6s.*

Hyne (C. J. Cutcliffe). MR. HORROCKS, PURSER. *Fifth Edition. Cr. 8vo. 6s.*
PRINCE RUPERT, THE BUCCANEER. Illustrated. *Third Edition. Cr. 8vo. 6s.*

Jacobs (W. W.). MANY CARGOES. *Thirty-first Edition. Cr. 8vo. 3s. 6d.*
SEA URCHINS. *Fifteenth Edition. Cr. 8vo. 3s. 6d.*
A MASTER OF CRAFT. Illustrated. *Ninth Edition. Cr. 8vo. 3s. 6d.*
LIGHT FREIGHTS. Illustrated. *Eighth Edition. Cr. 8vo. 3s. 6d.*
THE SKIPPER'S WOOING. *Ninth Edition. Cr. 8vo. 3s. 6d.*
AT SUNWICH PORT. Illustrated. *Tenth Edition. Cr. 8vo. 3s. 6d.*
DIALSTONE LANE. Illustrated. *Seventh Edition. Cr. 8vo. 3s. 6d.*
ODD CRAFT. Illustrated. *Third Edition. Cr. 8vo. 3s. 6d.*
THE LADY OF THE BARGE. Illustrated. *Eighth Edition. Cr. 8vo. 3s. 6d.*
SALTHAVEN. Illustrated. *Second Edition. Cr. 8vo. 3s. 6d.*
SAILORS' KNOTS. Illustrated. *Fourth Edition. Cr. 8vo. 3s. 6d.*

James (Henry). THE SOFT SIDE. *Second Edition. Cr. 8vo. 6s.*
THE BETTER SORT. *Cr. 8vo. 6s.*
THE GOLDEN BOWL. *Third Edition. Cr. 8vo. 6s.*

Le Queux (William). THE HUNCHBACK OF WESTMINSTER. *Third Edition. Cr. 8vo. 6s.*
THE CLOSED BOOK. *Third Edition. Cr. 8vo. 6s.*
THE VALLEY OF THE SHADOW. Illustrated. *Third Edition. Cr. 8vo. 6s.*
BEHIND THE THRONE. *Third Edition. Cr. 8vo. 6s.*
THE CROOKED WAY. *Second Edition. Cr. 8vo. 6s.*

*****Lindsey (William).** THE SEVERED MANTLE. *Cr. 8vo. 6s.*

London (Jack). WHITE FANG. *Seventh Edition. Cr. 8vo. 6s.*

Lubbock (Basil). DEEP SEA WARRIORS. Illustrated. *Third Edition.* Cr. 8vo. 6s.

Lucas (St John). THE FIRST ROUND. Cr. 8vo. 6s.

Lyall (Edna). DERRICK VAUGHAN, NOVELIST. 44*th Thousand.* Cr. 8vo. 3s. 6d.

Maartens (Maarten). THE NEW RELIGION: A MODERN NOVEL. *Third Edition.* Cr. 8vo. 6s.
BROTHERS ALL; MORE STORIES OF DUTCH PEASANT LIFE. *Third Edition.* Cr. 8vo. 6s.
THE PRICE OF LIS DORIS. *Second Edition.* Cr. 8vo. 6s.

M'Carthy (Justin H.). THE DUKE'S MOTTO. *Fourth Edition.* Cr. 8vo. 6s.

Macnaughtan (S.). THE FORTUNE OF CHRISTINA M'NAB. *Fifth Edition.* Cr. 8vo. 6s.

Malet (Lucas). COLONEL ENDERBY'S WIFE. *Fourth Edition.* Cr. 8vo. 6s.
A COUNSEL OF PERFECTION. *Second Edition.* Cr. 8vo. 6s.
THE WAGES OF SIN. *Sixteenth Edition.* Cr. 8vo. 6s.
THE CARISSIMA. *Fifth Ed.* Cr. 8vo. 6s.
THE GATELESS BARRIER. *Fifth Edition.* Cr. 8vo. 6s.
THE HISTORY OF SIR RICHARD CALMADY. *Seventh Edition.* Cr. 8vo. 6s.

Mann (Mrs. M. E.). THE PARISH NURSE. *Fourth Edition.* Cr. 8vo. 6s.
A SHEAF OF CORN. *Second Edition.* Cr. 8vo. 6s.
THE HEART-SMITER. *Second Edition.* Cr. 8vo. 6s.
AVENGING CHILDREN. *Second Edition.* Cr. 8vo. 6s.

Marsh (Richard). THE COWARD BEHIND THE CURTAIN. Cr. 8vo. 6s.
THE SURPRISING HUSBAND. *Second Edition.* Cr. 8vo. 6s.
A ROYAL INDISCRETION. *Second Edition.* Cr. 8vo. 6s.
LIVE MEN'S SHOES. Cr. 8vo. 6s.

Marshall (Archibald). MANY JUNES. *Second Edition.* Cr. 8vo. 6s.
THE SQUIRE'S DAUGHTER. *Third Edition.* Cr. 8vo. 6s.

Mason (A. E. W.). CLEMENTINA. Illustrated. *Third Edition.* Cr. 8vo. 6s.

Maud (Constance). A DAUGHTER OF FRANCE. *Second Edition.* Cr. 8vo. 6s.

Maxwell (W. B.). VIVIEN. *Ninth Edition.* Cr. 8vo. 6s.
THE RAGGED MESSENGER. *Third Edition.* Cr. 8vo. 6s.
FABULOUS FANCIES. Cr. 8vo. 6s.

THE GUARDED FLAME. *Seventh Edition.* Cr. 8vo. 6s.
ODD LENGTHS. *Second Ed.* Cr. 8vo. 6s.
HILL RISE. *Fourth Edition.* Cr. 8vo. 6s.
THE COUNTESS OF MAYBURY: BETWEEN YOU AND I. *Fourth Edition.* Cr. 8vo. 6s.

Meade (L. T.). DRIFT. *Second Edition.* Cr. 8vo. 6s.
RESURGAM. *Second Edition.* Cr. 8vo. 6s.
VICTORY. Cr. 8vo. 6s.
A GIRL OF THE PEOPLE. Illustrated. *Fourth Edition.* Cr. 8vo. 3s. 6d.
HEPSY GIPSY. Illustrated. Cr. 8vo. 2s. 6d.
THE HONOURABLE MISS: A STORY OF AN OLD-FASHIONED TOWN. Illustrated. *Second Edition.* Cr. 8vo. 3s. 6d.

Mitford (Bertram). THE SIGN OF THE SPIDER. Illustrated. *Seventh Edition.* Cr. 8vo. 3s. 6d.

Molesworth (Mrs.). THE RED GRANGE. Illustrated. *Second Edition.* Cr. 8vo. 3s. 6d.

Montague (C. E.). A HIND LET LOOSE. Cr. 8vo. 6s.

Montgomery (K. L.). COLONEL KATE. *Second Edition.* Cr. 8vo. 6s.

Morrison (Arthur). TALES OF MEAN STREETS. *Seventh Edition.* Cr. 8vo. 6s.
A CHILD OF THE JAGO. *Fifth Edition.* Cr. 8vo. 6s.
THE HOLE IN THE WALL. *Fourth Edition.* Cr. 8vo. 6s.
DIVERS VANITIES. Cr. 8vo. 6s.

Nesbit (E.), (Mrs. H. Bland). THE RED HOUSE. Illustrated. *Fourth Edition.* Cr. 8vo. 6s.

Noble (Edward). LORDS OF THE SEA. *Third Edition.* Cr. 8vo. 6s.

Ollivant (Alfred). OWD BOB, THE GREY DOG OF KENMUIR. With a Frontispiece. *Eleventh Ed.* Cr. 8vo. 6s.

Oppenheim (E. Phillips). MASTER OF MEN. *Fourth Edition.* Cr. 8vo. 6s.

Oxenham (John). A WEAVER OF WEBS. Illustrated. *Fourth Ed.* Cr. 8vo. 6s.
THE GATE OF THE DESERT. *Fourth Edition.* Cr. 8vo. 6s.
PROFIT AND LOSS. *Fourth Edition.* Cr. 8vo. 6s.
THE LONG ROAD. *Fourth Edition.* Cr. 8vo. 6s.
THE SONG OF HYACINTH, AND OTHER STORIES. *Second Edition.* Cr. 8vo. 6s.
MY LADY OF SHADOWS. *Fourth Edition.* Cr. 8vo. 6s.

*****Pain (Barry).** THE EXILES OF FALOO. *Crown 8vo.* 6s.

Parker (Gilbert). PIERRE AND HIS PEOPLE. *Sixth Edition.* Cr. 8vo. 6s.

Fiction

MRS. FALCHION. *Fifth Edition. Cr. 8vo. 6s.*
THE TRANSLATION OF A SAVAGE. *Third Edition. Cr. 8vo. 6s.*
THE TRAIL OF THE SWORD. Illustrated. *Tenth Edition. Cr. 8vo. 6s.*
WHEN VALMOND CAME TO PONTIAC: The Story of a Lost Napoleon. *Sixth Edition. Cr. 8vo. 6s.*
AN ADVENTURER OF THE NORTH. The Last Adventures of 'Pretty Pierre.' *Fourth Edition. Cr. 8vo. 6s.*
THE SEATS OF THE MIGHTY. Illustrated. *Sixteenth Edition. Cr. 8vo. 6s.*
THE BATTLE OF THE STRONG: a Romance of Two Kingdoms. Illustrated. *Sixth Edition. Cr. 8vo. 6s.*
THE POMP OF THE LAVILETTES. *Third Edition. Cr. 8vo. 3s. 6d.*
NORTHERN LIGHTS. *Fourth Edition. Cr. 8vo. 6s.*

Pasture (Mrs. Henry de la). THE TYRANT. *Fourth Edition. Cr. 8vo. 6s.*

Patterson (J. E.). WATCHERS BY THE SHORE. *Third Edition. Cr. 8vo. 6s.*

Pemberton (Max). THE FOOTSTEPS OF A THRONE. Illustrated. *Third Edition. Cr. 8vo. 6s.*
I CROWN THEE KING. Illustrated. *Cr. 8vo. 6s.*
LOVE THE HARVESTER: A STORY OF THE SHIRES. Illustrated. *Third Edition. Cr. 8vo. 3s. 6d.*
THE MYSTERY OF THE GREEN HEART. *Second Edition. Cr. 8vo. 6s.*

Phillpotts (Eden). LYING PROPHETS. *Third Edition. Cr. 8vo. 6s.*
CHILDREN OF THE MIST. *Fifth Edition. Cr. 8vo. 6s.*
THE HUMAN BOY. With a Frontispiece. *Seventh Edition. Cr. 8vo. 6s.*
SONS OF THE MORNING. *Second Edition. Cr. 8vo. 6s.*
THE RIVER. *Third Edition. Cr. 8vo. 6s.*
THE AMERICAN PRISONER. *Fourth Edition. Cr. 8vo. 6s.*
THE SECRET WOMAN. *Fourth Edition. Cr. 8vo. 6s.*
KNOCK AT A VENTURE. *Third Edition. Cr. 8vo. 6s.*
THE PORTREEVE. *Fourth Edition. Cr. 8vo. 6s.*
THE POACHER'S WIFE. *Second Edition. Cr. 8vo. 6s.*
THE STRIKING HOURS. *Second Edition. Cr. 8vo. 6s.*
THE FOLK AFIELD. *Crown 8vo. 6s.*

Pickthall (Marmaduke). SAID THE FISHERMAN. *Seventh Edition. Cr. 8vo. 6s.*

'Q' (A. T. Quiller Couch). THE WHITE WOLF. *Second Edition. Cr. 8vo. 6s.*
THE MAYOR OF TROY. *Fourth Edition. Cr. 8vo. 6s.*
MERRY-GARDEN AND OTHER STORIES. *Cr. 8vo. 6s.*

MAJOR VIGOUREUX. *Third Edition. Cr. 8vo. 6s.*

Querido (Israel). TOIL OF MEN. Translated by F. S. ARNOLD. *Cr. 8vo. 6s.*

Rawson (Maud Stepney). THE ENCHANTED GARDEN. *Fourth Edition. Cr. 8vo. 6s.*
THE EASY GO LUCKIES : OR, ONE WAY OF LIVING. *Second Edition. Cr. 8vo. 6s.*
HAPPINESS. *Second Edition. Cr. 8vo. 6s.*

Rhys (Grace). THE BRIDE. *Second Edition. Cr. 8vo. 6s.*

Ridge (W. Pett). ERB. *Second Edition. Cr. 8vo. 6s.*
A SON OF THE STATE. *Second Edition. Cr. 8vo. 3s. 6d.*
A BREAKER OF LAWS. *Cr. 8vo. 3s. 6d.*
MRS. GALER'S BUSINESS. Illustrated. *Second Edition. Cr. 8vo. 6s.*
THE WICKHAMSES. *Fourth Edition. Cr. 8vo. 6s.*
NAME OF GARLAND. *Third Edition. Cr. 8vo. 6s.*
SPLENDID BROTHER. *Fourth Edition. Cr. 8vo. 6s.*

Ritchie (Mrs. David G.). MAN AND THE CASSOCK. *Second Edition. Cr. 8vo. 6s.*

Roberts (C. G. D.). THE HEART OF THE ANCIENT WOOD. *Cr. 8vo. 3s. 6d.*

Robins (Elizabeth). THE CONVERT. *Third Edition. Cr. 8vo. 6s.*

Rosenkrantz (Baron Palle). THE MAGISTRATE'S OWN CASE. *Cr. 8vo. 6s.*

Russell (W. Clark). MY DANISH SWEETHEART. Illustrated. *Fifth Edition. Cr. 8vo. 6s.*
HIS ISLAND PRINCESS. Illustrated. *Second Edition. Cr. 8vo. 6s.*
ABANDONED. *Second Edition. Cr. 8vo. 6s.*
MASTER ROCKAFELLAR'S VOYAGE. Illustrated. *Fourth Edition. Cr. 8vo. 3s. 6d.*

Sandys (Sydney). JACK CARSTAIRS OF THE POWER HOUSE. Illustrated. *Second Edition. Cr. 8vo. 6s.*

Sergeant (Adeline). THE PASSION OF PAUL MARILLIER. *Cr. 8vo. 6s.*

*Shakespear (Olivia). UNCLE HILARY. *Cr. 8vo. 6s.*

Sidgwick (Mrs. Alfred). THE KINSMAN. Illustrated. *Third Edition. Cr. 8vo. 6s.*
THE SEVERINS. *Fourth Edition. Cr. 8vo. 6s.*

Stewart (Newton V.). A SON OF THE EMPEROR. : BEING PASSAGES FROM THE LIFE OF ENZIO, KING OF SARDINIA AND CORSICA. *Cr. 8vo. 6s.*

Swayne (Martin Lutrell). THE BISHOP AND THE LADY. *Second Edition. Cr. 8vo. 6s.*

Thurston (E. Temple). MIRAGE. *Fourth Edition. Cr. 8vo. 6s.*

Underhill (Evelyn). THE COLUMN OF DUST. *Cr. 8vo. 6s.*

Vorst (Marie Van). THE SENTIMENTAL ADVENTURES OF JIMMY BULSTRODE. *Cr. 8vo. 6s.*
IN AMBUSH. *Second Edition. Cr. 8vo. 6s.*

Waineman (Paul). THE WIFE OF NICHOLAS FLEMING. *Cr. 8vo. 6s.*

Watson (H. B. Marriott). TWISTED EGLANTINE. Illustrated. *Third Edition. Cr. 8vo. 6s.*
THE HIGH TOBY. *Third Edition. Cr. 8vo. 6s.*
A MIDSUMMER DAY'S DREAM. *Third Edition. Cr. 8vo. 6s.*
THE CASTLE BY THE SEA. *Third Edition. Cr. 8vo. 6s.*
THE PRIVATEERS. Illustrated. *Second Edition. Cr. 8vo. 6s.*
A POPPY SHOW: BEING DIVERS AND DIVERSE TALES. *Cr. 8vo. 6s.*
THE FLOWER OF THE HEART. *Third Edition. Cr. 8vo. 6s.*

Webling (Peggy). THE STORY OF VIRGINIA PERFECT. *Third Edition. Cr. 8vo. 6s.*
*THE SPIRIT OF MIRTH. *Cr. 8vo. 6s.*

Wells (H. G.). THE SEA LADY. *Cr. 8vo. 6s. Also Medium 8vo. 6d.*

Weyman (Stanley). UNDER THE RED ROBE. Illustrated. *Twenty-Second Edition. Cr. 8vo. 6s.*

Whitby (Beatrice). THE RESULT OF AN ACCIDENT. *Second Edition. Cr. 8vo. 6s.*

White (Edmund). THE HEART OF HINDUSTAN. *Cr. 8vo. 6s.*

White (Percy). LOVE AND THE WISE MEN. *Third Edition. Cr. 8vo. 6s.*

Williamson (Mrs. C. N.). THE ADVENTURE OF PRINCESS SYLVIA. *Second Edition. Cr. 8vo. 6s.*
THE WOMAN WHO DARED. *Cr. 8vo. 6s.*
THE SEA COULD TELL. *Second Edition. Cr. 8vo. 6s.*
THE CASTLE OF THE SHADOWS. *Third Edition. Cr. 8vo. 6s.*
PAPA. *Cr. 8vo. 6s.*

Williamson (C. N. and A. M.). THE LIGHTNING CONDUCTOR: The Strange Adventures of a Motor Car. Illustrated. *Seventeenth Edition. Cr. 8vo. 6s. Also Cr. 8vo. 1s. net.*
THE PRINCESS PASSES: A Romance of a Motor. Illustrated. *Ninth Edition. Cr. 8vo. 6s.*
MY FRIEND THE CHAUFFEUR. Illustrated. *Tenth Edition. Cr. 8vo. 6s.*
LADY BETTY ACROSS THE WATER. *Tenth Edition. Cr. 8vo. 6s.*
THE CAR OF DESTINY AND ITS ERRAND IN SPAIN. Illustrated. *Fourth Edition. Cr. 8vo. 6s.*
THE BOTOR CHAPERON. Illustrated. *Fifth Edition. Cr. 8vo. 6s.*
SCARLET RUNNER. Illustrated. *Third Edition. Cr. 8vo. 6s.*
SET IN SILVER. Illustrated. *Second Edition. Cr. 8vo. 6s.*
LORD LOVELAND DISCOVERS AMERICA. *Second Edition. Cr. 8vo. 6s.*

Wyllarde (Dolf). THE PATHWAY OF THE PIONEER (Nous Autres). *Fourth Edition. Cr. 8vo. 6s.*

Books for Boys and Girls.

Illustrated. Crown 8vo. 3s. 6d.

THE GETTING WELL OF DOROTHY. By Mrs. W. K. Clifford. *Second Edition.*

ONLY A GUARD-ROOM DOG. By Edith E. Cuthell.

MASTER ROCKAFELLAR'S VOYAGE. By W. Clark Russell. *Fourth Edition.*

SYD BELTON: Or, the Boy who would not go to Sea. By G. Manville Fenn. *Second Edition.*

THE RED GRANGE. By Mrs. Molesworth. *Second Edition.*

A GIRL OF THE PEOPLE. By L. T. Meade. *Fourth Edition.*

HEPSY GIPSY. By L. T. Meade. *2s. 6d.*

THE HONOURABLE MISS. By L. T. Meade. *Second Edition.*

THERE WAS ONCE A PRINCE. By Mrs. M. E. Mann.

WHEN ARNOLD COMES HOME. By Mrs. M. E. Mann.

FICTION

The Novels of Alexandre Dumas.

Medium 8vo. Price 6d. Double Volumes, 1s.

ACTÉ.
THE ADVENTURES OF CAPTAIN PAMPHILE.
AMAURY.
THE BIRD OF FATE.
THE BLACK TULIP.
THE CASTLE OF EPPSTEIN.
CATHERINE BLUM.
CÉCILE.
THE CHATELET.
THE CHEVALIER D'HARMENTAL. (Double volume.)
CHICOT THE JESTER.
THE COMTE DE MONTGOMERY.
CONSCIENCE.
THE CONVICT'S SON.
THE CORSICAN BROTHERS; and OTHO THE ARCHER.
CROP-EARED JACQUOT.
DOM GORENFLOT.
THE FATAL COMBAT.
THE FENCING MASTER.
FERNANDE.
GABRIEL LAMBERT.
GEORGES.
THE GREAT MASSACRE.
HENRI DE NAVARRE.
HÉLÈNE DE CHAVERNY.
THE HOROSCOPE.
LOUISE DE LA VALLIÈRE. (Double volume.)
THE MAN IN THE IRON MASK. (Double volume.)
MAÎTRE ADAM.
THE MOUTH OF HELL.
NANON. (Double volume.)
OLYMPIA.
PAULINE; PASCAL BRUNO; and BONTEKOE.
PÈRE LA RUINE.
THE PRINCE OF THIEVES.
THE REMINISCENCES OF ANTONY.
ROBIN HOOD.
SAMUEL GELB.
THE SNOWBALL AND THE SULTANETTA.
SYLVANDIRE.
THE TAKING OF CALAIS.
TALES OF THE SUPERNATURAL.
TALES OF STRANGE ADVENTURE.
TALES OF TERROR.
THE THREE MUSKETEERS. (Double volume.)
THE TRAGEDY OF NANTES.
TWENTY YEARS AFTER. (Double volume.)
THE WILD-DUCK SHOOTER.
THE WOLF-LEADER.

Methuen's Sixpenny Books.

Medium 8vo.

Albanesi (E. Maria). LOVE AND LOUISA.
I KNOW A MAIDEN.
Anstey (F.). A BAYARD OF BENGAL.
Austen (J.). PRIDE AND PREJUDICE.
Bagot (Richard). A ROMAN MYSTERY.
CASTING OF NETS.
DONNA DIANA.
Balfour (Andrew). BY STROKE OF SWORD.

Baring-Gould (S.). FURZE BLOOM.
CHEAP JACK ZITA.
KITTY ALONE.
URITH.
THE BROOM SQUIRE.
IN THE ROAR OF THE SEA.
NOÉMI.
A BOOK OF FAIRY TALES. Illustrated.
LITTLE TU'PENNY.
WINEFRED.
THE FROBISHERS.
THE QUEEN OF LOVE.

ARMINELL.
BLADYS OF THE STEWPONEY.

Barr (Robert). JENNIE BAXTER.
IN THE MIDST OF ALARMS.
THE COUNTESS TEKLA.
THE MUTABLE MANY.

Benson (E. F.). DODO.
THE VINTAGE.

Brontë (Charlotte). SHIRLEY.

Brownell (C. L.). THE HEART OF JAPAN.

Burton (J. Bloundelle). ACROSS THE SALT SEAS.

Caffyn (Mrs.). ANNE MAULEVERER.

Capes (Bernard). THE LAKE OF WINE.

Clifford (Mrs. W. K.). A FLASH OF SUMMER.
MRS. KEITH'S CRIME.

Corbett (Julian). A BUSINESS IN GREAT WATERS.

Croker (Mrs. B. M.). ANGEL.
A STATE SECRET.
PEGGY OF THE BARTONS.
JOHANNA.

Dante (Alighieri). THE DIVINE COMEDY (Cary).

Doyle (A. Conan). ROUND THE RED LAMP.

Duncan (Sara Jeannette). A VOYAGE OF CONSOLATION.
THOSE DELIGHTFUL AMERICANS.

Eliot (George). THE MILL ON THE FLOSS.

Findlater (Jane H.). THE GREEN GRAVES OF BALGOWRIE.

Gallon (Tom). RICKERBY'S FOLLY.

Gaskell (Mrs.). CRANFORD.
MARY BARTON.
NORTH AND SOUTH.

Gerard (Dorothea). HOLY MATRIMONY.
THE CONQUEST OF LONDON.
MADE OF MONEY.

Gissing (G.). THE TOWN TRAVELLER.
THE CROWN OF LIFE.

Glanville (Ernest). THE INCA'S TREASURE.
THE KLOOF BRIDE.

Gleig (Charles). BUNTER'S CRUISE.

Grimm (The Brothers). GRIMM'S FAIRY TALES.

Hope (Anthony). A MAN OF MARK.
A CHANGE OF AIR.
THE CHRONICLES OF COUNT ANTONIO.
PHROSO.
THE DOLLY DIALOGUES.

Hornung (E. W.). DEAD MEN TELL NO TALES.

Ingraham (J. H.). THE THRONE OF DAVID.

Le Queux (W.). THE HUNCHBACK OF WESTMINSTER.

Levett-Yeats (S. K.). THE TRAITOR'S WAY.
ORRAIN.

Linton (E. Lynn). THE TRUE HISTORY OF JOSHUA DAVIDSON.

Lyall (Edna). DERRICK VAUGHAN.

Malet (Lucas). THE CARISSIMA.
A COUNSEL OF PERFECTION.

Mann (Mrs. M. E.). MRS. PETER HOWARD.
A LOST ESTATE.
THE CEDAR STAR.
ONE ANOTHER'S BURDENS.
THE PATTEN EXPERIMENT.
A WINTER'S TALE.

Marchmont (A. W.). MISER HOADLEY'S SECRET.
A MOMENT'S ERROR.

Marryat (Captain). PETER SIMPLE.
JACOB FAITHFUL.

March (Richard). A METAMORPHOSIS.
THE TWICKENHAM PEERAGE.
THE GODDESS.
THE JOSS.

Mason (A. E. W.). CLEMENTINA.

Mathers (Helen). HONEY.
GRIFF OF GRIFFITHSCOURT.
SAM'S SWEETHEART.
THE FERRYMAN.

Meade (Mrs. L. T.). DRIFT.

Miller (Esther). LIVING LIES.

Mitford (Bertram). THE SIGN OF THE SPIDER.

Montresor (F. F.). THE ALIEN

Morrison (Arthur). THE HOLE IN THE WALL.

Nesbit (E.). THE RED HOUSE.

Norris (W. E.). HIS GRACE.
GILES INGILBY.
THE CREDIT OF THE COUNTY.
LORD LEONARD THE LUCKLESS.
MATTHEW AUSTEN.
CLARISSA FURIOSA.

Oliphant (Mrs.). THE LADY'S WALK.
SIR ROBERT'S FORTUNE.
THE PRODIGALS.
THE TWO MARYS.

Oppenheim (E. P.). MASTER OF MEN.

Parker (Gilbert). THE POMP OF THE LAVILETTES.
WHEN VALMOND CAME TO PONTIAC.
THE TRAIL OF THE SWORD.

Pemberton (Max). THE FOOTSTEPS OF A THRONE.
I CROWN THEE KING.

Phillpotts (Eden). THE HUMAN BOY.
CHILDREN OF THE MIST.
THE POACHER'S WIFE.
THE RIVER.

'Q' (A. T. Quiller Couch). THE WHITE WOLF.

Ridge (W. Pett). A SON OF THE STATE.
LOST PROPERTY.
GEORGE and THE GENERAL.

ERB.

Russell (W. Clark). ABANDONED.
A MARRIAGE AT SEA.
MY DANISH SWEETHEART.
HIS ISLAND PRINCESS.

Sergeant (Adeline). THE MASTER OF BEECHWOOD.
BALBARA'S MONEY.
THE YELLOW DIAMOND.
THE LOVE THAT OVERCAME.

Sidgwick (Mrs. Alfred). THE KINSMAN.

Surtees (R. S.). HANDLEY CROSS.
MR. SPONGE'S SPORTING TOUR.
ASK MAMMA.

Walford (Mrs. L. B.). MR. SMITH.
COUSINS.
THE BABY'S GRANDMOTHER.
TROUBLESOME DAUGHTERS.

Wallace (General Lew). BEN-HUR.
THE FAIR GOD.

Watson (H. B. Marriott). THE ADVENTURERS.
*CAPTAIN FORTUNE.

Weekes (A. B.). PRISONERS OF WAR.

Wells (H. G.). THE SEA LADY.

White (Percy). A PASSIONATE PILGRIM.

For Product Safety Concerns and Information please contact our EU representative GPSR@taylorandfrancis.com
Taylor & Francis Verlag GmbH, Kaufingerstraße 24, 80331 München, Germany

www.ingramcontent.com/pod-product-compliance
Lightning Source LLC
Chambersburg PA
CBHW071711300426
44115CB00010B/1381